SOCIAL PROBLEMS TODAY

Coping with the Challenges of a Changing Society

JAMES M. HENSLIN

PRENTICE HALL
Englewood Cliffs, New Jersey 07632

Library of Congress Cataloging-in-Publication Data

Social problems today : coping with the challenges of a changing
  society / [edited by] James M. Henslin.
        p.   cm.
    ISBN 0-13-815523-2 :
    1. United States--Social conditions--1980- 2. Social problems.
  I. Henslin, James M.
  HN59.2.S64 1990
  361.1--dc20   89-25535
                                                      CIP

Editorial/production supervision: Evalyn Schoppet
Cover design: Bruce Kenselaar
Manufacturing buyer: Ed O'Dougherty

Cover: Vasily Kandinsky, Painting No. 200, 1914,
oil on canvas, 64 x 31½ in. (162.5 x 80 cm.).
Collection, The Museum of Modern Art, New York,
Mrs. Simon Guggenheim Fund. Photograph © 1990
The Museum of Modern Art, New York.

 © 1990 by Prentice-Hall, Inc.
A Division of Simon & Schuster
Englewood Cliffs, New Jersey 07632

Printed in the United States of America
10 9 8 7 6 5 4 3 2 1

ISBN 0-13-815523-2

Prentice-Hall International (UK) Limited, *London*
Prentice-Hall of Australia Pty. Limited, *Sydney*
Prentice-Hall Canada, Inc., *Toronto*
Prentice-Hall Hispanoamericana, S. A., *Mexico*
Prentice-Hall of India Private Limited, *New Delhi*
Prentice-Hall of Japan, Inc., *Tokyo*
Simon & Schuster Asia Pte. Ltd., *Singapore*
Editora Prentice-Hall do Brazil, Ltda., *Rio de Janeiro*

For my son, Paul, whose exuberance for the future inspires me.

CONTENTS

Rape

2. DRUG ABUSE

The liquid drug

Profits and violence

3. MENTAL ILLNESS

Can the psychiatric profession tell the sane from the insane?

4. SUICIDE

Why do people take their own lives?

When the young kill themselves

1. PROSTITUTION

The international sex tour industry

The social organization of prostitution

2. HOMOSEXUALITY

Situational homosexual behavior

3. PORNOGRAPHY

Outlets for pornography

PREFACE

Social problems come in a dazzling variety—from sexual discrimination and suicide to sexual abuse in day care and warfare between nations. And it seems that everyone has favorite solutions for most problems—"gut" feelings of what is wrong, of what underlies the problems we see on the surface, as well as strong opinions of what ought to be done about those problems. But no pat answer holds *the* solution. Social problems are too complex, too intricately interrelated with social arrangements, to be amenable to simple solutions. And no sooner does one social problem decline—or, more likely, recede from view—than another takes its place, seemingly more ominous than the preceding one.

This book is dedicated to making clearer the interrelationships of social problems, both to one another and to the social institutions of society. It is intended to impress upon students that social problems do not stand in isolation but are deeply embedded in our culture. The corresponding message is that no little tinkering will provide the solution to any social problem, but that solutions require fundamental change in our culture, and that we *can* make those changes if we collectively desire to solve our problems. The nagging question, of course, is: Are we willing to pay the costs that those solutions demand, or are we content merely to cope with the problems?

ORGANIZATION

This anthology is intended to be compatible with any of the major social problems texts, so its organization parallels those texts. The *correlation chart* in Appendix B provides specific guidelines for integrating these selections with other texts. The initial readings introduce theoretical considerations in the sociology of social problems. From there, the focus is placed on problems that are usually thought of in individualistic terms, such as sexual abuse, drug abuse, mental illness, and suicide. The middle group of readings take on wider dimension, examining problems of social inequality and discrimination and problems relating to specific social institutions. The final readings focus on problems of a more global nature.

This organizational device is intended to help make the classroom task easier, but it does not, of course, adequately reflect the real world, for social problems do not lend themselves to such neat classification. Rather, there is much overlap between problems, so much so that articles can usually be classified in several ways. Consequently, for the instructor who may wish to present these selections in a different order, a *topical index* for alternative classifications is provided in Appendix A. Topics that are not specifically singled out in the table of contents are also indicated in the topical index. For example, because so many selections focus on urban problems, this topic does not appear as a separate category in the table of contents. The topical index, however, identifies articles that focus on urban problems.

A FINAL WORD

If you have any suggestions for improving this anthology, either in its organization or content, please contact me. Your feedback will help make this book work better in the classroom. I look forward to hearing from you.

James M. Henslin
Department of Sociology
Southern Illinois University
Edwardsville, Illinois 62026

PART I

THEORETICAL CONSIDERATIONS

Although this first part of the book presents an overview of three major social problems in American society—poverty, crime, and the inequitable distribution of power to which many social problems owe their origin—its primary purpose is to introduce the sociological perspective on social problems. To do this, we examine the major theories that sociologists use to interpret social problems.

THE SOCIOLOGICAL IMAGINATION

When people have problems, they usually see them in highly personal terms. Their perspective is limited primarily to their immediate situation, and they fail to see the broader context in which those problems exist. People seldom connect their personal lives with the larger social context, and so they tend to blame themselves and one another for their troubles.

The *sociological imagination* is a term that refers to looking at human behavior and attitudes in the context of the social forces and institutional arrangements that shape them. C. Wright Mills, the sociologist who developed this concept, emphasized that change in society exerts direct and profound influence on the people living in it. As a society changes, people get caught on various sides of social issues, making social problems a dynamic part of their lives.

Mills used the term *personal troubles* to refer to an individual's experience of a social problem, stressing that we must understand the social context that influences people's perceptions, attitudes, and behaviors. He referred to this emphasis on the social context of people's lives as the sociological imagination (or perspective), a way of thinking that helps make visible the larger forces that underlie personal troubles.

To illustrate this concept, we can use the example of abortion. When the older people in our society grew up, not only was abortion illegal, but people did not even talk openly about abortion. Social attitudes were such that every woman was expected to be a mother, and almost all girls grew up with motherhood as their foremost goal. Almost everyone agreed that abortion was murder, and women who sought abortions kept their debasing crime a secret, enduring blindfolded taxi rides, kitchen-table surgery, and risk of postoperative infection. In contrast, broad social approval of abortion is a recent development in our society, resulting in large part from the women's movement, which has stressed that each woman has the right to make choices and exercise judgment about her own body.

People growing up in either era—or in groups that emphasize one or the other set of opinions and attitudes—tend to adopt the perspective of their group. Consequently, people over fifty are more likely to favor abortion than are younger people. The sociological perspective helps reveal this underlying social basis of their attitudes. Looking at social issues in this broader context, we also see that race, education, income, and politics are significant underlying factors—blacks, college graduates, Democrats, and people who earn more than $25,000 a year are likely to favor abortion.

Sociologists stress the need to use the sociological imagination in evaluating social problems, to understand how the times and social forces influence people's ideas, behaviors, and personal troubles. To use the sociological perspective is to see how our own views of what is or is not a social problem, and of what we think should be done about it, are shaped by our personal experiences of broad social forces and institutional arrangements.

WHAT IS A SOCIAL PROBLEM?
OBJECTIVE CONDITIONS AND SUBJECTIVE CONCERNS

Social problems begin with an *objective condition*, some aspect of society that can be measured or experienced. With abortion, this objective condition would include whether or not abortions are legal, who obtains them, and under what circumstances. The second key element of the definition is the *subjective concern* that a significant number of people have about the objective condition. On the one hand, subjective concern about abortion includes some people's distress that abortion is not more freely available and that some women must give birth to unwanted children. On the other hand, it includes other people's distress that pregnant women would willfully terminate the lives of their unborn children.

A social problem, then, *is some aspect of society* (the objective condition) *about which large numbers of people are concerned* (the subjective condition). In addition, the objective condition must also be one that lends itself to change as a result of people's efforts; for example, concern about the weather is not a social problem, but being upset about the high murder rate in American society is.

SOCIOLOGY AND COMMON SENSE

We all have "gut feelings" about the world around us. Based on our experiences, we "just know" what is and is not true. *Common sense*, the ideas common to a society that are used to make sense out of human experience, include ideas about social problems. Everybody develops opinions about why people do what they do, what causes a social problem, and what ought to be done about it.

Because it is based on impressions that may or may not be correct, common sense is not enough to develop adequate social policies for dealing with social problems. Consequently, sociologists investigate social problems in order to determine people's experience with a problem, their attitudes and opinions, and underlying causes of the problem. They use the sociological perspective and place particular social problems in the context of the larger picture. To explain the objective conditions of a social problem, as well as the subjective concerns that arouse people to action, sociologists use theories.

SOCIOLOGICAL THEORIES AND SOCIAL PROBLEMS

A *theory* explains the relationship between two or more concepts, such as attitudes toward abortion and age or education. (An explanation of why Republicans, whites, Hispanics, people with less money, and high school graduates [as compared to Democrats, blacks, the wealthier, and college graduates] are more likely to oppose abortion is an example of a theory.) Theories help us make sense of objective conditions by providing a framework for interpreting them. However, no theory encompasses all of reality, and each theory has both strengths and weaknesses. One theory may stress social conflict, another social harmony. This makes one theory more useful in one situation and another more useful in a different situation.

Three major theories that sociologists use to analyze social problems, as well as to interpret social life in general, are symbolic interactionism, functionalism, and conflict theory. Let us look at how each provides a different perspective on social problems.

SYMBOLIC INTERACTIONISM

The essence of the symbolic interactionist perspective is that we see the world through *symbols*, such as language, to which we attach meanings and that we then use to communicate with one another. *Symbolic interactionism* is the sociological theory that examines the symbols and definitions that people use to communicate with one another and that provide people with their view of the world.

For example, if we hear that Joan has had an abortion, attitudes arise within us. Some of us feel sorry that she had the abortion, others encouraged that she made a difficult choice, and still others angry, incensed, or disgusted. On the basis of what abortion means to us, each of us classifies Joan and then sees her through those symbols that we have used to classify her. In other words, we tend to perceive both ourselves and others—as well as all of life and everything that people do—according to the symbols that our culture provides, especially the symbols that we have learned in our particular corners of life. This is what symbolic interactionists stress: the contrasting and changing definitions that underlie the way we interpret the world. They emphasize that for understanding a social problem, it is essential that we search for the underlying definitions, or symbols, by which people view their social worlds.

That a characteristic of society may be considered a social problem by some groups but not by others embodies the symbolic interactionist perspective. So does the idea that at one point in time people will take some condition for granted, but at another will define it as a problem. Symbolic interactionists emphasize that social problems do not exist like stones, independent of whoever observes them. Rather, some objective condition must be defined as seriously problematic, or it will not be regarded as a social problem. *From the perspective of symbolic interactionism, then, social conditions do not automatically constitute a social problem. Rather, it all depends on how those conditions are viewed.*

Symbolic Interactionism and Social Problems: A Summary

Symbolic interactionists emphasize that social problems do not exist "out there," independent of how people define their world. Social problems are socially constructed as people determine whether or not to consider some objective condition a social problem—and how to react to it. Symbolic interactionists also stress that to understand any social problem adequately, be it abortion or crime or war, we must take into account the meanings that the problem has for those who are involved in it. To understand social problems, then, it is essential that we focus on how objective conditions become socially constructed into social problems and how they are experienced by those who are directly involved in them.

FUNCTIONALISM

The second major theory sociologists use to interpret social problems is *functionalism* (also called *functional analysis*). Functionalists stress that society is made up of various parts. Each part fulfills a *function* that contributes to society's equilibrium, or it would not exist. When working properly, each part contributes to the stability of the whole.

Just as in a machine, however, the parts of a social system sometimes fail, and this creates problems for the system. These failures, called *dysfunctions*, can create instability or disequilibrium in society. If they do, they are social problems. *From the functionalist perspective, then, social problems are conditions or failures that impede the fulfillment of society's goals or that interfere with its smooth functioning.* For example, if the 1.5 million abortions each year in the United States should create a shortage of workers, that result would be a dysfunction, and it would be part of a social problem. If, however, it allows women to participate more equally in the work force and increases their social status, then in that respect it will not have been part of a social problem. Whether or not something is a social problem depends on its social consequences.

From this perspective, society is seen as a functioning unit, and when a part does not meet its function, it contributes to society's disequilibrium, to some sort of maladjustment within that society. It is then part of a social problem.

Functionalists use the term *manifest function* to refer to the beneficial consequence that people intend when they do something. If their action turns out to have some unintended beneficial consequence, that is its *latent function*. If it has some unintended harmful consequence, that is its *latent dysfunction*. From the functionalist perspective, social problems are latent dysfunctions on a large scale.

Functionalism sensitizes us to think in terms of systems, to see whatever we are studying as part of a larger unit. When we examine a smaller part, functionalists stress that we should look for its functions in order to see how it is related to the larger unit.

Functionalism and Social Problems: A Summary

Functionalists emphasize that the parts of a system are interrelated, so that when change occurs in some part of a social system it affects other parts. With their focus on the social system and its interrelated parts, functionalists stress that a particular social problem is only part of a larger whole. In order to understand a social problem, they stress that one must place it in this broader context. Functionalists view a social problem as a consequence of the way a social system is put together.

CONFLICT THEORY

Conflict theorists look at things in a very different light. They stress that life is a struggle. Each person, each group, and each nation strives to gain control over a larger share of scarce resources. Although this struggle sometimes requires that groups cooperate with others or even form alliances, we are all essentially in competition with one another. Competition, or survival of the fittest, is the cornerstone of Charles Darwin's theory of evolution. Competition is also an essential element of the marketplace. The primary fact of social life, stress conflict theorists, is competition, for it lies at the root of the relationships of the groups that make up society.

The trouble with functionalists, conflict theorists argue, is that they regard the parts of society as working together, harmoniously contributing to a larger whole. Instead, those parts are in competition with one another, ready to break into open conflict at any time. Moreover, the guiding principle of social life is disequilibrium and change, not equilibrium and harmony. Whether people recognize it or not, they are enmeshed in a basic struggle, with each group in society attempting to make gains for itself at the expense of other groups. This inherent conflict over limited resources threatens to throw society into turmoil.

From the conflict perspective, then, social problems are the natural and inevitable outcomes of social struggle, not, as the functionalists think, sand accidentally lodged in the smoothly meshing gears of society. Whatever the surface appearance of a social problem, at its essence is always this: people in power pitted against those they control, and those being controlled attempting to overcome their various forms of oppression and to gain more resources for themselves.

Social problems evolve naturally from this inherent conflict between the powerful and the powerless, between the controllers and the controlled, between the exploiters and the exploited. The powerful seize as much of a society's resources for themselves as they can, and in the process exploit the powerless and create problems such as poverty, discrimination, and oppression. The reactions of the exploited to their oppression create still other social problems, such as rebellion, crime, and suicide. To understand a social problem, then, we need to penetrate such surface manifestations as violence or escapist drug abuse and pierce through to the basic conflict that underlies them.

From the conflict perspective, then, *social problems are the troubles experienced by the exploited when the powerful push them around, or the troubles experienced by the powerful as the exploited resist, rebel, or appeal to higher values of justice.* Although their options are limited, the exploited are not without resources of their own. Depending on how they perceive their situation— their relationship to the powerful and their options within that relationship—they may cooperate with their own exploitation, attempt to bring about social change through demonstrations and the ballot box, or drag their feet through work stoppages and hunger strikes. In some instances, the exploited feel that they can no longer live within the framework of their limited options, that an entire new social structure is required. They then take up arms against the prevailing social order, and bloody revolution is the result.

Only rarely is the reaction of the exploited so severe, for most people who occupy the lower rungs of society accept the legitimacy of the social order to which they belong. Discontent grows easily, however, for the exploited witness at least some of the inequalities of their society. In order to reduce discontent and keep the lid from boiling over, from time to time the controllers of society grant concessions to the poor. Consequently, conflict theorists look for the trade-offs that the powerful make as they deal with the less powerful, for they view the social policies that benefit the less privileged not only as concessions forced from the powerful, but also as actions designed to keep the privileged in their positions of power.

Conflict Theory and Social Problems: A Summary

The conflict perspective emphasizes that power, privilege, and other resources are limited and that they are distributed unequally among the various groups in a society. Conflict, then, is both natural and inevitable, for as each group pursues its own interests and values, it comes in conflict with other groups that are doing the same. This makes social equilibrium only temporary, something that is always in the process of tipping out of balance. Thus, stress conflict theorists, whenever you examine a social problem you should look at the distribution of power and privilege, for social problems always center around the conflicting interests and values of a society's groups.

Finally, conflict theorists point out that social change always brings social problems. The ways in which a problem unfolds, what groups line up on which sides, and the solutions that are developed to deal with conflict tell us much about how a society is evolving.

IN SUM

As you read these selections, it should become apparent how each theory provides a complementary perspective on social problems. This foundation will help prepare you for understanding the social problems examined in the later parts of the book, enabling you to appreciate the sociological understanding of social problems.

1

Social Problems
As Collective Behavior

HERBERT BLUMER

My thesis is that social problems are fundamentally products of a process of collective
definition instead of existing independently
as a set of objective social arrangements with
an intrinsic makeup. This thesis challenges
the premise underlying the typical sociological study of social problems. The thesis, if
true, would call for a drastic reorientation of
sociological theory and research in the case
of social problems.

Let me begin with a brief account of the
typical way in which sociologists approach
the study and analysis of social problems.
The approach presumes that a social problem exists as an objective condition or arrangement in the texture of a society. The
objective condition or arrangement is seen
as having an intrinsically harmful or malignant nature standing in contrast to a normal
or socially healthful society. In sociological
jargon it is a state of dysfunction, pathology,

disorganization, or deviance. The task of
the sociologist is to identify the harmful
condition or arrangement and to resolve it
into its essential elements or parts. This
analysis of the objective makeup of the
social problem is usually accompanied by an
identification of the conditions which cause
the problem and by proposals as to how the
problem might be handled. In having analyzed the objective nature of the social problem, identified its causes, and pointed out
how the problem could be handled or
solved, the sociologist believes that he has
accomplished his scientific mission. The
knowledge and information which he has
gathered can, on the one hand, be added to
the store of scholarly knowledge and, on the
other hand, be placed at the disposal of
policy makers and the general citizenry.

This typical sociological approach seems
on its face to be logical, reasonable, and

justifiable. Yet, in my judgment, it reflects a gross misunderstanding of the nature of social problems and, accordingly, is very ineffectual in providing for their control. To give an initial indication of the deficiency of the approach, let me indicate briefly the falsity or unproven character of several of its key assumptions or claims.

First, current sociological theory and knowledge, in themselves, just do not enable the detection or identification of social problems. Instead, sociologists discern social problems only after they are recognized as social problems by and in a society. Sociological recognition follows in the wake of societal recognition, veering with the winds of the public identification of social problems. Illustrations are legion—I cite only a few of recent memory. Poverty was a conspicuous social problem for sociologists a half-century ago, only to practically disappear from the sociological scene in the 1940s and early 1950s, and then to reappear in our current time. Racial injustice and exploitation in our society were far greater in the 1920s and 1930s than they are today; yet the sociological concern they evoked was little until the chain of happenings following the Supreme Court decision on school desegregation and the riot in Watts. Environmental pollution and ecological destruction are social problems of very late vintage for sociologists, although their presence and manifestation date back over many decades. The problem of the inequality of women's status, emerging so vigorously on our current scene, was of peripheral sociological concern a few years back. Without drawing on other illustrations, I merely assert that in identifying social problems sociologists have consistently taken their cue from what happens to be in the focus of public concern. This conclusion is supported further by the indifference of sociologists and the public, alike, to many questionable and harmful dimensions of modern life. Such injurious dimensions may be casually noted, but despite their gravity are given the status of social problems by sociologists. A few instances that come to mind are: the vast overorganization that is developing in modern society, the unearned increment in land values which Henry George campaigned against three-quarters of a century ago, the injurious social effects of our national highway system, the pernicious social consequences of an ideology of "growth," the unsavory side of established business codes; and may I add for my State of California, a state water plan with hidden social consequences of a repelling character. I think that the empirical record is clear that the designation of social problems by sociologists is derived from the public designation of social problems.

Let me add that, contrary to the pretensions of sociologists, sociological theory, *by itself*, has been conspicuously impotent to detect or identify social problems. This can be seen in the case of the three most prestigeful sociological concepts currently used to explain the emergence of social problems, namely, the concepts of "deviance," "dysfunction," and "structural strain." These concepts are useless as means of identifying social problems. For one thing, none of them has a set of benchmarks that enables the scholar to identify in the empirical world the so-called instances of deviance, dysfunction, or structural strain. Lacking such clear identifying characteristics, the scholar cannot take up each and every social condition or arrangement in society and establish that it is or is not an instance of deviance, dysfunction, or structural strain. But this deficiency, however serious, is of lesser importance in the matter I am considering. Of far greater significance is the inability of the scholar to explain why some of the instances of deviance, dysfunction, or structural strain noted by him fail to achieve the status of social problems, whereas other instances do reach this status. There are all kinds of deviance that do not gain recognition as social problems; we are never told how or when deviance becomes a social problem. Similarly, there are many alleged dysfunctions or structural strains that never come to be seen as social problems; we are not told how and when so-called dysfunctions or structural strains become social problems. Obviously, deviance, dysfunction, and structural strain on one side and social problems on the other side are not equivalent.

If conventional sociological theory is so decisively incapable of detecting social problems and if sociologists make this detection by following and using the public recognition of social problems, it would seem logical that students of social problems ought to study the process by which a society comes to recognize its social problems. Sociologists have conspicuously failed to do this.

A *second* deficiency of the conventional sociological approach is the assumption that a social problem exists basically in the form of an identifiable objective condition· in a society. Sociologists treat a social problem as if its being consisted of a series of objective items, such as rates of incidence, the kind of people involved in the problem, their number, their types, their social characteristics, and the relation of their condition to various selected societal factors. Is it assumed that the reduction of a social problem into such objective elements catches the problem in its central character and constitutes its scientific analysis. In my judgment this assumption is erroneous. As I will show much clearer later, a social problem exists primarily in terms of how it is defined and conceived in a society instead of being an objective condition with a definitive objective makeup. The societal definition, and not the objective makeup of a given social condition, determines whether the condition exists as a social problem. The societal definition gives the social problem its nature, lays out how it is to be approached, and shapes what is done about it. Alongside these decisive influences, the so-called objective existence or makeup of the social problem is very secondary indeed. A sociologist may note what he believes to be a malignant condition in a society, but the society may ignore completely its presence, in which event the condition will not exist as a social problem for that society regardless of its asserted objective being. Or, the objec-

tive breakdown made by a sociologist of a societally recognized social problem may differ widely from how the problem is seen and approached in the society. The objective analysis made by him may have no influence on what is done with the problem and consequently have no realistic relation to the problem. These few observations suggest a clear need to study the process by which a society comes to see, to define, and to handle their social problems. Students of social problems notoriously ignore this process; and it scarcely enters into sociological theory.

There is a third highly questionable assumption underlying the typical orientation of sociologists in the study of social problems. It is that the findings resulting from their study of the objective makeup of a social problem provide society with the solid and effective means for remedial treatment of that problem. All that society has to do, or should do, is to take heed of the findings and to respect the lines of treatment to which the findings point. This assumption is largely nonsense. It ignores or misrepresents how a society acts in the case of its social problems. A social problem is always a focal point for the operation of divergent and conflicting interests, intentions, and objectives. It is the interplay of these interests and objectives that constitutes the way in which a society deals with any one of its social problems. The sociological account of the objective makeup of the problem stands far outside of such interplay—indeed, may be inconsequential to it. This distant removal of the sociological study from the real process through which a society acts towards its social problem is a major explanation of the ineffectiveness of sociological studies of social problems.

The three central deficiencies that I have mentioned are only a sketch of a needed full-fledged criticism of the typical sociological treatment of social problems. But they serve as a clue and hence as an introduction to the development of my thesis that social problems lie in and are products of a process of collective definition. The process of collective definition is responsible for the emergence of social problems, for the way in which they are seen, for the way in which they are approached and considered, for the kind of official remedial plan that is laid out, and for the transformation of the remedial plan in its application. In short, the process of collective definition determines the career and fate of social problems, from the initial point of their appearance to whatever may be the terminal point in their course. They have their being fundamentally in this process of collective definition, instead of in some alleged objective area of social malignancy. The failure to recognize and respect this fact constitutes, in my opinion, the fundamental weakness in the sociological study of social problems and in sociological knowledge of social problems. Let me proceed to develop my thesis.

To lodge the emergence, the career, and the fate of social problems in a process of collective definition calls for an analysis of the course of this process. I find that the process passes through five stages. I shall label these: (1) the emergence of a social problem, (2) the legitimation of the problem, (3) the mobilization of action with regard to the problem, (4) the formation of an official plan of action, and (5) the transformation of the official plan in its empirical implementation. I propose to discuss briefly each of these five stages.

THE EMERGENCE OF SOCIAL PROBLEMS

Social problems are not the result of an intrinsic malfunctioning of a society but are the result of a process of definition in which a given condition is picked out and identified as a social problem. A social problem does not exist for a society unless it is recognized by that society to exist. In not being aware of a social problem, a society does not perceive it, address it, discuss it, or do anything about it. The problem is just not there. It is necessary, consequently, to consider the question of how social problems arise. Despite its crucial importance, this question has been essentially ignored by sociologists.

It is a gross mistake to assume that any kind of malignant or harmful social condition or arrangement in a society becomes automatically a social problem for that society. The pages of history are replete with instances of dire social conditions unnoticed and unattended in the societies in which they occurred. Intelligent observers, using the standards of one society, may perceive abiding harmful conditions in another society that just do not appear as problems to the membership of the latter society. Further, individuals with keen perceptions of their own society, or who as a result of distressing experience may perceive given social conditions in their society as harmful, may be impotent in awakening any concern with the conditions. Also, given social conditions may be ignored at one time yet, without change in their makeup, become matters of grave concern at another time. All of these kinds of instances are so drearily repetitive as not to require documentation. The most casual observation and reflection shows clearly that the recognition by a society of its social problems is a highly selective process, with many harmful social conditions and arrangements not even making a bid for attention and with others falling by the wayside in what is frequently a fierce competitive struggle. Many push for societal recognition, but only a few come out of the end of the funnel.

I would think that students of social problems would almost automatically see the need to study this process by which given social conditions or arrangements come to be recognized as social problems. But, by and large, sociologists do not either see the need or detour around it. Sociological platitudes, such as that the perception of social problems depend on ideologies or on traditional beliefs, tell us practically nothing about what a society picks out as its social problems and how it comes to pick them out. We have scarcely any studies, and pitifully limited knowledge, of such relevant matters as the following: the role of agitation in getting recognition for a problem; the role of violence in gaining such recognition; the play of interest groups who seek to shut off recognition of a problem; the role of other interest groups who foresee material gains by elevating a given condition to a problem (as in the case of police with the current problem of crime and drugs); the role of political figures in fomenting concern with certain problems and putting the damper on concern with other conditions; the role of powerful organizations and corporations doing the same thing; the impotency of powerless groups to gain attention for what they believe to be problems; the role of the mass media in selecting social problems; and the influence of adventitious happenings that shock public sensitivities. We have here a vast field which beckons study and which needs to be studied if we are to understand the simple but basic matter of how social problems emerge. And I repeat that if they don't emerge, they don't even begin a life.

LEGITIMATION OF SOCIAL PROBLEMS

Societal recognition gives birth to a social problem. But if the social problem is to move along on its course and not die aborning, it must acquire social legitimacy. It may seem strange to speak of social problems having to become legitimated. Yet after gaining initial recognition, a social problem must acquire social endorsement if it is to be taken seriously and move forward in its career. It must acquire a necessary degree of respectability which entitles it to consideration in the recognized arenas of public discussion. In our society such arenas are the press, other media of communication, the church, the school, civic organizations, legislative chambers, and the assembly places of officialdom. If a social problem does not carry the credential of respectability necessary for entrance into these arenas, it is doomed. Do not think because a given

social condition or arrangement is recognized as grave by some people in a society—by people who indeed attract attention to it by their agitation—that this means that the problem will break through into the arena of public consideration. To the contrary, the asserted problem may be regarded as insignificant, as not worthy of consideration, as in the accepted order of things and thus not to be tampered with, as distasteful to codes of propriety, or as merely the shouting of questionable or subversive elements in a society. Any of these conditions can block a recognized problem from gaining legitimacy. If the social problem fails to get legitimacy, it flounders and languishes outside of the arena of public action.

I want to stress that among the wide variety of social conditions or arrangements that are recognized as harmful by differing sets of people, there are relatively few that achieve legitimacy. Here again we are confronted with a selective process in which, so to speak, many budding social problems are choked off, others are ignored, others are avoided, others have to fight their way to a respectable status, and others are rushed along to legitimacy by a strong and influential backing. We know very little of this selective process through which social problems have to pass in order to reach the stage of legitimacy. Certainly such passage is not due merely to the intrinsic gravity of the social problem. Nor is it due to merely the prior state of public interest or knowledge; nor to the so-called ideologies of the public. The selective process is far more complicated than is suggested by these simple, commonplace ideas. Obviously, many of the factors which operate to affect the recognition of social problems continue to play a part in the legitimation of social problems. But it seems evident that there are other contributing factors through which the elusive quality of social respectability comes to be attached to social problems. We just do not have much knowledge about this process, since it is scarcely studied. It is certainly a cardinal matter that should be engaging the concern of students of social problems.

MOBILIZATION OF ACTION

If a social problem manages to pass through the stages of societal recognition and of social legitimation, it enters a new stage in its career. The problem now becomes the object of discussion, of controversy, of differing depictions, and of diverse claims. Those who seek changes in the area of the problem clash with those who endeavor to protect vested interests in the area. Exaggerated claims and distorted depictions, subserving vested interests, become commonplace. Outsiders, less involved, bring their sentiments and images to bear on their framing of the problem. Discussion, advocacy, evaluation, falsification, diversionary tactics, and advancing of proposals take place in the media of communication, in casual meetings, organized meetings, legislative chambers, and committee hearings. All of this constitutes a mobilization of the society for action on the social problem. It seems scarcely necessary to point out that the fate of the social problem depends greatly on what happens in this process of mobilization. How the problem comes to be defined, how it is bent in response to awakened sentiment, how it is depicted to protect vested interests, and how it reflects the play of strategic position and power—all are appropriate questions that suggest the importance of the process of mobilization for action.

Again, as far as I can see, students of social problems bypass concern with and consideration of this stage of the collective defining process. Our best knowledge of this stage has come from students of public opinion. Yet their contribution is fragmentary and woefully inadequate, primarily because of a lack of detailed empirical analysis of the process. The students of the public opinion process tell us little about how given social problems come to survive in their confrontations and how they are redefined in order to achieve such survival. Similarly, they tell us next to nothing about how other social problems languish, perish, or just fade away in this stage. That students of

social problems should overlook this crucial stage in the fate of social problems seems to me to be extraordinarily shortsighted.

FORMATION OF AN OFFICIAL PLAN OF ACTION

This stage in the career of social problems represents the decision of a society as to how it will act with regard to the given problem. It consists of the hammering together of an official plan of action, such as takes place in legislative committees, legislative chambers, and executive boards. The official plan is almost always a product of bargaining, in which diverse views and interests are accommodated. Compromises, concessions, trade-offs, deference to influence, response to power, and judgments of what may be workable—all play a part in the final formulation. This is a defining and redefining process in a concentrated form—the forming, reworking and the recasting of a collective picture of the social problem, so that what emerges may be a far cry from how the problem was viewed in the earlier stage of its career. The official plan that is enacted constitutes, in itself, the official definition of the problem; it represents how the society through its official apparatus perceives the problem and intends to act toward the problem. These observations are commonplace. Yet, they point to the operation of a defining process that has telling significance for the fate of the problem. Surely, effective and relevant study of social problems should embrace what happens to the problem in the process of agreeing on official action.

IMPLEMENTATION OF THE OFFICIAL PLAN

To assume that an official plan and its implementation in practice are the same is to fly in the face of facts. Invariably to some degree, frequently to a large degree, the plan as put into practice is modified, twisted and reshaped, and takes on unforeseen accretions. This is to be expected. The implementation of the plan ushers in a new process of collective definition. It sets the stage for the formation of new lines of action on the part of those involved in the social problem and those touched by the plan. The people who are in danger of losing advantages strive to restrict the plan or bend its operation to new directions. Those who stand to benefit from the plan may seek to exploit new opportunities. Or both groups may work out new accommodative arrangements unforeseen in the plan. The administration and the operating personnel are prone to substitute their policies for the official policy underlying the plan. Frequently, various kinds of subterranean adjustments are developed which leave intact central areas of the social problem or transform other of its areas in ways that were never officially intended. The kind of accommodations, blockages, unanticipated accretions, and unintended transformations of which I am speaking can be seen abundantly in the case of many past attempts to put official plans into actual practice. Such consequences were conspicuous in the implementation of the prohibition amendment. They are notorious in the case of the regulatory agencies in our country. They are to be seen in the case of most new law enforcement programs designed to combat the problem of crime. I scarcely know of any facet of the general area of social problems that is more important, less understood, and less studied than that of the unforeseen and unintended restructuring of the area of a social problem that arises from the implementation of an official plan of treatment. I am unable to understand why students of social problems, in both their studies and their formulation of theory, can afford to ignore this crucial step in the life-being of social problems.

I hope that my discussion of the five discernible stages in the full career of social problems brings out the need for developing a new perspective and approach in the sociological study of social problems. It seems to me to be indubitably necessary to place social problems in the context of a process of collective definition. It is this process which determines whether social problems are recognized to exist, whether they qualify for consideration, how they are to be considered, what is to be done about them, and how they are reconstituted in the efforts undertaken to control them. Social problems have their being, their career, and their fate in this process. To ignore this process can yield only fragmentary knowledge and a fictitious picture of social problems.

My discussion should not be construed as denying value to the conventional way in which sociologists approach the topic of social problems. Knowledge of the objective makeup of social problems (which is their aim) should be sought as a corrective for ignorance or misinformation concerning this objective makeup. Yet, such knowledge is grossly inadequate with regard either to the handling of social problems or to the development of sociological theory.

In the handling of social problems, knowledge of the objective makeup of the social problem area is of significance only to the extent that the knowledge enters into the process of collective definition which determines the fate of social problems. In this process the knowledge may be ignored, distorted, or smothered by other considerations. For me, it is self-evident that sociologists who wish their studies of social problems to bring about improved conditions had better study and understand the process of collective definition through which changes are made.

On the side of sociological theory, knowledge of the objective makeup of social problems is essentially useless. It is useless because, as I have sought to show, social problems do not lie in the objective areas to which they point, but in the process of being seen and defined in the society. All the empirical evidence that I can find points indubitably to this conclusion. I would welcome any evidence to the contrary. Sociologists who seek to develop theory of social problems on the premise that social problems are lodged in some kind of objective social structure are misreading their world. To attribute social problems to presumed structural strains, upsets in the equilibrium of the social system, dysfunctions, breakdown of social norms, clash of social values, or deviation from social conformity, is to unwittingly transfer to a suppositious social structure what belongs to the process of collective definition. As I have said earlier, no one of these concepts is capable of explaining why some of the empirical instances covered by the concept become social problems and others do not. This explanation must be sought in the process of collective definition. If sociological theory is to be grounded in knowledge of the empirical world of social problems, it must heed and respect the nature of that empirical world.

2

Social Problems
as Claims-Making Activities

Malcolm Spector
John I. Kitsuse

We want to define the subject matter of the sociology of social problems so that a researcher may carry through the analysis with the same reasonable procedure as the student of work and occupations. Just as the study of occupations examines how people earn their living, the study of social problems must look at how people define social problems. If a sociologist of occupations studying prostitution would look for people earning their livings at it, the sociologist of social problems would look for people engaged in defining (or promoting) the prostitution problem. The student of occupations sets out to describe work activity, elaborating its various forms and organization, and inventing concepts to make sense of and explain its variations. In the same way, the student of social problems should discover the nature of social problem activities and develop concepts that will most clearly and succinctly account for their special character. In each case, a distinctive kind of activity is singled out for attention: in the former case, the technical term for the activity is *work*. In the latter case, we must propose, define, and elaborate the technical term which we call claims-making activity.

A DEFINITION OF SOCIAL PROBLEMS

Our definition of social problems focuses on the process by which members of a society define a putative condition as a social problem. Thus, we define social problems as *the activities of individuals or groups making assertions of grievances and claims with respect to some putative conditions.* The emergence of a social problem is contingent upon the organization of activities asserting the need for eradicating, ameliorating, or otherwise changing some condition. *The central problem for a theory of social problems is to account for the emergence, nature, and maintenance of claims-making and responding activities.* Such a theory should address the activities of any group making claims on others for ameliorative action, material remuneration, alleviation of social, political, legal, or economic disadvantage.

Let us comment briefly on the word *putative* in the above definition. The dictionary defines this word as "reputed, hypothesized, or inferred." We use the word to emphasize that any given claim or complaint is about a condition *alleged* to exist, rather than about a condition whose existence we, as sociologists, are willing to verify or certify. That is, in focusing attention on the claims-making process, we set aside the question of whether those claims are true or false. . . .

We are interested in constructing a theory of claims-making activities, not a theory of conditions. Thus, the significance of objective conditions for us is *the assertions made about them*, not the validity of those assertions as judged from some independent standpoint, as for example, that of a scientist. To guard against the tendency to slip back into an analysis of the condition, we assert that even the existence of the condition itself is irrelevant to and outside of our analysis. We are not concerned whether or not the imputed condition exists. If the alleged condition were a complete hoax—a fabrication—we would maintain a noncommittal stance toward it unless those to whom the claim were addressed initiated their own analysis and uncovered it as a hoax.

Having stated the matter in the most extreme, and seemingly unreasonable, fashion, let us try to make it appear more sensible. Some objection to this position may stem from the fact that certain conditions do exist in the real world—out there. Objections may also be based on the view that some putative conditions appear to be just the phenomena that sociologists are trained to discover and verify. Let us discuss the second point first.

Suppose the following claims are made by three different groups:

1. The admission policy of Paramount University Medical School systematically discriminates against female and minority applicants; thus it violates affirmative action guidelines.
2. The water in Brown River is polluted and constitutes an acute health hazard for the city's residents.
3. Interplanetary beings have landed and established bases in the remote mountain areas of Wyoming. They are preparing a massive strike against the United States.

A sociologist might feel competent to make a direct assessment of the validity of the first group's assertion, refer the second to a natural scientist, and assert that the claims of the third group are groundless, perhaps investigating the *activities* of this group as an instance of collective delusion. But let us phrase each of these questions differently: Is the admission policy of Paramount University a social problem? Is water quality of the Brown River a social problem? Is the existence of interplanetary visitors a social problem? Phrased in this way, the verification of assertions about conditions is not a fundamental aspect of the sociologist's analysis of social problems. On what theoretical grounds are the facts of some conditions investigated and others dismissed as nonexistent? It would rarely occur to the sociologist to independently attempt to verify the alleged pollution of the river; still less to attempt to objectively confirm a claim about an interplanetary invasion. The fact that the sociologist has become qualified to certify the factual character of *some* claims about conditions does not provide the theoretical warrant for the view that certification of claims is a fundamental feature of social problems analysis. Yet, if the subject matter of social problems is claims-making activity, the *factual basis* of assertions about racist or sexist policies of medical schools is not any more relevant to their status as social problems than the factual basis of assertions about interplanetary invasions. . . .

On these grounds, it is not such an extreme position to urge that sociologists of social problems set aside the issue of the objective basis of alleged conditions, even to the extent of remaining indifferent to their existence. Does this mean that we maintain such conditions do not exist, or that the sociologist or any other scientist should not attempt to document their existence and study their causes? Not at all. Whatever the factual basis of the various conditions imputed to exist, the claims-making and responding activities themselves are the subject matter of the sociology of social problems. We contend that these activities exist, and can be documented and analyzed from a sociological perspective.

CLAIMS-MAKING ACTIVITIES

The activity of making claims, complaints, or demands for change is the core of what we call social problems activities. Claims-making is always a form of interaction: a demand made by one party to another that something be done about some putative condition. A claim implies that the claimant has a right at least to be heard, if not to receive satisfaction. A letter from a constituent to a member of Congress urging support of some measure is a claim. So is a petition to the city council to fix potholes in the streets. So, also, is a resolution of a professional body calling for the end of a war in Indochina. Mundanely, claims-making consists of demanding services, filling out forms, lodging complaints, filing lawsuits, calling press conferences, writing letters of protest, passing resolutions, publishing exposés, placing ads in newspapers, supporting or opposing some governmental practice or policy, setting up picket lines or boycotts; these are integral features of social and political life. . . .

All those who involve themselves in these activities participate in the process of defining social problems. This may include a great variety of persons such as protest groups or moral crusaders who make demands and complaints; the officials or agencies to whom such complaints are directed; members of the media who publicize and disseminate news about such activities (as well as participate in them); commissions of inquiry; legislative bodies and executive or administrative agencies that respond to claims-making constituents; members of the helping professions, such as physicians, psychiatrists, social workers; and sometimes, social scientists who contribute to the definition and development of social problems.

Usually it is not difficult for the sociologist to recognize and classify activities cited as claims because *they are so recognized and interpreted by members as well.* That is, claims are a common-sense category, understood by members of a society and often associated with such terms as demands, complaints, gripes, and requests.

There are several reasons to stress that the technical term *claim* is also a member's category. However routine and ordinary an event may be, the participants in an activity must construct its meaning as a claim. A complaint presented in the most conventional manner may sometimes be interpreted and dismissed as senseless, just as a bizarre act, such as the delivery of an amputated human ear, may be interpreted as a terrorist's demand for the release of political prisoners. Or, what might be presented as a claim from the participant's point of view may be defined by institutional authorities as symptoms of mental illness or insanity. Such a construction can effectively defuse the claims-making activity, relegating it to surveillance and control by law enforcement or psychiatric agencies.

Other examples more forcefully demonstrate the socially constructed nature of the category "claim." Activities outside of the usual conventions may be used to make claims, or may be interpreted as claims, whatever their intent. Members may succeed or fail to sustain a definition of these events as an instance of claims-making. For example, a journalist writes a story on the filthy conditions found in the kitchens of local restaurants. While the story neither explicitly criticizes the health department or the proprietors of the restaurants, nor calls for action to be taken, both health officials and proprietors may respond to the charges and demands that they see as implicit in the story. The journalist's reportage is interpreted as a claim.

On the other hand, when firefighters are ambushed by snipers at a fire set to lure them to a particular location, the act may be attributed to or claimed by a local organization. But it may also remain undefined and unclaimed. If the group engaging in such activities issues no communication claiming credit or making demands, on what basis could we say that they were "calling on another for something due?" In such instances, the press, police, and public officials often attempt to make sense of events by attributing them to some known terrorist group. Thus, a claim may be created by observers and added to the actual events in which no claims were, in fact, presented. In the same way, groups may claim credit for an event (a skyjacking, for example) where there is no evidence that they were actually responsible for it. . . .

What kinds of questions might we ask about claims-making activities? First, let us consider what a claim consists of, what its elemental parts are. A claim is a demand that one party makes upon another. How do these two parties get together so that one is the claimant and the other the recipient of the claim? Second, how does the claimant decide where to lodge a complaint? Given the vast array of jurisdictions, authorities, and referral networks, this selection or funneling process itself is problematic and requires our attention. We cannot take for granted, or being our analysis with, the claimant and respondent interacting in claims-making activity. Much work has already taken place before they come together. Claimants construct notions about the causes of the conditions they find onerous, assign blame, and locate officials responsible for rectifying the conditions. Alternatively, claimants may decide that no one is in charge of doing something about the condition, and *that* may become the substance of their complaints. Consequently, they may seek out those they think are in charge of creating and assigning such responsibility. Third, they may ask who benefits from the condition in question and look for vested interests—groups that actively perpetuate and profit from it or support it for personal pleasure or convenience. These options, not necessarily mutually exclusive, may lead to different strategies about how the claim should be phrased and to whom it should be directed.

Value judgments lead people to experience conditions as offensive and to define them as social problems. Social problems activities are heavily freighted with morality and values. People making claims often express indignation, phrasing their claims as demands for more equitable, orderly, humane, or convenient arrangements. Claims are normative phenomena. They are statements about conditions that *ought not* to exist; something *ought* to be done to improve conditions. The concept of values, therefore, is clearly relevant for the analysis of social problems. . . .

To ask what are the effective causes of social problems, or what keeps social problems activities going, is to ask what sustains the participants in these activities. Some groups may be led to the social problems arena through moral indignation, for example, humanitarian reformers, crusaders of various persuasion, and garden-variety "do-gooders." However, not all social problems activities spring from this sort of disinterested, principled activity. Humanitarian crusaders by definition set out to improve the lot of disadvantaged others. They are not themselves victims of the conditions they set out to ameliorate. When those who complain *claim to be* the victims of the conditions, we call them an *interest group.* Thus, interest groups are those who claim to have something to gain or lose over and above the way everyone else in the society might be affected. For example, in their efforts to decriminalize homosexual acts, the Gay Activists Alliance is involved in legislative processes as an interest group, while legal, church, and other organizations in support of such legislation do so on disinterested, principled grounds. . . .

We define interests as *any real and material advantage or stake that an individual or group claims, or is imputed by others to have, in the outcome of activity.* The scope of this definition is intentionally broad to suggest that almost any aspect or object in social life may become the focal point for social problems activity. Not all groups that enter the social problems arena do so to defend some interest; their impetus may be altruistic. Similarly, not all activities of interest groups are directed toward defining social problems. For example, a significant portion of the work of the National Association for the Advancement of Colored People, a group that is frequently involved in claims-making activity, deals with organizational problems as raising funds for scholarships, recruiting members, and planning their annual convention.

Groups defining conditions as social problems may be sustained by interests or values, or a combination of them. Some of the interesting varieties might include the following:

1. Value groups find that as they raise a condition as a social problem, they gain as allies other groups who have a vested interest in their claim.

2. Interest groups may find that public debate must take place in terms of values or ideals. Thus, in order to present claims effectively or argue a position, groups must acquire a set of values that legitimate their claims. Clinical psychologists, pressing their claims against the psychiatric profession's monopoly over the practice of psychotherapy, may find their case strengthened by a statement of their concern about the lack of attention and service given to the mental health of the poor.

3. A protest group may find a convenient overlap between their interest and their publicly espoused values. That is, their claims as an interest group are easily articulated with statements of values to legitimate those claims. An adoption agency concerned about the encroachment onto their domain of other organizations is able to espouse the importance of professional counseling services for unmarried mothers in the adoption process, services that only this agency may be organized and staffed to provide.

4. Alternatively, a group may find itself cross-pressured when its interest requires it to sacrifice or ignore some publicly stated value, or its values may require it to work against its own interests. School administrators who are doctrinally committed to integrated education sometimes find themselves compromising these values while opposing school bussing in the name of "orderly" educational processes.

5. To the extent that a disinterested value-oriented group is successful in its activity, it may develop various interests to protect: organizations, careers, reputations. It may face a crisis of the "routinization of disinterest" when others charge they are self-serving, rather than altruistic. An anticruelty-to-animals group may be reluctant to investigate charges that pet-shop owners who contribute money to their organization fail to maintain health standards in the care of the animals they sell.

This distinction between interested and value-oriented social problems activities goes beyond the bald assertion that value judgments cause people to define conditions as social problems. It provides a place for pure, value-driven participants while, at the same time, it allows that many engaged in social problems activities are there to defend vested interests. In addition, it provides for the possibility that groups may disingenuously espouse value positions and take pragmatic views to protect their interests. Values and interests constitute rival or complementary explanations of the activities of social problem groups or individuals.

Claims express demands within a moral universe. Values are those statements that express *the grounds or the basis* of the complaint. They are used to justify a demand, to explain not simply what is wrong, but why it is wrong. Like motives, values are the resource in the language; they are used to justify a line of conduct. In social problems, values are invoked to justify claims or demands, or express dissatisfaction, indignation, or outrage. They are answers to the questions, "Why does this make you angry?" or, "What's wrong with the way we handle this now?" Viewed in this way, values are part of the data of social problems rather than explanations of them. To say that social problem activities are heavily freighted with values is not to say that values cause social problems, or that values lead people to define conditions as problems. Rather, values are a constituent feature of social problems activities that are observable in what participants do and say.

A wide choice of values may be used to articulate a claim. These may be chosen very strategically according to the agency, organization, or institution to which the claim is directed. Strategy in the choice of values may rest on an analysis of the previous success of phasing a complaint in specified ways. For example, a group protesting the firing of a popular professor might debate whether they should phrase their claim as a question of academic freedom, civil liberties, racism, sexism, or due process. Each of these is a value position that might be used to legitimate a particular claim. None is inherent in the event that activated their protest; thus, none is the cause of its definition as a problem. Vocabularies of values to express dissatisfactions provide participants with a range of choices, choices that are not mechanically determined by the condition itself.

3

Social Structure and Anomie

Robert K. Merton

There persists a notable tendency in sociological theory to attribute the malfunctioning of social structure primarily to those of man's imperious biological drives which are not adequately restrained by social control. In this view, the social order is solely a device for "impulse management" and the "social processing" of tensions. These impulses which break through social control, be it noted, are held to be biologically derived. Nonconformity is assumed to be rooted in original nature.[1] Conformity is by implication the result of an utilitarian calculus or unreasoned conditioning. This point of view, whatever its other deficiencies, clearly begs one question. It provides no basis for determining the nonbiological conditions which induce deviations from prescribed patterns of conduct. In this paper, it will be suggested that certain phases of social structure generate the circumstances in which infringement of social codes constitutes a "normal" response.[2]

The conceptual scheme to be outlined is designed to provide a coherent, systematic approach to the study of sociocultural sources of deviate behavior. Our primary aim lies in discovering how some social structures *exert a definite pressure* upon certain persons in the society to engage in nonconformist rather than conformist conduct. The many ramifications of the scheme cannot all be discussed; the problems mentioned outnumber those explicitly treated.

Among the elements of social and cultural structure, two are important for our purposes. These are analytically separable although they merge imperceptibly in concrete situations. The first consists of culturally defined goals, purposes, and interests. It comprises a frame of aspirational reference. These goals are more or less inte-

From American Sociological Review, Vol. 3, October 1938, pp. 672-682.
Reprinted by permission of the author.

grated and involve varying degrees of prestige and sentiment. They constitute a basic, but not the exclusive, component of what Linton aptly has called "designs for group living." Some of these cultural aspirations are related to the original drives of man, but they are not determined by them. The second phase of the social structure defines, regulates, and controls the acceptable modes of achieving these goals. Every social group invariably couples its scale of desired ends with moral or institutional regulation of permissible and required procedures for attaining these ends. These regulatory norms and moral imperatives do not necessarily coincide with technical or efficiency norms. Many procedures which from the standpoint of *particular individuals* would be most efficient in securing desired values, e.g., illicit oil-stock schemes, theft, fraud, are ruled out of the institutional area of permitted conduct. The choice of expedients is limited by the institutional norms.

To say that these two elements, culture goals and institutional norms, operate jointly is not to say that the ranges of alternative behaviors and aims bear some constant relation to one another. The emphasis upon certain goals may vary independently of the degree of emphasis upon institutional means. There may develop a disproportionate, at times, a virtually exclusive, stress upon the value of specific goals, involving relatively slight concern with the institutionally appropriate modes of attaining these goals. The limiting case in this direction is reached when the range of alternative procedures is limited only by technical rather than institutional considerations. Any and all devices which promise attainment of the all important goal would be permitted in this hypothetical polar case.[3] This constitutes one type of cultural malintegration. A second polar type is found in groups where activities originally conceived as instrumental are transmuted into ends in themselves. The original purposes are forgotten and ritualistic adherence to institutionally prescribed conduct becomes virtually obsessive.[4] Stability is largely ensured while change is flouted. The range of alternative behaviors is severely limited. There develops a tradition-bound, sacred society characterized by neophobia. The occupational psychosis of the bureaucrat may be cited as a case in point. Finally, there are the intermediate types of groups where a balance between culture goals and institutional means is maintained. These are the significantly integrated and relatively stable, though changing, groups.

An effective equilibrium between the two phases of the social structure is maintained as long as satisfactions accrue to individuals who conform to both constraints, viz., satisfactions from the achievement of the goals and satisfactions emerging directly from the institutionally canalized modes of striving to attain these ends. Success, in such equilibrated cases, is twofold. Success is reckoned in terms of the product and in terms of the process, in terms of the outcome and in terms of activities. Continuing satisfactions must derive from sheer *participation* in a competitive order as well as from eclipsing one's competitors if the order itself is to be sustained. The occasional sacrifices involved in institutionalized conduct must be compensated by socialized rewards. The distribution of statuses and roles through competition must be so organized that positive incentives for conformity to roles and adherence to status obligations are provided *for every position* within the distributive order. Aberrant conduct, therefore, may be viewed as a symptom of dissociation between culturally defined aspirations and socially structured means.

Of the types of groups which result from the independent variation of the two phases of the social structure, we shall be primarily concerned with the first, namely, that involving a disproportionate accent on goals. This statement must be recast in a proper perspective. In no group is there an absence of regulatory codes governing conduct, yet groups do vary in the degree to which these folkways, mores, and institutional controls are effectively integrated with the more diffuse goals which are part of the culture matrix. Emotional convictions may cluster about the complex of socially acclaimed ends, meanwhile shifting their support from the culturally defined implementation of these ends. As we shall see, certain aspects of the social structure may generate countermores and antisocial behavior precisely because of differential emphases on goals and regulations. In the extreme case, the latter may be so vitiated by the goal-emphasis that the range of behavior is limited only by considerations of technical expediency. The sole significant question then becomes, which available means is most efficient in netting the socially approved value?[5] The technically most feasible procedure, whether legitimate or not, is preferred to the institutionally prescribed conduct. As this process continues, the integration of the society becomes tenuous and anomie ensues.

Thus, in competitive athletics, when the aim of victory is shorn of its institutional trappings and success in contests becomes construed as "winning the game" rather than "winning through circumscribed modes of activity," a premium is implicitly set upon the use of illegitimate but technically efficient means. The star of the opposing football team is surreptitiously slugged; the wrestler furtively incapacitates his opponent through ingenious but illicit techniques; university alumni covertly subsidize "students" whose talents are largely confined to the athletic field. The emphasis on the goal has so attenuated the satisfactions deriving from sheer participation in the competitive activity that these satisfactions are virtually confined to a successful outcome. Through the same process, tension generated by the desire to win in a poker game is relieved by successfully dealing oneself four aces, or, when the cult of success has become completely dominant, by sagaciously shuffling the cards in a game of solitaire. The faint twinge of uneasiness in the last instance and the surreptitious nature of public delicts indicate clearly that the institutional rules of the game *are known* to those who evade them, but that the emo-

tional supports of these rules are largely vitiated by cultural exaggeration of the success-goal.[6] They are microcosmic images of the social macrocosm.

Of course, this process is not restricted to the realm of sport. The process whereby exaltation of the end generates a *literal demoralization*, i.e., a deinstitutionalization, of the means is one which characterizes many[7] groups in which the two phases of the social structure are not highly integrated. The extreme emphasis upon the accumulation of wealth as a symbol of success[8] in our own society militates against the competely effective control of institutionally regulated modes of acquiring a fortune.[9] Fraud, corruption, vice, crime, in short, the entire catalogue of proscribed behavior, becomes increasingly common when the emphasis on the *culturally induced* success-goal becomes divorced from a coordinated institutional emphasis. This observation is of crucial theoretical importance in examining the doctrine that antisocial behavior most frequently derives from biological drives breaking through the restraints imposed by society. The difference is one between a strictly utilitarian interpretation which conceives man's ends as random and an analysis which finds these ends deriving from the basic values of the culture.[10]

Our analysis can scarcely stop at this juncture. We must turn to other aspects of the social structure if we are to deal with the social genesis of the varying rates and types of deviate behavior characteristic of different societies. Thus far, we have sketched three ideal types of social orders constituted by distinctive patterns of relations between culture ends and means. Turning from these types of *culture patterning*, we find five logically possible, alternative modes of adjustment or adaptation *by individuals* within the culture-bearing society or group.[11] These are schematically presented in the following table, where (**+**) signifies "acceptance," (**−**) signifies "elimination" and (**±**) signifies "rejection and substitution of new goals and standards."

Our discussion of the relation between

		Culture Goals	Institutionalized Means
I.	Conformity	+	+
II.	Innovation	+	−
III.	Ritualism	−	+
IV.	Retreatism	−	−
V.	Rebellion[12]	±	±

these alternative responses and other phases of the social structure must be prefaced by the observation that persons may shift from one alternative to another as they engage in different social activities. These categories refer to role adjustments in specific situations, not to personality *in toto*. To treat the development of this process in various spheres of conduct would introduce a complexity unmanageable within the confines of this paper. For this reason, we shall be concerned primarily with economic activity in the broad sense, "the production, exchange, distribution and consumption of goods and services" in our competitive society, wherein wealth has taken on a highly symbolic cast. Our task is to search out some of the factors which exert pressure upon individuals to engage in certain of these logically possible alternative responses. This choice, as we shall see, is far from random.

In every society, Adaptation I (conformity to both culture goals and means) is the most common and widely diffused. Were this not so, the stability and continuity of the society could not be maintained. The mesh of expectancies which constitutes every social order is sustained by the modal behavior of its members falling within the first category. Conventional role behavior oriented toward the basic values of the groups is the rule rather than the exception. It is this fact alone which permits us to speak of a human aggregate as comprising a group or society.

Conversely, Adaptation IV (rejection of goals and means) is the least common. Persons who "adjust" (or maladjust) in this fashion are, strictly speaking, *in* the society but not *of* it. Sociologically, these constitute the true "aliens." Not sharing the common

frame of orientation, they can be included within the societal population merely in a fictional sense. In this category are *some* of the activities of psychotics, psychoneurotics, chronic autists, pariahs, outcasts, vagrants, vagabonds, tramps, chronic drunkards and drug addicts.[13] These have relinquished, in certain spheres of activity, the culturally defined goals, involving complete aim-inhibition in the polar case, and their adjustments are not in accord with institutional norms. This is not to say that in some cases the source of their behavioral adjustments is not in part the very social structure which they have in effect repudiated, nor that their very existence within a social area does not constitute a problem for the socialized population.

This mode of "adjustment" occurs, as far as structural sources are concerned, when both the culture goals and institutionalized procedures have been assimilated thoroughly by the individual and imbued with affect and high positive value, but where those institutionalized procedures which promise a measure of successful attainment of the goals are not available to the individual. In such instances, there results a twofold mental conflict insofar as the moral obligation for adopting institutional means conflicts with the pressure to resort to illegitimate means (which may attain the goal) and inasmuch as the individual is shut off from means which are both legitimate *and* effective. The competitive order is maintained, but the frustrated and handicapped individual who cannot cope with this order drops out. Defeatism, quietism and resignation are manifested in escape mechanisms which ultimately lead the individual to "escape" from the requirements of the society. It is an expedient which arises from continued failure to attain the goal by legitimate measures and from an inability to adopt the illegitimate route because of internalized prohibitions and institutionalized compulsives, *during which process the supreme value of the success-goal has as yet not been renounced.* The conflict is resolved by eliminating *both* precipitating elements, the goals and means.

The escape is complete, the conflict is eliminated and the individual is asocialized.

Be it noted that where frustration derives from the inaccessibility of effective institutional means for attaining economic or any other type of highly valued "success," that Adaptations II, III and V (innovation, ritualism and rebellion) are also possible. The result will be determined by the particular personality, and thus, the *particular* cultural background, involved. Inadequate socialization will result in the innovation response whereby the conflict and frustration are eliminated by relinquishing the institutional means and retaining the success-aspiration; an extreme assimilation of institutional demands will lead to ritualism wherein the goal is dropped as beyond one's reach but conformity to the mores persists; and rebellion occurs when emancipation from the reigning standards, due to frustration or to marginalist perspectives, leads to the attempt to introduce a "new social order."

Our major concern is with the illegitimacy adjustment. This involves the use of conventionally proscribed but frequently effective means of attaining at least the simulacrum of culturally defined success— wealth, power, and the like. As we have seen, this adjustment occurs when the individual has assimilated the cultural emphasis on success without equally internalizing the morally prescribed norms governing means for its attainment. The question arises, Which phases of our social structure predispose toward this mode of adjustment? We may examine a concrete instance, effectively analyzed by Lohman,[14] which provides a clue to the answer. Lohman has shown that specialized areas of vice in the near north side of Chicago constitute a "normal" response to a situation where the cultural emphasis upon pecuniary success has been absorbed, but where there is little access to conventional and legitimate means for attaining such success. The conventional occupational opportunities of persons in this area are almost completely limited to manual labor. Given our cultural stigmatization of manual labor, and its correlate, the pres-

tige of white collar work, it is clear that the result is a strain toward innovational practices. The limitation of opportunity to unskilled labor and the resultant low income can not compete *in terms of conventional standards of achievement* with the high income from organized vice.

For our purposes, this situation involves two important features. First, such antisocial behavior is in a sense "called forth" by certain conventional values of the culture *and* by the class structure involving differential access to the approved opportunities for legitimate, prestige-bearing pursuit of the culture goals. The lack of high integration between the means-and-end elements of the cultural pattern and the particular class structure combine to favor a heightened frequency of antisocial conduct in such groups. The second consideration is of equal significance. Recourse to the first of the alternative responses, legitimate effort, is limited by the fact that actual advance toward desired success-symbols through conventional channels is, despite our persisting open-class ideology,[15] relatively rare and difficult for those handicapped by little formal education and few economic resources. The dominant pressure of group standards of success is, therefore, on the gradual attenuation of legitimate, but by and large ineffective, strivings and the increasing use of illegitimate, but more or less effective, expedients of vice and crime. The cultural demands made on persons in this situation are incompatible. On the one hand, they are asked to orient their conduct toward the prospect of accumulating wealth and on the other, they are largely denied effective opportunities to do so institutionally. The consequences of such structural inconsistency are psychopathological personality, and/or antisocial conduct, and/or revolutionary activities. The equilibrium between culturally designed means and ends becomes highly unstable with the progressive emphasis on attaining the prestige-laden ends by any means whatsoever. Within this context, Capone represents the triumph of amoral intelligence over morally prescribed "failure," when the channels of vertical mobility are closed or narrowed[16] *in a society which places a high premium on economic affluence and social ascent for* all *its members.*[17]

This last qualification is of primary importance. It suggests that other phases of the social structure besides the extreme emphasis on pecuniary success, must be considered if we are to understand the social sources of antisocial behavior. A high frequency of deviate behavior is not generated simply by "lack of opportunity" or by this exaggerated pecuniary emphasis. A comparatively rigidified class structure, a feudalistic or caste order, may limit such opportunities far beyond the point which obtains in our society today. It is only when a system of cultural values extols, virtually above all else, certain *common* symbols of success *for the population at large* while its social structure rigorously restricts or completely eliminates access to approved modes of acquiring these symbols *for a considerable part of the same population*, that antisocial behavior ensues on a considerable scale. In other words, our egalitarian ideology denies by implication the existence of noncompeting groups and individuals in the pursuit of pecuniary success. The same body of success-symbols is held to be desirable for all. These goals are held to *transcend class lines*, not to be bounded by them, yet the actual social organization is such that there exist class differentials in the accessibility of these *common* success-symbols. Frustration and thwarted aspiration lead to the search for avenues of escape from a culturally induced intolerable situation; or unrelieved ambition may eventuate in illicit attempts to acquire the dominant values.[18] The American stress on pecuniary success and ambitiousness for all thus invites exaggerated anxieties, hostilities, neuroses and antisocial behavior.

This theoretical analysis may go far toward explaining the varying correlations between crime and poverty.[19] Poverty is not an isolated variable. It is one in a complex of interdependent social and cultural variables. When viewed in such a context, it represents quite different states of affairs. Poverty as such, and consequent limitation of opportunity, are not sufficient to induce a conspicuously high rate of criminal behavior. Even the often mentioned "poverty in the midst of plenty" will not necessarily lead to this result. Only insofar as poverty and associated disadvantages in competition for the culture values approved for *all* members of the society is linked with the assimilation of a cultural emphasis on monetary accumulation as a symbol of success is antisocial conduct a "normal" outcome. Thus, poverty is less highly correlated with crime in southeastern Europe than in the United States. The possibilities of vertical mobility in these European areas would seem to be fewer than in this country, so that neither poverty *per se* nor its association with limited opportunity is sufficient to account for the varying correlations. It is only when the full configuration is considered, poverty, limited opportunity and a commonly shared system of success symbols, that we can explain the higher association between poverty and crime in our society than in others where rigidified class structures is coupled with *differential class symbols of achievement.*

In societies such as our own, then, the pressure of prestige-bearing success tends to eliminate the effective social constraint over means employed to this end. "The-end-justifies-the-means" doctrine becomes a guiding tenet for action when the cultural structure unduly exalts the end and the social organization unduly limits possible recourse to approved means. Otherwise put, this notion and associated behavior reflect a lack of cultural coordination. In international relations, the effects of this lack of integration are notoriously apparent. An emphasis upon national power is not readily coordinated with an inept organization of legitimate, i.e., internationally defined and accepted, means for attaining this goal. The result is a tendency toward the abrogation of international law, treaties become scraps of paper, "undeclared warfare" serves as a technical evasion, the bombing of civilian populations is rationalized,[20] just as the same societal situation induces the same sway of illegitimacy among individuals.

The social order we have described necessarily produces this "strain toward dissolution." The pressure of such an order is upon outdoing one's competitors. The choice of means within the ambit of institutional control will persist as long as the sentiments supporting a competitive system, i.e., deriving from the possibility of outranking competitors and hence enjoying the favorable response of others, are distributed throughout the entire system of activities and are not confined merely to the final result. A stable social structure demands a balanced distribution of affect among its various segments. When there occurs a shift of emphasis from the satisfactions deriving from competition itself to almost exclusive concern with successful competition, the resultant stress leads to the breakdown of the regulatory structure.[21] With the resulting attenuation of the institutional imperatives, there occurs an approximation of the situation erroneously held by utilitarians to be typical of society generally wherein calculations of advantage and fear of punishment are the sole regulating agencies. In such situations, as Hobbes observed, force and fraud come to constitute the sole virtues in view of their efficiency in attaining goals— which were for him, of course, not culturally derived.

It should be apparent that the foregoing discussion is not pitched on a moralistic plane. Whatever the sentiments of the writer or reader concerning the ethical desirability of coordinating the means-and-goals phases of the social structure, one must agree that lack of such coordination leads to anomie. Insofar as one of the most general functions of social organization is to provide a basis for calculability and regularity of behavior, it is increasingly limited in effectiveness as these elements of the structure become dissociated. At the extreme, predictability virtually disappears and what may be properly termed cultural chaos or anomie intervenes.

This statement, being brief, is also incomplete. It has not included an exhaustive treatment of the various structural elements which predispose toward one rather than another of the alternative responses open to individuals; it has neglected, but not denied the relevance of, the factors determining the specific incidence of these responses; it has not enumerated the various concrete responses which are constituted by combinations of specific values of the analytical variables; it has omitted, or included only by implication, any consideration of the social functions performed by illicit responses; it has not tested the full explanatory power of the analytical scheme by examining a large number of group variations in the frequency of deviate and conformist behavior; it has not adequately dealt with rebellious conduct which seeks to refashion the social framework radically; it has not examined the relevance of cultural conflict for an analysis of culture-goal and institutional-means malintegration. It is suggested that these and related problems may be profitably analyzed by this scheme.

NOTES

1. E.g., Ernest Jones, *Social Aspects of Psychoanalysis*, 28, London, 1924. If the Freudian notion is a variety of the "original sin" dogma, then the interpretation advanced in this paper may be called the doctrine of "socially derived sin."

2. "Normal" in the sense of a culturally oriented, if not approved, response. This statement does not deny the relevance of biological and personality differences which may be significantly involved in the *incidence* of deviate conduct. Our focus of interest is the social and cultural matrix; hence we abstract from other factors. It is in this sense, I take it, that James S. Plant speaks of the "normal reaction of normal people to abnormal conditions." See his *Personality and the Cultural Pattern*, 248, New York, 1937.

3. Contemporary American culture has been said to tend in this direction. See André Siegfried, *America Comes of Age*, 26–37, New York, 1927. The alleged extreme (?) emphasis on the goals of monetary success and material prosperity leads to dominant concern with technological

and social instruments designed to produce the desired result, inasmuch as institutional controls become of secondary importance. In such a situation, innovation flourishes as the *range of means* employed is broadened. In a sense, then, there occurs the paradoxical emergence of "materialists" from an "idealistic" orientation. Cf. Durkheim's analysis of the cultural conditions which predispose toward crime and innovation, both of which are aimed toward efficiency, not moral norms. Durkheim was one of the first to see that "contrairement aux idées courantes le criminel n'apparait plus comme un etre radicalement insociable, comme une sorte d'element parasitaire, de corps etranger et inassimilable, introduit au sein de la societe; c'est un agent regulier de la vie sociale." See *Les Regles de la Methode Sociologique*, 86–89, Paris, 1927.

4. Such ritualism may be associated with a mythology which rationalizes these actions so that they appear to retain their status as means, but the dominant pressure is in the direction of strict ritualistic conformity, irrespective of such rationalizations. In this sense, ritual has proceeded farthest when such rationalizations are not even called forth.

5. In this connection, one may see the relevance of Elton Mayo's paraphrase of the title of Tawney's well known book, "Actually the problem *is not that of the sickness of an acquisitive society; it is that of the acquisitiveness of a sick society.*" *Human Problems of an Industrial Civilization*, 153, New York, 1933. Mayo deals with the process through which wealth comes to be a symbol of social achievement. He sees this as arising from a state of anomie. We are considering the unintegrated monetary-success goal as an element in producing anomie. A complete analysis would involve both phases of this system of interdependent variables.

6. It is unlikely that interiorized norms are completely eliminated. Whatever residuum persists will induce personality tensions and conflict. The process involves a certain degree of ambivalence. A manifest rejection of the institutional norms is coupled with some latent retention of their emotional correlates. "Guilt feelings," "sense of sin," "pangs of conscience" are obvious manifestations of this unrelieved tension; symbolic adherence to the nominally repudiated values or rationalizations constitute a more subtle variety of tensional release.

7. "Many," and not all, unintegrated groups, for the reason already mentioned. In groups where the primary emphasis shifts to institutional means, i.e., when the range of alternatives is very limited, the outcome is a type of ritualism rather than anomie.

8. Money has several peculiarities which render it particularly apt to become a symbol of prestige divorced from institutional controls. As Simmel emphasized, money is highly abstract and impersonal. However acquired, through fraud or institutionally, it can be used to purchase the same goods and services. The anonymity of metropolitan culture, in conjunction with this peculiarity of money, permits wealth, the sources of which may be unknown to the community in which the plutocrat lives, to serve as a symbol of status.

9. The emphasis upon wealth as a success-symbol is possibly reflected in the use of the term "fortune" to refer to a stock of accumulated wealth. This meaning becomes common in the late sixteenth century (Spenser and Shakespeare). A similar usage of the Latin *fortuna* comes into prominence during the first century B.C. Both these periods were marked by the rise to prestige and power of the "bourgeoisie."

10. See Kingsley Davis, "Mental Hygiene and the Class Structure," *Psychiatry*, 1928, I, esp. 62–63; Talcott Parsons, *The Structure of Social Action*, 59–60, New York, 1937.

11. This is a level intermediate between the two planes distinguished by Edward Sapir; namely, culture patterns and personal habit systems. See his "Contribution of Psychiatry to an Understanding of Behavior in Society," *Amer. J. Sociol.*, 1937, 42:862–70.

12. This fifth alternative is on a plane clearly different from that of the others. It represents a *transitional* response which seeks to *institutionalize* new procedures oriented toward revamped cultural goals shared by the members of the society. It thus involves efforts to *change* the existing structure rather than to perform accommodative actions *within* this structure, and introduces additional problems with which we are not at the moment concerned.

13. Obviously, this is an elliptical statement. These individuals may maintain some orientation to the values of their particular differentiated groupings within the larger society or, in part, of the conventional society itself. Insofar as they do so, their conduct cannot be classified in the "passive rejection" category (IV). Nels Anderson's description of the behavior and attitudes of the bum, for example,

can readily be recast in terms of our analytical scheme. See *The Hobo*, 93–98, *et passim*, Chicago, 1923.

14. Joseph D. Lohman, "The Participant Observer in Community Studies," *Amer. Sociol. Rev.*, 1937, 2:890–98.

15. The shifting historical role of this ideology is a profitable subject for exploration. The "office-boy-to-president" stereotype was once in approximate accord with the facts. Such vertical mobility was probably more common then than now, when the class structure is more rigid. (See the following note.) The ideology largely persists, however, possibly because it still performs a useful function for maintaining the *status quo*. For insofar as it is accepted by the "masses," it constitutes a useful sop for those who might rebel against the entire structure, were this consoling hope removed. This ideology now serves to lessen the probability of Adaptation V. In short, the role of this notion has changed from that of an approximately valid empirical theorem to that of an ideology, in Mannheim's sense.

16. There is a growing body of evidence, though none of it is clearly conclusive, to the effect that our class structure is becoming rigidified and that vertical mobility is declining. Taussig and Joslyn found that American business leaders are being *increasingly* recruited from the upper ranks of our society. The Lynds have also found a "diminished chance to get ahead" for the working classes in Middletown. Manifestly, these objective changes are not alone significant; the individual's subjective evaluation of the situation is a major determinant of the response. The extent to which this change in opportunity for social mobility has been recognized by the least advantaged classes is still conjectural, although the Lynds present some suggestive materials. The writer suggests that a case in point is the increasing frequency of cartoons which observe in a tragi-comic vein that "my old man says everybody can't be President. He says if ya can get three days a week steady on W.P.A. work ya ain't doin' so bad either." See F. W. Taussig and C. S. Joslyn, *American Business Leaders*, New York, 1932; R. S. and H. M. Lynd, *Middletown in Transition*, 67 ff., chap. 12, New York, 1937.

17. The role of the Negro in this respect is of considerable theoretical interest. Certain elements of the Negro population have assimilated the dominant caste's values of pecuniary success and social advancement, but they also recognize that social ascent is at present restricted to their own caste almost exclusively. The pressures upon the Negro which would otherwise derive from the structural inconsistencies we have noticed are hence not identical with those upon lower class whites. See Kingsley Davis, *op. cit.*, 63; John Dollard, *Caste and Class in a Southern Town*, 66 ff., New Haven, 1936; Donald Young, *American Minority Peoples*, 581, New York, 1932.

18. The psychical coordinates of these processes have been partly establishes by the experimental evidence concerning *Ansbruchsniveaus* and levels of performance. See Kurt Lewin, *Vorsatz, Willie and Bedurfnis*, Berlin, 1926; N. F. Hoppe, "Erfolg und Misserfolg," *Psychol. Forschung*, 1930, 14:1–63; Jerome D. Frank, "Individual Differences in Certain Aspects of the Level of Aspiration," *Amer. J. Psychol.*, 1935, 47:119–28.

19. Standard criminology texts summarize the data in this field. Our scheme of analysis may serve to resolve some of the theoretical contradictions which P. A. Sorokin indicates. For example, "not everywhere nor always do the poor show a greater proportion of crime . . . many poorer countries have had less crime than the richer countries . . . The [economic] improvement in the second half of the nineteenth century, and the beginning of the twentieth, has not been followed by a decrease of crime." See his *Contemporary Sociological Theories*, 560–61, New York, 1928. The crucial point is, however, that poverty has varying social significance in different social structures, as we shall see. Hence, one would not expect a linear correlation between crime and poverty.

20. See M. W. Royse, *Aerial Bombardment and the International Regulation of War*, New York, 1928.

21. Since our primary concern is with the socio-cultural aspects of this problem, the psychological correlates have been only implicitly considered. See Karen Horney, *The Neurotic Personality of Our Time*, New York, 1937, for a psychological discussion of this process.

4

The Uses of Poverty:
The Poor Pay All

Herbert J. Gans

Some 20 years ago, Robert K. Merton applied the notion of functional analysis to explain the continuing though maligned existence of the urban political machine: If it continued to exist, perhaps it fulfilled latent—unintended or unrecognized—positive functions. Clearly it did. Merton pointed out how the political machine provided central authority to get things done when a decentralized local government could not act, humanized the services of the impersonal bureaucracy for fearful citizens, offered concrete help (rather than abstract law or justice) to the poor, and otherwise performed services needed or demanded by many people but considered unconventional or even illegal by formal public agencies.

Today, poverty is more maligned than the political machine ever was; yet it, too, is a persistent social phenomenon. Conse-quently, there may be some merit in applying functional analysis to poverty, in asking whether it also has positive functions that explain its persistence.

Merton defined functions as "those observed consequences [of a phenomenon] which make for the adaptation of adjustment of a given [social] system." I shall use a slightly different definition; instead of identifying functions for an entire social system, I shall identify them for the interest groups, socioeconomic classes, and other population aggregates with shared values that "inhabit" a social system. I suspect that in a modern heterogeneous society, few phenomena are functional or dysfunctional for the society as a whole, and that most result in benefits to some groups and costs to others. Nor are any phenomena indispensable; in most instances, one can suggest what Merton calls "functional alternatives" or equivalents for

Social Policy, published by Social Policy Corporation, New York, NY 10036.
Copyright 1971 by Social Policy Corporation.

them, i.e., other social patterns or policies that achieve the same positive functions but avoid the dysfunction.[1]

Associating poverty with positive functions seems at first glance to be unimaginable. Of course, the slumlord and the loan shark are commonly known to profit from the existence of poverty, but they are viewed as evil men, so their activities are classified among the dysfunctions of poverty. However, what is less often recognized, at least by the conventional wisdom, is that poverty also makes possible the existence or expansion of respectable professions and occupations, for example, penology, criminology, social work, and public health. More recently, the poor have provided jobs for professional and paraprofessional "poverty warriors," and for journalists and social scientists, this author concluded, who have supplied the information demanded by the revival of public interest in poverty.

Clearly, then, poverty and the poor may well satisfy a number of positive functions for many nonpoor groups in American society. I shall describe 13 such functions—economic, social, and political—that seem to me most significant.

THE FUNCTIONS OF POVERTY

First, the existence of poverty ensures that society's "dirty work" will be done. Every society has such work: physically dirty or dangerous, temporary, dead-end and underpaid, undignified, and menial jobs. Society can fill these jobs by paying higher wages than for "clean" work, or it can force people who have no other choice to do the dirty work—and at low wages. In America, poverty functions to provide a low-wage labor pool that is willing—or rather, unable to be *un*willing—to perform dirty work at low

---

[1]I shall henceforth abbreviate positive functions as functions and negative functions as dysfunctions. I shall also describe functions and dysfunctions, in the planner's terminology, as benefits and costs.

cost. Indeed, this function of the poor is so important that in some Southern states, welfare payments have been cut off during the summer months when the poor are needed to work in the fields. Moreover, much of the debate about the Negative Income Tax and the Family Assistance Plan has concerned their impact on the work incentive, by which is actually meant the incentive of the poor to do the needed dirty work if the wages therefrom are no larger than the income grant. Many economic activities that involve dirty work depend on the poor for their existence: restaurants, hospitals, parts of the garment industry, and "truck farming," among others, could not persist in their present form without the poor.

Second, because the poor are required to work at low wages, they subsidize a variety of economic activities that benefit the affluent. For example, domestics subsidize the upper-middle and upper classes, making life easier for their employers and freeing affluent women for a variety of professional, cultural, civic, and partying activities. Similarly, because the poor pay a higher proportion of their income in property and sales taxes, among others, they subsidize many state and local governmental services that benefit more affluent groups. In addition, the poor support innovation in medical practice as patients in teaching and research hospitals and as guinea pigs in medical experiments.

Third, poverty creates jobs for a number of occupations and professions that serve or "service" the poor, or protect the rest of society from them. As already noted, penology would be miniscule without the poor, as would the police. Other activities and groups that flourish because of the existence of poverty are the numbers game, the sale of heroin and cheap wines and liquors, pentecostal ministers, faith healers, prostitutes, pawn shops, and the peacetime army, which recruits its enlisted men mainly from among the poor.

Fourth, the poor buy goods others do not want and thus prolong the economic usefulness of such goods—day-old bread, fruit and vegetables that would otherwise have to be thrown out, secondhand clothes, and deteriorating automobiles and buildings. They also provide incomes for doctors, lawyers, teachers, and others who are too old, poorly trained, or incompetent to attract more affluent clients.

In addition to economic functions, the poor perform a number of social functions.

Fifth, the poor can be identified and punished as alleged or real deviants in order to uphold the legitimacy of conventional norms. To justify the desirability of hard work, thrift, honesty, and monogamy, for example, the defenders of these norms must be able to find people who can be accused of being lazy, spendthrift, dishonest, and promiscuous. Although there is some evidence that the poor are about as moral and law-abiding as anyone else, they are more likely than middle-class transgressors to be caught and punished when they participate in deviant acts. Moreover, they lack the political and cultural power to correct the stereotypes that other people hold of them and thus continue to be thought of as lazy, spendthrift, etc., by those who need living proof that moral deviance does not pay.

Sixth, and conversely, the poor offer vicarious participation to the rest of the population in the uninhibited sexual, alcoholic, and narcotic behavior in which they are alleged to participate and which, being freed from the constraints of affluence, they are often thought to enjoy more than the middle classes. Thus, many people—some social scientists included—believe that the poor not only are more given to uninhibited behavior (which may be true, although it is often motivated by despair more than by lack of inhibition), but derive more pleasure from it than affluent people (which research by Lee Rainwater, Walter Miller, and others shows to be patently untrue). However, whether the poor actually have more sex and enjoy it more is irrelevant; so long as middle-class people believe this to be true, they can participate in it vicariously when

instances are reported in factual or fictional form.

Seventh, the poor also serve a direct cultural function when culture created by or for them is adopted by the more affluent. The rich often collect artifacts from extinct folk cultures of poor people; and almost all Americans listen to the blues, Negro spirituals, and country music, which originated among the Southern poor. Recently they have enjoyed the rock styles that were born, like the Beatles, in the slums; and in the last year, poetry written by ghetto children has become popular in literary circles. The poor also serve as culture heroes, particularly, of course, to the left; but the hobo, the cowboy, the hipster, and the mythical prostitute with a heart of gold have performed this function for a variety of groups.

Eighth, poverty helps to guarantee the status of those who are not poor. In every hierarchical society someone has to be at the bottom; but in American society, in which social mobility is an important goal for many and people need to know where they stand, the poor function as a reliable and relatively permanent measuring rod for status comparisons. This is particularly true for the working class, whose politics is influenced by the need to maintain status distinctions between themselves and the poor, much as the aristocracy must find ways of distinguishing itself from the *nouveaux riches*.

Ninth, the poor also aid the upward mobility of groups just above them in the class hierarchy. Thus, a goodly number of Americans have entered the middle class through the profits earned from the provision of goods and services in the slums, including illegal or nonrespectable ones that upper-class and upper-middle-class businessmen shun because of their low prestige. As a result, members of almost every immigrant group have financed their upward mobility by providing slum housing, entertainment, gambling, narcotics, etc., to later arrivals—most recently to blacks and Puerto Ricans.

Tenth, the poor help to keep the aristocracy busy, thus justifying its continued existence. "Society" uses the poor as clients of settlement houses and beneficiaries of charity affairs; indeed, the aristocracy must have the poor to demonstrate its superiority over other elites who devote themselves to earning money.

Eleventh, the poor, being powerless, can be made to absorb the costs of change and growth in American society. During the nineteenth century, they did the backbreaking work that built the cities; today, they are pushed out of their neighborhoods to make room for "progress." Urban renewal projects to hold middle-class taxpayers in the city and expressways to enable suburbanites to commute downtown have typically been located in poor neighborhoods, since no other group will allow itself to be displaced. For the same reason, universities, hospitals, and civic centers also expand into land occupied by the poor. The major costs of the industrialization of agriculture have been borne by the poor, who are pushed off the land without recompense; and they have paid a large share of the human cost of the growth of American power overseas, for they have provided many of the foot soldiers for Vietnam and other wars.

Twelfth, the poor facilitate and stabilize the American political process. Because they vote and participate in politics less than other groups, the political system is often free to ignore them. Moreover, since they can rarely support Republicans, they often provide the Democrats with a captive constituency that has no other place to go. As a result, the Democrats can count on their votes, and be more responsive to voters—for example, the white working class—who might otherwise switch to the Republicans.

Thirteenth, the role of the poor in upholding conventional norms (see the *fifth* point, above) also has a significant political function. An economy based on the ideology of laissez-faire requires a deprived population that is allegedly unwilling to work or that can be considered inferior because it must accept charity or welfare in order to survive. Not only does the alleged moral deviancy of the poor reduce the moral pressure on the present political economy to eliminate poverty, but socialist alternatives can be made to look quite unattractive if those who will benefit most from them can be described as lazy, spendthrift, dishonest, and promiscuous.

THE ALTERNATIVES

I have described 13 of the more important functions poverty and the poor satisfy in American society, enough to support the functionalist thesis that poverty, like any other social phenomenon, survives in part because it is useful to society or some of its parts. This analysis is not intended to suggest that because it is often functional, poverty *should* exist, or that it *must* exist. For one thing, poverty has many more dysfunctions than functions; for another, it is possible to suggest functional alternatives.

For example, society's dirty work could be done without poverty, either by automation or by paying "dirty workers" decent wages. Nor is it necessary for the poor to subsidize the many activities they support through their low-wage jobs. This would, however, drive up the costs of these activities, which would result in higher prices to their customers and clients. Similarly, many of the professionals who flourish because of the poor could be given other roles. Social workers could provide counseling of the affluent, as they prefer to do anyway; and the police could devote themselves to traffic and organized crime. Other roles would have to be found for badly trained or incompetent professionals now relegated to serving the poor, and someone else would have to pay their salaries. Fewer penologists would be employable, however. And pentecostal religion could probably not survive without the poor—nor would parts of the second- and third-hand-goods market. And in many cities, "used" housing that no one else wants would then have to be torn down at public expense.

Alternatives for the cultural functions of the poor could be found more easily and cheaply. Indeed, entertainers, hippies, and adolescents are already serving as the deviants needed to uphold traditional morality and as devotees of orgies to "staff" the fantasies of vicarious participation.

The status functions of the poor are another matter. In a hierarchical society, some people must be defined as inferior to everyone else with respect to a variety of attributes, but they need not be poor in the absolute sense. One could conceive of a society in which the "lower class," though last in the pecking order, received 75 percent of the median income, rather than 15–40 percent, as is now the case. Needless to say, this would require considerable income redistribution.

The contribution the poor make to the upward mobility of the groups that provide them with goods and services could also be maintained without the poor's having such low incomes. However, it is true that if the poor were more affluent, they would have access to enough capital to take over the provider role, thus competing with, and perhaps rejecting, the "outsiders." (Indeed, owing in part to antipoverty programs, this is already happening in a number of ghettos, where white storeowners are being replaced by blacks.) Similarly, if the poor were more affluent, they would make less willing clients for upper-class philanthropy, although some would still use settlement houses to achieve upward mobility, as they do now. Thus "Society" could continue to run its philanthropic activities.

The political functions of the poor would be more difficult to replace. With increased affluence, the poor would probably obtain more political power and be more active politically. With higher incomes and more political power, the poor would be likely to resist paying the costs of growth and change. Of course, it is possible to imagine urban renewal and highway projects that properly reimbursed the displaced people, but such projects would then become considerably more expensive, and many might never be built. This, in turn, would reduce the comfort and convenience of those who now benefit from urban renewal and expressways. Finally, hippies could serve also

as more deviants to justify the existing political economy—as they already do. Presumably, however, if poverty were eliminated, there would be fewer attacks on that economy.

In sum, then, many of the functions served by the poor could be replaced if poverty were eliminated, but almost always at higher costs to others, particularly more affluent others. Consequently, a functional analysis must conclude that poverty persists not only because it fulfills a number of positive functions but also because many of the functional alternatives to poverty would be quite dysfunctional for the affluent members of society. A functional analysis thus ultimately arrives at much the same conclusion as radical sociology, except that radical thinkers treat as manifest what I describe as latent: that social phenomena that are functional for affluent or powerful groups and dysfunctional for poor or powerless ones persist; that when the elimination of such phenomena through functional alternatives would generate dysfunctions for the affluent or powerful, they will continue to persist; and that phenomena like poverty can be eliminated only when they become dysfunctional for the affluent or powerful, or when the powerless can obtain enough power to change society.

Author's Postscript[2]

Over the years, this article has been interpreted as either a direct attack on functionalism or a tongue-in-cheek satirical comment on it. Neither interpretation is true. I wrote the article for two reasons. First and foremost, I wanted to point out that there are, unfortunately, positive functions of poverty, which have to be dealt with by antipoverty policy. Second, I was trying to show that functionalism is not the inherently conservative approach for which it has often been criticized, but that it can be employed in liberal and radical analyses.

---

[2]The author requested that I add this postscript to his article–*Ed.*

5

The Structure of Power
in American Society

C. Wright Mills

I

Power has to do with whatever decisions men make about the arrangements under which they live, and about the events which make up the history of their times. Events that are beyond human decision do happen; social arrangements do change without benefit of explicit decision. But insofar as such decisions are made, the problem of who is involved in making them is the basic problem of power. Insofar as they could be made but are not, the problem becomes, who fails to make them?

We cannot today merely assume that in the last resort men must always be governed by their own consent. For among the means of power which now prevail is the power to manage and to manipulate the consent of men. That we do not know the limits of such power, and that we hope it does have limits, does not remove the fact that much power today is successfully employed without the sanction of the reason or the conscience of the obedient.

Surely nowadays we need not argue that, in the last resort, coercion is the "final" form of power. But then, we are by no means constantly at the last resort. Authority (power that is justified by the beliefs of the voluntary obedient) and manipulation (power that is wielded unbeknown to the powerless) must also be considered, along with coercion. In fact, the three types must be sorted out whenever we think about power.

In the modern world, we must bear in mind, power is often not so authoritative as it seemed to be in the medieval epoch: Ideas which justify rulers no longer seem so necessary to their exercise of power. At least for many of the great decisions of our time—

especially those of an international sort—mass "persuasion" has not been "necessary"; the fact is simply accomplished. Furthermore, such ideas as are available to the powerful are often neither taken up nor used by them. Such ideologies usually arise as a response to an effective debunking of power; in the United States, such opposition has not been effective enough recently to create the felt need for new ideologies of rule.

There has, in fact, come about a situation in which many who have lost faith in prevailing loyalties have not acquired new ones, and so pay no attention to politics of any kind. They are not radical, not liberal, not conservative, not reactionary. They are inactionary. They are out of it. If we accept the Greek's definition of the idiot as an altogether private man, then we must conclude that many American citizens are now idiots. And I should not be surprised, although I do not know, if there were not some such idiots even in Germany. This—and I use the word with care—this spiritual condition seems to me the key to many modern troubles of political intellectuals, as well as the key to much political bewilderment in modern society. Intellectual "conviction" and moral "belief" are not necessary, in either the rulers or the ruled, for a ruling power to persist and even to flourish. So far as the role of ideologies is concerned, their frequent absences and the prevalence of mass indifference are surely two of the major political facts about the western societies today.

How large a role any explicit decisions do play in the making of history is itself an historical problem. For how large that role may be depends very much upon the means of power that are available at any given time in any given society. In some societies, the innumerable actions of innumerable men modify their milieux, and so gradually modify the structure itself. These modifications—the course of history—go on behind the backs of men. History is drift, although in total "men make it." Thus, innumerable entrepreneurs and innumera-

ble consumers by ten-thousand decisions per minute may shape and reshape the free-market economy. Perhaps this was the chief kind of limitation Marx had in mind when he wrote, in *The 18th Brumaire* that: "Men make their own history, but they do not make it just as they please; they do not make it under circumstances chosen by themselves. . . ."

But in other societies—certainly in the United States and in the Soviet Union today—a few men may be so placed within the structure that by their decisions they modify the milieux of many other men, and in fact nowadays the structural conditions under which most men live. Such elites of power also make history under circumstances not chosen altogether by themselves, yet compared with other men, and compared with other periods of world history, these circumstances do indeed seem less limiting.

I should contend that "men are free to make history," but that some men are indeed much freer than others. For such freedom requires access to the means of decision and of power by which history can now be made. It has not always been so made; but in the later phases of the modern epoch it is. It is with reference to this epoch that I am contending that if men do not make history, they tend increasingly to become the utensils of history-makers as well as the mere objects of history.

The history of modern society may readily be understood as the story of the enlargement and the centralization of the means of power—in economic, in political, and in military institutions. The rise of industrial society has involved these developments in the means of economic production. The rise of the nation-state has involved similar developments in the means of violence and in those of political administration.

In the western societies, such transformations generally have occurred gradually, and many cultural traditions have restrained and shaped them. In most of the Soviet societies, they are happening very

rapidly indeed and without the great discourse of western civilization, without the
Renaissance and without the Reformation,
which so greatly strengthened and gave
political focus to the idea of freedom. In
those societies, the enlargement and the
coordination of all the means of power has
occurred more brutally, and from the beginning under tightly centralized authority.
But in both types, the means of power have
now become international in scope and similar in form. To be sure, each of them has its
own ups and downs; neither is as yet absolute; how they are run differs quite sharply.

Yet so great is the reach of the means of
violence, and so great the economy required
to produce and support them, that we have
in the immediate past witnessed the consolidation of these two world centers, either of
which dwarfs the power of Ancient Rome.
As we pay attention to the awesome means
of power now available to quite small groups
of men we come to realize that Caesar could
do less with Rome than Napoleon with
France; Napoleon less with France than
Lenin with Russia. But what was Caesar's
power at its height compared with the
power of the changing inner circles of Soviet Russia and the temporary administra-
tions of the United States? We come to
realize—indeed they continually remind
us—how a few men have access to the means
by which in a few days continents can be
turned into thermonuclear wastelands.
That the facilities of power are so enormously enlarged and so decisively centralized surely means that the powers of quite
small groups of men, which we may call
elites, are now of literally inhuman consequence.

My concern here is not with the international scene but with the United States in the
twentieth century. I must emphasize "in the
twentieth century" because in our attempt to
understand any society we come upon images which have been drawn from its past
and which often confuse our attempt to
confront its present reality. That is one
minor reason why history is the shank of
any social science: we must study it if only to

rid ourselves of it. In the United States,
there are indeed many such images and
usually they have to do with the first half of
the nineteenth century. At that time the
economic facilities of the United States were
very widely dispersed and subject to little or
to no central authority. The state watched in
the night but was without decisive voice in
the day. One man meant one rifle and the
militia were without centralized orders.

Any American, as old-fashioned as I, can
only agree with R. H. Tawney that "Whatever the future may contain, the past has
shown no more excellent social order than
that in which the mass of the people were
the masters of the holdings which they
ploughed and the tools with which they
worked, and could boast . . . 'It is a quietness
to a man's mind to live upon his own and to
know his heir certain.' "

But then we must immediately add: all
that is of the past and of little relevance to
our understanding of the United States today. Within this society, three broad levels
of power may now be distinguished. I shall
begin at the top and move downward.

II

The power to make decisions of national
and international consequence is now so
clearly seated in political, military, and economic institutions that other areas of society
seem off to the side and, on occasion,
readily subordinated to these. The scattered
institutions of religion, education, and family are increasingly shaped by the big three,
in which history-making decisions now regularly occur. Behind this fact there is all the
push and drive of a fabulous technology;
for these three institutional orders have
incorporated this technology and now guide
it, even as it shapes and paces their development.

As each has assumed its modern shape,
its effects upon the other two have become
greater, and the traffic between the three
has increased. There is no longer, on the
one hand, an economy, and, on the other, a

political order, containing a military establishment unimportant to politics and to
money-making.There is a political economy
numerously linked with military order and
decision. This triangle of power is now a
structural fact, and it is the key to any
understanding of the higher circles in
America today. For as each of these domains has coincided with the others, as
decisions in each have become broader, the
leading men of each—the high military, the
corporation executives, the political
directorate—have tended to come together
to form the power elite of America.

The political order, once composed of
several dozen states with a weak federal
center, has become an executive apparatus
which has taken up into itself many powers
previously scattered, legislative as well as
administrative, and which now reaches into
all parts of the social structure. The long-
time tendency of business and government
to become more closely connected has, since
World War II, reached a new point of
explicitness. Neither can now be seen clearly
as a distinct world. The growth of executive
government does not mean merely the "enlargement of government" as some kind of
autonomous bureaucracy; under American
conditions, it has meant the ascendancy of
the corporation man into political emi-
nence. Already during the New Deal, such
men had joined the political directorate; as
of World War II, they came to dominate it.
Long involved with government, now they
have moved into quite full direction of the
economy of the war effort and of the postwar era.

The economy, once a great scatter of
small productive units in somewhat automatic balance, has become internally dominated by a few hundred corporations, ad-
ministratively and politically interrelated,
which together hold the keys to economic
decision. This economy is at once a
permanent-war economy and a private-
corporation economy. The most important
relations of the corporation to the state now
rest on the coincidence between military
and corporate interests, as defined by the
military and the corporate rich, and accepted by politicians and public. Within the
elite as a whole, this coincidence of military
domain and corporate realm strengthens
both of them and further subordinates the
merely political man. Not the party politician but the corporation executive, is now
more likely to sit with the military to answer
the question: what is to be done?

The military order, once a slim establishment in a context of civilian distrust, has
become the largest and most expensive feature of government; behind smiling public
relations, it has all the grim and clumsy
efficiency of a great and sprawling bureaucracy. The high military have gained decisive political and economic relevance. The
seemingly permanent military threat places
a premium upon them and virtually all
political and economic actions are now
judged in terms of military definitions of
reality; the higher military have ascended to
a firm position within the power elite of our
time.

In part, at least, this is a result of an
historical fact, pivotal for the years since
1939: the attention of the elite has shifted
from domestic problems—centered in the
thirties around slump—to international
problems—centered in the forties and fifties
around war. By long historical usage, the
government of the United States has been
shaped by domestic clash and balance; it
does not have suitable agencies and traditions for the democratic handling of international affairs. In considerable part, it is in
this vacuum that the power elite has grown.

1. To understand the unity of this
power elite, we must pay attention to the
psychology of its several members in their
perspective milieux. Insofar as the power
elite is composed of men of similar origin
and education, of similar career and style of
life, their unity may be said to rest upon the
fact that they are of similar social type, and
to lead to the fact of their easy intermingling. This kind of unity reaches its frothier
apex in the sharing of that prestige which is
to be had in the world of the celebrity. It
achieves a more solid culmination in the fact

of the interchangeability of positions between the three dominant institutional orders. It is revealed by considerable traffic of personnel within and between these three, as well as by the rise of specialized go-betweens as in the new-style high-level lobbying.

2. Behind such psychological and social unity are the structure and the mechanics of those institutional hierarchies over which the political directorate, the corporate rich, and the high military now preside. How each of these hierarchies is shaped and what relations it has with the others determine in large part the relations of their rulers. Were these hierarchies scattered and disjointed, then their respective elites might tend to be scattered and disjointed; but if they have many interconnections and points of coinciding interest, then their elites tend to form a coherent kind of grouping. The unity of the elite is not a simple reflection of the unity of institutions, but men and institutions are always related; that is why we must understand the elite today in connection with such institutional trends as the development of a permanent war-establishment, alongside a privately incorporated economy, inside a virtual political vacuum. For the men at the top have been selected and formed by such institutional trends.

3. Their unity however, does not rest solely upon psychological similarity and social intermingling, nor entirely upon the structural blending of commanding positions and common interests. At times it is the unity of a more explicit coordination.

To say that these higher circles are increasingly coordinated, that this is *one* basis of their unity, and that at times—as during open war—such coordination is quite willful, is not to say that the coordination is total or continuous, or even that it is very sure-footed. Much less is it to say that the power elite has emerged as the realization of a plot. Its rise cannot be adequately explained in any psychological terms.

Yet we must remember that institutional trends may be defined as opportunities by those who occupy the command posts. Once

such opportunities are recognized, men may avail themselves of them. Certain types of men from each of these three areas, more farsighted than others, have actively promoted the liaison even before it took its truly modern shape. Now more have come to see that their several interests can more easily be realized if they work together, in informal as well as in formal ways, and accordingly they have done so.

The idea of the power elite is of course an interpretation. It rests upon and it enables us to make sense of major institutional trends, the social similarities and psychological affinities of the men at the top. But the idea is also based upon what has been happening on the middle and lower levels of power, to which I now turn.

III

There are of course other interpretations of the American system of power. The most usual is that it is a moving balance of many competing interests. The image of balance, at least in America, is derived from the idea of the economic market: in the nineteenth century, the balance was thought to occur between a great scatter of individuals and enterprises; in the twentieth century, it is thought to occur between great interest blocs. In both views, the politician is the key man of power because he is the broker of many conflicting powers.

I believe that the balance and the compromise in American Society—the "countervailing powers" and the "veto groups," of parties and associations, of strata and unions—must now be seen as having mainly to do with the middle levels of power. It is these middle levels that the political journalist and the scholar of politics are most likely to understand and to write about—if only because, being mainly middle class themselves, they are closer to them. Moreover, these levels provide the noisy content of most "political" news and gossip; the images of these levels are more or less in accord with the folklore of how democracy works;

and, if the master image of balance is accepted, many intellectuals, especially in their current patrioteering, are readily able to satisfy such political optimism as they wish. Accordingly, liberal interpretations of what is happening in the United States are now virtually the only interpretations that are widely distributed.

But to believe that the power system reflects a balancing society is, I think, to confuse the present era with earlier times, and to confuse its top and bottom with its middle levels.

By the top levels, as distinguished from the middle, I intend to refer, first of all, to the scope of the decisions that are made. At the top today, these decisions have to do with all the issues of war and peace. They have also to do with slump and poverty which are now so very much problems of international scope. I intend also to refer to whether or not the groups that struggle politically have a chance to gain the positions from which such top decisions are made, and indeed whether their members do usually hope for such top national command. Most of the competing interests which make up the clang and clash of American politics are strictly concerned with their slice of the existing pie. Labor unions, for example, certainly have no policies of an international sort other than those which given unions adopt for the strict economic protection of their members; neither do farm organizations. The actions of such middle-level powers may indeed have consequence for top-level policy; certainly at times they hamper these policies. But they are not truly concerned with them, which means of course that their influence tends to be quite irresponsible.

The facts of the middle levels may in part be understood in terms of the rise of the power elite. The expanded and centralized and interlocked hierarchies over which the power elite preside have encroached upon the old balance and relegated it to the middle level. But there are also independent developments of the middle levels. These, it seems to me, are better understood as an affair of entrenched and provincial demands than as a center of national decision. As such, the middle level often seems much more of a stalemate than a moving balance.

1. The middle level of politics is not a forum in which there are debated the big decisions of national and international life. Such debate is not carried on by nationally responsible parties representing and clarifying alternative policies. There are no such parties in the United States. More and more, fundamental issues never come to any point of decision before the Congress, much less before the electorate in party campaigns. In the case of Formosa, in the spring of 1955 the Congress abdicated all debate concerning events and decisions which surely bordered on war. The same is largely true of the 1957 crisis in the Middle East. Such decisions now regularly bypass the Congress, and are never clearly focused issues for public decision.

The American political campaign distracts attention from national and international issues but that is not to say that there are no issues in these campaigns. In each district and state, issues are set up and watched by organized interests of sovereign local importance. The professional politician is of course a party politician, and the two parties are semifeudal organizations: they trade patronage and other favors for votes and for protection. The differences between them so far as national issues are concerned, are very narrow and very mixed up. Often each seems to be fifty parties, one for each state; and accordingly, the politician as campaigner and as Congressman is not concerned with national party lines, if any are discernible. Often he is not subject to any effective national party discipline. He speaks for the interests of his own constituency, and he is concerned with national issues only insofar as they affect the interests effectively organized there, and hence his chances of re-election. That is why, when he does speak of national matters, the result is so often such an empty rhetoric. Seated in his sovereign locality, the politician is not at the national summit. He is on and of the middle levels of power.

2.   Politics is not an arena in which free and independent organizations truly connect the lower and middle levels of society with the top levels of decision. Such organizations are not an effective and major part of American life today. As more people are drawn into the political arena, their associations become mass in scale, and the power of the individual becomes dependent upon them; to the extent that they are effective, they have become larger, and to that extent they have become less accessible to the influence of the individual. This is a central fact about associations in any mass society; it is of most consequence for political parties and for trade unions.

In the thirties, it often seemed that labor would become an insurgent power independent of corporation and state. Organized labor was then emerging for the first time on an American scale, and the only political sense of direction it needed was the slogan, "organize the unorganized." Now without the mandate of the slump, labor remains without political direction. Instead of economic and political struggles it has become deeply entangled in administrative routines with both corporation and state. One of its major functions, as a vested interest of the new society, is the regulation of such irregular tendencies as may occur among the rank and file.

There is nothing, it seems to me, in the make-up of the current labor leadership to allow us to expect that it can or that it will lead, rather than merely react. Insofar as it fights at all, it fights over a share of the goods of a single way of life and not over that way of life itself. The typical labor leader in the U.S.A. today is better understood as an adaptive creative creature of the main business drift than as an independent actor in a truly national context.

3.   The idea that this society is a balance of powers requires us to assume that the units in balance are of more or less equal power and that they are truly independent of one another. These assumptions have

rested, it seems clear, upon the historical importance of a large and independent middle class. In the latter nineteenth century and during the Progressive Era, such a class of farmers and small businessmen fought politically—and lost—their struggle for a paramount role in national decision. Even then, their aspirations seemed bound to their own imagined past.

This old, independent middle class has of course declined. On the most generous count, it is now 40 percent of the total middle class (at most 20 percent of the total labor force). Moreover, it has become politically as well as economically dependent upon the state, most notably in the case of the subsidized farmer.

The *new* middle class of white-collar employees is certainly not the political pivot of any balancing society. It is in no way politically unified. Its unions, such as they are, often serve merely to incorporate it as hanger-on of the labor interest. For a considerable period, the old middle class *was* an independent base of power; the new middle class cannot be. Political freedom and economic society *were* anchored in small and independent properties; they are not anchored in the worlds of the white-collar job. Scattered property holders were economically united by more or less free markets; the jobs of the new middle class are integrated by corporate authority. Economically, the white-collar classes are in the same condition as wage workers; politically, they are in a worse condition, for they are not organized. They are no vanguard of historic change; they are at best a rear guard of the welfare state.

The agrarian revolt of the eighteen-nineties, the small-business revolt that has been more or less continuous since the eighteen-eighties, the labor revolt of the thirties—each of these has failed as an independent movement which could countervail against the powers that be; they have failed as politically autonomous third parties. But they have succeeded, in varying degrees, as interests vested in the expanded corporation and state; they have succeeded as parochial interests seated in particular districts, in local divisions of the two parties, and in the Congress. What they would become, in short, are well-established features of the *middle* levels of balancing power, on which we may now observe all those strata and interests which in the course of American history have been defeated in their bids for top power or which have never made such bids.

In the earlier part of this century, many observers thought of the American state as a mask behind which an invisible government operated. But nowadays, much of what was called the old lobby, visible or invisible, is part of the quite visible government. The "governmentalization of the lobby" has proceeded in both the legislative and the executive domain, as well as between them. The executive bureaucracy becomes not only the center of decision but also the arena within which major conflicts of power are resolved or denied resolution. "Administration" replaces electoral politics; the maneuvering of cliques (which include leading Senators as well as civil servants) replaces the open clash of parties.

The shift of corporation men into the political directorate has accelerated the decline of the politicians in the Congress to the middle levels of power; the formation of the power elite rests in part upon this relegation. It rests also upon the semi-organized stalemate of the interests of sovereign localities, into which the legislative function has so largely fallen; upon the virtually complete absence of a civil service that is a politically neutral but politically relevant, depository of brainpower and executive skill; and it rests upon the increased official secrecy behind which great decisions are made without benefit of public or even of Congressional debate.

IV

There is one last belief upon which liberal observers everywhere base their interpretations and rest their hopes. That is the idea of the public and the associated idea of public opinion. Conservative thinkers, since the French Revolution, have of course Viewed With Alarm the rise of the public, which they have usually called the masses, or something to that effect. "The populace is sovereign," wrote Gustave LeBonn, "and the tide of barbarism mounts." But surely those who have supposed the masses to be well on their way to triumph are mistaken. In our time, the influence of publics or masses within political life is in fact decreasing, and such influence as on occasion they do have tends, to an unknown but increasing degree, to be guided by the means of mass communication.

In a society of publics, discussion is the ascendant means of communication, and the mass media, if they exist, simply enlarge and animate this discussion, linking one face-to-face public with the discussions of another. In a mass society, the dominant type of communication is the formal media, and publics become mere markets for these media: the "public" of a radio program consists of all those exposed to it. When we try to look upon the United States today as a society of publics, we realize that it has moved a considerable distance along the road to the mass society.

In official circles, the very term, "the public," has come to have a phantom meaning, which dramatically reveals its eclipse. The deciding elite can identify some of those who clamor publicly as "Labor," others as "Business," still others as "Farmer." But these are not the public. "The public" consists of the unidentified and the nonpartisan in a world of defined and partisan interests. In this faint echo of the classic notion, the public is composed of these remnants of the old and new middle classes whose interests are not explicitly defined, organized, or clamorous. In a curious adaptation, "the public" often becomes, in administrative fact, "the disengaged expert," who, although never so well informed, has never taken a clear-cut and public stand on controversial issues. He is the "public" member of the board, the commission, the committee. What "the public" stands for, accordingly, is often a vagueness of policy (called "openmindedness"), a lack of involvement in public affairs (known as "reasonableness"), and a professional disinterest (known as "tolerance").

All this is indeed far removed from the eighteenth century idea of the public of public opinion. The idea parallels the economic idea of the magical market. Here is the market composed for freely competing entrepreneurs; there is the public composed of circles of people in discussion. As price is the result of anonymous, equally weighted, bargaining individuals, so public opinion is the result of each man's having thought things out for himself and then contributing his voice to the great chorus. To be sure, some may have more influence on the state of opinion than others, but no one group monopolizes the discussion, or by itself determines the opinions that prevail.

In this classic image, the people are presented with problems. They discuss them. They formulate viewpoints. These viewpoints are organized, and they compete. One viewpoint "wins out." Then the people act on this view, or their representatives are instructed to act it out, and this they promptly do.

Such are the images of democracy which are still used as working justifications of power in America. We must now recognize this description as more a fairy tale than a useful approximation. The issues that now shape man's fate are neither raised nor decided by any public at large. The idea of a society that is at bottom composed of publics is not a matter of fact; it is the proclamation of an ideal, and as well the assertion of a legitimation masquerading as fact.

I cannot here describe the several great forces within American society as well as elsewhere which have been at work in the debilitation of the public. I want only to remind you that publics, like free associations, can be deliberately and suddenly smashed, or they can more slowly wither away. But whether smashed in a week or withered in a generation, the demise of the public must be seen in connection with the rise of centralized organizations, with all their new means of power, including those of the mass media of distraction. These, we now know, often seem to expropriate the rationality and the will of the terrorized or—as the case may be—the voluntarily indifferent society of masses. In the more democratic process of indifference, the remnants of such publics as remain may only occasionally be intimidated by fanatics in search of "disloyalty." But regardless of that, they lose their will for decision because they do not possess the instruments for decision; they lose their sense of political belonging because they do not belong; they lose their political will because they see no way to realize it.

The political structure of a modern democratic state requires that such a public as is projected by democratic theorists not only exist but that it be the very forum within which a politics of real issues is enacted.

It requires a civil service that is firmly linked with the world of knowledge and sensibility, and which is composed of skilled men who, in their careers and in their aspirations, are truly independent of any private, which is to say, corporate, interests.

It requires nationally responsible parties which debate openly and clearly the issues which the nation, and indeed the world, now so rigidly confronts.

It requires an intelligentsia, inside as well as outside the universities, who carry on the big discourse of the Western world, and whose work is relevant to and influential among parties and movements and publics.

And it certainly requires, as a fact of power, that there be free associations standing between families and smaller communities and publics, on the one hand, and the state, the military, the corporation, on the other. For unless these do exist, there are no vehicles for reasoned opinion, no instruments for the rational exertion of public will.

Such democratic formations are not now ascendant in the power structure of the United States, and accordingly the men of decision are not selected and formed by careers within such associations and by their performance before such publics. The top of modern American society is increasingly unified, and often seems willfully coordinated: at the top there has emerged an elite whose power probably exceeds that of any small group of men in world history. The middle levels are often a drifting set of stalemated forces: the middle does not link the bottom with the top. The bottom of this society is politically fragmented, and even as a passive fact, increasingly powerless: at the bottom there is emerging a mass society.

These developments, I believe, can be correctly understood neither in terms of the liberal nor the Marxian interpretation of politics and history. Both these ways of thought arose as guidelines to reflection about a type of society which does not now exist in the United States. We confront there a new kind of social structure, which embodies elements and tendencies of all modern society, but in which they have assumed a more naked and flamboyant prominence.

That does not mean that we must give up the ideals of these classic political expectations. I believe that both have been concerned with the problem of rationality and of freedom: liberalism, with freedom and rationality as supreme facts about the individual; Marxism, as supreme facts about man's role in the political making of history. What I have said here, I suppose, may be taken as an attempt to make evident why the ideas of freedom and of rationality now so often seem so ambiguous in the new society of the United States of America.

6

Crime and the Development of Capitalism

RICHARD QUINNEY

An understanding of crime in our society begins with the recognition that the crucial phenomenon to be considered is not crime per se, but the historical development and operation of capitalist society (Hirst, 1972). The study of crime involves an investigation of such natural products and contradictions of capitalism as alienation, inequality, poverty, unemployment, spiritual malaise, and the economic crisis of the capitalist state. To understand crime we have to understand the development of the political economy of capitalist society.

DOMINATION, EXPLOITATION, AND THE CLASS STRUGGLE

The necessary condition for any society is that its members produce their material means of subsistence. Social production is therefore the primary process of all social life. Furthermore, in the social production

of our existence we enter into relations that are appropriate to the existing forces of production. According to Karl Marx (1970), it is this "economic" structure that provides a grounding for social and political institutions, for everyday life, and for social consciousness.

The capitalist class survives by appropriating the labor of the working class, and the working class as an exploited class exists as long as labor is required in the productive process: each class depends on the other for its character and existence.

The amount of labor appropriated, the techniques of labor exploitation, the conditions of working-class life, and the level of working-class consciousness have all been an integral part of the historical development of capitalism (Kuczynski, 1967). In like manner, the degree of antagonism and conflict between classes has varied at different stages in the development. Nevertheless, it is the basic contradiction between classes,

From Richard Quinney, *Class, State, and Crime* (2d ed.). New York: Longman, 1980. Reprinted by permission of the author.

generalized as class conflict, that typifies the developmennt of capitalism. Class conflict permeates the whole of capitalist development, represented in the contradiction between those who own property and those who do not, and by those who oppress and those who are oppressed (Heiss, 1957). All past history that involves the development of capitalism is the history of class struggle.

THE CAPITALIST STATE AND LEGAL REPRESSION

The state arose to protect and promote the interests of the dominant class, the class that owns and controls the means of production. The state exists as a device for controlling the exploited class, the class that labors, for the benefit of the ruling class. Modern civilization, as epitomized in capitalist societies, is founded on the exploitation of one class by another. Moreover, the capitalist state is oppressive not only because it supports the interests of the dominant class but also because it is responsible for the design of the whole system within which the capitalist ruling class dominates and the working class is dominated (Gold, Lo, & Wright, 1975). The capitalist system of production and exploitation is secured and reproduced by the capitalist state.

The coercive force of the state, embodied in law and legal repression, is the traditional means of maintaining the social and economic order. Contrary to conventional wisdom, law, instead of representing the community custom, is an instrument of the state that serves the interests of the developing capitalist class (Diamond, 1971; Tigar, 1977). Law emerged with the rise of capitalism. As human labor became a commodity, human relations in general began to be the object of the commodity form. Human beings became subject to juridic regulation; the capitalist mode of production called forth its equivalent mode of regulation and control, the legal system (Pashukanis, 1951; Balbus, 1977) and criminal law developed as the most appropriate form of control for capitalist society. Criminal law and legal repression continue to serve the interests of the capitalist class and the perpetuation of the capitalist system.

Through the legal system, then, the state forcefully protects its interests and those of the capitalist class. Crime control becomes the coercive means of checking threats to the existing social and economic order, threats that result from a system of oppression and exploitation. As a means of controlling the behavior of the exploited population, crime control is accomplished by a variety of methods, strategies, and institutions (see Quinney, 1974). The state, especially through its legislative bodies, establishes official policies of crime control. The administrative branch of the state formulates and enforces crime-control policies, usually setting the design for the whole nation. Specific agencies of law enforcement, such as the Federal Bureau of Investigation and the recent Law Enforcement Assistance Administration, determine the nature of crime control, and the state is able through its Department of Justice officially to repress the "dangerous" and "subversive" elements of the population. Together, these state institutions attempt to rationalize the legal system by employing the advanced methods of science and technology. And whenever any changes are to be attempted to reduce the incidence of crime, rehabilitation of the individual or reform within the existing institutions is suggested (Liazos 1974). To drastically alter the society and the crime-control establishment would be to alter beyond recognition the capitalist system.

Yet the coercive force of the state is but one means of maintaining the social and economic order. A more subtle reproductive mechanism of capitalist society is the perpetuation of the capitalist concept of reality, a nonviolent but equally repressive means of domination. As Alan Wolfe (1971) has shown, in the manipulation of consciousness the existing order is legitimated and secured:

The most important reproductive mechanism which does not involve the use of state violence is consciousness-manipulation. The liberal state has an enormous amount of violence at its disposal, but it is often reluctant to use it. Violence may breed counter-violence, leading to instability. It may be far better to manipulate consciousness to such an extent that most people would never think of engaging in the kinds of action which could be repressed. The most perfectly repressive (though not violently so) capitalist system, in other words, would not be a police state, but the complete opposite, one in which there were no police because there was nothing to police, everyone having accepted the legitimacy of that society and all its daily consequences.

Those who rule in capitalist society—with the assistance of the state—not only accumulate capital at the expense of those who work but impose their ideology as well. Oppression and exploitation are legitimized by the expropriation of consciousness; since labor is expropriated, consciousness must also be expropriated (Wolfe, 1974). In fact, *legitimacy* of the capitalist order is maintained by controlling the consciousness of the population.

CRIMES OF DOMINATION

The crimes of domination most characteristic of capitalist domination are those crimes that occur in the course of securing the existing economic order. These *crimes of economic domination* include the crimes committed by corporations, ranging from price fixing to pollution of the environment in order to protect and further capital accumulation. Also included are the economic crimes of individual businessmen and professionals. In addition, the crimes of the capitalist class and the capitalist state are joined in organized crime. The more conventional criminal operations of organized crime are linked to the state in the present stage of capitalist development. The operations of organized crime and the criminal operations of the state are united in the attempt to assure the survival of the capitalist system.

Then there are the *crimes of government* committed by the elected and appointed officials of the capitalist state. The Watergate crimes, carried out to perpetuate a particular governmental administration, are the most publicized instances of these crimes. There are also those offenses committed by the government against persons and groups who would seemingly threaten national security. Included here are the crimes of warfare and the political assassination of foreign and domestic leaders.

Crimes of domination also occur in the course of state control. These are the *crimes of control*. They include the felonies and misdemeanors that law-enforcement agents, especially the police, carry out in the name of the law, usually against persons accused of other violations. Violence and brutality have become a recognized part of police work. In addition to these crimes of control, there are crimes of a more subtle nature in which agents of the law violate the civil liberties of citizens, as in the various forms of surveillance, the use of provocateurs, and the illegal denial of due process.

Finally, many *social injuries* committed by the capitalist class and the capitalist state are not usually defined as criminal in the legal codes of the state (Platz, 1974; Schwendinger & Schwendinger, 1970). These systematic actions, involving the denial of basic human rights (resulting in sexism, racism, and economic exploitation), are an integral part of capitalism and are important to its survival.

Underlying all the capitalist crimes is the appropriation of the surplus value created by labor. The working class has the right to possess the whole of this value. The worker creates a value several times greater than the labor power purchased by the capitalist. The excess value created by the worker over and above the value of labor power is the surplus value appropriated by the capitalist, being the source of accumulation of capital and expansion of production.

Domination and repression are basic to class struggle in the development of capitalism. The capitalist class and the state protect and promote the capitalist order by controlling those who do not own the means of production. The labor supply and the conditions for labor must be secured. Crime control and crimes of domination are necessary features and natural products of a capitalist political economy.

CRIMES OF ACCOMMODATION AND RESISTANCE

The contraditions of developing capitalism heighten the level of class struggle and thereby increase (1) the need to dominate by the capitalist class and (2) the need to accommodate and resist by the classes exploited by capitalism, particularly the working class. Most of the behavior in response to domination, including actions of the oppressed defined as criminal by the capitalist class, is a product of the capitalist system of production. In the course of capitalist appropriation of labor, for the accumulation of capital, conditions are established that call for behaviors that may be defined as criminal by the capitalist state. These behaviors become eligible for crime control when they disturb or threaten in some way the capitalist order (Spitzer, 1975).

Hence, the class that does not own or control the means of production must adapt to the conditions of capitalism. Accommodation and resistance to the conditions of capitalism are basic to the class struggle. The argument here is that action by people who do not own and control the means of production, those who are exploited and oppressed, is largely an accommodation or resistance to the conditions produced by capitalist production. Thus, criminality among the oppressed classes is action (conscious or otherwise) in relation to the capitalist order of exploitation and oppression. Crime, with its many historical variations, is an integral part of class struggle in the development of capitalism.

Many crimes of accommodation are of this nature. Nevertheless, these actions occur within the context of capitalist oppression, stemming from the existing system of production. Much criminal behavior is of a parasitical nature, including burglary, rob-

bery, drug dealing, and hustling of various sorts (Hill, 1975). These are *predatory crimes.* The behavior, although pursued out of the need to survive, is a reproduction of the capitalist system. The crimes are nevertheless antagonistic to the capitalist order. Most police activity is directed against these crimes.

In addition to predatory crimes there are *personal crimes*, which are usually directed against members of the same class. These are the conventional criminal acts of murder, assault, and rape. They are pursued by those who are already brutalized by the conditions of capitalism. These actions occur in immediate situations that are themselves the result of more basic accommodations to capitalism.

Aside from these crimes, actions are carried out, largely by the working class, that are in resistance to the capitalist system. These actions, sometimes directed against the work situation, are direct reflections of the alienation of labor—a struggle, conscious or unconscious, against the exploitation of the life and activity of the worker. For example, workers may engage in concrete political actions against their employers:

On the assembly lines of the American automobile industry, this revolt extends as far as clandestine acts of sabotage against a product (the automobile body) which appears to the worker as the detestable materialization of the social uselessness and individual absurdity of his toil. Along the same lines is the less extreme and more complex example of miners fighting with admirable perseverance against the closing of the mines where they are exploited under inferior human and economic conditions—but who, individually, have no difficulty in recognizing that even if the coal they produced were not so bad and so expensive, their job, under the prevailing conditions, would still be abominable (Gorz, 1967, pp. 57–58).

These defensive actions by workers are likely to become even more politically motivated and organized in the future, for built into the capitalist economy is the contradiction that increased economic growth necessitates the kind of labor that further alienates workers from their needs. Further economic expansion can bring with it only an increase in crimes of resistance. For the purpose of class struggle, leading to socialist revolution, a Marxist analysis of crime gives attention to *crimes of resistance*, committed primarily by members of the working class.

The effects of the capitalist mode of production for the worker are all-inclusive, going far beyond the workplace. The worker can no longer be at home anyplace in the everyday world. The alienation experienced in the workplace now represents the condition of the worker in all other areas of life. Ownership and control of life in general have been surrendered to alien hands (Marx, 1971). The production of life itself is alienated under capitalism.

Moreover, large numbers of workers under advanced capitalism become expendable. For the capitalist the problem becomes that of the kind and size of labor force necessary to maximize production and realize surplus value. The physical well-being and spiritual needs of the worker are not the concern; rather, capitalism requires an "industrial reserve army" that can be called into action when necessary and relieved when no longer needed—but that is always available. Marx observed in *Capital* (1967):

But if a surplus laboring population is a necessary product of accumulation or of the development of wealth on a capitalist basis, this surplus population becomes, conversely, the lever of capitalist accumulation, nay, a condition of existence of the capitalist mode of production. It forms a disposable industrial reserve army that belongs to capital quite as absolutely as if the latter had bred it at its own cost. Independently of the limits of the actual increase of population, it creates, for the changing needs of the self-expansion of capital, a mass of human material always ready for exploitation. (p. 632)

Under these conditions, "the labor force consists of two parts, the employed and the unemployed, with a gray area in between continuing the part-time or sporadically employed. Furthermore, all these categories of workers and potential workers continuously expand or contract with technological change, the ups and downs of the business cycle, and the vagaries of the market, all inherent characteristics of capitalist production" ("Economic Crisis," 1975, p. 2). Many workers are further exploited by being relegated to the degradations and uncertainties of a reserve army of labor.

For the unemployed, as well as for those who are always uncertain about their employment, this life condition has its personal and social consequences. Basic human needs are thwarted when the life-giving activity of work is lost or curtailed. This form of alienation gives rise to a multiplicity of psychosocial maladjustments and psychic disorders (Kapp, 1975). In addition, unemployment means the loss of personal and family income. Choices, opportunities, and even life maintenance are jeopardized. For many people, the appropriate reaction consists not only of mental disturbance but also of outright acts of personal and social destruction.

Crimes of economic gain increase whenever the jobless seek ways to maintain themselves and their families. Crimes of violence rise when the problems of life are further exacerbated by the loss of life-supporting activity. Anger and frustration at a world that punishes rather than supports produce their own forms of destruction. Permanent unemployment—and the acceptance of that condition—can result in a form of life where criminality is an appropriate and consistent response.

Hence, crime under capitalism has become a response to the conditions of life (Gordon, 1973). Nearly all crimes among the working class in capitalist society are actually a means of *survival*, an attempt to exist in a society where survival is not assured by other, collective means. Crime is inevitable under capitalist conditions.

Yet understanding crime as a reaction to capitalist conditions, whether as acts of frustration or means of survival, is only one side of the picture. The other side involves the problematics of the consciousness of *criminality* in capitalist society (Taylor, Walton &

Young, 1973). The history of the working class is in large part one of rebellion against the conditions of capitalist production, as well as against the conditions of life resulting from work under capitalism. Class struggle involves, after all, a continuous war between two dialectically opposed interests: on one hand, capital accumulation for the benefit of a nonworking minority class that owns and controls the means of production and, on the other hand, control and ownership of production by those who actually labor. Since the capitalist state regulates this struggle, the institutions and laws of the social order are intended to assure the victory of the capitalist class over the working class. Yet the working class constantly struggles against the capitalist class, as shown in the long history of labor battles against the conditions of capitalist production (Lens, 1973; Brecher, 1972; Yellin, 1936; Boyer & Morais, 1955). The resistance continues as long as there is need for class struggle, that is, as long as capitalism exists.

With the instruments of force and coercion on the side of the capitalist class, much of the activity in the working-class struggle is defined as criminal. Indeed, according to the legal codes, whether in simply acting to relieve the injustices of capitalism or in taking action against the existence of class oppression, actions against the interests of the state are crimes. With an emerging consciousness that the state represses those who attempt to tip the scales in favor of the working class, working-class people engage in actions against the state and the capitalist class. This is crime that is politically conscious.

Crimes of accommodation and resistance thus range from unconscious reactions to exploitation, to conscious acts of survival within the capitalist system, to politically conscious acts of rebellion. These criminal actions, moreover, not only cover the range of meaning but actually evolve or progress from *unconscious reaction* to *political rebellion*. Finally, the crimes may eventually reach the ultimate stage of conscious political action—*revolt*. In revolt, criminal actions are not only

against the system but are also an attempt to overthrow it.

The movement toward a society can occur only with political consciousness on the part of those oppressed by capitalist society. The alternative to capitalism cannot be willed into being but requires the conscious activity of those who seek new conditions of existence. Political consciousness develops in an awareness of the alienation suffered under capitalism. The contradiction of capitalism—the disparity between actuality and human possibility—makes large portions of the population ready to act in ways that will bring about a new existence. When people become conscious of the extent to which they are dehumanized under the capitalist mode of production, when people realize the source and nature of their alienation, they become active in a movement to build a new society. Many of the actions taken result in behaviors defined as criminal by the capitalist state.

CONCLUSION

An understanding of crime, as developed here, begins with an analysis of the political economy of capitalism. The class struggle endemic to capitalism is characterized by a dialectic between domination and accommodation. Those who own and control the means of production, the capitalist class, attempt to secure the existing order through various forms of domination, especially crime control by the capitalist state. Those who do not own and control the means of production, especially the working class, accommodate to and resist the capitalist domination in various ways. Crime is related to this process. Crime control and criminality (consisting of the crimes of domination and the crimes of accommodation) are understood in terms of the conditions resulting from the capitalist appropriation of labor.

The only lasting solution to the crisis of capitalism is socialism. Under late, advanced capitalism, socialism will be achieved in the struggle of all people who are oppressed by the capitalist mode of production, namely, the workers and all elements of the surplus population. An alliance of the oppressed must take place (O'Connor, 1973). Given the objective conditions of a crisis in advanced capitalism, and the conditions for an alliance of the oppressed, a mass socialist movement can be formed, cutting across all divisions in the working class.

The objective of our analysis is to promote a further questioning of the capitalist system, leading to a deeper understanding of the consequences of capitalist development. The *essential meaning* of crime in the development of capitalism is the need for a socialist society. And as the preceding discussion indicates, in moving toward the socialist alternative, our study of crime is necessarily based on a social and moral analysis of capitalist society. Crime is essentially a product of the material and spiritual contradictions of capitalism.

REFERENCES

Balbus, I. D. (1977, Winter). Commodity form and legal form: An essay on the "relative autonomy" of the law. *Law and Society Review, 11*, 571–588.

Boyer, R. O., & Morais, H. M. (1955). *Labor's untold story*. New York: Cameron Associates.

Brecher, J. (1972). *Strike!* Greenwich, CT: Fawcett.

Diamond, S. (1971, Spring). The rule of law versus the order of custom. *Social Research, 38*, 42–72.

The economic crisis in historical perspective. (1975, June). *Monthly Review, 26*, 2.

Gold, D. A., Lo, C. Y. H., & Wright, E. R. (1975, November). Recent developments in Marxist Theories of the State. *Monthly Review, 27*, 36–51.

Gordon, D. M. (1973, April). Capitalism, class, and crime in America. *Crime and Delinquency, 19*, 163–186.

Gorz, A. (trans. by M. A. Nicolaus & V. Ortiz). *Strategy for labor: A radical proposal* (pp. 131–132). Boston: Beacon.

Heiss, R. (1957). *Engels, Kierkegaard, and Marx* (p. 390). New York: Dell.

Hill, J. (1975). *Class analysis: United States in the 1970's* (pp. 86–87). Emeryville, CA: Class Analysis.

Hirst, P. Q. (1972, February). Marx and Engels on law, crime and morality. *Economy and Society, 1*, 28–56.

Kapp, K. W. (1975, March). Socio-economic effects of law and high employment. *Annals of the American Academy of Political and Social Science, 418*, 60–71.

Kuczynski, J. (1967). *The rise of the working class*. New York: McGraw-Hill.

Lens, S. (1973). *The labor wars: From the Molly Maguires to the sitdowns*. New York: Doubleday.

Liazos, A. (1974, Fall). Class oppression: The functions of juvenile justice. *Insurgent Sociologist, 5*, 2–24.

Marx, K. (1967). *Capital* (Vol. 1, p. 632). New York: International Publishers.

Marx, K. (1970). *A contribution to the critique of political economy*, M. Dobb (Ed.), pp. 20–21. New York: International Publishers.

Marx, K. (1971). *The Gundrisse*. David McLellan (Ed.), pp. 132–143. New York: Harper & Row.

O'Connor, J. (1973). *The fiscal crisis of the state* (pp. 221–256). New York: St. Martin's Press.

Pashukanis, E. B. (1951). The general theory of law and Marxism. In H. W. Babb (Ed./Trans.), *Soviety legal philosophy* (pp. 111–225). Cambridge, MA: Harvard University Press.

Platt, T. (1974, Spring-Summer). Prospects for a radical criminology in the United States. *Crime and Social Justice, 1*, 2–10.

Quinney, R. (1974). *Critique of legal order: Crime control in capitalist society* (pp. 95–135). Boston: Little, Brown.

Schwendinger, H., & Schwendinger, J. (1970, Summer). Defenders of order or guardians of human rights? *Issues in Criminology, 5*, 123–157.

Spitzer, S. (1975, June). Toward a Marxian theory of deviance. *Social Problems, 22*, 638–651.

Taylor, I., Walton, P., & Young, J. (1973). *The new criminology: For a social theory of deviance* (pp. 217–220). London: Routledge & Kegan Paul.

Tigar, M. (with the assistance of Levy, M.). (1977). *Law and the Rise of capitalism*. New York: Monthly Review Press.

Wolfe, A. (1971, December). Political repression and the liberal state. *Monthly Review, 23*, 20.

Wolfe, A. (1974, Winter). New directions in the Marxist theory of politics. *Politics and Society, 4*, 155–157.

Yellin, S. (1936). *American labor struggles*. New York: Russell.

PART II

THE SO-CALLED PERSONAL PATHOLOGIES

When it comes to some social problems, it is difficult not to think almost exclusively in terms of personal problems. Often what is visible to us is only our own personal involvement in a problem; its sociological roots lie far beyond our perception. Sociologists, however, stress the *social* aspects of human behavior, and search for causes that lie beyond the individual. They stress that people's participation in group life motivates their behaviors, whether those activities be approved and encouraged or disapproved and punished, as are those we consider in this second part of the book.

The sociological base for people's behaviors is perhaps the most difficult to see in the sexual abuse of children, for most of us see only perverted people. But does the sexual abuse of children center around only bizarre personal tendencies or strange psychological characteristics? It may seem so since it is extremely difficult for us to look past the act and the actors in this human drama, for they are such powerful social symbols. Yet here too social factors are at work. Sociologists have discovered underlying social patterns; for example, that a child's chances of sexual victimization are related to such factors as household income, the child's relationship to the adult male in the household, and differences in education between the mother and that adult male. Certainly these social factors take us far beyond personal proclivity or psychological characteristics.

The social basis for violating sexual mores is more evident when it comes to sexual harassment. Indeed, sociological examination of sexual harassment shows that two systems of mores come into conflict with one another: the one from the female world—ideas of sexual privacy, personal freedom, and dignity, and developing conceptions of one's rightful participation in the work world; the other revolving around a male subculture of machismo, powerful subgroup reinforcers for pressuring women to have sex, and a feeling that it is permissible to use one's more powerful position to extract sexual benefits. Similarly, some male subcultures encourage rape, as interviews with convicted rapists show.

In other areas of what often are considered personal pathologies, the social basis is much more evident. For example, alcohol-related automobile accidents claim from 20,000 to 25,000 Americans each year. Most of these "accidents" are caused by young, male, drunk drivers. Why are they not evenly distributed with young females or older persons? Sociologists find the answer in our culture's association of masculinity with heavy alcohol consumption, which leads many young males to identify excessive drinking as a sign of sexuality. Still in the "proving" stages of their manhood, young males find drinking and driving a particularly valued expression of bravado, a form of risk-taking that validates their developing sense of male identity.

Similarly, the social basis of drug abuse becomes more apparent when we note its dependence on social norms. For example, in our culture, smoking a joint of marijuana is generally considered drug abuse, while drinking a glass of wine is not. What is it that makes one drug "bad" and the other "good"? Sociologists stress that no drug is good or bad in and of itself. The good and evil of drugs, or their perceived desirability or undesirability, are matters of social definition—the ways that a group of people view a particular drug and then react to it. Those definitions arise from the drug's social history, its patterns of use in a society. People project their fantasies and fears onto drugs, defining a drug as socially desirable at one time and as part of a social problem at another. For example, the social climate for drug use in the United States today is quite unlike what it was in the 1800s, when one could legally buy opium and morphine from drug stores, grocery stores, and general stores, or, if more convenient, could order them by mail. With labels such as Mrs. Winslow's Soothing Syrup, McMunn's Elixir, and Dover's Powder, housewives were encouraged to purchase opium, to use it themselves, and even to give it to cranky children. At that point in our history, smoking cigaretes and drinking alcohol were far more offensive than the use of opium or its derivatives.

As symbolic interactionists stress, it is not the objective nature of human behavior that makes something a social problem—who has sex with whom and under what conditions, who uses what drugs, whether or not one commits suicide, and so forth. Rather, like other social problems, these more personal behaviors are social problems if people so define them as social problems. What is considered a sexual violation, an inappropriate taking of one's life, or drug abuse in one place or at one historical time, then, may be looked at as normal in another place or at another time. In short, all social problems are part of social controversy, with people adopting different definitions and lining up on different sides of the issue.

You may find it difficult to apply this principle to some social problems, especially those about which you feel utter contempt and even moral revulsion. Sociologists strive for this value-neutral perspective, but they too find it difficult to apply sometimes, especially to behavior such as the sexual abuse of children. Nevertheless, from the sociological perspective the good or evil of behavior is seen as a matter of social definition, which in turn influences how people react to one another.

To this point of view, which is central to the symbolic interactionist perspective, conflict theorists would add that definitions flow downward. That is, those in positions of power in a society are primarily the ones who determine what is acceptable and unacceptable for the members of that society. It is they, for example, who define rape, and it is they who enforce those definitions—or do not enforce them if they so choose. Those in power are men, and if, for instance, men find it to their advantage to maintain the virginity of "marriageable females" until marriage, perhaps in order to protect their line of descent, they will do so. Under such conditions, rape will be severely punished, unless, that is, the social class barrier is broken from higher above, such as a male from the ruling class raping a female from the lower class. In such instances, there is likely to be little or no consequence—for the male, that is—since the males in power wield greater control over the rules.

The matter is much more complicated than this, as conflict theorists would point out, but the principle is intact: Those in power utilize their more privileged positions to set the rules, design them to benefit themselves, and manipulate them to their advantage. Consequently, social change comes only with great resistance from those in power, for they stand to lose if the rules are changed by those beneath them.

7

Sexual Abuse of Children

DAVID FINKELHOR

[The following findings are based on a study of 796 college students and the sexual abuse some of them had experienced. In this sample, 19 percent of the women and 9 percent of the men had sexual encounters under age 13 with persons at least 5 years older than themselves or between the ages of 13 and 16 with persons at least 10 years older. Sexual encounters were intercourse, oral-genital contact, fondling, or an encounter with an exhibitionist. The analysis is limited to the girls in the study because the sample turned up too few boy victims. The background factors on the girls are presented in Table 1.]

FATHERS AND STEPFATHERS

As Table 1 shows, the background factors most strongly associated with sexual victim-ization involved characteristics of the child's parents. For example, having a stepfather, one of the strongest risk factors, more than doubled a girl's vulnerability. Virtually *half* the girls with stepfathers were victimized by someone (not necessarily their stepfather). Moreover, this risk factor remained the strongest correlate of victimization, even when all other variables were statistically controlled.

Apparently there is substance to the notion that stepfathers are more sexually predatory toward their daughters than are fathers (de Young, 1982; Gruber & Jones, 1983). In our study, a stepfather was five times more likely to sexually victimize a daughter than was a natural father. This corresponds with findings of other studies (de Young, 1982; Gruber and Jones, 1983), particularly Russell's (1984). Russell found that one out of six women who had a

TABLE 1. Family Characteristics and Sexual Victimization of Girls

Family Characteristic	Association Yes (+)	Association No (0)	% Victimized[a]	N
Whole Family Characteristics				
Income under $10,000	+		33	(72)
Lived on farm	+		44	(16)
Religious background		0		
Ethnic background		0		
Family size		0		
Crowded home		0		
Parents had unhappy marriage	+		25	(155)
Parents showed little mutual affection	+		27	(162)
Father's Characteristics				
Child ever lived without father	+		29	(86)
Child had a stepfather	+		47	(30)
Child not close to father		0		
Blue collar	+		26	(179)
Never finished high school		0		
Often ill		0		
Often drank		0		
General inadequacy		0		
Little affection toward child	+		31	(42)
Conservative family values	+		38	(37)
Conservative sexual values		0		
Sexually modest or immodest		0		
Gave no sex education		0		
Punitive sexually		0		
Violent toward child or mother		0		
Spanked child at age 12		0		
Mother's Characteristics				
Child ever lived without mother	+		58	(19)
Child had a stepmother	+		35	(17)
Child not close to mother	+		34	(105)
Employed		0		
Never finished high school	+		38	(77)
Often ill	+		35	(134)
Often drank		0		
General inadequacy		0		
Little affection toward child	+		32	(108)
Conservative family values		0		
Conservative sexual values		0		
Sexually modest or immodest		0		
Gave no sex education		0		
Punitive sexually	+		35	(97)
Violent toward child or father		0		
Spanked child at age 12	+		24	(241)
N =			530	

[a]The total rate of victimization for all girls was 19%. A positive association was considered to exist only if subgroup in table had significantly higher percentage of victimized children than the rest of the sample, as tested by chi-square at p < .05.

stepfather as a principal figure in her child-hood was sexually abused by him, compared to a rate of one out of forty for abuse by biological fathers.

Stepdaughters are even more vulnerable than these comparisons might suggest. Only a quarter of their added vulnerability in the present study was due to the intrusions of their stepfathers. Girls with stepfathers are also more likely than other girls to be vic-timized by other men. In particular, they are five times more likely to be victimized by a friend of their parents.

Why do girls with stepfathers suffer at the hands of parents' friends? Two things appear to be going on. Being a stepdaugh-ter puts a girl into contact with other sexu-ally predatory men besides her stepfather. Some of these men are friends of her step-father, men who may not feel the same kind of restraint they might if this were the *real* (rather than the step) daughter of a friend.

But paradoxically some of these step-daughters were victimized prior even to meeting their stepfather. The parents' friends who took advantage of them were probably friends of their mothers. Thus, a mother who is courting may bring sexually opportunistic men into the home who may have little compunction about sexually ex-ploiting the daughter if the chance arises. So the high vulnerability of girls who have stepfathers is a function of both the pres-ence of a stepfather and the earlier expo-sure to a mother who was dating actively and may have put her daughter in jeopardy through the men she brought into the home.

The study also suggests that the quality of a daughter's relationship to a father, whether natural or stepfather, makes a dif-ference in her vulnerability to abuse. When a father has particularly conservative family values, for example, believing strongly in children's obedience and in the subordina-tion of women, a daughter is more at risk. Moreover, when he gives her little physical affection, the same is true. Such daughters have a harder time refusing the intrusions of an older man, even when they suspect

them to be wrong, because they have been taught to obey. Moreover, a child who is starved for physical affection from a father may be less able to discriminate between a genuine affectional interest on the part of an adult and a thinly disguised sexual one.

IMPORTANCE OF THE MOTHER

The study also confirmed the idea that mothers are very important in the protec-tion of daughters. Girls who had ever lived without their natural mother were three times more vulnerable to sexual abuse than the average girl. Similarly, if a girl reported that her mother was emotionally distant, often ill, or unaffectionate, the girl was also at much higher risk. Part of the problem here may be a lack of adequate supervision. However, daughters of mothers who worked were *not* at higher risk, so it is not simply a matter of a mother's not being around the house.

Another part of the problem of absent and unavailable mothers may be a lack of communication. When daughters report to interested mothers about their activities, such mothers may alert them to potential dangers in their environment. Girls without mothers or with distant, ill, or unaffection-ate mothers may not get such assistance. However, it wasn't simply a matter of sex education, because victimized daughters got just as much (or, more accurately, just as little) sex information from their mothers as any daughters.

It may have been that girls with absent or unavailable mothers have many unmet emo-tional needs that make them vulnerable. This is not to say that they seek out victim-ization. But they may be more susceptible to the ploys of a sexual offender. Their need-iness may make them conspicuous as poten-tial victims of such men.

The study also suggests a connection be-tween the oppression of wives and the vic-timization of daughters. Girls whose moth-ers are powerless may more easily fall into the victim role themselves. Although no direct measure of marital power was available, we could look at relative distribution between husbands and wives of one important power resource: education. A wife who has substantially less education than her husband is much more likely to be subordinate to and dependent on him. The lesson a daughter learns from observing her parents may be that she, too, is powerless and must obey.

Educational inferiority in a wife did indeed prove to be an important correlate of a daughter's sexual victimization. The most dangerous parental combination for a daughter is not when her mother and father are both poorly educated, but when her father is well educated and her mother is not (see Table 2). If a poorly educated mother is married to a well-educated father (a situation indicating that she is on the short end of a power relationship), her daughter is significantly more vulnerable than if both parents have little education (44% vs. 30% victimized).

A mother's importance may also lie in the specifically sexual messages that she transmits to her daughter. Victimized girls were much more likely to have mothers who were punitive about sexual matters. These mothers warned, scolded, and punished their daughters much more often than usual for asking sex questions, for masturbating, and for looking at sexual pictures. A girl with a sexually punitive mother was 76% more vulnerable to sexual victimization than the "typical" girl in the sample. It was the second most powerful predictor of victimization, after having a stepfather, and was still highly significant when all other variables were controlled.

This indication makes clear that sexually repressive practices backfire, although we can only speculate about why. It is possible that girls most bombarded with sexual prohibitions and punishments have the hardest time developing realistic standards about what constitutes danger. Blanket taboos often incite rebelliousness, and such girls may discard all the warnings they receive from their mothers about sex, including ones about sexual victimization. Moreover, if mothers have repressed all the healthier ways of satisfying sexual curiosity, these daughters may be more vulnerable to an adult or authority figure who appears to give them permission and opportunity to

TABLE 2. Mother's and Father's Education and Sexual Victimization of Girls

Parent's Education	% Victimized	(N)
Father finished high school Mother *did not* finish high school	44	(34)
Father *did not* finish high school Mother *did not* finish high school	30	(47)
Father *did not* finish high school Mother finished high school	28	(43)
Father finished high school Mother finished high school	16	(394)

Analysis of Variance

Source of variance	F	df	p
Father's education	0.35	1	N.S.
Mother's education	10.20	1	.001
Father's × mother's	5.80	1	.020

explore sex, albeit in the process of being exploited.

Whatever the precise mechanism, it is clear from this finding that it is not sexually lax, but sexually severe, families that foster a high risk for sexual exploitation, and some priority should be given to investigating this connection further.

OTHER FACTORS

Besides some of the factors that seemed to be associated with abuse, it is important to mention a few that appeared not to be associated. Perhaps most important, there was not much evidence of physical abuse being connected with sexual abuse. Girls who were victimized did not report any higher levels of violence in their family (either directed against themselves, or between their parents) than did nonvictims. There was somewhat more spanking in the background of victimized girls, but the difference was slight and it washed out when other factors such as social class and parental education were controlled. Many people have wondered whether physical abuse and sexual abuse are closely related, and on the basis of these data and other research (Finkelhor & Hotaling, 1983), the conclusion we would make is that they are not.

We also note that religion, ethnicity, family size, and crowdedness were not related to victimization. These are all factors which have, at times, been speculated about in the literature, but which had no relationship to sexual abuse in the sample we surveyed.

RISK FACTORS CHECKLIST

Putting some of the above findings together, we were able to construct a tool that is surprisingly effective in helping to identify children at risk for sexual victimization: The Sexual Abuse Risk Factor Checklist. The checklist includes eight of the strongest independent predictors of sexual victimization. Figure 1 shows that among children

with none of the factors present in their backgrounds, victimization was virtually absent. Among those with five factors, two-thirds had been victimized. The presence of each additional factor increased a child's vulnerability between 10% and 20%. The relationship is fairly linear and quite dramatic.

The factors included in the checklist were arrived at by using a stepwise multiple regression analysis. These were the factors which made the strongest independent contribution to the explanation of sexual victimization. A checklist containing only four or five factors would have had about equivalent predictive value, but a longer list was viewed as preferable because in using such a checklist in field situations, information on some of the variables may be missing.

The checklist is still in the process of formulation and refinement. It needs to be validated on a sample different from the one from which it was derived. It should not be seen as an instrument for predicting precisely in advance who will be sexually victimized. We are skeptical of the possibility or advisability of ever devising such a screening test for the problem of physical or sexual abuse (Light, 1974). However, it can be a device for sensitizing professionals about the kinds of backgrounds which put a child at risk for sexual victimization. Also, it can be a tool for further research and theorizing about the causes of abuse.

BLAMING THE VICTIM

An important caveat needs to be raised about the approach taken in this chapter. The research reported here is on victimization as seen through the eyes of the victim. Large quantities of information were gathered on the victims and their families. Little information was gathered directly, nor could be, given the research design, about the offenders, their backgrounds, or their family situations. Hence the findings tend to overemphasize the victims' role in the experience. The role of the perpetrators is ob-

FIGURE 1. Likelihood of Girls' Sexual Victimization by Presence of Eight Vulnerability Factors in Childhood

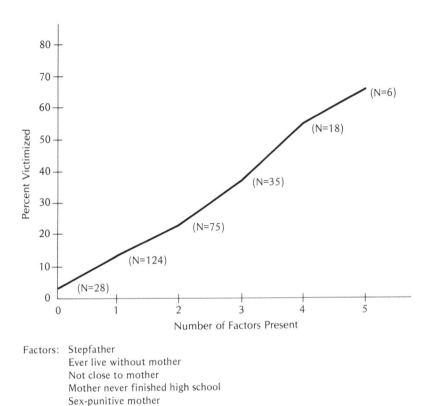

Factors: Stepfather
Ever live without mother
Not close to mother
Mother never finished high school
Sex-punitive mother
No physical affection from father
Income under $10,000
2 friends or less in childhood

scured. This type of emphasis can create the impression of blaming the victims for their own victimization.

It is important to keep in mind that moral and factual responsibility for the victimization experiences studied here lies with the offenders. They initiated the activities in 97% of the cases, according to our respondents. The most immediate and relevant "cause" of the victimization was a decision made by an offender.

Some might argue on the basis of this logic that, not to implicate victims unfairly, we should only study offenders. However, that is not a satisfactory solution. Offenders are harder to study, especially offenders who have not been caught. To limit our studies to offenders would severely curtail the amount of information we could obtain about sexual abuse. Victims can give us a lot of knowledge about the problem, knowledge we would be foolish to ignore, but even more important, we have to learn to identify children who may be at high risk. It is only through identifying characteristics of children at high risk that we can develop prevention programs targeted at the populations which are the most vulnerable. We have to do this by studying victims.

Clearly we cannot confine ourselves to

studies of victims. One of the evident short-comings of a great deal of research on child sexual abuse is that knowledge about offenders and victims is rarely brought together. Studies are done on victims, and the conclusions make it appear that the victims were the cause of the abuse. Or studies are done on offenders, and we get no useful information on what might have put some potential victims at greater risk than others. Obviously a melding of these two approaches is needed.

REFERENCES

de Young, M. (1982). *The sexual victimization of children*. Jefferson, NC: McFarland.

Finkelhor, D., & Hotaling, G. (1983). Sexual abuse in the National Incidence Study of Child Abuse and Neglect. Report to the National Center for Child Abuse and Neglect.

Gruber, K., & Jones, R. (1983). Identifying determinants of risk of sexual victimization of youth. *Child Abuse and Neglect, 7,* 17–24.

Light, R. (1974). Abused and neglected children in America: A study of alternative policies. *Harvard Educational Review, 43,* 556–598.

Russell, D. (1984). *Sexual exploitation: Rape, child sexual abuse, and sexual harassment.* Beverly Hills: Sage.

8

Sexual Extortion

Julia R. Schwendinger
Herman Schwendinger

Sexual harassment is often linked to extortion whenever it is perpetrated by men who can affect an important aspect of a woman's life. Harassment frequently includes many of the more subtle forms of sexism that occur at places where women work. Very few women report or complain of harassment on their jobs, because resistance involves humiliation and economic penalties. Women who complain are ridiculed and since they are usually harassed by managers or other high-ranking men, risk being fired. If sex is stipulated as part of a new job and a woman refuses, the chances are that she will not be hired.

Therefore, before taking action—either complaining or quitting—a working woman is also forced to calculate the risks to her independence and livelihood. Farley (1978) says:

To make a decision women must weigh in the balance economic necessity, prospects for other jobs, a good recommendation rather than a poor one, the chances of being fired, the attitudes of husband, friends, lovers or parents, interest in the job and rate of pay, the number of times the abuse has been experienced and countless other factors. (p. 23)

If her job is a good one, she risks sliding down to a less desirable one. If she cannot find suitable new work, she forfeits unemployment payments because she left the job "voluntarily."

Regardless of the risk, some women do complain, but they do so informally. One congressional aide told a congresswoman that she had to date "that dirty old man" [a congressman] twice a week to keep her job. This congresswoman was further informed that, in order to get a job, "kinky sex" was demanded of certain women employees. The congresswoman also discovered that women were asked, as a job requirement, if they engaged in oral sex.

Women may come up against such work requirements in institutions with either high or low prestige, in traditional and nontraditional occupations. About 20 employees on Capitol Hill alone reportedly complained that sex is an expected part of their jobs. Although usually such complaints are made only to one's closest circle of friends, most of the twenty spoke out despite their fears of "severe job repercussions." They were interested in developing a grievance procedure to protect their economic security.

Occupational coercion to provide sex on demand is also revealed by women employed in nontraditional jobs. Bitzy Gomez is a truck driver who handles big rigs. After ten years of fighting off passes in the sleeper compartment of tractor-trailer rigs, Gomez formed the Los Angeles Coalition of Women Truck Drivers in 1976 to defend working women against both unions and employers who regard them as prostitutes. Approximately 100 women responded to an advertisement for a coalition. Gomez reported that all the women were faced with job discrimination in finding work and sexual abuse when they were on the job.

More explicit economic motives for harassment may be involved here. Sexual harassment may be motivated by the desire to discourage women who are competing for men's jobs. Gomez added that some union locals will not allow women to join because their members see women as competition. According to Gomez, women on a road test often find that it becomes a "sleeper test." After you drive 20 miles out of town the man giving the test tells you to "put out or get out."

A further example is sexual extortion by police. There are obvious parallels here to the extortion experienced by women truck drivers. In the District of Columbia, policewomen have complained of sexual harassment by male officers who frequently out-

ranked the women. The women said the male officers punished those who did not submit to sexual advances and that rewards, in the form of better assignments and better treatment, were given to those who did submit.

Women in other occupations—stenographers, waitresses, singers, actresses, jockeys, and there are more—are also coerced to provide sex on demand. Their bosses in business, bureaucracy, and entertainment are their oppressors. Complaining about "systematic sexual abuse," a group of 35 student actresses and their NOW supporters protested against their acting director in New York City in October 1979. The director, who was their source of training, support, and job offers, had reportedly used his position and power to manipulate them into engaging in sex with him. The women organized, shared their victimization experiences and brought a criminal suit against the director. It was dismissed because they could not prove that physical force was used to compel them to submit to his sexual advances.

Although men with supervisory authority, political power, and economic means have used their power and resources to coerce women sexually, sometimes harassment is indirect. Bitzy Gomez, for instance, contended that many trucking firms try to discourage women truckers by placing them with male partners and using them as "sexual rewards" for the men's good performance records. Management, therefore, encourages sexual abuse in order to maintain highly profitable discriminatory labor markets. Even though management may not abuse the women directly, such policies are responsible for the continuation of this abuse.

REFERENCE

Farley, L. (1978). *Sexual shakedown: The sexual harassment of women on the job.* New York: McGraw-Hill.

9

"Riding the Bull at Gilley's": Convicted Rapists Describe the Rewards of Rape

Diana Scully
Joseph Marolla

Over the past several decades, rape has become a "medicalized" social problem. That is to say, the theories used to explain rape are predicated on psychopathological models. They have been generated from clinical experiences with small samples of rapists, often the therapists' own clients. Although these psychiatric explanations are most appropriately applied to the atypical rapist, they have been generalized to all men who rape and have come to inform the public's view on the topic.

Two assumptions are at the core of the psychopathological model; that rape is the result of idiosyncratic mental disease and that it often includes an uncontrollable sexual impulse (Scully & Marolla, 1985). For example, the presumption of psychopathology is evident in the often cited work of Nicholas Groth (1979). While Groth emphasizes the nonsexual nature of rape (power, anger, sadism), he also concludes, "Rape is

always a symptom of some psychological dysfunction, either temporary and transient or chronic and repetitive" (Groth, 1979:5). Thus, in the psychopathological view, rapists lack the ability to control their behavior; they are "sick" individuals from the "lunatic fringe" of society.

In contradition to this model, empirical research has repeatedly failed to find a consistent pattern of personality type or character disorder that reliably discriminates rapists from other groups of men (Fisher & Rivlin, 1971; Hammer & Jacks, 1955; Rada, 1978). Indeed, other research has found that fewer than 5 percent of men were psychotic when they raped (Abel et al., 1980).

Evidence indicates that rape is not a behavior confined to a few "sick" men, but many men have the attitudes and beliefs necessary to commit a sexually aggressive act. In research conducted at a midwestern

From *Social Problems*, Vol. 32, No. 3, pp. 251–263. Copyright © 1985 by the Society for the Study of Social Problems. Reprinted by permission.

university, Koss and her coworkers reported that 85 percent of men defined as highly sexually aggressive had victimized women with whom they were romantically involved (Koss & Leonard, 1984). A recent survey quoted in *The Chronicle of Higher Education* estimates that more than 20 percent of college women are the victims of rape and attempted rape (Meyer, 1984). These findings mirror research published several decades earlier which also concluded that sexual aggression was commonplace in dating relationships (Kanin, 1957, 1965, 1967, 1969; Kirkpatrick & Kanin, 1957). In their study of 53 college males, Malamuth, Haber and Feshback (1980) found that 51 percent indicated a likelihood that they, themselves, would rape if assured of not being punished.

In addition, the frequency of rape in the United States makes it unlikely that responsibility rests solely with a small lunatic fringe of psychopathic men. Johnson (1980), calculating the lifetime risk of rape to girls and women aged twelve and over, makes a similar observation. Using Law Enforcement Assistance Association and Bureau of Census Crime Victimization Studies, he calculated that, excluding sexual abuse in marriage and assuming equal risk to all women, 20 to 30 percent of girls now 12 years old will suffer a violent sexual attack during the remainder of their lives. Interestingly, the lack of empirical support for the psychopathological model has not resulted in the de-medicalization of rape, nor does it appear to have diminished the belief that rapists are "sick" aberrations in their own culture. This is significant because of the implications and consequences of the model.

A central assumption in the psychopathological model is that male sexual aggression is unusual or strange. This assumption removes rape from the realm of the everyday or "normal" world and places it in the category of "special" or "sick" behavior. As a consequence, men who rape are cast in the role of outsider and a connection with normative male behavior is avoided. Since, in this view, the source of the behavior is thought to be within the psychology of the individual, attention is diverted away from culture or social structure as contributing factors. Thus, the psychopathological model ignores evidence which links sexual aggression to environmental variables and which suggests that rape, like all behavior, is learned.

CULTURAL FACTORS IN RAPE

Culture is a factor in rape, but the precise nature of the relationship between culture and sexual violence remains a topic of discussion. Ethnographic data from pre-industrial societies show the existence of rape-free cultures (Broude & Green, 1976; Sanday, 1979), although explanations for the phenomenon differ. Sanday (1979) relates sexual violence to contempt for female qualities and suggests that rape is part of a culture of violence and an expression of male dominance. In contrast, Blumberg (1979) argues that in pre-industrial societies women are more likely to lack important life options and to be physically and politically oppressed where they lack economic power relative to men. That is, in pre-industrial societies relative economic power enables women to win some immunity from men's use of force against them.

Among modern societies, the frequency of rape varies dramatically, and the United States is among the most rape-prone of all. In 1980, for example, the rate of reported rape and attempted rape for the United States was eighteen times higher than the corresponding rate for England and Wales (West, 1983). Spurred by the Women's Movement, feminists have generated an impressive body of theory regarding the cultural etiology of rape in the United States. Representative of the feminist view, Griffin (1971) called rape "The All American Crime."

The feminist perspective views rape as an act of violence and social control which functions to "keep women in their place" (Brownmiller, 1975; Kasinsky, 1975; Russell, 1975). Feminists see rape as an extension of normative male behavior, the result of conformity or overconformity to the values and prerogatives which define the traditional male sex role. That is, traditional socialization encourages males to associate power, dominance, strength, virility and superiority with masculinity, and submissiveness, passivity, weakness, and inferiority with femininity. Furthermore, males are taught to have expectations about their level of sexual needs and expectations for corresponding female accessibility which function to justify forcing sexual access. The justification for forced sexual access is buttressed by legal, social, and religious definitions of women as male property and sex as an exchange of goods (Bart, 1979). Socialization prepares women to be "legitimate" victims and men to be potential offenders (Weis & Borges, 1973). Herman (1984) concludes that the United States is a rape culture because both genders are socialized to regard male aggression as a natural and normal part of sexual intercourse.

Feminists view pornography as an important element in a larger system of sexual violence; they see pornography as an expression of a rape-prone culture where women are seen as objects available for use by men (Morgan, 1980; Wheeler, 1985). Based on his content analysis of 428 "adults only" books, Smith (1976) makes a similar observation. He notes that, not only is rape presented as part of normal male/female sexual relations, but the woman, despite her terror, is always depicted as sexually aroused to the point of cooperation. In the end, she is ashamed but physically gratified. The message—women desire and enjoy rape—has more potential for damage than the image of the violence *per se*.

The fusion of these themes—sex as an impersonal act, the victim's uncontrollable orgasm, and the violent infliction of pain—is commonplace in the actual accounts of rapists. Scully and Marolla (1984) demonstrated that many convicted rapists denied their crime and attempted to justify their rapes by arguing that their victim enjoyed herself despite the use of a weapon and the infliction of serious injuries, or even death. In fact, many argued, they had been instrumental in making *her* fantasy come true.

The images projected in pornography contribute to a vocabulary of motive which trivializes and neutralizes rape and which might lessen the internal controls that otherwise would prevent sexually aggressive behavior. Men who rape use this culturally acquired vocabulary to justify their sexual violence.

Another consequence of the application of psychopathology to rape is that it leads one to view sexual violence as a special type of crime in which the motivations are subconscious and uncontrollable rather than overt and deliberate as with other criminal behavior. Black (1983) offers an approach to the analysis of criminal and/or violent behavior which, when applied to rape, avoids this bias. Black suggests that it is theoretically useful to ignore that crime is criminal in order to discover what such behavior has in common with other kinds of conduct. From his perspective, much of the crime in modern societies, as in pre-industrial societies, can be interpreted as a form of "self help" in which the actor is expressing a grievance through aggression and violence. From the actor's perspective, the victim is deviant and his own behavior is a form of social control in which the objective may be conflict management, punishment, or revenge. For example, in societies where women are considered the property of men, rape is sometimes used as a means of avenging the victim's husband or father (Black, 1983). In some cultures rape is used as a form of punishment. Such was the tradition among the puritanical, patriarchal Cheyenne, where men were valued for their ability as warriors. It was Cheyenne custom that a wife suspected of being unfaithful could be "put on the prairie" by her husband. Military confreres then were invited to "feast" on the prairie (Hoebel, 1954; Llewellyn & Hoebel, 1941). The ensuing mass rape was a husband's method of punishing his wife.

Black's (1983) approach is helpful in understanding rape because it forces one to examine the goals that some men have learned to achieve through sexually violent means. Thus, one approach to understanding why some men rape is to shift attention from individual psychopathology to the important question of what rapists gain from sexual aggression and violence in a culture seemingly prone to rape. In this paper, we address this question using data from interviews conducted with 114 convicted, incarcerated rapists.

METHODS

Sample

During 1980 and 1981 we interviewed 114 convicted rapists. All of the men had been convicted of the rape or attempted rape (n = 8) of an adult woman and subsequently incarcerated in a Virginia prison. Men convicted of other types of sexual offense were omitted from the sample.

In addition to their convictions for rape, 39 percent of the men also had convictions for burglary or robbery, 29 percent for abduction, 25 percent for sodomy, 11 percent for first or second degree murder, and 12 percent had been convicted of more than one rape. The majority of the men had previous criminal histories, but only 23 percent had a record of past sex offenses and only 26 percent had a history of emotional problems. Their sentences for rape and accompanying crimes ranged from ten years to seven life sentences plus 380 years for one man. Twenty-two percent of the rapists were serving at least one life sentence. Forty-six percent of the rapists were white, 54 percent black. In age, they ranged from 18 to 60 years, but the majority were between 18 and 35 years. Based on a statistical profile of felons in all Virginia prisons prepared by the Virginia Department of Corrections, it appears that this sample of rapists was disproportionately white and, at the time of the research, somewhat better educated and younger than the average inmate.

All participants in this research were volunteers. In constructing the sample, age, education, race, severity of current offense and past criminal record were balanced within the limitations imposed by the characteristics of the volunteer pool. Obviously the sample was not random and thus may not be typical of all rapists, imprisoned or otherwise.

HOW OFFENDERS VIEW THE REWARDS OF RAPE

Revenge and Punishment

As noted earlier, Black's (1983) perspective suggests that a rapist might see his act as a legitimized form of revenge or punishment. Additionally, he asserts that the idea of "collective liability" accounts for much seemingly random violence. "Collective liability" suggests that all people in a particular category are held accountable for the conduct of each of their counterparts. Thus, the victim of a violent act may merely represent the category of individual being punished.

These factors—revenge, punishment, and the collective liability of women—can be used to explain a number of rapes in our research. Several cases will illustrate ways in which these factors combined in various types of rape. Revenge-rapes were among the most brutal and often included beatings, serious injuries, and even murder.

Typically, revenge-rapes included the element of collective liability. This is, from the rapist's perspective, the victim was a substitute for the woman he wanted to avenge. As explained elsewhere, (Scully & Marolla, 1984), an upsetting event, involving a woman, preceded a significant number of rapes. When they raped, these men were angry because of a perceived indiscretion, typically related to a rigid, moralistic standard of sexual conduct, which they required from "their woman" but, in most cases, did not abide by themselves. Over and over these rapists talked about using rape "to get even" with their wives or other significant woman. Typical is a young man who, prior to the rape, had a violent argument with his wife over what eventually proved to be her misdiagnosed case of venereal disease. She assumed the disease had been contracted through him, an accusation that infuriated him. After fighting with his wife, he explained that he drove around "thinking about hurting someone." He encountered his victim, a stranger, on the road where her car had broken down. It appears she accepted his offered ride because her car was out of commission. When she realized that rape was pending, she called him "a son of a bitch," and attempted to resist. He reported flying into a rage and beating her, and he confided,

I have never felt that much anger before. If she had resisted, I would have killed her . . . The rape was for revenge. I didn't have an orgasm. She was there to get my hostile feelings off on.

Although not the most common form of revenge rape, sexual assault continues to be used in retaliation against the victim's male partner. In one such case, the offender, angry because the victim's husband owed him money, went to the victim's home to collect. He confided, "I was going to get it one way or another." Finding the victim alone, he explained, they started to argue about the money and,

I grabbed her and started beating the hell out of her. Then I committed the act. I knew what I was doing. I was mad. I could have stopped but I didn't. I did it to get even with her and her husband.

Griffin (1971) points out that when women are viewed as commodities, "In raping another man's woman, a man may aggrandize his own manhood and concurrently reduce that of the other man (p. 33).

Revenge-rapes often contained an element of punishment. In some cases, while the victim was not the initial object of the

revenge, the intent was to punish her because of something that transpired after the decision to rape had been made or during the course of the rape itself. This was the case with a young man whose wife had recently left him. Although they were in the process of reconciliation, he remained angry and upset over the separation. The night of the rape, he met the victim and her friend in a bar where he had gone to watch a fight on TV. The two women apparently accepted a ride from him, but after taking her friend home, he drove the victim to his apartment. At his apartment, he found a note from his wife indicating she had stopped by to watch the fight with him. This increased his anger because he preferred his wife's company. Inside his apartment, the victim allegedly remarked that she was sexually interested in his dog, which he reported, put him in a rage. In the ensuing attack, he raped and pistol-whipped the victim. Then he forced a vacuum cleaner hose, switched on suction, into her vagina and bit her breast, severing the nipple. He stated:

I hated at the time, but I don't know if it was her (the victim). (Who could it have been?) My wife? Even though we were getting back together, I still didn't trust her.

During his interview, it became clear that this offender, like many of the men, believed men have the right to discipline and punish women. In fact, he argued that most of the men he knew would also have beaten the victim because "that kind of thing (referring to the dog) is not acceptable among my friends."

Finally, in some rapes, both revenge and punishment were directed at victims because they represented women whom these offenders perceived as collectively responsible and liable for their problems. Rape was used "to put women in their place" and as a method of proving their "manhood" by displaying dominance over a female. For example, one multiple rapist believed his actions were related to the feeling that women thought they were better than he was.

Rape was a feeling of total dominance. Before the rapes, I would always get a feeling of power and anger. I would degrade women so I could feel there was a person of less worth than me.

Another, especially brutal, case involved a young man from an upper middle class background, who spilled out his story in a seven-hour interview conducted in his solitary confinement cell. He described himself as tremendously angry, at the time, with his girlfriend, who he believed was involved with him in a "storybook romance," and from whom he expected complete fidelity. When she went away to college and became involvd with another man, his revenge lasted eighteen months and involved the rape and murder of five women, all strangers who lived in his community. Explaining his rape-murders, he stated:

I wanted to take my anger and frustration out on a stranger, to be in control, to do what I wanted to do. I wanted to use and abuse someone as I felt used and abused. I was killing my girl friend. During the rapes and murders, I would think about my girl friend. I hated the victims because they probably messed men over. I hated women because they were deceitful and I was getting revenge for what happened to me.

An Added Bonus

Burglary and robbery commonly accompany rape. Among our sample, 39 percent of the rapists had also been convicted of one or the other of these crimes committed in connection with rape. In some cases, the original intent was rape and robbery was an afterthought. However, a number of men indicated that the reverse was true in their situation. That is, the decision to rape was made subsequent to their original intent, which was burglary or robbery.

This was the case with a young offender who stated that he originally intended only to rob the store in which the victim happened to be working. He explained that when he found the victim alone,

I decided to rape her to prove I had guts. She was just there. It could have been anybody.

Similarly, another offender indicated that he initially broke into his victim's home to burglarize it. When he discovered the victim asleep, he decided to seize the opportunity "to satisfy an urge to go to bed with a white woman, to see if it was different." Indeed a number of men indicated that the decision to rape had been made after they realized they were in control of the situation. This was also true of an unemployed offender who confided that his practice was to steal whenever he needed money. On the day of the rape, he drove to a local supermarket and paced the parking lot, "staking out the situation." His pregnant victim was the first person to come along alone and "she was an easy target." Threatening her with a knife, he reported the victim as saying she would do anything if he didn't harm her. At that point, he decided to force her to drive to a deserted area, where he raped her. He explained:

I wasn't thinking about sex. But when she said she would do anything not to get hurt, probably because she was pregnant, I thought, 'why not?'

The attitude of these men toward rape was similar to their attitude toward burglary and robbery. Quite simply, if the situation is right, "why not?" From the perspective of these rapists, rape was just another part of the crime—an added bonus.

Sexual Access

In an effort to change public attitudes that are damaging to the victims of rape and to reform laws seemingly premised on the assumption that women both ask for and enjoy rape, many writers emphasize the violent and aggressive character of rape. Often such arguments appear to discount the part that sex plays in the crime. The data clearly indicate that from the rapists' point of view, rape is in part sexually motivated. Indeed, it is the sexual aspect of rape that distinguishes it from other forms of assault.

Rape as a means of sexual access also

shows the deliberate nature of this crime. When a woman is unwilling or seems unavailable for sex, the rapist can seize what isn't volunteered. In discussing his decision to rape, one man made this clear.

All the guys wanted to fuck her . . . a real fox, beautiful shape. She was a beautiful woman and I wanted to see what she had.

The attitude that sex is a male entitlement suggests that when a woman says "no," rape is a suitable method of conquering the "offending" object. If, for example, a woman is picked up at a party or in a bar or while hitchhiking (behavior which a number of the rapists saw as a signal of sexual availability), and the woman later resists sexual advances, rape is presumed to be justified. The same justification operates in what is popularly called "date rape." The belief that sex was their just compensation compelled a number of rapists to insist they had not raped. Such was the case of an offender who raped and seriously beat his victim when, on their second date, she refused his sexual advances.

I think I was really pissed off at her because it didn't go as planned. I could have been with someone else. She led me on but wouldn't deliver . . . I have a male ego that must be fed.

The purpose of such rapes was conquest, to seize what was not offered.

Despite the cultural belief that young women are the most sexually desirable, several rapes involved the deliberate choice of a victim relatively older than the assailant. Since the rapists were themselves rather young (26 to 30 years of age on the average), they were expressing a preference for sexually experienced, rather than elderly, women. Men who chose victims older than themselves often said they did so because they believed that sexually experienced women were more desirable partners. They raped because they also believed that these women would not be sexually attracted to them.

Finally, sexual access emerged as a factor in the accounts of black men who consciously chose to rape white women. The majority of rapes in the United States are intraracial. However, for the past 20 years, according to national data based on reported rapes as well as victimization studies, which include unreported rapes, the rate of black on white (B/W) rape has significantly exceeded the rate of white on black (W/B) rape (La Free, 1982). Indeed, we may be experiencing a historical anomaly, since, as Brownmiller (1975) has documented, white men have freely raped women of color in the past. The current structure of interracial rape, however, reflects contemporary racism and race relations in several ways.

First, the status of black women in the United States today is relatively lower than the status of white women. Further, prejudice, segregation and other factors continue to militate against interracial coupling. Thus, the desire for sexual access to higher status, unavailable women, an important function in B/W rape, does not motivate white men to rape black women. Equally important, demographic and geographic barriers interact to lower the incidence of W/B rape. Segregation as well as the poverty expected in black neighborhoods undoubtedly discourages many whites from choosing such areas as a target for housebreaking or robbery. Thus, the number of rapes that would occur in conjunction with these crimes is reduced.

Reflecting in part the standards of sexual desirability set by the dominant white society, a number of black rapists indicated they had been curious about white women. Blocked by racial barriers from legitimate sexual relations with white women, they raped to gain access to them. They described raping white women as "the ultimate experience" and "high status among my friends. It gave me a feeling of status, power, macho." For another man, raping a white woman had a special appeal because it violated a "known taboo," making it more dangerous and, thus more exciting, to him than raping a black woman.

Impersonal Sex and Power

The idea that rape is an impersonal rather than an intimate or mutual experience appealed to a number of rapists, some of whom suggested it was their preferred form of sex. The fact that rape allowed them to control rather than care encouraged some to act on this preference. For example, one man explained,

Rape gave me the power to do what I wanted to do without feeling I had to please a partner or respond to a partner. I felt in control, dominant. Rape was the ability to have sex without caring about the woman's response. I was totally dominant.

Another rapist commented:

Seeing them laying there helpless gave me the confidence that I could do it. . . .With rape, I felt totally in charge. I'm bashful, timid. When a woman wanted to give in normal sex, I was intimidated. In the rapes, I was totally in command, she totally submissive.

During his interview, another rapist confided that he had been fantasizing about rape for several weeks before committing his offense. His belief was that it would be "an exciting experience—a new high." Most appealing to him was the idea that he could make his victim "do it all for him" and that he would be in control. He fantasized that she "would submit totally and that I could have anything I wanted." Eventually, he decided to act because his older brother told him, "forced sex is great, I wouldn't get caught and, besides, women love it." Though now he admits to his crime, he continues to believe his victim "enjoyed it." Perhaps we should note here that the appeal of impersonal sex is not limited to convicted rapists. The amount of male sexual activity that occurs in homosexual meeting places as well as the widespread use of prostitutes suggests that avoidance of intimacy appeals to a large segment of the male population. Through rape men can experience power and avoid the emotions related to intimacy

and tenderness. Further, the popularity of violent pornography suggests that a wide variety of men in this culture have learned to be aroused by sex fused with violence (Smith, 1976). Consistent with this observation, experimental research conducted by Malamuth et al. (1980) demonstrates that men are aroused by images that depict women as orgasmic under conditions of violence and pain. They found that, for female students, arousal was high when the victim experienced an orgasm and *no* pain, whereas male students were highly aroused when the victim experienced an orgasm and pain. On the basis of their results, Malamuth et al. suggest that forcing a woman to climax despite her pain and abhorrence of the assailant makes the rapist feel powerful, he has gained control over the only source of power historically associated with women, their bodies. In the final analysis, dominance was the objective of most rapists.

Recreation and Adventure

Among gang rapists, most of whom were in their late teens or early twenties when convicted, rape represented recreation and adventure, another form of delinquent activity. Part of rape's appeal was the sense of male camaraderie engendered by participating collectively in a dangerous activity. To prove one's self capable of "performing" under these circumstances was a substantial challenge and also a source of reward. One gang rapist articulated this feeling very clearly,

We felt powerful, we were in control. I wanted sex and there was peer pressure. She wasn't like a person, no personality, just domination on my part. Just to show I could do it—you know, macho.

One research revealed several forms of gang rape. A common pattern was hitchhike-abduction for the purpose of having sex. Though the intent was rape, a number of men did not view it as such because they were convinced that women hitchhiked primarily to signal sexual availability and only secondarily as a form of transportation. In these cases, the unsuspecting victim was driven to a deserted area, raped, and in the majority of cases physically injured. Sometimes, the victim was not hitchhiking; she was abducted at knife or gun point from the street, usually at night. Some of these men did not view this type of attack as rape either, because they believed a woman walking alone at night to be a prostitute. In addition, they were often convinced "she enjoyed it."

"Gang date" rape was another popular variation. In this pattern, one member of the gang would make a date with the victim. Then, without her knowledge or consent, she would be driven to a predetermined location and forcibly raped by each member of the group. One young man revealed this practice was so much a part of his group's recreational routine, they had rented a house for the purpose. From his perspective, the rape was justified because "usually the girl had a bad reputation, or we knew it was what she liked."

During his interview, another offender confessed to participating in twenty or thirty such "gang date" rapes because his driver's license had been revoked, making it difficult for him to "get girls." Sixty percent of the time, he claimed, "they were girls known to do this kind of thing," but "frequently, the girls didn't want to have sex with all of us." In such cases, he said, "It might start out as rape, but, then, the (the women) would quiet down and none ever reported it to the police." He was convicted for a gang rape, which he described as "the ultimate thing I ever did," because unlike his other rapes, the victim, in this case, was a stranger whom the group abducted as she walked home from the library. He felt the group's past experience with "gang date" rape had prepared them for this crime in which the victim was blindfolded and driven to the mountains where, though it was winter, she was forced to remove her clothing. Lying on the snow, she was raped by each of the four men several times before being abandoned

near a farm house. This young man continued to believe that if he had spent the night with her, rather than abandoning her, she would not have reported to the police.

Solitary rapists also used terms like "exciting," "a challenge," "an adventure" to describe their feelings about rape. Like the gang rapists, these men found the element of danger made rape all the more exciting. Typifying this attitude was one man who described his rape as intentional. He reported:

It was exciting to get away with it (rape), just being able to beat the system, not women. It was like doing something illegal and getting away with it.

Another rapist confided that for him "rape was just more exciting and compelling" than a normal sexual encounter because it involved forcing a stranger. A multiple rapist asserted, "it was the excitement and fear and the drama that made rape a big kick."

Feeling Good

When the men were asked to recall their feelings immediately following the rape, only eight percent indicated that guilt or feeling bad was part of their emotional response. The majority said they felt good, relieved, or simply nothing at all. Some indicated they had been afraid of being caught or felt sorry for themselves. Only two men out of 114 expressed any concern or feeling for the victim. Feeling good or nothing at all about raping women is not an aberration limited to men in prison. Smithyman (1978), in his study of "undetected rapists"—rapists outside of prison—found that raping women had no impact on their lives, nor did it have a negative effect on their self-image.

Significantly, a number of men volunteered the information that raping had a positive impact on their feelings. For some, the satisfaction was in revenge. For example, the man who had raped and murdered five women:

It seems like so much bitterness and tension had built up and this released it. I felt like I had just climbed a mountain and now I could look back.

Another offender characterized rape as habit forming: "Rape is like smoking. You can't stop once you start." Finally one man expressed the sentiments of many rapists when he stated,

After rape, I always felt like I had just conquered something, like I had just ridden the bull at Gilley's.

CONCLUSIONS

This paper has explored rape from the perspective of a group of convicted, incarcerated rapists. The purpose was to discover how these men viewed sexual violence and what they gained from their behavior.

We found that rape was frequently a means of revenge and punishment. Implicit in revenge-rapes was the notion that women were collectively liable for the rapists' problems. In some cases, victims were substitutes for significant women on whom the men desired to take revenge. In other cases, victims were thought to represent all women, and rape was used to punish, humiliate, and "put them in their place." In both cases women were seen as a class, a category, not as individuals. For some men, rape was almost an afterthought, a bonus added to burglary or robbery. Other men gained access to sexually unavailable or unwilling women through rape. For this group of men, rape was a fantasy come true, a particularly exciting form of impersonal sex which enabled them to dominate and control women, by exercising a singularly male form of power. These rapists talked of the pleasures of raping—how for them it was a challenge, an adventure, a dangerous and "ultimate" experience. Rape made them feel good and, in some cases, even elevated their self image.

The pleasure these men derived from raping reveals the extreme to which they objectified women. Women were seen as sexual commodities to be used or conquered rather than as human beings with rights and feelings. One young man expressed the extreme of the contemptful view of women when he confided to the female researcher.

Rape is a man's right. If a women doesn't want to give it, the man should take it. Women have no right to say no. Women are made to have sex. It's all they are good for. Some women would rather take a beating, but they always give in; it's what they are for.

This man murdered his victim because she wouldn't "give in."

Undoubtedly, some rapes, like some of all crimes, are idiopathic. However, it is not necessary to resort to pathological motives to account for all rape or other acts of sexual violence. Indeed, we find that men who rape have something to teach us about the cultural roots of sexual aggression. They force us to acknowledge that rape is more than an idiosyncratic act committed by a few "sick" men. Rather, rape can be viewed as the end point in a continuum of sexually aggressive behaviors that reward men and victimize women. In the way that motives for committing any criminal act can be rationally determined, reasons for rape can also be determined. Our data demonstrate that some men rape because they have learned that in this culture, sexual violence is rewarding. Significantly, the overwhelming majority of these rapists indicated they never thought they would go to prison for what they did. Some did not fear imprisonment because they did not define their behavior as rape. Others knew that women frequently do not report rape and of those cases that are reported, conviction rates are low, and therefore they felt secure. These men perceived rape as a rewarding, low-risk act. Understanding that otherwise normal men can and do rape is critical to the development of strategies for prevention.

We are left with the fact that all men do not rape. In view of the apparent rewards and cultural supports for rape, it is important to ask why some men do not rape. Hirschi (1969) makes a similar observation about delinquency. He argues that the key question is not "Why do they do it?" but rather "Why don't we do it?" (p. 34). Likewise, we may be seeking an answer to the wrong question about sexual assault of women. Instead of asking men who rape "Why?" perhaps we should be asking men who don't "Why not?"

REFERENCES

Abel, G., Becker, J., & Skinner, L. (1980). Aggressive behavior and sex. *Psychiatric Clinics of North America, 3*, 133–151.

Bart, P. (1979). Rape as a paradigm of sexism in society—victimization and its discontents. *Women's Studies International Quarterly, 2*, 347-57.

Black, D. (1983). Crime as social control. *American Sociological Review, 48*, 34–45.

Blumberg, R. L. (1979). A paradigm for predicting the position of women: policy implications and problems. In J. Lipman-Blumen & J. Bernard (Eds.), *Sex roles and social policy* (pp. 113–142). London: Sage Studies in International Sociology.

Broude, G., Green, S. (1976). Cross-cultural codes on twenty sexual attitudes and practices. *Ethnology, 15*, 409–428.

Brownmiller, S. (1975). *Against our will.* New York: Simon & Schuster.

Fisher, G., & Rivlin, E. (1971). Psychological needs of rapists. *British Journal of Criminology, 11*, 182–185.

Griffin, S. (1971, September 10). Rape: The all American crime. *Ramparts*, pp. 26–35.

Groth, N. (1979). *Men who rape.* New York: Plenum Press.

Hammer, E., & Jacks, I. (1955). A study of Rorschach flexnor and extensor human movements. *Journal of Clinical Psychology, 11*, 63–67.

Herman, D. (1984). The rape culture. In J. Freeman (Ed.), *Women: A feminist perspective* (pp. 20–39). Palo Alto, CA: Mayfield.

Hirschi, T. (1969). *Causes of delinquency.* Berkeley: University of California Press.

Hoebel, E. A. (1954). *The law of primitive man.* Boston: Harvard University Press.

Johnson, A. G. (1980). On the prevalence of rape in the United States. *Signs, 6*, 136–146.

Kanin, E. (1957). Male aggression in dating-courtship relations. *American Journal of Sociology, 63*, 197–204.

Kanin, E. (1965). Male sex aggression and three psychiatric hypotheses. *Journal of Sex Research, 1*, 227–229.

Kanin, E. (1967). Reference groups and sex conduct norm violation. *Sociological Quarterly, 8*, 495–504.

Kanin, E. (1969). Selected dyadic aspects of male sex aggression. *Journal of Sex Research, 5*, 12–28.

Kasinsky, R. (1975, September) Rape: A normal act? *Canadian Forum*, pp. 18–22.

Kirkpatrick, C., & Kanin, E. (1957). Male sex aggression on a university campus. *American Sociological Review, 22*, 52–58.

Koss, M. P., & Leonard, K. E. (1984). Sexually aggressive men: Empirical findings and theoretical implications. In N. M. Malamuth & E. Donnerstein (Eds.), *Pornography and sexual aggression* (pp. 213–232). New York: Academic Press.

LaFree, G. (1980). The effect of sexual stratification by race on official reactions to rape. *American Sociological Review, 45*, 824–854.

LaFree, G. (1982). Male power and female victimization: Towards a theory of interracial rape. *American Journal of Sociology, 88*, 311–328.

Llewellyn K. N., & Hoebel, E. A. (1941). *They Cheyenne way: Conflict and case law in primitive jurisprudence.* Norman: University of Oklahoma Press.

Malamuth, N., Haber, S., & Feshback, S (1980). Testing hypotheses regarding rape: Exposure to sexual violence, sex difference, and the "normality" of rapists. *Journal of Research in Personality, 14*, 121–137.

Malamuth, N., Heim, M., & Feshback, S (1980). Sexual responsiveness of college students to rape depictions: Inhibitory and disinhibitory effects. *Social Psychology, 38*, 399–408.

Meyer, T. J. (1984, December 5). "Date rape": A serious problem that few talk about. *Chronicle of Higher Education.*

Morgan, R. (1980). Theory and practice: Pornography and rape. In L. Lederer, (Ed.), *Take back the night: Women on pornography* (pp. 134–140). New York: William Morrow.

Rada, R. (1978). *Clinical aspects of rape.* New York: Grune & Stratton.

Russell, D. (1975). *The politics of rape.* New York: Stein & Day.

Sanday, P. R. (1979). *The socio-cultural context of rape.* Washington, DC: U.S. Dept. of Commerce, National Technical Information Service.

Scully, D., & Marolla, J. (1984). Convicted rapists' vocabulary of motive: Excuses and justifications. *Social Problems, 31,* 530–544.

Scully, D., & Marolla, J. (1985). Rape and psychiatric vocabulary of motive: Alternative perspectives. In A. W. Burgess (Ed.), *Rape and sexual assault: A research handbook* (pp. 294–312). New York: Garland Publishing.

Smith, D. (1976). The social context of pornography. *Journal of Communications, 26,* 16–24.

Smithyman, S. (1978). *The undetected rapist.* Unpublished dissertation, Claremont Graduate School.

West, D. J. (1983). Sex offenses and offending. In M. Tonry & N. Morris (Eds.), *Crime and justice: An annual review of research* (pp. 1–30). Chicago: University of Chicago Press.

Weis, Kr., & Borges, S (1973). Victimology and rape: The case of the legitimate victim. *Issues in Criminology, 8,* 71–115.

Wheeler, H. (1985). Pornography and rape: A feminist perspective. In A. W. Burgess (Ed.), *Rape and sexual assault: A research handbook* (pp. 374–391). New York: Garland Publishing.

10

Alcoholism in the Family

Joan K. Jackson

Over a three-year period, this investigator has been an active participant in the Alcoholics Anonymous Auxiliary in Seattle. This group is composed partly of women whose husbands are or were members of Alcoholics Anonymous, and partly of women whose husbands are excessive drinkers but have never contacted Alcoholics Anonymous.

Verbatim shorthand notes have been taken of all discussions, at the request of the group, who also make use of the notes for the group's purposes. Informal contact has been maintained with past and present members. In the past three years, 50 women have been members of this group. In addition, in connection with research on hospitalized alcoholics, many of their wives have been interviewed. The interviews with the hospitalized alcoholics, as well as with male members of Alcoholics Anonymous, have also provided information on family interactions. Further information has been derived from another group of wives, not connected with Alcoholics Anonymous, and from probation officers, social workers and court officials.

The families represented in this study are from the middle and lower classes. The occupations of the husbands prior to excessive drinking included small business owners, salesmen, business executives, skilled and semiskilled workers. Prior to marriage, the wives were nurses, secretaries, teachers, saleswomen, cooks, or waitresses. The economic status of the childhood families of these husbands and wives ranged from very wealthy to very poor.

STATEMENT OF THE PROBLEM

For purposes of this presentation, the family is seen as involved in a cumulative crisis. All family members behave in a manner which they hope will resolve the crisis and

Reprinted by permission, from *Quarterly Journal of Studies on Alcohol,* Vol. 15, pp. 562–594, 1954. Copyright by Journal of Studies on Alcohol, Inc., Rutgers Center of Alcohol Studies, New Brunswick, NJ 08903 permit a return to stability. Each member's action is influenced by his previous personality structure, by his previous role and status in the family group, and by the history of the crisis and its effects on his personality, roles and status up to that point. Action is also influenced by the past effectiveness of that particular action as a means of social control before and during the crisis. The behavior of family members in each phase of the crisis contributes to the form which the crisis takes in the following stages and sets limits on possible behavior in subsequent stages.

Family members are influenced, in addition, by the cultural definitions of alcoholism as evidence of weakness, inadequacy, or sinfulness; by the cultural prescriptions for the roles of family members; and by the cultural values of family solidarity, sanctity, and self-sufficiency. Alcoholism in the family poses a situation defined by the culture as shameful but for the handling of which there are no prescriptions which are effective or which permit direct action not in conflict with other cultural prescriptions. Thus, in facing alcoholism, the family is in an unstructured situation and must find the techniques for handling it through trial and error.

STAGES IN FAMILY ADJUSTMENT TO AN ALCOHOLIC MEMBER

The Beginning of the Marriage

At the time marriage was considered, the drinking of most of the men was within socially acceptable limits. In a few cases the men were already alcoholics but managed to hide this from their fiancées. They drank only moderately or not at all when on dates and often avoided friends and relatives who might expose their excessive drinking. The relatives and friends who were introduced to the fiancée were those who had hopes that "marriage would straighten him out" and thus said nothing about the drinking. In a small number of cases, the men spoke with their fiancées of their alcoholism. The

women who had no conception of what alcoholism meant, other than it involved more than the usual frequency of drinking, and they entered the marriage with little more preparation than if they had known nothing about it.

Stage 1. Attempts to Deny the Problem

Usually the first experience with drinking as a problem arises in a social situation. The husband drinks in a manner which is inappropriate to the social setting and the expectations of others present. The wife feels embarrassed on the first occasion and humiliated as it occurs more frequently. After several such incidents, she and her husband talk over his behavior. The husband either formulates an explanation for the episode and assures her that such behavior will not occur again, or he refuses to discuss it at all. For a time afterward he drinks appropriately and drinking seems to be a problem no longer.

Eventually another inappropriate drinking episode occurs and the pattern is repeated. The wife worries but takes action only in the situations in which inappropriate drinking occurs, as each long intervening period of acceptable drinking behavior convinces her that a recurrence is unlikely. As times goes on, in attempting to cope with individual episodes, she runs the gamut of possible trial and error behaviors, learning that none is permanently effective.

On the whole, a man reacts to his wife's suggestion that he has not adequately controlled his drinking with resentment, rebelliousness, and a display of emotion which makes rational discussion difficult. The type of husband-wife interaction outlined in this stage has occurred in many American families in which the husband never became an excessive drinker.

Stage 2. Attempts to Eliminate the Problems

Stage 2 begins when the family experiences social isolation because of the husband's drinking. Invitations to the homes of friends become less frequent. When the couple does visit friends, drinks are not served or are limited, thus emphasizing the reason for exclusion from other social activities of the friendship group. Discussions of drinking, begin to be sidestepped awkwardly by friends, the wife, and the husband.

By this time the periods of socially acceptable drinking are becoming shorter. The wife, fearing that the full extent of her husband's drinking will become known, begins to withdraw from social participation, hoping to reduce the visibility of his behavior, and thus the threat to family status.

Attempts to cover up increase. The employer who calls to inquire about the husband's absence from work is given excuses. The wife is afraid to face the consequences of the loss of the husband's pay check in addition to her other concerns. Questions from the children are evaded or they are told that their father is ill. The wife lives in terror of the day when the children will be told by others of the nature of the "illness." She is also afraid that the children may describe the father's symptoms to teachers or neighbors.

During this stage, husband and wife are drawing further apart. Each feels resentful of the behavior of the other. When this resentment is expressed, further drinking occurs. When it is not, tension mounts and the next drinking episode is that much more destructive of family relationships. The reasons for drinking are explored frantically. Both husband and wife feel that if only they could discover the reason, all members of the family could gear their behavior to making drinking unnecessary. The discussions become increasingly unproductive, as it is the husband's growing conviction that his wife does not and cannot understand him.

All attempts to stabilize or structure the situation to permit consistent behavior fail. Threats of leaving, hiding his liquor away, emptying the bottles down the drain, curtailing his money, are tried in rapid succession, but none is effective. Less punitive methods, as discussing the situation when

he is sober, babying him during hangovers, and trying to drink with him to keep him in the home, are attempted and fail. Long-term goals become secondary to just keeping the husband from drinking today.

There is still an attempt to maintain the illusion of husband-wife-children roles. When the father is sober, the children are expected to give him respect and obedience. The wife also defers to him in his role as head of the household. Each drinking event thus disrupts family functioning anew. The children begin to show emotional disturbances as a result of the inconsistencies of parental behavior. During periods when the husband is drinking, the wife tries to shield them from the knowledge and effects of his behavior, at the same time drawing them closer to herself and deriving emotional support from them. In sober periods, the father tries to regain their favor. Due to experiencing directly only pleasant interactions with their father, considerable affection is often felt for him by the children. This affection becomes increasingly difficult for the isolated wife to tolerate, and an additional source of conflict. She feels that she needs and deserves the love and support of her children and, at the same time, she feels it is important to maintain the children's picture of their father. She counts on the husband's affection for the children to motivate a cessation of drinking as he comes to realize the effects of his behavior on them.

Stage 3. Disorganization

The wife begins to adopt a "What's the use?" attitude and to accept her husband's drinking as a problem likely to be permanent. Attempts to understand one another become less frequent. Sober periods still engender hope, but hope qualified by skepticism; they bring about a lessening of anxiety and this is defined as happiness.

The children are increasingly torn in their loyalties as they become tools in the struggle between mother and father. If the children are at an age of comprehension, they have usually learned the true nature of their family situation, either from outsiders or from their mother, who has given up attempts to bolster her husband's position as father. The children are often bewildered but questioning their parents brings no satisfactory answers, as the parents themselves do not understand what is happening. Some children become terrified; some have increasing behavior problems within and outside the home; others seem on the surface to accept the situation calmly.

When the wife looks at her present behavior, she worries about her "normality." In comparing the person she was in the early years of her marriage with the person she has become, she is frightened. She finds herself nagging and unable to control herself. She resolves to stand up to her husband when he is belligerent but instead finds herself cringing in terror and then despises herself for her lack of courage. If she retaliates with violence, she is filled with self-loathing at behaving in an "unwomanly" manner. She is confused about where her loyalty lies, whether with her husband or her children. She feels she is a failure as a wife, mother, and person. She believes she should be strong in the face of adversity, and instead feels herself weak.

The wife begins to find herself avoiding sexual contact with her husband when he has been drinking. Sex under these circumstances, she feels, is sex for its own sake rather than an indication of affection for her. Her husband's lack of consideration of her needs to be satisfied leaves her feeling frustrated. The lack of sexual responsiveness reflects her emotional withdrawal from him in other areas of family life. Her husband, on his parts, feels frustrated and rejected; he accuses her of frigidity and this adds to her concern about her adequacy as a woman.

In Stage 3 all is chaos. Few problems are met constructively. The husband and wife both feel trapped in an intolerable, unstructured situation which offers no way out. The wife's self-assurance is almost completely gone. She is afraid to take action and

afraid to let things remain as they are. Fear is one of the major characteristics of this stage: fear of violence, fear of personality damage to the children, fear for her own sanity, fear that relatives will interfere, and fear that they will not help in an emergency. Added to this, the family feels alone in the world and helpless. The problems, and the behavior of family members in attempting to cope with them, seem so shameful that help from others is unthinkable. They feel that attempts to get help would meet only with rebuff, and that communication of the situation will engender disgust.

Stage 4. Attempts to Reorganize in Spite of the Problems

Stage 4 begins when a crisis occurs which necessitates that action be taken. There may be no money or food in the house; the husband may have been violent to the children; or life on the level of Stage 3 may have become intolerable. At this point some wives leave, thus entering directly into Stage 5.

The wife who passes through Stage 4 usually begins to ease her husband out of his family roles. She assumes husband and father roles. This involves strengthening her role as mother and putting aside her role as wife. She becomes the manager of the home, the discipliner of the children, the decision-maker. She either ignores her husband as much as possible or treats him as her most recalcitrant child. Techniques are worked out for getting control of his pay check, if there still is one, and money is doled out to her husband on the condition of his good behavior. Where her obligations to her husband conflict with those to her children, she decides in favor of the latter.

In this stage the husband often tries to set his will against hers in decisions about the children. If the children have been permitted to stay with a friend overnight, he may threaten to create a scene unless they return immediately. He may make almost desperate efforts to gain their affection and respect, his affection and respect, his behavior ranging from getting them up in the middle of the night to fondle them to giving them stiff lectures on children's obligations to fathers. Sometimes he will attempt to align the males of the family with him against the females. He may openly express resentment of the children and become belligerent toward them physically or verbally.

Much of the husband's behavior can be conceptualized as resulting from an increasing awareness of his isolation from the other members of the family and their steady withdrawal of respect and affection. It seems to be a desperate effort to regain what he has lost, but without any clear idea of how this can be accomplished—an effort to change a situation in which everyone is seen as against him; and, in reality, this is becoming more and more true. As the wife has taken over control of the family with some degree of success, he feels, and becomes, less and less necessary to the ongoing activity of the family. There are fewer and fewer roles left for him to play. He becomes aware that members of the family enjoy each other's company without him. When he is home he tries to enter this circle of warmth or to smash it. Either way he isolates himself further. He finds that the children discuss with the mother how to manage him and he sees the children acting on the basis of their mother's idea of him. The children refuse to pay attention to his demands: they talk back to him in the same way that they talk back to one another, adding pressure on him to assume the role of just another child. All this leaves him frustrated and, as a result, often aggressive or increasingly absent from home.

Often the wife has had a talk with an Alcoholics Anonymous member and has begun to look into what is known about alcoholism. If she has attended a few Alcoholics Anonymous meetings, her sense of shame has been greatly alleviated as she finds so many others in the same boat. She learns that her husband is ill rather than merely "ornery," and this often serves to quell for the time being thoughts about leaving him which have begun to germinate as she has gained more self-confidence. She learns

that help is available, but also that her efforts to push him into help are unavailing.

Stage 5. Efforts to Escacpe the Problems

Stage 5 may be the terminal one for the marriage. In this stage the wife separates from her husband. Sometimes the marriage is reestablished after a period of sobriety, when it appears certain that the husband will not drink again. If he does revert to drinking, the marriage is sometimes finally terminated, but with less emotional stress than the first time. If the husband deserts, being no longer able to tolerate his lack of status in his family, Stage 6 may be entered abruptly.

The events precipitating the decision to terminate the marriage may be near-catastrophic, as when there is an attempt by the husband to kill the wife or children, or they may appear trivial to outsiders, being only the last straw to an accumulation of years.

The wife must come to terms with her own mixed feelings about her husband, her marriage, and herself before she can decide on such a step as breaking up the marriage. She must give up hope that she can be of any help to her husband. She must command enough self-confidence, after years of having it eroded, to be able to face an unknown future and leave the security of an unpalatable but familiar past and present. She must accept that she has failed in her marriage, not an easy thing to do after having devoted years to stopping up the cracks in the family structure as they appeared. Breaking up the marriage involves a complete alteration in the life goals toward which all her behavior has been oriented. It is hard for her to rid herself of the feeling that she married him and he is her responsibility. Having thought and planned for so long a day-to-day basis, it is difficult to plan for a long-term future.

Some events, however, help her to arrive at a decision. During the absences of her husband, she has seen how manageable life can be and how smoothly her family can run. She finds that life goes on without him. The wife who is working comes to feel that "my husband is a luxury I can no longer afford." After a few short-term separations in which she tries out her wings successfully, leaving comes to look more possible. Another step on the path to leaving is the acceptance of the idea that, although she cannot help her husband, she can help her family.

Stage 6. Reorganization of Part of the Family

This wife is without her husband and must reorganize her family on this basis. Substantially the process is similar to that in other divorced families, but with some additions. The divorce rarely cuts her relationships to her husband. Unless she and her family disappear, her husband may make attempts to come back. When drunk, he may endanger her job by calls at her place of work. He may attempt violence against members of the family, or he may contact the children and work to gain their loyalty so that pressure is put on the mother to accept him again. Looking back on her marriage, she forgets the full impact of the problem situation on her and on the children and feels more warmly toward her husband, and these feelings can still be manipulated by him. The wide circulation of information on alcoholism as an illness engenders guilt about having deserted a sick man. Gradually, however, the family becomes reorganized.

Stage 7. Recovery and Reorganization of the Whole Family

Stage 7 is entered if the husband achieves sobriety, whether or not separation has preceded. It was pointed out that in earlier stages most of the problems in the marriage were attributed to the alcoholism of the husband, and thus problems in adjustment not related directly to the drinking were unrecognized and unmet. Also, the "sober personality" of the husband was thought of

as the "real" personality, with a resulting lack of recognition of other factors involved in his sober behavior, such as remorse and guilt over his actions, leading him to act to the best of his ability like "the ideal husband" when sober. Irritation or other signs of growing tension were viewed as indicators of further drinking, and hence the problems giving rise to them were walked around gingerly rather than faced and resolved. Lack of conflict and lack of drinking were defined as indicating a perfect adjustment. For the wife and husband facing a sober marriage after many years of an alcoholic marriage, the expectations of what marriage without alcoholism will be are unrealistically idealistic, and the reality of marriage almost inevitably brings disillusionment. The expectation that all would go well and that all problems be resolved with the cessation of the husband's drinking cannot be met, and this threatens the marriage from time to time.

The beginning of sobriety for the husband does not bring too great hope to the family at first. They have been through this before but are willing to help him along and stand by him in the new attempt. As the length of sobriety increases, so do the hopes for its permanence and efforts to be of help. The wife at first finds it difficult to think more than in terms of today, waking each morning with fear of what the day will bring and sighing with relief at the end of each sober day.

With the continuation of sobriety, many problems begin to crop up. Mother has for years managed the family, and now father again wishes to be reinstated in his former roles. Usually the first role reestablished is that of breadwinner, and the economic problems of the family begin to be alleviated as debts are gradually paid and there is enough left over for current needs. With the resumption of this role, the husband feels that the family should also accept him at least as a partner in the management of the family. Even if the wife is willing to hand over some of the control of the children, for example, the children often are not able to accept this change easily. Their mother has been both parents for so long that it takes time to get used to the idea of consulting their father on problems and asking for his decisions. Often the father tries too hard to manage this change overnight, and the very pressure put on the children toward this end defeats him. In addition, he is unable to meet many of the demands the children make on him because he has never really become acquainted with them or learned to understand them and is lacking in much necessary background knowledge of their lives.

The wife, who finds it difficult to conceive of her husband as permanently sober, feels an unwillingness to let control slip from her hands. At the same time she realizes that reinstatement of her husband in his family roles is necessary to his sobriety. She also realizes that the closer his involvement in the family, the greater the probability of his remaining sober. Yet she remembers events in the past in which his failure to handle his responsibilities was catastrophic to the family.

Gradually, however, the drinking problem sinks into the past and marital adjustment at some level is achieved. Even when this has occurred, the drinking problem crops up occasionally, as when the time comes for a decision about whether the children should be permitted to drink. The mother at such times becomes anxious, sees in the child traits which remind her of her husband, worries whether these are the traits which mean future alcoholism. At parties, at first, she is watchful and concerned about whether her husband will take a drink or not. Relatives and friends may, in a party mood, make the husband the center of attention by emphasizing his nondrinking. They may unwittingly cast aspersions on his character by trying to convince him that he can now "drink like a man." Some relatives and friends have gone so far as secretly to "spike" a nonalcoholic drink and then cry "bottoms up!" without realizing the risk of reactivating the patterns from the past.

If sobriety has come through Alcoholics Anonymous, the husband frequently throws himself so wholeheartedly into AA activities that his wife sees little of him and feels neglected. As she worries less about his drinking, she may press him to cut down on these activities. Also, the wife discovers that although she has a sober husband, she is by no means free of alcoholics. In his Twelfth Step work, he may keep the house filled with men he is helping. In the past her husband has avoided self-searching; and now he may become excessively introspective, and it may be difficult for her to deal with this.

SUMMARY

The onset of alcoholism in a family member has been viewed as precipitating a cumulative crisis for the family. Seven critical stages have been delineated. Each stage affects the form which the following one will take. The family finds itself in an unstructured situation which is undefined by the culture. Thus it is forced to evolve techniques of adjustment by trial and error. The unpredictability of the situation, added to its lack of structure, engenders anxiety in family members which gives rise to personality difficulties. Factors in the culture, in the environment, and within the family situation prolong the crisis and deter the working out of permanent adjustment patterns. With the arrest of the alcoholism, the crisis enters its final stage. The family attempts to reorganize to include the ex-alcoholic and makes adjustments to the changes which have occurred in him.

11

The Drug Gangs

TOM MORGANTHAU

Bleak by day and terrifying by night, south-central Los Angeles could be the set for some B-picture about the world after a nuclear apocalypse—a nightmare landscape inhabited by marauding thugs and hard-nosed cops, a world in which innocence is hostage to violence and bystanders too often wind up as victims. When darkness comes to Watts, law-abiding citizens cower behind locked doors. Shadowy groups of young men pad quietly down the alleyways while police crusiers roam the streets and helicopters clatter overhead. The police presence is overwhelmimg: anyone on the street is liable to be stopped and questioned. *"Hands on the car, homeboy! Where's your ID? What's that in your pocket? Got any dope? Seen any gang bangers? Where you been, where you going? Answer me, homes—I'm talkin' to YOU."*

The name of this tough and dangerous game is suppression—a massive attempt by the outnumbered Los Angeles police and sheriff's departments to keep the estimated 70,000 gang members in Los Angeles County off balance and on the defensive. It isn't working. Despite years of experience combating street crime, few L.A. cops will deny that their war against the groups has taken a decisive turn for the worse. The gangs are better armed and more violent than ever before; they are also more adept at evading the law. It's like Vietnam, says one prosecutor: "The cops are winning all the battles, but we're still losing the war."

The reason is drugs—particularly crack, or "rock," concaine. The crack trade, built on the enormous influx of cocaine from Latin America, is now transforming some of the country's toughest street gangs into ghetto-based drug-trafficking organizations. Equally ominous, according to law-enforcement sources, is the fact that at least some L.A. gangs have now established direct connections to major Colombian smugglers, thus ensuring a continous supply of top-quality cocaine.

Dangerous as it is, the situation on the West Coast is just part of a much larger problem. Big-city gangs in New York, Chicago, Miami, and Washington, D.C., are breaking into the crack business as well, and some are actively spreading drugs and violence to other cities all across the country. In Chicago, where gang membership has now reached an estimated 13,000 after a lull in the 1970s, the infamous El Rukns are under active investigation for drug trafficking. In New York, where a rookie cop was assassinated by a cocaine kingpin's hit men three weeks ago, police are struggling to contain an explosion of drug-related violence that has left more than 500 persons dead in upper Manhattan alone during the past five years. A Miami-based gang called the Untouchables is pushing crack northward to Atlanta, Savannah, and other cities of the Southeast, where the group is known and feared as the Miami Boys.

There are black gangs, Hispanic gangs, Asian gangs, and gangs drawn from specific nationality groups. Police from Boston to Houston are alarmed by the emergence of Jamaican gangs known as "posses." According to federal sources, there are 30 to 40 posses with a total of about 5,000 members now operating in the United States. Clannish, cunning, and extraordinarly violent, the Jamaicans are dominating the drug trade in carefully chosen cities from Texas to Alaska. "The bigger crack becomes, the bigger the posses get," says special agent James Watterson of the U.S. Bureau of Alcohol, Tobacco and Firearms. "And what's scary is that the crack problem just keeps getting worse."

The ghetto gangs' entry into drug trafficking on a major scale may be creating the nation's biggest crime problem in decades. Drug profits are soaring—and so is the drug-related homicide rate in cities where the gangs are most entrenched. It is arguable, in fact, that the emergence of drug gangs from coast to coast is very similar to what occurred during the early years of Prohibition, when La Costa Nostra—the Mafia—consolidated its status as an under-

world cartel by building on the profits of illicit alcohol. "Look at the development of organized crime in the United States," says Thomas Reppetto, president of the Citizen's Crime Commission of New York, a privately funded group. "If we've learned anything, it's that once we let these guys get too big, we've got a situation that will take decades to [control]. The [ghetto] gangs now have an opportunity provided by the crack explosion and the breakup of [traditional] organized-crime groups. These gangs are where the [Italian] gangs were when they moved into bootlegging. We can't let that happen again."

"KILL HIM"

The analogy to Prohibition, as Reppetto notes, has one significant flaw: today's ghetto gangs, especially the Jamaican posses, are far more violent than the Mafia. In part, the extraordinary level of violence is the result of the ready availability of military and paramilitary weapons. Guns like Uzis, AK-47 assault rifles, and AR-15 semiautomatics are widely bought (some even legally in gun shops) by gang members, who finance their high-tech arsenals with profits from the drug trade. Another factor, experts agree, is the sociopathic recklessness of these youth: big-city ghettos and barrios are full of teenagers whose poverty and deprivation have immunized them to both hope and fear. The result is a casual acceptance of—and sometimes enthusiasm for —torture and murder, "drive by" shootings and public mayhem. "If they don't kill you, they'll kill your mother," BATF's Watterson says of the Jamaican gangs. "The Cubans and Colombians don't want to deal with them because they're so dangerous." But the point applies to New York's black and Dominican drug gangs as well. Investigators say these gangs make a point of staging their assassinations in broad daylight whenever possible. "You don't kill no mother------ from across the street," one young hit man explained to undercover agents. "You walk up to him, you kill him in his head."

Gang culture—the mock-feudal tradition of inner-city kids banding together for comfort, support and mutual protection—has a long and, some would say, romantic history in America. Think of "West Side Story." It is still true that many gangs are little more than collections of neighborhood youths with a penchant for macho posturing, petty crime, and street brawls over girls or turf. Recruitment begins early, in the grade-school years: gang veterans call their young acolytes "peewees" or "wannabees" (want-to-be's). Though old hands say the custom is dying out, initiation by a Los Angeles gang is supposed to be a brutal ritual known as being "courted in" or "jumped in." To be jumped in is to receive a beating administered by three or four gang members: the candidate is expected to show his fighting spirit. If he passes the test, the peewee then becomes a "banger" or "gangbanger" and is entitled to share in the gang's fortunes or, more commonly, misfortunes.

COLORS AND SIGNS

The two most notorious L.A. gangs—the Bloods and the Crips—are not really gangs at all. Instead, the names denote legendary confederations among hundreds of sub-groups, or "sets." Sets are formed along neighborhood lines, and only a few have more than 100 bangers; 20 to 30 members is commonplace. Leadership is usually collective, and internal organization is rudimentary. One gang expert with the Los Angeles Police Department, Deputy Chief Glenn Levant, says most sets are as casually organized as a pickup basketall game. Bloods wear red and Crips wear blue; traditionally, each gang member wears or carries a bandanna (his "rag") to show his colors. (Many gangs also use "signs," which are hand gestures like a letter of the deaf alphabet, for identification when the members are not wearing their colors.) But local variations on the theme are endless, and Crip gangs are almost as likely to fight each other as they are to fight the Bloods.

The days when rival gangs fought each other only over turf and colors are fading fast. In Los Angeles, Chicago, New York and dozens of other cities, gang conflicts have become a form of urban-guerrilla warfare over drug trafficking. Informers, welshers and competitors are ruthlessly punished; many have been assassinated. Gang turf, which is still demarcated with graffiti in Los Angeles, now involves more than bragging rights; it is sales territory. Some gang graffiti are coded threats. One in south-central L.A. reads as follows: "Big Hawk 1987 BSVG c 187." To translate, Big Hawk is a gang member's street name. BSVG stands for Blood Stone Villains Gang, a Bloods set. The lower-case c, which is deliberately x'd out, indicates that the writer kills Crips, and the number 187 refers to the section of the California criminal code for murder.

"ROLLERS" AND "O.G.'S"

The variety of drugs sold by big-city gangs includes heroin, marijuana, PCP, hallucinogens, and designer drugs like fentanyl, a synthetic heroin that is even more potent than the real thing and just as addictive. But crack cocaine is the rage—and the scourge—of the ghetto. Crack is a drug peddler's dream: it is cheap, easily concealed and provides a short-duration high that invariably leaves the user craving more. It was probably inevitable that street gangs, observing crack's arrival in their neighborhoods over the past several years, would be drawn into trafficking themselves. South-central Los Angeles today, like Miami and New York, is flooded with crack. It is sold on street corners by peewees and in rock houses operated by bangers. Somewhere behind the scenes, much of the ghetto cocaine trade is controlled by what Los Angeles calls "rollers" and "O.G.'s"—old gangsters, a term that usually refers to gang veterans, many of them still in their twenties, who have been to prison.

Rollers, short for "high rollers," are gang members who have made it big in the drug trade, whether or not they are actually at the top of the distribution pyramid. Typically, rollers are in their teens or twenties. They tend to wear gold jewelry and drive flashy cars: Datsun sports coupes, five-liter Mustangs, BMW's and Mercedes-Benzes are among the most popular models. Roger Hamrick, a community-relations worker in Miami, remembers a gang member who moved to Daytona Beach, Florida, to peddle crack. "When he left [Miami], he was on a bicycle," Hamrick says. "When he came back, he wore more gold than Mr. T. and he was sitting in a white Mercedes. He's not even 24 years old and he has two Mercedeses and a Rolex watch." Says Bill Blanco, another gang specialist in Miami: "Who you are is dictated by the gold chains, the Rolex, the car. And everybody's got a car phone." Cellular telephones are more than decoration, of course: they are extremely useful in the drug trade. Beepers, which are equally useful to dealers, are now so common among ghetto teenagers that Los Angeles public schools have banned them.

Some gang veterans say the cocaine trade in south-central L.A. is controlled by 15 to 20 O.G.'s—an assessment that is shared by knowledgeable law-enforcement officials. Deputy Chief Levant, who commands a newly formed LAPD unit that specializes in major drug traffickers among the street gangs, says 75 to 100 gangs are now actively involved in cocaine distribution. Some of these groups, he says, now have sales totaling up to $1 million a week. "There is a link between the South Americans and the street gangs," Levant says.

That link—the strategic nexus between the Colombian cocaine cartel and street-level distribution in the United States—is becoming increasingly visible to investigators in southern California and elsewhere. There is little question that some black drug traffickers have now established direct relationships with top-level Colombian smugglers. According to Los Angeles County officials, the Colombians are even willing to sell drugs to O.G.'s and rollers on a consignment basis, a strong indicator of the cartel's

trust. One example of the increasingly close connection between the Colombians and the ghetto dealers was uncovered during Operation Pisces II, a two-year investigation run jointly by the U.S. Drug Enforcement Administration and state and local authorities in California and Florida. Pisces II was a money-laundering sting aimed at identifying both smugglers and dealers. In a video-taped conversation between two Colombian smugglers and detectives who operated the fake money "laundry," the Colombians admiringly describe a black trafficker in south Florida. "That s.o.b., he just ordered and ordered; it was hard to keep him stocked," one smuggler exclaimed. "Those blacks are really the best ones," the second smuggler agreed.

EAST AND WEST

There is equally little question that some of the more aggressive big-city gangs have begun to spread the drug trade into the heartland. Police from Denver to Vancouver report that Los Angeles gangs are moving in to establish branch operations selling rock cocaine. In Atlanta, Savannah, and Montgomery, Alabama, authorities say the Miami Boys are following the same expansionary pattern. Chicago gangs have appeared in Milwaukee, Minnneapolis and Racine, Wisconsin, and the Jamaican posses seem to be organizing crack outlets almost everywhere. Kansas City authorities recently managed to break a Jamaican posse that began importing crack from its East Coast base. The posse was operating 75 crack houses that grossed $400,000 a day. After that success, however, Kansas City was invaded from the West Coast as well. Four members of an L.A.-based Bloods gang were indicted for selling cocaine, and investigators say they have identified 15 L.A. gang members in their city. "This is the first time we've seen an *American* gang move into town," says U.S. Attorney Robert Larsen. "They're great entrepreneurs."

The big-city boys have two things going for them. First, they are usually able to buy top-quality cocaine directly from major smugglers at wholesale prices—as little as $10,000 per kilo. The second is that they are better armed and far more violent than the gangs or drug rings they encounter in smaller cities. As a result, they can compete successfully on price and quality—and if those classic business advantages are insufficient to establish a beachhead, they intimidate the competition with mayhem and murder. In Atlanta, says police Lt. John Woodward, the invading Miami Boys demonstrated the attitude that "we're *bad* and we'll prove it to you . . . [they'll] walk up to [their competitors] and just kill 'em. It's not, 'I'm going to out-macho you,' It's 'I'm going to *kill you*'."

Enriched by their drug profits, big-city gangs can now easily afford the overhead of far-flung operations. The gang may send a scout—often a younger memger—to test the market in the target city. If the first expedition pans out, a larger group will follow to rent a ghetto apartment as a stash house for volume sales. Woodward says the lookouts and runners are often local. Bodyguards may be either locals or out-of-towners. But the higher-ups, who control the stash and count the money, are always members of the invading gang. The amount of cocaine involved, Woodward also says, need not be large—a kilo or so every few days. Bring in "one kilo and you've got 10,000 bags of crack, and that will supply quite a few little housing areas for a few days," he says. "You're talking about $25 a bag, or $250,000 per kilo. The kilo costs [the Miami Boys] $10,000 to $12,000 in Miami, so there is a great, great profit margin here."

THE POSSES

Although there is still some controversy over just how well organized the American drug gangs are, no one doubts that the Jamaican posses are as disciplined as they are violent. Many members are believed to be illegal aliens, and the groups themselves are usually based in Jamiacan-immigrant communities on the East Coast—New York, Miami, Washington, D.C., among others. But their nationwide spread over the past several years has been staggering. The posses are major factors in the crack trade in most East Coast cities. They are also active in Dallas and Houston, in cities across the Midwest and, remarkably enough, they have recently been spotted in Anchorage, Alaska. Like most American drug gangs, the Jamaicans are known to hire local helpers when they open a crack house in a new city. But the core group is always from the island, and no outsiders are allowed to penetrate the upper echelons of the ring.

U.S. lawmen say many of the posses have their roots in the slums around Kingston, Jamaica. Their names reflect that genealogy. The Riverton City posse is named after a Kingston neighborhood, and so are the Maverly and Waterhouse posses. (The Jamaicans call themselves posses after the armed bands in American Westerns.) Some, like the Shower and Spangler gangs, claim vague affiliations with Jamaican political parties: the Spangler posse aligns itself with the People's National Party of former prime minister Michael Manley, while the Showers identify with the Jamaican Labor Party of current Prime Minister Edward Seaga. Jamaican politicians, however, disavow any connection to the groups.

In reality, most posses were probably marijuana-smuggling rings in Jamaica. But the crack explosion of the 1980s offers unlimited profits to the posses just as it does to American gangs, and Jamaicans have been even quicker than the American gangs to exploit the opportunity. South Florida, with its Colombian drug connections, is the adopted home for an estimated 1,000 posse members. The Shower and Spangler posses are the two main groups, and some lawmen say all other gangs are offshoots of these two. The lesser posses have exotic names like Dog, Jungle and Okra Slime. One group, the Jungle Lites, is reputed to be expert in guerrilla-warfare tactics, and police suspect they may have received military training in Cuba.

A Jamaican Invasion in West Virginia

With its tidy clapboard houses and neat apple and peach orchards on land George Washington surveyed centuries ago, Martinsburg, West Virginia (population: 13,000), seems far from the mean streets normally patrolled by drug gangs. But over the last three years, an invasion of Jamaican drug dealers has turned the home of the Mountain State Apple Harvest Festival into a mecca for cocaine.

The Jamaicans first arrived in Martinsburg as migrant workers to pick apples and peaches at harvest time, but many stayed on to peddle coke and crack. Hundreds squeezed into small apartments in a poor neighborhood called "the Hill" and transformed several blocks near the center of town into an open-air drug supermarket. Supplied by couriers shuttling between Jamaican gangs in Washington, Miami, and New York, as many as 50 dealers could be found brazenly hawking dope in broad daylight, just three blocks from the police station. At times business was so brisk that intersections were clogged with traffic; many cars bore out-of-state license plates. The customers "were all ethnic groups, age groups and every profession," says police chief Jack Strobridge. "They came riding up on skateboards, on bikes, in Mercedes-Benz cars, in pickup trucks." Stores in the region mysteriously sold out of vitamin B; police soon figured out that dealers were using it to "cut" the cocaine. Then the Jamaicans introduced crack—and started a run on plastic food-storage bags used to package the drug.

Martinsburg's 28-man police force carried out small raids but were overwhelmed by the dealers. In a region where one or two murders per years was the norm, 20 homicides, all drug related, occurred in 18 months as rival dealers fought for control. Cases of venereal disease shot up as prostitutes imported by the dealers worked the streets. At local schools, students hired as drug couriers strutted around in expensive Nike jogging suits and gold chains, intimidating classmates and teachers. A police raid of a Jamaican dealer's house turned up crude photographs of a former homecoming queen posing half nude, pieces of crack lying about her. According to law-enforcement authorities, she later gave birth to a baby fathered by the dealer.

Needles and Knives

Residents were virtually besieged in their homes. Theresa Shamburg was unable to leave her driveway without being offered "crack, cocaine or reefer" by pushers. Discarded needles and knives littered her front yard. She called police but they were unable to drive away the dealers. One night, when the Jamaicans outside became particularly raucous, Shamburg woke to see her husband crouched with a shotgun in one hand and a pistol in the other, grimly waiting for a break-in.

Under pressure from the community, local police asked the federal authorities for help. Some 200 agents from a special federal drug task force and local police raided 26 drug dens, arresting 35 dealers and seizing a cache of high-powered weapons. Police also found a "hit list" with the names of local judges and law-enforcement officials. The suspects arrested insisted the names were targeted only for a mystical curse by Jamaican witch doctors. Even so, three county magistrates began carrying guns for self-protection.

Street Action

The raid pushed the most blatant dealers off the streets—at least for a while. Much of the street action moved down the road to Charles Town, 16 miles away. But many Jamaican dealers have kept up a flourishing underground trade in Martinsburg. On warm days, Theresa Shamburg once again sees dealers congregating across the street. The Shamburgs will not wait to see what happens next. After three years of trying, they have finally found an out-of-town buyer for their home. They are moving to a house in the country, but Shamburg suspects there is no escape. She says: "I really don't think it's safe anywhere anymore."

MARK MILLER

REGGAE AND DEATH

But every posse has a fearful reputation for violence. Nationwide, according to U.S. experts, the Jamaican gangs have been linked to 800 murders, including more than 350 last year alone. Posse gunmen are known to prefer shooting their victims in public, and reggae clubs in major cities have a well-deserved reputation for frequent homicides. A dispute between posse members at a reggae club in Houston last October led to a fatal shooting in front of nearly 100 witnesses, and New York police report that homicides occur almost weekly at a popular Brooklyn nightspot known as the Love People disco. Torture and maimings are posse trademarks as well. "They don't mind shooting people. We've had numerous cases of Jamaicans who were shot in the knee or leg," says Dallas police investigator Charles Storey." A lot of groups have a potential for violence, but [the Jamaicans] demonstrate it daily."

The explosive growth of the drug gangs nationwide is putting enormous pressure on police all across the country. Cocaine and heroin traffickers are now deeply entrenched in the ghettos of many larger cities, and drug profits are a powerful incentive to hundreds of thousands of unemployed black and Hispanic teenagers. In addition, many gang members are increasingly expert in exploiting loopholes in the law. As a result, California and New York authorities are considering new anti-gang legislation patterned after the federal RICO (Racketeer-Influenced Corrupt Organization) law; such state RICO statues will enable prosecutors to seek longer prison terms for gang leaders convicted on other charges. Officials in cities like New York, San Francisco, and Washington, D.C.—to say nothing of Los Angeles—are also being forced to reorganize their police departments to meet the threat of drugs, which means cutting back on manpower for other crimes. "We need more resources—people and equipment," says Frank Storey, the FBI's chief drug official. "Resources are the most critical problem at the federal, state, and local level."

Outmanned, outgunned and outspent, the cops are fighting back as best they can. Officers who must deal with the gangs routinely wear armored vests (which often will not stop an assault-rifle round), and many departments now equip all their officers with automatic pistols to increase their firepower. But ghetto busts are extremely dangerous anyway: in Boston, for example, Police Lt. Det. Mel Ahearn has trained a special "Jamaican entry squad" to take on the posses in their strongholds.

There is every indication, meanwhile, that the gang/drug problem will get worse. If the analogy to Prohibition is accurate, the gangs have only begun to consolidate their hold on drug trafficking—and given their growth so far, it seems reasonable to expect that they, like the Mafia before them, will become even more skillful in evading law enforcement. The supply of smuggled drugs—Asian heroin, Mexican heroin, and cocaine most of all—seems almost limitless. At the same time, the federal government, which has scattered the responsibility for combating drugs among dozens of different agencies, seems to lack a coordinated national strategy. Who's running the war, America's hard-pressed cops are asking—and when are the good guys finally going to win?

12

On Being Sane in Insane Places

David L. Rosenhan

If sanity and insanity exist, how shall we know them? The question is neither capricious nor itself insane. However much we may be personally convinced that we can tell the normal from the abnormal, the evidence is simply not compelling. It is commonplace, for example, to read about murder trials wherein eminent psychiatrists for the defense are contradicted by equally eminent psychiatrists for the prosecution on the matter of the defendant's sanity. More generally, there are a great deal of conflicting data on the reliability, utility, and meaning of such terms as "sanity," "insanity," "mental illness," and "schizophrenia." Finally, as early as 1934, Benedict suggested that normality and abnormality are not universal.[1] What is viewed as normal in one culture may be seen as quite aberrant in another. Thus, notions of normality and abnormality may not be quite as accurate as people believe they are.

To raise questions regarding normality and abnormality is in no way to question the fact that some behaviors are deviant or odd. Murder is deviant. So, too, are hallucinations. Nor does raising such questions deny the existence of the personal anguish that is often associated with "mental illness." Anxiety and depression exist. Psychological suffering exists. But normality and abnormality, sanity and insanity, and the diagnoses that flow from them may be less substantive than many believe them to be.

At its heart, the question of whether the sane can be distinguished from the insane (and whether degrees of insanity can be distinguished from each other) is a simple matter: Do the salient characteristics that lead to diagnoses reside in the patients themselves or in the environments and contexts in which observers find them? From Bleuler, through Kretchmer, through the formulators of the recently revised *Diagnos-*

Science, Vol. 179, pp. 250-258, January 19, 1973. © 1973 by the American Association for the Advancement of Science.

tic and Statistical Manual of the American Psychiatric Association, the belief has been strong that patients present symptoms, that those symptoms can be categorized, and, implicitly, that the sane are distinguishable from the insane. More recently, however, this belief has been questioned. Based in part on theoretical and anthropological considerations, but also on philosophical, legal, and therapeutic ones, the view has grown that psychological categorization of mental illness is useless at best and downright harmful, misleading, and pejorative at worst. Psychiatric diagnoses, in this view, are in the minds of the observers and are not valid summaries of characteristics displayed by the observed.

Gains can be made in deciding which of these is more nearly accurate by getting normal people (that is, people who do not have, and have never suffered, symptoms of serious psychiatric disorders) admitted to psychiatric hospitals and then determining whether they were discovered to be sane and, if so, how. If the sanity of such pseudopatients were always detected, there would be *prima facie* evidence that a sane individual can be distinguished from the insane context in which he is found. Normality (and presumably abnormality) is distinct enough that it can be recognized wherever it occurs, for it is carried within the person, If, on the other hand, the sanity of the pseudopatients were never discovered, serious difficulties would arise for those who support traditional modes of psychiatric diagnosis. Given that the hospital staff was not incompetent, that the pseudopatient had been behaving as sanely as he had been outside of the hospital, and that it had never been previously suggested that he belonged in a psychiatric hospital, such an unlikely outcome would support the view that psychiatric diagnosis betrays little about the patient but much about the environment in which an observer finds him.

This article describes such an experiment. Eight sane people gained secret admission to twelve different hospitals. Their diagnostic experiences constitute the data of the first part of this article: the remainder is devoted to a description of their experiences in psychiatric institutions. Too few psychiatrists and psychologists, even those who have worked in such hospitals, know what the experience is like. They rarely talk about it with former patients, perhaps because they distrust information coming from the previously insane. Those who have worked in psychiatric hospitals are likely to have adapted so thoroughly to the settings that they are insensitive to the impact of that experience. And while there have been occasional reports of researchers who submitted themselves to psychiatric hospitalization, these researchers have commonly remained in the hospitals for short periods of time, often with the knowledge of the hospital staff. It is difficult to know the extent to which they were treated like patients or like research colleagues. Nevertheless, their reports about the inside of the psychiatric hospital have been valuable. This article extends those efforts.

PSEUDOPATIENTS AND THEIR SETTINGS

The eight pseudopatients were a varied group. One was a psychology graduate student in his twenties. The remaining seven were older and "established." Among them were three psychologists, a pediatrician, a psychiatrist, a painter, and a housewife. Three pseudopatients were women, five were men. All of them employed pseudonyms, lest their alleged diagnoses embarrass them later. Those who were in mental health professions alleged another occupation in order to avoid the special attentions that might be accorded by staff, as a matter of courtesy or caution, to ailing colleagues.[2] With the exception of myself (I was the first pseudopatient and my presence was known to the hospital administrator and chief psychologist and, so far as I can tell, to them alone), the presence of pseudopatients and the nature of the research program were not known to the hospital staffs.[3]

The settings were similarly varied. In order to generalize the findings, admission into a variety of hospitals was sought. The twelve hospitals in the sample were located in five different states on the East and West coasts. Some were old and shabby, some were quite new. Some were research-oriented, others not. Some had good staff-patient ratios, others were quite under-staffed. Only one was a strictly private hospital. All of the others were supported by state or federal funds, or in one instance, by university funds.

After calling the hospital for an appoint-ment, the pseudopatient arrived at the ad-missions office complaining that he had been hearing voices. Asked what the voices said, he replied that they were often un-clear, but as far as he could tell they said "empty," "hollow," and "thud." The voices wer unfamiliar and were of the same sex as the pseudopatient. The choice of these symptoms was occasioned by their apparent similarity to existential symptoms. Such symptoms are alleged to arise from painful concerns about the perceived meaningless-ness of one's life. It is as if the hallucinating person were saying, "My life is empty and hollow." The choice of these symptoms was also determined by the *absence* of a single report of existential psychoses in the litera-ture.

Beyond alleging the symptoms and falsi-fying name, vocation, and employment, no further alterations of person, history, or circumstances were made. The significant events of the pseudopatient's life history were presented as they had actually oc-curred. Relationships with parents and sib-lings, with spouse and children, with people at work and in school, consistent with the aforementioned exceptions, were described as they were or had been. Frustrations and upsets were described along with joys and satisfactions. These facts are important to remember. If anything, they strongly biased the subsequent results in favor of detecting sanity, since none of their histories or cur-rent behaviors were seriously pathological in any way.

Immediately upon admission to the psy-chiatric ward, the pseudopatient ceased sim-ulating *any* symptoms of abnormality. In some cases, there was a brief period of mild nervousness and anxiety, since none of the pseudopatients really believed that they would be admitted so easily. Indeed, their shared fear was that they would be immedi-ately exposed as frauds and greatly embar-rassed. Moreover, many of them had never visited a psychiatric ward; even those who had, nevertheless had some genuine fears about what might happen to them. Their nervousness, then, was quite appropriate to the novelty of the hospital setting, and it abated rapidly.

Apart from that short-lived nervousness, the pseudopatient behaved on the ward as he "normally" behaved. The pseudopatient spoke to patients and staff as he might ordinarily. Because there is uncommonly little to do on a psychiatric ward, he at-tempted to engage others in conversation. When asked by staff how he was feeling, he indicated that he was fine, that he no longer experienced symptoms. He responded to instructions from attendants, to calls for medication (which was not swallowed), and to dining-hall instructions. Beyond such ac-tivities as were available to him on the ad-missions ward, he spent his time writing down his observations about the ward, its patients, and the staff. Initially these notes were written "secretly," but as it soon be-came clear that no one much cared, they were subsequently written on standard tab-lets of paper in such public places as the dayroom. No secret was made of these ac-tivities.

The pseudopatient, very much as a true psychiatric patient, entered a hospital with no foreknowledge of when he would be discharged. Each was told that he would have to get out by his own devices, essen-tially by convincing the staff that he was sane. The psychological stresses associated with hospitalization were considerable, and all but one of the pseudopatients desired to be discharged almost immediately after be-ing admitted. They were, therefore, motivated not only to behave sanely, but to be paragons of cooperation. That their behavior was in no way disruptive is confirmed by nursing reports, which have been obtained on most of the patients. These reports uniformly indicate that the patients were "friendly," "cooperative," and "exhibited no abnormal indications."

THE NORMAL ARE NOT DETECTABLY SANE

Despite their public "show" of sanity, the pseudopatients were never detected. Admitted, except in one case, with a diagnosis of schizophrenia,[4] each was discharged with a diagnosis of schizophrenia "in remission." The label "in remission" should in no way be dismissed as a formality, for at no time during any hospitalization had any question been raised about any pseudopatient's simulation. Nor are there any indications in the hospital records that the pseudopatient's status was suspect. Rather, the evidence is strong that, once labeled schizophrenic, the pseudopatient was stuck with that label. If the pseudopatient was to be discharged, he must naturally be "in remission"; but he was not sane, nor, in the institution's view, had he ever been sane.

The uniform failure to recognize sanity cannot be attributed to the quality of the hospitals, for, although there were considerable variations among them, several are considered excellent. Nor can it be alleged that there was simply not enough time to observe the pseudopatients. Length of hospitalization ranged from seven to fifty-two days, with an average of nineteen days. The pseudopatients were not, in fact, carefully observed, but this failure clearly speaks more to traditions within psychiatric hospitals than to lack of opportunity.

Finally, it cannot be said that the failure to recognize the pseudopatients' sanity was due to the fact that they were not behaving sanely. While there was clearly some tension present in all of them, their daily visitors could detect no serious behavioral consequences—nor, indeed, could other patients. It was quite common for the patients to "detect" the pseudopatients' sanity. During the first three hospitalizations, when accurate counts were kept, 35 of a total of 188 patients on the admissions ward voiced their suspicions, some vigorously. "You're not crazy. You're a journalist, or a professor [referring to the continual note-taking]. You're checking up on the hospital." While most of the patients were reassured by the pseudopatient's insistence that he had been sick before he came in but was fine now, some continued to believe that the pseudopatient was sane throughout his hospitalization.[5] The fact that the patients often recognized normality when staff did not raises important questions.

Failure to detect sanity during the course of hospitalization may be due to the fact that physicians operate with a strong bias toward what statisticians call the type 2 error. This is to say that physicians are more inclined to call a healthy person sick (a false positive, type 2) than a sick person healthy (a false negative, type 1). The reasons for this are not hard to find: It is clearly more dangerous to misdiagnose illness than health. Better to err on the side of caution, to suspect illness even among the healthy.

But what holds for medicine does not hold equally well for psychiatry. Medical illnesses, while unfortunate, are not commonly pejorative. Psychiatric diagnoses, on the contrary, carry with them personal, legal, and social stigmas. It was therefore important to see whether the tendency toward diagnosing the sane insane could be reversed. The following experiment was arranged at a research and teaching hospital whose staff had heard these findings but doubted that such an error could occur in their hospital. The staff was informed that at some time during the following three months, one or more pseudopatients would attempt to be admitted into the psychiatric hospital. Each staff member was asked to rate each patient who presented himself at admissions or on the ward according to the likelihood that the patient was a pseudopatient. A 10-point scale was used, with a 1 and 2 reflecting high confidence that the patient was a pseudopatient.

Judgments were obtained on 193 patients who were admitted for psychiatric treatments. All staff who had had sustained contact with or primary responsibility for the patient—attendants, nurses, psychiatrists, physicians, and psychologists—were asked to make judgments. Forty-one patients were alleged, with high confidence, to be pseudopatients by at least one member of the staff. Twenty-three were considered suspect by at least one psychiatrist. Nineteen were suspected by one psychiatrist and one other staff member. Actually, no genuine pseudopatient (at least from my group) presented himself during this period.

The experiment is instructive. It indicates that the tendency to designate sane people as insane can be reversed when the stakes (in this case, prestige and diagnostic acumen) are high. But what can be said of the nineteen people who were suspected of being "sane" by one psychiatrist and another staff member? Were these people truly "sane," or was it rather the case that in the course of avoiding the type 2 error the staff tended to make more errors of the first sort—calling the crazy "sane"? There is no way of knowing. But one thing is certain: Any diagnostic process that lends itself so readily to massive errors of this sort cannot be a very reliable one.

THE STICKINESS OF PSYCHODIAGNOSTIC LABELS

Beyond the tendency to call the healthy sick—a tendency that accounts better for diagnostic behavior on admission than it does for such behavior after a lengthy period of exposure—the data speak to the massive role of labeling in psychiatric assessment. Having once been labeled schizophrenic, there is nothing the pseudopatient can do to overcome the tag. The tag profoundly colors others' perceptions of him and his behavior.

From one viewpoint, these data are hardly surprising, for it has long been known that elements are given meaning by the context in which they occur. Gestalt psychology made this point vigorously, and Asch[6] demonstrated that there are "central" personality traits (such as "warm" versus "cold") which are so powerful that they markedly color the meaning of other information in forming an impression of a given personality. "Insane," "schizophrenic," "manic-depressive," and "crazy" are probably among the most powerful of such central traits. Once a person is designated abnormal, all of his other behaviors and characteristics are colored by that label. Indeed, that label is so powerful that many of the pseudopatients' normal behaviors were overlooked entirely or profoundly misinterpreted. Some examples may clarify this issue.

Earlier I indicated that there were no changes in the pseudopatient's personal history and current status beyond those of name, employment, and, where necessary, vocation. Otherwise, a veridical description of personal history and circumstances was offered. Those circumstances were not psychotic. How were they made consonant with the diagnosis of psychosis? Or were those diagnoses modified in such a way as to bring them into accord with the circumstances of the pseudopatient's life, as described by him?

As far as I can determine, diagnoses were in no way affected by the relative health of the circumstances of a pseudopatient's life. Rather, the reverse occurred: The perception of his circumstances was shaped entirely by the diagnosis. A clear example of such translation is found in the case of a pseudopatient who had had a close relationship with his mother but was rather remote from his father during his early childhood. During adolescence and beyond, however, his father became a close friend, while his relationship with his mother cooled. His present relationship with his wife was characteristically close and warm. Apart from occasional angry exchanges, friction was minimal. The children had rarely been spanked. Surely there is nothing especially pathological about such a history. Indeed, many readers may see a similar pattern in their own experiences, with no markedly deleterious consequences. Observe, however, how such a history was translated in the psychopathological context, this from the case summary prepared after the patient was discharged.

This white 39-year-old male . . . manifests a long history of considerable ambivalence in close relationships, which begins in early childhood. A warm relationship with his mother cools during adolescence. A distant relationship to his father is described as becoming very intense. Affective stability is absent. His attempts to control emotionality with his wife and children are punctuated by angry outbursts and, in the case of the children, spankings. And while he says that he has several good friends, one senses considerable ambivalance embedded in those relationships also. . . .

The facts of the case were unintentionally distorted by the staff to achieve consistency with a popular theory of the dynamics of schizophrenic reaction. Nothing of an ambivalent nature had been described in relations with parents, spouse, or friends. To the extent that ambivalence could be inferred, it was probably not greater than is found in all human relationships. It is true the pseudopatient's relationships with his parents changed over time, but in the ordinary context that would hardly be remarkable—indeed, it might be very well expected. Clearly, the meaning ascribed to his verbalizations (that is, ambivalence, affective instability) was determined by the diagnosis: schizophrenia. An entirely different meaning would have been ascribed if it were known that the man was "normal."

All pseudopatients took extensive notes publicly. Under ordinary circumstances, such behavior would have raised questions in the minds of observers, as, in fact, it did among patients. Indeed, it seemed so certain that the notes would elicit suspicion that elaborate precautions were taken to remove them from the ward each day. But the precautions proved needless. The closest any staff member came to questioning these notes occurred when one pseudopatient asked his physician what kind of medication he was receiving and began to write down the response. "You needn't write it," he was told gently. "If you have trouble remembering, just ask me again."

If no questions were asked of the pseudopatients, how was their writing interpreted? Nursing records for three patients indicate that the writing was seen as an aspect of their pathological behavior. "Patient engages in writing behavior" was the daily nursing comment on one of the pseudopatients who was never questioned about his writing. Given that the patient is in the hospital, he must be psychologically disturbed. And given that he is disturbed, continuous writing must be a behavioral manifestation of that disturbance, perhaps a subset of the compulsive behaviors that are sometimes correlated with schizophrenia.

One tacit characteristic of psychiatric diagnosis is that it locates the sources of aberration within the individual and only rarely within the complex of stimuli that surrounds him. Consequently, behaviors that are stimulated by the environment are commonly misattributed to the patient's disorder. For example, one kindly nurse found a pseudopatient pacing the long hospital corridors. "Nervous, Mr. X?" she asked. "No, bored," he said.

The notes kept by pseudopatients are full of patient behaviors that were misinterpreted by well-intentioned staff. Often enough, a patient would go "berserk" because he had, wittingly or unwittingly, been mistreated by, say, an attendant. A nurse coming upon the scene would rarely inquire even cursorily into the environmental stimuli of the patient's behavior. Rather, she assumed that his upset derived from his pathology, not from his present interactions with other staff members. Occasionally, the staff might assume that the patient's family (especially when they had recently visited) or other patients had stimulated the outburst. But never were the staff found to assume that one of themselves or the structure of the hospital had anything to do with a patient's behavior. One psychiatrist pointed to a group of patients who were sitting outside the cafeteria entrance half an hour before lunchtime. To a group of young residents he indicated that such behavior was characteristic of the oral-acquisitive nature of the syndrome. It seemed not to occur to him that there were very few things to anticipate in the psychiatric hospital besides eating.

A psychiatric label has a life and an influence of his own. Once the impression has been formed that the patient is schizophrenic, the expectation is that he will continue to be schizophrenic. When a sufficient amount of time has passed, during which the patient has done nothing bizarre, he is considered to be in remission and available for discharge. But the label endures beyond discharge, with the unconfirmed expectation that he will behave as a schizophrenic again. Such labels, conferred by mental health professionals, are as influential on the patient as they are on his relatives and friends, and it should not surprise anyone that the diagnosis acts on all of them as a self-fulfilling prophecy. Eventually, the patient himself accepts the diagnosis, with all of its surplus meanings and expectations, and behaves accordingly.

The inferences to be made from these matters are quite simple. Much as Zigler and Phillips have demonstrated that there is enormous overlap in the symptoms presented by patients who have been variously diagnosed,[7] so there is enormous overlap in the behaviors of the sane and the insane. The sane are not "sane" all of the time. We lose our tempers "for no good reason." We are occasionally depressed or anxious, again for no good reason. And we may find it difficult to get along with one or another person—again for no reason that we can specify. Similarly, the insane are not always insane. Indeed, it was the impression of the pseudopatients while living with them that they were sane for long periods of time—

that the bizarre behaviors upon which their diagnoses were allegedly predicated constituted only a small fraction of their total behavior. If it makes no sense to label ourselves permanently depressed on the basis of an occasional depression, then it takes better evidence than is presently available to label all patients insane or schizophrenic on the basis of bizzare behaviors or cognitions. It seems more useful, as Mischel[8] has pointed out, to limit our discussions to *behaviors*, the stimuli that provoke them, and their correlates.

It is not known why powerful impressions of personality traits, such as "crazy" or "insane," arise. Conceivably, when the origins of and stimuli that give rise to a behavior are remote or unknown, or when the behavior strikes us as immutable, trait labels regarding the *behavior* arise. When, on the other hand, the origins and stimuli are known and available, discourse is limited to the behavior itself. Thus, I may hallucinate because I am sleeping, or I may hallucinate because I have ingested a peculiar drug. These are termed sleep-induced hallucinations, or dreams, and drug-induced hallucinations, respectively. But when the stimuli to my hallucinations are unknown, that is called craziness, or schizophrenia—as if that inference were somehow as illuminating as the others. . . .

THE CONSEQUENCES OF LABELING AND DEPERSONALIZATION

Whenever the ratio of what is known to what needs to be known approaches zero, we tend to invent "knowledge" and assume that we understand more than we actually do. We seem unable to acknowledge that we simply don't know. The needs for diagnosis and remediation of behavioral and emotional problems are enormous. But rather than acknowledge that we are just embarking on understanding, we continue to label patients "schizophrenic," "manic-depressive," and "insane," as if in those words we had captured the essence of understanding. The facts of the matter are that we have known for a long time that diagnoses are often not useful or reliable, but we have nevertheless continued to use them. We now know that we cannot distinguish insanity from sanity. It is depressing to consider how that information will be used.

Not merely depressing, but frightening. How many people, one wonders, are sane but recognized as such in our psychiatric institutions? How many have been needlessly stripped of their privileges of citizenship, from the right to vote and drive to that of handling their own accounts? How many have feigned insanity in order to avoid the criminal consequences of their behavior, and, conversely, how many would rather stand trial than live interminably in a psychiatric hospital—but are wrongly thought to be mentally ill? How many have been stigmatized by well-intentioned, but nevertheless erroneous, diagnoses? On the last point, recall again that a "type 2 error" in psychiatric diagnosis does not have the same consequences it does in medical diagnosis. A diagnosis of cancer that has been found to be in error is cause for celebration. But psychiatric diagnoses are rarely found to be in error. The label sticks, a mark of inadequacy forever.

NOTES

1. R. Benedict, *J. Gen. Psychol. 10*, 59(1934).
2. Beyond the personal difficulties that the pseudopatient is likely to experience in the hospital, there are legal and social ones that, combined, require considerable attention before entry. For example, once admitted to a psychiatric institution, it is difficult, if not impossible, to be discharged on short notice, state law to the contrary notwithstanding. I was not sensitive to these difficulties at the outset of the project, nor to the personal and situational emergencies that can arise, but later a writ of habeas corpus was prepared for each of the entering pseudopatients and an attorney was kept "on call" during every hospitalization. I am grateful to John Kaplan and Robert Bartels for legal advice and assistance in these matters.

3. However distasteful such concealment is, it was a necessary first step to examining these questions. Without concealment, there would have been no way to know how valid these experiences were; nor was there any way of knowing whether whatever detections occurred were a tribute to the diagnostic acumen of the staff or to the hospital's rumor network. Obviously, since my concerns are general ones that cut across individual hospitals and staffs, I have respected their anonymity and have eliminated clues that might lead to their identification.

4. Interestingly, of the twelve admissions, eleven were diagnosed as schizophrenic and one, with the identical symptomatology, as manic-depressive psychosis. This diagnosis has a more favorable prognosis, and it was given by the only private hospital in our sample. On the relations between social class and psychiatric diagnosis, see A. B. Hollingshead and F. C. Redlich, *Social Class and Mental Illness: A Community Study* (New York: Wiley, 1958).

5. It is possible, of course, that patients have quite broad latitudes in diagnosis and therefore are inclined to call many people sane, even those whose behavior is patently aberrant. However, although we have no hard data on this matter, it was our distinct impression that this was not the case. In many instances, patients not only singled us out for attention, but came to imitate our behaviors and styles.

6. S. E. Asch, *J. Abnorm. Soc. Psychol. 41*, 258 (1946); *Social Psychology* (New York: Prentice-Hall, 1952).

7. E. Zigler and L. Phillips, *J. Abnorm. Soc. Psychol. 63*, 69 (1961). See also R. K. Freudenberg and J. P. Robertson, *A.M.A. Arch. Neurol. Psychiatr. 76*, 14 (1956).

8. W. Mischel, *Personality and Assessment* (New York: Wiley, 1968).

13

When Life Seems Hopeless: Suicide in American Society

James M. Henslin

Mary's eyes were fixed on the razor poised over her outstretched wrist. She shuddered, thinking of the pain it wound bring. As she began to draw the razor, she felt herself becoming sick at the thought of blood gushing from her wrist.

"Oh, well, Plan B will have to do," Mary said aloud, as she laid the razor down. "It's a little slower, but much more peaceful," she added, as if announcing her intentions to the empty room. Methodically, she began to swallow the sleeping tablets, emptying the entire bottle. Then, slowly, deliberately, she settled back into her inviting bed.

Bill stared intently at the mirror. He didn't like what he saw. The reflection seemed to taunt him endlessly, conjuring fleeting images of cruel rejection.

"No more of that. No one is ever going to laugh at me again," Bill thought as he raised his dad's .32 to his temple, his finger slowly tightening around the trigger. Bill watched his reflection grimace in anticipation. The explosion still reverberated as his body collapsed against the sink, shuddered, and fell lifeless to the floor.

SEX AND SUICIDE

Mary and Bill illustrate three remarkable patterns in American suicide. Let's look at those patterns before moving on to the broader picture.

First, females are much more likely to *attempt* suicide. For every male who attempts to kill himself, about 5 or 6 females try to do the same thing.

Second, in spite of their fewer attempts, males are much more likely to *commit* suicide. In the United States, for every female who takes her life, three or four males take theirs. In every other country for which we have data, the male ratio also runs considerably higher, reaching a low of 1.7:1 in Denmark and a high of 5:1 in Poland [*Statistical Abstract, 1989.*]

Third, as shown in Table 1, males are more than one and one-half times as likely to shoot themselves, while women are two and a half times as likely to poison themselves.

Table 1. Method of American Suicide, by Sex

	MALE		FEMALE	
	Number	*Percent*	*Number*	*Percent*
Guns	15,518	64.1	2,635	39.5
Poison[1]	3,516	14.5	2,520	37.7
Hanging and Strangulation[2]	3,761	15.5	845	12.7
Other	1,431	5.9	678	10.1
Total Suicides	24,226	100	6,678	100

[1]Includes solids, liquids, and gases
[2]Includes suffocation
  Source: *Statistical Abstract of the United States* 1989, Table 126.

Let's look at each of these patterns. First, why do females attempt suicide more than males? Researchers interpret these attempts as "a cry for help," a sort of desperate, last-minute, bid for the attention of significant others, a dramatic attempt to secure help in crisis (Farberow & Shneidman, 1965). If so, this may indicate basic differences in male-female socialization, with females asking for help more than males, albeit in a highly striking fashion.

But why do so many more males succeed in killing themselves, although they attempt suicide so much less often? Apparently, male-female socialization is also critical here. Guns are "male" objects, associated with power, brutality, and violence—key male characteristics in our society. Males are more likely to learn to use guns during their youth, and then to select guns when they decide to end their lives. The choice is critical, for guns are more likely to be fatal: Most poisons allow a period of time during which attempters can be found and "saved." Also, many attempters communicate their intentions—obliquely, as by cleaning out their locker on a Friday afternoon and giving away prized possessions (Frymier, 1988), or directly, by telephoning a friend or relative, saying they have just taken sleeping pills—providing a "life-line," which, though tenuous, often thwarts the attempt. (This leads to the interesting possibility that many suicides by poison are, in reality, "accidents," for the individual may not really have wanted to die, but rather hoped to obtain help by means of dramatic display. Unfortunately, the "clues" were not picked up, the message didn't get through, or emergency personnel arrived too late.)

Researchers also believe that women are more likely to take their appearance into consideration when they plan suicide, imagining what they will look like when someone finds them. An image of their head blown open, their brains splattered against the wall, and blood covering their upper bodies does not match the image they want to present in their "final scene" (Henslin, 1970; 1972). This conjecture is supported by the finding that when females do choose guns, they are more likely than males to shoot themselves in the body than in the head (Lester, 1972).

THE SOCIOLOGICAL PERSPECTIVE

These differences in male-female suicide patterns are of central sociological significance, for they indicate that *suicide follows social patterns*. That is, suicide is not simply a matter of individuals choosing to take their lives due to some sort of "suicidal impulse" that is evenly distributed throughout the population. If it were, we could expect that men and women would kill themselves in about equal numbers; that in some months more women would commit suicide and in other months more men; and that more young people would kill themselves at some times and more elderly people at others.

However, suicide does not work this way. *Characteristics of society underlie suicide, leading to the same patterns in suicide month after month and year after year.* For example, look at Figure 1. First, note that, males kill themselves much more frequently than do females. Then note that this is true regardless of race. This pattern of race and sex in self-inflicted death holds true year after year, even decade after decade. It is not that blacks have higher suicide rates in some years, women in other years, and so on. It is similarly the case with age—the elderly are more likely to commit suicide than the young. From such patterns, sociologists conclude that characteristics of society—the ways in which whites and blacks and females and males are treated—underlie their different rates of suicide.

In other words, *sociologists look for social factors to explain social events.* That is, to explain differences in people's behaviors,

FIGURE 1. Suicide Rate by Race and Sex

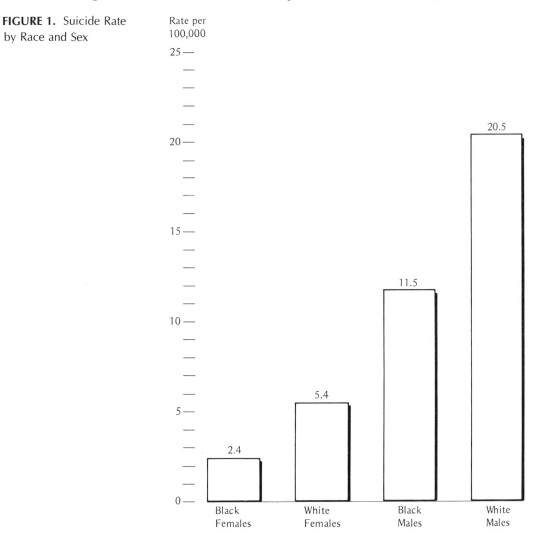

Source: *Statistical Abstract of the United States, 1989, Table 119.*

sociologists do not look for differences within people (such as "personality" or genetic factors of race or sex). Rather, they examine differences in how people are socialized (how they are brought up), their social location (amount of income or education, type of jobs, general beliefs and ideas, and so on), and their relationship with other groups in society (dominant, in control, greater or lesser access to wealth, and so on).

This brings us to theories and hypotheses, ideas that attempt to explain the patterns between suicide and demographics such as race and age. Let's look first at race and then at age, paying special attention to youthful suicide.

RACE AND SUICIDE

Following their perspective of examining *social* characteristics, when it comes to racial differences in suicide, sociologists stress not race, but social differences between the races. Compared with whites, for example, blacks are disproportionately deprived of income, education, marital stability, and access to good jobs. Therefore, one would expect them to have a higher suicide rate, that they would be more likely to kill themselves out of greater desperation. As we have seen, however, the figures run in just the opposite direction, a phenomenon which has been most perplexing for sociologists. The most likely reason for this unexpected finding is that the homicide rate of blacks is several times greater than the homicide rate of whites. Although blacks make up only 12 percent of the American population, they account for 48 percent of all homicides (Zawitz, 1988). If there is a certain amount of propensity for violence—the desire to strike out—that builds up due to frustrations in social life, and if one is going to act on that propensity, one has the choice of striking out against others or against oneself. Apparently blacks are more likely to strike out against others in the form of homicide, while whites are more likely to turn aggressive rage inward in the form of suicide.

But why should such differences in choosing targets exist? Sociologists Andrew F. Henry and James F. Short, Jr. (1954) explain the differences this way: On the one hand, people who have relatively high status in society and more access to the means to reach their goals experience a sense of control. When they fail, they tend to blame themselves, so they are more likely to make themselves the target of aggression. On the other hand, people who experience relatively low status and fewer advantages feel a sense of powerlessness. They therefore tend to blame others for their failures, and are more likely to make others the target of their aggressions.

While that explanation may be correct, I am convinced there are vital cultural differences that have not been explored. For example, there may be elements in our culture, and in the racial subcultures, that encourage some people to strike out against others and other people to strike inward. If so, we do not know what those factors are. It also would be important to know if blacks and whites in the same social classes have similar rates of homicide and suicide, for one would assume that feelings of status, blaming the self or others, and consequent outward or inward aggression would be similar. Unfortunately, we currently face many unanswered questions.

SUICIDE AND AGE

We should first note that, in spite of all the publicity given to increases in suicide among our youth, the suicide rate of the young is *less* than the suicide rate of the elderly. Indeed, as Figure 2 shows, suicide generally *increases* with age. The reasons for this increase are not clear-cut. I suggest that there is a gradual loss of optimism and hope and a growing sense of despair among the elderly. As the years pass, larger numbers of people experience a sense of being "beaten down," their competitive and combative energies waning in the face of accumulating problems. If this is true, however, the specifics of the process remain to be discovered.

FIGURE 2. The American Suicide Rate by Age

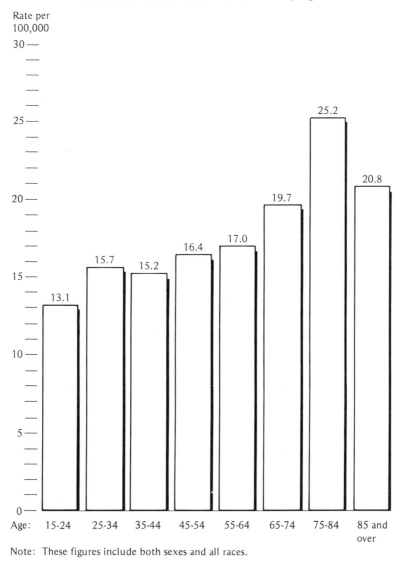

Note: These figures include both sexes and all races.

Source: Statistical Abstract of the United States, 1989, Table 119.

The basic reason that suicide jumps after the age of 64 is likely *status displacement*. A basic tenet of symbolic interactionism is that each of us receives a sense of identity by how others relate to us. Our jobs and families build ties to the larger social group and help give us a sense of identity and belonging. When those vital ties are ruptured, our identity, our sense of belonging and well being, and our feelings of purpose are threatened. Sociologist Emile Durkheim (1897/1951) referred to this as decreased *social integration*. Consequently, the potential for suicide increases at such times—at divorce or the breakup of some other significant relationship, at the death of a loved one, or upon being fired from a job, flunking out of school, getting kicked out of home, and so on. We can also catch a glimpse of this underlying pattern by noting that those who are married and those who have children have a lower suicide rate (Conklin & Simpson, 1987).

When older people retire, they withdraw from social roles that had provided them a valued identity and sense of usefulness. Their occupational roles, along with their friendship networks at work, had given them a sense of purpose in life, often considerably more than they realized when they were working. Upon disengagement from those roles, they are left facing a void. For some, that void is adequately filled by other friendships, by hobbies, golf, fishing, travel, and so on. For others, the void is never filled, and they experience a sense of emptiness, of purposelessness, of drifting, and of despair—conditions that Durkheim termed *anomie*. Anomic persons, of course, are more subject to suicide.

As Figure 2 shows, the rate of self-inflicted death takes an even larger leap after the age of 74. We can assume that decreased social integration also underlies this increase, for at this age very few individuals remain in occupational roles that provide a sense of self-worth or purpose in life. A sense of anomie is also fostered by declining participation in other social roles, such as in church or other social organizations. Two other factors also significantly decrease a sense of belonging at this age: First, death may have disrupted marital and friendship bonds, leaving many with a sense of isolation. Second, health is often failing at this time. When friends or a spouse dies, and when health deteriorates, the future looks very bleak. The elderly are especially fearful of cancer, and if they see their friends die—one by one, often in lingering pain—they may find little purpose in continuing the struggle called life.

Although the suicide rate drops after the age of 84—likely indicating that problems of living have stabilized somewhat, or that peo-ple of this age have worked out adjustments to the situations they face—it never drops very far. Note that it still remains higher than all age groups except that of 75–84.

SUICIDE AMONG YOUTH

As Figure 3 shows, between 1970 and 1986, suicide among young Americans increased sharply, the rate more than doubling among the youngest group. Let us look first at how the patterns of youthful suicide are similar to those of older people, then at how they differ, and, finally, at possible reasons for the increase in suicide among the young.

Many patterns of young people's suicide parallel those of older people. For example, adolescent females are more likely to attempt suicide, but adolescent males, like their older counterparts, are more likely to use guns and to succeed in the attempt (Brent, Perper, & Allman, 1987). Also, like the older people who kill themselves, a young person's suicide is likely to be preceded by a rupture of a primary relationship or some other crisis (Peck, 1987).

Unlike other age groups, however, young people who are married are *more* likely to commit suicide. This contradictory pattern has been explained by noting that people who marry young are likely to be using marriage as a way to escape an unhappy home life, and unhappy homes are a common background characteristic of people who commit suicide (Petzel & Cline, 1978).

Another contradictory pattern is shown by college students who commit suicide. Unlike the general population, in which failure often precedes suicide, college students who kill themselves generally have higher than average grades. It has been suggested that suicidal college students who make good grades don't feel they are successful, but that their success is an accident and eventually people will find out what they are really like. Munter (1966) refers to this nagging anxiety about one's ability and self worth, even in the face of outward signs of success, as "The Fraud Complex."

Many people find it difficult to under-

FIGURE 3. Suicide Rate of American Youth

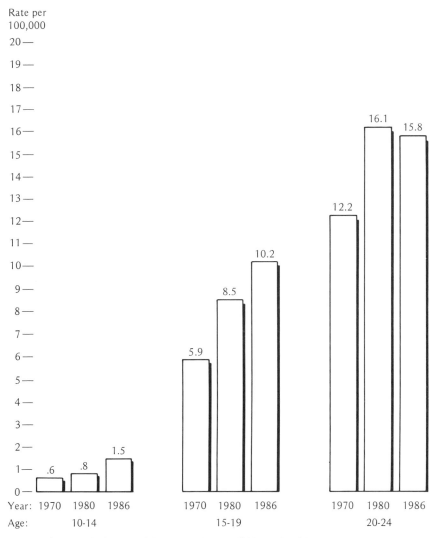

Rate per
100,000

Year: 1970 1980 1986   1970 1980 1986   1970 1980 1986
Age: 10-14   15-19   20-24

Source: Statistical Abstract of the United States, 1989, Table 125.

stand why young people would ever commit suicide. Comparing the situation of today's youth with what life was like when they were young, they reason like this:

What do the young have to worry about? Education is more readily available now than ever, we live in times of relative prosperity, entertainment is ubiquitous in the forms of television, movies, home videos, and video games. And even sex is considerably more open than it used to be.

What that thinking overlooks, however, are root causes, the fundamental anxieties and concerns that plague today's youth.

Durkheim's (1897, 1951) concept of social integration also provides the key to understanding the growing suicide rate of our youth. Durkheim's principal reasoning is that social integration tends to prevent suicide. Where social ties are strong, suicide tends to decrease; where social ties are weak, suicide tends to increase. Accordingly, since the rate of suicide by youth has increased, it is likely that integration among the youth has decreased. This, I believe, is the explanatory avenue that holds the best possibility.

Why would social integration of the young be lessening? What major changes have occurred in our society to bring about such a result? To this sociological recorder of the human scene, although limited to a small corner of the Western world, there seems to have been a fundamental change in orientation. No longer is there as much agreement about purposes in life (much less *the* purpose), or convictions about overarching reasons for one's activities. For many, even to mention such a topic seems but a quaint relic from the past. The radical reformulations of society, of life's purpose, of patriotism, and even of God, have left the young confused, bereft of overarching purposes, of heroes, of something worthwhile to cling to in order to justify making sacrifices, or even of continuing when the odds look bleak. Material goods, which seem to have become the primary focus of our society, are simply not an adequate substitute for God, or for heroes that instill allegiance and make the blood run hot in dedication to larger causes. The heroes of television are transitory and unreal, always ready to be replaced by other images which, in their turn, will come and go. This is certainly not comparable to legends of daring, nor to the firm belief that larger purposes govern the world, much less of conviction of one's own proper place within that larger scheme of things.

Even drugs, I submit, are not a basic cause of suicide, although they do contribute to it. Rather, they are merely a symptom of the lingering malaise that plagues our culture—indeed, Western civilization itself. There is also a second fundamental reason, not unrelated to the first. This is the breakdown of community. Certainly, community never has ben perfect, and there is no mythical past in which everyone felt a strong sense of belonging—we have always had the homeless, transients, runaways, alcoholics, spouse abusers, rapists, murderers, deserters, traitors, and so forth. Nevertheless, I am convinced that in the not-so-distant past, most people experienced a greater sense of community, of belonging, than they do today. I am referring to greater identifications with one's ethnic roots (ties with people who just a generation or two before had spoken a different language); with religion (in the small and even medium-sized towns that dotted our landscape, the church or synagogue was a powerful central, integrating force); with family (although American families have always been small [Blumstein & Schwartz, 1985], identifications extended farther beyond the nuclear family than they do today, and there certainly was considerably less divorce and illegitimacy).

Young people face a dazzling array of choices: occupation, lifestyle, geographical area in which to live, college to attend. Yet even this presence of choices, which would appear to offer attractions to life, not to death, creates problems, for it fosters rising expectations, as sociologists call them, that are not easily satisfied. On the contrary, they are easily crushed, leading to frustration and despair.

The material display of our culture—sometimes puffed up as the grandest accomplishment of humanity—does not replace poverty of spirit. The youth are still left with the perplexing question of the purpose of it all. If our culture cannot answer that basic question (beyond saying that one is born to be a consumer!), then alternatives are an absence of purpose, experimentation with dangerous drugs, despair, and suicide.

I submit, therefore, that the moral bankruptcy of our present culture is at the crux of the rise in the suicide rate of our young.

SUICIDE PREVENTION

On an individual level, each of us can be sensitive to the people around us, alert for the "cry for help" that the potential suicide may give, and willing to do our best to meet that person's needs. However, just as the problem is broad-based, so must the solution be. The analysis I have made of the fundamentals underlying our increased suicide rate among youth is controversial. Many will heartily disagree with me, pointing out that I cannot prove that we have less community, fewer ties, and so on. In any meaningful scientific sense, that argument is correct, but there are times when we need to move away from strict science in order to evaluate what we observe and to try to propose solutions. Otherwise, we will forever measure, eternally argue the merits of those measures, and never make any headway toward finding solutions.

While the particulars of my analysis need to be modified in any number of ways, I am convinced of the accuracy of the broad sketch. It has a solid theoretical base, going back to the earliest sociological analysis of the causes of suicide: that decreasing social integration leads to higher rates of suicide. If, then, the argument has merit, the basic solution would be to foster social integration, to create community, to make ties to society stronger. Specifics could include encouraging religious participation, ethnic identities, family ties, family activities, strong marriages, childbearing, patriotism, and identification with heroes that provide positive role models. Steps that strengthen such aspects of the social world will tend to strengthen people's social integration and thereby reduce their proclivity to suicide.

REFERENCES

Blumstein, P., & Schwartz, P. (1985). *American couples.* New York: Pocket Books.

Brent, D. A., Perper, J. A., & Allman, C. J. (1987). Alcohol, firearms, and suicide among youth. *Journal of the American Medical Association, 257,* 3369–3372.

Conklin, G. H., & Simpson, M. E. (1987). The family, socio-economic development and suicide: A 52 nation comparative study. *Journal of Comparative Family Studies, 18,* 99–112.

Durkheim, E. *Suicide.* (1951). (First published in 1897, John A. Spaulding & George Simpson, trans.). New York: Free Press.

Farberow, N. L., & Shneidman, E. S. (Eds.). (1965). *The cry for help.* New York: McGraw-Hill.

Frymier, J. (1988, December). Understanding and preventing teen suicide: An interview with Barry Garfinkel. *Phi Delta Kappan,* 290–293.

Henry, A. F., & Short, J. F., Jr. (1954). *Suicide and homicide: Some economic, sociological, and psychological aspects of aggression.* New York: Free Press.

Henslin, J. M. (1970). Guilt and guilt neutralization: Response and adjustment to suicide. In J. D. Douglas (Ed.), *Deviance and respectability: The Social construction of moral meanings* (pp. 192–228). New York: Basic Books.

Henslin, J. M. (1972). Studying deviance in four settings: Research experiences with cabbies, suicides, drug users, and abortionees. In J. D. Douglas (Ed.), *Research on deviance* (pp. 35–70). New York: Random House.

Lester, D. (1972). *Why people kill themselves: A summary of research findings on suicidal behavior.* Springfield, IL: Charles C Thomas.

Munter, P. K. (1966). Depression and suicide in college students. In L. McNeer (Ed.), *Proceedings of Conference on Depression and Suicide in Adolescents and Young Adults* (pp. 20–25). Fairlee, VT: Vermont Department of Mental Health.

Peck, D. L. (1987). Social-psychological correlates of adolescent and youthful suicide. *Adolescence, 22,* 863–879.

Petzel, S. V., & Cline, D. W. (1978). Adolescent suicide: epidemiological and biological aspects. *Adolescent Psychiatry, 6,* 239–266.

Statistical Abstract of the United States. (1989). Table 1408. Washington, DC: U.S. Government Printing Office.

Zawitz, M. W. (Ed.). (1988, July) *Report to the nation on crime and justice* (2nd ed.). Washington, DC: U.S. Department of Justice, Bureau of Justice Statistics.

14

Teenage Suicide

Jack Frymier

Barry Garfinkel, M.D., is director of the division of Child and Adolescent Psychiatry at the University of Minnesota Hospital and Clinic in Minneapolis. Dr. Garfinkel is an authority in the areas of mental health, learning disorders, psychopharmacology, and child and adolescent suicide and has published extensively in these fields. He also headed the Phi Delta Kappa Task Force on Adolescent Suicide. Born in Winnipeg, Manitoba, Dr. Garfinkel has worked in the Departments of Psychiatry at the University of Toronto, Brown University, and the University of Minnesota.

Frymier: To some people, the problem of adolescent suicide seems to have sprung up from nowhere. Just how bad is the problem?

Garfinkel: In understanding teenage suicide today, we have to explain a number of specific concerns that have emerged over the past 30 years. First, the total number of youngsters who kill themselves has increased 300% during this time. What's more, suicide attempts have jumped between 350% and 700%. Clearly, one of the questions we must try to answer is, What has caused these increases? At the same time, there has been a dramatic rise in the number of severely and profoundly depressed high school students, amounting to between 6% and 8% of junior and senior high schoolers at any point in time.

Frymier: Can you tell us anything about who these young people at risk of suicide are, and how parents and educators might identify them?

Garfinkel: Researchers have been working to develop a profile of the young person likely to become involved in self-destructive behavior. Unfortunately, we haven't completely succeeded in our attempts to identify such individuals. We know that the three strongest social correlates of suicidal behavior in youth are family breakdown, a youth's

Reprinted by permission of *Phi Delta Kappan.*

unemployment, and the decreasing religious observance among the young. However, we have been more successful in identifying some characteristics of those least likely to commit suicide.

For instance, we know that girls kill themselves much less often than do boys—at a rate somewhere between one-third to one-quarter that of boys. We also know that race is a factor. The rate of suicide for black youth is about one-fifth that for whites, while Native Americans kill themselves 10 times more often than whites. Geography seems to play a role, as well. Rural youth kill themselves at a higher rate than do urban youth.

Then there are the factors associated with family life. Family breakdown is associated with higher rates of suicide among young people, and a family history of chemical dependency or of completed or attempted suicide is also associated with higher rates among young people. Thus it appears that suicide runs in families, though it's not possible to say precisely whether social learning and modeling of such behaviors as substance abuse is at work or whether some sort of genetic link exists. We also know that religion is a factor. The traditional conservative religions seem to have some preventive effect; Catholic and Jewish young people commit suicide less often than do Protestant youth.

Frymier: You say that researchers have not been wholly successful in describing individuals who are apt to commit suicide, but can you give us the best profile researchers have been able to develop?

Garfinkel: We see four specific patterns in youngsters who do engage in self-destructive behavior. First, we see the youngsters who are isolated and who passively avoid issues and demands placed on them. Signs of this pattern might be deteriorating academic performance, trouble complying with rules in school or at home, and, generally, avoidance of association with one's peer group.

Second, we see youngsters who are highly irritable, who seem to have a chip on their shoulder. These youngsters tend to push people away and prevent others from being effective helpers. Whether consciously or not, the result is that these young people are alone.

Third, we see a tendency to exhibit aggressive behaviors. These young people engage in petty crime and vandalism, but they are more nuisances than delinquents or dangerous criminals. On the surface, they tend to look like the truly antisocial youngsters who normally go through the juvenile system. But it is important that their needs be addressed by the mental health system rather than the courts.

Finally, we see youngsters who use maladaptive coping strategies to deal with their problems. Rather than resolve their difficulties, they'll pick up methods that give them temporary relief, e.g., experimentation with alcohol and other drugs or engaging in thrill-seeking behavior. In the end, however, these behaviors do not resolve the difficulties these young prople face.

Frymier: Clearly, these young people have trouble dealing with the difficulties of growing up. Are the stresses teenagers face today, both in the family and in school, greater than they were previously? Are we placing more demands on young people than ever before?

Garfinkel: It is apparent that those youngsters who commit suicide or who attempt to do so are experiencing significant stress in their lives, including failing grades, difficulties with peers, trouble at home, and so on. But the stressors themselves are not, by and large, unique to suicidal individuals. Rather, an accumulation of various stresses ultimately overwhelms these youngsters and leaves them believing that suicide is the only solution available to them. Now we have found a few stressors that stand out as very difficult to adjust to and accept. One such is a history of physical and sexual abuse. The abuse of teenagers, boys and girls alike, is associated with a higher rate of self-destructive behaviors.

One striking finding of the research on teenage suicide is that, while some of the stresses that youngsters face do seem to cause suicidal behavior and depression, a whole set of stressors are a consequence of already being depressed. Thus deteriorating school performance and a drop in the level of participation in sports or in social activities are characteristics of a young person who is already depressed. Additional stresses simply compound and worsen the already-existing depression.

Frymier: What can we hope to do to prevent suicidal behavior in our young people?

Garfinkel: One of the things that we would like to achieve is for youngsters to be able to monitor themselves, to recognize when they are under stress or when they are beginning to feel depressed. Instead of letting the pressure build until they need massive amounts of help—possibly even hospitalization and medication—young people could then seek help sooner. In other words, we want youngsters to learn to recognize and admit to being troubled. We have found that girls are more willing than boys to say that they're depressed and to seek help. Perhaps boys are culturally conditioned to view this as unmasculine, as an acknowledgment of weakness, but for every adolescent boy who seeks help, three girls do so.

Frymier: Are there some other things that mental health professionals would like to see young people doing for themselves?

Garfinkel: Yes, we would like to help youngsters understand coping styles and coping mechanisms. We would like them to be better able to adapt to stress and feelings of depression. We would like to teach them to replace ineffective coping styles with more effective ones.

Frymier: What are some of the ineffective coping styles that young people resort to?

Garfinkel: Among the most common ineffective coping styles in this age group are experimentation with alcohol, the use of illicit drugs, promiscuity, delinquency, and school failure. Through such coping behaviors young people may find temporary social approval in certain peer groups, and this in turn may yield temporary relief from the discomfort of depression. But in the long run these behaviors only worsen the existing depression.

Frymier: What about more effective ways of coping with stress and depression?

Garfinkel: The effective coping styles all relate to an area in which we would like to educate our young people, and that is the importance of communication. Assertive, direct, and clear communication when one is troubled is a central goal of those of us who are trying to help troubled youth. Of course, this kind of communication depends on whether a troubled youngster knows and can trust specific adults or peers. Many troubled youngsters feel that they alone are burdened with a specific problem, when many young people probably share similar problems.

Once youngsters are able to communicate their feelings and are willing to share them, we would like them to become logical problem solvers, so that, when personal problems arise with their families or peer groups, they can sort them out logically and try to arrive at a reasonable solution. They can then try to find real solutions, rather than resort to the temporary relief offered by such artificial ways of handling stress as the use of illicit drugs and alcohol.

Frymier: Let me move to some more specific questions. Do depression and suicidal tendencies develop slowly over an extended period of time? And what behaviors might a teacher observe that would suggest seeking professional assistance for a child?

Garfinkel: First, there's a group of young people, mostly boys, who act impulsively and kill themselves in response to their very first bout of depression. One-fourth of all adolescent suicides fall into this category, and that number is growing. In such cases, there's very little planning involved, no suicide note, and no indicators.

As far as the rest of the potential teenage suicides are concerned, there are three clusters of identifying symptoms that I've referred to obliquely before. First, look for any signs of academic deterioration: grades falling from A's and B's to C's and D's, tardiness, incomplete assignments. Second, at-risk youngsters seem to slow down physically. They may have trouble staying awake, or they may suddenly drop out of athletic activities. Third, they may withdraw from other kinds of involvement with their peers. They may drop out of the drama club or the band and begin to seem socially isolated. These three clusters of symptoms are almost universal, but other symptoms may also appear.

Themes of suicide may appear in student writing or artwork. A youngster may begin to give away possessions. The student who cleans out a locker on Friday afternoon and gives away all of his or her possessions must be taken seriously. Finally, talking about suicide can be a sign that a young person is in trouble. Such pessimistic and self-deprecatory remarks as "I'm dead meat" or "I'm not worth a plug nickel" are not by themselves surefire signs of trouble, but they do occur at a much higher rate among youngsters who are suicidal.

Frymier: The subject of suicide is not one that teachers can easily broach with parents. If a teacher has serious concerns about a youngster, what would be some appropriate ways to bring up the topic and encourage the parents to seek help for their child?

Garfinkel: A teacher can take a number of steps. First, a teacher should not try to handle such a burden alone. Even in the best medical centers, in which handling suicidal youngsters is practically routine, we involve a network of people. Teachers in schools must tell the guidance counselor, the school social worker, or the school psychologist. Establishing that support network within the school is the first thing the teacher should do.

Second, with one of these other people, the teacher should confront the student to discuss what is causing him or her to contemplate suicide. If the student recognizes the need for help, that's when the family should be alerted. And it's important that the mental health professionals in the school, perhaps in conjunction with the principal or another administrator, should sit down with the family and discuss the concerns of the school staff about the child.

But the school's efforts shouldn't stop there. It's essential for the school to maintain a policy of monitoring and following up on youngsters who have been identified as suicidal. Just asking how things are going, just showing interest and concern, may be all that is required. Youngsters routinely get over periods of depression. But if things aren't getting better, then the school officials must once again alert the family.

Frymier: Let me follow up on the development of depression in young people. Is there a particular length of time that it takes for depression to develop in adolescents? Might a teacher become aware of it gradually? How long might a depression last?

Garfinkel: There has been a lot of research on this subject recently. Untreated depression appears to last anywhere from 6 months to 18 months. Because depression lasts a long time, a great many bad things can happen to young people while they're depressed.

When should a teacher begin to worry? Well, I don't have to tell teachers that adolescents are moody by definition, so every time students look grumpy or seem irritable doesn't mean that they're clinically depressed. But if that moodiness, grumpiness, or irritablity persists and is generally consistent for longer than two weeks, then I would say it's time to get the school mental health network involved, meet with the student, and alert the family.

Frymier: I've heard that peer counseling is popular in high schools today. Does this offer some hope for dealing with suicidal youngsters?

Garfinkel: Peer counseling is something of a two-edged sword. Certainly, when they're depressed or are contemplating suicide, teenagers routinely seek out their peer group. But what this means is that the people who are most able to help, who have the expertise, and who have a mature perspective on the problem are not being asked to help. Our research has shown that 75% of teenagers who are severely depressed or suicidal turn to their peers, about 18% turn to their parents, and only 7% turn to mental health professionals. While peers offer what support they can, their limited perspective on the emotional problems of their age-mates usually won't help to resolve the difficulties.

We present teenagers with something of a puzzle. We tell them that they must become more independent and develop autonomy when they go off to high school or college or join the work force. Unfortunately, we don't often remind them that it's okay to ask for help when they're in trouble. Turning to someone for help isn't a sign of weakness or of being effeminate; it's a sign of good judgment, if you turn to the right person.

One final point about peer counseling: teenagers make very good diagnosticians, but they make terrible therapists. They're very good at recognizing issues that trouble members of their peer group, but they simply don't have the mature perspective to provide the most effective help.

Frymier: We've been talking almost exclusively about teenagers. Are depression and suicidal tendencies simply less of a problem in the elementary grades?

Garfinkel: Yes. There are a few epidemiological studies, both in the United States and in New Zealand, that have shown that depression isn't a major problem before puberty. The rate of depression in 10-year-olds, for example, is around 1.5%. Yet, as I mentioned before, in the high school years it runs to between 6% and 8%. Something happens during and following the onset of physical maturation that is associated with a greatly increased rate of depression.

Frymier: Are there certain people in the school who, by virtue of the roles they play or the skills they have, would be most likely to be particularly aware of and helpful to young people who are depressed? Guidance counselors seem like the obvious candidates, but in many schools guidance counselors are so overburdened that they aren't able to spend much time with each student.

Garfinkel: First, anyone who has the opportunity to hear what young people are thinking and feeling is in a position to help by alerting others to a potential problem. And that means any teacher. What we have found is that physical education teachers and health teachers are often the first ones to become aware of a student's problem. They may notice that a student lacks energy or doesn't seem able to put forth as much effort as before. After them, we have found that those who work with mental health care, including school nurses, guidance counselors, school social workers, and school psychologists, are often in a position to learn of a problem firsthand, and, of course, they are often the people who can be of most help. After them, English teachers and art teachers get the opportunity to hear or see student's artistic expressions, which sometimes include themes of death and self-destruction.

Frymier: Is there any kind of closing statement that you would like to offer?

Garfinkel: I think that the most important thing to do is to recognize that we have a problem and that we must take action. The situation is worsening, and we aren't changing course. Moreover, I think that the school district is the appropriate level for action. Superintendents are the ones who must take the lead in raising the level of staff awareness and in committing the school district to respond with the appropriate resources and policies. Without their efforts to control and direct school policy, the needed changes will never occur.

PART III

PROSTITUTION, HOMOSEXUALITY, AND PORNOGRAPHY

A basic sociological principle is that sex is never a personal matter only. All societies control or channel human sexual behavior. One way this is done is by shaping people's ideas of what is right and wrong sexually. As a consequence, behavior that people see as "simply natural" is really the result of years of learning what one's culture expects.

As functionalists stress, to shape people's sexuality, all societies use the social institutions of marriage and family. Uniting in marriage and having children, men and women form families, the basic unit of society. The family performs such important functions as legitimizing birth, socializing the young, ascribing status, and transmitting property across generations. The family also serves the vital function of introducing children to the basic expectations of what it means to be a member in good standing of one's society. Some of these expectations concern acceptable sexual behavior. As they learn the ways of their social group, most people learn to identify strongly with the sexual behavior that is considered acceptable. In short, most people become conforming members of society.

But not everyone conforms. Some learn to become *sexual deviants*, people who violate the sexual norms of their society. When sexual deviance is mild, it is generally tolerated. However, when society feels threatened by sexual deviance, and especially when it sees it as a threat to the family, the deviant behavior is likely to be considered a social problem. In our society, for example, the prostitution of children or their appearance in pornography poses strong threats to our norms of family and acceptable sexual behavior. Americans generally find sexual deviance involving children more troubling than the same forms of behavior engaged in by adults. Our society often tolerates adult prostitution and pornography, but recoils in horror at child prostitution and pornography.

Our society is currently undergoing sweeping changes that are transforming our basic orientation to sexual behavior and causing a fundamental questioning of traditional morality. Prostitution, homosexuality, and pornography—the vanguard of the changes in sexual deviance that are shaking our society—are the focus of this third part of the book. They are social problems in the same way that other issues are social problems in that large numbers of people are concerned about them and would like to see a change in them.

Prostitution, homosexuality, and pornography similarly reflect the relative nature of social problems. Due to a lack of moral consensus on these issues, Americans are divided into opposing camps based on their personal experiences and values. While some people consider these activities a serious threat to social life, others find them eminently acceptable.

It is not in the realm of science, however, to pronounce moral judgments as to which "camp" is right. Rather, it is the function of science to report on attitudes and social controversy—the concerns that make contempoary society so exciting.

PROSTITUTION

It is no accident that *prostitution*, the selling of one's body for sexual purposes, has been called "the world's oldest profession." Accounts of prostitution reach back to the beginnings of recorded history. It exists in one form or another almost everywhere.

It is impossible to state with precision just how many "hookers" there are in the United States (the term comes from the Civil War camp followers of General Joseph Hooker), but estimates range from 250,000 to about a half million (Winick & Kinsie, 1971; Sheehy, 1973). It is also estimated that the average prostitute performs approximately 40 sexual acts each week (Sheehy, 1973). If this estimate is anywhere near accurate, in the United States somewhere between 10 and 20 million acts of commercial sex take place each week.

Although some of the prostitutes' customers (whom they call "johns" or "tricks") have bizarre sexual desires, most are average middle-aged men, most of whom are married (Wells, 1970). That so many married men visit prostitutes brings us to the relationship of prostitution to marriage and family, a key to the functionalist explanation of why prostitution seems to occur in all societies. Sociologist Kingsley Davis (1937; 1966), a functionalist, observed that prostitution serves to channel male sexual dissatisfaction into a sexual outlet that poses little threat to marriage. Prostitution does this by providing sexual gratification:

1. within a setting of anonymity;
2. that takes only a short time;

3. without requiring elaborate rituals of seduction;
4. without emotional commitment;
5. that includes sexual variety on request;
6. that is relatively inexpensive, often costing less than would a date.

Conflict theorists provide a sharp contrast to this functional interpretation. They emphasize that most women are dependent on men for their livelihood. This places them at an extreme disadvantage and makes them highly exploitable. In many areas of social life, men degrade women, using them as objects for their own pleasure. Prostitution is simply part of the essential degradation of women in a sexist society, another manifestation of the basic exploitation of women by men.

Conflict theorists point out that two themes run through the background of most prostitutes. The first is poverty. Reseachers have found few prostitutes who come from privileged backgrounds; almost all come from homes that are deprived both materially and emotionally. The second theme is abuse: It is common for prostitutes to come from families in which the father or stepfather beat and sexually abused them. Running consistently through the accounts that prostitutes give of their early home life are poverty, sexual abuse, and emotional deprivation (James & Davis, 1982; Silbert & Pines, 1982, 1983; Williams & Kornblum, 1985).

As children, those who later become prostitutes are generally regarded by their parents, teachers, and neighbors as troublemakers and misfits. In the face of alienation from school and parents, prostitution becomes a way out, a seeming escape from an unbearable life. It appears to offer the glamour of a fast life, easy money, and the emotional gratification of being accepted by men.

Finding that most prostitutes were abused as children, most often by males, conflict theorists stress that prostitutes have become locked into a way of life in which they continue to be victimized by males—by pimps who exploit their bodies for a profit and by "johns" who degrade their bodies for their own sexual pleasure.

We should also note that prostitution is not limited to females. Some men serve as prostitutes for women (gigolos), some for other men (male hustlers). While there are many male hustlers, being a gigolo is "an infrequent behavior, for which there is little demand and probably more folklore than reality" (Sagarin, 1980). Male hustlers most frequently operate on the streets, out of bars, and out of private escort services (Luckenbill, 1986). A much rarer location is the house of male prostitution, located in some large cities (Pittman, 1971).

HOMOSEXUALITY

What do we know about the causes of homosexuality? In seeking an answer to this question, researchers have been unable to find anything more than sexual preference to definitively set homosexuals apart from heterosexuals. No chemical, biological, or even psychological differences have been isolated that distinguish homosexuals and heterosexuals.

Consequently, sociologists do not view homosexuality as the result of glandular malfunction, hormonal imbalance, genetic predisposition, or the inevitable consequence of patterns of family relations (such as a "weak" father and a "dominant" mother). Rather, they view homosexuality as a learned identity. Researcher Vivienne C. Cass (1979) has distinguished six stages in this process:

1. *Identity confusion.* Finding his or her feelings at odds with heterosexual orientations, the individual is thrown into confusion and turmoil. He or she asks the burning question, "Who am I?" and in reply says, *"My behavior or feelings could be called homosexual."*

2. *Identity comparison.* The individual begins to feel "different," alienated, as though he or she does not belong. He or she makes the first tentative commitment to a homosexual identity by saying, *"I may be a homosexual."*

3. *Identity tolerance.* During this stage, the individual turns the self-image further away from a heterosexual identity and more toward a homosexual identity. This increased commitment is commonly expressed in the statement, *"I am probably a homosexual."*

4. *Identity acceptance.* In this stage the individual moves from tolerating a homosexual self-image to accepting a homosexual identity. Afer increasing contact with others who define themselves as homosexual, he or she concludes, *"I am a homosexual."*

5. *Identity pride.* During this stage, the individual thinks of homosexuality as good and heterosexuality as bad. He or she makes a strong commitment to a homosexual group, which generates a firm sense of group identity. The individual may become politically active to fight the "heterosexual establishment" and thinks, "I am gay and good" or "I am a homosexual and proud of it."

6. *Identity synthesis.* In this last stage, the individual decides that the "them and us" philosophy does not hold true and concludes that there is no clear dichotomy between the heterosexual and homosexual worlds. The individual begins to feel much similarity between himself or herself and heterosexuals as well as some dissimilarity between himself or herself and homosexuals. Although homosexuality remains essential to the individual's identity, it becomes merely one aspect of that identity. The individual is likely to say, *"I am a homosexual—and I am also a lot of other things in life."*

In line with symbolic interactionism, this analysis stresses that people actively construct their own self-image. Individuals who have begun to understand their feelings and behavior in terms of homosexuality may stop at any stage, either going no further or even moving toward a heterosexual identity. For example, in stage 1, faced with the possibility that one's behavior could be *called* homosexual, a person could either stop the behavior or continue it but define it as situational, that is, a characteristic of the situation rather than a part of one's own makeup. People in the third stage may feel positive about the probability of being homosexual and eagerly move to the fourth stage, or they may intensely dislike such a probability and take steps that move them away from a homosexual identification. In metaphorical terms, one could get off the train at the station marked "Identification Stops Here," or even the one marked "Return to Heterosexuality." To have begun the journey does not mean that someone is fated to continue it to a final destination of "Homosexuality" (Bell, Weinberg, & Hammersmith, 1981).

According to symbolic interactionism, identities, including one's sexual identity, are not fixed in nature or an inherent part of one's birth. Instead, this theory indicates that we are born with an undirected sexual potential that becomes channeled by our experiences into a homosexual or heterosexual direction. A heterosexual or homosexual identity does not simply automatically unfold from within, like an acorn planted inside an individual that can only become an oak tree. Rather, sexual preferences are learned and matching sexual identities are then acquired.

Like prostitution, homosexuality is a social problem because of subjective concern, public evaluation of the behavior. However, Americans are seriously divided on this issue. Many are convinced that homosexual behavior is wrong, a perversion of the natural sexual order between men and women, and that it poses a threat to the family and to basic decency and values. Others believe that homosexuality is simply an alternative lifestyle, that any problem that exists is due to narrow-minded people who insist on imposing their sexual orientations on others. There are extremists on one side who argue that homosexuals should be punished with severe legal and social sanctions, and extremists on the other side who argue that homosexuality should be encouraged among our youth.

PORNOGRAPHY

The production and distribution of pornography has become a major economic enterprise in American society. Pornography has flourished from a marginal, underground cottage industry into an open and aggressive $4 billion a year business. Behind it lies a network of people who profit from pornography: financiers, writers, publishers, actors, film makers, bookstore and theater owners, the independent operators of corner newsstands, and the chain-operated supermarkets.

Like homosexuality, pornography has become a controversial and emotional issue. On the one hand, those who denounce pornography argue that:

1. Pornography is *wrong in and of itself.*
2. Exposure to pornography *changes the viewer's ideas or standards* of what is right and wrong sexually. For example, watching the portrayal of rape, sex with children, sex with animals, and homosexual copulation will make those activities appear normal.
3. Exposure to pornography *changes sexual desires,* often stimulating the sexual appetite into deviant directions, such as enhancing the desire for rape and other sexual violence.

4. Pornography *"triggers" sexual deviance*. Watching deviant sexual activities encourages participation in similar activities.
5. Much pornography *dehumanizes women,* depicting them as mere sex objects, little more than bodies to be abused and exploited for the pleasure of men.

On the other hand, those who defend pornography argue that:

1. If pornograpy is not in and of itself a *good* thing, then it is at least *morally neutral.*
2. Pornography can indeed *change sexual attitudes,* and in the interest of greater sexual freedom this is *desirable.*
3. Pornography *does not lead to involvement in deviant sex.* Those who would involve themselves in such activities will do so anyway, without the prodding of pornography.
4. Pornography is a *"safety valve,"* allowing the private release of sexual fantasies. Thus, it protects people from those who would otherwise select unwilling victims to act out their fantasies.
5. Pornography provides *pleasure,* and, in the absence of demonstrable harm to others, this source of sexual excitement should be *permissible* in a free society.
6. Although some find pornography objectionable, it is simply one of the costs of a free society. *It is censorship that is the greater evil.*

The thorny question that bothers many people is: Does pornography cause sex crimes? Ted Bundy was convinced that pornography was the basic reason that he became a serial rapist-murderer. However, scientific proof (objective, consistent, verifiable) of a causal relationship remains elusive, for ethics forbid the experiments that could settle this question once and for all: under controlled conditions, exposing some children but not others to various types of pornography, and then studying their later patterns of sex crimes. Hence, as with most of life's questions ("Will my marriage work out? Will I like this job? What will my children be like?"), we must make decisions in the absence of full information.

After a period of vacillation, most feminists have taken an anti-pornography position, having become convinced that pornography teaches men to view women as "pieces of meat" that can be dealt with by males however they desire. Whether or not it can be proven that pornography causes sex crimes is not the point, they insist, for this portrayal creates hatred for women and thus is a vicious element contributing to the general victimization of women in society.

REFERENCES

Bell, A. P., Weinberg, M. S., & Hammersmith, S. E. (1981). *Sexual preference: Its development in men and women. Bloomington: Indiana University Press.*
Cass, V. C. (1979, Spring). Homosexual identity formation: A theoretical model. *Journal of Homosexuality, 4,* 219–235.
Davis, K. (1937, October). The sociology of prostitution. *American Sociological Review, 2,* 744–755.
Davis, K. (1966). Sexual behavior. In *Contemporary social problems* (2nd ed.), R. Merton & R. Nisbet (Eds.). New York: Harcourt.

James, J., & Davis, N. J. (1982, Winter). Contingencies in female sexual role deviance: The case of prostitution. *Human Organization, 41*(4), 345–350.

Luckenbill, D. F. (1986, April). Deviant career mobility: The case of male prostitutes. *Social Problems 33*(4), 283–296.

Pittman, D. J. (1971, March-April). The male house of prostitution. *Transaction, 8,* 21–27.

Sagarin, E. (1980, April 7). Communication to the author.

Sheehy, G. (1973). *Hustling: Prostitution in our wide-open society.* New York: Deli.

Silbert, M. H., & Pines, A. M. (1982, June). Entrance into prostitution. *Youth and Society, 13*(4), 471–500.

Silbert, M. H., & Pines, A. M. (1983, July-August). Early sexual exploitation as an influence in prostitution. *Social Work, 28,* 285–289.

Wells, J. W. (1970). *Tricks of the trade.* New York: New American Library.

Williams, T. M., & Kornblum, W. (1985). *Growing up poor.* Lexington: Lexington Books.

Winick, C., & Kinsie, P. M. (1971). *The lively commerce: Prostitution in the United States.* Chicago: Quadrangle.

15

The 'Patriotic' Prostitute

Jill Gay

Germany's Rosie Travel sells sex tours to Thailand. "Anything goes in this exotic country," says the company's brochure. "Especially when it comes to girls. Still, it appears to be a problem for visitors to Thailand to find the right places where they can indulge in unknown pleasures. . . . Rosie has done something about this. . . . You can book a trip to Thailand with erotic pleasures included in the price."

Japan Air Lines (JAL) is a little more subtle. "In order to embellish and relish better the nights of Korea," its brochure advises, "you must start above all else with a Kisaeng party." In South Korea, Kisaeng women were traditionally hired to sing and dance at parties; today, however, the word is synonymous with prostitute. "A night spent with a consummate Kisaeng girl dressed in a gorgeous Korean blouse and skirt is just perfect," continues the JAL pamphlet. Kisaeng parties, it adds, have "become one of the nation's most charming attractions."

"I felt I was picking out a slave girl at a slave market," says one Japanese tourist about his visit to Korea.

The international sex trade has reached shocking proportions. Between 70 and 80 per cent of male tourists who travel from Japan, the United States, Australia, and Western Europe to Asia do so solely for the purpose of sexual entertainment, according to *World View 1984*, a French political almanac. The Thai police estimated in 1982 that there were 700,000 prostitutes in the country—about 10 per cent of all Thai women between the ages of fifteen and thirty. A 1982 International Labor Organization (ILO) study found some 500,000 prostitutes in Bangkok alone. In the Philippines, an estimated 200,000 prostitutes operate; in South Korea, 260,000.

Reprinted by permission from *The Progressive,* 409 East Main Street, Madison, Wisconsin 53703. Copyright © 1985, The Progressive, Inc.

But far from being alarmed by these figures, leaders of the countries affected are spurring the trade along. "Within the next two years, we are going to need money," said Thailand's vice premier, talking to a meeting of provincial governors in 1980. "Therefore, I ask of all governors to consider the natural scenery in your provinces, together with some forms of entertainment that some of you might consider disgusting and shameful because they are forms of sexual entertainment that attract tourists.

"Such forms of entertainment should not be prohibited . . . because you are morally fastidious. . . . We must do this because we have to consider the jobs that will be created for the people."

In South Korea, the government sponsors an "orientation program"; prostitutes are issued identification cards that serve as hotel passes. The card is a "Certificate of Employment in Entertainment Service."

"You girls must take pride in your devotion to your country," the women are told at the orientation sessions. "Your carnal conversations with foreign tourists do not prostitute either yourself or the nation, but express your heroic patriotism."

Though prostitution is called the world's oldest profession, the boom in Southeast Asia started with the U.S. presence in Vietnam. There were 20,000 prostitutes in Thailand in 1957; by 1964, after the United States established seven bases in the country, that number had skyrocketed to 400,000. Throughout the war, Bangkok was a favorite "rest-and-recreation" (R&R) spot for GIs. Similarly, the number of R&R centers in the Phillippines increased from twenty to 600. And in South Vietnam itself, there were about 400,000 prostitutes at the height of the war—almost one for every GI.

"Saigon has become an American brothel." Senator J. William Fulbright noted. And the South Vietnamese government didn't seem to mind. "The Americans need girls; we need dollars," one official said. "Why should we refrain from the exchange? It's an inexhaustible source of U.S. dollars for the State."

When the American soldiers left in the mid-1970s, "the post-Vietnam slack was picked up by tourism," says an activist with Friends of Women, an organization based in Bangkok. The area around the U.S. military base at Subic Bay and the R&R center in Olongapo—both in the Philippines—are the largest bases for prostitution in Asia. But something other than the mere presence of soldiers and tourists accounts for the flourishing business.

"Sex tourism in the Philippines really took off during the period after 1972 when martial law was declared, and the government gave priority to export promotion," says Irene Santiago, a Filipina community organizer. "We needed a lot of dollars in order to pay off the foreign debt, so tourism was a major thrust for dollar earning. And with that, came the sex tourists—mainly from Japan." Currently, as the economy of the Philippines deteriorates, "the government feels there is a more urgent need to earn foreign exchange," adds Santiago, "so there's been a proliferation of prostitutes now."

The Manila Midtown Ramada Inn hands out a printed sheet "to our Japanese guests with ladies" that lists the charges for taking a woman to a room. One source reported in 1979 that the Manila Ramada made 40 per cent of its income from extra fees for prostitutes.

When Japan severed diplomatic ties with Taiwan in 1973, much of the Japanese sex trade shifted from Taiwan to South Korea, a move welcomed by the South Korean government. Massive investments have been made in resort areas, and the government is counting on billions of dollars in tourism revenues to help cover a foreign debt that exceeds $20 billion.

The sex trade has also figured in Thailand's economic development strategy, which calls for reducing investment in agriculture and aggressively pushing the export of goods produced in the cities. In a typical village in the north, as many as one-third of the families have no land, and three-quarters have less than the two acres needed for subsistence. Many send their daughters to Bangkok to work as prostitutes.

And some women opt for the profession because they don't care to work in the hazardous export-oriented plants. "You get cancer working in factories, we get abortion and VD working as prostitutes," one woman says. Prostitution now vies with sugar as Thailand's second largest producer of foreign exchange.

Taew grew up as one of eight children in northern Thailand. Her two elder sisters worked as prostitutes to American GIs at the base at Udon. When the U.S. Air Force left in 1975, her sisters came back to farm the land. But the soil was too poor to support them, so they went back to work as prostitutes in the cities. Then they got married, and the family lost its major source of income.

So Taew was sent to Bangkok to find work. She made a $1.50 a day mixing cement and steel, then $20 a month as a housemaid. Later she tried waitressing. Still struggling, she was finally persuaded to sell her virginity for $400, of which she received $100. "Taew did not like it a bit," the ILO study reported. "She cried for several days afterward." Taew sent her earnings home so her family could build a well for drinking water.

After her parents kept writing Taew letters asking for more money, Taew relented and went back to work as a prostitute, frequenting the Grace Hotel.

The Grace Hotel does not employ prostitutes, but it makes its coffee shop available as a marketplace. The owner charges an entrance fee of $2. Women who come to the Grace Hotel are usually on the way down in the market. They are not so attractive, having lost the sweet and innocent look, and are heavily made up. Men who come to the Grace Hotel are searching for specific styles of sex which they have difficulty finding elsewhere. They bargain. In the lounge of the hotel, men in their sixties can be seen propositioning girls in their teens.

Taew's story is not an aberration. Indeed, the ILO study found that of fifty prostitutes interviewed, all but four sent money home. Most remit one-third to one-half of their earnings, sums essential to their rural families' survival.

Pasuk Phongpaichit, author of the ILO study, says she first met a woman named Lek in a so-called massage parlor, which was actually a brothel. "She still had the look of a little girl, and her figure was not fully developed," recalls Phongpaichit. "When asked if she liked the job, she said she did not. She would like to go home."

But she couldn't go home. Lek's employer had lent her parents some money; it was up to Lek to work for the employer as repayment for the loan. She figured she would have to work 150 hours more, but then her parents took out another loan to pay for medical bills her grandparents had incurred. Lek was their only source of income. One day, her father went to see her at work. He said he wanted to make sure his daughter was in a good place. In fact, he went to ask her employer for more money.

"I have done my best to make money," one prostitute says, "even going to the extreme of selling my one and only asset, but all in vain. Isn't it strange that it is always someone else that reaps what one sows?" Airlines, travel agencies, hotels, madams, pimps—all take a chunk of the prostitutes' earnings. Korea Church Women United estimates that prostitutes receive less than one-thirtieth of the fees their patrons pay.

But the hazards are all their own. "After having my body ravaged by several customers in a row, I just get too tired to move my limbs," one prostitute says. "At times like this, a shot of heroin is needed. This enables me to handle five or six men in a single night. I can't help but take the drug in order to keep myself in working condition."

A study by the United Nations Fund for Population Activities disclosed that out of 1,000 prostitutes in Thailand, one quarter were regular users of drugs, particularly speed, barbiturates, and heroin. Forty-one per cent of the prostitutes had venereal disease and 19 per cent had undergone abortions, which are prohibited by law in Thailand (and therefore often hazardous).

Suicides are not uncommon. One woman killed herself after observing her own naked body in a mirror. It was covered with scars inflicted by a man who used lit cigarettes. Another woman, as recounted in a Korean newspaper story a few years ago, tried unsuccessfully to escape, but failed.

"At one o'clock every night, a guard locked the door of my room and took away the key," the woman said. "In the daytime, a receptionist kept a constant watch over the entrance. Since all ground floor windows were covered with iron grids, it was impossible to think of escaping through them. Even when I went to the bathhouse, someone was sent along to guard me." So she jumped out of a second-story window—and now is paralyzed from the waist down.

Women's groups around the world have begun to mobilize against the international big business of prostitution. In 1982, Dutch women held a militant protest at the Amsterdam airport for the departing plane to Bangkok, dubbed the "gonorrhea express." When the jet landed in Bangkok, it was greeted by another demonstration, held by Friends of Women and other Thai feminists.

In the Philippines as well, women have protested the sex trade. When then–Prime Minister Zenko Suzuki of Japan visited the Philippines in 1981, "the Japanese women's groups were able to link up with Philippine women's groups," recalls community organizer Santiago. The protest was coordinated by the Filipina organization, Third World Movement Against the Exploitation of Women, and it "really embarrassed the Prime Minister on his state visit," Santiago says. "They presented him with a letter of protest saying that this is a shame on the Japanese people, and that he should put a stop to the whole thing. That really got the attention of the press. And it actually stopped Japanese sex tours for a while."

Currently, "the Catholic Women's League, other church groups, and even the mayor have been holding rallies against sex tourism" in Sebu, the Philippines, a new center of the trade, says Santiago.

Such demonstrations are essential if the sex trade is to come to a halt. But they are not likely to succeed unless there are more profound changes, both in the presence of the U.S. military and in the export-oriented development strategies of Asian countries that depend on foreign exchange—at the expense of their most impoverished women.

16

Bell Desk Prostitution

LOREN D. REICHERT
JAMES H. FREY

Prostitution, whether on the streets of New York (Cohen, 1980) or within the milieu of "rough-area" hotels of a Canadian city (Prus & Irini, 1980), is a highly organized activity. This organization includes more than the "underworld" activities of prostitutes, pimps, and other "deviants." Rather, the prostitute's activity exists within a larger, organized network of relationships embracing actors of diverse licit and illicit statuses who control entry and exit into the network and who are governed by agreed-upon rules. Thus, bell-desk prostitution takes the form of "organized deviance" rather than being an apparently random, disorganized activity.

METHOD

The Las Vegas, Nevada, area provides an excellent research site for the investigation of prostitution, particularly organized hotel prostitution (Frey, Reichert, & Russell, 1981). Even though prostitution is illegal within the city and its contiguous county, every form of prostitution flourishes. Police files list over 10,000 prostitutes who have worked Las Vegas since 1970. This is a conservative figure, since a good proportion of prostitutes never come into contact with law enforcement, and fewer are arrested. Every form of prostitution, including streetwalkers, clandestine bordellos, high-class call girls, and quasi-legal massage parlors and escort services is found in Las Vegas. "Bell girls" obtain "dates" through bell desk personnel who act as intermediaries. In a hierarchy of types of prostitution, the bell girls would rank near the top; their status is exceeded only by call girls who maintain a restricted list of wealthy clients and by girls who are on call to service a very select clientele who are identified by upper management.

From *Sociology and Social Research*, Vol. 69, July 1985, 516-526. Reprinted by permission of the authors and publisher.

Using a referral process, we conducted intensive personal interviews with fifteen prostitutes plus several bellmen, bell captains, and hotel security guards. Two hotel executives and eight vice squad officers were also interviewed. Interviews lasted from one to two and one-half hours; some informants were interviewed more than once. It was difficult to obtain informants from the ranks of bell personnel. The few interviewed spoke freely, but many bellmen and captains approached by us directly, or by referral, declined to be interviewed.

We found prostitutes to be willing and candid interview subjects once rapport was established. In some cases, a student was trained to interview an acquaintance who was part of a network, but who was unwilling to be interviewed by either author. Additionally, an ex-prostitute volunteered to interview her contacts. The reliability of her interviews, and those obtained by students, was checked by post-interview briefings and by comparison with the results of other interviews. Information from all sources was routinely compared and crosschecked for validity with key informants.

BELL DESK NETWORKS

The jobs of bell captain and bellman are very desirable, even though these positions are among the lowest paid in the hotel. A union bellman receives $36.45 per eight-hour shift ($4.55 per hour). A bell captain receives $60.00 per shift. The bellman's hourly wage is exceeded by just about every other job category in the hotel, including maids ($6.68 per hour) and restroom attendants ($5.68 per hour). However, the gross annual income of a bellman is estimated to be three to five times that of his fellow service employees because of the substantial gratuities he receives. These take the form of commissions that originate in legal sources such as car rental arrangement, baggage transfers for groups, and show-room reservations. With the assistance of management, at one hotel it was calculated

that a bellman could make from $25,000 to $40,000 per year from legal gratuities. Earnings increase another 25 percent when illegal income is calculated. The attractiveness of this job is verified by the fact that bell desk personnel have the lowest quit rates and highest average years in service of any category of hotel employee. In fact, the average length of stay of members of one hotel bell crew was between eighteen and nineteen years.

The insulated organizational position of bell personnel, low contractual pay, and their position as "first greeters" for the hotel put the bell crew in an excellent position to service the needs of hotel patrons, which could include requests for prostitutes. The control of all bell activities, legal or illegal, rests with the bell captain.

Bell captains maintain a list of prostitutes. These lists range from roughly twenty names in smaller establishments to more than seventy in the larger hotels. Methods of getting on these lists vary. Some prostitutes enter a network through personal contacts and recommendations from women already on the list, or from hotel employees. Coercion is also a means of recruitment. A bell captain stated that, on occasion, he stopped freelancers on their way to guest rooms. They were given the choice of working for him (and giving him forty percent of their fees), or being taken to the security office. In addition, some prostitutes will take a more direct approach by introducing themselves to bell captains and requesting placement on their lists.

At the beginning of each shift (day, swing, graveyard), bell girls choosing to work during that shift call and report their availability to the bell desk. After receiving a request from a would-be client (directly or through a bellman), the captain verifies that the guest is registered in the hotel. He does this to obtain additional information from the front desk personnel about the guest. This information is important since the guest could be a policemen or the guest could be potentially threatening to the girl. If either determination is made the bell captain will call the room and inform the guest that no girls are available at this time. If the guest's status is cleared, the captain calls an available bell girl who matches, or approximates the characteristics (e.g., age, size, hair color, range of services) specified by the guest. During this call the captain gives her the room number and a capsule description of the client. If the "action" is to be other than standard fare ($100 for one hour, or one male ejaculation—whichever is first) he may relay this information to her as well. The prostitute can accept or refuse the date on the basis of this information. However, such refusals are infrequent because that could mean the removal of her name from the captain's list.

The prostitute will make every effort to arrive within a short time, 10–20 minutes, after the bell captain's call. She enters the hotel and alerts the captain, who notes her time of arrival as she passes his desk on her way to the guest's room. Depending upon the hotel, she may call the captain from the room to verify the arrival time, the "action" desired, and the fee to be charged. This fee is collected before she undresses. After the guest has been satisfied or the time limit is reached, the prostitute calls the captain to report that she is leaving. She will be met by the captain or a bellman at a predetermined location (e.g., outside the guest's room, near the elevators on that floor, or in a service room), where she gives him forty percent of the fee. She then leaves the hotel to return home to await another call or she goes on to another prearranged client. Many bell girls are listed at more than one hotel and manage their calls with the aid of answering service "beepers," or home answering recorders.

The captain's forty percent share is locked in the captain's drawer and, at the end of the day, the accumulation of fees from the three shifts is divided equally among participating captains. This method of disbursing reduces competition for assignments among bell captains to the most lucrative evening shift. Any other participants, such as bellmen or security guards, in

specific transactions get their share "off the top." For example, a bellman who helped to arrange a date receives one-half of the captain's share from that date, typically twenty dollars.

Risk Management and Exchange Among Network Participants

Prostitution can be risky business. Threats of violent assault, robbery, arrest, and public exposure may be felt by prostitute and patron alike. The casino hotels of Las Vegas, and the local economy, benefit from prostitution that is controlled and discreet (Skolnick, 1978; Frey, Reichert, & Russell, 1981). The point of control is a reduction of risk—risk being the antithesis of discretion. Organizing prostitution to reduce its risks not only results in its *de facto* acceptability in the local context, it also provides—along with sex or money—a major inducement for maintaining participation in the network.

Guest/Bell Captain Exchange

A hotel guest who desires a prostitute may approach the bell captain as a potential procurer. A guest, especially one indicating interest in obtaining a prostitute, is attractive to the captain as a source of money. A bellman may propose procurement by saying something like: "Hey, do you want company? Don't get it on the street, man." A guest who knows the ropes may simply call the bell captain and request that a prostitute be sent to his room.

The cost to guest, in terms of value given to the captain directly, is, at most, a tip. The value given indirectly to the captain is his cut of the prostitute's fee. This amount is significant to the captain, but of little or no consequence to the client. The fee a client would pay a freelancer picked up in the hotel bar is not significantly different than that demanded by a bell girl. A streetwalker's rate might be substantially lower, but we are inclined to doubt that a significant proportion of bell girls' clients consider street pick-ups as an alternative. In exchange, the captain's client receives services that reduce his non-monetary costs and risks. He saves time and effort, and he runs no risk of error or rebuff in misidentifying a woman as a prostitute. More importantly, there is the sharply reduced risk of being robbed or possibly blackmailed by the prostitute. A freelancer is a total unknown. If she victimizes a client, he can only complain to the police, and this he is unlikely to do, given the fear of costly stigma. Even if he does complain, he is unlikely to get his stolen money or property returned.

Procurement sevice as provided by the bell captain provides an inherent deterrent to the "trick roll." The prostitute's identity is known to the captain. A victimized guest is more likely to complain to the captain rather than to the police. A complaint to the captain is "off the record" since it involved no signed complaints or statements confessing to the illegality and impropriety of sex with a prostitute. Such a complaint is not very costly to the guest, and it is quite likely to be brought to bear upon the prostitute. Moreover, the guest has a "right" to complain to the captain, not only because the captain arranged the date, but also because his legitimate role is that of serving hotel guests and attending to their needs. Bell girls know that a victimized client is likely to complain to the captain who, in turn, will punish them for robbing clients.

A bell captain receives little or nothing from a client directly, but he knows that in serving the client he will later collect his portion of the prostitute's fee. His direct cost in serving the client is correspondingly slight—a minute or two spent on the telephone. How profitable his involvement proves to be, given that the reward is substantially fixed, depends upon his ability to collect his share from the prostitute and to minimize other potential risks. For example, the client could be a vice officer or someone who is potentially dangerous to the bell girl, but the captain (or bellman) depends on his ability to "size up" a customer on the basis of appearance and guest registration informa-

tion to minimize these risks. If the client is a police officer, not only will there be no percentage to collect, but the captain could also lose the respect of his peers for carelessness, be arrested on a pandering charge, and be terminated from his job.

To summarize the position of the captain, his direct costs, although potentially substantial (a felony arrest and job loss) are reduced to a very low order of probability with a moderate exercise of caution. The direct reward from a client is modest (if obtained at all), but the indirect, eventual reward for his speculation is substantial. Bell captains have been known to make up to $500 per week from their prostitution activities.

Bell Captain/Bell Girl Exchange

While freelancers and independent call girls spurn work through the bell desk as excessively costly and overrated as a source of protection, bell girls are attracted by the perceived or real benefits offered by captains in exchange for forty percent of their fees. One rather obvious benefit is the volume of business. "If a girl is in good with the captains at [hotel name], they really keep you going. You can really make a lot of money." Then too, there are obvious cost reductions. Just as the captain relieves a client of having to leave his room to go hunting, he relieves the bell girl of having to leave her apartment to hustle on the street or in bars. "I don't like sitting around in bars. This way I just stay home and wait for the phone to ring," noted one informant.

Participation in the bell network also reduces the risk of violence against a bell girl in the same way that the risk of a "trick roll" is reduced. The guest's identity is known to the captain, and the guest knows he can be traced by the police if he harms the prostitute. Knowledge of the client not only reduces risk to the captain, but it is also viewed as a basis for protection he offers to the bell girl.

It is obvious that bell girls benefit from risk reduction. But is this a benefit offered to them by the bell captains, and is it protection given to them in exchange for a percentage of their fees? One bell girl specifically noted that her captain regularly met her at the guest's room (she called him when she was ready to leave) and "he escorts me down to the lobby." She interpreted this as protection, as seeing her safely away from the room. Another bell girl was sure that, "If I was late in leaving the room, he would send security—or come up himself—to see what was going on. He did this once. I was late and he was snooping around by the door when I came out." A bell captain gave a different interpretation of the first prostitute's observation, but confirmed the statement of the second one. He offered that the reason for the bell girl's call to the desk before leaving the room is:

So you can meet her on the floor. You can't transact money in a lobby full of people with a woman who looks like a hooker, you know. That is as much as saying that you are pandering. . . . You meet her on the floor by the elevators and escort her down.

Escorting, then, does not exist for the purpose of protection of the bell girl (though it might serve that end), but for the protection of the captain as he collects his cut. On the other hand,

QUESTION: So if a girl doesn't cheat on you, and she doesn't take action away from you . . .

BELL CAPTAIN: She makes good money and we protect her, we make sure that there is no Freaky Freddies in there and there is nothing bad that happens to her.

QUESTION: How do you protect her from Freaky Freddie?

BELL CAPTAIN: We know what room the guy is in, and we know that he is upstairs with a girl and if he comes downstairs before the girl comes downstairs, then there is something funny. We check it out. If he wants something weird, then we get a weird girl for him. We are the protectors because she makes the call down before she does the trick. If she doesn't call down within the hour after she calls the first time, then security goes up.

QUESTION: Security will actually go to the room if she is overdue?

BELL CAPTAIN: Sure. Usually at that point you can say I saw this bimbo go into 546 with this guy and she ain't been out. Or you can say there has been a complaint from the guy next door.

The data suggest that the captains do actively offer some protection to their bell girls, but at least part of their motivation is self-protection and only incidentally protection for the prostitute. A prostitute is actively protected by her captain if that activity does not put the captain at risk, and, more certainly, if that protection reduces his risk. Otherwise she must "take it on the chin." The more generalized risk reduction that benefits bell girls is the result of their participation in a covertly sheltered facet of the local economy which includes a network of relationships managed in terms of rules and procedures designed to maintain the network's existence.

Bell Network Rules

Over and above their percentages of the fees, the captains demand compliance if their services are to be obtained. The bell network has rules and the captains enforce them. These rules, and the captains' authority, are rationally justified by network participants and rest upon the same values that mediate exchanges within employer-employee relations and the labor market generally. While all of these rules were not mentioned by all respondents, what follows represents an aggregate statement of rules for bell girls—expressed in their own words: (1) Be neat and clean. (2) Take care of yourself physically—stay in shape. (3) Arrive promptly—within about ten minutes of your call. (4) Don't come to work loaded on downers (mood depressants) or drunk. These rules are justified primarily in terms of an expected standard for client service, although rule four also has protective connotations. Several prostitutes and the bell captain said that a "loaded" bell girl is viewed as unreliable, or as "not smart." Consistent violation of these rules means a loss of business, i.e., being removed from the bell captain's list.

Rules five through nine may be seen as rules to maintain the operation itself—rules establishing obligations to, and reciprocity with, one's exchange partner: (5) Collect the money from the client first. (6) Call the desk within the agreed-upon time, usually one hour, and leave the client's room promptly. (7) Don't cheat the bell captain. This rule was universally mentioned, and said to be fundamental in its importance. (8) Be available for work; don't turn down too many dates. Rule eight varies considerably in its interpretation from hotel to hotel. In any hotel, however, a bell girl who is not sufficiently available, or who turns down too many requests, will be dropped from the list. (9) Don't give your phone number to clients. A prostitute who gives her telephone number to clients is competing with the bell network. The next time a client wants that woman, he can call her directly, thus depriving the captain of a client and a cut of the fee. A bell captain noted:

It is inevitable that if a girl gets a good trick, a guy that is going to come in, let's say, three or four times a year and drop them $7,000 for company for three days . . . they are going to nail their phone number. "Here, next time you are in town, you call me at this number. Don't even bother with the bell captain."

But you see, I don't have control over that. That is the only way that they can really get you. . . . They would just eliminate us getting our 40% by having him go to their apartment or their house.

The only control you have over it is that you fire on the guy again and say, "Have I got something for you!". . . Then he might say, "Why should I call this one? I will try someone new, same amount of money."

[If you know a girl on your list has given her number to a big spender] You will dump her for that. No more calls from our hotel, and when the guy comes to town we say, "Remember that girl you were with the last time? Did you have any trouble? We had two guys get social disease from her." We undermine her whole base.

But, as these statements indicate, the rule is nearly unenforceable. A bell girl told us, "That is another rule, no phone numbers. But I do and so do all the girls, because this is the only way we are going to make money."

The last group of rules, ten through fourteen, appear to require behavior of the bell girl that protects the network from the police or from hotel security in the performance of their legitimate enforcement responsibilities: (10) If you are busted in the hotel, take the rap alone. Don't implicate others. (11) Don't trick roll. Don't steal from clients. (12) Don't hang around the hotel. Come in only when you are called and leave directly when you are done. (13) Don't look like a hooker by wearing too much makeup or dressing in an outrageous or flamboyant manner. Some clients do not want their prostitute to fit the image of the hooker. Also, abnormal appearance is more likely to draw the attention of security or other hotel personnel who might take action to investigate just why this person is in the hotel. (14) Be smart, Have brains enough to follow the rules, to not get tricked by clients, to size up clients as vice cops or freaks, and to do the right thing. The twelfth rule does double duty as well. It not only serves to keep the operation discreet, but its performance keeps the captain from thinking that the bell girl is freelancing in competition with bell operations.

Rule Enforcement

Captains have discretionary powers on the frequency and extent to which a rule is enforced. A bell girl may be reprimanded for a first infraction of a minor rule or a violation without intent to deceive the captain.

Escalation of the severity of sanctions moves from a verbal reprimand to not giving the prostitute dates. This latter sanction may be exerted by only one captain, but, as each captain has favorites on the list, the number of her dates received can be reduced if the girl is not dropped from the list, but removed from a "favored" status to one of lower rank. More extreme, a bell girl can be crossed off the list at the captain's hotel, or, as a further step, at other hotels where he has contacts. Such action might be taken against a woman who is a chronic "ding head," a "doper," or a suspected cheat. To blatantly cheat a captain may not only result in her being removed from lists, but in being "eighty-sixed" or removed as well. A bell girl said, "Don't rip off the bell captains. If you get caught, you are eighty-sixed; not just at that hotel, the whole Las Vegas. They spread the word. Bell captains are friendly with other bell captains in each hotel." In the event of a "trick roll," or even a cheating violation, the captain may have a prostitute set up for a vice arrest, but the mechanics by which that is accomplished are unknown.

Finally, the captain may enforce rules through physical coercion and violence. One prostitute told us:

I remember one girl at [hotel]. She got paid something like $700 to spend the night there. She didn't call the bell captain. She just zoomed off and the bell captain called upstairs and the guy said she had been gone for half an hour. That bell captain sent two bellmen to her house and told her, "Well, what happened to the cut?" And the girl said, "Well, I am leaving town and I need this, so there is no cut." They beat the hell out of her and got the whole $700. You just don't fool around with the bell.

A captain working at a large hotel may have a list of seventy-five women to select from. If he drops a prostitute from the list, or has her "eighty-sixed," he is still in business. Conversely, he may be her only, or major, source of dates. She may be on several hotel lists, but "each captain has his favorites that he calls regularly" and the loss of a favoring captain will seriously decrease a bell girl's ability to obtain dates. Moreover, in terms of finding an alternative source of valued services, we note that there are many more prostitutes than there are bell captains (though some proportion of the prostitute population lacks the reliability or other traits required of bell girls).

Favoritism and Exploitation

A captain can easily reward a bell girl for being a "good" prostitute by giving her more dates, or he can punish her by withholding calls. A prostitute who is given frequent dates in exchange for compliance to the captain is more likely to accept the relationship as fair and, so, also give him respect. A relationship of mutual approval may result and mitigate his demands for compliance. But dates given to her are not given to others. Although he provides fewer dates for these other bell girls, he cannot demand less from them in terms of rule compliance. Yet, they may have to strive harder than before to obtain his services. They may have to offer him additional inducements (free sex), or stand ready to accept additional costs (greater availability, complimentary sex) to obtain dates through him. Being a captain's favorite can, then, be a powerful asset in getting dates. A favorite may also be obliged to give sex to the captain, but he has obligated by giving her a disproportionate number of dates.

Exploitive use of bell girls is sometimes mentioned when a captain uses his power for personal and unbusinesslike ends, or when his demands for business services from bell girls do not produce rewards for them. Exploitive personal use of bell girls is seen in a captain's demand for sex—a "freebee." It is not the "freebee" given by a favorite in exchange for good service from the captain that is problematic, but the sexual services demanded as a condition of working at all. The exploitation, and the values and sense of fairness in terms of which it is defined, is analogous to sexual harassment in legitimate organizations. The second situation seen as exploitive by some bell girls is one in which they are directed by a captain who does not favor them to provide sex to a client without a fee—a "comp" (complimentary sex). "Comping" a client such as a junket (gambling tour) organizer may be good business as far as the captains are concerned, and for the hotel in general, but those longer-range business interests seem pretty remote to the prostitute who is doing the "comping." It is the favorite bell girls who will especially profit from future junket business, while the less favored prostitutes provide the "comp."

CONCLUSION

The desired but unreal image of the resort city is protected by the covert organization of prostitution. This organization simultaneously offers prostitution services in volume, conceals that prostitution from non-participants, reduces the probability of participant vicitimization, and benefits from police efforts to eliminate street prostitution and open solicitation that are contrary to the desirable image of community.

However, the organizaiton is not that of "organized crime" as such. Rather, the organization of hotel prostitution involves several legitimate entities. Members of hotel bell crews participate directly in the operation. Other entities, including the police department, the general management of the resorts, and resort security units, are implicated in the organization through tolerant inaction, selective enforcement, and, on occasion, public disavowal of organized bell desk prostutiton. Our findings do not suggest that these entities, or their personnel as individuals, are normally bound to one another in conspiracy or relations of bribery and extortion. To be sure, individual security guards may be "tipped" for a service rendered—including looking the other way. This seems incidental, though. It greases the wheel, but it does not make it go around. The usual relationship among participants appears as an exchange of benefits linking them together in a symbiotic community of interests.

REFERENCES

Cohen, B. (1980). *Deviant street networks: Prostitution in New York City.* Lexington, MA: Heath.

Frey, J. H., Reichert, L., & Russell, K. (1981, July-September). Prostitution, business, and police: The maintenance of an illegal economy. *The Police Journal, 54,* 239–249.

Prus, R., & Irini, S. (1980). *Hookers, rounders, and desk clerks.* Toronto: Cage.

Skolnick, J. (1978). *House of cards.* Boston: Little, Brown.

17

Homosexuality in Prison
GEORGE L. KIRKHAM

It has been suggested many times that being without women is by far the most difficult aspect of imprisonment for most men. Certainly, the loss of liberty, the requirement to live in a restricted and insecure environment, and the absence of certain goods and services are frustrating to all prisoners; yet it is the complete unavailability of sexual and social relations with women which is almost intolerable for the average man in prison.

As if such sexual and psychological "pain" were not already sufficiently stressful for men whose backgrounds amply attest to an inability to adaptively handle frustration, the memory of woman is kept painfully alive by a multiplicity of stimuli. In addition to the sexual themes so common in prison humor and conversation, and the sub-rosa body of pornographic literature which is always in circulation, the mass media play an important role in aggravating the prisoner's psychosexual condition. Television, radio, newspapers, motion pictures—all combine to provide unrelenting titillation by keeping inmates exposed to the sexually charged atmosphere which characterizes contemporary American society. Mail and visits from wives and girlfriends only exacerbates the frustration which men in prison must endure daily.

Granted the fact of prolonged heterosexual deprivation, there exist only three possible adaptations open to members of the inmate community: sexual abstinence, masturbation, or involvement in institutional homosexuality. The individual reactions of abstinence and masturbation warrant only brief consideration here, since the problems which arise from "sex in prison" are primarily sociological products of the interaction of inmates with one another. Suffice it to say that an inmate may take the ascetic task of complete abstinence during his incarceration, or the more common one of regular or sporadic masturbation. Successful self-imposed continence is usually associated with an extremely short sentence and rigidly internalized notions of the inherent evilness of both masturbation and homosexuality. While it is true that individual differences in age and physiology enable some inmates to serve even long periods of confinement without any sexual outlet, the pressures on the average prisoner are such that he enages in at least periodic masturbation.

Homosexuality represents a third possible reaction to the deprivation of heterosexual intercourse. The small number of prisoners who engage in institutional homosexuality comprise a subterranean world, a kind of subculture within a subculture, which has profound consequences for the entire prison community. A homosexually oriented system of values, norms, argot, and statuses is so inextricably interwoven with the larger inmate social structure as to render the subject of sex between an inescapable reality of daily life for all prisoners. Homosexuality in prison becomes something with respect to which every man must constantly define himself as long as he is incarcerated.

Inmate society makes many complex distinctions between both acts and actors when evaluating any sexual activity which involves two or more prisoners. Members of inmate society exempt certain of their peers who indulge in homosexuality while incarcerated from the odious ascription of a "homosexual" status. There exist two criteria, both of which must be fulfilled, for an inmate to escape such stigmatization: (1) the homosexual act or acts must represent only a situational reaction to the deprivation of heterosexual intercourse, and (2) such behavior must involve a complete absence of emotionality and effeminacy—both of which are regarded as signs of "weakness" and "queerness." An inmate who engages in homosexual activity must present a convincing façade of toughness and sterotypical "manliness" in order to escape being defined as a homosexual. It is only because of the unrelenting "pain" of being totally de-

prived of sexual contact with women, something which is felt by all men in prison, that inmates are willing to take into consideration situational determinants of homosexuality. They therefore make a sharp distinction between homosexual behavior which is preferential and that which is believed to be only a substitutive response to heterosexual deprivation.

METHODOLOGY

I studied the inmate population of a major California medium security prison—the Correctional Training Facility, Soledad—while I was employed there over a two-year period as both a Student Professional Assistant and, later, as a Correctional Counselor. In gathering data for this period, I employed several methods: analysis of case files of homosexuality involved inmates: examination of incident reports relating to homosexual acts and actors (many of these yielded information on the subculture nature of "homosexual violence" and "pressure cliques"); and, thirdly, I developed a 43-item questionnaire using a Likert Scale which was designed to tap attitudes of the general inmate population with respect to various kinds of institutional homosexuality, as well as information on masturbation, abstinence, and so forth. This questionnaire was administered to a random sample of 150 Soledad inmates.

THE "QUEEN" OR "FAG": PREFERENTIAL HOMOSEXUALITY

The expression "queen" is used by both inmates and staff to refer to the inmate who closely approaches the popular stereotype of the "flaming faggot," the classically effeminate homosexual. It is believed that the queen engages in prison homosexuality solely out of a preference for male sexual partners. The behavior of such an inmate, rather than being rationalized as a situational reaction to being deprived of women, is felt to be merely the logical continuation of a preexisting pattern of "righteous homosexuality." Even if women were available, inmates aver, the queen would continue to play a "passive" homosexual role; nor is his homosexuality felt to derive primarily from either a desire to secure prison amenities, or protection, though these motives are recognized as sometimes being of secondary importance.

While prison queens form the smallest category of homosexually involved inmates, they are quickly identifiable solely on the basis of their overt appearances and mannerisms. Exaggerated limp-wristed effeminacy, a bizarre caricature of real femininity, serves to set them apart from the majority of inmates who engage in homosexuality. In every nuance of appearance, attitude, and behavior, the queen seeks to make "herself" attractive to a heterosexually deprived population of men as the closest approximation to a much desired but unobtainable sexual object: Woman.

Queens, who are usually referred to in the feminine gender by both inmates and staff, usually adopt nicknames which are unequivocally feminine; not infrequently, the selection of names such as Dee-Dee, Chee-Chee, and Peaches, betrays a sardonic mockery of females, which is also apparent in dress and other mannerisms. Even the casual visitor will easily notice the queen's "swishy" gait. If necessity is truly the mother of invention, then the queen has done well in using what the environment offers in approaching a feminine appearance: back pockets are torn out of tight prison denims to make them form fitting, makeshift cosmetics are fashioned from smuggled medical and food supplies, and jewelry is produced in hobby shops. Hair is grown as long as officials will tolerate, and eyebrows and whiskers often plucked. Like "her" counterpart in free society, the institutional "drag queen" is easily recognized.

The ostensible contempt and ridicule with which members of the inmate population speak of the queen belie the fact that "she" actually enjoys the position of a scarce object of high functional utility; for with the passage of time in prison, the flagrant differences which exist between male and female reach such a point of situational convergence for many sexually deprived men that the queen possesses a very real substitutive appeal. As one inmate confided, "Some of them look and act so damn much like real women!" The queen's effeminacy thus often evokes a memory and longing for females, a longing which sometimes leads otherwise exclusive heterosexual men to seek sexual relief from the queen.

Usually the queen will enter into a number of prison sexual liaisons which perhaps are best described as approaching serial monogamy. The use of the term "marriage" to describe these evanescent liaisons is no misnomer, for such relationships often reveal many of the elements common to heterosexual marriage. The queen brings to a marriage a desire for esteem, security, and affection, as well as for sexual gratification. She will usually continue the relationship for only as long as a preponderance of these needs are fulfilled. Like the heterosexual marriage, there is usually a stringent demand for sexual fidelity in such relationships.

Despite the general proscription of infidelity, two marriage partners may arrive at an agreement whereby the queen will prostitute herself to other inmates in return for certain goods and services. Some prison queens are able to amass considerable institutional affluence through selective prostitution; obviously, such activity also may serve the latent function of providing variety in sexual partners as a means of gratifying the queen's narcissism.

The brittle marriage of the queen results from a tacit, symbiotic contract in which she agrees to provide another inmate, usually known in prison parlance as a "wolf" or "jocker," with both sexual gratification and status among his peers as a "daddy." The "jocker," in addition to reciprocating sexual favors, acts as a protector and provides the queen with a measure of security in a highly predatory environment. The symbiosis thus revolves primarily about sex and security. Security, in the form of physical protection, is particularly important to the weak and effeminate queen. It is for this reason that most queens move from marriage to marriage, seldom terminating one relationship unless another is immediately available. By thus remaining always with a strong "daddy," she becomes relatively immune to the institutional phenomenon known as "sex pressuring" (coercion into homosexual activity). An unattached queen is constantly liable to sexual assault by lone predators, gang rape, and coercion into indiscriminate prostitution. Without a protective marriage, as one queen put it," . . . the traffic gets too heavy to bear." While a married queen may occasionally be "hit on" (approached for sexual favors), the knowledge that any aggressive overture may elicit a reprisal from her "daddy" serves to largely insulate her from the fate which befalls other weak and sexually vulnerable inmates.

THE "PUNK": CANTEEN AND PRESSURE

Those members of the inmate community who are regarded by their peers as "punks" occupy a status which is the very nadir of prison life. With the possible exception of the "rat," or informer, the punk is uniformly the most despised of inmates, a pariah who occupies at most a precarious position on the margin of inmate society. Unlike the queen who openly chooses a life of passive homosexuality and even embraces the stigma of effeminacy as desirable, the punk is hated because his involvement in prison homosexuality is believed to result from either personal weakness in the face of pressure or from a mercenary willingness to sacrifice his manhood for certain goods and services.

It is possible to discern two subcategories of institutional punks; in the language of the prison, these are (1) the "canteen punk," and (2) the "pressure punk."

The Canteen Punk

Inmates who are ascribed membership in this status are believed to engage in homosexual acts out of a desire for personal aggrandizement. They are men whose homosexuality represents an attempt to mitigate the frustration which results from being deprived of certain goods and services; thus, canteen punks form a class of prison prostitutes who perform fellatio and submit to pederasty in return for gratuities such as candy, cigarettes, money, or personal favors. As such, they represent a sexual outlet which is available to the inmate who desires homosexual release, but who is unable either to win a queen or to successfully coerce a weaker inmate into performing homosexual acts without cost.

The Pressure Punk

This category includes most of those who are disparagingly referred to by inmates and staff as punks. The "pressure punk" is one who submits to a homosexually passive role because of either threatened or actual physical force. As a group, such inmates are predominantly younger, less "prisonized"[1] individuals who have been singled out as "weak" by more sophisticated and sexually aggressive peers; usually, such men evince little or no prior history of homosexual behavior.

Sometimes a man enters prison with a "punk jacket." The dynamics of this process are often as follows: a rumor, often completely false, is circulated by one or more inmates at the institution that a prisoner who is scheduled to arrive has already been "ripped off" or "turned out" at the county jail or the prison transferring him; often this is done with the cooperation of inmate clerks at the other end, who have placed a prearranged pen mark or other symbol on the prisoner's file card to denote that he can probably be successfully "pressured" for sex. Soon word spreads throughout the institution, through an amazingly intricate communications system, that the inmate in question is "stuff," or a "broad." By the time the new prisoner arrives, the matter of the truth or falsity of this belief will be sociologically irrelevant. This entire process may be set in motion by nothing more than a "hunch" based upon an inmate's youthful or weak appearance. Sometimes, however, it results from a calculated desire on the part of others to even up a score for some real or imagined wrong committed outside the prison.

Whatever the reason, an inmate defined as amenable to sexual "pressure" will be tested by sexually predatory prisoners for the purpose of verifying his "punk" status as a preliminary to securing homosexual favors. The burden of proving that he is not a "pressure punk" rests entirely with the new inmate.

A very real *rite de passage* confronts all new arrivals at the adult male prison. Unless a man is a well-known returnee or has friends or "homeboys" who will help define him as a "solid con" to other prisoners, he may be in serious trouble. An imate who lacks such resources, and who does not possess a sufficient level of prisonization to enable him to navigate in a normatively acceptable manner, will very often have to run a terrifying gauntlet of sexual "pressuring" at the hands of other prisoners.

From the moment a new busload of inmates arrives at the prison, institutional "jockers" make a careful review of all "fish," or newcomers, in the hope of discovering which men will likely prove vulnerable to sexual coercion. Inmates who are regarded as potential pressure punks often will be first approached in the yard or cellblock with a friendly offer of goods or services. The new inmate, alone and frightened in a strange environment, is all too eager to accept the offer of assistance, candy or cigarettes, from the man who appears to know his way around. Because of his lack of familiarity with prison life, he does not realize that a "real con" never accepts anything from another prisoner—goods or services—without a clear statement of what

is expected in return. He likewise fails to grasp that the acceptance of favors under such circumstances is regarded by those proffering them as tantamount of a willingness to reciprocate in the currency of homosexual behavior.

Another common means of ensnaring the unwary "fish" is the invitation to enter a card game, or other gambling activity—which is predictably crooked—for the purpose of getting him into debt. The "fish," who usually has nothing to gamble with, at first is told that he can owe until canteen draw; however, suddenly he is deeply in debt and his fellow gamblers are no longer willing to wait until commissary time for settlement of the debt. As Lindner states:

When the showdown arrives and payment is demanded, he [the pressure victim] may be unwilling to come across. Then a startling transformation comes over his benefactor and erstwhile friend, and the harassed neophyte finds himself backed against a wall with a knife pressed to his stomach, and he hears the demand to "fuck or fight."[2]

The approaches of bribery and gambling are often expediently bypassed if any inmate is regarded as especially weak and frightened. Such men are often bluntly informed to submit to homosexual acts or else. One young inmate was approached less than five minutes after his arrival by a prison "jocker" who stated, "Listen, you need a 'daddy' and I'm it!"

Other inmates avoid those of their peers who are being subjected to sex pressuring; they refuse to help either out of fear of suffering the same fate or because of a very real danger of being beaten or even killed for interfering. Nor can the inmate under pressure go to staff for help because of the proscription against "ratting."

"Wolves" and "jockers" are able to wield sanctions ranging from threats to cold-blooded murder with the confidence that virtually no one will inform on them out of fear of being labeled a "rat." The code exhortation to "do your own time" also serves to reinforce the unwillingness of other inmates to become involved in the punk's problem. The subcultural belief that the pressure victim "brings it on himself" out of weakness or stupidity enables other prisoners to rationalize their noninvolvement in preventing behavior which they actually disapprove of.

Pressure punks are usually "owned" by one or more of the predatory groups of "jockers" which exist in prison. In addition to being used for homosexuality by the "pressure clique," the punk is often forced by such groups into prison prostitution or to "burn," that is, rob, the cells of other inmates. These groups of "wolves" or "jockers," each of which may range in size from three or four to twenty or more inmates, divide the proceeds of such activity on a businesslike basis. Sometimes the clique, or one of its members who has come into sole ownership of a "punk," will sell him to another group or individual, a "good punk" bringing perhaps fifteen to twenty cartons of commercial cigarettes. Like the queen, a punk may form a symbiotic alliance with a strong "jocker" in the hope of escaping homosexual assaults and control by pressure cliques.

THE "WOLF" OR "JOCKER": LONERS AND PRESSURE CLIQUES

Under certain circumstances a homosexually involved inmate may be defined by his peers as a "wolf," "jocker," or "daddy." These expressions each refer to a single status which involves a minimum of stigmatization. Men who are placed in this category by the inmate community are not regarded as "real homosexuals," since their behavior is felt to be the result of heterosexual deprivation, and conspicuously lacks effeminacy and emotional attachment.

The wolf or jocker plays the stereotyped "male" role in sexual activity. He views himself, and needs to be viewed by his fellow inmates, as "a man"; and within prison to be "a man" and still engage in homosexual acts one must present an image of exaggerated toughness and unequivocal masculinity. The jocker, by consistently wielding force over or raping his sexual partners, maintains for himself and others a perception of his behavior as basically masculine under the circumstances. The more violence that surrounds his sexual acts, the closer the jocker comes to actually engaging in an emotionless act of rape, thereby escaping both homosexual anxiety and the imputation of "queerness" by his peers.

The "jocker's" personality and background are usually characterized by an impulsive and hedonistic concern with securing personal gratification. When combined with the psychopathy which often pervades his personality, imprisonment in a world without women leads him to adopt a "take sex where you can get it" philosophy. While the jocker ostensibly has a strong preference for heterosexual partners, homosexual intercourse means little more to him than the difference between intravaginal and intra-anal penetration. He usually evinces little if any concern for the attitudes or feelings of his partners, whether they are heterosexual or homosexual. While most prisoners disapprove of his behavior, the jocker usually escapes the public scorn and derision which are meted out to punks and queens. A notable exception to this, however, is the jocker who "takes a queen." Other inmates are aware of the emotional elements likely to be involved in such a relationship, if only because of the nature of queens. Rather than being regarded by peers as consistently playing the masculine sex role, jockers who marry queens are often believed to "flip-flop," that is, sometimes play a passive sex role. Prisoners have a saying, directed toward such liaisons, that "when you make the team, you agree to play any position." One will sometimes hear jibes, such as "Who's playing the daddy tonight?" derisively flung at the jocker who has "courted and married a queen." The possibility of homosexual panic appearing is very real for the would-be masculine jocker who finds himself becoming emotionally involved with a queen.

The jocker is painfully aware that the

slightest suggestion of weakness, or emotional involvement in homosexual relations—the smallest chink in his armor of tough masculinity—may instantly topple him to the lowly status of "punk." He constantly must face the possibility that someone will successfully challenge the legitimacy of his claimed status. It is because of this that most prison jockers do not operate as loners; instead, such men usually form predatory alliances with other wolves. The manifest reason for the existence of such groups is the belief that extortion of homosexual favors requires the "muscle" of more than one inmate if it is to be successful; however, the formation of such groups actually serves the latent function of providing security for individuals who often are quite frightened themselves. For the jocker who is running scared, the best defense is a good offense.

The inability to effectively control prison pressure cliques proves both frustrating and embarrassing to the staff of a correctional institution. Even in those few instances where a pressure victim initially agrees to testify against his attackers, a sudden "lapse of memory" often occurs just before the case goes to court. Typical of such situations was the statement made by a young inmate who had resisted a group of jockers, only to be knifed by one of their number. He initially agreed to name the inmate who assaulted him, but soon backed down, stating to a prison official from his hospital bed, "You and I both know who 'shanked' [knifed] me, but nothing could make me testify. If I did, my life wouldn't be work two cents."

CONCLUSION

The author's two-year period of reseach at a major California prison led him ineluctably to the conclusion that the "homosexual problem" derives largely from the fear and violence which are produced by the attempt of a relatively small number of men to secure substitutive sexual gratification. To reiterate an earlier point, its existence in prison must be constantly dealt with on both a psychological and sociological level by every inmate. The typology of homosexual roles discussed here is certainly neither exhaustive nor immutable; hopefully, however, it provides a reasonably inclusive overview of a highly complex and constantly changing system of social behavior, and will also serve to encourage further research on the subject.

NOTES

1. The expression "prisonization" was originated by Donald Clemmer, *The Prison Community* (New York: Holt, Rinehart and Winston, 1958) to denote the extent to which an inmate has taken on, or internalized, the value system of the prisons.
2. Robert M. Lindner, *Stone Walls and Men* (New York: Odyssey Press, 1946), p. 454.

18

The Production and Distribution of Sexually Explicit Materials

THE ATTORNEY GENERAL'S COMMISSION ON PORNOGRAPHY

MOTION PICTURES AND VIDEO CASSETTES

Production

The average cost of producing a feature-length, 16mm or 35mm sexually explicit movie for theatrical release is $75,000. The costs may range from $30,000 to $150,000. A 16mm film that will be marketed on videotape costs between $10,000 and $30,000 to produce.

The sexually explicit film industry is presently in a state of transition from a theater-centered base to one dominated by videotape cassettes viewed in the home. Not surprisingly, the most rapidly growing method of production is to shoot a sexually explicit movie directly on videotape. A 60-minute video can be produced in two days at a cost of $4,000 to $8,000. A 90-minute video is often taped within three days at a cost of $10,000 to $20,000. The costs primarily consist of performer and crew fees.

Most sexually explicit movies begin by the producer choosing a title. The producer attempts to choose a title that will attract the customer's eye and make the movie more marketable. One current trend is to take popular general release movies and develop sexually explicit "takeoffs" based on the titles and plots of the general release movies.

After a title has been selected, the script is written to suit the title. Sometimes, however, the script has no relationship to the title. In addition, it is not uncommon for producers to use the same script for more than one movie.

Once a title is chosen and a script written, the producer finds a location at which to shoot the movie. Films may be shot in motel rooms, private homes, or on sound stages. The primary consideration for the type of

Final Report of The Attorney General's Commission on Pornography, U.S. Department of Justice.

location used is often the budget allotted to the particular film.

After a location is selected, the producer chooses the performers. Producers sometimes contact performers through agents. The producer usually looks through the agent's book listing performers along with their photographs. The producer may choose a performer on the basis of appearance alone or on the basis of previous performances. The producer may select performers by using a "cattle call," in which ten or fifteen performers are asked to appear at his location for an interview. In Los Angeles there are two agents who specialize in providing performers for sexually explicit films. The agent reeives $45 to $50 a day for each performer that he provides.

The producer is looking for several things when choosing the performers. The most important factor is appearance. Producers may want performers who have certain anatomical characteristics or who look particularly youthful. The second criterion is that the performer must be able to do the sexual acts called for in the script. These acts may include sadomasochistic activities, anal sex, group sex, urination, and defecation.

Female performers earn $350 to $500 per day of performance. Male performers earn $250 to $450 per day of performance. Better known "stars" of sexually explicit movies earn from $1,000 to $2,500 per day of performance. Performers may also be paid on the basis of the number and type of sex acts in which they engage. Some performers receive $250 per sex act.

As with any filming, the producer must own or rent lights, cameras and props. The necessary equipment costs $500 to $1,000 per day to rent. Larger production companies usually own their own equipment.

When the producer is ready to begin filming, he will often contact the agent and instruct the agent to have the performers meet the producer at a designated location. The producer sometimes transports the performers to the shooting location to avoid attracting the attention of the police or others. The police often learn of sexually explicit movie shootings when a neighbor complains about activities next door. The producer may also have security personnel check for police surveillance while the shooting is in progress.

Once on site, the performers go through makeup and wardrobe, and have a script review. The script is usually minimal and is rewritten during the filming.

Dialogue scenes are usually shot in the first two or three takes. The sex scenes are usually filmed in one take. The director will usually tell the performers exactly what he wants them to do. The director will tell them which way to turn their heads and what positions to use while they engage in sexual activity.

The most important part of the movies is considered by the trade to be the male ejaculation scene. This scene is always filmed when the male's penis is outside the partner's body. The male usually ejaculates on the buttocks, breast, or face of his partner.

Still photographs may also be taken during the shooting and are used for promotional material such as fliers, film or video package covers, posters, as well as unrelated magazine layouts.

It is also common for two versions of a movie to be produced during the filming. One version contains more sexually explicit scenes than the other. The less sexually explicit film is sometimes introduced into the subscription television market.

A day's shooting may last from seven in the morning until two o'clock the following morning. During this time, the performers and crew are literally locked into the location. The meals are prepared or brought in and lunch and dinner breaks are taken on site.

At the conclusion of the shooting the performers are asked to sign a "model release." The performers are then paid for their work, generally in cash. After the shooting is complete, the producers prepares a master print to be sold to the distributor.

The distributor first edits the movie and then adds the soundtrack. There are basically three types of sexually explicit films marketed: 8mm, 16mm, and 35mm. The 8mm films are usually made into loops. A "loop" is a 7- to 8-minute excerpt of a feature-length film.

The master tape is used to produce thousands of videotapes in order to supply the thousands of "adults only" pornographic outlets and general videotape retailers across the country. The distributor also packages the videotape and prepares his advertising and promotional material. The cost to the distributor for the purchase, reproduction, packaging and advertising of a videotape is on average between $8,000 and $15,000. The distributor then sells the videotape to a wholesaler for about $31. Generally, the distributor's profit margin is between 100–400% for a videotape.

Recently, the major distributors of sexually explicit films have rapidly entered the national videotape market. This is not surprising in light of the fact that the sexually explicit video industry's profits are in the hundreds of millions of dollars annually.

The wholesalers sell the videotapes to retailers across the country. Each wholesaler may carry thousands of titles from different distributors and sell the videotapes to retailers at a $2 to $6 profit.

Many times the distributor and the wholesaler are one and the same. Sometimes, the producer, distributor, and wholesaler are the same individual or corporation.

Sexually explicit videotapes can be purchased in "adults only" pornographic outlets as well as a significant number of general video retail outlets. One source estimated that at least 12,000 of the over 20,000 general video retail outlets across the United States distribute sexually explicit videotapes.

Sexually explicit videotapes are advertised on posters inside "adults only" pornographic outlets as well as trade magazines such as *Adult Video News*. These videos are also advertised in sexually explicit tabloids, magazines, and paperback books. In addi-tion, some video clubs advertise "X" rated videos in their publications, and some general video retailers also advertise these sexually explicit videos.

MAGAZINES

Production

Mainstream sexually explicit magazines have grown in number since the arrival of the first of this genre, *Playboy*, in 1953. These magazines generally follow a formula of sexually explicit photographs featuring primarily nude females in a variety of sexual activities interspersed with textual content that is either also sexually oriented or covers general-interest topics.

The content of the April 1986 issues of twelve of the most widely circulated of these magazines was examined and analyzed to more systematically portray this material. The magazines examined were: *Cheri, Chic, Club International, Gallery, Genesis, High Society, Hustler, Oui, Penthouse, Playboy,* and *Swank*.

To get a better understanding of the range of material available in one issue of these magazines, frequency counts were obtained of the advertising, editorial, and pictorial content.

Each advertisement was counted regardless of whether it was a display or a classified advertisement. In terms of the percentage of sexually oriented advertising, the amounts ranged from 100% of the advertising being sex-related, as was the case with *Club International* and *High Society*, to 20% in *Penthouse* and 10% in *Playboy*.

Phone sex was the product/service most heavily advertised across these magazines, with 49% of the advertising featuring this service. This was followed by sexually explicit video (16%) and sexually oriented magazine (10%) advertisements.

Editorial content in these magazines similarly varied from being totally or almost totally sex-related (*Club International* has 100% sex-oriented content, followed by

Cheri with 94%, and *High Society* with 91%), to having a greater proportion of general-interest topics (67% in *Playboy* and 60% in *Penthouse* were on nonsex-related topics).

Pictorial matter generally consisted of a "centerfold," other photographs of females posed alone, with other females, or with one or two males, and featured a variety of sexual activities. The most common of the acts portrayed was that of a nude female in what the jargon of the trade calls the "split beaver" shot, a shot of a female with her legs spread apart and in many instances, also spreading open her vaginal lips with her fingers. One in five of the acts portrayed in these magazines were of this variety. Nineteen percent of the activities depicted showed some type of touching or fondling, followed by oral-genital (12%) and sexual activities between two women (9%).

In 1983, a similar content analysis was carried out on one issue of eleven of these magazines by Canadian National Commission studying sexual offenses against children.[1] Included in this analysis were *Playboy, Penthouse, Hustler, Gallery, Cheri, Playgirl, Forum, Oui, Club, Swank,* and *Genesis.* The results showed that

- A large majority of the photographs depicted partially dressed females.
- The largest category of photographic depictions was for female body parts, primarily breasts, nipples (17%), followed by genitals (14%).
- The most common sexual act depicted in the text was masturbation (21%) followed by oral-genital contact (14%).
- The use of force in these textual depictions (anal penetration, bondage equipment, weapons, rape, and murder) accounted for 10% of the sexual acts depicted.
- Sexually oriented products featuring children were most heavily advertised in *Hustler* magazine.

In 1980, Malamuth and Spinner conducted a more specific study that analyzed the content of all *Playboy* and *Penthouse* cartoons and pictorials from 1973 through 1977. Pictorial violent sexuality was found to have increased significantly over the five years analyzed both in absolute numbers and as a percentage of the total number of pictorials. However, pictorials rated sexually violent were still a small percentage of the total pictorial material, reaching about 5% in 1977. Throughout this period, *Penthouse* was also found to have a greater percentage of sexually violent cartoons than *Playboy* (13% vs. 6%).

The sexually explicit magazines which are not included in the studies discussed above and are primarily available at "adults only" pornographic outlets portray masturbation as well as group, lesbian, gay, and transvestite sexual activities. Actual anal and vaginal intercourse as well as fellatio, cunnilingus and sodomy are also prevalent. There are depictions of rape, incest, bondage and discipline, sadomasochism, urination and defecation, bestiality, and simulated sexual activity with juveniles. Additionally, they cater to every type of paraphernalia which has been currently identified.[2]

In 1982, Dietz and Evans classified 1760 heterosexual pornographic magazines according to the imagery portrayed on the cover photographs.[3] Four shops were randomly selected from the 42nd Street district in New York City and every magazine-format publication with a female or cross-dress male on the cover was categorized. Depictions of a woman posed alone predominated these covers in 1970, according to the authors, but only constituted 11% of the authors' 1980 sample. Bondage and domination imagery was the most prevalent imagery (17% of the covers), while smaller proportions of material were devoted to group sexual activity (10%). The authors suggested that pornographic imagery is an unobtrusive measure of the relative prevalence of those paraphilias associated with preferences for specific types of visual imagery.

CABLE AND SATELLITE TELEVISION

Production

Cable television is a subscription service that first appeared in the United States in the 1940s to serve areas where broadcast television signals could not be received. The cable television industry expanded slowly until the 1970s, when the Federal Communications Commission (FCC) adopted a deregulatory philosophy to allow cable services to offer a greater number of channels and to foster program diversity. Cable subscriptions also increased when satellites were used by cable programming networks to distribute programming to local cable operators across the country. As a result of these developments, cable operators were able to offer programming from a wide variety of sources.

Today there are 6500 cable television systems in the United States serving over 40 million subscribing households. Cable television is currently available to 70% of the 85 million television households in the country.

Individual local cable operators control what programming will be offered on their systems. One of the basic attributes of cable television is "narrowcasting," or presenting programming designed for a particular audience, such as children's programs, educational programs, "adults only" programs, and foreign-language programs. Most cable systems offer a basic service package consisting of local broadcast channels and other nationally or regionally distributed channels such as Cable News Network (CNN), Christian Broadcasting Network (CBN), and the sports channel (ESPN). Cable systems usually offer at least one of the "pay television" channels such as Home Box Office (HBO), Cinemax, Showtime, or the Disney Channel. These channels usually carry unedited movies without commercial interruption and are sold to subscribers on a per-channel or per-program basis. The subscriber pays a monthly fee for the basic service and an additional fee for the "pay television" channels.

Distribution

An analysis of the various forms of television transmission discloses that most of the sexually explicit programs appear on "pay television." This programming includes movies that have been given an "R" rating by the Motion Picture Association of America (MPAA) and self-designated "triple X" films. Movies in the "R" category may depict violence, nudity, or sexuality, and contain sexually explicit or profane language. Unedited programs with these ratings are generally not shown over regular broadcast television; therefore, cable and satellite television programs often contain more sexually explicit scenes than those shown over broadcast television.

The difference in fare offered over regular broadcast television and cable and satellite television is due in part to the different legal restriction placed on each. Under current law, regular broadcast television cannot offer indecent or obscene programs.

Channels which carry "R" rated programming reach in excess of 14.5 million homes over 6900 cable and satellite systems. In addition to the sexual activity, the violence depicted in "R" rated movies can also be very explicit. Many times the violence depicted is of a sexual nature.

Other pay television channels carry programming that is exclusively "adult oriented" or sexually explicit. One such channel began in December of 1980 and currently has over 700,000 subscribers over 580 cable television systems. The channel's sexually explicit programs are shown during the hours of 8:00 p.m. and 6:00 a.m. In addition to "R" rated movies, the channel programming includes original adult programs and unrated movies.

In addition to this channel, there are two satellite networks which distribute sexually oriented programs to cable and satellite systems. One of the networks began operations in January 1985 and delivers sexually explicit movies over both cable and satellite television. Programs are shown between 11:00 p.m. and 4:00 a.m. over six cable systems.

Another network shows "triple X," unedited adult programming. A "triple X" rating is attached by the movie producer and generally covers the same material as the "X" rating but is meant to connote very explicit fare. This network has been in existence since 1983 and its programs are shown to 26,400 subscribers over eleven cable and satellite systems.

In addition to the cable-transmitted pay television channels, "X" rated and other sexually explicit movies are also available on direct satellite channels. Some of the "X" rated movies shown over satellite television include "The Opening of Misty Beethoven," "Sex Wish," "Easy," "Talk Dirty to Me," "Vista Valley PTA," "Insatiable," "Taboo," "Insatiable II," and "The Devil in Miss Jones." Although citizen complaints about obscene programming have been filed with the Federal Communications Commission, no action has yet been taken to regulate this programming.

Cable television operators have taken some precautions regarding the showing of sexually explicit programs. Some cable programmers and operators offer detailed program guides giving specific information about the content of upcoming programs. Some provide on-screen notices or warnings before sexually explicit programs are shown. Most operators limit such programming to the late evening hours and transmit the material in a scrambled mode to ensure against inadvertent reception by non-subscribers. Finally, all cable systems are required by federal law to provide lockboxes, upon request, for either lease or sale. This device enables a subscriber to lock out a particular channel or channels during certain periods.

DIAL-A-PORN

Production

In the 1920s, the Bell Telephone Company began providing recorded messages which gave the time of day and weather to its customers. The technology developed for such message services enabled Bell to provide these services at reduced costs because an operator did not have to handle the calls and give the information. Such recorded messages were called "Dial-it" services.

By the 1970s, this service had expanded and included recordings such as dial-a-joke and sports score lines. The telephone company was solely responsible for the content, distribution and advertising of the recorded messages.

In the early 1980s, the Federal Communications Commission ruled that providing information by recorded messages was a service beyond the permissible scope of the telephone companies' authority. As a result of this ruling, the entire telephone Dial-it service network was transformed.

Today, the delivery of all recorded message services involves two entities: the information provider, which is responsible for the content, distribution, and advertising of the message; and, the telephone company, which is responsible for transmitting the calls and billing the caller.

The recorded messages referred to as "Dial-A-Porn" began in 1982 after the deregulation of the Dial-it service. With the advent of telephone deregulation, some telephone companies began holding lotteries to select providers of recorded messages or Dial-it services. One provider of Dial-A-Porn Services was a winner in the lottery conducted in New York State and by February 1983 was offering Dial-A-Porn services over three telephone lines. It had acquired the lines either through the lottery process or by leasing them from other lottery winners. While this company has become one of the leading providers of Dial-A-Porn services, there are now many other Dial-A-Porn providers in the market.

There are two types of Dial-A-Porn calls. The first involves the customer dialing a number and carrying on a conversation with a paid performer on the other end of the line. The performer who answers the call will talk to the caller in terms as sexually explicit as the caller desires and may encourage him to perform sexual acts during the course of the phone conversation. The call may last up to 45 minutes and the caller is billed on his credit card for an amount usually between $15 and $30.

The second type of Dial-A-Porn call involves the receipt of a prerecorded message when the caller dials the designated number. These calls are a part of the Mass Announcement Network Service (MANS) and all begin with the prefix "976." MANS recorded messages provide other information such as prayers, racetrack results, weather forecasts, sports scores, time of day, and childrens' stories. The caller is charged for each call to this service on his monthly telephone bill.

The Dial-A-Porn recorded messages often consist of verbal illustrations of sex acts. These acts are frequently described by the performer as though they were actually occurring during the call with the caller and the performer was an actual participant in the acts. The acts described may include lesbian sexual activity, sodomy, rape, incest, excretory functions, bestiality, sadomasochistic abuse, and sex acts with children. One Dial-A-Porn number in California offers the caller a choice of five "pleasures," including descriptions of sadomasochistic abuse, urination, and anal intercourse.

COMPUTERS

Production

The personal home computer provides individuals with an extraordinary new form of communication and information access. Providers of sexually explicit materials have taken advantage of this new technology by making computer subscription services the most recent advance in "sexually explicit communications."

In order to set up a computer information service, the information provider must have a computer facility with the capability of handling a number of incoming calls to the information service. The computers used by information providers can cost from $20,000 to $30,000 for a microcomputer (which can handle approximately ten calls at one time) to timeshare computers costing $100,000 or more (which can handle significantly more calls). The basic cost of providing an information service of any type depends on the magnitude and complexity of the service offered. Computer services offering sexually explicit communications run the gamut from small bulletin board operations to large-scale, multifaceted services.

The types of information provided also vary. The computer services are similar to Dial-A-Porn telephone services in that some offer live conversations with an employee of the service, prerecorded messages, or an open line where individuals can communicate with other subscribers. Sexually explicit services may offer one or all of these features. Other, general-information providers may offer open "adult" channels where subscribers can carry on sexually explicit conversations with others on the system.

PEEP SHOWS

Production

The aveage peep show booth has dimensions of about three by five feet. The booths are partitioned four-sided cubicles generally made out of wood or plastic. Often, a bench is built onto one of the walls. On the wall next to the bench is the coin- or token-operated box. A customer places coins or tokens into the box and the movie inside the booth is activated.

If a film is shown, the booth is equipped with a movie projector. If a video is shown, the peep-show booth is wired so that a selected video appears on the television screen. Sometimes, the video system in the booths is computer operated. If the peep show involves live performances, there is usually a clear partition between the performer and viewer.

Peep-show movies come in 8mm, 16mm or VHS format. The 8mm films do not have sound and are shorter in length than the videos. The movies include homosexual, heterosexual, and sadomasochistic sexual activities between two women, coprophilia, bestiality, or simulated juvenile sexual activities.

Distribution

Some "adults only" pornographic outlet owners buy their peep show booths outright, while others rent their booths. The initial cost of purchasing a peep-show booth is between $20,000 and $30,000. If booths are rented, the store owner usually shares the profits of the booths with the lessors in exchange for the lessor's installation and maintenance of the booths.

Inside the booths the viewer may see approximately two minutes of the movie for twenty-five cents. As the number of sexually explicit scenes or diversity of sexual acts increases, the viewing time decreases. Tokens or quarters needed to operate the peep shows can be obtained at the outlet's sales counter.

The average peep-show booth has enough room for two adults to stand shoulder to shoulder. The inside of the booth is dark, when the door is closed, except for the light which emanates from the screen or enters from the bottom of the door.

The inside walls of the peep-show booths are often covered with graffiti and messages. The graffiti is generally of a sexual nature and consists of telephone numbers, names, requests and offers for homosexual acts, anatomical descriptions, and sketches. The booth may also contain a chart which is used to schedule appointments and meetings in that particular booth. In some cases, this arrangement has been used for the solicitation of prostitutes.

After purchasing tokens from the store clerk, the patron selects the type of movie he wishes to view. A brief description of the film is usually posted on the door of the peep-show booth. A number or letter is assigned to each film and indicates which coin box inside the booth corresponds with the selected movie.

The film or videotape is operated by placing a quarter or token into the coin box, which activates the movie projector or videotape player to begin the movie. Quarters or tokens must be repeatedly inserted to continue viewing the movie, which may last from 10 to 90 minutes.

In addition to movie viewing, the booths also provide places for anonymous sexual relations. Many booths are equipped with a hole in the side wall between the booths to allow patrons to engage in anonymous sex. The holes are used for oral and anal sexual acts. Sexual activity in the booths involves mostly males participating in sexual activities with one another. However, both heterosexual and homosexual men engage in these activities. The anonymity provided by the "glory holes" allows the participants to fantasize about the gender and other characteristics of their partners.

The booth is sometimes equipped with a lock on the door. Many patrons intentionally leave the door unlocked. Some patrons look inside the booths in an attempt to find one already occupied. It is commonplace for a patron to enter an occupied booth, close the door behind him, and make advances toward the occupant. He may grab the occupant's genitals in an effort to invoke sexual activity or attempt to arrange a later sexual encounter. The sexual activities reported in peep show booths include masturbation, anal intercourse, and fellatio.

Inside the booths, the floors and walls are often wet and sticky with liquid or viscous substances, including semen, urine, feces, used prophylactics, gels, saliva, or alcoholic beverages. The soles of a patron's shoes may stick to certain areas of the floor. The booths are also often littered with cigarette butts and tobacco. The trash and sewage and the application of disinfectants or ammonia on occasion create a particularly nauseating smell in the booths.

It has been estimated that peep shows are the biggest moneymaking portion of this industry. Annual net profits for peep-show booths alone have been projected at two billion dollars.

NOTES

1. Malamuth and Spinner. A Longitudinal Content Analysis of Sexual Violence in the Best-Selling Erotic Magazines, *16, The Journal of Sex Research, 226,* 1980.
2. Paraphilias are pychosexual disorders where "unusual or bizarre imagery or other acts are necessary for sexual excitement. Such imagery or acts tend to be insistently and involuntarily repetitive and generally involve either: (1) preference for use of a nonhuman object for sexual arousal; (2) repetitive sexual activity with humans involving real or simulated suffering or humiliation, or (3) repetitive sexual activity with nonconsenting partners. In other classifications these disorders are referred to as "Sexual Deviations." American Psychiatric Association, *Diagnostic and Statistical Manual of Mental Disorders,* (3rd ed. 1983), p. 266.
3. Dietz and Evans, *Pornographic Imagery and Prevalence of Paraphilia,* 139 American Journal of Psychiatry (1982), p. 1493.

19

The Mind of a Killer: The Ted Bundy Case

THE DOBSON-BUNDY INTERVIEW

Ted Bundy spent ten years on death row in Florida. He had killed at least 23 young women, perhaps as many as 36. He did most of his killing in Washington, Utah, Idaho, and Colorado, sexually abusing and mutilating his victims before killing them and disposing of their bodies. One of his most infamous crimes was breaking into the Chi Omega sorority house in Tallahassee and murdering two Florida State University students as they slept in their beds.

Bundy, of course, did not begin his life as a killer. In fact, his early life makes him sound like the "All-American Boy." He had been a Boy Scout and studied law after completing college. At the age of 28, however, he began the killing that eventually took him to death row.

On January 23, 1989, the day before his execution, Bundy asked to speak to James Dobson, a psychologist and the host of the national radio program, *Focus on the Family.*

Dr. Dobson had been a member of the Attorney General's Commission on Pornography. This is a transcript of that interview.

A few house after he spoke to Dobson, Bundy, at the age of 42, was executed for killing a 12-year-old girl in 1980. Outside the prison, hundreds of people cheered his death.

Dobson: Ted, it is about 2:30 in the afternoon. You are scheduled to be executed tomorrow morning at seven o'clock if you don't receive another stay. What is going through your mind? What thoughts have you had in these last few days?

Bundy: Well, I won't kid you to say that it's something that I feel that I'm in control of, or something that I've come to terms with, because I haven't. It's a moment-by-moment thing. Sometimes I feel very tranquil, and other times I don't feel tranquil at all. What's going through my mind right now is to use the minutes and hours that I have left as fruitfully as possible, and see what happens. It helps to live in the moment in the essence that we use is it productively. Right now, I'm feeling calm and in large part because I'm here with you.

Dobson: For the record, you are guilty of killing many women and girls.

Bundy: Yes. Yes. That's true.

Dobson: Ted, how did it happen? Take me back. What are the antecedents of the behavior that we've seen? So much grief, so much sorrow, so much pain for so many people. Where did it start? How did this moment come about?

Bundy: That's the question of the hour and one that not only people much more intelligent than I have been working on for years, but one that I've been working on for years and trying to understand. Is there enough time to explain it all? I don't know. I think I understand it though . . . understand what happened to me to the extent that I can see how certain feelings and ideas that developed in me to the point where I began to act out on them—certain very violent and very destructive feelings.

Dobson: Let's go back, then, to those roots. First of all, you, as I understand it, were raised in what you consider to have been a healthy home.

Bundy: Absolutely.

Dobson: You were not physically abused; you were not sexually abused; you were not emotionally abused.

Bundy: No. No way. That's part of the tragedy of this whole situation, because I grew up in a wonderful home with two dedicated and loving parents. I'm one of five brothers and sisters. [It was] a home where we as children were the focus of my parents' lives, where we regularly attended church; [I had] two Christian parents who did not drink, they did not smoke, there was no gambling, there was no physical abuse or

fighting in the home. I'm not saying this was "Leave It to Beaver."

Dobson: It wasn't a perfect home.

Bundy: No, I don't know that such a home even exists, but it was a fine, solid, Christian home, and I hope no one will try to take the easy way out and blame or otherwise accuse my family of contributing to this because I know, and I'm trying to tell you as honestly as I know how, what happened. I think this is the message I want to get across. But as a young boy—and I mean a boy of 12 or 13 certainly—I encountered outside the home again . . . in the local grocery store and the local drug stores, the soft-core pornography, what people call "soft core." But as I think I explained to you last night, Dr. Dobson, in an anecdote, that as young boys do, we explored the back roads and side ways and byways of our neighborhood, and oftentimes people would dump the garbage and whatever they were cleaning out of the house. From time to time we'd come across pornographic books of a harder nature, more graphic you might say, [of] a more explicit nature than we would encounter, let's say, in your local grocery store. And this also included such things as detective magazines. . . .

Dobson: And those that involved violence, then.

Bundy: Yes, this is something I think I want to emphasize as the most damaging kinds of pornography, and again I'm talking from personal experience—hard, real, personal experience. The most damaging kinds of pornography are those that involve violence and sexual violence. Because the wedding of those two forces, as I know only too well, brings about behavior that is just too terrible to describe.

Dobson: Now walk me through that. What was going on in your mind at that time?

Bundy: Okay, but before we go any further, I think it's important to me that people believe what I'm saying. I'm not blaming pornography; I'm not saying that it caused me to go out and do certain things. And I take full responsibility for whatever I've done and all the things that I've done. That's not the question here. The question and the issue is how this kind of literature contributed and helped mold and shape the kinds of violent behavior.

Dobson: It fueled your fantasies.

Bundy: In the beginning it fuels this kind of thought process. Then at a certain time it's instrumental in what I would say crystallizing it, making it into something which is almost like a separate entity inside. At that point you're at the verge, or I was at the verge of acting out on these kinds of thoughts.

Dobson: Now I really want to understand that. You had gone about as far as you could go in your own fantasy life with printed material, and then there was the urge to take that little step or big step over to a physical event.

Bundy: Right. And it happened in stages, gradually. It doesn't necessarily, not to me at least, happen overnight. My experience with pornography that deals on a violent level with sexuality is that once you become addicted to it—and I look at this as a kind of addiction—like other kinds of addiction. . . . I would keep looking for more potent, more explicit, more graphic kinds of materials. Like an addiction, you keep craving something which is harder, harder. Something which gives you a greater sense of excitement. Until you reach the point where the pornography only goes so far. You reach that jumping-off point where you begin to wonder if maybe actually doing it will give you that which is beyond just reading about it or looking at it.

Dobson: How long did you stay at that point before you actually assaulted someone?

Bundy: That is a very delicate point in my own development. And we're talking about something . . . we're talking about

having reached the point or a gray area that surrounded that point over a course of years.

Dobson: You don't remember how long that was?

Bundy: I would say a couple of years. What I was dealing with there were strong inhibitions against criminal behavior—violent behavior—that had been conditioned into me, bred into me, in my environment, in my neighborhood, in my church, in my school. Things which said no, this is wrong. I mean, even to think of this is wrong, but certainly to do it is wrong. And I'm on that edge, and these last . . . you might say, the last vestiges of restraint—the barriers to actually doing something were being tested constantly, and assailed through the kind of fantasy life that was fueled largely by pornography.

Dobson: Do you remember what pushed you over that edge? Do you remember the decision to go for it? Do you remember where you decided to throw caution to the wind?

Bundy: Again, when you say pushed, I know what you're saying. . . . I don't want to infer again that I was some helpless kind of victim. And yet, we're talking about an influence which—that is the influence of violent types of media and violent pornography—which was an indispensable link in the chain of behavior, the chain of events that led to the behavior, to the assaults, to the murders, and what have you. It's a very difficult thing to describe. The sensation of reaching that point where I knew that it was like something had snapped, that I knew that I couldn't control it anymore, that these barriers that I had learned as a child, that had been instilled in me, were not enough to hold me back with respect to seeking out and harming somebody.

Dobson: Would it be accurate to call that a frenzy, a sexual frenzy?

Bundy: Well, yes. That's one way to describe it. A compulsion, a building up of destructive energy. Again, another fact here that I haven't mentioned is the use of alcohol. But I think that what alcohol did in conjunction with, let's say, my exposure to pornography [is that] alcohol reduced my inhibitions, at the same time. The fantasy life that was fueled by pornography eroded them further, you see.

Dobson: In the early days, you were nearly always about half-drunk when you did these things. Is that right?

Bundy: Yes. Yes.

Dobson: Was that always true?

Bundy: I would say that was generally the case. Almost without exception.

Dobson: Alright, if I can understand it now, there's this battle going on within. There are the conventions that you've been taught. There's the right and wrong that you learned as a child. And then there is this unbridled passion fueled by your plunge into hard-core, violent pornography. And those things ar at war with each other.

Bundy: Yes.

Dobson: And then with the alcohol diminishing the inhibitions, you let go.

Bundy: Well, yes. And you can summarize it that way, and that's accurate, certainly. And it just occurred to me that some people would say that, well, I've seen that stuff, and it doesn't do anything to me. And I can understand that. Virtually everyone can be exposed to so-called pornography, and while they were aroused to it one degree or another, not go out and do anything wrong.

Dobson: Addictions are like that. They affect some people more than they affect others. But there is a percentage of people affected by hard-core pornography in a very violent way, and you're obviously one of them.

Bundy: That was a major component, and I don't know why I was vulnerable to it. All I know is that it had an impact on me that was just so essential to the development of the violent behavior that I engaged in.

Dobson: Ted, after you committed your first murder, what was the emotional effect on you? What happened in the days after that?

Bundy: Again, please understand that even all these years later, it's very difficult to talk about it, and reliving it through talking about it. It's difficult, to say the least, but I want you to understand what happened. It was like coming out of some kind of horrible trance or dream. I can only liken it to, and I don't want to overdramatize it, but to have been possessed by something so awful and so alien, and then the next morning wake up from it, remember what happened and realize that basically, I mean, in the eyes of the law, certainly, and in the eyes of God, you're responsible. To wake up in the morning and realize what I had done, with a clear mind and all my essential moral and ethical feelings intact at that moment. [I was] absolutely horrified that I was capable of doing something like that.

Dobson: You really hadn't known that before?

Bundy: There is just absolutely no way to describe—first the brutal urge to do that kind of thing, and then what happens. I want people to understand this, too, and I'm not saying this gratuitously because it's important that people understand this. That basically, I was a normal person. I wasn't some guy hanging out at bars, or a bum. Or I wasn't a pervert in the sense that people look at somebody and say I know there's something wrong with him and just tell. But I was essentially a normal person. I had good friends. I lived a normal life, except for this one small, but very potent, very destructive segment that I kept very secret, very close to myself, and didn't let anybody know about it. And part of the shock and horror for my dear friends and family, years ago when I was first arrested, was that there was no clue. They looked at me, and they looked at the All-American boy. I mean, I wasn't perfect, but I want to be quite candid with you. I was okay. The basic humanity and basic spirit that God gave me was intact, but it unfortunately became overwhelmed at times. And I think people need to recognize that those of us who have been so much influenced by violence in the media—in particular pornographic violence—are not some kind of inherent monsters. We are your sons, and we are your husbands. And we grew up in regular families. And pornography can reach out and snatch a kid out of any house today. It snatched me out of my home 20, 30 years ago, as diligent as my parents were, and they were diligent in protecting their children. And as good a Christian home as we had—and we had a wonderful Christian home—there is no protection against the kinds of influences that there are loose in a society that tolerates.

Dobson: You feel this really deeply, don't you? Ted, outside these walls right now are several hundred reporters that wanted to talk to you.

Bundy: Yeah.

Dobson: And you asked me to come here from California because you had something you wanted to say. This hour that we have together is not just an interview with a man who is scheduled to die tomorrow morning. I'm here and you're here because of this message that you're talking about right here. You really feel that hard-core pornography and the doorway to it, soft-core pornography, is doing untold damage to other people, and causing other women to be abused and killed the way you did it.

Bundy: Listen. I'm no social scientist, and I haven't done a survey. I mean, I don't pretend that I know what John Q. Citizen thinks about this. But I've lived in prison for a long time now. And I've met a lot of men who were motivated to commit violence just like me. And without exception, every one of them was deeply involved in pornography—without question, without exception—deeply influenced and con-

sumed by an addiction to pornography. There's no question about it. The FBI's own study on serial homicide shows that the most common interest among serial killers is pornography.

Dobson: That's true.

Bundy: And it's real. It's true.

Dobson: Ted, what would your life have been like without that influence? You can only speculate.

Bundy: I know it would have been far better, not just for me—and excuse me for being so self-centered here, [but] it would have been a lot better for me and lots of other people. It would have been a lot better. There is no question but that it would have been a fuller life. Certainly a life that would not have involved—I'm absolutely certain—would not have involved this kind of violence that I have committed.

Dobson: I'm sure, Ted if I were able to ask you the questions that are being asked out there. One of the most important as you come down to perhaps your final hours: Are you thinking about all those victims out there and their families who are wounded? You know, years later their lives have not returned to normal. They will never return to normal.

Bundy: Absolutely.

Dobson: Are you carrying that load, that weight? Is there remorse there?

Bundy: Again, I know that people will accuse me of being self-serving, but we're beyond that now. I mean, I'm just telling you how I feel. But through God's help, I have been able to come to the point where I—much too late, but better late than never—feel the hurt and the pain that I am responsible for. Yes, absolutely. In the past few days, myself and a number of investigators have been talking about unsolved cases—murders that I was involved in. And it's hard to talk about all these years later because it revives in me all those terrible feelings and those thoughts that I have steadfastly and diligently dealt with—I think successfully, with the love of God. And yet, it's reopened that. And I felt the pain, and I've felt the horror again of all that. And I can only hope that those who I have harmed and those who I have caused so much grief—even if they don't believe my expression of sorrow and remorse—will believe what I'm saying now, that there is loose in their towns, in their communities, people like me today whose dangerous impulses are being fueled day in and day out by violence in the media in its various forms, particularly sexualized violence. And what scares me—and let's come into the present now because what I'm talking about happened 20, 30 years ago, that is, in my formative stages. And what scares and appalls me, Dr. Dobson, is when I see what's on cable TV, some of the movies, some of the violence in the movies that come into homes today was stuff that they wouldn't show in X-rated adult theaters 30 years ago.

Dobson: The slasher movies that you're talking about.

Bundy: That stuff is—I'm telling you from personal experience—the most graphic violence on the screen. Particularly as it gets into the home to the children who may be unattended or unaware that they may be a Ted Bundy who has that vulnerability, that predisposition to be influenced by that kind of behavior, by that kind of movie and that kind of violence. There are kids sitting out there switching the TV dial around and come upon these movies late at night, or I don't know when they're on, but they're on, and any kid can watch them. It's scary when I think what would have happened to me if I had seen [them]. [Or] to know that children are watching that kind of thing today, or can pick up their phone and dial away for it, or send away for it.

Dobson: Can you help me understand this desensitization process that took place? What was going on in your mind?

Bundy: Well, by desensitization, I describe it in specific terms. Each time I

harmed someone, each time I killed someone, there would be an enormous amount of—especially at first—enormous amount of horror, guilt, remorse afterward. But then that impulse to do it again would come back even stronger. The unique thing about how this worked, Dr. Dobson, is that I still felt in my regular life, the full range of guilt and remorse about other things. Regret and . . .

Dobson: You had this compartmentalized . . .

Bundy: . . . compartmentalized, very well focused, very sharply focused area where it was like a black hole. It was like a crack. And everything that fell into that crack just disappeared. Does that make sense?

Dobson: Yes, it does. One of the final murders that you committed, of course, was apparently little Kimberly Leach, 12 years of age. I think the public outcry is greater there because an innocent child was taken from a playground. What did you feel after that? Were there the normal emotions three days later? Where were you, Ted?

Bundy: I can't really talk about that right now. I would like to be able to convey to you what that experience is like, but I can't. I won't be able to talk about that. I can't begin to understand. Well, I can try, but I, I'm aware that I can't begin to understand the pain that the parents of these children that I have—and these young women—that I have harmed feel. And I can't restore really much to them, if anything. And I won't pretend to. And I don't even expect them to forgive me, and I'm not asking for it. That kind of forgiveness is of God. And if they have it, they have it. And if they don't, well, maybe they'll find it someday.

Dobson: Do you deserve the punishment the state has inflicted upon you?

Bundy: That's a very good question, and I'll answer it very honestly. I don't want to die. I'm not going to kid you. I'll kid you not. I deserve, certainly, the most extreme punishment society has, and I think society deserves to be protected from me and from others like me. That's for sure. What I hope will come of our discussion is [that] I think society deserves to be protected from itself because as we've been talking there are forces at loose in this country—particularly again, this kind of violent pornography—where on the one hand, well-meaning, decent people will condemn behavior of a Ted Bundy, while they're walking past a magazine rack full of the very kinds of things that send young kids down the road to be Ted Bundys. That's the irony. We're talking here not just about morals. What I'm talking about is going beyond retribution, which is what people want with me. Going beyond retribution and punishment, because there is no way in the world that killing me is going to restore those beautiful children to their parents and correct and soothe the pain. But I'll tell you, there are lots of other kids playing in streets around this country today who are going to be dead tomorrow and the next day and the next day and next month, because other young people are reading the kinds of things and seeing the kinds of things that are available in the media today.

PART IV

INEQUALITY AND DISCRIMINATION

TYPES OF POVERTY

The definition of poverty is neither simple nor obvious. First, there is the lowest level, what some call *biological poverty*. This refers to physical suffering, to malnutrition causing brain damage in young children, to starvation, or to housing and clothing being so inadequate that people are harmed from exposure to the elements. Our homeless suffer from biological poverty.

Much more common is *relative poverty*, that is, deprivation as measured by the standards of one's society. The meaning of income and resources varies considerably from group to group. Some members of country clubs feel "poor" because they are among the few who don't drive a new Jaguar or because they have fewer jewels to parade at formal dinner dances. More seriously impoverished are people whose income is only half or one quarter the average of their society. On a world scale, what is relative poverty in the United States would mean comfortable living in China or Africa, where families generally live in a couple of rooms and consume a third of the calories that Americans eat. Yet by the standards of our own culture, Americans who live on half the average American income are relatively poor.

Relative poverty has two dimensions. One is objective. *Objective poverty* refers to the proportion of people in a society who lack something, be it running water or adequate protein or even telephones or VCRs, depending on the criteria one uses to define poverty. The other dimension is subjective. *Subjective poverty* refers to feelings of being deprived, which depend on one's *reference groups*, the groups we use as a basis for measuring ourselves. Since our reference groups change over time, so too does subjective poverty.

Many countries also have *official poverty*, the government's definition of what income level (or "threshold") makes people eligible for welfare benefits. Because the American poor spend about one-third of their income on food, official poverty in the United States is three times a very low, emergency-level food budget. That figure is adjusted for how many dependents a person has, how old he or she is, and whether he or she is disabled. In order to try to represent the same level of material comfort year after year, the figure is adjusted annually to match the Consumer Price Index, our official gauge of inflation.

Although experts disagree about the absolute numbers, two facts stand out: Millions of Americans do live in poverty, and this social problem is closely associated with many of the other problems facing our nation, such as prostitution, rape, murder, and alcoholism and other forms of drug addicition.

SOCIAL INEQUALITY

Despite our ideals, we have considerable inequality in the United States. The poorest fifth of the nation receive less than $5,000 a year, while the richest fifth average almost $60,000. We can express this contrast in this way: The richest 20 percent of all families receive 44 percent of America's income, while the poorest 20 percent get only 5 percent. Despite all our social legislation, this disparity remains, and the proportions run fairly constant year after year.

While differences in income are large, far more important is inequality of wealth. Income from salaries is only a small part of the money that people have. *Wealth* consists of all income, savings, property, investments, and other economic assets. To examine wealth is to see just how skewed the distribution of resources is.

Overall, Americans are worth about $11 trillion, mostly in the form of real estate, corporate stock, and business assets. However, the vast majority of that wealth, 68 percent, is owned by only *one-tenth* of our families. "They own half of the value of all real estate, plus 90 percent of corporate stocks and business assets and 95 percent of bonds" (Stafford et al., 1986–87, p. 3). Yet our wealth is even more concentrated than this, for the top one-half of 1 percent of the richest Americans—about 400,000 households—owns 27 percent of our country's entire wealth, including 14 percent of all real estate. Their ownership of 40 percent of all corporate stock and business assets means that they virtually control corporate America (Stafford et al., 1986–87; *Wall Street Journal*, 1986).

In addition to interlocking experiences in business and politics, members of this powerful group come from similar backgrounds. Most, like President Bush, are white, Anglo-Saxon Protestants who have attended exclusive prep schools and Ivy League colleges. They share ideologies and values and are likely to belong to the same private clubs, hire the same bands for their debutante balls, and vacation at the same exclusive resorts. This sharing of backgrounds, contacts, ideologies, and vested interests reinforces each member of the group, and thus the group as a whole (Domhoff, 1978).

THE POWER ELITE

C. Wright Mills (1959) called these relatively few, powerful people with shared backgrounds and coinciding interests the *power elite*. While the circumstantial evidence that these people actually work together to wield power is persuasive, proof is difficult to find. Consequently, not all sociologists agree with the idea of a power elite. One group of sociologists, called *pluralists*, argue that social, economic, and political power are dispersed among a wide variety of competing interest groups in our society, such as unions, industries, professional associations, ecologists, hawks, doves, and so forth. They conclude that *no one group is in control*. Sociologist David Riesman and his colleagues (1951) maintained that these diverse and frequently conflicting interest groups make a united policy or action impossible. While Mills argued that members of the power elite settle differences among themselves, Riesman maintained that differences are decided through a bargaining process, that the exercise of power is distributed among many groups, which competitively work out their differences. This matter is still an open question.

WHAT IS PROBLEMATIC ABOUT SOCIAL INEQUALITY?

Is the concentration of power a problem? As symbolic interactionists would say, that depends on your point of view. I would simply point out that it can contravene the democratic processes on which our country is founded. Such an interlocking management can result in inordinate control over America by a few individuals, with a business elite controlling the destiny of American commerce and politics. Unless one trusts the few thousand people who make up the economic and political elite to make all the right decisions for the rest of America's 240 million people, such concentration of power is a national social problem that undermines the principles of a democratic society.

What is problematic about our concentration of wealth? Part of the problem is the tremendous power that wealth carries with it. Since owning 10 or 20 percent of a company's stock can give one a controlling block of votes, the 400,000 or so households who own nearly half of all corporate stock wield immense power over the economy. This tiny elite can close down factories and throw thousands of people out of work, or they can decide to move corporate enterprises from one city to another, or even to relocate operations to a foreign land where labor is cheaper. The point is that these decisions are not made by the people who stand to lose their jobs—the workers—but by a small elite whose prime interest is in increasing their wealth, and the rest of society has to live with the consequences.

Thus, underlying the problems of social inequality, the unequal distribution of options and opportunities, is the extensive inequality of wealth I have described. Because the rich can hire the best minds to represent them in Washington, in the state legislatures, and before the bar of justice, and because they can pay for the best financial advice, they perpetuate their advantages. It is the poor, not they, who live in fear of unemployment, the breakdown of the family car, injustice in the courts, and political candidates and lobbyists who ignore their values and interests (Stafford et al., 1986–87).

The consequences of social inequality extend deeply into people's lives. Wealth and income represent privileges—received or denied—and quality of life. For example, people with higher incomes have job security, company paid pensions, and better health insurance coverage than people with lower paying jobs. People with low-paying jobs commonly suffer periods of unemployment, receive few if any medical benefits, have no pension funds, and are laid off if they become sick. Such differences show up in stark results: Those at the lower end of the scale don't eat as well, they are more likely to have accidents at work and at home, and their children are more likely to die during infancy.

Conflict theorists stress that social inequality arises from the struggle of the many for limited resources, especially for wealth and power. Those who win hold on to what they gain, using their power to make the losers dependent on them. The social class system that arises enables those who are affluent to pass on their advantages to their children, often under the banner of equal opportunity and democracy.

Race is a critical factor in social inequality, as some ethnic minorities are more likely than whites to be poor. Blacks, for example, are almost three times as likely as whites to live in poverty, while Hispanics are about two and one-half times as likely to be poor. In recent years, many blacks have moved out of poverty, leaving behind an underclass of undereducated and unskilled persons. This has resulted in a major division between blacks with good jobs and blacks who remain in poverty.

Another major aspect of inequality and discrimination in American society is *sexism*, singling people out on the basis of their sex for unfair treatment. Sex is *the* major sorting factor in our society. Males continue to be paid more for the same work, and they continue to dominate politics and public life. Because females are discriminated against economically, politically, and socially, sociologists apply the term *minority group* to them, in spite of the fact that females make up slightly more than half of our population. They are considered by sociologists to be a minority group because of their position relative to males, the dominant group.

The most common sociological position is that, whatever differences in temperament, personality, or predisposition to act one way or another that biology *might* provide the sexes, culture overrides those differences and shapes people into the types of men and women that are common in a particular society. People everywhere, however, wear cultural blinders that mask the workings of their own culture, and each considers the characteristics implanted into their males and females to be overwhelming evidence of the "natural" differences between the sexes. They see the effects of social inequality and discrimination, while the causes of those effects remain invisible to them.

REFERENCES

Domhoff, G. W. (1978). *The powers that be.* New York: Random House.

Mills, C. W. (1959). *The power elite.* New York: Oxford University Press.

Riesman, D. , Glazer, N., & Denney, R. (1951). *The lonely crowd: A study of the changing American character.* New Haven, CT: Yale University Press.

Stafford, L., Kennedy, R., Lehman, J. E., & Arnold, G. (1986-87, Winter). Wealth in America. *ISR Newsletter.*

The Wall Street Journal. (1986, July 28), p. 38.

20

Diary of a Homeless Man

John R. Coleman

WEDNESDAY, 1/19

Somehow, 12 degrees at 6 a.m. was colder than I had counted on. I think of myself as relatively immune to cold, but standing on a deserted sidewalk outside Penn Station with the thought of ten days ahead of me as a homeless man, the immunity vanished. When I pulled my collar closer and my watch cap lower, it wasn't to look the part of a street person; it was to keep the wind out.

My wardrobe wasn't much help. I had bought my "new" clothes—flannel shirt, baggy sweater, torn trousers, the cap and the coat—the day before on Houston Street for $19. "You don't need to buy shoes," the shopkeeper had said. "The ones you have on will pass for a bum's." I was hurt: they were shoes I often wore to the office.

Having changed out of my normal clothes in the Penn Station's men's room and stowed them in a locker, I was ready for the street. Or thought so.

Was I imagining it, or were people looking at me in a completely different way? I felt that men, especially the successful-looking ones in their forties and over, saw me and wondered. For the rest, I wasn't there.

At Seventh Avenue and 35th Street, I went into a coffee shop. The counterman looked me over carefully. When I ordered the breakfast special—99 cents plus tax—he told me I'd have to pay in advance. I did (I'd brought $40 to see me through my ten days), but I noticed that the other customers were given checks, and paid only when they left.

By 9:30, I had read a copy of the *Times* retrieved from a trash basket; I had walked most of the streets around the station; I had watched the construction at the new convention center. There was little else to do.

Later, I sat and watched the drug sales going on in Union Square. Then I went into the Income Maintenance Center on 14th

Street and watched the people moving through the welfare lines. I counted the trucks on Houston Street.

I vaguely remembered a quote to the effect that "idleness is only enjoyable when you have a lot to do." It would help to be warm, too.

There was ample time and incentive to stare at the other homeless folk on the street. For the most part, they weren't more interesting than the typical faces on Wall Street or upper Madison Avenue. But the extreme cases caught and held the eye. On Ninth Avenue, there was a man on the sidewalk directing an imaginary (to me) flow of traffic. And another, two blocks away, tracing the flight of planes or birds—or spirits—in the winter sky. And there was a woman with gloves tied to her otherwise bare feet.

Standing outside the Port Authority Bus Terminal was a man named Howard. He was perhaps my age, but the seasons had left deeper marks on his face. "Come summertime, it's all going to be different," he told me. "I'm going to have a car to go to the beach. And I'm going to get six lemons and make me a jug of ice-cold lemonade to go with the car.

"This whole country's gone too far with the idea of one person being at the top. It starts with birthday parties. Who gets to blow out the candles? One person. And it takes off from there. If we're ever going to make things better, we gotta start with those candles."

Was there any chance of people like us finding work?

"Jobs are still out there for the young guys who want them," Howard said. "But there's nothing for us. Never again. No, I stopped dreaming about jobs a long time ago. Now I dream about cars. And lemonade."

Drugs and alcohol are common among the homeless. The damage done by them was evident in almost every street person I saw. But which was cause and which was effect? Does it matter, once this much harm has been done?

My wanderings were all aimless. There was no plan, no goal, no reason to be anywhere at any time. Only hours into this role, I felt a useless part of the city streets. I wasn't even sure why I was doing this. . . .

A weathered drifter told me about a hideaway down in the bowels of the station, where it was warm and quiet. I found my way there and lay down on some old newspapers to sleep.

How long did I sleep? It didn't seem long at all. I was awakened by a flashlight shining in my eyes, and a voice, not an unkind one, saying, "You can't sleep here. Sorry, but you have to go outside."

I hadn't expected to hear that word "sorry." It was touching.

I left and walked up to 47th Street, between Fifth and Madison Avenues, where I knew there was a warm grate in the sidewalk. (I've been passing it every morning for over five years on my way to work.) One man was asleep there already. But there was room for two, and he moved over.

THURSDAY, 1/20

When you're spending the night on the street, you learn to know morning is coming by the kinds of trucks that roll by. As soon as there are other than garbage trucks—say, milk or bread trucks—you know the night will soon be over.

I went back to Penn Station to clean up in the washroom. The care with which some of the other men with me bathed themselves at the basins would have impressed any public-health officer. And I couldn't guess from the appearance of their clothes who would be the most fastidious.

I bought coffee and settled back to enjoy it out of the main traffic paths in the station. No luck. A cop found me and told me to take it to the street.

After breakfast ($1.31 at Blimpie), I walked around to keep warm until the public library opened. I saw in a salvaged copy of the *Times* that we had just had our coldest night of the year, well below zero with the windchill factor, and that a record 4,635 people had sought shelter in the city's hostels.

The library was a joy. The people there treated me the same as they might have had I been wearing my business suit. To pass the time, I got out the city's welfare reports for 50 years ago. In the winter of 1933, the city had 4,524 beds available for the homeless, and all were said to be filled every night. The parallel to 1983 was uncanny. But, according to the reports, the man in charge of the homeless program in 1933, one Joseph A. Manning, wasn't worried about the future. True, the country was in the midst of a depression. But there had been a slight downturn in the numbers served in the shelters in the two months immediately preceding his report. This mean, wrote Manning, that "the depression, in the parlance of the ring, is K.O.'d."

Already, I notice changes in me. I walk much more slowly. I no longer see a need to beat a traffic light or to be the first through a revolving door. Force of habit still makes me look at my wrist every once in a while. But there's no watch there, and it wouldn't make any difference if there were. The thermometer has become much more important to me now than any timepiece could be.

The temperature rose during the day. Just as the newspaper headlines seem to change more slowly when you're on the streets all day long, so the temperature seems to change more rapidly and tellingly.

At about 9 P.M., I went back to the heated grate on 47th Street. The man who had been there last night was already in place. He made it clear that there was again room for me.

I asked him how long he had been on the streets.

"Eleven years, going on twelve." he said.

"This is only my second night."

"You may not stick it out. This isn't for every man."

"Do you ever go into the shelters?"

"I couldn't take that. I prefer this anytime."

FRIDAY, 1/21

When I left my grate mate—long before dawn—he wished me a good day. I returned the gesture. He meant his, and I meant mine.

In Manhattan's earliest hours, you get the feeling that the manufacture and removal of garbage is the city's main industry. So far, I haven't been lucky or observant enough to rescue much of use from the mounds of trash waiting for the trucks and crews. The best find was a canvas bag that will fit nicely over my feet at night.

I'm slipping into a routine: Washing up at the station. Coffee on the street. Breakfast at Blimpie. A search for the *Times* in the trash baskets. And then a leisurely stretch of reading in the park.

Some days bring more luck than others. Today I found 20 cents in a pay-phone slot, and heard a young flutist playing the music of C. P. E. Bach on Sixth Avenue between 9th and 10th streets. A lot of people ignored her, even stepped over her flute case as if it were litter on the sidewalk. More often than not, those who put money in the case looked embarrassed. They seemed to be saying, "Don't let anyone see me being appreciative."

By nightfall, the streets were cruelly cold once again.

I headed for the 47th Street grate again but found my mate gone. There was no heat coming up through it. Do they turn it off on Friday nights? Don't we homeless have any rights?

On the northwest corner of Eighth Avenue and 33rd Street, there was a blocked-off subway entrance undergoing repair. I curled up against the wall there under some cardboard sheets. Rain began to fall, but I stayed reasonably dry and was able to get to sleep.

At some point, I was awakened by a man who had pulled back the upper piece of cardboard.

"You see my partner here. You need to give us some money."

I was still half-asleep. "I don't have any."

"You must have something, man."

"Would I be sleeping here in the rain if I did?"

His partner intervened. "C'mon. Leave the old bastard alone. He's not worth it."

"He's got something. Get up and give it to us."

I climbed to my feet and began fumbling in my pocket. Both men were on my left side. That was my chance. Suddenly I took off and ran along 33rd Street toward Ninth Avenue. They gave no chase. And a good thing, too, because I was too stiff with cold to run a good race.

SATURDAY, 1/22

A man I squatted next to in a doorway on 29th Street said it all: "The onliest thing is to have a warm place to sleep. That and having somebody care about you. That'd be even onlier."

He had what appeared to be rolls of paper toweling wrapped around one leg and tied with red ribbon. But the paper, wet with rain by now, didn't seem to serve any purpose.

I slept a little. The forecast was for more rain tomorrow, so why wish the night away?

The morning paper carried news of Mayor Koch's increased concern about the homeless.

But what can he do? He must worry that the more New York does to help, the greater the numbers will grow. At the moment he's berating the synagogues for not doing anything to take street people in.

Watching people come and go at the Volvo tennis tournament at Madison Square Garden, I sensed how uncomfortable they were at the presence of the homeless. Easy to love in the abstract, not so easy face to face.

It's no wonder that the railway police are under orders to chase us out of sight.

Perhaps a saving factor is that we're not individuals. We're not people anybody knows. So far I've had eye contact with only three people who know me in my other life.

None showed a hint of recognition. One was the senior auditor at Arthur Andersen & Company, the accounting firm that handles the Clark Foundation, my employer. One was a fellow lieutenant in the Auxiliary Police Force, a man with whom I had trained for many weeks. And one was an owner in the cooperative apartment building where I live.

Early in the evening I fell asleep on the Seventh Avenue steps outside the Garden. Three Amtrak cops shook me awake to ask if two rather good looking suitcases on the steps were mine. I said that I had never seen them.

One cop insisted that I was lying, but then a black man appeared and said they belonged to a friend of his. The rapid-fire questioning from two of the cops soon made that alibi rather unlikely. The third cop was going through the cases and spreading a few of the joints he found inside on the ground.

As suddenly as it had begun, the incident was over. The cops walked away, and the man retrieved the bags. I fell back to sleep. Some hours later when I woke up again, the black man was still there, selling.

SUNDAY, 1/23

A new discovery of a warm and dry, even scenic, place to sit on a rainy day: the Staten Island Ferry.

For one 25-cent fare, I had four crossings of the harbor, read all I wanted of the copy of the Sunday *Times* I'd found, and finished the crossword puzzle.

When I got back to the Garden, where the tennis tournament was in its last hours, I found the police were being extra diligent in clearing us away from the departing crowds. One older woman was particularly incensed at being moved. "You're ruining my sex life," she shouted. "That's what you're doing. My sex life. Do you hear?"

A younger woman approached me to ask if I was looking for love. "No, ma'am. I'm just trying to stay out of the rain."

So, back to the unused subway entrance, because there was still no heat across town on the 47th Street grate.

The night was very cold. Parts of me ached as I tried to sleep. Turning over was a chore, not only because the partially wet cardboard had to be rearranged with such care, but also because the stiffer parts of my body seemed to belong to someone else. Whatever magic there was in those lights cutting down through the fog was gone by now. All I wanted was to be warm and dry once more. Magic could wait.

MONDAY, 1/24

Early this morning I went to the warren of employment agencies on 14th Street to see if I could get a day's work. There was very little action at most of these last-ditch offices, where minimum wages and sub-minimum conditions are the rule.

But I did get one interview and thought I had a dishwashing job lined up. I'd forgotten one thing. I had no identification with me. No identification, no job.

There was an ageless, shaggy woman in Bryant Park this morning who delivered one of the more interesting monologues I've heard. For a full ten minutes, with no interruption from me beyond an occasional "Uh-huh," she analyzed society's ills without missing a beat.

Beginning with the complaint about the women's and men's toilets in the park being locked ("What's a poor body to do?"), she launched into the strengths of the Irish, who, though strong, still need toilets more than others, and the weaknesses of the English and the Jews, the advantages of raising turkeys over other fowl, and the wickedness of Eleanor Roosevelt in letting the now Queen Mother and that stuttering king of hers rave so much about the hot dogs served at Hyde Park that we had no alternative but to enter World War II on their side. The faulty Russian satellite that fell into the Indian Ocean this morning was another example of shenanigans, she said. It turns out the Russians and Lady Diana, "that so-called Princess of Wales," are in cahoots to keep us so alarmed about such things far away from home that we don't get anything done about prayer in schools or the rest of it. But after all, what would those poor Protestant ministers do for a living if the children got some real religion in school, like the kind we got from the nuns, God bless them?

That at least was the gist of what she said. I know I've missed some of the finer points.

At 3:30 P.M., with more cold ahead, I sought out the Men's Shelter at 8 East 3rd Street. This is the principal entry point for men seeking the city's help. It provides meals for 1,300 or so people every day and beds for some few of those. I had been told that while there was no likelihood of getting a bed in this building, I'd be given a meal here and a bed in some other shelter.

I've seen plenty of drawings of London's workhouses and asylums in the times of Charles Dickens. Now I've seen the real thing, in the last years of the twentieth century in the world's greatest city.

The lobby and the adjacent "sitting room" were jammed with men standing, sitting, or stretched out in various positions on the floor. It was as lost a collection of souls as I could have imagined. Old and young, scarred and smooth, stinking and clean, crippled and hale, drunk and sober, ranting and still, parts of another world and parts of this one. The city promises to take in anyone who asks. Those rejected everywhere else find their way to East 3rd Street.

The air was heavy with the odors of Thunderbird wine, urine, sweat, and, above all, nicotine and marijuana. Three or four Human Resources Administration police officers seemed to be keeping the violence down to tolerable levels, but barely so.

After a long delay, I got a meal ticket for dinner and was told to come back later for a lodging ticket.

It was time to get in line to eat. This meant crowding into what I can only compare to a cattle chute in a stockyard. It ran along two walls of the sitting room and was already jammed. A man with a bullhorn kept yelling at us to stand up and stay in line. One very old and decrepit (or drunk?) man couldn't stay on his feet. He was helped to a chair, from which he promptly fell onto the floor. The bullhorn man had some choice obscenities for him, but they didn't seem to have any effect. The old man just lay there; and we turned our thoughts back to the evening meal.

I made a quick, probably grossly unfair, assessment of the hundreds of men I could see in the room. Judging them solely by appearance, alertness, and body movements, I decided that one-quarter of them were perfectly able to work; they, more likely than not, were among the warriors who helped us win the battle against inflation by the selfless act of joining the jobless ranks. Another quarter might be brought back in time into job-readiness by some counseling and some caring for them as individuals. But the other half seemed so ravaged by illness, addiction, and sheer neglect that I couldn't imagine them being anything but society's wards from here on out to—one hopes—a peaceful end.

At the appointed hour, we were released in groups of twenty or thirty to descend the dark, filthy steps to the basement eating area. The man with the bullhorn was there again, clearly in charge and clearly relishing the extra power given to his voice by electric amplification. He insulted us collectively and separately without pause, but because his vocabulary was limited it tended to be the same four-letter words over and over.

His loudest attack on me came when I didn't move fast enough to pick up my meal from the counter. His analysis of certain flaws in my white ancestry wasn't hard to follow, even for a man in as much of a daze as I was.

The shouting and the obscenities didn't stop once we had our food. Again and again we were told to finish and get out. Eating took perhaps six minutes, but those minutes removed any shred of dignity a man might have brought in with him from the street.

Back upstairs, the people in charge were organizing the people who were to go to a shelter in Brooklyn. Few had volunteered, so there was more haranguing.

In the line next to the one where I was waiting for my lodging ticket a fight suddenly broke out. One man pulled a long knife from his overcoat pocket. The other man ran for cover, and a police officer soon appeared to remove the man with the knife from the scene. The issue, it seems, was one of proper places in the line.

There still weren't enough Brooklyn volunteers to suit the management, so they brought in their big gun: Mr. Bullhorn. "Now, listen up," he barked. "There aren't any buses going to Ft. Washington [another shelter] until 11:30, so if you want to get some sleep, go to Brooklyn. Don't ask me any questions. Just shut up and listen. It's because you don't listen up that you end up in a place like this."

I decided to ask a question anyway, about whether there would still be a chance for me to go to Brooklyn once I got my lodging ticket. He turned on me and let me have the full force of the horn: "Don't ask questions, I said. You're not nobody."

The delays at the ticket-issuing window went on and on. Three staff members there seemed reasonably polite and even efficient. The fourth and heaviest one—I have no idea whether it was a man or woman—could not have moved more slowly without coming to a dead halt. The voice of someone who was apparently a supervisor came over the public-address system from time to time to apologize for the delay in going to the Ft. Washington shelter, which was in an armory, but any good he did from behind the scenes was undone by the staff out front and a "see-no-work, hear-no-work, do-no-work" attendant in the office.

As 11:30 approached, we crowded back into the sitting room to get ready to board the buses. A new martinet had appeared on the scene. He got as much attention through his voice, cane, and heavy body as Mr. Bullhorn had with his amplifying equipment. But this new man was more openly vile and excitable; he loved the power that went with bunching us all up close together and then ordering us to stretch out again in a thinner line. We practiced that routine several times.

Long after the scheduled departure, the lines moved. We sped by school buses to the armory at Ft. Washington Avenue and 168th Street. There we were met, just before 2:30 A.M., by military police, social workers, and private guards. They marched us into showers (very welcome), gave us clean underwear, and sent us upstairs to comfortable cots arranged in long rows in a room as big as a football field.

There were 530 of us there for the night, and we were soon quiet.

TUESDAY, 1/25

We were awakened at 6 A.M. by whistles and shouting, and ordered to get back onto the buses for the return trip to lower Manhattan as soon as possible.

Back at 8 East 3rd Street, the worst of the martinets were off duty. So I thought breakfast might be a bit quieter than dinner had been. Still, by eight, I had seen three incidents a bit out of the ordinary for me.

A man waiting for breakfast immediately ahead of me in the cattle chute suddenly grabbed a chair from the adjoining area and prepared to break it over his neighbor's head. In my haste to get out of the way, I fell over an older man sleeping against the wall. After some shouts about turf, things cooled off between the fighters, and the old man forgave me.

In the stairwell leading down to the eating area, a young man made a sexual advance to me. When I withdrew from him and stupidly reached for my coat pocket, he thought I was going for a weapon. He at once pinned me against the wall and searched my pockets; there was nothing there.

As I came out of the building onto East 3rd Street, two black Human Resources Administration policemen were bringing two young blacks into the building. One officer has his man by the neck. The other officer had his man's hands cuffed behind his back and repeatedly kicked him hard in the buttocks.

My wanderings were still more aimless today. I couldn't get East 3rd Street out of my mind. What could possibly justify some of that conduct? If I were a staff member there, would I become part of the worst in that pattern? Or would I simply do as little, and think as little, as possible?

At day's end I can't recall much of where I went or why I went there.

Only isolated moments remain with me. Like staring at the elegant crystal and silver in the shops just north of Madison Square Park and wondering what these windows say to the people I'd spent the night with.

Much too soon it was time to go back to the shelter for dinner and another night. At first I thought I didn't have the guts to do it again. Does one have to do *this* to learn who the needy are? I wanted to say, "Enough! There's only so much I need to see."

But I went back to the shelter anyway, probably because it took more guts to quit than it did to go ahead.

A man beside me in a tense dinner line drove one truth of this place home to me. "I never knew hell came in this color," he said.

I was luckier in my assignment for the night. I drew the Keener Building, on Wards Island, a facility with a capacity of 416 men. The building was old and neglected, and the atmosphere of a mental hospital, which it once was, still hung over it. But the staff was polite, the rooms weren't too crowded (there were only twelve beds in Room 326), the single sheet on each bed was clean, and there was toilet paper in the bathroom.

There were limits and guards and deprivations, but there was also an orderliness about the place. Here, at least, I didn't feel I had surrendered all of my dignity at the door.

WEDNESDAY, 1/26

Back to the shelter on East 3rd Street for dinner.

There is simply no other situation I've

seen that is so devoid of any graces at all, so tense at every moment, or so empty of hope. The food isn't bad, and the building is heated; that's all it has going for it.

The only cutlery provided is a frail plastic spoon. With practice you can spread hard oleo onto your bread with the back of one. If there's liver or ham, you don't have to cut it; just put it between the two pieces of bread that go with each meal. Everything else—peas, collard greens, apple pudding, plums—can be managed with the spoon. And talk over dinner or sipping, rather than gulping, coffee isn't all that important.

What is hardest to accept is the inevitable jungle scene during the hour you stand in line waiting to eat. Every minute seems to be one that invites an explosion. You know instinctively that men can't come this often to the brink without someone going over. One person too many is going to try to jump ahead in line. One particular set of toes is going to be stepped on by mistake. And the lid is going to blow.

The most frightening people here are the many young, intensely angry blacks. Hatred pours out in all of their speech and some of their actions. I could spend a lot of time imagining how and why they became so completely angry—but if I were the major, the counselor, or the man with the bullhorn, I wouldn't know how to divert them from that anger any more. Hundreds and hundreds of men have been destroyed by alcohol or drugs. A smaller, but for me more poignant, number are being destroyed by hate.

Their loudest message—and because their voices are so strong it is very loud indeed—is "Respect me, man." The constant theme is that someone or some group is putting them down, stepping on them, asking them to conform to a code they don't accept, getting in their way, writing them off.

So most of the fights begin over turf. A place in line. A corner to control. The have-nots scrapping with the have-nots.

Tonight, I chose the Brooklyn shelter because I thought the buses going there would leave soonest. The shelter, a converted school, is on Williams Avenue and has about 400 beds.

We left in fairly good time but learned when we got to the shelter that no new beds would be assigned until after 11 P.M. We were to sit in the auditorium until then.

At about ten, a man herded as many of us newcomers as would listen to him into a corner of the auditorium. There he delivered an abusive diatribe outlining the horror that lay ahead for our possessions and our bodies during the night to come. It made the ranting at East 3rd Street seem tame.

It's illustrative of what the experience of homelessness and helplessness does to people that all of us—regardless of age, race, background, or health—listened so passively.

Only at midnight, when some other officials arrived, did we learn that this man had no standing whatsoever. He was just an underling who strutted for his time on the stage before any audience cowed enough to take what he dished up.

THURSDAY, 1/27

Back on the street this morning, I became conscious of how little time I had left to live this way. There seemed so much still to do, and so little time in which to do it.

One part of me tells me I have been fully a part of this. I know I walk with slower steps and bent shoulders. I know I worry a lot more about keeping clean.

But then I recall how foolish that is. I'm acting. This will end tomorrow night. I can quit any time I want to. And unlike my mate from 47th Street, I haven't the slightest idea of what eleven years of sleeping on a grate amount to.

Early this afternoon, I went again to the Pavilion restaurant, where I had eaten five times before. I didn't recognize the man at the cash register.

"Get out," he said.

"But I have money."

"You heard me. Get out." His voice was stronger.

"That man knows me," I said, looking toward the owner in the back of the restaurant.

The owner nodded, and the man at the register said, "Okay, but sit in the back."

If this life in the streets had been real, I'd have gone out the door at the first "Get out." And the assessment of me as not worthy would have been self-fulfilling; I'd have lost so much respect for myself that I wouldn't have been worthy of being served the next time. The downward spiral would have begun.

Until now I haven't understood the extent of nicotine addiction. Dependencies on drugs and alcohol have been around me for a long time, but I thought before that smoking was a bad habit rather easy to overcome.

How many times have I, a nonsmoker, been begged for a cigarette in these days? Surely hundreds. Cigarettes are central. A few folks give them away, a small number sell them for up to 8 cents apiece, and almost all give that last pathetic end of a butt to the first man who asks for what little bit is left. I know addiction now as I didn't before.

Tonight, after a repeat of the totally degrading dinner-line scene at East 3rd Street, I signed up for Keener once again. No more Brooklyn for me.

Sitting upstairs with the other Keener-bound men, I carelessly put my left foot on the rung of the chair in front of me, occupied by a young black.

"Get your foot off, yo."

("Yo" means "Hey, there," "Watch yourself," "Move along," and much more.)

I took it off. "Sorry," I said.

But it was too late. I had broken a cardinal rule. I had violated the man's turf. As we stood in the stairwell waiting for the buses, he told a much bigger, much louder, much angrier friend what I had done.

That man turned on me.

"Wait till we get you tonight, whitey. You stink. Bad. The worst I've ever smelled. And when you put your foot on that chair, you spread your stink around. You better get yourself a shower as soon as we get there, but it won't save you later on. And don't sit near me or him on the bus. You hear, whitey?"

I didn't reply.

The bombardment went on as we mounted the bus. No one spoke up in my defense. Three people waved me away when I tried to sit next to them. The next person, black and close to my age, made no objection when I sat beside him.

The big man continued the tirade for a while, but he soon got interested in finding out from the driver how to go about getting a bus-driver's license. Perhaps he had come down from a high.

I admit I was scared. I wrote my name, address, and office telephone number on a piece of paper and slipped it into my pocket. At least someone would know where to call if the threats were real. I knew I couldn't and wouldn't defend myself in this setting.

While we stood in line on Wards Island waiting for our bed assignments, there were plenty of gripes about the man who was after me. But no one said anything directly to him. Somehow it didn't seem that this was the night when the meek would inherit the earth.

I slept fitfully. I don't like lying with the sheet hiding my face.

FRIDAY, 1/28

I was up and out of Keener as early as possible. That meant using some of my little remaining money for a city-bus ride back to Manhattan, but it was worth it to get out of there.

After breakfast on East 3rd Street, I was finished with the public shelters. That was an easy break for me to make, because I had choices and could run.

The day was cold and, for the early hours, clear. I washed the memory of the big man at 3rd Street out of my mind by wandering through the Fulton Fish Market. I walked across the Brooklyn Bridge and even sang as I realized how free I was to relax and enjoy its beauty.

With a cup of coffee and the *Times*, I sat on a cinder block by the river and read. In time, I wandered through the Wall Street district and almost learned the lay of some of the streets.

I walked up to the Quaker Meeting House at Rutherford Place and 15th Street. Standing on the porch outside, I tried hard to think how the doctrine that "there is that of God in every person" applied to that man last night and to some of the others I had encountered in these ten days. I still think it applies, but it isn't always easy to see how.

Darkness came. I got kicked out of both the bus terminal and Grand Central. I got my normal clothes out of the locker at Penn Station, changed in the men's room, and rode the AA train home.

My apartment was warm, and the bed was clean.

That's the onliest thing.

21

The Bohemian Grove
and Other Retreats

G. WILLIAM DOMHOFF

THE BOHEMIAN GROVE

Picture yourself comfortably seated in a beautiful open-air dining hall in the midst of 2700 acres of giant California redwoods. It is early evening and the clear July air is still pleasantly warm. Dusk has descended, you have finished a sumptuous dinner, and you are sitting quietly with your drink and your cigar, listening to nostalgic welcoming speeches and enjoying the gentle light and eerie shadows that are cast by the two-stemmed gaslights flickering softly at each of the several hundred outdoor banquet tables.

You are part of an assemblage that has been meeting in this redwood grove 65 miles north of San Francisco for over a hundred years. It is not just any assemblage, for you are a captain of industry, a well-known television star, a banker, a famous

artist, or maybe a member of the President's Cabinet. You are one of fifteen hundred men gathered together from all over the country for the annual encampment of the rich and the famous at the Bohemian Grove.

"Bohemians" of the 1970s and 1980s include such personages as former President Ronald Reagan; President George Bush; former Attorney General William French Smith; former Secretary of State George P. Schultz; former President Richard Nixon; former President Gerald Ford; former Supreme Court Justice Potter Steward; Herbert Hoover, Jr.; Herbert Hoover III; newspaperman William R. Hearst, Jr.; five members of the Dean Witter family of investment bankers; entertainers Art Linkletter and Edgar Bergen; presidents and chairmen of several oil companies such as Marathon Oil and Standard Oil; the presi-

From G. William Domhoff, The Bohemian Grove and Other Retreats: A Study in Ruling-Class Cohesiveness. New York: Harper & Row, 1974. Reprinted by permission of the author.

dent of Rockefeller University; officers of Anheuser-Busch breweries; the president of Kaiser Industries; bank presidents from California to New York; the president and chairman of Hewlett-Packard Co.; and many other representatives of American industry, finance, government, and entertainment. When these participants arrive for the annual "campout," an elaborate ritual called the Cremation of Care welcomes them and instructs them to leave all cares behind while they join together for two weeks of lavish entertainment, fellowship, and "communion with nature."

The Cremation of Care is the most spectacular event of the midsummer retreat that members and guests of San Francisco's Bohemian Club have taken every year since 1878. However, there are several other entertainments in store. Before the Bohemians return to the everyday world, they will be treated to plays, variety shows, song fests, shooting contests, art exhibits, swimming, boating, and nature rides.

A cast for a typical Grove play easily runs to seventy-five or one hundred people. Add in the orchestra, the stagehands, the carpenters who make the sets, and other supporting personnel, and over three hundred people are involved in creating the High Jinks each year. Preparations begin a year in advance, with rehearsals occurring two or three times a week in the month before the encampment, and nightly in the week before the play.

Costs are on the order of $20,000 to $30,000 per High Jinks, a large amount of money for a one-night production which does not have to pay a penny for salaries (the highest cost in any commercial production). "And the costs are talked about, too," reports my informant. "Hey, did you hear the High Jinks will cost $25,000 this year? one of them will say to another. The expense of the play is one way they can relate to its worth."

Entertainment is not the only activity at the Bohemian Grove. For a little change of pace, there is intellectual stimulation and political enlightenment every day at 12:30

p.m. Since 1932 the meadow from which people view the Cremation of Care also has been the setting for informal talks and briefings by people as varied as Dwight David Eisenhower (before he was President), Herman Wouk (author of *The Caine Mutiny*), Bobby Kennedy (while he was Attorney General), and Neil Armstrong (after he returned from the moon).

Cabinet officers, politicians, generals, and governmental advisers are the rule rather than the exception for Lakeside Talks, especially on weekends. Equally prominent figures from the worlds of art, literature, and science are more likely to make their appearance during the weekdays of the encampment, when Grove attendance may drop to four or five hundred (many of the members only come up for one week or for the weekends because they cannot stay away from their corporations and law firms for the full two weeks).

The Grove is an ideal off-the-record atmosphere for sizing up politicians. "Well, of course when a politician comes here, we all get to see him, and his stock in trade is his personality and his ideas," a prominent Bohemian told a *New York Times* reporter who was trying to cover Nelson Rockefeller's 1963 visit to the Grove for a Lakeside Talk. The journalist went on to note that the midsummer encampments "have long been a major showcase where leaders of business, industry, education, the arts, and politics can come to examine each other."[1]

For 1971, then-President Nixon was to be the featured Lakeside speaker. However, when newspaper reporters learned that the President planned to disappear into a redwood grove for an off-the-record speech to some of the most powerful men in America, they objected loudly and vowed to make every effort to cover the event. The flap caused the club considerable embarrassment, and after much hemming and hawing back and forth, the club leaders asked the President to cancel his scheduled appearance. A White House press secretary then announced that the President had decided not to appear at the Grove rather than risk the tradition that speeches there are strictly off the public record.[2]

However, the President was not left without a final word to his fellow Bohemians. In a telegram to the president of the club, which now hangs at the entrance to the reading room in the San Francisco club-house, he expressed his regrets at not being able to attend. He asked the club president to continue to lead people into the woods, adding that he in turn would redouble his efforts to lead people out of the woods. He also noted that, while anyone could aspire to be President of the United States, only a few could aspire to be president of the Bohemian Club.

Not all the entertainment at the Bohemian Grove takes place under the auspices of the committee in charge of special events. The Bohemians and their guests are divided into camps which evolved slowly over the years as the number of people on the retreat grew into the hundreds and then the thousands. These camps have become a significant center of enjoyment during the encampment.

At first the camps were merely a place in the woods where a half-dozen to a dozen friends would pitch their tents. Soon they added little amenities like their own special stove or a small permanent structure. Then there developed little camp "traditions" and endearing camp names like Cliff Dwellers, Moonshiners, Silverado Squatters, Woof, Zaca, Toyland, Sundodgers, and Land of Happiness. The next steps were special emblems, a handsome little lodge or specially constructed tepees, a permanent bar, and maybe a grand piano.[3] Today there are 129 camps of varying sizes, structures, and statuses. Most have between 10 and 30 members, but there are one or two with about 125 members and several with less than 10. A majority of the camps are strewn along what is called the River Road, but some are huddled in other areas within five or ten minutes of the center of the Grove.

The entertainment at the camps is mostly informal and impromptu. Someone will decide to bring together all the jazz musicians in the Grove for a special session. Or maybe all the artists or writers will be invited to a luncheon or a dinner at a camp. Many camps have their own amateur piano players and informal musical and singing groups which perform for the rest of the members.

But the joys of the camps are not primarily in watching or listening to performances. Other pleasures are created within them. Some camps become known for their gastronomical specialties, such as a particular drink or a particular meal. The Jungle Camp features mint juleps, Halcyon has a three-foot-high martini maker constructed out of chemical glassware. At the Owl's Nest [Ronald Reagan's club] it's the gin-fizz breakfast—about a hundred people are invited over one morning during the encampment for eggs Benedict, gin fizzes, and all the trimmings.

The men of Bohemia are drawn in large measure from the corporate leadership of the United States. They include in their numbers directors from major corporations in every sector of the American economy. An indication of this fact is that one in every five resident members and one in every three nonresident members is found in Poor's *Register of Corporations, Executives, and Directors*, a huge volume which lists the leadership of tens of thousands of companies from every major business field except investment banking, real estate, and advertising.

Even better evidence for the economic prominence of the men under consideration is that at least one officer or director from 40 of the 50 largest industrial corporations in America was present, as a member or a guest, on the lists at our disposal. Only Ford Motor Company and Western Electric were missing among the top 25! Similarly, we found that officers and directors from 20 of the top 25 commercial banks (including all of the 15 largest) were on our lists. Men from 12 of the first 25 life insurance companies were in attendance (8 of these 12 were from the top 10). Other business sectors were represented somewhat less: 10 of 25 in transportation, 8 of 25 in utilities, 7 of 25 in conglomerates, and only 5 of 25 in retailing. More generally, of the top-level businesses ranked by *Fortune* for 1969 (the top 500 industrials, the top 50 commercial banks, the top 50 life insurance companies, the top 50 transportation companies, the top 50 utilities, the top 50 retailers, and the top 47 conglomerates), 29 *percent of these 797 corporations were "represented" by at least one officer or director.*

OTHER WATERING HOLES

Other camps and retreats were founded by wealthy and powerful men, bsed on the model provided by the Bohemian Grove. One example is the Rancheros Visitadores (Visiting Ranchers), who meet each May for horseback rides through the California ranch land. These are accompanied by feasts, entertainment, and general merry-making with a Spanish-ranch motif.

Among the Rancheros a common interest in horses and horseplay provides a social setting in which men with different forms of wealth get to know each other better. *Sociologically speaking, the Rancheros Visitadores is an organization which serves the function (whether the originators planned it that way or not) of helping to integrate ranchers and businessmen from different parts of the country into a cohesive social class.*

The Rancheros had to divide into camps because of a postwar increase in membership. There are seventeen camps, sporting such Spanish names as Los Amigos, Los Vigilantes, Los Tontos (bums), Los Bandidos, and Los Flojos (lazy ones). They range in size from fifteen to ninety-three, with the majority of them listing between twenty and sixty members. Most camps have members from a variety of geographical locations, although some are slightly specialized in that regard. Los Gringos, the largest camp, has the greatest number of members from out of state. Los Borrachos, Los Picadores, and Los Chingadores, the next largest camps, have a predominance of people from the Los Angeles area. Los Vigilantes,

with twenty members, began as a San Francisco group, but now includes riders from Oregon, Washington, New York, and southern California.

In 1928 the Bohemian Grove provided John J. Mitchell with the inspiration for his retreat on horseback, the Rancheros Visitadores. Since 1930 the Rancheros have grown to the point where they are an impressive second best to the Grove in size, entertaiment, and stature. Their combination of businessmen and ranchers is as unique as the Bohemian's amalgamation of businessmen and artists. It is hardly surprising that wealthy men from Los Angeles, San Francisco, Honolulu, Spokane, and Chicago would join Mitchell in wanting to be membes of both.

Another club, the Colorado-based Roundup Riders of the Rockies, imitates the Rancheros in its emphasis on "roughing it" and socializing.

The riders do not carry their fine camp with them. Instead, twenty camp-hands are employed to move the camp in trucks to the next campsite. Thus, when the Roundup Riders arrive at their destination each evening they find fourteen large sleeping tents complete with cots, air mattresses, portable toilets, and showers. Also up and ready for service are a large green dining tent and an entertainment stage. A diesel-powered generator provides the camp with electricity.

Food service is provided by Martin Jetton of Fort Worth, Texas, a caterer advertised in the Southwest as "King of the Barbecue." Breakfasts and dinners are said to be veritable banquets. Lunch is not as elaborate, but it does arrive to the riders on the trail in a rather unusual fashion that only those of the higher circles could afford: "lunches in rugged country are often delivered by light plane or helicopter."[4] One year the men almost missed a meal because a wind came up and scattered the lunches, which were being parachuted from two Cessna 170s.

In addition to the twenty hired hands who take care of the camp, there are twenty wranglers to look after the horses. The horses on the ride—predominantly such fine breeds as Arabian, Quarter Horse, and Morgan—are estimated to be worth more than $200,000. Horses and riders compete in various contests of skill and horsemanship on a layover day in the middle of the week. Skeet shooting, trap shooting, and horseshoes also are a part of this event.

The Roundup Riders, who hold their trek at the same time the Bohemians hold their encampment, must be reckoned as a more regional organization. Although there are numerous millionaires and executives among them, the members are not of the national stature of most Bohemians and many Rancheros. They can afford to invest thousands of dollars in their horses and tack, to pay a $300 yearly ride fee, and to have their lunch brought to them by helicopter, but they cannot compete in business connections and prestige with those who assemble at the Bohemian Grove. Building from the Denver branch of the upper class, the Roundup Riders reach out primarily to Nebraska (six), Texas (five), Illinois (five), Nevada (three), California (three), and Arizona (three). There are no members from New York, Boston, Philadelphia, or other large Eastern cities.

Several other regional rides have been inspired by the Rancheros, rides such as the Desert Caballeros in Wickenburg, Arizona, and the Verde Vaqueros in Scottsdale, Arizona. These groups are similar in size and membership to the Roundup Riders of the Rockies. Like the Roundup Riders, they have a few overlapping members with the Rancheros. But none are of the status of the Rancheros Visitadores. They are minor legacies of the Bohemian Grove, unlikely even to be aware of their kinship ties to the retreat in the redwoods.

DO BOHEMIANS, RANCHEROS, AND ROUNDUP RIDERS RULE AMERICA?

The foregoing material on upper-class retreats, which I have presented in as breezy a manner as possible, is relevant to highly emotional questions concerning the distribution of power in modern America. In this final section, I will switch styles somewhat and discuss these charged questions in a sober, simple, and straightforward way.

It is my hypothesis that there is a ruling social class in the United States. This class is made up of the owners and managers of large corporations, which means the members have many economic and political interests in common, and many conflicts with ordinary working people. Comprising at most 1 percent of the total population, members of this class own 25 to 30 percent of all privately held wealth in America, own 60 to 70 percent of the privately held corporate wealth, receive 20 to 25 percent of the yearly income, direct the large corporations and foundations, and dominate the federal government in Washington.

Most social scientists disagree with this view. Some dismiss it out of hand, others become quite vehement in disputing it. The overwhelming majority of them believe that the United States has a "pluralistic" power structure, in which a wide variety of "veto groups" (e.g., businessmen, farmers, unions, consumers) and "voluntary associations" (e.g., National Association of Manufacturers, Americans for Democratic Action, Common Cause) form shifting coalitions to influence decisions on different issues. These groups and associations are said to have differing amounts of interest and influence on various questions. Contrary to my view, pluralists assert that no one group, not even the owners and managers of large corporations, has the cohesiveness and ability to determine the outcome of a large variety of social, economic, and political issues.

As noted, I believe there is a national upper class in the United States. This means that wealthy families from all over the country, and particularly from major cities like New York, San Francisco, Chicago, and Houston, are part of interlocking social circles which perceive each other as equals, belong to the same clubs, interact frequently, and freely intermarry.

Whether we call it a "social class" or a

"status group," many pluralistic social scientists would deny that such a social group exists. They assert that there is no social "cohesiveness" among the various rich in different parts of the country. For them, social registers, blue books, and club membership lists are merely collections of names which imply nothing about group interaction.

There is a wealth of journalistic evidence which suggests the existence of a national upper class. It ranges from Cleveland Armory's *The Proper Bostonians* and *Who Killed Society?* to Lucy Kavaler's *The Private World of High Society* and Stephen Birmingham's *The Right People*. But what is the systematic evidence which I can present for my thesis? There is first of all the evidence that has been developed from the study of attendance at private schools. It has been shown that a few dozen prep schools bring together children of the upper class from all over the country. From this evidence it can be argued that young members of the upper class develop lifetime friendship ties with like-status mates in every section of the country.[5]

There is second the systematic evidence which comes from studying high-status summer resorts. Two such studies show that these resorts bring together upper-class families from several different large cities.[6] Third, there is the evidence of business interconnections. Several studies have demonstrated that interlocking directorships bring wealthy men from all over the country into face-to-face relationships at the board meetings of banks, insurance companies, and other corporations.[7]

And finally, there is the evidence developed from studying exclusive social clubs. Such studies have been made in the past, but the present investigation of the Bohemian Club, the Rancheros Visitadores, and the Roundup Riders of the Rockies is a more comprehensive effort. *In short, I believe the present study to be significant evidence for the existence of a cohesive American upper class.*

The Bohemian Grove, as well as other watering holes and social clubs, is relevant to the problem of class cohesiveness in two ways. First, the very fact that rich men from all over the country gather in such close circumstances as the Bohemian Grove is evidence for the existence of a socially cohesive upper class. It demonstrates that many of these men do know each other, that they have face-to-face communications, and that they are a social network. In this sense, we are looking at the Bohemian Grove and other social retreats as a *result* of social processes that lead to class cohesion. But such institutions also can be viewed as *facilitators* of social ties. Once formed, these groups become another avenue by which the cohesiveness of the upper class is maintained.

In claiming that clubs and retreats like the Bohemians and the Rancheros are evidence for my thesis of a national upper class, I am assuming that cohesion develops within the settings they provide. Perhaps some readers will find that assumption questionable. So let us pause to ask: Are there reasons to believe that the Bohemian Grove and its imitators lead to greater cohesion within the upper class?

For one thing, we have the testimony of members themselves. There are several accounts by leading members of these groups, past and present, which attest to the intimacy that develops among members. John J. Mitchell, El Presidente of Los Rancheros Visitadores from 1930 to 1955, wrote as follows on the twenty-fifth anniversary of the group:

All the pledges and secret oaths in the universe cannot tie men, our kind of men, together like the mutual appreciation of a beautiful horse, the moon behind a cloud, a song around the campfire or a ride down the Santa Ynez Valley. These are experiences common on our ride, but unknown to most of our daily lives. Our organization, to all appearances, is the most informal imaginable. Yet there are men here who see one another once a year, yet feel a bond closer than between those they have known all their lives.[8]

F. Burr Betts, chairman of the board of Security Life of Denver, says the following about the Roundup Riders:

I think you find out about the Roundup Riders when you go to a Rider's funeral. Because there you'll find, no matter how many organizations the man belonged to, almost every pallbearer is a Roundup Rider. I always think of the Roundup Riders as the first affiliation. We have the closest knit fraternity in the world.[9]

A second reason for stressing the importance of retreats and clubs like the Bohemian Grove is a body of research within social psychology which deals with group cohesion. "Group dynamics" suggests the following about cohesiveness. (1) *Physical proximity is likely to lead to group solidarity.* Thus, the mere fact that these men gather together in such intimate physical settings implies that cohesiveness develops. (The same point can be made, of course, about exclusive neighborhoods, private schools, and expensive summer resorts). (2) *The more people interact, the more they will like each other.* This is hardly a profound discovery, but we can note that the Bohemian Grove and other watering holes maximize personal interactions. (3) *Groups seen as high in status are more cohesive.* The Bohemian Club fits the category of a high-status group. Further, its stringent membership requirements, long waiting lists, and high dues also serve to heighten its valuation in the eyes of its members. Members are likely to think of themselves as "special" people, which would heighten their attractiveness to each other and increase the likelihood of interaction and cohesiveness. (4) *The best atmosphere for increasing group cohesiveness is one that is relaxed and cooperative.* Again the Bohemian Grove, the Rancheros, and the Roundup Riders are ideal examples of this kind of climate. From a group-dynamics point of view, then, we could argue that one of the reasons for upper-class cohesiveness is the fact that the class is organized into a wide variety of small groups which encourage face-to-face interaction and ensure status and security for members.[10]

In summary, if we take these several common settings together—schools, resorts, corporation directorships, and social clubs—and assume on the basis of members'

testimony and the evidence of small-group research that interaction in such settings leads to group cohesiveness, then I think we are justified in saying that wealthy families from all over the United States are linked together in a variety of ways into a national upper class.

Even if the evidence and arguments for the existence of a socially cohesive national upper class are accepted, there is still the question of whether or not this class has the means by which its members can reach policy consensus on issues of importance to them.

A five-year study based upon information obtained from confidential informants, interviews, and questionnaires has shown that social clubs such as the Bohemian Club are an important consensus-forming aspect of the upper class and big-business environment. According to sociologist Reed Powell, "the clubs are a repository of the values held by the upper-level prestige groups in the community and are a means by which these values are transferred to the business environment." Moreover, the clubs are places where problems are discussed:

On the other hand, the clubs are places in which the beliefs, problems, and values of the industrial organization are discussed and related to other elements in the larger community. Clubs, therefore, are not only effective vehicles of informal communication, but also valuable centers where views are presented, ideas are modified, and new ideas emerge. Those in the interview sample were appreciative of this asset; in addition, they considered the club as a valuable place to combine social and business contacts.[11]

The revealing interview work of Floyd Hunter, an outstanding pioneer researcher on the American power structure, also provides evidence for the importance of social clubs as informal centers of policy making. Particularly striking for our purposes is a conversation he had with one of the several hundred top leaders that he identified in the 1950s. The person in question was a conservative industrialist who was ranked as a top-level leader by his peers:

Hall [pseudonym] spoke very favorably of the Bohemian Grove group that met in California every year. He said that although over the entrance to the Bohemian Club there was a quotation, "Weaving spiders come not here," there was a good deal of informal policy made in this association. He said that he got to know Herbert Hoover in this connection and that he started work with Hoover in the food administration of World War I.[12]

Despite the evidence presented by Powell and Hunter that clubs are a setting for the development of policy consensus, I do not believe that such settings are the only, or even the primary, locus for developing policy on class-related issues. For policy questions, other organizations are far more important, organizations like the Council on Foreign Relations, the Committee for Economic Development, the Business Council, and the National Municipal League. These organizations, along with many others, are the "consensus-seeking" and "policy-planning" organizations of the upper class. Directed by the same men who manage the major corporations, and financed by corporation and foundation monies, these groups sponsor meetings and discussions wherein wealthy men from all over the country gather to iron out differences and formulate policies on pressing problems.

No one discussion group is *the* leadership council within the upper class. While some of the groups tend to specialize in certain issue areas, they overlap and interact to a great extent. Consensus slowly emerges from the interplay of people and ideas within and among the groups.[13] This diversity of groups is made very clear in the following comments by Frazar B. Wilde, chairman emeritus of Connecticut General Life Insurance Companny and a member of the Council on Foreign Relations and the Committee for Economic Development. Mr. Wilde was responding to a question about the Bilderbergers, a big-business meeting group which includes Western European leaders as well as American corporation and foundation directors:

Business has had over the years many different seminars and discussion meetings. They run all the way from large public gatherings like NAM [National Association of Manufacturers] to special sessions such as those held frequently at Arden House. Bilderberg is in many respects one of the most important, if not the most important, but this is not to deny that other strictly off-the-record meetings and discussion groups such as those held by the Council on Foreign Relations are not in the front rank.[14]

Generally speaking, then, it is in these organizations that leaders within the upper class discuss the means by which to deal with problems of major concern. Here, in off-the-record settings, these leaders try to reach consensus on general issues that have been talked about more casually in corporate boardrooms and social clubs. These organizations, aided by funds from corporations and foundations, also serve several other functions:

1. They are a training ground for new leadership within the class. It is in these organizations, and through the publications of these organizations, that young lawyers, bankers, and businessmen become acquainted with general issues in the areas of foreign, domestic, and municipal policy.
2. They are the place where leaders within the upper class hear the ideas and findings of their hired experts.
3. They are the setting wherein upper-class leaders "look over" young experts for possible service as corporation or governmental advisers.
4. They provide the framework for expert studies on important issues. Thus, the Council on Foreign Relations undertook a $1 million study of the "China question" in the first half of the 1960s. The Committee for Economic Development created a major study of money and credit about the same time. Most of the money for these studies was provided by the Ford, Rockefeller, and Carnegie foundations.[15]
5. Through such avenues as books, journals, policy statements, discussion groups, press releases, and speakers, the policy-planning organizations greatly influence the "climate of opinion" within which major issues are con-

sidered. For example, *Foreign Affairs*, the journal of the Council on Foreign Relations, is considered the most influential journal in its field, and the periodic policy statements of the Committee for Economic Development are carefully attended to by major newspapers and local opinion leaders.

It is my belief, then, that the policy-planning groups are essential in developing policy positions which are satisfactory to the upper class as a whole. As such, I think they are a good part of the answer to any social scientist who denies that members of the upper class have institutions by which they deal with economic and political challenges.

However, the policy-planning groups could not function if there were not some common interests within the upper class in the first place. The most obvious, and most important, of these common interests have to do with the shared desire of the members to maintain the present monopolized and subsidized business system which so generously overrewards them and makes their jet setting, fox hunting, art collecting, and other extravagances possible. But it is not only shared economic and political concerns which made consensus possible. The Bohemian Grove and other upper-class social institutions also contribute to this process: *Group-dynamics research suggests that members of socially cohesive groups are more open to the opinions of other members, and more likely to change their views to those of fellow members.*[16] Social cohesion is a factor in policy consensus because it creates a desire on the part of group members to reconcile differences with other members of the group. It is not enough to say that members of the upper class are bankers, businessmen, and lawyers with a common interest in profit maximization and tax avoidance who meet together at the Council on Foreign Relations, the Committee for Economic Development, and other policy-planning organizations. We must add that they are Bohemians, Rancheros, and Roundup Riders.

NOTES

1. Wallace Turner, "Rockefeller Faces Scrutiny of Top Californians: Governor to Spend Weekend at Bohemian Grove among State's Establishment," *New York Times*, July 26, 1963, p. 30. In 1964 Senator Barry Goldwater appeared at the Grove as a guest of retired General Albert C. Wedemeyer and Herbert Hoover, Jr. For that story see Wallace Turner, "Goldwater Spending Weekend in Camp at Bohemian Grove," *New York Times*, July 31, 1964, p. 10.
2. James M. Naughton, "Nixon Drops Plan for Coast Speech," *New York Times*, July 31, 1971, p. 11.
3. There is a special moisture-proof building at the Grove to hold a dozen of expensive Steinway pianos belonging to the club and various camps.
4. Robert Pattridge, "Closer to Heaven on Horseback," *Empire Magazine, Denver Post*, July 9, 1972, p. 12. I am grateful to sociologist Ford Cleere for bringing this article to my attention.
5. E. Digby Baltzell, *Philadelphia Gentlemen* (New York: Free Press, 1958), chapter 12, and G. William Domhoff, *The Higher Circles* (New York: Random House, 1970), p. 78.
6. Baltzell, *Philadelphia Gentleman*, pp. 248–51, and Domhoff, *The Higher Circles*, pp. 79–82. For recent anecdotal evidence on this point, see Stephen Birmingham, *The Right People* (Boston: Little, Brown, 1968), Part 3.
7. *Interlocks in Corporate Management* (Washington: U.S. Government Printing Office, 1965) summarizes much of this information and presents new evidence as well. See also Peter Dooley, "The Interlocking Directorate," *American Economic Review*, December 1969.
8. Neill C. Wilson, *Los Rancheros Visitadores: Twenty-Fifth Anniversary* (Rancheros Visitadores, 1955), p. 2.
9. Pattridge, "Closer to Heaven on Horseback," p. 11.
10. Dorwin Cartwright and Alvin Zander, *Group Dynamics* (New York: Harper & Row, 1960), pp. 74–82; Albert J. Lott and Bernice E. Lott, "Group Cohesiveness as Interpersonal Attraction," *Psychological Bulletin 64* (1965):259–309; Michael Argyle, *Social Interaction* (Chicago: Aldine Publishing Company, 1969), pp.

220–23. I am grateful to sociologist John Sonquist of the University of California, Santa Barbara, for making me aware of how important the small-groups literature might be for studies of the upper class. Findings on influence processes, communication patterns, and the development of informal leadership also might be applicable to problems in the area of upper-class research.

11. Reed M. Powell, *Race, Religion, and the Promotion of the American Executive*, College of Administrative Science Monograph No. AA–3, Ohio State University, 1969, p. 50.

12. Floyd Hunter, *Top Leadership, U.S.A.* (Chapel Hill: University of North Carolina Press, 1959), p. 109. Hunter also reported (p. 199) that the most favored clubs of his top leaders were Metropolitan, Links, Century, University (New York), Bohemian, and Pacific Union. He notes (p. 223 n.) that he found clubs to be less important in policy formation on the national level than they are in communities.

13. For a detailed case study of how the process works, see David Eakins, "Business Planners and America's Postwar Expansion," in David Horowitz (ed.), *Corporations and the Cold War* (New York: Monthly Review Press, 1969). For other examples and references, see Domhoff, *The Higher Circles*, chapters 5 and 6.

14. Carl Gilbert, personal communication, June 30, 1972. Mr. Gilbert has done extensive research on the Bilderberg group, and I am grateful to him for sharing his detailed information with me. For an excellent discussion of this group, whose role has been greatly distorted and exaggerated by ultraconservatives, see Eugene Pasymowski and Carl Gilbert, "Bilderberg, Rockefeller, and the CIA," *Temple Free Press*, No. 6, September 16, 1968. The article is most conveniently located in a slightly revised form in the *Congressional Record*, September 15, 1971, E9615, under the title "Bilderberg: The Cold War Internationale."

15. The recent work of arch-pluralist Nelson Polsby is bringing him dangerously close to this formulation. Through studies of the initiation of a number of new policies, Polsby and his students have tentatively concluded that "innovators are typically professors or interest group experts." Where Polsby goes wrong is in failing to note that professors are working on Ford Foundation grants and/or Council on Foreign Relations fellowships. If he would put his work in a sociological framework, people would not gain the false impression that professors are independent experts sitting in their ivory towers thinking up innovations for the greater good of humanity. See Nelson Polsby, "Policy Initiation in the American Political System," in Irving Louis Horowitz (ed.), *The Use and Abuse of Social Science* (New Brunswick, N.J.: TransAction Books, 1971), p. 303.

16. Cartwright and Zander, *Group Dynamics*, p. 89; Lott and Lott, "Group Cohesiveness as Interpersonal Attraction," pp. 291–96.

22

Outlaw Motorcyclists

J. MARK WATSON

Walter Miller's (1958) typology of focal concerns of lower-class culture as a generating milieu for gang delinquency is by most standards a classic in explaining gang behavior among juvenile males. Its general heuristic value is here demonstrated by the striking parallel between this value system and that of adult outlaw motorcyclists.

The reader may remember Miller's general schema, which concerned the strain between the value system of youthful lower class males and the dominant, middle-class system of those in a position to define delinquent behavior. Because the typology itself is contained in the discussion of biker values, it will not be discussed separately here.

METHODOLOGY

The findings of the paper are based on my three years of participant observation in the subculture of outlaw motorcyclists. Although I am not a member of any outlaw clubs, I am or have been acquainted with members and officers of various clubs, as well as more loosely organized groups of motorcyclists for ten years. I am myself a motorcycle enthusiast, which facilitated a natural entry into the biker scene. I both build and ride bikes and gained direct access to local biker groups by frequenting places where bikers congregate to work on their bikes. Building a bike gave me legitimation and access to local biker groups and eventually led to contact with other bikers, including outlaws. Groups observed varied from what could be classified as clubs to loose-knit groups of associated motorcyclists. Four groups were studied in depth. Two small local groups in middle Tennessee were subjects of direct participation. Here they are given the fictional names of the Brothers and the Good Old Boys. In addition, one regional group from North Carolina, given the fictional name of Bar Hop-

Reprinted by permission of the author and publisher, Hemisphere Publishing Corporation.

pers, was studied through interviews with club officers and members. One national-level group, one of the largest groups of outlaw motorcyclists, was extensively observed and interviewed, primarily at regional and national events. This group is given the fictional name of the Convicts.

Interviews were informally administered in the sense that no formal interview schedule was used. Instead, bikers were queried in the context of what would pass for normal conversation. Notes and impressions were taken at night and/or after the events. Groups and individuals were generally not aware that they were being studied, although I made no attempt to hide my intentions. Some bikers who came to know me were curious about a university professor participating in such activities and accordingly were told that a study was being conducted. This honesty was prompted by fear of being suspected of being a narcotics agent. Such self-revelation was rarely necessary, as the author affected the clothing and jargon of bikers and was accepted as such. Frequent invitations to engage in outrageous and illegal behavior (e.g., drug use and purchase of stolen parts) that would not be extended to outsiders were taken as a form of symbolic acceptance. My demeanor and extensive association with lower-class gangs in adolescence combined with the type of mechanical skills necessary to build bikes mentioned earlier may have contributed to an ability to blend in. Reactions to self-revelation, when necessary, generally ranged from amazement to amusement. I suspect that, as is true with the general population, most bikers had no idea what a sociologist was, but the presence of a professor in their midst was taken as a sort of legitimation for the group.

It must be kept in mind that research conducted with this kind of deviant subculture can be dangerous. Because many outlaws do not welcome scrutiny and carefully avoid those who they feel may not be trusted, which includes most nonbikers, I remained as unobtrusive as possible. Generally, I felt my presence was accepted. This acceptance can be symbolized by my receiving a nickname (Doc) and eventually being defined as an expert in a certain type of obsolete motorcycle (the Harley-Davidson 45-cubic-inch side-valve model). I assumed the role of an inside outsider.

THE BIKER SUBCULTURE

We may locate outlaw bikers in the general spectrum of bikers as the most "outrageous" (their own term, a favorite modifier indicating something distinctively appealing to their own jaded sense of values) on the continuum of bikers, which extends from housewives on mopeds to clubs that actually engage in illegal behavior with a fair degree of frequency, thus the term "outlaws" (Thompson, 1967). Outlaws generally adopt certain symbols and lead a lifestyle that is clearly defined and highly visible to other bikers. Symbols include extensive tattooing, beard, dirty jeans, earrings, so-called stroker caps and quasi-military pins attached, engineer's boots, and cut-off jackets with club emblems, called "colors," sewn on the back. Weapons, particularly buck knives and guns of any sort, and chains (motorcycle or other types) are favorite symbols as well (*Easyriders*, 1977a). By far the most important symbol, however, is the Harley-Davidson V-twin motorcycle. It should be kept in mind that many other motorcyclists affect these symbols, although they are by no means outlaws.

OUTLAW LIFE-STYLE

This lifestyle is in many respect a lower-class variation of bohemian, "dropout" subcultures. Such similarities include frequent unemployment and disdain for cleanliness, orderliness, and other concerns of conventional culture. For example, I have observed bikes being built and stored in living rooms or kitchens, two nonessential rooms in the subculture. This is apparently a common practice. Parts may be stored in an oil bath in the bathtub, also a nonessential device.

Although individual freedom and choice are also emphasized, the club actually suppress individual freedom, while using the value to defend their lifestyle from outsiders. For example, when the Convicts take a club trip called a "run," all members must participate. Those whose bikes are "down" for repairs are fined and must find a ride in a truck with the women. Many club rules require members to follow orders as prescribed by club decisions upon threat of violence and expulsion. Club rules generally include a constitution and bylaws that are surprisingly elaborate and sophisticated for groups of this nature. Many club members express pride in their written regulations. It seems likely that the basic format is borrowed from that developed by the Hell's Angels (Thompson, 1967). Most club decisions are made in a democratic way, but minority rights are not respected. Once such a decision is made, it is imperative to all members, with risk of physical retribution for failure to conform. Typical rules include care of colors, which are to never touch the ground or be washed. They are treated essentially as a flag.

Masculinity as a dominant value is expressed in many ways, including toughness and a general concern with looking mean, dirty, and "outrageous." Some other biker-associated values include racism, concern with Nazism, and in-group superiority. "Righteousness" is achieved through adherence to these values. One celebrity member of the Brothers had been convicted of killing a young black man in a street confrontation. He is reported to have jumped bail and lived with a Nazi couple in South America, where he worked as a ranch hand. This particular member spoke some German and frequently spouted racist and Nazi doctrine. A typical righteous outlaw belongs to a club, rides an American-made motorcycle, is a white male, displays the subculture's symbols, hates most if not all nonwhites and Japanese motorcycles, works irregularly at best, dresses at all times in dirty jeans, cut-off denim jacket, and engineer's boots, drinks beer, takes whichever drugs are available, and treats women as objects of contempt.

OUTLAW BIKER WORLD VIEW AND SELF-CONCEPT

The outlaw biker generally views the world as hostile, weak, and effeminate. Perhaps this view is a realistic reaction to a working-class socialization experience. However, the reaction contains certain elements of a self-fulfilling prophecy. Looking dirty, mean, and generally undesirable may be a way of frightening others into leaving one alone, although, in many senses such an appearance arouses anger, hostility, and related emotions in the observer and results in the persecution that such qualities are intended to protect one from.

Bikers tend to see the world in terms of here and now. They are not especially hostile toward most social institutions such as family, government, and education. Most of the local group members had finished high school and had been employed from time to time, and some had been college students. Some were veterans, and nearly all had been married more than once. Few had been successful in these endeavors, however. They are generally not capable of establishing the temporal commitments necessary for relating to such institutions. For example, marriages and similar relationships rarely last more than a few years, and education requires concentrated effort over a time span that they are generally not willing or in many cases not capable of exerting. Most of them drift from one job to another or have no job at all. Simply keeping up with where the informants were living proved to be a challenge. I frequently had a call from a local biker relating that he was "on his way over" only to find that he did not arrive at all or arrived hours or days later. I have been on runs that were to depart in the early morning and that did not in fact depart until hours later. The biker's sense of time and commitment to it is not only lower class, but more typical of preliterate societies. The result is frequent clashes with bureaucratically organized institutions, such as government and economy, which are oriented toward impulse control, commitment, and punctuality, and failure in organizations that require long-term commitments or interpersonal relations, such as family and education.

Outlaw bikers generally view themselves as outsiders. I have on occasion invited local bikers to settings that would place them in contact with members of the middle class. Their frequent response is that they would "not fit in" or would "feel out of place." Basically, they seem to feel that they cannot compete with what sociologists define as the middle class although I have never heard the term used by bikers. Outlaws see themselves as losers, as symbolized by tattoos, patches, and even their humor, which portrays them as ignorant. "One percenter" is a favorite patch, referring to its wearers as the most deviant fraction of the biker fraternity. In effect, the world that they create for themselves is an attempt to suspend the rules of competition that they cannot win by and create a world where one does not compete but simply exists (Montgomery, 1976, 1977). Pretense and self-importance are ways to lose acceptance quickly in such a situation. One does not compete with or "put down" a fellow biker, for he is a "brother."

It is not that bikers are uniformly hostile toward the outside world; they are indifferent toward, somewhat threatened by, and contemptuous of it.

MILLER'S FOCAL CONCERNS AS EXPRESSED IN OUTLAW BIKER CULTURE

Trouble

Trouble is a major theme of the outlaw biker culture, as illustrated by the very use of the term "outlaw." The term refers to one who demonstrates his distinctiveness (righteousness) by engaging in outrageous and even illegal behavior. Trouble seems to serve several purposes in this subculture. First, flirting with trouble is a way of demonstrating masculinity—trouble is a traditionally male prerogative. Trouble also enforces group solidarity through emphasizing the outsider status of the outlaw, a status that can be sustained only by the formation of counterculture. Given the outlaw biker's world view and impulsiveness, trouble comes without conscious effort. Trouble may come over drug use, stolen bikes or parts, possession of firearms, or something as simple as public drunkenness. Some of the local bikers whom I knew well had prison records for manslaughter (defined as self-defense by the subjects), receiving stolen property, drug possession, statutory rape, and assault on an officer. All saw these sentences as unjust and claimed that the behavior was justifiable or that they were victims of a case of overzealous regulation of everyday activities or deliberate police harassment.

Toughness

In addition to trouble, toughness is at the heart of the biker emphasis on masculinity and outrageousness. To be tough is to experience trouble without showing signs of weakness. Therefore, the objective of trouble is to demonstrate the masculine form of toughness. Bikers have contempt for such comforts as automobiles or even devices that increase biking comfort or safety such as eye protection, helmets, windshields, farings, or even frames with spring rear suspension (a so-called hardtail is the preferred frame). Bikers wear denim or leather, but the sleeves are generally removed to show contempt for the danger of "road rash," abrasions caused by contact with the road surface at speed, which protective material can prevent.

Part of toughness is the prohibition against expressing love for women and children in any but a possessive way. Women are viewed with contempt and are regarded as a necessary nuisance (generally referred to as "cunts," "whores," or "sluts"), as are children ("rug rats"). Curiously, bikers seem to attract an adequate supply of women despite the poor treatment they receive from them. When asked about the female's motivation for participation in the subculture, one (male) informant stated simply "they're looking for excitement." The women attracted to such a scene are predictably tough and hard-bitten themselves. Not all are unattractive, but most display signs of premature aging typical of lower-class and deviant lifestyles. All work to keep up their mate and his motorcycle. I must admit that my interviews with biker women were limited lest my intentions be misinterpreted. I could have hired some of them under sexual pretenses, as many may be bought, but ethical and financial considerations precluded this alternative. My general impression is that these women generally come from lower-class families in which the status of the female is not remarkably different from that they currently enjoy. Being a biker's "old lady" offers excitement and opportunities to engage in exhibitionist and outlandish behavior that in their view contrasts favorably with the lives of their mothers. Many are mothers of illegitimate children before they resort to bikers and may view themselves as fallen women who have little to lose in terms of respectability. Most seem to have fairly low self-concepts, which are compatible with their status as bikers' old ladies.

Of course, the large, heavy motorcycles bikers ride are symbolic of their toughness as well. Not everyone can ride such a machine because of its sheer weight. Many models are "kick start," and require some strength and skill just to start. A certain amount of recklessness is also used to express toughness. To quote Bruce Springsteen: "It's a death trap, a suicide rap" (Springsteen, 1976), and the ability to ride it, wreck it, and survive demonstrates toughness in a very dramatic way. An example of my experience in this regard may be illuminating. Although I had ridden motorcycles for years, I became aware of the local biker group while building my first Harley-Davidson. Full acceptance by this group was not extended until my first and potentially fatal accident, however. Indeed, local bikers who had only vaguely known me offered the gift of parts and assistance in reconstructing my bike and began to refer to me by a new nickname, "Doc." I sensed and was extended to a new degree of acceptance after demonstrating my "toughness" by surviving the accident. Toughness, in this sense, is a combination of stupidity and misfortune, and hardly relates to any personal virtue.

Smartness

On this characteristic, biker values seem to diverge from general lower-class values as described by Miller. The term "dumb biker" is frequently used as a self-description. Given the choice of avoiding, outsmarting, or confronting an opponent, the biker seems to prefer avoidance or confrontation. Confrontation gives him the opportunity to demonstrate toughness by generating trouble. Avoidance is not highly valued, but no one can survive all the trouble he could generate, and the stakes are frequently the highest—life itself or at least loss of freedom. The appearance of toughness and outlandishness mentioned above make confrontation a relatively infrequent occurrence, as few outsiders will challenge a group of outlaw bikers unless the issue is of great significance. Smartness, then, does not seem to be an emphasized biker value or characteristic. Gambling on outsmarting an opponent is for low stakes such as those faced by the adolescents Miller studied.

Excitement

One of the striking things about the outlaw lifestyle is its extremes. Bikers hang out at chopper (motorcycle) shops, clubhouses, or bars during the day, except when they are in prison or jail, which is not uncommon. Places frequented by bikers are generally located in lower-class neighborhoods.

A clubhouse, for example, is generally a rented house which serves as a headquarters, party location, and place for members to "crash" when they lack more personal accommodations. They are not unlike a lower-class version of a fraternity house. Outlaws tend to designate bars as their own. This involves taking over bars to the exclusion of their usual lower- or working-class clientele. Such designations are frequently short-lived, as the bars may be closed as a public nuisance or the proprietor may go out of business for economic or personal reasons as a result of the takeover. I know of at least one such bar that was burned by local people to rid the neighborhood of the nuisance. Its owner relocated the business some 40 miles away.

Local bikers who worked generally had unskilled and semi-skilled jobs, which are dull in themselves. Examples include laborers, factory workers, construction workers, and hospital orderlies. Many do not work regularly, being supported by their women.[1] In any case most of their daylight hours are spent in deadly dull environment where the most excitement may be a mechanical problem with a bike. Escape from this dull lifestyle is dramatic in its excesses. Drugs, alcohol, and orgiastic parties are one form of escape. Other escapes include the run or simply ridding the bikes for which the subculture is named. Frequently both forms of escape are combined, and such events as the Daytona and Sturgis runs are remarkable, comparing favorably to Mardis Gras as orgiastic events. Living on the edge of trouble, appearing outlandish, fierce, and tough, itself yields a form of self-destructive excitement, especially when it can be used to outrage others.

Unlike the situation that Miller studied, excitement and trouble rarely seem to center around women, as their status among bikers is even lower than in the lower class in general. I have never seen a conflict over a woman among bikers and am struck by the casual manner in which they move from one biker to another. The exchange of women seems to be the male's prerogative, and women appear to be traded or given away as casually as pocket knives are exchanged among old men. I have on occasion been offered the use of a female for the duration of a run. This offer was always made by the male and was made in the same manner that one might offer the use of a tool to a neighbor. (I have never been offered the loan of a bike, however.) The low regard for women combined with the traditional biker's emphasis on brotherhood seems to minimize conflicts over women. Those conflicts that do occur over women seem to occur between clubs and are a matter of club honor rather than jealousy or grief over the loss of a relationship.

Fate

Because bikers do not emphasize smartness to the extent that Miller perceived it among the lower class, the role of fate in explaining failure to succeed is somewhat different for them. In Miller's analysis, fate was a rationalization used when one was outsmarted. The biker's attitude toward fate goes much deeper and could be described as figuratively and literally fatalistic. The theme of death is central to their literature and art.[2] A biker who becomes economically successful or who is too legitimate is suspect. He is no longer one of them. He has succeeded in the outside and in a sense has sold out. His success alone shows his failure to subscribe to the basic values that they hold. He is similar to a rich Indian—no longer an Indian but a white man with red skin. Members of local groups, the Brothers and Good Old Boys, came and went. Membership fluctuated. Few members resigned because of personal difficulty. However, many former members were still around. The single characteristic that they all shared was economic success. Although these former members tended to be older than the typical member, many current members were as old or older. Success in small businesses were typical. Some former members had been promoted to lower management positions in local factories and related businesses, apparently were no longer comfortable in their former club roles, and so resigned. Some kept their bikes, others exchanged them for more respectable touring bikes, and others sold their bikes. In any case, although some maintained limited social contact and others participated in occasional weekend runs, their success appeared to make them no longer full participants in group activities and resulted ultimately in their formal resignation from the clubs. Bikers basically see themselves as losers and affect clothing, housing, and other symbols of the embittered and dangerous loser. They apparently no longer dream the unrealistic adolescent dreams of the "big break." Prison and death are seen as natural concomitants of the biker lifestyle. Fate is the grim reaper that so often appears in biker art.

Autonomy

Autonomy in the form of freedom is central to the outlaw biker's expressed philosophy and in this respect closely parallels the lower-class themes outlined by Miller. A studied insistence that they be left alone by harassing law enforcement agencies and overregulating bureaucrats is a common theme in biker literature and personal expressions. The motorcycle itself is an individual thing, begrudgingly including an extra seat for an "old lady" or "down" brother. Ironically, the outlaw biker lifestyle is so antisocial vis-à-vis the wider society that it cannot be pursued individually. A lone outlaw knows he is a target, an extremely visible and vulnerable one. Therefore, for purposes of self-protection, the true outlaw belongs to a club and rarely makes a long trip without the company of several brothers.

Outlaw clubs are themselves both authoritarian and democratic. Members may vote on issues or at least select officers, but club policy and rules are absolute and may be enforced with violence (*Choppers*, March 1978). Antisocial behavior associated with the outlaw lifestyle itself frequently results in loss of autonomy. Most prisons of any size

not only contain substantial biker population but may contain local (prison) chapters of some of the larger clubs (*Life*, 1979). *Easyriders*, a biker magazine, regularly contains sections for pen pals and other requests from brothers in prison (*Easyriders*, 1977b). So, although autonomy in the form of the right to be different is pursued with a vengeance, the ferocity with which it is pursued ensures its frequent loss.

Miller noted an ambivalent attitude among lower-class adolescents toward authority: They both resented it and sought situations in which it was forced on them. The structure of outlaw clubs and the frequent incarceration that is a result of their lifestyle would seem to be products of a similar ambivalence. Another loss of autonomy that Miller noted among lower-class gangs was a dependence on females that caused dissonance and was responsible for lower-class denigration of female status. Outlaws take the whole process a step further, however. Many of their women engage in prostitution, topless waitressing, or menial, traditionally; female labor. Some outlaws live off the income of several women and in this sense are dependent on them but only in the sense that a pimp is dependent on his string of girls. From their point of view, the females see themselves as protected by and dependent on the male rather than the other way around.

CONCLUSION

Miller's topology of lower-class focal concerns appears to be a valid model for analyzing outlaw biker cultures, just as it was for analyzing some forces behind juvenile gang delinquency. Although there are some differences in values and their expression, the differences are basically those occurring by the transferring of the values from streetwise adolescents to adult males. My experiences with bikers indicate a working-class family background with downward mobility. A surprising portion of the bikers interviewed indicated respectable working-class or lower-middle-class occupations for their fathers. Examples included postal worker, forestry and lumber contractor, route sales business owner, and real estate agency owner. They are definitely not products of multigenerational poverty. I would classify them as nonrespectable working-class marginals.

The study is presented primarily as an ethnographic description of a difficult and sometimes dangerous subculture to study, which when viewed from the outside appears as a disorganized group of deviants but when studied carefully with some insider's insights is seen to have a coherent and reasonably consistent value system and a lifestyle based on that value system.

NOTES

1. Outlaw bikers sometimes support themselves by dealing in drugs, bootleg liquor, and prostitution of their women.

2. Of the fiction of the entire 1977 issue of *Easyriders*, 40 percent of the articles concerned themselves with death.

REFERENCES

Choppers. (1978, March). Club profile: Northern Indiana invaders M/C, pp. 36–39.

Easyriders. (1977a, February). Gun nut report, pp. 28, 29, 55.

Easyriders. (1977b, October). Man is the ruler of woman, p. 15.

Life. (1979, August). Prison without stripes, pp. 80–81.

Miller, W. B. (1958). Lower class culture as a generating milieu for gang delinquency. *Journal of Social Issues, 4,* 5–19.

Montgomery, R. (1976). The outlaw motorcycle subculture. *Canadian Journal of Criminology and Corrections, 18.*

Montgomery, R. (1977). The outlaw motorcycle subculture II. *Canadian Journal of Criminology and Corrections, 19.*

Springsteen, B. (1976). "Born to Run." Columbia Records.

Thompson, H. (1967). *Hell's Angels: A strange and terrible saga.* New York: Random House.

23

Covert Sex Discrimination

Nijole V. Benokraitis
Joe R. Feagin

Covert sex discrimination refers to unequal and harmful treatment of women that is hidden, clandestine, and maliciously motivated. Unlike overt and subtle sex discrimination, covert sex discrimination is very difficult to document and prove because records are not kept or are inaccessible, the victim may not even be aware of being a "target," or the victim may be ignorant of how to secure, track, and record evidence of covert discrimination.

Six types of covert sex discrimination are discussed in this chapter—tokenism, containment, manipulation, sabotage, revenge, and co-optation.

TOKENISM

For our purposes, tokenism refers to the unwritten and usually unspoken policy or practice of hiring, promoting, or otherwise including a miniscule number of individuals from underrepresented groups—women, minorities, the handicapped, the elderly. Through tokenism, organizations maintain the semblance of equality because no group is totally excluded. Placing a few tokens in strategically visible places precludes the necessity of practicing "real" equality—that is, hiring and promoting individuals regardless of their sex.

General Characteristics

Across almost all occupational areas and often regardless of age, degree of experience, religion, color, level of education, intelligence, and ability, female tokens are marginal/alienated members of the work groups, highly visible, and excluded from entering upwardly mobile opportunities. They experience continuous stress because

Benokraitis/Feagin, *Modern Sexism: Blatant, Subtle, and Covert Discrimination*, © 1986, pp. 99–113. Reprinted by permission of Prentice-Hall, Englewood Cliffs, N.J.

they are always on display and rarely recognize tokenistic maneuvers.

There is a close relationship between tokenism and powerlessness. For example, Rich (1979) characterizes female tokenism as a "false power which masculine society offers to a few women who 'think like men.' " And, according to Laws (1975), "tokenism is likely to be found wherever a dominant group is under pressure to share privilege, power, or other desirable commodities with a group which is excluded." Tokenism is a conscious, calculated effort to avoid charges of discrimination and possible subsequent investigations that might uncover widespread and effective exclusionary policies and practices.

How Tokenism Works

There are three types of commonly practiced tokenism that limit women's equal participation in the labor force. A popular form is based on *numerical exclusion*, which uses quotas to maintain a predominantly male work force:

As soon as they come into my office, a lot of recruiters tell me exactly how many women they plan to hire and in which departments. They say things like, "This year we need two women in accounting, one in marketing, and one in data processing." Some [of the recruiters] have fairly detailed data showing exactly how many women they should be hiring for their company. (What if the most qualified candidates are all women?)

Most recruiters automatically assume that women are *not* the most qualified—they got high grades because they slept around, they're not serious about long-term job commitments, they don't understand the business world and so on. . . . They interview the [women] students we schedule, but rarely hire more than one or two they're told to hire. (College job placement director)

Because male quotas are high—95 to 99 percent—it is not difficult to fill the low percentage of slots allocated to token women.

Pragmatic tokenism hires and retains women as long as it is cost effective to do so. As long as there is a large pool of talented women who are happy to get any job, have high productivity rates, do not protest about serving as window dressing, and do not demand genuine progress, tokenism runs smoothly. If tokens push for real improvement—especially in salaries—they are often fired. Turnover is inexpensive because there is a plentiful supply of replacements, even at higher levels:

. . . levels of management, as business sees it, that's not a problem. There are already more candidates for management than business could ever use. And the benefits of a cheap labor force far outweigh the dubious value of having a larger pool of managerial talent (LaRouche & Ryan, 1984).

This "revolving door" brand of tokenism is profitable for companies because it ensures a continuous flow of hardworking and competent employees at low costs.

CONTAINMENT

"Containment" refers to the unwritten and usually unspoken policy or practice of restricting women's entry into designated jobs and positions so as not to threaten or displace the composition of dominant—that is, white male—group members. While tokenism establishes the limits on how many women will be allowed entry into (especially nonfemale) jobs, containment specifies where the entry will take place. Thus, tokenism ensures *quantitative* exclusion, whereas containment ensures *qualitative* exclusion.

Establishing Male-Female Domains

Most of us spend the first twenty years of our lives learning and internalizing norms and values that will later make containment in employment perfectly natural, normal, acceptable, and even comfortable. Using the term in a broader context, women's (and men's) behavior is limited, that is, "contained," from the time they are born. Both sexes learn that girls and boys (and, later, men and women) speak, think, act, dress, smell, feel, play, work, pray, fight, drink, eat, smoke, sit, stand, bend, walk, drive, shop, sleep, make love, write, urinate, belch, and argue *differently*. In these and other activities, men are or should be independent, in control, knowledgeable, and in command; women are or should be dependent, submissive, uninformed, and controlled. What is important is not that men and women are taught to be different, but that women's "different" is seen as *inferior* to men's "different."

Maintaining Male-Female Domains

Upon entering adulthood, some individuals have the opportunity and resources to dig their way out of the avalanche of sexist rhetoric and behavior in which they grew up. Many do not. They do not, in large part, because containment procedures, especially in employment, effectively maintain male-female domains through such activities as stalling, demotions/promotions, and exclusion from important decision-making functions.

Stalling. An effective containment procedure is stalling. When women try to move beyond their token positions (especially in male-dominated areas), supervisors and peers discourage such ambitions through a variety of delaying techniques:

I worked in the shipping and receiving department but wanted to drive the trucks for more money. My supervisor claimed that he couldn't spare me, that the trucks were difficult to drive (even though I had driven eighteen-wheelers in the past) and that driving a truck would cause trouble with the rest of the women in the department. (Female employee in a parcel service company)

Women's applications for promotion are often "misplaced" or are sent to the "wrong department." After completing the necessary training or educational requirements, women are told that there is a "hiring freeze," even though men are hired. Or, women may give up after waiting, sometimes for several months, because "the committee hasn't met," a key decision maker is "in Europe," or "we can't make a decision until the department has been reorganized."

Demotions/promotions. Another method for maintaining boundaries between men's and women's jobs is to hire women at relatively high levels and later move them into lower-paying or less responsible positions:

When I was hired, I needed job training to meet the specialized computer needs of the department. Several months went by—no training. I learned some things on my own through trial-and-error, but the progress was slow and I made mistakes. Every time I reminded my boss about the training, he'd say, "In a couple of weeks," but nothing happened. Eight months into the job I was told that my position was being terminated but that I could move into similar positions in other departments. The other positions turned out to be word-processing jobs—at lower levels and lower salaries. After I left I heard that [Company X] hired a guy in my job and started training him the first day. (Data processor at a large department store)

Thus, an initially promising job can deteriorate, quietly and almost imperceptibly, into a demotion.

Promotions are also used to maintain established male-female employment domains. A female chancellor at a large state university noted that the departments that deal with money and budgets (comptrollers, fund-raising, grants) are led by men; women are promoted as "assistant to" but not "director of" such departments. In legal firms, similarly, women attorneys are "promoted," regardless of specialization, to female-dominated areas:

My specialty is labor law. The only promotion offers I've gotten were in domestic and family law. The promotions would have meant more money initially, but not in the long run. Divorces, child custody, and all of that are important, but our company sees it as a service, a throwaway. (Female attorney in a large legal firm)

When the draft ended in the early 1970s, the military recruited women to meet projected manpower shortages. The typical route to high ranks in the military is through combat. Because women are not allowed to serve in combat, promotion opportunities are limited to command of support units and other peripheral positions. In the Navy, for example, the 175 women surface-warfare officers who are preparing for sea duty can serve on only 33 of the Navy's 527 ships, and those 33 operate only on the fringes of the fleet—as repair vessels, research ships, tenders (small ships that service larger ships), and the like. As one female officer states, "To spend twenty years to get to be a captain of a tender isn't enough incentive" (Schwadel, 1985).

Thus, promotions can maintain containment by ensuring sex segregation—especially at supervisory and managerial levels.

Exclusion from decision-making groups. Even if an individual has been hired into or promoted to an objectively powerful position, another method of maintaining male-female authority is to exclude women from important decision-making processes.

One form of exclusion is not to elect or appoint women to decision-making bodies. In a study of university governance, for example, Muller (1978) found that although women were equally interested in governance and were equally willing to serve on committees, men were "far more likely to be involved" because women were not asked to serve on committees or were not nominated to represent their peers.

Another common exclusionary device is to set up "separate but equal" male-female programs. The women's programs are headed by women, are visible, and sometimes get public attention. However, because the women are not involved in bud-

getary decisions or because the women's program is subsumed under men's programs, the equality is only cosmetic. In the area of athletics, for example, regardless of level (high school, college) or locus of control (county recreation departments, state government, education boards), the allocation of resources of girls' and women's athletic budgets are male controlled and male dominated (Huckle, 1978).

Finally, screening by gatekeepers also creates and maintains containment. Gatekeepers are individuals who examine an applicant's credentials and decide who is qualified or unqualified for employment consideration. They may act independently (as a personnel director) or within a larger collectivity (as a union or referral agency). According to Harragan (1977), "employment agencies and executive-search agencies serve as the screening agent to eliminate women from companies which cannot be caught doing it themselves. This goes on in a very underhanded, covert way, so ambitious women have to play a most sophisticated form of corporate politics when dealing with placement firms."

Whether it is a university search committee or a job interviewer in business or industry, the gatekeepers are typically men who are uncomfortable in dealing with women. According to a consultant for several Fortune 500 companies, the biggest hurdle women face is fitting in with male managers: "At senior management levels, competence is assumed. . . . What you're looking for is someone who fits, someone who gets along, someone you trust. . . . How does a group of men feel that a woman is going to fit in? I think it's very hard" (Fraker, 1984). Similarly, in a study of 173 male and female managers at two companies, Harlan and Weiss (1981) found that women managers felt that male managers excluded women from informal mentoring situations:

Sometimes I see store managers that invite the guys for coffee in the morning because they feel comfortable and they can talk sports with the guys or whatever it might be. But they leave out their women department managers. And when you do that, the guys are getting more information than the girls are to work with because while you're sitting there having coffee, you might be talking about the Red Sox, but most of the time you're talking about what we're going to do with the department here or whatever we're going to do with this . . . or business in general.

Because women are excluded from informal get-togethers by gatekeepers, they can be contained more easily within entry-level positions.

As noted earlier, tokenism and containment determine *how many* women will enter certain occupational positions and *where* they will be located. Whereas tokenism and containment limit women's entry, manipulation, sabotage, and revenge discourage their occupational *progression* and actively encourage job *exits*.

MANIPULATION

There are a number of effective manipulative strategies that discourage women's economic progress. Questioning or casting aspersions on a woman's qualifications or ability will threaten, weaken, or subvert a woman's power, credibility, and usefulness. If, especially, the woman is seen as a "troublemaker," male superiors "may insinuate that the misbehaving woman is basically incompetent, which may lead other women to fear being associated with her cause" (Pendergrass et al., 1976).

I've been working for this operation for six years. Our supervisor makes a point of reminding me and the other women of our routes and transfers almost every week even though the written schedules are posted on the bulletin board. He treats us as though we can't remember what we're supposed to be doing. (MTA bus driver)

If a woman holds a formal position of power and authority, men (and women) subordinates can manipulate the female superior into not recognizing and not using her power by bypassing her in the organizational structure. Bayes and Newton (1978)

provide an example of this in their analysis of a mental health organization where, in one department, male staff members were subordinates and a woman was the superior:

When senior male staff spoke to her [Dr. A., the female superior] about their work, it was in the spirit of obtaining her consultation to them, thereby obfuscating their subordinacy. They struggled to be independent of her, to distance themselves from her authority. They had difficulties in accepting criticism from Dr. A. and would go to great lengths to defend their work. For her part, Dr. A. found herself being excessively cautious in offering a negative assessment of male staff members' work.

Another manipulative strategy is to give women undesirable jobs under the guise of "equal treatment":

Some of us [women] have more seniority than men but our schedules are changed more often, we get the undesirable routes, and the buses we're assigned are in the worst possible working order. When we go to the union meetings to complain, there is always a male driver who complains that women are "too soft for the job" and reminds us that we can't expect any "special treatment." (MTA bus driver)

SABOTAGE

Through sabotage, employers and employees purposely and consciously undermine or undercut a woman's position. Sabotage strategies vary by degree of sophistication, which depends on whether the woman is in a traditionally female job, a traditionally male job, or a job in which boundaries are, in principle, nonexistent because they are, in practice, not job related.

Traditionally Female Jobs

In traditionally female jobs (domestic, service, clerical), male sabotage is normative, because men at a comparable job level have higher status (owing to higher wages) or because men have supervisory positions. In comparable job levels, men can use sabotage because their job functions are less vulnerable to inspection and represent higher control than those of women:

I was hassled by the bartender and the male kitchen staff. When you're a waitress, you have to keep in the good books of the guys backing you up. If the bartender takes a dislike to you, he can slow down on your orders to the point where you get no tips at all. The kitchen staff can sabotage you in other ways. The food can be cold, it can arrive late and orders can be all mixed up. (Backhouse & Cohen, 1981)

In traditionally female jobs, male sabotage is blatant, unmasked, raw, and unsophisticated. It is used openly to control and take advantage of women's inferior job status.

Traditionally Male Jobs

In traditionally male-dominated jobs, sabotage strategies are more sophisticated. In contrast to the "good ole boys" mentality, which literally and proudly espouses a "women-are-good-for-only-one-thing" rhetoric, male job occupants traditionally react to women negatively because women are seen as potentially threatening the "old gang" cohesion, camaraderie, and esprit de corps. In an effort to preserve long-accepted strongholds over men's jobs, men use a variety of sabotage techniques to discourage women's participation and success in traditionally male jobs:

I've been in this job nine years and I still have problems with the guys. About a year ago, whenever I returned from my route, I'd find a bunch of mail that I hadn't picked up. The district manager said I wasn't doing my job and gave me an undesirable [high crime] route. I found out later that the district manager gave my route to a new guy who was a friend of the family. (Black female mail carrier)

My co-workers would watch me talking to customers. When I went in to get the paperwork, they'd ridicule me to the customers. "She hasn't been here that long." "Women don't know much about cars." Then, they'd go over the same questions with the customers and get the sale. (Automobile salesperson)

In contrast to women in female-dominated jobs, women in male-dominated jobs find that they are "set up" to fail but are not told, openly, that this is due to their gender.

Sex-Neutral Jobs

The most sophisticated sabotage strategies occur in professional, technical, and administrative (and sometimes sales) jobs where sex is totally irrelevant to job performance. The sabotage techniques are so subtle and covert that women see the sabotage long after it is too late to do anything about the discrimination.

One mid-level manager [at a nationally known company] said she had gotten excellent ratings from her supervisors throughout her first year of employment. In the meantime, the company psychologist had called her in about once a month and inquired "how things were going." She was pleased by the company's interest in its employees. At the end of the year, one of her male peers (whose evaluations were known to be very mediocre) got the promotion and she didn't. When she pursued the reasons for her non-promotion, she was told, by one of the company's vice presidents, that "anyone who has to see the company psychologist once a month is clearly not management material." She had no way of proving she had been sabotaged. (Benokraitis, 1983)

In other examples, a female insurance agent is directed by the manager to nonelitist client accounts (in contrast to her male counterparts) and then not promoted because her clients take out only "policies for the poor"; an urban renewal administrative assistant who is more qualified than her supervisor (and is frank about wanting his job) finds the information in her folders scrambled over a period of months and is told that her "administrative chaos" will lead to a demotion; and a faculty member in an all-male political science department is thanked for her committee and advising work but dismissed because of insufficient publications, while her male counterpart, who has several publications (because he has been protected from committee or advising work), is promoted.

REVENGE

Revenge, especially when it is done creatively, is effective in limiting women's upward mobility. Revenge punishes vocal women who complain about sex inequality and discourages open criticism from observers. A study of women in the newsroom (Schultz-Brooks, 1984) showed that women who sued their employers found themselves writing more obituaries, working more graveyard shifts, and passed over in promotions. Even when out-of-court settlements have included promises to remedy discriminatory practices, management has pursued such vengeful activities as moving women laterally but listing the moves as promotions in the house letter and giving inflated experience ratings to new male employees so that men's starting salaries were higher than those of women with equal experience.

Women who sympathize or appear to sympathize with the complainant(s) or their colleagues may also become targets of revenge:

After [Company X] settled out-of-court, there was a great deal of resentment. Even the women who benefited from the settlement were hostile toward them [the women who had filed the class action suit]. To ease some of the tension, I got permission and some money to organize a workshop to discuss future opportunities. I was very careful. . . . I hired some men as speakers, provided a light lunch, and sent out attractive, carefully worded but upbeat invitations. The turnout was modest, but not a single man showed up—not even the guys in management who had approved the workshop and paid for it! About three months later, my position was abolished. They changed the title and hired a man. (Assistant director of personnel and labor relations in manufacturing)

Besides being punished for her seemingly sympathetic stance toward the women who sued the company, in this case the respondent may also have been sabotaged. By

supporting the workshop on paper, management had proof that the company was not bitter about the settlement and was showing an interest in improving the work climate for women. Yet the "troublemaker" was fired. After she lost the job, some of her co-workers said, privately, that the workshop had been described as "creating even more conflict," "divisive," and "anti-management." As in other forms of covert discrimination, there was no "hard evidence."

Men, and especially non-minority men, who endorse women's rights may be seen as "biting the hand that feeds them" and "betraying the system" and may be punished accordingly. Some reprisals are economic: salaries may be frozen, prestigious jobs taken away, and fringe benefits decreased (Schultz-Brooks, 1978). Other reprisals, equally effective, include social ostracism, name-calling and jokes about being "a sissy" or being "gay," and polite exclusion from "the boys'" basketball games during lunch or drinks after work. Most men are very aware of such reprisals and avoid incurring the wrath of their male peers. They are especially careful about their relationships with feminists:

Of the [43] male faculty, I'm pretty good friends with two of the men. We read each other's work, go out to lunch once in a while, drop by each other's office and call each other almost on a daily basis. But, you know, if they're going to lunch with a couple of the other guys and I bump into them, they *never* ask me to join them. They're cool and businesslike and act as though they barely know me. Even worse, when they're in my office, they criticize sexist remarks that they laughed at during a committee meeting two hours earlier. . . . [Pause] . . . Maybe you should be doing research on unpaid whores. . . . (Woman faculty member in a computer science department)

Both at home and especially in the workplace, promoting women's equality or associating with women who are fighting for women's rights often results in social and economic reprisals for both men and women. Revenge is a clandestine but very effective way of keeping the status quo.

CO-OPTATION

Co-optation refers to the process of bringing selected women into the system and then using these women to control the entry and promotion of other women—through subtle and covert sex discrimination mechanisms.

Co-optation can be a source of upward mobility. Because mobility is severely limited (there are always more applicants than available positions), the co-opted typically attribute their progress to their own intelligence, success, and hard work. That is, they identify themselves with a handful of "deserving elite":

The token woman is encouraged to see herself as different from most other women; as exceptionally talented and deserving; and to separate herself from the wider female condition; and she is perceived by 'ordinary' women as separate also. . . . (Rich, 1979)

By improving the position of a few women, co-optation reinforces the subordinate position of the majority of women. Scattering a few women throughout seemingly powerful positions gives the appearance that the institution recognizes talent and is "sex blind" and egalitarian; it also implies that there are few women in top levels because most women are unqualified or not competitive enough. Co-optation encourages blaming the self rather than the social structure. Thus, the status quo is maintained.

If, moreover, the co-opted are also gatekeepers, the responsibility for sex equality shifts from the dominant group to the co-opted. Thus, the dominant group can be "innocent bystanders" while the (few) women maintain group solidarity against "outsiders" (that is, other women) (Laws, 1975).

Finally, co-optation provides false role models to other women. Women who are newcomers to the job market, are unaware of covert sex discrimination, or are in isolated positions may assume, mistakenly, that the co-opted *really* did "make it" on their abilities, are powerful, and are worthy of imitation, respect, and admiration.

REFERENCES

Backhouse, C., & Cohen, L. (1981). *Sexual harassment on the job* (p. 9). Englewood Cliffs, NJ: Prentice-Hall.

Bayes, M., & Newton, P. M. (1978, November). Women in authority: A sociopsychological analysis. *Journal of Applied Behavioral Science, 14,* 15.

Benokraitis, N. (1983). Sex discrimination in the 80s. In *Maryland Women* (p. 4). Baltimore, MD: Maryland Commission for Women.

Fraker, S. (1984, April 16). Why top jobs elude female executives. *Fortune,* p. 46.

Harlan, A., & Weiss, C. (1981). *Moving up: Women in managerial careers* (p. 53). Wellesley, MA: Wellesley College Center for Research on Women.

Harragan, B. L. (1977). *Games mother never taught you: Corporate gamesmanship for women* (p. 158). New York: Warner Books.

Huckle, P. Back to the starting line. (1978, January-February). *American Behavioral Scientist, 121,* 379–392.

LaRouche, J., & Ryan, R. (1984). *Strategies for women at work* (p. 113). New York: Avon Books.

Laws, J. L. (1975, January). The psychology of tokenism: An analysis. *Sex Roles, 1,* 51.

Muller, J. K. (1978). Interest and involvement of women in university governance. *Journal of NAWDAC, 42,* 10–15.

Pendergrass, V. E., Kimmel, E., Joestring, J., Peterson, J., & Bush, E. (1976, January). Sex discrimination in counseling. *American Psychologist, 31,* p. 38.

Rich, A. (1979, September). Privilege, power, and tokenism. *Ms,* pp. 42–44.

Schultz-Brooks, T. (1984, March-April). Getting there: Women in the newsroom. *Columbia Journalism Review,* pp. 27, 29.

Schwadel, F. (1985, March 14). Women move up in the military, but many jobs remain off limits. *The Wall Street Journal,* p. 33.

24

The Black Underclass

William Julius Wilson

It is no secret that the social problems of urban life in the United States are, in great measure, associated with race.

While rising rates of crime, drug addiction, out-of-wedlock births, female-headed families, and welfare dependence have afflicted American society generally in recent years, the increases have been most dramatic among what has become a large and seemingly permanent black underclass inhabiting the cores of the nation's major cities.

And yet, liberal journalists, social scientists, policy makers, and civil-rights leaders have for almost two decades been reluctant to face this fact. Often, analysts of such issues as violent crime or teenage pregnancy deliberately make no reference to race at all, unless perhaps to emphasize the deleterious consequences of racial discrimination or the institutionalized inequality of American society.

Some scholars, in an effort to avoid the appearance of "blaming the victim," or to protect their work from charges of racism, simply ignore patterns of behavior that might be construed as stigmatizing to particular racial minorities.

Such neglect is a relatively recent phenomenon. Twenty years ago, during the mid-1960s, social scientists such as Kenneth B. Clark (*Dark Ghetto*, 1965), Daniel Patrick Moynihan (*The Negro Family*, 1965), and Lee Rainwater (*Behind Ghetto Walls*, 1970) forthrightly examined the cumulative effects on inner-city blacks of racial isolation and class subordination. They vividly described aspects of ghetto life that, as Rainwater observed, "are usually forgotten or ignored in polite discussions." All of these studies attempted to show the connection between the economic and social environment into which many blacks are born and the creation of patterns of behavior that, in Clark's

From the *Wilson Quarterly*, Spring 1984. Copyright © 1984 by The Woodrow Wilson International Center for Scholars.

words, frequently amounted to a "self-perpetuating pathology."

Why have scholars lately shied away from this line of research? One reason has to do with the vitriolic attacks by many black leaders against Moynihan upon publication of his report in 1965—denunciations that generally focused on the author's unflattering depiction of the black family in the urban ghetto rather than on his proposed remedies or his historical analysis of the black family's special plight. The harsh reception accorded to *The Negro Family* undoubtedly dissuaded many social scientists from following in Moynihan's footsteps.

The "black solidarity" movement was also emerging during the mid-1960s. A new emphasis by young black scholars and intellectuals on the positive aspects of the black experience tended to crowd out older concerns. Indeed, certain forms of ghetto behavior labeled pathological in the studies of Clark et al. were redefined by some during the early 1970s as "functional" because, it was argued, blacks were displaying the ability to survive and in some cases flourish in an economically depressed environment. Scholars such as Andrew Billingsley (*Black Families in White America*, 1968), Joyce Ladner (*Tomorrow's Tomorrow*, 1971), and Robert Hill (*The Strengths of Black Families*, 1971) described the ghetto family as resilient and capable of adapting creatively to an oppressive, racist society.

In the end, the promising efforts of the early 1960s—to distinguish the socioeconomic characteristics of different groups within the black community, and to identify the structural problems of the U.S. economy that affected minorities—were cut short by calls for "reparations" or for "black control of institutions serving the black community." In his 1977 book, *Ethnic Chauvinism*, sociologist Orlando Patterson lamented that black ethnicity had become "a form of mystification, diverting attention from the correct kinds of solutions to the terrible economic condition of the group."

Meanwhile, throughout the 1970s, ghetto life across the nation continued to deterio-

rate. The situation is best seen against the backdrop of the family.

In 1965, when Moynihan pointed with alarm to the relative instability of the black family, one-quarter of all such families were headed by women; 15 years later, the figure was a staggering 42 percent. (By contrast, only 12 percent of white families and 22 percent of Hispanic families in 1980 were maintained by women.) Not surprisingly, the proportion of black children living with both their father and their mother declined from nearly two-thirds in 1970 to fewer than half in 1978.

In the inner city, the trend is more pronounced. For example, of the 27,178 families with children living in Chicago Housing Authority projects in 1980, only 2,982, or 11 percent, were husband-and-wife families.

TEENAGE MOTHERS

These figures are important because even if a woman is employed full-time, she almost always is paid less than a man. If she is not employed, or employed only part-time, and has children to support, the household's situation may be desperate. In 1980, the median income of families headed by black women ($7,425) was only 40 percent of that of black families with both parents present ($18,593). Today, roughly five out of 10 black children under the age of 18 live below the poverty level; the vast majority of these kids have only a mother to come home to.

The rise in the number of female-headed black families reflects, among other things, the increasing incidence of illegitimate births. Only 15 percent of all births to black women in 1959 were out of wedlock; the proportion today is well over one-half. In the cities, the figure is invariably higher: 67 percent in Chicago in 1978, for example. Black women today bear children out of wedlock at a rate nine times that for whites. In 1982, the number of black babies born out of wedlock (328,879) nearly matched the number of illegitimate white babies

(337,050). White or black, the women bearing these children are not always mature adults. Almost half of all illegitimate children born to blacks today will have a teenager for a mother.

The effect on the welfare rolls is not hard to imagine. A 1976 study by Kristin Moore and Steven B. Cardwell of Washington's Urban Institute estimated that, nationwide, about 60 percent of the children who are born outside of marriage and are not adopted receive welfare; furthermore, "more than half of all AFDC (Aid to Families with Dependent Children) assistance in 1975 was paid to women who were or had been teenage mothers." A 1979 study by the Department of City Planning in New York found that 75 percent of all children born out of wedlock in that city during the previous 18 years were recipients of AFDC.

WHY NOT PROGRESS?

I have concentrated on young, female-headed families and out-of-wedlock births among blacks because these indices have become inextricably connected with poverty and welfare dependency, as well as with other forms of social dislocation (including joblessness and crime).

As James Q. Wilson observed in *Thinking About Crime* (1975), these problems are also associated with a "critical mass" of young people, often poorly supervised. When that mass is reached, or is increased suddenly and substantially, "a self-sustaining chain reaction is set off that creates an explosive increase in the amount of crime, addiction, and welfare dependency." The effet is magnified in densely populated ghetto neighborhoods, and further magnified in the massive public housing projects.

Consider Robert Taylor Homes, the largest such project in Chicago. In 1980, almost 20,000 people, all black, were officially registered there, but according to one report "there are an additional 5,000 to 7,000 who are not registered with the Housing Authority." Minors made up 72 percent of the

population and the mother alone was present in 90 percent of the families with children. The unemployment rate was estimated at 47 percent in 1980, and some 70 percent of the project's 4,200 official households received AFDC. Although less than one-half of one percent of Chicago's population lived in Robert Taylor Homes, 11 percent of all the city's murders, nine percent of its rapes, and 10 percent of its aggravated assaults were committed in the project in 1980.

Why have the social conditions of the black underclass deteriorated so rapidly?

Racial discrimination is the most frequently invoked explanation, and it is undeniable that discrimination continues to aggravate the social and economic problems of poor blacks. But is discrimination really greater today than it was in 1948, when black unemployment was less than half of what it is now, and when the gap between black and white jobless rates was narrower?

As for the black family, it apparently began to fall apart not before but after the mid-20th century. Until publication in 1976 of Herbert Gutman's *The Black Family in Slavery and Freedom*, most scholars had believed otherwise. "Stimulated by the bitter public and academic controversy over the Moynihan report," Gutman produced data demonstrating that the black family was not significantly disrupted during slavery or even during the early years of the first migration to the urban North, beginning after the turn of the century. The problems of the modern black family, he implied, were a product of modern forces.

Those who cite racial discrimination as the root cause of poverty often fail to make a distinction between the effeccts of *historic* discrimination (that is, discrimination prior to the mid-20th century) and the effects of *contemporary* discrimination. That is why they find it so hard to explain why the economic position of the black underclass started to worsen soon after Congress enacted, and the White House began to enforce, the most sweeping civil-rights legislation since Reconstruction.

MAKING COMPARISONS

My own view is that historic discrimination is far more important than contemporary discrimination in understanding the plight of the urban underclass; that, in any event, there is more to the story than discrimination (of whichever kind).

Historic discrimination certainly helped to create an impoverished urban black community in the first place. In *A Piece of the Pie: Black and White Immigrants since 1880* (1980), Stanley Lieberson shows how, in many areas of life, including the labor market, black newcomers from the rural South were far more severely discriminated against in Northern cities than were the new white immigrants from southern, central, and eastern Europe. Skin color was part of the problem, but it was not all of it.

The disadvantage of skin color—the fact that the dominant whites preferred whites over non-whites—is one that blacks shared with Japanese, Chinese, and others. Yet the experience of the Asians, whose treatment by whites "was of the same violent and savage character in areas where they were concentrated," but who went on to prosper in their adopted land, suggests that skin color per se was not an insurmountable obstacle." Indeed, Lieberson argues that the greater success enjoyed by Asians may well be explained largely by the different context of their contact with whites. Because changes in immigration policy cut off Asian migration to America in the late 19th century, the Japanese and Chinese populations did not reach large numbers and therefore did not pose as great a threat as did blacks.

Furthermore, the discontinuation of large-scale immigration from Japan and China enabled Chinese and Japanese to solidify networks of ethnic contacts and to occupy particular occupational niches in small, relatively stable communities. For blacks, the situation was different. The 1970 census recorded 22,580,000 blacks in the United States, but only 435,000 Chinese and 591,000 Japanese. "Imagine," Lieberson exclaims, "22 million Japanese Americans trying to carve out initial niches through truck farming."

THE YOUTH EXPLOSION

If different population sizes accounted for a good deal of the difference in the economic success of blacks and Asians, they also helped determine the dissimilar rates of progress of urban blacks and the new *European* arrivals. European immigration was curtailed during the 1920s, but black migration to the urban North continued through the 1960s. With each passing decade, Lieberson writes, there were many more blacks who were recent migrants to the North, whereas the immigrant component of the new Europeans dropped off over time. Eventually, other whites muffled their dislike of the Poles and Italians and Jews and saved their antagonism for blacks. As Lieberson notes, "The presence of blacks made it harder to discriminate against the new Europeans because the alternative was viewed less favorably."

The black migration to New York, Philadelphia, Chicago, and other Northern cities—the continual replenishment of black populations there by poor newcomers—predictably skewed the age profile of the urban black community and kept it relatively young. The number of central-city black youths aged 16–19 increased by almost 75 percent from 1960 to 1969. Young black adults (ages 20–24) increased in number by two-thirds during the same period, three times the increase for young white adults. In the nation's inner cities in 1977, the median age for whites was 30.3, for blacks 23.9. The importance of this jump in the number of young minorities in the ghetto, many of them lacking one or more parent, cannot be overemphasized.

Age correlates with many things. For example, the higher the median age of a group, the higher its income; the lower the median age, the higher the unemployment rate and the higher the crime rate. (More than half of those arrested in 1980 for violent and property crimes in American cities were under 21.) The younger a woman is, the more likely she is to bear a child out of wedlock, head up a new household, and depend on welfare. In short, much of what has gone awry in the ghetto is due in part to the sheer increase in the number of black youths. As James Q. Wilson has argued, an abrupt rise in the proportion of young people in *any* community will have an "exponential effect on the rate of certain social problems."

The population explosion among minority youths occurred at a time when changes in the economy were beginning to pose serious problems for unskilled workers. Urban minorities have been particularly vulnerable to the structural economic changes of the past two decades: the shift from goods-producing to service-providing industries, the increasing polarization of the labor market into low-wage and high-wage sectors, technololgical innovations, and the relocation of manufacturing industries out of the central cities. During the 1970s, Chicago lost more than 200,000 jobs, mostly in manufacturing, where many inner-city blacks had traditionally found employment. New York City lost 600,000 jobs during the same period, even though the number of white-collar professional, managerial, and clerical jobs increased in Manhattan. Today, as John D. Kasarda has noted, the nation's cities are being transformed into "centers of administration, information exchange, and service provision." Finding work now requires more than a willing spirit and a strong back.

BEYOND RACE

Roughly 60 percent of the unemployed blacks in the United States reside within the central cities. Their situation, already more difficult than that of any other major ethnic group in the country, continues to worsen. Not only are there more blacks without jobs every year; many, especially young males, are dropping out of the labor force entirely.

The percentage of blacks who were in the labor force fell from 45.6 in 1960 to 30.8 in 1977 for those aged 16–17 and from 90.4 to 78.2 for those aged 20–24. (During the same period, the proportion of white teenagers in the labor force actually *increased*.)

More and more black youths, including many who are no longer in school, are obtaining no job experience at all. The proportion of black teenager males who have *never* held a job increased from 32.7 to 52.8 percent between 1966 and 1977; for black males under 24, the percentage grew from 9.9 to 23.3. Research shows, not surprisingly, that joblessness during youth has a harmful impact on one's future success in the job market.

There have been recent signs, though not many, that some of the inner city's ills may have begun to abate. For one, black migration to urban areas has been minimal in recent years; many cities have experienced net migration of blacks *to* the suburbs. For the first time in the twentieth century, a heavy influx from the countryside no longer swells the ranks of blacks in the cities. Increases in the urban black population during the 1970s, as demographer Philip Hauser has pointed out, were mainly due to births. This means that one of the major obstacles to black advancement in the cities has been removed. Just as the Asian and European immigrants benefited from a cessation of migration, so too should the economic prospects of urban blacks improve now that the great migration from the rural South is over.

Even more significant is the slowing growth in the number of *young* blacks inhabiting the central cities. In metropolitan areas generally, there were six percent fewer blacks aged 13 or under in 1977 than there were in 1970; in the inner city, the figure was 13 percent. As the average age of the urban black community begins to rise, lawlessness, illegitimacy, and unemployment should begin to decline.

Even so, the problems of the urban black underclass will remain crippling for years to come. And I suspect that any significant reduction of joblessness, crime, welfare dependency, single-parent homes, and out-of-wedlock pregnancies would require far more comprehensive social and economic change than Americans have generally deemed appropriate or desirable. It would require a radicalism that neither the Republican nor the Democratic Party has been bold enough to espouse.

The existence of a black underclass, as I have suggested, is due far more to historic discrimination and to broad demographic and economic trends than it is to radical discrimination in the present day. For that reason, the underclass has not benefited significantly from "race specific" antidiscrimination policies, such as affirmative action, that have aided so many trained and educated blacks. If inner-city blacks are to be helped, they will be helped not by policies addressed primarily to inner-city minorities, but by policies designed to benefit all of the nation's poor.

I am reminded in this connection of Bayard Rustin's plea during the early 1960s that blacks recognize the importance of *fundamental* economic reform (including a system of national economic planning along with new education, manpower, and public works programs to help achieve full employment) and the need for a broad-based coalition to achieve it. Politicians and civil-rights leaders should, of course, continue to fight for an end to racial discrimination. But they must also recognize that poor minorities are profoundly affected by problems that affect other people in America as well, and that go beyond racial considerations. Unless those problems are addressed, the underclass will remain a reality of urban life.

25

Searching for Roots in a Changing World

RICHARD RODRIGUEZ

Today I am only technically the person I once felt myself to be—Mexican-American, a Chicano. Partly because I had no way of comprehending my racial identity except in this technical sense, I gave up long ago the cultural consequences of being a Chicano.

The change came gradually but early. When I was beginning grade school, I noted to myself the fact that the classroom environment was so different in its styles and assumptions from my own family environment that survival would essentially entail a choice between both worlds. When I became a student, I was literally "remade"; neither I nor my teachers considered anything I had known before as relevant. I had to forget most of what my culture had provided, because to remember it was a disadvantage. The past and its cultural values became detachable, like a piece of clothing grown heavy on a warm day and finally put away.

Strangely, the discovery that I have been inattentive to my cultural past has arisen because others—student colleagues and faculty members—have started to assume that I am a Chicano. The ease with which the assumption is made forces me to suspect that the label is not meant to suggest cultural, but racial, identity. Nonetheless, as a graduate student and a prospective university faculty member, I am routinely expected to assume intellectual leadership *as a member of a racial minority*. Recently, for example, I heard the moderator of a panel discussion introduce me as "Richard Rodriguez, a Chicano intellectual." I wanted to correct the speaker—because I felt guilty representing a nonacademic cultural tradition that I had willingly abandoned. So I can ony guess what it would have meant to have retained my culture as I entered the classroom, what it would mean for me to be today a *Chicano intellectual.* (The two words juxtaposed excite me; for years I thought a Chicano had to decide between being one or the other.)

Does the fact that I barely spoke any English until I was nine, or that as a child I felt a surge of *self*-hatred whenever a passing teenager would yell a racial slur, or that I saw my skin darken each summer—do any of these facts shape the ideas which I have or am capable of having? Today, I suspect they do—in ways I doubt the moderator who referred to me as a "Chicano intellectual" intended. The peculiar status of being a "Chicano intellectual" mades me grow restless at the thought that I have lost at least as much as I have gained through education.

I remember when, 20 years ago, two grammar-school nuns visited my childhood home. They had come to suggest—with more tact than was necessary, because my parents accepted without question the church's authority—that we make a greater effort to speak as much English around the house as possible. The nuns realized that my brothers and I led solitary lives largely because we were barely able to comprehend English in a school where we were the only Spanish-speaking students. My mother and father complied as best they could. Heroically, they gave up speaking to us in Spanish—the language that formed so much of the family's sense of intimacy in an alien world—and began to speak a broken English. Instead of Spanish sounds, I began hearing sounds that were new, harder, less friendly. More important, I was encouraged to respond in English.

The change in language was the most dramatic and obvious indication that I would become very much like the "gringo"—a term which was used descriptively rather than pejoratively in my home—and unlike the Spanish-speaking relatives who largely constituted my preschool world. Gradually, Spanish became a sound freighted with only a kind of sentimental significance, like the sound of the bedroom clock I listened to in my aunt's house when I spent the night. Just as gradually, English beame the language I came not to *hear* because it was the language I used every day, as I gained access to a new, larger society. But the memory of Spanish persisted as a reminder of the society I had left. I can remember occasions when I entered a room and my parents were speaking to one another in Spanish, seeing me, they shifted into their more formalized English. Hearing them speak to me in English troubled me. The bonds their voices once secured were loosened by the new tongue.

This is not to suggest that I was being *forced* to give up my Chicano past. After the initial awkwardness of transition, I committed myself, fully and freely, to the culture of the classroom. Soon what I was learning in school was so antithetical to what my parents knew and did that I was careful about the way I talked about myself at the evening dinner table. Occasionally, there were moments of childish cruelty: a son's condescending to instruct either one of his parents about a "simple" point of English pronunciation or grammar.

Social scientists often remark, about situations such as mine, that children feel a sense of loss as they move away from their working-class identifications and models. Certainly, what I experienced, others have also—whatever their race. Like other generations of, say, Polish-American or Irish-American children coming home from college, I was to know the silence that ensues so quickly after the quick exchange of news and the dwindling of common interests.

In addition, however, education seemed to mean not only a gradual dissolving of familial and class ties, but also a change of racial identity. The new language I spoke was only the most obvious reason for my associating the classroom with "gringo" society. The society I knew as Chicano was barely literate—in English *or* Spanish—and so impatient with either prolonged reflection or abstraction that I found the academic environment a sharp contrast. Sharpening the contrast was the stereotype of the Mexican as a mental inferior. (The fear of this stereotype has been so deep that only recently have I been willing to listen to those, like D. H. Lawrence, who celebrate the "noncerebral" Mexican as an alternative to the rational and scientific European man.) Because I did not know how to distinguish the healthy nonrationality of Chicano culture from the mental incompetency of which Chicanos were unjustly accused, I was willing to abandon my nonmental skills in order to disprove the racist's stereotype.

I was wise enough not to feel proud of the person education had helped me to become. I knew that education had led me to repudiate my race. I was frequently labeled a *pocho*, a Mexican with gringo pretentions, not only because I could not speak Spanish but also because I would respond in English with precise and careful sentences. Uncles would laugh good-naturedly, but I detected scorn in their voices. For my grandmother, the least assimilated of my relations, the changes in her grandson since entering school were especially troubling. She remains today a dark and silently critical figure in my memory, a reminder of the Mexican-Indian ancestry that somehow my educational success has violated.

Nonetheless, I became more comfortable reading or writing careful prose than talking to a kitchen filled with listeners, withdrawing from situations to reflect on their significance rather than grasping for meaning at the scene. I remember, one August evening, slipping away from a gathering of aunts and uncles in the backyard, going into a bedroom tenderly lighted by a late sun, and opening a novel about life in nineteenth-century England. There, by an open window, reading, I was barely conscious of the sounds of laughter outside.

With so few fellow Chicanos in the university, I had no chance to develop an alternative consciousness. When I spent occasional weekends tutoring lower-class Chicano teenagers or when I talked with Mexican-American janitors and maids around the campus, there was a kind of sympathy—a sense, however privately held—that we knew something about one another. But I regarded them all primarily as people from my past. The maids reminded me of my aunts (similarly employed); the students I tutored reminded me of my cousins (who also spoke English with barrio accents).

When I was young, I was taught to refer to my ancestry as Mexican-American. *Chicano* was a word used among friends or relatives. It implied a familiarity based on shared experience. Spoken casually, the term easily became an insult. In 1968 the word *Chicano* was about to become a political term. I heard it shouted into microphones as Third World groups agitated for increased student and faculty representation in higher education. It was not long before I *became* a Chicano in the eyes of students and faculty members. My racial identity was assumed for only the simplest reasons: my skin color and last name.

On occasion I was asked to account for my interests in Renaissance English literature. When I explained them, declaring a need for cultural assimilation on the campus, my listener would disagree. I sensed suspicion on the part of a number of my fellow minority students. When I could not imitate Spanish pronunciations of the dialect of the barrio, when I was plainly uninterested in wearing ethnic costumes and could not master a special handshake the minority students often used with one another, they knew I was different. And I was. I was assimilated into the culture of a graduate department of English. As a result, I watched how in less than five years nearly every minority graduate student I knew dropped out of school, largely for cultural reasons. Often they didn't understand the value of analyzing literature in professional jargon, which others around them readily adopted. Nor did they move as readily to lofty heights of abstraction. They became easily depressed by the seeming uselessness of the talk they heard around them. "It's not for real," I still hear a minority student murmur to herself and perhaps to me, shaking her head slowly, as we sat together in a class listening to a discussion on punctuation in a Renaissance epic.

I survived, thanks to the accommodation I had made long before. In fact, I prospered, partly as a result of the political movement designed to increase the enrollment of minority students less assimilated than I in higher education. Suddenly grants, fellowships, and teaching offers became abundant.

In 1972, I went to England on a Fulbright scholarship. I hoped months of brooding about racial identity were behind me. I wanted to concentrate on my dissertation, which the distractions of an American campus had not permitted. But the freedom I anticipated did not last for long. Barely a month after I had begun working regularly in the reading room of the British Museum, I was surprised, and even frightened, to have to acknowledge that I was not at ease living the rarefied life of the academic. With my pile of research file cards growing taller, the mass of secondary materials and opinions was making it harder for me to say anything original about my subject. Every sentence I wrote, every thought I had, became so loaded with qualifications and footnotes that it said very little. My scholarship became little more than an exercise in caution. I had an accompanying suspicion that whatever I did manage to write and call my dissertation would be of little use. Opening books so dusty that they must not have been used in decades, I began to doubt the value of writing what only a few people would read.

Obviously, I was going through the fairly typical crisis of the American graduate student. But with one difference: After four years of involvement with questions of racial identity, I now saw my problems as a scholar in the context of the cultural issues that had been raised by my racial situation. So much of what my work in the British Museum lacked, my parents' culture possessed. They were people not afraid to generalize or to find insights in their generalities. More important, they had the capacity to make passionate statements, something I was beginning to doubt my dissertation would ever allow me to do. I needed to learn how to trust the use of "I" in my writing the way they trusted its use in their speech. Thus developed a persistent yearning for the very Chicano culture that I had abandoned as useless.

Feelings of depression came occasionally but forcefully. Some days I found my work so oppressive that I had to leave the reading room and stroll through the museum. One afternoon, appropriately enough, I found myself in an upstairs gallery containing Mayan and Aztec sculptures. Even there the sudden yearning for a Chicano past seemed available to me only as nostalgia. One morning, as I was reading a book about Puritan autobiography, I overheard two Spaniards whispering to one another. I did not hear what they said, but I did hear the sound of their Spanish—and it embraced me, filling my mind with swirling images of a past long abandoned.

I returned from England, disheartened, a few months later. My dissertation was coming along well, but I did not know whether I wanted to submit it. Worse, I did not know whether I wanted a career in higher education. I detested the prospect of spending the rest of my life in libraries and classrooms, in touch with my past only through the binoculars nostalgia makes available. I knew that I could not simply re-create a version of what I would have been like had I not become an academic. There was no possibility of going back. But if the culture of my birth was to survive, it would have to animate my academic work. That was the lesson of the British Museum.

I frankly do not know how my academic autobiography will end. Sometimes I think I will have to leave the campus, in order to reconcile my past and present. Other times, more optimistically, I think that a kind of negative reconciliation is already in progress, that I can make creative use of my sense of loss. For instance, with my sense of the cleavage between past and present, I can, as a literary critic, identify issues in Renaissance pastoral—a literature which records the feelings of the courtly when confronted by the alternatives of rural and rustic life. And perhaps I can speak with unusual feeling about the price we must pay, or have paid, as a rational society for confessing seventeenth-century Cartesian faiths. Likewise, because of my sense of cultural loss, I may be able to identify more readily than another the ways in which language has meaning simply as sound and what the printed word can and cannot give us. At the very least, I can point up the academy's tendency to ignore the cultures beyond its own horizons.

*   *   *

On my job interview, the department chairman has been listening to an oral version of what I have just written. I tell him he should be very clear about the fact that I am not, at the moment, confident enough to call myself a Chicano. Perhaps I never will be. But as I say all this, I look at the interviewer. He smiles softly. Has he heard what I have been trying to say? I wonder. I repeat: I have lost the ability to bring my past into my present; I do not know how to be a Chicano reader of Spenser or Shakespeare. All that remains is a desire for the past. He sighs, preoccupied, looking at my records. Would I be interested in teaching a course on the Mexican novel in translation? Do I understand that part of my duties would require that I become a counselor of minority students? What was the subject of that dissertation I did in England? Have I read the book on the same subject that was published this month?

Behind the questioner, a figure forms in my imagination: my grandmother, her face solemn and still.

26

Facing Old Age in American Society

James M. Henslin

"No one wants to grow old." Most of us would accept such a statement as true, for to most people, to grow old is to gradually lose one's physical capacities and eventually to die. Few people look forward to such events.

Growing old is a *biological* event, essential to humanity. Aging, however, is more than biology. It is also a *sociological* event; that is, growing old takes place within a particular society at a certain point in time, and each society treats its elderly in its own way. That unique treatment, accompanied by some standardized set of attitudes, imbues aging with its meaning. Thus, it *means* one thing to grow old in one society, but something entirely different in another society. Growing old can be good, bad, or somewhere in between, depending on how the elderly are treated in a society and the social meanings that society places on aging.

In our society, the social aspects of growing old make this biological event a less desirable state of affairs than it otherwise would be. Let us examine two sociological aspects of aging that make it difficult for most Americans to face growing old: negative stereotypes and social death. Following this, we shall look at the elderly's struggle for economic resources, and then try to glimpse the future.

THE BURDEN OF STEREOTYPES

Imagine yourself facing negative stereotypes. You are judged negatively, not because of anything you have done, but simply because you belong to a group. Fairness is pushed aside by otherwise reasonable people as they judge *you* to be dirty, lazy, dishonest, and incapable. There is nothing you can do about the stereotype because it is a *cultural idea*, a generalized, firmly established belief about the way the world is. People only have to *look* at you and they have already made up their minds.

Some people, bearing physical stigmata, face such *stereotypical perceptions* on a daily basis: members of some ethnic groups, the crippled, the disfigured, the obese, the ugly, to name just a few. The unfairness of the perception—and its matching dehumanizing treatment—is a fact of life. The individual is powerless in the face of such cultural bias. His or her life is turned upside down as opportunities are denied, social injustices routinized.

Worst of all, however, is the internal wrenching, the disabling of the self concept. To face the constant message that one is less worthy than others is to confront regular disconfirmation of the self. This challenge to one's basic humanity, to one's own value as a human being, strikes deep into the soul.

Among the groups that face such negative stereotypical perception is the aged. It is not enough that they must wrestle with declining physical capacities; they must also struggle against an onslaught of negative stereotypes. *Simply because they are old*, they are seen as dottering, feeble, incapable, rigid, cantankerous, ugly, dull, useless, and parasitical.

As with the groups mentioned above, the perception comes through the stereotype. Again, place yourself in that situation. You may be healthy, physically capable, mentally alert, talented, and able, have a good attitude and a healthy outlook on life, be friendly, congenial, and giving. It does not matter. People will still tend to see you through cultural stereotypes.

It is up to you to prove that you do not match the stereotype, that you are an exception and should be viewed differently. Like other disparaged groups, that becomes the challenge the elderly face, to constantly disprove "what everyone knows." And that is a burden.

CULTURAL ROOTS OF STEREOTYPES

Our society has turned into a youth cult. Americans worship youth, acknowledging the vibrant health and bright future of youth as the quintessence of social life. How did we come to plaster the walls of society with posters of youth?

Sociologically, the answer to why we do not revere the aged, as in classic Chinese society, goes back to economic production (Achenbaum, 1978). In societies that change only slowly, in which the generations replicate one another as children repeat the activities and lifestyles of their parents, the elderly tend to be looked up to *because they represent accumulated knowledge*. They have confronted, successfully, the very same problems that the youth now face. The elderly have acquired answers that work. As possessors of an invaluable stockpile of knowledge, perhaps even wisdom, they deserve respect, for throughout their lives the information they share can help ease the burdens of life.

The above picture, although overdrawn, for it represents tendencies, not inevitable outcomes, does not apply to industrialized society. Here life changes rapidly. Technologies appear overnight that render people's knowledge and skills outmoded. We find ourselves constantly adapting to ever-changing situations as our learning and competencies, though valuable just a short time before, fail to match the shifting requirements of contemporary life.

In such a society, the knowledge of the young soon outpaces that of the elderly. For example, it is not unusual for students in good high schools to realize that their parents are unable to be of much help with their homework in mathematics, science, or composition. Consequently, the *social* basis for intergenerational respect is undermined. Our attitude tends to become that what our parents know may fit their needs, but it certainly does not match ours. We live in a distinct world, our needs are unique, and we must have different answers. Solutions of an older generation simply will not do.

Attitudes, rooted in an economic base, are promoted by our mass media, which reflect and amplify cultural stereotypes. To be sure, change occurs in the media's portrayals. Without a shrill outcry and an immediate consumer boycott, the media can no longer broadly paint blacks as incompetent, Jews as greedy exploiters, the Irish as drunkards, or women as scatterbrained. When it comes to the elderly, however, there are no such restrictions, and media personnel can manipulate negative images to their heart's content.

Usually, however, the message is subtle. It is the young who are portrayed as enjoying leisure, demonstrating sexual capacities, lustily feasting on a cornucopia of consumer products, and moving confidently toward a vibrant future. In contrast, the media inform us that we should remove any and all telltale signs of approaching old age: We should disguise the gray in our hair, use wrinkle creams, get our faces lifted, have our hair transplanted. The upshot is that the characteristics of youth are valued and those of the elderly are devalued.

However, a fresh breath of air that may dispel this negative stereotyping has blown into the mass media. For example, some television programs, such as "The Golden Girls" and "Knight and Daye," portray old men and women as vibrant people who have interests beyond failing health: They live vibrantly, keep abreast of current events, and even enjoy sensual and sexual relationships.

For the media to portray a variety of conceptions of the elderly is to encourage multiple views and individualized perception. This will result in less stereotyping, and, eventually, perhaps the removal of stigma. Consequently, as it picks up more positive elements, the term "old" will take on new meaning. I believe that this is the direction in which we are headed, for just as negative meaning was given old age due to changed economic relationships, so shifting economic conditions are leading to a contrasting portrayal of the elderly. The economic strides the elderly have made in recent decades have made them more visible in a variety of positive settings. It is this shift which is being reflected in the media. I wish to explore the changing economic situation

of the elderly, but first let us turn to the second severe problem the elderly face— being groomed for social death.

GROOMING FOR SOCIAL DEATH: THE PROCESS OF DECULTURATION

Life expectancy has increased dramatically in this century. In 1900, the life expectancy of Americans was only 47. Today it is 75. In 1900, one of eleven Americans was 65 or over; today there is one in eight. In 1965, 18 million Americans were 65 or over; today there are 30 million. And the average person who lives to the age of 65 can expect to see 82 (Anderson, 1972; *Statistical Abstract*, 1989a). Because the future is expected to bring even longer life expectancy, the elderly will make up an even larger proportion of our population.

Our treatment of the elderly, however, has not kept pace with the technological developments that have made it possible for so many people to reach advanced years. Accompanied by negative stereotypes, aging Americans are gradually groomed for social death. This process is often the reverse of the enculturative process of childhood. During childhood the individual learns the customary ways of society in order to be able to function as a full member within it, but during old age the individual is made to unlearn those ways so he or she can eventually cease to function culturally (Anderson, 1972).

In traditional society, old people represent the same culture as the young. As mentioned earlier, their accumulated experience is taken as wisdom gained through living and is respected because it can help the young adjust to the demands of life. In our technologically driven society, in contrast, old people represent a "lost generation": They are carriers of an outmoded and bypassed culture, displaced persons who are being replaced by the young standard-bearers of a new culture. With their experiences deemed insignificant for the present, the elderly themselves are judged insignificant.

The destination of old people is clear to all, including the aged. Seen as irrelevant and insignificant for contemporary life, they are supposed to enter a period of "temporary tangential identity" that is soon followed by "dissolution and social death" (Anderson, 1972, p. 211). To be groomed for social death is to be distanced from the traditional activities, goals, and even ideologies of our culture. The elderly learn that it is the young who have taken the reins of social life. It is they who are to be hard-working, acquisitive, and immersed in pleasures and plans. The old are expected to withdraw from the mainstream, to sit back and let those who are capable run things. The no-longer-capable are to be resigned to their fate and to move to a less active, less responsible, and more dependent role—even to become as children. Deemed no longer competent, unable to care for themselves or their affairs, a group of younger, though also aging, heirs breathlessly awaits the outcome, fearful that the aged will somehow squander their inheritance by inappropriately enjoying life.

THE BATTLE FOR SOCIAL SECURITY

In order to understand the present financial situation of the elderly, it is useful to first examine the history of Social Security in the United States. The industrialization of America came at a high cost to the aged, transforming them from a productive and respected group to a deprived and disgraced group. Although industrialization increased the life span (between 1870 and 1930, the number of people over 65 increased at twice the rate of the rest of the population), it undermined basic social relations so that the elderly received less support from family and farm than ever before. One of the more startling statistics of the period before Social Security legislation is that, in the 1920s, two-thirds of all citizens over 65 had no savings and could not support themselves (Holtzman, 1963; Hudson, 1978).

The Great Depression, making matters worse, led to a significant perceptual shift: The elderly no longer saw themselves as unfortunate *individuals*, but as a deprived *social group*. They then consolidated into a powerful political lobby whose goal was to attain social security. In 1930 Robert C. Townsend, a physician and social reformer, began to rally older citizens into a political force. He soon had one-third of all Americans over 65 enrolled in his Townsend clubs, demanding benefits from the federal government (Holtzman, 1963). His idea was for the federal government to impose a national sales tax of 2 percent to provide $200 a month for every person over 65 (Gordon, 1987). This is equivalent to about $1,700 a month today. Townsend tried to sell his idea by stressing that this would vastly increase spending and help the depressed economy by generating new business.

In 1934, the Townsend Plan went before Congress, and the Townsend clubs gathered hundreds of thousands of signatures on petitions in support of the plan. In that election year, Congress was particularly vulnerable to a grass-roots revolt by old people across the country. Nevertheless, the Townsend Plan frightened Congress because it called for such a high fixed income per month, and many were afraid that it would remove the incentive to work and save for the future (Schottland, 1963). Congress looked for a way to reject the plan without appearing to be opposed to old-age pensions. When President Roosevelt announced his own, more modest Social Security plan in June 1934, Congress embraced it.

Older citizens were not satisfied. Seeing flaws in the Social Security Act, they successfully fought to change them. For instance, old-age pensions were not scheduled to begin until 1942, which would have left millions of workers uncovered. Moreover, the depression continued to drag even more old people into poverty. (The average old-age assistance from the states was $19.21 a month, about $163 in today's dollars.) During the presidential elections of 1940, the Republicans supported the Townsend lobby as a way to criticize President Roosevelt's Social Security Act. The Townsend proposals failed in Congress once again, but the political pressure from the clubs led Congress to begin paying Social Security benefits sooner—in 1940—and to increase old-age assistance grants.

Contrary to common ideas, the Social Security benefits we have today are not the result of generous hearts in Congress. They are, rather, the result of conflict between competing interest groups. The aged banded together to push their own interests. When Congress perceived a threat in terms of votes against incumbents, they gave in and awarded benefits to the elderly. They gave as little as they thought they could get away with, however, and had to be politically threatened again before they reluctantly increased benefits. Those benefits came at a price to the elderly, however, for they were removed from the labor market. Thus, in this conflict, employers also won their goal of employing a younger work force (Williamson, Shindul, & Evans, 1985).

Social Security, along with expanded federal programs, has produced a turnaround situation for the elderly. Let's look at that change—and its unexpected consequences.

CHANGING FINANCIAL RESOURCES AND WHY ANOTHER BATTLE IS SHAPING UP

As I indicated, changes are occurring in the ways that the elderly are stereotyped, and I am convinced that altered economic circumstances underlie those changes. The image of poor, ill, neglected grandparents that has been used to promote programs to benefit elderly Americans is no longer broadly accurate. The expansion of federal programs and general economic growth have led to one of the greatest success stories of public policy. Since the late 1960s, the poverty rate for the aged declined so rapidly that it now is *less* than that of the nonaged population. The elderly have seen their proportion in poverty decline from 35 percent in 1959, to

15 percent in 1975, to 12 percent in 1987 (Hudson, 1978; *Statistical Abstract*, 1989b).

The aged have turned their situation around so radically that some people now believe that the substantial benefits the elderly receive constitute an inequity—a social problem of the 1990s. While people are pleased at the reduction of poverty among the elderly—in 30 years the ratio dropped from 1 in 3 to 1 in 8—they are concerned that it may have come at the cost of other groups. The elderly reply that their moving out of poverty has not caused anyone else to move into poverty, that no one should live in poverty, and that they favor programs to reduce the poverty of other groups.

Some, however, feel that the elderly have taken more than their share of society's resources. They are especially alarmed at the costs of Social Security (Old Age and Survivors Insurance). The cost of this program, which was $784 million in 1950, has mushroomed to $272 billion today. In 1986, payments ran about *350 times* the amount paid out in 1950. If this increase were to continue at the same rate during the next 36 years, the annual amount would total more than $90 trillion—an impossible figure since the entire annual income of the United States is only $4.5 trillion, including all the salaries, interest, and rents paid to individuals as well as all profits to businesses and corporations (*Statistical Abstracts*, 1989c).

Medicare and Medicaid costs for the elderly have similarly soared. They now account for more than *80 percent* of all federal money spent on health care (*Statistical Abstracts*, 1989d). If the growth of Medicare were to continue at its present rate, by the year 2000 it would cost more than Social Security—another impossible figure, of course, but one that shows the collision course we are on.

The growing proportion of the elderly in our population adds pressure to increase expenditures for Social Security, Medicare, and Medicaid. That the elderly make up a larger proportion of our population is due to two factors: improvements in sanitation and health care that allow people to live longer, and the effects abortion and other forms of birth control are having on our population distribution. Consequently, between the years 1990 and 2000, the population of people 65 and over is expected to *grow* by 3,300,000, while our college-age population, 18 to 24, will *shrink* by 910,000 (*Statistical Abstracts*, 1989e).

This changing balance of age groups only intensifies the problem, and an intergenerational struggle for resources is shaping up. Proposals have already been made to trim Social Security, Medicare, and other programs for the elderly on the basis that they are "beyond the nation's ability to pay" (Otten, 1988). Some fear that Congress may "pick between old people and kids" (Davidson, 1985). Others predict that in about 25 years, when the baby boom generation begins to retire, the far smaller baby bust generation will rebel against paying the heavy taxes needed to support huge numbers of elderly Americans (Otten, 1986).

To protect their remarkable gains, as well as to demand even more resources, older Americans have organized a powerful political lobby. This group, the American Association of Retired Persons (AARP), boasts 28 million members. Their power has already begun to arouse resentment (Samuelson, 1988), providing further indication that an intergenerational conflict will erupt in the 1990s.

Some form of conflict seems inevitable, for the interests of younger and older groups are running on a collision course. As America ages, the number of people who collect Social Security benefits grows, while the proportion of working people—those who pay for those benefits out of their wages—shrinks. The problem is that the money a worker "contributes" to Social Security is not put into the worker's own account but is paid out to those who are already retired—a sort of chain-letter arrangement by which the young support the old (Smith, 1987). We are seeing a major shift in our *dependency ratio*, the number of workers compared with the number of Social Security recipients. Presently, five working-age Americans pay Social Security taxes to support each person who is over 65. In approximately another generation, the ratio will drop to less than 3 to 1, and by the year 2035, to 2 to 1.

Because of a 1983 increase in the Social Security tax, however, increased revenues are projected to produce a surplus of several trillions of dollars in excess of payments to retirees (Sweet, 1984). Many hope that this surplus will enable us to avoid an intergenerational showdown. It could, however, fuel the fires of intergenerational conflict if the younger demand that it be put to work *for them* by funding federal programs more to their liking (Malabre, 1988).

CONCLUSION

In recent decades, the situation of the elderly in American society has changed for the better. This has come about through Social Security legislation and the expansion of other federal programs. One consequence is that the proportion of the elderly who live in poverty has decreased markedly. Another is that the negative stereotyping of the elderly is changing, with positive imagery being added to our cultural stereotypes. While these are positive changes, all does not glitter in the golden years. Discrimination on the basis of age is endemic to our society; even medical treatment routinely given the young is denied people simply because they are elderly (Becker & Kaufman, 1988). The 12 percent of those 65 and over who remain in poverty represents 3,700,000 people who are ill-clothed, ill-housed, and who face a constant struggle to survive. The continued negative stereotypes and the grooming for social death, accompanied by the constant worry that one may outlive one's financial resources, take a severe toll. An indication is the suicide rate of the elderly. Of all age groups in the United States, people over 65 are the most likely to kill themselves (*Statistical Abstracts*, 1989f). Whereas about 13 of every 100,000 Americans between 15 and 24 commit suicide each year, this figure jumps to 19 for those between the ages of 65 and 74 and to 25 for those 75 to 84. More than 10,000 Americans over 60 take their own lives each year.

In short, in spite of improvements, there is much left to be done if we hope to offer a life of social worth and self-respect to our elderly Americans.

REFERENCES

Achenbaum, W. A. (1978). *Old age in the new land: The American experience since 1970.* Baltimore: Johns Hopkins University Press.

Anderson, B. G. (1972, October). The process of deculturation—Its dynamics among United States aged. *Anthropological Quarterly, 45,* 209–216.

Becker, G., & Kaufman, S. (1988). Old age, rehabilitation, and research: A review of the issues. *The Gerontologist, 28* (4), 459–468.

Davidson, J. (1985, June 27). Differing social programs for young, old result in contrasting poverty levels for two groups. *Wall Street Journal,* p. 56.

Gordon, R. J. (1987). *Macroeconomics* (4th ed.). Boston: Little Brown.

Holtzman, A. (1963). *The Townsend movement: A political study.* New York: Bookman.

Hudson, R. B. (1978, October). The "graying" of the federal budget and its consequences for old-age policy. *The Gerontologist, 18,* 428–440.

Malabre, A. L., Jr. (1988, October 17). *Wall Street Journal,* p. A1.

Otten, A. L. (1986, January 13). Warning of generational fighting draws critics—led by the elderly. *Wall Street Journal,* p. 36.

Otten, A. L. (1988, January 22). Ethicist draws fire with proposal for limiting health care to aged. *Wall Street Journal,* p. 22.

Samuelson, R. J. (1988, March 21). The elderly aren't needy. *Newsweek,* p. 68.

Schottland, C. I. (1963). *The social security plan in the U.S.* New York: Appleton.

Smith, L. (1987, July 20). The war between the generations. *Fortune,* p. 78–82.

Statistical Abstract of the United States. (1989a). Tables 17, 109. Washington, DC: U.S. Government Printing Office.

Statistical Abstract of the United States. (1989b). Table 743. Washington, DC: U.S. Government Printing Office.

Statistical Abstract of the United States. (1989c). Tables 566, 686. Washington, DC: U.S. Government Printing Office.

Statistical Abstract of the United States. (1989d). Table 570. Washington, DC: U.S. Government Printing Office.

Statistical Abstract of the United States. (1989e). Table 17. Washington, DC: U.S. Government Printing Office.

Statistical Abstract of the United States. (1989f). Table 119. Washington, DC: U.S. Government Printing Office.

Sweet, S. J. (1984, March 28). A looming federal surplus. *Wall Street Journal,* p. 28.

Williamson, J. B., Shindul, J. A., & Evans, L. (1985). *Aging and social policy: Social control or social justice?* Springfield, IL: Charles C. Thomas.

27

Widowhood

Starr Roxanne Hiltz

The death of a spouse is one of the most serious life crises a person faces. The immediate emotional crisis of bereavement, if not fully worked through, may result in symptoms of mental disorder. During the first few days of bereavement, sacred and secular guidelines define the proper mourning role for the widow. Over the longer term, however, there is generally a need for a total restructuring of the widow's life, as she finds herself much poorer, socially isolated, and left without a meaningful life pattern. Widowhood is best conceptualized as a negatively evaluated social category where the individual loses the central source of identity, financial support, and social relationships. It is a "roleless role."

Currently, American women have a life expectancy of 79, about seven years longer than American men. If demographic patterns were used to suggest marital arrangements, it would make sense for older women to marry younger males. However, our cultural norms and opportunities are such that the initial mortality differences are compounded by the tendency for women to marry older men.

WIDOWHOOD ROLES

Most preindustrial societies have very clear roles for widows. For example, in traditional Indian society, [in the past] a Brahmin widow was supposed to commit *suttee* by throwing herself on her husband's funeral pyre. If she did not do this, she was condemned to live out her life dressed in a single coarse garment, with shaven head, eating only one meal a day, and shunned by others as "unlucky." Another extreme solution, practiced in many African societies, was an immediate (automatic) remarriage, in which the wife and children were "inher-

From *Marriage and Family Review*, November/December 1978, Vol. 1, No. 6
Copyright © 1978 The Haworth Press, 12 West 32nd St., New York, NY 10001.

ited" by a younger brother of the deceased or by some other heir, and the widow became one of his wives in a polygamous family. Even if such prescribed actions and roles were not particularly desirable from the widow's point of view, at least it was clear what she was to do with the rest of her life.

The new widow in American and other (Western) industrialized societies has lost not only a husband, but her own main functions, reason for being, and self-identity. In spite of the large number of women in the work force, most women who are becoming widows have defined themselves primarily as wives and mothers. Lopata sums up the situation in *Widowhood in an American City*, a study of Chicago widows:

In spite of the rapid industrialization, urbanization, and increasing complexity of the social structure of American society, the basic cluster of social roles available to, and chosen by, its women has been that of wife-mother-housewife. This fact imposes some serious problems upon the last stage of their lives, similar to the problems of retirement in the lives of men who had concentrated upon their occupational roles. The wife-mother-housewife often finds herself with children who are grown, absent from her home, and independent of her as a basic part of their lives; her husband has died, and her household no longer contains a client segment. (Lopata, 1973, pp. 87–88)

Caine, in her poignant account of her own bereavement and eventual readjustment with professional help, has written a most moving description of the effects of the wrenching away of one's social and self-identity that occurs with the death of a husband:

"Widow" is a harsh and hurtful word. It comes from the Sanskrit and means "empty." . . .

After my husband died, I felt like one of those spiraled shells washed up on the beach. Poke a straw through the twisting tunnel, around and around, and there is nothing there. No flesh. No life. Whatever lived there is dried up and gone.

Our society is set up so that most women lose their identities when their husbands die. Marriage is a symbolic relationship for most of us. We draw our identities from our husbands. We add ourselves to our men, pour ourselves into them and their lives. We exist in their reflection. And then . . . ? If they die . . . ? What is left? It's wrenching enough to lose the man who is your lover, your companion, your best friend, the father of your children, without losing yourself as well. (Caine, 1974, pp. 181)

It should be noted that Caine had a fine job for many years before her husband died, but this did not alleviate the necessity and pain of totally restructuring her social role.

Remarriage is not a likely solution. There are fewer than two million widowers in the United States, one for every five widows, and they are likely to marry younger women. Cleveland and Gianturco (1976), in a retrospective study of North Carolina data, for instance, concluded that less than 5% of women widowed after age 55 ever remarry.

As Lopata points out:

Life styles for American widows are generally built upon the assumption that they are young and can soon remarry or that they are very old and removed from the realm of actual involvement. The trouble is that most widows are neither, but the society has not taken sufficient cognizance of this fact to modify the facilities and roles available to them. (Lopata, 1973, p. 17)

A woman is likely to spend as much time as a widow as she does raising children. Although she was socialized all through her early life for the wife-and-motherhood role, she typically has had no preparation at all for the widowhood role. The whole subject has been taboo, and few women prepare ahead of time for widowhood.

GRIEF AS A KIND OF ILLNESS: EFFECTS ON ROLE PERFORMANCE

The emotional and psychological traumas of grief and mourning involve "letting go" of the emotional ties and roles centered on the husband. If this working through of grief is successfully accomplished, the widow can face a second set of problems having to do with building a new life, a new set of role relationships, and a new identity.

Much of the psychological literature on grief represents an elaboration of Freud's theories. For Freud, grief or "grief work" is the process by which bereaved persons struggle to disengage the loved object. The emotional bond is fused with energy, bound to memories and ideas related to former interactions with the loved person. The mourner has to spend time and effort to bring to consciousness all of these memories in order to set free the energy, to break the tie (Freud, 1917/1957).

At one time "grief," as in the extended "pining away," was recognized as a cause of death and listed on death certificates. As Glick et al. (1974, p. 10) have concluded from their extensive studies of bereavement, "the death of a spouse typically gives rise to a reaction whose duration must be measured in years rather than in weeks."

A variety of grief reactions may occur when the mourner does not express emotion or refuses to deal with the loss. These include delay of the grief reactions for months or even years; overactivity without a sense of loss; indefinite irritability and hostility toward others; sense of the presence of the deceased; acquisition of the physical symptoms of the deceased's last illness; insomnia; apathy; psychosomatically based illnesses such as ulcerative colitis; and such intense depression and feelings of worthlessness that suicide is attempted (Parkes, 1972, p. 211).

One tendency is to reconstruct an idealized version of one's deceased husband and of the role relationship with him before the death. Referred to as "husband sanctification," Lopata (1976) reports that three-quarters of the Chicago area current and former beneficiaries of Social Security define their late husband as having been "extremely good, honest, kind, friendly, and warm" (pp. 4–5). Sanctification is especially likely among women who rank the role of wife above all others. It is an attempt to

continue defining oneself primarily in terms of the now-broken role relationship. Lopata views this as an effort to "remove the late husband into an other-worldly position as an understanding but purified and distant observer" (p. 30), so that the widow is able to go about reconstructing old role relationships and forming new ones.

There are several factors related to severe or prolonged grief. Sixty-eight widows and widowers under the age of 45 were interviewed shortly after the spouse died and again a year later [for] the Harvard Bereavement Study. An "outcome score" was obtained from depth interview material and answers to questions on health; increased consumption of alcohol, tranquilizers, and tobacco; self-assessment as "depressed or very unhappy"; and "wondering whether anything is worthwhile anymore." Three classes of strongly correlated and intercorrelated variables predict continued severe bereavement reactions 13 months after the death:

1. Low socioeconomic status, i.e., low weekly income of the husband, Spearman's rho correlation of .44; low occupational status, .28.
2. Lack of preparation for loss due to noncancer deaths, short terminal illness, accident or heart attack, or failure to talk to the spouse about the coming death, correlations of .26 to .29.
3. Other life crises preceding spouse's death, such as infidelity and job loss, correlations of .25 to .44. (Parkes, 1975, pp. 308–309)

It is interesting that a poor outcome is likely if the marriage relationship was troubled before the death; folk wisdom would have it that the widow would be "glad to be rid of him." Psychologically debilitating guilt over having wished the death of the husband seems to be very strong in such cases, however. Another problem is the amount of "unfinished business" (Blauner, 1966) left by the removal of the husband through death. Parkes concludes that for his young respondents, including widowers as well as widows, "When advance warning was short and the death was sudden, it seemed to have a much greater impact and to lead to greater and more lasting disorganization" (Parkes, 1975, p. 313).

Emotional problems related to grief or bereavement are not independent of the problems relating to income, friends, and family. Disturbance and dissolution of the widow's main social relationships and removal of the main source of income require finding new friends and activities, a job, often less expensive housing; and similar adjustments. Any major change in role relationships and living patterns is stressful, and causes emotional disturbance. But many changes in one's life circumstances and behavior patterns simultaneously are especially likely to be associated with extreme emotional stress and such symptoms as mental illness, heart attacks, and suicide.

FINANCIAL PROBLEMS

The subsequent life changes and problems faced by the widow indicate that widowhood is a role for which there is no comparable role among males. Glick et al. (1974) summarize the difference between their samples of widows and of widowers: "Insofar as the men reacted simply to the *loss of a loved other*, their responses were *similar* to those of widows, but insofar as men reacted to the *traumatic disruption of their lives*, their responses were *different*" (p. 262). This differential impact is found in the financial impact of the death. For the widow, it almost always means the loss of the main source of financial support for the family and a consequent lowering of the standard of living.

By two or three years after the onset of widowhood, the incomes of the widows' families were down an average of 44% from previous levels, and 58% had incomes that fell below the amount that would have been necessary to maintain their family's former standard of living. This occurred even among those who received life insurance benefits. After final expenses, 44% had used up part of this for living expenses, and 14% had consumed all of it.

In addition to financially devastating final expenses which wipe out savings, widows are entitled to no Social Security benefits at all unless they have dependents or are over 60. After 60 years of age, they are entitled only to a portion of what would have been their husband's benefits. The final explanation for the high probability of poverty among widows is that because of age, low level of skill and education, and lack of experience, they are often unable to obtain employment. In other words, neither the private economy nor the public welfare system is currently structured to provide economic support to widows in late middle age.

FINDING NEW SOCIAL ROLES

Before widowhood, a married woman defines herself and relates to others mainly in terms of her status as somebody's wife. At widowhood, most of her role relationships will have to adjust and some will terminate. She will have to establish new role relationships if her life is to be a satisfying one. For example, she is unlikely to maintain close ties with friends and relatives who belonged to social circles maintained with her husband. Changes in finances can require changes in other spheres of life, such as movement into the work force. A change in residence may result in loss of contact with neighbors. Often, in settling her husband's estate, she has to deal with lawyers and insurance agents and has to take on the role of businesswoman (Lopata, 1975).

The difficulties an older woman in our society is likely to encounter in establishing such a new set of role relationships are affirmed by Professor Lopata. She found that half of the widows in her sample considered loneliness their greatest problem, and another third listed it second. Social isolation was listed by 58%, who agreed with the statement "One problem of being a widow is feeling like a 'fifth wheel' " (Lopata, 1972, pp. 91, 346).

Lopata's work focuses on the widow's

role relationships in regard to motherhood, kin relationships, friendship, and community involvement, including employment. Among her findings are that "women who develop satisfactory friendships, who weather the transition period and solve its problems creatively, tend to have a higher education, a comfortable income, and the physical and psychic energy needed to initiate change" (p. 216). These women are not the "average" widow, who is likely to have a high school education or less, low income, depleted physical energy due to advancing age, and depleted psychic energy due to the trauma to bereavement and its associated problems.

The importance of maintaining or establishing supportive role relationships with an understanding "other," such as an old friend, neighbor, or supportive professional or paraprofessional, has been emphasized in many studies. For instance, Maddison and Raphael (1975) emphasize their "conviction that the widow's perception of her social network is an extremely important determinant of the outcome of her bereavement crisis" (p. 29). "Bad outcome" women had no one to whom they could freely express their grief and anger.

DISRUPTION OF FAMILY RELATIONSHIPS

The death of the husband tends to cause strain in relationships with children, in-laws, and even one's own siblings and other relatives. The problems with children were twofold: a perceived coldness or neglect to give the widow as much "love" and support and time as she thought she was entitled to (17%), and what the widow considered serious behavioral problems with the children, such as taking drugs or withdrawing from employment and from communication with the mother (15%) (Hiltz, 1977).

What is seen as "neglect" or "coldness" by the widow may be viewed as an unfair and unpleasant burden by the child, especially

sons. For example, Adams (1968) found that grown middle-class sons perceived their obligations to their mother as a "one-way" or unreciprocated pattern of aid and support-giving. This typically results in a son's loss of affection for the mother and his resentment of her dependence upon him.

For younger widows with dependent children, there are difficulties in maintaining the maternal role of effectively responding to the child's needs. Silverman and Englander (1975) found that most parents and children avoided talking about the death to one another. Common reactions of the child were fear that they would lose the surviving parent, too; the assumption by the child of new family responsibilities; and poor school work related to rebellion and social withdrawal.

INTERVENTION STRATEGIES AND THEIR EFFECTIVENESS

Findings from recent research projects have sustained the premise that social service or intervention programs to help the widow cope and build a satisfactory network of role relationships do work. One such project involving intervention in the life of the widow is the "Widow-to-Widow" program. Five widows were originally recruited as aides, chosen as having personal skills in dealing with people and as representatives of the dominant racial and religious groups in the community. The aide wrote the new widow a letter saying that she would call on her at a particular time. This usually occurred three weeks after the death, unless the widow telephoned and requested no visit. Of the 91 widows located in the first seven months of the program, 64 accepted contact, half by visit and half by telephone, an overall acceptance rate of 60%. The aides offered friendship as well as advice and assistance with specific problems. In addition, group discussion meetings and social events such as a cookout were organized to which all of the widows were invited (Silverman, 1969). As Silverman describes the role of the aide, she "encourages, prods, insists, and sometimes even takes the widow by the hand and goes through the motions with her" (1972, p. 101).

On the basis of this project and one other, Silverman and Cooperband (1975) conclude that "the evidence points to another widow as the best caregiver. . . . This other widow . . . can provide a perspective on feelings; she provides a role model; she can reach out as a friend and neighbor" (p. 11).

Some psychiatrists and social workers question the advisability of using untrained recent widows to give aid to other widows, without available referral to professionals. For instance, they point to abnormal grief reactions experienced by widows visited by aides, including two who died, who may have responded to professional intervention. Also, unresolved elements of her own grief might lead the widow-aide to excessive reliance upon her own methods of coping, overlooking or negatively responding to other possibilities (Kahana, 1975). "The danger is that unresolved or unrecognized grief may adversely influence the aide in trying to assist the newly bereaved widow. . . . Some of the people who say 'I know how you feel' may really mean 'I know how I feel' " (Blau, 1975, pp. 36–37).

Group discussion or therapy sessions, with groups of three to ten widows, met weekly with a professional leader [from the Casework Service of the Widows Consultation Center, New York City]. They varied, depending upon the participants, from fairly casual sharing of experiences as widows to explicitly therapeutic groups. (See Hiltz, 1975, for a description of these groups.)

Social activities and recreational events were organized for the Center's clients. These social get-togethers were initiated slowly, with the first year's activities most typically a monthly tea at the Center preceded by a brief lecture on some topic of apparent interest to widows, such as a book on widowhood. By the third year, a part-time social worker was hired to organize and conduct social activities, such as Sunday afternoon sessions at the local "Y," weekend bus trips, and free theater parties.

Special professional consultation about legal or financial problems was arranged through caseworkers, who made appointments for clients who seemed to need expert advice. The financial consultant was a well-known writer on personal finance, who did not recommend specific investments but gave generalized advice on types of investments, budgeting, and allocation of funds.

The main criterion of effectiveness used in this study was the widows' own feelings about whether or not the [Center] had helped them with each problem area identified by each widow at the time she came to the Center.

When asked "Overall, would you say that the Widows Consultation Center was a great deal of help to you, of some help, or no help at all?"; 33% said "of some help,"; and 30% said "no help." These results become more favorable as the number of private interviews, group therapy sessions, or social activities attended increases. For example, less than a third of those who had only one or two private interviews felt that the Center had given them a "great deal of help," compared to 79% of those who had five or more private consultation sessions. These findings support the feelings of the caseworkers that they achieved much more success in helping their clients with a supportive casework process that extended over some period of time, rather than a one- or two-visit process.

SUMMARY

Studies of widowhood during the last decade have given us an understanding of the fact that widows in American society must forge a total emotional, financial, and social reorganization of their lives, at a time when their resources for such a task are generally inadequate. There are many areas in which the "broad picture" of the problems faced by widows must be filled in by much more detail. Strategies to prevent deterioration in communication and quality of relationship between the newly widowed mother and her dependent or grown children is one example of an area in which such research would be particularly valuable. At the societal level, we need to explore what mix of private and public efforts can replace the likelihood of poverty created by the current Social Security "blackout period" and lack of job opportunities for older widows with some assurance of financial security. Finally, we need to forge a stronger relationship between social service programs and social research, so that knowledge of successful and unsuccessful strategies in helping widows to build a socially and financially supportive set of role relationships becomes cumulative and shared.

REFERENCES

Adams, B. (1968). The middle-class adult and his widowed or still-married mother. *Social Problems, 16*, 50–59.

Blau, D. (1975). On Widowhood: Discussion. *Journal of Geriatric Psychiatry, 8*, 29–40.

Blauner, R. (1966). Death and social structure. *Psychiatry, 29*, 387–394.

Caine, L. (1974). *Widow.* New York: Wm. Morrow & Co.

Cleveland, W. P., & Gianturco, D. T. (1976). Remarriage probability after widowhood: A retrospective method. *Journal of Gerontology, 31*, 99–103.

Freud, S. (1957). Mourning and melancholia. In J. Strachey (Ed. and trans.), *The Standard Edition of the Complete Psychological Works of Sigmund Freud* (Vol. XIV). London: The Hogarth Press and the Institute for Psycho Analysis. (Originally published 1917).

Glick, I. O., Weiss, R., & Parkes, C. M. (1974). *The first year of bereavement.* New York: John Wiley & Sons.

Hiltz, S. R. (1975). Helping widows: Group discussions as a therapeutic technique. *The Family Coordinator, 24*, 331–336.

Hiltz, S. R. (1977). *Creating community services for widows: A pilot project.* Port Washington, N.Y.: Kennikat Press, pp. 64–65.

Kahana, R. J. (1975). On widowhood: Introduction. *Journal of Geriatric Psychiatry, 8*, 5–8.

Lopata, H. Z. (1972). Role changes in widowhood: A world perspective. In D. Cowgill & L. Holmes (Eds.), *Aging and modernization.* New York: Appleton-Century-Crofts.

Lopata, H. Z. (1973). *Widowhood in An American City.* Cambridge, MA.: Schenkman Publishing Co.

Lopata, H. Z. (1975). On widowhood: Grief, work, and identity reconstruction. *Journal of Geriatric Psychiatry, 8*, 41–55.

Lopata, H. Z. (1976, August). *Widowhood and husband sanctification.* Paper presented at the 71st annual meeting of the American Sociological Association, New York City.

Maddison, D., & Raphael, B. (1975). Conjugal bereavement and the social network. In B. Schoenberg, I. Gerber, A. Wiener, A. Kutscher, D. Peretz, & C. Carr. (Eds.), *Bereavement: Its psychological aspects.* New York: Columbia University Press.

Parkes, C. M. (1972). *Bereavement: Studies of grief in adult life.* New York: International Press.

Parkes, C. M. (1975). Determinants of outcome following bereavement. *Omega: Journal of Death and Dying, 6*, 303–323.

Silverman, P. R. (1969). The widow-to-widow program: An experiment in preventive intervention. *Mental Hygiene, 53*, 333–337.

Silverman, P. R. (1972). Widowhood and preventive intervention. *The Family Coordinator, 21*, 95–102.

Silverman, P. R., & Cooperband, A. (1975). On widowhood: Mutual help and the elderly widow. *Journal of Geriatric Psychiatry, 8*, 9–27.

Silverman, P. R., & Englander, S. (1975). The widow's view of her dependent children. *Omega: Journal of Death and Dying, 6*, 3–20.

PART V

CRIME, DELINQUENCY, AND THE CRIMINAL JUSTICE SYSTEM

CRIME IN THE UNITED STATES

Crime is a social problem when rules that are considered essential to a society are violated. In such cases, crime threatens people's lives, property, and general well-being. It undermines their security, peace, and quality of life. In considering crime as a social problem, sociologists do not only study the doings of criminals, but they also look at a less obvious aspect: the *criminal justice system* itself—the network of agencies that respond to crime, including the police, courts, jails, and prisons. The criminal justice system is a social problem when it fails to prevent, contain, or rehabilitate offenders and when, instead of providing justice, it discriminates against certain groups of citizens.

How extensive is crime in American society? The *crime rate*—the number of crimes per some unit of the population—is an effective way to measure its extent. In 1987, 35 million Americans reported being the victims of crimes, and 12 million Americans were arrested (Zawitz, 1988b). In addition to 19,000 murders and 87,000 forcible rapes, there were about 500,000 robberies, 725,000 aggravated assaults, 1 million automobile thefts, 3 million burglaries, and 7 million larcenies (Zawitz, 1988a). America apparently has the highest rate of robbery in the Western world. Our burglary rate is so high that more burglaries occur in the city of Chicago alone than in all of Japan. Another way of putting it is to say that each year about one of every 15 Americans is robbed, assaulted, murdered, raped, or burgled. At this rate, at least on average, you can expect everyone on your block to fall victim to one of these crimes within the next 15 years.

The U.S. Department of Justice has summarized the extent of our crime by saying that

> *. . . the chance of being the victim of a violent crime is greater than that of being hurt in a traffic accident" . . . [A]t current crime rates, almost everyone will be a victim of crime during his or her lifetime.* (Zawitz, 1988a, pp. 24, 29).

Although there are societies with lower crime rates than ours, are there societies without crime? By definition, that would be impossible. As Durkheim (1897) pointed out almost a century ago, crime is universal by its very nature. As we just noted, crime is the violation of law. Each society passes laws against acts that it considers threatening to its well-being. The behaviors which the laws are directed against already exist. When there are rules (or laws), there will always be rule breakers (criminals). Consequently, no society, country, or political system is exempt from crime.

THE CRIMINAL JUSTICE SYSTEM

If we accept the notion that one goal of the judicial system is to rehabilitate people, our *recidivism rate*—the percentage of people released from prison who are rearrested—shows how inadequate our criminal justice system really is: More than half the inmates released from prison will return to prison, most coming back within three years of when they were released (Zawitz, 1988a). (Some researchers indicate that 85 to 90 percent is more accurate [Blumstein & Cohen, 1987].) Despite repeated prison stays, up to 50 percent of inmates answer yes when they are asked, "Do you think you could do the same crime again without getting caught?" (Zawitz, 1988a).

Here are some of the specifics that researchers have uncovered:

1. The more serious one's involvement in juvenile delinquency, the greater the chances of adult arrest.
2. The more often someone is arrested, the greater the chances of that person being arrested again.
3. The more often someone has been arrested before going to prison, the sooner that person will be arrested upon release.

And this finding, which illustrates the abject failure of prison:

4. The more often someone has been put in prison, the greater are that person's chances of going back to prison.

It should be stressed that the recidivism rate does not represent the true crime rate among former prisoners; it only represents how many of them are caught. Their crime rate is much, much higher, for each one who is rearrested is likely to have committed many crimes before being apprehended.

JUVENILE DELINQUENCY

The vast majority of crimes by juveniles are committed by males. Juvenile males commit *eight times* as many crimes of violence and about *four times* as many property crimes as do females. Female juveniles, however, are closing the gap—another factor that alarms people (Federal Bureau of Investigation, 1987).

In a study of over 69,000 juveniles who had come before the courts in Phoenix, Arizona, sociologist Howard Snyder (1988) discovered these patterns of the "delinquent career":

1. After their first arrest, most youth (59 percent) never return to juvenile court.
2. Juveniles referred to court a second time before age 16 are those most likely to continue their delinquent behavior.
3. Those charged with a violent offense (murder, rape, robbery, or aggravated assault) are likely to have engaged in a wide range of delinquent behaviors.
4. Although only 5 percent of youth are ever charged with a violent offense, the younger a juvenile is when first charged, the greater the likelihood that he or she will later be charged with a violent offense. (Those first charged at age 13 are *twice* as likely to be arrested for a later violent offense than those first charged at age 16).
5. The youth *most* likely to have a second referral to court are those originally charged with burglary, truancy, motor vehicle theft, or robbery.
6. The youth *least* likely to have a second referral are those originally charged with underage drinking, running away, or shoplifting.
7. Girls (29 percent) are much less likely to recidivate (to come before the courts again) than are boys (46 percent).

PLEA BARGAINING

As sociologist James Coleman (1989) has noted, since most people accused of street crimes have little money to pay lawyers, defense attorneys have a strong interest in quickly processing each case and moving on to the next client. This motivates them to encourage *plea bargaining*, to plead guilty to a lesser offense in return for saving the state the expense and bother of a trial. Plea bargaining is also a result of our criminal justice system being slow and inefficient. Courtroom schedules are jammed and courtroom hours short. Rules for presenting evidence under our constitutional system are complex. The snail's pace at which the criminal justice system creeps means that some innocent people are detained behind bars for months and even years while some guilty people are released and able to commit more crimes while free and awaiting a distant trial.

Such delays subvert the constitutional guarantee of a speedy trial and encourage plea bargaining. If they were to actually defend their clients, the courts would be so jammed that they could not handle the cases (Mills, 1974). Judges punish attorneys who don't go along with the "routine," interrupting their defense and making them wait while they tend to other business (Lipetz, 1984). Public defenders, then, are turned into regular team players that keep the system going. They develop "implicit understandings" about what their job really is—team playing to produce "assembly-line justice" for the poor (Blumberg, 1967).

Plea bargaining has become so prevalent that the majority of people accused of a serious crime do not receive a trial, but instead plead guilty to a lesser offense. On average, only 5 percent of criminal cases are heard before a jury (Zawitz, 1988a). Plea bargaining subverts the constitutionality of our criminal justice system, for the Sixth Amendment to the Constitution declares that "the accused shall enjoy the right to a speedy and public trial, by an impartial jury of the State and district wherein the crime shall have been committed." Often what is supposed to be a trial, then, becomes merely the perfunctory validation of pretrial interrogation and investigation.

ORGANIZED CRIME

Although our knowledge of organized crime in the United States is far from complete, we do know that crime is their business, that the structure of their organization resembles that of legitimate businesses, that their crime empire is extensive and has international connections, that they infiltrate legitimate businesses, and that violence remains part of their way of doing business—their public relations claim to the contrary notwithstanding.

In spite of the United States government continuously waging a "war" against the Mafia, this form of organized crime not only survives but flourishes. The Mafia operates the principal loan sharking operation (making illegal loans at high rates of interest) in the United States. They are the major importers and wholesalers of narcotics. They control large labor unions and much of the construction trade of New Jersey. In New York City, they control private bus companies that transport school children, sanitation companies that cart garbage, large parts of the garment industry, and major labor unions. They have also gained control over some banks and Teamster pension funds.

Why has the Mafia been so successful, growing to such levels of prosperity and power? We can cite the following reasons:

1. It is highly *organized*, operating a bureaucracy with capable, full-time specialists engaged in a wide array of criminal pursuits.
2. It provides illegal *services that are in high demand* (for example, prostitution, gambling, and loan sharking)—"victimless crimes" with no complainant.
3. It wields influence in a vast system of *political corruption*.
4. It has *little organized opposition*. (The attention of the FBI, for example, has been sporadic, subject to political whim, and hampered by limited budget and personnel.)
5. At the center of its operation is *violence and intimidation*, directed against victims and used to control and discipline its own members. (*Organized Crime*, 1976)

Conflict theorists add a *sixth* reason for the success of organized crime in the United States—that it serves the economic and political goals of the American ruling class. According to sociologist David R. Simon (1981), the ruling class uses organized crime to control the working class. The Mafia has helped to keep labor from becoming too organized or too "radical." During periods of labor unrest between the 1920s and the 1940s, he observes, owners of large corporations hired gangsters as strikebreakers and union infiltrators, especially in auto manufacturing and longshoremen unions. He cites other evidence of under-the-table cooperation between the ruling elite and organized crime in order to accomplish political goals. For example, during World War II, U.S. Navy Intelligence officials apparently arranged with Lucky Luciano to spy out German agents in the New York docks.

Perhaps the most ludicrous level of this connection between our political elite and the Mafia is represented by the revelations of one of President John F. Kennedy's former lovers. Judith Campbell Exner says that in 1960 and 1961 she delivered numerous envelopes between Kennedy and Sam Giancana, the head of the Chicago Mafia (Kelley, 1988). Supposedly, the mobster delivered votes to Kennedy in key states and plotted the assassination of Fidel Castro.

Regardless of the extent to which organized crime, the power elite, and political officials have cooperated with one another, or the degree to which the ruling class has found it useful to allow the Mafia to continue its activities, many sociologists emphasize that organized crime poses a threat to the well-being of American society. They see the most serious threat not as gambling, prostitution, or loan sharking, but the corruption of our social institutions. With their vast sums of untaxed dollars, the Mafia bribe police, judges, and politicians and force their way into the control of labor unions and legitimate businesses. This threatens the social order, as it provides a broad base of power for the Mafia and simultaneously subverts the institutions and organizations intended to deal with crime. Thus, violence, bribery, and other corruption work their way into the social system, leaving us with the frightening possibility that large parts of our society may eventually come under the control of organized crime.

REFERENCES

Blumstein, A. & Cohen, J. (1987, August) Characterizing criminal careers. *Science, 237*, 985–991.

Blumberg, A. S. (1967). The practice of law as confidence game: Organizational cooptation of a profession. *Law and Social Review, 1*, 15–39.

Coleman, J. W. (1989). *The criminal elite: The sociology of white collar crime*. New York: St. Martin's Press.

Durkheim, E. (1951). *Suicide*. John A. Spaulding and George Simpson (trans.). New York: Free Press. (Originally published in 1897.)

Federal Bureau of Investigation. (1987). *FBI uniform crime reports*, Table 28. Washington, DC: Author.

Kelley, K. (1988, February 28). "The dark side of Camelot." *People Magazine*, pp. 107–114.

Lipetz, M. J. (1984). *Routine justice: Processing cases in women's court.* New Brunswick, NJ: Transaction Books.

Mills, James. (1974). *One just man.* New York: Simon and Schuster.

Organized crime: Report of the Task Force on Organized Crime. (1976). Washington, DC: National Advisory Committee on Criminal Justice Standards and Goals.

Snyder, H. (1988). *Court careers of juvenile offenders.* Washington, DC: Office of Juvenile Justice and Delinquency Prevention.

Simon, D. R. (1981). The political economy of crime. In S. G. McNall (Ed.), *Political economy: A critique of American society.* Glenview, IL: Scott Foresman.

Zawitz, M. W. (Ed.). (1988a). *Report to the Nation on Crime and Justice* (2nd ed.) (pp. 12, 24, 29, 84). Washington, DC: U.S. Department of Justice, Bureau of Justice Statistics.

Zawitz, Marianne W. (Ed.). (1988b, July). *Technical appendix to report to the Nation on Crime and Justice* (2nd ed.) (pp. 5, 44). Washington, DC: U.S. Department of Justice, Bureau of Justice Statistics.

28

Identity and the Shoplifter

Mary Owen Cameron

It seems probable that most adult pilferers start their careers as children or adolescents in groups where the techniques of successful pilfering are learned from other, more experienced children. Later as group activity is abandoned, some of the group members continue the practices they learned as adolescents. The lavish displays of merchandise which department stores exhibit to encourage "impulse buying" are, for the experienced pilferer, there for the taking.

Adult women pilferers, generally belonging to families of rather modest income, enter department stores with a strong sense of the limitations of their household budgets. They do not steal merchandise which they can rationalize purchasing: household supplies, husband's clothes, children's wear. But beautiful and luxury goods for their personal use can be purchased legitimately only if some other member of the family is deprived. Although pilferers often have guilt feelings about their thefts, it still seems to them less wrong to steal from a rich store than to take from the family budget. Pilferers seem to be, thus, narcissistic individuals in that they steal for their own personal use, but, on the other hand, they do not use the limited family income for their own luxury goods.

Pilferers differ in one outstanding respect, at least, from other thieves: They generally do not think of themselves as thieves. In fact, even when arrested, they resist strongly being pushed to admit their behavior is theft. This became very clear as I observed a number of interrogations of shoplifters by the store detective staff, and it was supported in conversations with the detectives who drew on their own wider experience. It is quite often difficult for the store staff to convince the arrested person that he or she has actually been arrested, even when the detectives show their licenses and badges. Again and again store police explain to pilferers that they are under arrest as thieves, that they will, in the normal course of events, be taken in a police van to jail, held in jail until bond is raised, and tried in a court before a judge and sentenced. Much of the interview time of store detectives is devoted to establishing this point; in making the pilferer understand that what happens to him from the time of his arrest is a legal question, but it is still a question for decision, first of all, by the store staff.

Store detectives use the naivete of pilferers as an assistance in arrest procedures while the pilferer is in the presence of legitimate customers on the floor of the store. The most tactful approach possible is used. The store detective will say, for example, "I represent the store office, and I'm afraid the office will have to see what's in your shopping bag. Would you care to come with me, please?" If the pilferer protests, the detective adds, "You wouldn't want to be embarrassed in front of all these people, would you? In the office we can talk things over in private."

Edwards (1958) states that the method of making an arrest is important in preventing excitement and even disorder.

A gentle approach will usually disarm any shoplifter, amateur or professional, while a rough seizure or loud accusation may immediately put him on the defensive. At other times it may result in a nervous or hysterical condition accompanied by an involuntary discharge which may be embarrassing to both the arrestor and the arrested. (p. 134)

Inbau (1952) adds the thought that the gentle approach is helpful too in forestalling suits for false arrest.

The finesse with which defendant accosts plaintiff is a definite factor also affecting the temper with which the court approaches a case. The defendant acting in good faith with probable cause, whose attitude is quiet, non-threatening, and deferential to the plaintiff's feelings can weather an honest mistake much more cheaply than otherwise. At the most it may induce a court to find there was no imprisonment at all. At the least, it will relieve the defendant of punitive damages and reduce the amount of actual damages.

The "deference" of the arresting detective combined with the already existing rationalizations of the pilferer sustain in him the belief that whereas his behavior might be reprehensible, the objects taken were, after all, not of great value, he would be glad to pay for them and be on his way. "Yes, I took the dress," one woman sobbed as she was being closely interrogated, "but that doesn't mean I'm a thief."

Arrest forces the pilferer to think of himself as a thief. The interrogation procedure of the store is specifically and consciously aimed at breaking down any illusions the shoplifter may have that his behavior is regarded as merely "naughty" or "bad." The breakdown of illusions is, to the store detective staff, both a goal in itself and a means of establishing the fact that each innocent-appearing pilferer is not, in fact, a professional thief "putting on an act." In the interrogation the shoplifter is searched for other stolen merchandise and for identification papers. Pockets and pocketbooks are thoroughly examined. All papers, letters, tickets, bills, etc., are read in detail in spite of considerable protest from the arrested person. Each person is made to explain everything he has with him. If suspect items such as public locker keys, pawn tickets, etc., are found, he will have to explain very thoroughly indeed and agree to have the locker examined and the pawned merchandise seen to avoid formal charge. In any event, once name, address, and occupation have been established (and for women, the maiden name and names in other marriages), the file of names and identifying material of all persons who have, in the past years, been arrested in other department stores is consulted. The shoplifter is questioned at length if similarities of names or other identifying data are encountered.

While identification and prior record are being checked, store detectives, persons in charge of refunds, and even experienced sales clerks may be summoned to look at the arrested person to determine if he has been previously suspected of stealing merchandise or has been noted as behaving suspiciously.

In the course of all this investigation, it becomes increasingly clear to the pilferer that he is considered a thief and is in imminent danger of being hauled into court and publicly exhibited as such. This realization is often accompanied by a dramatic change in attitudes and by severe emotional disturbance. Occasionally even hysterical semi-attempts at suicide result.

The professional shoplifter who has been arrested and knows he is recognized, on the other hand, behaves quite differently. He does, of course, make every effort possible to talk his way out of the situation. But once he finds that this is impossible, he accepts jail and its inconveniences as a normal hazard of his trade.

"This is a nightmare," said one woman pilferer who had been formally charged with stealing an expensive handbag. "It can't be happening to me! Why, oh why can't I wake up and find that it isn't so," she cried later as she waited at a store exit, accompanied by a city and a store policemen, for the city police van to arrive. "Whatever will I do? Please make it go away," she pleaded with the officer. "I'll be disgraced forever. I can never look anyone in the face again."

Pilferers expect no "in-group" support for their behavior. As they become aware of the possible serious consequences of their arrest (trial, jail, etc.), pilferers obviously feel isolated from all supporting relationships. Store detectives report that the most frequent question women ask is, "Will my husband have to know about this?" Men, they say, express immediate fear that their employers will be informed of their arrest when questions about employment are

raised. Children are apprehensive of parental reaction. Edwards (1958) says,

The composure of juveniles being detained has never ceased to amaze me, that is, until notified that they must tell a parent of their misdemeanor. Then the tears flow and pleadings begin. The interviewer must be firm in his denial that notification will "kill" the parent, and he must sell the child on the idea that any deviation from accepted practice must be discussed with the person most interested in his welfare. (p. 135–136)

Pilferers feel that if their family or friends learn about their arrest they will be thoroughly disgraced. The fear, shame, and remorse expressed by arrested pilferers could not be other than genuine and a reflection of their appraisal of the attitudes they believe others will take toward them. One woman was observed who, thoroughly shaken as the realization of her predicament began to appear to her, interrupted her protestations of innocence from time to time, overwhelmed at the thought of how some particular person in her "in-group" would react to her arrest. Her conversation with the interrogator ran somewhat as follows: "I didn't intend to take the dress, I just wanted to see it in daylight. [She had stuffed it into a shopping bag and carried it out of the store.] Oh, what will my husband do? I *did* intend to pay for it. It's all a mistake. Oh, my God, what will my mother say! I'll be glad to pay for it. See, I've got the money with me. Oh, my children! They can't find out I've been *arrested!* I'd never be able to face them again."

Pilferers not only expect no in-group support, but they feel that they have literally *no* one to turn to. The problem of being embroiled in a wholly unfamiliar legal situation is obviously not only frightening but unexpected. Apparently they had anticipated being reprimanded; they had not anticipated being searched by a licensed detective, identified, etc., and on the whole, placed in a position in which the burden of argument for keeping out of jail is theirs.

The contrast in behavior between the

pilferer and the recognized and self-admitted thief is striking. The experienced thief either already knows what to do or knows precisely where and how to find out. His emotional reactions may involve anger directed at himself or at features in the situation around him, but he is not at a loss for reactions. He follows the prescribed modes of behavior, and knows, either because of prior experience or through the vicarious experiences of acquaintances, what arrest involves by way of obligations and rights. He has some familiarity with bonding practice and either already has or knows how to find a lawyer who will act for him.

Because the adult pilferer does not think of himself, prior to his arrest, as a thief and can conceive of no in-group support for himself in that role, his arrest forces him to reject the role (at least insofar as department store shoplifting is concerned). The arrest procedure, even though not followed by prosecution, is in itself sufficient to cause him to redefine his situation. He is, of course, informed that subsequent arrest by any store will be followed by immediate prosecution and probably by a considerable jail sentence. But since this does not act as a deterrent to the self-admitted thief, nor could this kind of admonition deter the compulsive neurotic, neither the fear of punishment nor the objective severity of the punishment in itself is the crucial point in relation to the change from criminal to law-abiding behavior. Rather, the threat to the person's system of values and prestige relationships is involved. Social scientists who have investigated criminal activities which have subcultural support are unanimous in pointing out the persistence of criminal activity, the high rate of recidivism and the resistance to reform shown by law violators. Pilfering seems to be the other side of the coin. Not having the support of a criminal subculture, pilferers are very "reformable" individuals. If the findings of this study are substantiated by studies of other offenses in which the offenders are similarly without support of a criminal subculture, there would be a strong argument in favor of keeping pilferers out of jail lest they receive there the kinds of knowledge and emotional support they need to become "successful" commercial thieves. Crime prevention would seem best achieved by helping the law violators retain their self-image of respectability while making it clear to them that a second offense will really mean disgrace.

REFERENCES

Edwards, L. (1958). *Shoplifting and shrinkage protection for stores.* Springfield, IL: Charles C. Thomas.

Inbau, F. E. (1952). Protection and recapture of merchandise from shoplifters. *Illinois Law Review, 46* (6).

29

The FBI's New Psyche Squad

Stephen G. Michaud

The police in a small Middle Western community were recently confronted with the case of a petite young nurse who vanished into the night from the parking lot of the local medical center. The next day, her car was found nearby, its interior bare, save for the nurse's white left shoe.

Twenty-four hours later, her body was discovered, partially covered by brush, along a little-used country lane not far from where she'd been abducted. The nurse had been raped and stabbed wildly, front and back, through her clothing. No murder weapon was found, but her wounds appeared to have been inflicted by a short-bladed instrument, such as a pocketknife. Missing, too, was the nurse's distinctive engagement ring.

It was the sort of brutal, random crime that lately has begun to plague police agencies across the country. (To protect the confidentiality of Federal Bureau of Investigation records, identities, dates, and locations

have been withheld.) Still, because murder in the United States remains primarily a matter involving people who know each other (58 percent of 1985's reported 18,980 homicides were slayings by relatives or acquaintances), in this case the police properly focused their investigation on the victim's fiancé, her family and her friends. When no good suspect emerged from this group, however, the local detectives were left to speculate that their Unsub, a police term for Unknown Subject, was either a transient serial killer or perhaps some recently released mental patient.

Only after two months of fruitless investigation did an inspiration prevent the nurse's murder from becoming one of the 5,000 or so homicides that go unsolved each year in this country. A police sergeant suggested a call for help to the FBI's National Center for the Analysis of Violent Crime, headquartered at the bureau's academy on the Quantico Marine Base in rural eastern

Reprinted by permission of the author.

Virginia. Within a month, the center's team of criminal personality profilers, as they are called, sent back their analysis. The nurse's killer, said the center's report, wasn't likely to be such a mysterious stranger after all. Look for a community resident, a youngish male of slight frame who lived within walking distance of the medical center. Chances were good he lived with a woman—his mother or a girlfriend—who helped support him. There was reason to believe that his name was already known to the police for chronic assaultive behavior. This probably was his most serious crime, but having killed once, he appeared to be someone who might kill again.

The FBI's Criminal profiling service, officially christened the National Center for the Analysis of Violent Crime in June 1985, has evolved from informal beginnings in the late 1960s to become the world's clearinghouse for the pursuit and capture of irrational, abnormal offenders, the most difficult of all criminals to apprehend. Working largely from police reports, autopsies, photos and the like—the center's nine profilers rarely visit the scene of a crime—they ferret out strictly behavioral clues to the identities of Unsubs and produce multipage, typewritten analyses, often in startling clarity and detail.

The analysis center's current cases range from the 1982 Tylenol murders in Illinois and one this year in New York, to arsons, bombings and a fearsome array of degenerate crimes. The bureau also accepts an increasing number of international cases, including the open investigation of a Florentine Unsub who has terrorized Tuscany for more than eight years, killing one or two victims a year.

According to two internal FBI studies, the center contributes significant aid in 80 percent of the more than 600 cases it now accepts each year. "It's the only service like this there is, or ever has been," says the center's senior profiler, 49-year-old Robert K. Ressler. "We're available to law enforcement on a 24-hour basis, 365 days a year."

None of the analysis center's profilers is a psychologist or psychiatrist, though all hold advanced degrees in one of the social sciences. "The thrust here is on the psychology of criminal behavior from the law enforcement side, not the therapeutic or diagnostic side," says Alan E. Burgess, 48, chief of the center's Behavioral Science Investigative Support Unit.

All the profilers have substantial investigative experience, and the key to their expertise is their unique familiarity with the workings of the irrational criminal mind. A forensic psychiatrist, Park Elliott Dietz, a professor of law and behavioral medicine and psychiatry at the University of Virginia, who served as the prosecution psychiatrist in the trial of John W. Hinckley Jr. for the attempted assassination of President Reagan, says the FBI's experts have no peers. "I think I know as much about criminal behavior as any mental-health professional," he says, "and I don't know as much as the bureau's profilers do."

In the United States, all violent crime has been on the increase, particularly deviant acts, such as forcible rape. Rape remains a seriously under-reported crime; Federal officials continue to believe that about half of these assaults are brought to police attention. The number of known incidents, however, rose from 17,190 cases in 1960 to more than 87,000 in 1985. Meanwhile, the percentage of those cases cleared by arrest has fallen off alarmingly. There are as yet no reliable figures to describe the precise dimensions of the problem posed by the offender who is a stranger to his victim, but the number of notorious recent cases of aberrant killers—names such as David (Son of Sam) Berkowitz, John Gacy, Wayne Williams and Ted Bundy come to mind—suggests a grim rising trend. "In my experience, there has been an increase in stranger homicides," says Lieut. Comdr. Vernon J. Geberth of the New York Police Department and the author of a standard police text, *Practical Homicide Investigation.* "And there has been an increase in sexually sadistic homicides."

Whatever its frequency—or cause—stranger, aberrant crime lately has come to trouble both small-town police forces unaccustomed to dealing with it, as well as big-city cops. "I believe that to a very large extent crime adjusts to the environment," says Roger Depue, the 48-year-old administrator of the National Center for the Analysis of Violent Crime. "We've become a highly-transient, stranger-to-stranger society. Criminals are going to take advantage of that."

At the FBI, educing an offender's general characteristics, such as sex and race, is often fairly simple. In the murder of the Middle Western nurse, profilers knew the Unsub was probaby a white male; rape-murders overwhelmingly are intraracial crimes. But achieving a higher order of precision requires considering evidence in the context of both the circumstances of the crime and the established patterns of criminal behavior.

The bureau's files bulge, for example, with detailed dossiers of serial killers, men who kill intermittently, often over the course of many years. (Mr. Ressler, in fact, started using the term because such an offender's behavior is so distinctly episodic, like the movie-house serials he enjoyed as a boy.) These case histories indicate that if a killer gets away with his first crime, his method in subsequent crimes is often more refined; his behavior pattern is marked by evolution. The serial killer habitually uses his own vehicle; not, as the nurse's killer had, his victim's. Further, this Unsub knew of a convenient, local lane in which to carry out his crime. And because the nurse's car was returned to the medical center's immediate vicinity, the killer likely had no vehicle of his own, and thus probably lived nearby.

Another important insight: "In our research projects, we're beginning to see that the most successful violent criminals are not crazies," says Mr. Depue, who was a police chief in Clare, Michigan, before he came to the bureau 18 years ago. The majority of them are intelligent." So the nurse's slayer was by no rule of experience an outwardly bizarre character.

The bureau has distinguished between what it terms Organized or Disorganized Unsub behavior. This offender appeared Organized; that is, he acted in a controlled methodical manner from the point of his abduction to the moment he raped his victim. This suggests that sexual assault was his primary motive, which, because rape is a deviant manifestation of aggression, makes it likely the Unsub was angry that night. The young nurse alone in the parking lot was a tragically opportune target.

From the evidence, however, he hadn't reckoned with *her* anger, or perhaps hysteria, following the rape. The shoe found in her car, plus the fact that the nurse was stabbed *through* her clothing, were consistent with the victim's having turned violently emotional as she dressed. The bureau profilers understand the Organized criminal's absolute need for mastery, and the panic he feels if he loses control. That's when he reaches—in fear—for a weapon, anything handy, such as a pocketknife.

Moreover, an experienced rape-slayer habitually brings with him a favored weapon. His method of murder has a practiced look to it, not the sloppy pattern of wounds found on the nurse. The front-and-back series of stabs suggested a pitched struggle. So the Unsub appeared not only youthful and inexperienced, but also not much larger than his diminutive victim.

The bureau's first serious student of the irrational offender was Agent Howard D. Teten, a veteran of the San Leandro, California, police department's evidence unit who joined the FBI in 1962, and in 1969 arrived as an instructor of applied criminology at the bureau's old training division in Washington. As an instructor, Mr. Teten added to his store of expertise whatever he thought useful, wherever he found it.

He made sure, for instance, to tap the wizardly Dr. James S. Brussel. A New York psychiatrist, Dr. Brussel had pioneered profiling in 1956 with his uncannily precise analysis of New York City's "Mad Bomber," who had intermittently terrorized the city with his homemade explosives for more than a decade. Dr. Brussel even accurately predicted that the bomber, George Metesky, would be brought in wearing a double-breasted suit, neatly buttoned. "Dr. Brussel and I spent a great deal of time together comparing notes and techniques," says Mr. Teten, now 53 and an independent investigator in northern Virginia.

Mr. Teten even absorbed some practical investigative philosophy from Sherlock Holmes. "Two points," he says. "The most obvious thing is probably the correct one. And, if you've eliminated all other "possibilities, whatever is left, however improbable, is what happened."

In 1972, Mr. Teten was joined at the new FBI academy at Quantico by Patrick J. Mullany, a one-time Christian brother who, as an FBI agent, has also conceived an interest in the aberrant criminal. Their students, agents, and selected police officers soon were bringing every manner of odd case to Mr. Teten and Mr. Mullany for behavioral analyses. "And the more we did it," says Mr. Mullany, now 51 and director of international security for First Interstate Bank in Los Angeles, "the more we realized the possibility of practical applications."

Their opportunity arose in early 1974. The previous June, 7-year-old Susan Jaeger, on a camping trip with her family in Montana, was snatched in the predawn hours from the children's tent as her parents slept nearby. The case came to Mr. Teten and Mr. Mullany and Mr. Ressler, then a new instructor-profiler at the academy, via Pete Dunbar, then an agent in the bureau's Bozeman office. Together, the three profilers concluded the Unsub has come upon the family during a habitual night prowl and impulsively took his victim by cutting through the tent with his knife. He appeared to be a young, white male, a loner who lived not far from the campsite. They warned Mr. Dunbar that Susan was probably dead. And from their knowledge of Organized criminal behavior, they came

to the grisly conclusion that her killer would be saving remembrances of his act, perhaps body parts.

Among Mr. Dunbar's early suspects was David Meirhofer, a 23-year-old Vietnam veteran whose name was offered by an informant. By coincidence, Mr. Dunbar, now the United States Attorney for Montana, knew the young man personally. "David was well groomed, courteous and exceptionally intelligent," he remembers. "He was the gentlest of persons, too."

Nothing substantive tied Mr. Meirhofer to the Jaeger murder. But then, in January 1974, an 18-year-old woman who had spurned his attentions was found incinerated in the woods. A suspect again, Mr. Meirhofer readily volunteered to take a polygraph exam and to be questioned under truth serum. "He passed them both with flying colors," says Mr. Dunbar. "After that, I didn't think he did it."

The Quantico profilers were unconvinced. The psychopath they believed had killed both females might easily pass any truth test. "We just kept going on him," says Mr. Mullany. "We kept saying, 'No! He's our boy!' "

On the first anniversary of Susan Jaeger's disappearance, a man who claimed to be keeping her, alive, telephoned Susan's parents at their home in Farmington, Michigan. As she had been advised by the bureau, Marietta Jaeger kept a tape recorder by the phone, and she flipped it on when the conversation began.

"He was very smug and taunting," Mrs. Jaeger recalls. "But my reaction was not what he was expecting. I felt truly able to forgive him. I had a great deal of compassion and concern, and that really took him aback. He let his guard down and finally just broke down and wept."

According to a voice analysis, the caller was Mr. Meirhofer. But such evidence was then insufficient in Montana to obtain a probable-cause search warrant. At this juncture, Mr. Mullany offered a bold suggestion. "It was a last-ditch thing," he says. "But after listening to that tape, I felt that

Meirhofer could be woman-dominated. I suggested that Mrs. Jaeger go to Montana and confront him."

Marietta Jaeger first met David Meirhofer at his lawyer's office, and begged him to tell her about Susan. But Mr. Meirhofer appeared unmoved. "He was very careful," says Mrs. Jaeger, "not to incriminate himself."

She returned to Michigan with her husband, William, both of them certain her pleas had had no effect. They were wrong. Presently there came a collect telephone call from Salt Lake City. A "Mr. Travis" wanted to explain that he, not this man up in Montana, had abducted Susan. But before Mr. Travis could go on with his confession, Mrs. Jaeger interrupted him. "Well, hello, David," she said.

Largely on the strength of Mrs. Jaeger's sworn affidavit, Mr. Dunbar got his search warrant. In Mr. Meirhofer's residence, Mr. Dunbar found remains of both Susan Jaeger and the older female. The young man then confessed to the murders, as well as to the unsolved killings of two local boys. Within a day, Mr. Meirhofer hanged himself in his jail cell.

By cracking Mr. Meirhofer's psychopathic shell, Mr. Teten and Mr. Mullany ratified their belief in behavioral analysis as an investigative tool. It was Mr. Ressler and another young agent at Quantico, John E. Douglas, who took the nascent craft the next step toward becoming an avowed FBI discipline.

As a boy in Chicago, Mr. Ressler eagerly followed local murder stories in the papers. He went on to earn a master's degree in criminology at Michigan State, and was an officer in the Army's Criminal Investigation Division before joining the FBI in 1970. Four years later, he came to the academy as an instructor.

Mr. Douglas, in contrast, never expected to become a Federal agent. Tall and dark, soft-spoken and one of the analysis center's nattier dressers, Mr. Douglas, 41, also joined the bureau in 1970, after being re-cruited out of graduate school at the University of Wisconsin. A native of Hempstead, Long Island, and an Air Force veteran, he had intended to become an industrial psychologist. "I knew nothing about the FBI or anything that it did," he says. By 1976, he was at Quantico.

In 1977, Mr. Ressler and Mr. Douglas began the bureau's first research survey into the aberrant mind. They wanted to test the validity of the Organized-Disorganized criminal models. They also wanted to examine some hoary truisms. Does, for instance, a killer always return to the scene of his crime?

"We wanted to find out factors that predisposed the guy," Mr. Ressler says. "What went on during the assault? What did he do after the crime? How did he cope? Did he take souvenirs? Take photographs? What part did pornography play? A lot of this stuff had been thrown around, but no one had ever really traced it right to the source."

So Mr. Ressler and Mr. Douglas embarked on an interview survey in the nation's prisons, visiting with a detailed questionnaire more than 50 notorious inmates, including Sirhan Sirhan, Charles Manson, Richard Speck, David Berkowitz, and John Gacy. Very few of the interviewees proved reticent to discuss their crimes. Many were flattered by the bureau's attention. And some were simply eager for the chance to relive their deeds. "They'd get all glassy-eyed," says Mr. Ressler. "One of the guys even wanted John and me to stay for dinner."

This altogether unique survey revealed the Organized offender to be of at least average intelligence, and socially and sexually competent. He was apt to be born early into a family in which the father held steady work, but in which parental discipline was inconsistent. This killer often lives with a woman. He drives a well-maintained car. He commonly commits his crimes after some stressful event.

His prey, almost always a stranger, nevertheless conforms to a type; one interviewee was drawn exclusively to solitary females driving two-door cars. The Organized offender often takes souvenirs, but he is very controlled. He doesn't leave his weapon or other incriminating evidence at the scene, and he takes care to hide his victim's body.

The Disorganized offender, as a rule, is not nearly so bright. He is often overtly inadequate, a deluded loner given to solo sex. He kills spontaneously, often brutally, with minimal thought for hiding the act.

These designations are not absolute. Mr. Meirhofer was a prototypical Organized killer, but the Unsub in the case of the Middle Western nurse was what the FBI calls "mixed," one who typically proceeds in an Organized-Disorganized-Organized pattern.

The killer survey and subsequent researches have greatly expanded the range of services of the National Center for the Analysis of Violent Crime. In the case of the 1979–81 Atlanta child murders, for instance, Mr. Ressler, Mr. Douglas, and another profiler, Robert (Roy) Hazelwood, described the personality of a man who might hunt and kill a number of young black males. Mr. Douglas then consulted in the prosecution of Wayne B. Williams.

"Douglas," says Jack Mallard, the Fulton County assistant district attorney who presented much of the case, "indicated to me he thought if we kept Williams on the stand as long as possible and cross-examined him in certain ways, he might break, he might show his true nature."

For two days, Mr. Mallard hammered relentlessly at the defendant. "Then he began lashing back," says the district attorney, "calling me names, the FBI 'goons' and so forth." Mr. Mallard calls this sudden eruption "the turning point in the cross-examination." He says, "It helped for the jury to see that Williams had another side to him."

The FBI's researches have continued to help sharpen the analysis center's profiles. Thus, in the case of the Middle Western nurse, the bureau was able to suggest that the Unsub possibly quarreled with his female companion the night of the murder,

and that he had probably been drinking. He would have returned home agitated, disheveled and possibly spattered with blood. The next day, the profile continued, the Unsub would invent some excuse to be taken to, or near, the scene of the crime to inspect his handiwork. And the killer had taken the victim's engagement ring, which he might later offer as a gift to his female companion. In the end, providing the local press with some of these indicators netted the police an informant. A telephone caller directed them to the doorstep of their astonished quarry, no longer an Unsub. He is now in prison.

The latest addition at Quantico is the Violent Criminal Apprehension Program, a computerized log of the unsolved cases reported to the National Center for the Analysis of Violent Crime by police agencies. Up to now, the bureau, like all law enforcement agencies, has had to track these criminals primarily by means of computerized newspaper indexes.

From this new program, it is hoped, the first clear picture of stranger violence in America will emerge. It is the brainchild of a former police detective, Pierce R. Brooks, now a criminal investigative consultant in Oregon, who also helped set up the system at Quantico. Mr. Ressler, now manager of the apprehension program, says that within a few years the system should contain as many as 10,000 cases, each fully described and cross-referenced for key clues and indicators.

The program, for example, might flag a murder in Pittsburgh if it is similar to one committed in Buffalo. If a third such killing is then reported in Akron, the system may have detected a serial killer. Then the evidence from all three cases can be examined together. Moreover, suspects can be eliminated—or focused upon—based on their whereabouts at the times of the thre killings. According to Robert D. Keppel, chief criminal investigator for the Washington State Attorney General, had the program been available to him in 1975, he might have stopped the serial killer Ted Bundy long before he was captured in Florida. Mr. Bundy began his murderous rampage in Seattle in the early 1970s; by his 1979 arrest, he was specifically linked to the killings of 23 females across the country.

Still another advantage of the program, says Mr. Ressler, will be to short-circuit grisly hoaxes like the one perpetrated by Henry Lee Lucas and Ottis Toole, a pair of drifters who startled the police in 1983 by confessing to upwards of 600 murders nationwide. It required an exhaustive review by a team of reporters at The Dallas Times Herald to determine that almost all of the confessions were fraudulent. Two or three years from now, Mr. Ressler says, a Henry Lucas won't be able to pass off fictitious information like that. "And theoretically," he says, "there aren't going to be any more Ted Bundys."

The National Center for the Analysis of Violent Crime also is now training selected police detectives to become profilers themselves. Five already are in place in Los Angeles, Austin, Texas, Washington, Baltimore and New York. "I thought I knew how to thoroughly investigate a crime before I went down there," reports Detective Raymond Pierce, New York City's newly trained profiler. "It was amazingly well done."

Mr. Pierce says he also discovered that profiling requires a sturdy psychic constitution, Mr. Mullany, a former profiler, agrees: "There are very serious emotional risks. Long-term ones. A person really can't stay with that stuff for very long."

Some profilers-in-training can't distance themselves from the horrors they analyze. "To assess these crimes," Mr. Ressler explains, "you have to *think* like the offender." Extreme weight loss and bouts of unruly emotion are not unknown at the National Center for the Analysis of Violent Crime.

Mr. Douglas, for example, remembers what happened to him two years ago in Seattle, under the enormous pressure of trying to capture the Green River Killer, who is still at large and thought to be responsible for the murders of at least 40 prostitutes from that area.

"I almost died," he says. "I came down with viral encephalitis, and the doctors said it was stress-related; the stress lowered my resistance. I was in a coma for a week. I was paralyzed. I was out of work for five months. My hand's still stiff today."

Such stresses may be the price of success; profiling's demonstrated value as an investigative tool has created a barely manageable workload at the National Center for the Analysis of Violent Crime. There is hope that in the future a newly begun artificial-intelligence project—a program to impart to computers at least some of the profilers' logic and expertise—will ease the burden.

Yet the better the bureau gets at detecting these offenders, the less its experts can foresee any future age of push-button sleuthing.

"Any time you're working with human behavior, you're going to find atypical situations and variables you haven't encountered before," says Mr. Hazelwood. "There's no cookbook, and there never will be a cookbook."

30

From Mafia to Cosa Nostra

ROBERT T. ANDERSON

Sicily has known centuries of inept and corrupt governments that have always seemed unconcerned about the enormous gap between the very rich minority and the incredibly poor majority. Whether from disinterest or from simple incapacity, governments have failed to maintain public order. Under these circumstances, local strong men beyond the reach of the government, or in collusion with it, have repeatedly grouped together to seek out their own interests. They have formed, in effect, little extra-legal principalities. A code of conduct, the code of *omertà*, justified and supported these unofficial regimes by linking compliance with a fabric of tradition that may be characterized as chivalrous. By this code, an "honorable" Sicilian maintained unbreakable silence concerning all illegal activities. To correct abuse, he might resort to feud

and vendetta. But never would he avail himself of a governmental agency. Sanctioned both by hoary tradition and the threat of brutal reprisal, this code in support of strong men was obeyed by the whole populace. The private domains thus established are old. After the 1860s they became known as "Mafias."

As an institution, the Mafia was originally at home in peasant communities as well as in pre-industrial towns and cities. (Sicilian peasants are notable for urban rather than village residence.) The Mafia built upon traditional forms of social interaction common to all Sicilians. Its functions were appropriate to face-to-face communities. Mafias persist and adapt in contemporary Sicily, which, to some extent, is industrializing and urbanizing. Mafias also took root in the United States, where industrialization and urbanization have created a new kind of society, and here, too, they have persisted and adapted. But can a pre-industrial peasant institution survive unchanged in an urban, industrial milieu? May we not anticipate major modifications of structure and function under such circumstances? The available evidence on secret organizations, though regrettably incomplete, inconsistent and inaccurate, suggests an affirmative answer. The Mafia has bureaucratized.

Formal organizations of a traditional type, whether castes in India, harvesting co-operatives in Korea, monasteries in Europe or other comparable groups, normally change as they increase the scale of their operations and as their milieu urbanizes. They often simply disappear, and their surviving activities are taken over by other institutions. Alternatively, however, these traditional associations may survive by being reconstituted as rational-legal associations or by being displaced or overlain by such associations, as castes in India, traditionally led by headmen and councils (panchayats), are now being reconstituted by the formation of caste associations. The substitution of rational-legal for traditional organization is of world-wide occurrence today. Because models of rational-legal organization are almost universally known, and because modern states provide the possibility of regulating organizations by law, bureaucratization rarely occurs now by simple evolution. The Mafia is one of the few exceptions. Because it is secret and illegal, it cannot reorganize by reconstituting itself as a rational-legal organization. Yet it has changed as it has grown in size and shifted to an urban environment. Analysis of this change assumes unusual importance, because the Mafia is a significant force in modern life and because, as a rare contemporary example of the reorganization of a traditional type of association without recourse to legal sanctions, it provides a basis for comparison with potential other examples. Much of the present controversy about the Mafia, particularly about whether such an organization exists in the United States,

is the result of confusing a modern, bureaucratic organization with the traditional institution from which it evolved.

THE TRADITIONAL MAFIA

A Mafia is not necessarily predatory. It provides law and order where the official government fails or is malfeasant. It collects assessments within its territory much as a legal government supports itself. While citizens everywhere often complain about taxation, these Mafia exactions have been defended as reasonable payment for peace. The underlying principle of Mafia rule is that it protects the community from all other strong men in return for regularized tribute.

To illustrate, the Grisafi band of the Agrigento countryside, led by a young, very large man called "Little Mark" (Marcuzzo Grisafi) formed a stable, though illicit, government that oversaw every event in his area for a dozen years (1904–16). An excellent marksman, he was able by his strength and with the aid of four to eight gunmen to guarantee freedom from roving bandit and village sneak alike.

On a larger scale, between approximately 1895 and 1924, a group of eleven villages in the Madonie Mountains were also ruled by a Mafia. The head and his assistants had private police force of as many as 130 armed men. A heavy tax resembling official annual taxes was imposed upon all landowners. As with the Grisafi band, this Mafia was not a roving body of terrorists. Their leaders, at least, were well-established citizens, landowners, and farmers. While they might mount up as a body to enforce their tax collections, they stayed for the most part in their homes or on their farms. They assumed supervision of all aspects of local life, including agricultural and economic activities, family relations, and public administration. As elsewhere, the will of the Mafia was the law. The head, in fact, was known locally as the "prefect" (*"U Prefetto"*).

Although not necessarily predatory, Mafias seem always to be so, despotisms possessed of absolute local power. Many in the band or collaborating with it may find it a welcome and necessary institution in an otherwise lawless land. But multitudes suffer gross injustice at its hands. No one dares offend the Mafia chief's sense of what is right. The lines between tax and extortion, between peace enforcement and murder, blur under absolutism. Many would claim that the Agrigento and Madonie *mafiosi* were mostly involved in blackmail, robbery, and murder. An overall inventory of Mafia activities leaves no doubt that it is a criminal institution, serving the interests of its membership at the expense of the larger population.

In organizational terms, the Mafia is a social group that combines the advantages of family solidarity with the membership flexibility of a voluntary association.

The most enduring and significant social bond in Sicily is that of the family. Its cohesiveness is reinforced by a strong tendency to village endogamy. Only along the coast, where communication was easier, was it common to marry outside of the locality. The tendency to family endogamy further included some cross-cousin marriage. Family bonds are not necessarily closely affectionate ones, but the tie has been the strongest social relationship known. It is the basic organizational group both economically and socially, functioning as a unit of production as well as of consumption.

Family ties often bind members of the Mafia together. The Mafia of the Madonie included two sets of brothers, as did the core membership of the Grisafi group. Not only are members of the Mafia frequently concealed and aided by their families, but their relatives commonly speculate on their activities and profit from them so that a clear line cannot be drawn between the criminal band on the one hand and the circle of kinsmen on the other.

Family ties have a certain utility for organizing social action. Brothers are accustomed to work together. They possess a complex network of mutual rights and obligations to cement their partnership. The father-son and uncle-nephew relationships, equally enduring and diffuse, possess in addition a well-established leader-follower relationship. Cousins and nephews may be part of the intimate family, and it has been suggested that the children of brothers are especially close as indicated by their designations as *fratelli-cugini* (brother-cousins) or *fratelli-carnale* (brothers of the flesh).

The family has one major drawback as a functioning group: its membership is relatively inflexible. Typically, family members vary in interests, capabilities, and temperaments. While this may be of little consequence for running a farm, it can constitute a serious handicap for the successful operation of a gang. Some offspring may be completely devoid of criminal capacity, while good potential *mafiosi* may belong to other families. To a certain degree this drawback is countered by the extension of ties through marriage. But often a desirable working alliance cannot be arranged through a suitable wedding.

Throughout Europe a technique is available for the artificial extension of kinship ties. The technique is that of fictive or ritual kinship. Godparenthood, child adoption, and blood brotherhood make it possible to extend kin ties with ease. These fictive bonds are especially notable for the establishment of kinlike dyadic relationships. Larger social groups have not commonly been formed in this way in Europe except as brotherhoods, the latter with variable, sometimes minimal, success. The Mafia constitutes an unusual social unit of this general type in that the fictive bond is that of godparenthood, elsewhere used for allying individuals, but only rarely for forming groups.

The godparenthood tie has had a variable history in Europe. In the Scandinavian countries it is a momentary thing, with few implications for future interaction. But in the Mediterranean area, and especially in Sicily, it is usually taken very seriously. An indissoluble lifetime bond, it is often claimed to be equal or even superior to the bond of true kinship. While the godparent-hood (*comparatico*) union may cross class lines to link the high and the low in a powerful but formal relationship, it is more often a tie of friends, affective in an overt way that contrasts with the lesser open affection of the domestic family. Above all, the relationship is characterized by mutual trust.

Sicilians in general, then, live with greatest security and ease in the atmosphere of the family with its fictive extensions. The Mafia is a common-interest group whose members are recruited for their special interests in and talents for the maintenance of a predatory satrapy. As noted above, this tie of shared interest often originates within a kinship parameter. When it does not, a kinlike tie is applied by the practice of becoming co-godparents. Although the Mafia *setta* (cell) may or may not be characterized by other structural features, it always builds upon real and fictive kinship.

The Mafia of nineteenth-century Sicily practiced a formal rite of initiation into the fictive-kin relationship. Joseph Valachi underwent the same rite in 1930 in New York. In addition to the "baptism of blood," the chief at the first opportunity normally arranges to become the baptismal godfather of the tyro's newborn child. Lacking that opportunity, he establishes a comparable tie in one of the numerous other *comparatico* relationships. The members among themselves are equally active, so that the passing years see a member more and more bound to the group by such ties.

Ritual ties seem to function in part as a temporizing device. Although efficacious in themselves, they are usually the basis for the later arrangement of marriages between sons and daughters, and thus ultimately for the establishment of affinal and consanguineous bonds. The resultant group is therefore very fluid. It utilizes to the utmost its potentialities for bringing in originally unrelated individuals. Yet it possesses the organizational advantages of a lasting body of kin.

Mafia family culture supports member-ship flexibility additionally by providing for the withdrawal of born members. The criminal family passes on Mafia tradition just as the farming family passes on farming traditions. Boys are taught requisite skills and attitudes. Girls are brought up to be inconspicuous, loyal, and above all silent. The problems of in-family recruitment are not greatly different from those of non-criminal groups. Just as a son without agricultural propensities or the chance to inherit land leaves the countryside to take up a trade or profession, the Mafia son lacking criminal interests or talents takes up a different profession. Indeed, sometimes Mafia family pride comes to focus upon a son who has left the fold to distinguish himself as a physician or professor. But while such an individual might not himself take up an illegal occupation, he is trained never to repudiate it for his kindred. In the Amoroso family, who controlled Porta Montalto near Palermo for many years in the nineteenth century, Gaspare Amoroso, a young cousin of the chief, degraded himself by joining the police force (*carabiniere*). When the youth was discharged and returned to his family home, the Amoroso leaders removed this dishonor by having him killed in cold blood.

The headship of a Mafia is well defined. Referred to as *capo* ("head") or *capomafia* ("Mafia head"), and addressed honorifically as *don*, the chief is clearly identified as the man in charge. Succession to this post, however, is not a matter of clear-cut procedure. In some cases family considerations may result in the replacement of a *capo* by his son or nephew. Commonly, an heir apparent, who may or may not be related consanguineously, is chosen on an essentially pragmatic basis and succeeds by co-optation. Generally, promotion is by intrigue and strength. It must be won by the most powerful and ruthless candidate with or without the blessing of family designation, or co-optation. Only the *capo*, in any case, is formally recognized. The appointment of secondary leaders and ranking within the membership are informal.

In sum, the traditional Mafia may be

described as family-like. It would not be considered a bureaucratic organization. Of the four basic characteristics of a bureaucracy outlined in Blau's *Bureaucracy in Modern Society* (Random House, 1956), the Mafia lacked three—a hierarchy of authority, specialization, and a system of rules. Impartiality, the fourth characteristic, requires a special note. Impartiality requires that promotion, reward, and job assignment ideally be uninfluenced by the pervasive ties of a primary group and determined solely by individual performance-achievement. The Mafia is a kind of kin group. The individual, once a member, belongs for life with a family member's ineluctable rights to group prerogatives. Yet the Mafia seems always to have been ruthlessly impersonal when it mattered. A criminal association survives by making its best marksmen assassins, its best organizers leaders, and by punishing those who are disloyal or not observant of *omertà*. Impartiality in the Mafia is not fully developed, but bureaucracy in this sense has no doubt always been present. The Amoroso murder of the *capo-mafia's* cousin, for example, illustrates extreme partiality for a family group.

BUREAUCRATIZATION OF THE MAFIA

Mafia formal organization seems at the turning point. The Mafia so far has remained essentially a hodgepodge of independent local units confined to the western part of the island, although cells have been established outside of Sicily. Cooperation among localities in Sicily has an old history. The more successful *capi* have at times established hegemony over wider areas. But it appears that large-scale groupings could not endure in an underdeveloped milieu with notoriously poor communication systems. Modernization, however, is breaking down this local isolation. The scale of operations is expanding. The face-to-face, family-like group in which relationships on the whole

are diffuse, affective, and particularistic is changing into a bureaucratic organization.

The best-documented example of early bureaucratization concerns the Mafia of Monreale. Known generally as the *Stoppaglieri*, or facetiously as a mutual-aid society (*società di mutuo soccorso*), and world famous later for the criminal success of some members who migrated to America, the group first formed in the 1870s, when one of Monreale's political factions, in danger of losing local power, formed a Mafia that succeeded in wresting control from the older Mafia of the area. The basic group consisted of 150 members in the city itself. As they prospered they expanded into the surrounding area. Affiliated chapters were established in Parco, San Giuseppe Iato, Santa Cristina, Montelepre, Borgetto, Piana dei Greci, and Misilmeri. A hierarchy of authority was created by the formal recognition of three ranked leadership roles rather than only one. The head of the whole organization was designated *capo*, but each area, including the various quarters of Monreale, was placed under the direct jurisdiction of a subhead or *sottocapo*. Each subhead in turn had an assistant, the *consiglio directivo*. The rules of the association were made somewhat more explicit than those of other Mafias in providing for the convocation of membership councils to judge members charged with breaking the regulations of the group. And these regulations, completely traditional in character, were very precise, binding members:

1. To help one another and avenge every injury of a fellow member;
2. To work with all means for the defense and freeing of any fellow member who had fallen into the hands of the judiciary;
3. To divide the proceeds of thievery, robbery, and extortion with certain considerations for the needy as determined by the *capo*;
4. To keep the oath and maintain secrecy on pain of death within twenty-four hours.

One may observe further bureaucratization of the Mafia in the United States.

Mafias were first established in America in the latter part of the nineteenth century. During the prohibition era they proliferated and prospered. Throughout this period, these groups continued to function essentially like the small traditional Mafia of western Sicily.

Recent decades in the United States have witnessed acceleration of all aspects of modernization. Here, if anywhere, the forces of urbanization impinge upon group life. But while American criminals have always been quick to capitalize upon technological advances, no significant organizational innovation occurred until the repeal of prohibition in 1932, an event that abruptly ended much of the lucrative business of the underworld. Small face-to-face associations gave way over subsequent decades to the formation of regional, national, and international combines, a change in which American *mafiosi* participated.

As always, information is incomplete and conflicting. Bureaucratization, however, seems to have increased significantly beyond that even of bureaucratized Sicilian groups. Specialization, generally undeveloped in Sicily, became prominent. Personnel now regularly specialize as professional gunmen, runners, executives, or adepts in other particular operations. Departmentalization was introduced and now includes an organizational breakdown into subgroups such as narcotics operations; gambling; the rackets; prostitution; and an enforcement department, the infamous Murder, Inc., with its more recent descendants.

The hierarchy of authority has developed beyond that of bureaucratized Sicilian Mafias. Bill Davidson describes a highly elaborated hierarchy of the Chicago Cosa Nostra, which he compares to the authority structure of a large business corporation. He points to the equivalent of a three-man board of directors, a president of the corporation, and four vice-presidents in charge of operations. He also notes a breakdown into three geographical areas, each headed by a district manager. District managers have executive assistants, who in turn have aids. Finally, at the lowest level are the so-called soldiers. National councils of the more important *capi* apparently meet from time to time to set up territories, co-ordinate tangential activities, and adjudicate disputes. They serve to minimize internecine strife rather than to administer co-operative undertakings. The problem of succession has still not been solved. The Valachi hearings revealed an equally complex hierarchy for the state of New York.

A written system of rules has not developed, although custom has changed. Modern *mafiosi* avoid the use of force as much as possible, and thus differ strikingly from old Sicilian practice. The old *"mustachios"* are being replaced by dapper gentlemen clothed in conservative business suits. But as a criminal organization, the Mafia cannot risk systematizing its rules in written statutes.

A major element of bureaucratization is the further development of impartiality. Mafiosi now freely collaborate on all levels with non-Sicilians and non-Italians. The Chicago association includes non-Italians from its "board of directors" down. In these relationships, consanguineous and affinal ties are normally absent and co-godparenthood absent or insignificant. Familistic organization, the structural characteristic that made for the combination of organizational flexibility with group stability in the traditional associations of Sicily—and that goes far to explain the success of Mafias there—apparently proved inadaptive in urban America. When it became desirable and necessary to collaborate with individuals of different criminal traditions, it sufficed to rely for group cohesion on the possibility of force and a businesslike awareness of the profits to be derived from co-operation. Family and ritual ties still function among Sicilian-American criminals to foster co-operation and mutual support within cliques, but pragmatic considerations rather than familistic Mafia loyalties now largely determine organizational arrangements.

CONCLUSION

The Mafia as a traditional type of formal organization has disappeared in America. Modern criminals refer to its successor as *Cosa Nostra*, "Our Thing." The Cosa Nostra is a lineal descendant of the Mafia, but it is a different kind of organization. Its goals are much broader as it exploits modern cities and an industrialized nation. The real and fictive kinship ties of the old Mafia still operate among fellow Sicilians and Italians, but these ties now coexist with bureaucratic ones. The Cosa Nostra operates above all in new and different terms. This new type of organization includes elaboration of the hierarchy of authority; the specialization and departmentalization of activities; new and more pragmatic, but still unwritten, rules; and a more developed impartiality. In America, the traditional Mafia has evolved into a relatively complex organization which perpetuates selected features of the older peasant organization but subordinates them to the requirements of a bureaucracy.

31

Techniques of Neutralization

Gresham M. Sykes
David Matza

As Morris Cohen once said, one of the most fascinating problems about human behavior is why men violate the laws in which they believe. This is the problem that confronts us when we attempt to explain why delinquency occurs despite a greater or lesser commitment to the usages of conformity. A basic clue is offered by the fact that social rules or norms calling for valued behavior seldom if ever take the form of categorical imperatives. Rather, values or norms appear as qualified guides for action, limited in their applicability in terms of time, place, persons, and social circumstances. The moral injunction against killing, for example, does not apply to the enemy during combat in time of war, although a captured enemy comes once again under the prohibition. Similarly, the taking and distributing of scarce goods in a time of acute social need is felt by many to be right, although under other circumstances private property is held

inviolable. The normative system of a society, then, is marked by what Williams has termed *flexibility*; it does not consist of a body of rules held to be binding under all conditions.[1]

This flexibility is, in fact, an integral part of the criminal law in that measures for "defenses to crimes" are provided in pleas such as nonage, necessity, insanity, drunkenness, compulsion, self-defense, and so on. The individual can avoid moral culpability for his criminal action—and thus avoid the negative sanctions of society—if he can prove that criminal intent was lacking. *It is our argument that much delinquency is based on what is essentially an unrecognized extension of defenses to crimes, in the form of justifications for deviance that are seen as valid by the delinquent but not by the legal system or society at large.*

These justifications are commonly described as rationalizations. They are viewed as following deviant behavior and as protecting the individual from self-blame and the blame of others after the act. But there is also reason to believe that they precede deviant behavior and make deviant behavior possible. It is this possibility that Sutherland mentioned only in passing and that other writers have failed to exploit from the viewpoint of sociological theory. Disapproval flowing from internalized norms and conforming others in the social environment is neutralized, turned back, or deflected in advance. Social controls that serve to check or inhibit deviant motivational patterns are rendered inoperative, and the individual is freed to engage in delinquency without serious damage to his self-image. In this sense, the delinquent both has his cake and eats it too, for he remains committed to the dominant normative system and yet so qualifies its imperatives that violations are "acceptable" if not "right." Thus, the delinquent represents not a radical opposition to law-abiding society, but something more like an apologetic failure, often more sinned against than sinning in his own eyes. We call these justifications of deviant behavior techniques of neutralization; and we believe these techniques make up a crucial component of Sutherland's "definitions favorable to the violation of law." It is by learning these techniques that the juvenile becomes delinquent, rather than by learning moral imperatives, values, or attitudes standing in direct contradiction to those of the dominant society. In analyzing these techniques, we have found it convenient to divide them into five major types.

THE DENIAL OF RESPONSIBILITY

Insofar as the delinquent can define himself as lacking responsibility for his deviant actions, the disapproval of self or others is sharply reduced in effectiveness as a restraining influence. As Justice Holmes has said, even a dog distinguishes between being stumbled over and being kicked, and modern society is no less careful to draw a line between injuries that are unintentional, i.e.,

where responsibility is lacking, and those that are intentional. As a technique of neutralization, however, the denial of responsibility extends much further than the claim that deviant acts are an "accident" or some similar negation of personal accountability. It may also be asserted that delinquent acts are due to forces outside of the individual and beyond his control such as unloving parents, bad companions, or a slum neighborhood. In effect, the delinquent approaches a "billiard ball" conception of himself in which he sees himself as helplessly propelled into new situations. From a psychodynamic viewpoint, this orientation toward one's own actions may represent a profound alienation from self, but it is important to stress the fact that interpretations of responsibility are cultural constructs and not merely idiosyncratic beliefs. The similarity between this mode of justifying illegal behavior assumed by the delinquent and the implications of a "sociological" frame of reference or a "humane" jurisprudence is readily apparent.[2] It is not the validity of this orientation that concerns us here, but its function of deflecting blame attached to violations of social norms and its relative independence of a particular personality structure.[3] By learning to view himself as more acted upon than acting, the delinquent prepares the way for deviance from the dominant normative system without the necessity of a frontal assault on the norms themselves.

THE DENIAL OF INJURY

A second major technique of neutralization centers on the injury or harm involved in the delinquent act. The criminal law has long made a distinction between crimes which are *mala in se* and *mala prohibita*—that is between acts that are wrong in themselves and acts that are illegal but not immoral—and the delinquent can make the same kind of distinction in evaluating the wrongfulness of his behavior. For the delinquent, however, wrongfulness may turn on the question of whether or not anyone has clearly been hurt by his deviance, and this matter is open to a variety of interpretations. Vandalism, for example, may be defined by the delinquent simply as "mischief"—after all, it may be claimed, the persons whose property has been destroyed can well afford it. Similarly, auto theft may be viewed as "borrowing," and gang fighting may be seen as a private quarrel, an agreed-upon duel between two willing parties, and thus of no concern to the community at large. We are not suggesting that this technique of neutralization, labeled the denial of injury, involves an explicit dialectic. Rather, we are arguing that the delinquent frequently, and in a hazy fashion, feels that his behavior does not really cause any great harm despite the fact that it runs counter to law. Just as the link between the individual and his acts may be broken by the denial of responsibility, so may the link between acts and their consequences be broken by the denial of injury. Since society sometimes agrees with the delinquent, e.g., in matters such as truancy, "pranks," and so on, it merely affirms the idea that the delinquent's neutralization of social controls by means of qualifying the norms is an extension of common practice rather than a gesture of complete opposition.

THE DENIAL OF THE VICTIM

Even if the delinquent accepts the responsibility for his deviant actions and is willing to admit that his deviant actions involve an injury or hurt, the moral indignation of self and others may be neutralized by an insistence that the injury is not wrong in light of the circumstances. The injury, it may be claimed, is not really an injury; rather, it is a form of rightful retaliation or punishment. By a subtle alchemy the delinquent moves himself into the position of an avenger and the victim is transformed into a wrongdoer. Assaults on homosexuals or suspected homosexuals, attacks on members of minority groups who are said to have gotten "out of

place," vandalism as revenge on an unfair teacher or school official, thefts from a "crooked" store owner—all may be hurts inflicted on a transgressor, in the eyes of the delinquent. As Orwell has pointed out, the type of criminal admired by the general public has probably changed over the course of years, and Raffles no longer serves as a hero;[4] but Robin Hood, and his latterday derivatives such as the tough detective seeking justice outside the law, still capture the popular imagination, and the delinquent may view his acts as part of a similar role.

To deny the existence of the victim, then, by transforming him into a person deserving injury is an extreme form of a phenomenon we have mentioned before, namely, the delinquent's recognition of appropriate and inappropriate targets for his delinquent acts. In addition, however, the existence of the victim may be denied for the delinquent, in a somewhat different sense, by the circumstances of the delinquent act itself. Insofar as the victim is physically absent, unknown, or a vague abstraction (as is often the case in delinquent acts committed against property), the awareness of the victim's existence is weakened. Internalized norms and anticipations of the reactions of others must somehow be activated, if they are to serve as guides for behavior; and it is possible that a diminished awareness of the victim plays an important part in determining whether or not this process is set in motion.

THE CONDEMNATION OF THE CONDEMNERS

A fourth technique of neutralization would appear to involve a condemnation of the condemners or, as McCorkle and Korn have phrased it, a rejection of the rejectors.[5] The delinquent shifts the focus of attention from his own deviant acts to the motives and behavior of those who disapprove of his violations. His condemners, he may claim, are hypocrites, deviants in disguise, or impelled by personal spite. This orientation toward the conforming world may be of particular importance when it hardens into a bitter cynicism directed against those assigned the task of enforcing or expressing the norms of the dominant society. Police, it may be said, are corrupt, stupid, and brutal. Teachers always show favoritism and parents always "take it out" on their children. By a slight extension, the rewards of conformity—such as material success—become a matter of pull or luck, thus decreasing still further the stature of those who stand on the side of the law-abiding. The validity of this jaundiced viewpoint is not so important as its function in turning back or deflecting the negative sanctions attached to violations of the norms. The delinquent, in effect, has changed the subject of the conversation in the dialogue between his own deviant impulses and the reactions of others; and by attacking others, the wrongfulness of his own behavior is more easily repressed or lost to view.

THE APPEAL TO HIGHER LOYALTIES

Fifth, and last, internal and external social controls may be neutralized by sacrificing the demands of the larger society for the demands of the smaller social groups to which the delinquent belongs, such as the sibling pair, the gang, or the friendship clique. It is important to note that the delinquent does not necessarily repudiate the imperatives of the dominant normative system, despite his failure to follow them. Rather, the delinquent may see himself as caught up in a dilemma that must be resolved, unfortunately, at the cost of violating the law. One aspect of this situation has been studied by Stouffer and Toby in their research on the conflict between particularistic and universalistic demands, between the claims of friendship and general social obligations, and their results suggest that "it is possible to classify people according to a predisposition to select one or the other horn of a dilemma in a role conflict."[6] For

our purposes, however, the most important point is that deviation from certain norms may occur not because the norms are rejected, but because other norms, held to be more pressing or involving a higher loyalty, are accorded precedence. Indeed, it is the fact that both sets of norms are believed in that gives meaning to our concepts of dilemma and role conflict.

The conflict between the claims of friendship and the claims of law, or a similar dilemma, has of course long been recognized by the social scientist (and the novelist) as a common human problem. If the juvenile delinquent frequently resolves his dilemma by insisting that he must "always help a buddy" or "never squeal on a friend," even when it throws him into serious difficulties with the dominant social order, his choice remains familiar to the supposedly law-abiding. The delinquent is unusual, perhaps, in the extent to which he is able to see the fact that he acts in behalf of the smaller social groups to which he belongs as a justification for violations of society's norms, but it is a matter of degree rather than of kind.

"I didn't mean it." "I didn't really hurt anybody." "They had it coming to them." "Everybody's picking on me." "I didn't do it for myself." These slogans or their variants, we hypothesize, prepare the juvenile for delinquent acts. These "definitions of the situation" represent tangential or glancing blows at the dominant normative system rather than the creation of an opposing ideology; and they are extensions of patterns of thought prevalent in society rather than something created *de novo*.

Techniques of neutralization may not be powerful enough to fully shield the individual from the force of his own internalized values and the reactions of conforming others, for as we have pointed out, juvenile delinquents often appear to suffer from feelings of guilt and shame when called into account for their deviant behavior. And some delinquents may be so isolated from the world of conformity that techniques of neutralization need not be called into play.

Nonetheless, we would argue that techniques of neutralization are critical in lessening the effectiveness of social controls and that they lie behind a large share of delinquent behavior.

NOTES

1. Cf. Williams, Robin Jr. (1951). *American society.* New York: Knopf, p. 28.
2. A number of observers have wryly noted that many delinquents seem to show a surprising awareness of sociological and psychological explanations for their behavior and are quick to point out the causal role of their poor environment.
3. It is possible, of course, that certain personality structures can accept some techniques of neutralization more readily than others, but this question remains largely unexplored.
4. Orwell, G. (1946). *Dickens, Dali, and others.* New York: Reynal.
5. McCorkle, L. W. & Korn, R. (1954, May). Resocialization within walls. *The Annals of the American Academy of Political and Social Science, 293,* 88–98.
6. See Stouffer, S. A. & Toby, J. (1951). Role conflict and personality. In *Toward a general theory of action,* Talcott Parsons and Edward A. Shils (Eds.). Cambridge: Harvard University Press, p. 494.

32

Lords of the Slums

Alex Kotlowitz

The Black Gangster Disciples have good sources of information.

Thus last week, when 60 uniformed officers raided a Disciple-controlled apartment building in a public-housing complex here, the street gang, tipped off, had already cleared out. For all their German shepherds and hand-held metal detectors, the police could find only one gun; they arrested no gang members.

As in other U.S. cities, street gangs have become a powerful presence in Chicago, menacing the lives of nearly every resident in the inner city. They prey particularly on the single women who occupy more than 70% of public-housing units here. Gang members move in on them and take over, using dwellings to store drugs and guns, and turning residents into virtual captives in their own homes.

Once entrenched, gang members convert buildings to private fortresses. To cloak their activities, they knock out lights in elevators and stairwells. They cut holes between apartments to make it easier to elude rival gangs and the police.

BUYING GOOD WILL

The gangs are even becoming adept at their own sort of public relations. They buy food for the elderly and sneakers for kids, making wary allies of both. They sponsor picnics, where they put up huge banners flaunting their names and colors.

"If you live here, you had better learn to get along with them," says Arrie Martin, who lives in Ogden Courts, a west-side development ruled by the Disciples. Adds Vincent Lane, the director of the beleaguered Chicago Housing Authority: "The gangs are the only formal structure out there that's effective. They control the social and economic environment of people in public housing."

Indeed, Mr. Lane and others talk about the need to win back the hearts and minds of tenants. He says his job now requires "changing the spirit of people in public housing."

Though the police have special units to deal with gang crimes and though individual officers bravely do what they can, their manpower remains limited. Members of the gang crimes unit, for instance, often are pulled away to work parades and local festivals. Uncooperative tenants also hamper their efforts. "The only way you get the gangs out is when the people get tired of them," says Hosea H. Crossley, the commander of the public-housing police unit. "Meanwhile, all we can do is hold them down."

BECOMING AN INSTITUTION

Gangs have so worked their way into the fabric of the community that no one—the police, the housing authority or the tenants—is certain how to get rid of them.

Says Irving Spergel, a University of Chicago professor of social-service administration, the gangs "are an institution, and we're just beginning to recognize that."

An unmarked police car wends its way up the narrow fire lane of the Robert Taylor Homes, 28 high-rises that stretch for two miles.

The warning whistles of young boys precede the gray sedan; sometimes they shout the number "seven," a signal that the police are nearby. Groups of teenagers stand around in the dark breezeways of the buildings. Most wear their baseball caps cocked to the right, a sign that they are Black Gangster Disciples.

Were it not for the full moon, they would be barely visible; they have punched out lights so that they can operate in the dark. They wait for the police to pass, then resume selling their drugs, mostly cocaine and heroin.

The three northernmost buildings at Robert Taylor and the two southernmost buildings at the adjacent Stateway Gardens are virtually owned by "Cold Black." The gang leader's real name is Robert L. Dordies. He served 11 years in prison for the murder of a 66-year-old man, from whom he stole $17. Now 32, he is a ranking member of the Black Gangster Disciples.

DORDIES'S TURF

From his house on Chicago's far south side, Mr. Dordies exercises iron-fisted control over his territory. He is so feared by residents that a woman contacted for this story was begged by her child to hang up the phone. A tenant tells of how Mr. Dordies once came to her door looking for her son, who owed Mr. Dordies money. A Disciple member put a gun to the son's head. The mother paid the $300 her son owed for drugs. "I've got grandkids, and I don't know what [the gangs] might do," she says.

Within the past year, police say, two men in their twenties have been slain by members of the Disciples for what police believe were actions that challenged Mr. Dordies's authority.

When a witness to one of the killings came forward, a would-be assassin shot at him from a rooftop with a high-powered rifle. The state's attorney's office moved the witness out of Illinois to protect him from further attempts on his life.

In recent years, Mr. Dordies has been charged with misdemeanors—criminal trespass, and a traffic violation. But in all cases, charges were dismissed. He is said never personally to handle guns or drugs. Stout and about six feet tall, he sports gold necklaces and carries a cellular telephone.

Incredibly, the managers and staff of the

Robert Taylor Homes and the Stateway Gardens say they have never heard of Cold Black. "No gangs have taken over any buildings in Stateway," insists Betty Walton, the former housing manager of the complex.

But residents here know otherwise. For Cold Black controls a small army of teenagers and men in their twenties, all members of the Disciples. He also recruits boys as young as 10, plying them with jogging suits and big radios. They run drugs for him and serve as bodyguards, according to tenants and the police.

OCCUPIED APARTMENTS

The "soldiers" in Cold Black's army often commandeer apartments in the high-rises, where they sell drugs and store guns. Some of these are vacant apartments, but others aren't. One man, afraid to have his name published, recounted one such takeover. His girlfriend owed Mr. Dordies several hundred dollars for cocaine, so one day Disciples showed up and announced that they intended to sell drugs from the man's two-bedroom apartment.

The arrangement quickly became total occupation, and for a nightmarish two months, the couple stayed in one of the back bedrooms while gang members watched TV and weighed and sold drugs from the front room. The Disciples, in groups of four to six, were there in shifts, 24 hours a day. Occasionally, Mr. Dordies himself is said to have visited the apartment.

The rightful tenant says his 12-year-old son often asked: "Daddy, why don't you make these men leave?" But, he says, "It wasn't my home anymore."

He feared retaliation if he called the police. He sent his son and two-year-old daughter to live with his sister's family while he gradually moved furniture and clothes out of the apartment. Late one night, he and his girlfriend left and didn't go back. The apartment, according to another tenant, now is boarded up.

LOST CHILDREN

While some families have lost their apartments to Mr. Dordies, others have lost their children. Tenants tell of one father who demanded that his 15-year-old son leave the gang. A group of Disciples told the man to mind his own business and then broke his arm.

But while Mr. Dordies is a loathsome presence to some, not everyone here wishes him ill. Some people believe the buildings have been safer under his control, police say. At night, they say, Mr. Dordies posts guards to protect his buildings. The police, meanwhile, continue to seek evidence that will help them put Cold Black back in prison.

Mr. Dordies couldn't be reached for comment. His attorney, William A. Swano, declined to comment on assertations in this story, except to say that two criminal-trespass charges and the traffic citation, all of which were dismissed, constituted "harassment by the police."

One reason police find it difficult to build cases is that tenants are so closely watched by the gangs. That is why, when there is trouble, residents of public housing often won't call the 911 emergency phone number. In Chicago, the caller's address automatically flashes at police headquarters, and police will sometimes then appear at the caller's home seeking more information.

RELUCTANT WITNESS

That happened once to Francine Washington, who lives in a part of Stateway Gardens controlled by a gang not affiliated with Mr. Dordies. From her second-floor apartment, she watched six gang members beat a young man with bricks and clubs. She immediately dialed 911, and within minutes, she says, six policemen were at her door.

"I have nothing to say to you," she told the officers, as one of the assailants stared up at her window, his arms defiantly crossed. "If you wanted to talk to me, you should have called me on the phone." The police do have a hot-line number, which promises confidentiality, but, they say, tenants rarely use it.

Witnesses to gang crimes typically refuse to come forward; if they do, retaliation is common. Even the most public and brutal of beatings go unreported.

Around one o'clock one steamy summer night, members of a gang called Vice Lords, police allege, beat 32-year-old Carl Maynard to death at Rockwell Gardens, using a baseball bat and belt buckles. It all happened in full view of tenants.

HOLDING COURT

Within hours, detectives were knocking on doors looking for witnesses. The Vice Lords' leader, Roy White, sat on a metal kitchen chair in the center of the basketball court, 10 to 15 of his soldiers surrounding him. From this central location, says Detective Bob Grapenthien, the gang leader directed his henchmen, who followed the police from floor to floor, standing in the hallway as a silent reminder to tenants that they were being watched.

The police have charged two gang members with the murder, but they worry that no witnesses will testify in court. Detectives concede that the case against the men may be iffy. "No one knows anything about nothing," says Detective Gar Eveland, one of the first police officers to try to interview witnesses.

In mid-July, residents of Robert Taylor Homes, which is Chicago's largest public-housing complex, received invitations to a picnic. Fliers promised free food and drink and softball for the children and a car show and wet T-shirt contest for adults.

The sponsors of the third annual Players Picnic: some of the city's top drug dealers and gang leaders. The flier identified some of them by name—Highsmith, Fat Cat, Bub and Disco.

Thus, on the last Sunday in July, about 2,000 Chicagoans convened in Dan Ryan Woods on the far south side. They danced to the funk rock of a live band and grilled hot dogs and ribs. Cars were so backed up going into the park that the police had to assign extra traffic details.

The kingpins showed off their glistening new Mercedes-Benzes, Rolls-Royces, and Jaguars. They danced and drank until 10 p.m., when the police broke up the festivities.

These days, the gangs are working harder than ever to ingratiate themselves with the neighbors. They have learned from the El Rukns gang, previously known as the Blackstone Rangers, who in the late 1960s and early 1970s were a political force, conducting federally financed job-training classes and organizing social events. They even sponsored their own singing group.

Gangs have held picnics for residents of Cabrini-Green and Ogden Courts, two big housing complexes here. At Cabrini-Green, one gang leader has distributed more than 1,000 pairs of sneakers each summer to children, according to city employees who work with the gangs. At Robert Taylor, according to the police, gang leaders give money to elderly residents in need. In Henry Horner Homes, one gang lieutenant hands out dollar bills to the children.

Al Kindle, of the Chicago Intervention Network, a city agency that works with gangs, says that all the politicking by gangs "makes it near impossible to fight them. People are hesitant to give information." The gangs, he says, have "an aura of knighthood."

Shortly before sunrise one morning, Evelyn Walker and her six children awoke to the sounds of shattering glass. A Molotov cocktail came hurtling through the children's bedroom window, quickly igniting the mattress of her 15-year-old daughter's bed. The children ran screaming from the fiery room, a hail of bullets following them. No one was killed, although one of the children was shot in the leg.

Until after the firebombing, Ms. Walker lived in the same high-rise that was raided by the 60 Chicago policemen last week. Located at 2417 W. Adams, the 135-unit complex is home to a faction of the Disciples not directly related to Cold Black's operations. The gang's insignia, the six-pointed star, adorns the breezeway of the building.

As Ms. Walker's experience attests, Chicago gangs have anything but a peaceful existence. Crime is so high at Rockwell Gardens, which is home to 4,100 people, that in 1987 more than eight violent crimes were committed there for every 100 residents.

KEEPING HEADS DOWN

Ms. Walker, a large woman whose hearty laugh often echoed through the cinderblock halls, had tried to organize her neighbors and to work with the gang controlling the building. But she hated that she and her six children had to eat their dinners on the floor of the children's bedroom because her dining-room table was exposed to the almost daily gunfire. She hated what the gang did to her building. (Earlier this year, she seriously injured her hand in a fall in the pitch-black stairwell, where lights had been broken by gang members.)

But the gangs, at times, assisted Ms. Walker. When she organized a barbecue, she requested protection from housing-authority security guards and the police. According to tenants, neither showed up. So, on the dirt lawn out back, parents grilled ribs and their children swirled around Ms. Walker, who was dressed as a clown. Three Disciples stood guard with walkie-talkies in hand.

"Since I can't get rid of them, I figured I might as well work with them and get some cooperation," she says.

Others who lived at the same address found that the only way to cope was to leave. One young woman, forced to pay protection money, fled the building on West Adams in terror, leaving behind dirty dishes in the sink and baby clothes drying on the balcony.

"I watched her leave and didn't even ask if I could help," recalls Celeste Deanes, a neighbor. "It happens so often that you fail to make normal reactions to abnormal situations." No one would help Ms. Deanes, either, when the gangs later came after her.

MOVING IN

Members of gangs often try to move into the high-rise apartments as boyfriends of single women living there. Once ensconced, they start moving in their buddies. The housing authority estimates that 60,000 people, many of them gang members, are living in its facilities illegally; 144,000 are there legally.

Ms. Deanes, 28 and recently divorced, moved into a sixth floor, two-bedroom apartment at this Rockwell Gardens building 18 months ago, while attending Chicago State University. Ms. Deanes says she kept to herself, usually rising at 3 a.m., to get her two children, who are five and three, to the baby sitter and then making the 1½-hour trip to school.

One day, a gang member in his thirties who lived illegally upstairs began making advances. When Ms. Deanes spurned them, she was harassed. First, her microwave oven was stolen. Then, about midnight one summer night, a pistol shot rang past her window, singeing her sheets. The next weekend her apartment was ransacked and her children's beds set afire. The washing machine and her Radio Shack computer also were stolen. Ms. Deanes finally packed and left.

According to residents, at least four other families fled the building during the summer because of gang harassment. Ms. Walker watched these tenants leave and felt an urgency to form a strong tenants' organization. If tenants didn't feel comfortable turning to the housing authority or the police, at least they have one another, she figured. "Everybody has failed," Ms. Walker told neighbors. Her handwritten announcement of a tenants' meeting was one of the few things to survive the firebombing of her apartment.

The Vice Lords, enemies of the Disciples, apparently had been gunning for a 15-year-old boy called "Pee Wee," who lived next door to Ms. Walker. They missed, hitting Ms. Walker's place instead.

They didn't let up, either. The firemen who arrived to put out the blaze had to take cover behind their trucks as the Vice Lords continued to shoot at the building. Ms. Walker herself took refuge under the fire truck.

When the shooting finally stopped and calm prevailed, the Disciples prepared for further battle. Members spent much of the day collecting money from tenants to buy guns. By early afternoon, they had filled a baseball cap with cash. They also put plywood in Ms. Walker's back windows because the housing-authority repairmen didn't show up until early afternoon. Even Pee Wee, for whom the attack was meant, came by to apologize to Ms. Walker and then helped sweep the water out of her blackened apartment.

Within the following five days, 21 windows on the first two floors of the building were shattered by bottles, bullets, and Molotov cocktails. At least six people were assaulted. The shooting between 2417 W. Adams and other buildings was so frequent that the local elementary-school principal requested and got police protection for the children going home from school. A killing the following weekend in front of the building was the last straw. The police, at the behest of the director of the housing authority, stormed the building the next day.

WINNING OVER TENANTS

Mr. Lane, the housing official, in his job only three months, had been making efforts to slowly win back the confidence of tenants. His assessment of how little control his agency actually has over its own real estate has been candid. But he has wanted to move cautiously, making every effort to assure tenants that his agency is on their side.

He held a series of public hearings at each of the city's 19 developments. Alleging that some of his own field managers have ignored problems or even cooperated with the gangs, he promised to transfer 22 of them. At least one manager is being investigated for possible drug ties.

But the urgency of problems at 2417 W. Adams pushed Mr. Lane to temporarily abandon his strategy and turn to an old tactic: police firepower. Mr. Lane led the police sweep: "Either [gangs] were going to run that building or I was."

Despite the failure of the raid to produce any arrests, Mr. Lane hopes his invasion of the Rockwell Gardens high-rise will set an example. Currently, five private security guards and one housing official keep watch day and night. The housing authority is erecting a steel gate and has issued tenants identification cards, which they now need in order to enter the building. No one but tenants can be on the premises after midnight. Mr. Lane says he plans to evict tenants who have a history of drug arrests or whose children are gang members. He will move in more law-abiding families, he says, and help build a tenants' council. He says he intends to repeat what he is doing here at 15 other Chicago high-rises.

Still, 2417 W. Adams is just one of many public-housing high-rises in Chicago, and neither the police nor the housing authority has the money or manpower to fully protect all the buildings in the city. Moreover, with the departure of Ms. Walker, the housing authority is losing its best tenant in the building. Her neighbors are losing their best friend.

But there has been at least one noticeable difference at 2417 W. Adams in the past few days. Last Friday evening, the playgound behind the building was full of children using the slides and hanging from the bars of the rusted Jungle Gym. That playground had been virtually abandoned, because children played indoors, afraid to be caught in the crossfire.

33

Rabble, Crime, and the Jail

John Irwin

The public and most criminal justice functionaries do not want to see the rabble treated any differently from the way they are now.

This attitude was clearly revealed when Goldfarb presented his reform ideas in a court that was hearing a suit against a medium-sized jail outside the city of New Orleans. According to Goldfarb (1975), the defense counsel began to ask him a long line of questions:

[He inquired] whether I would allow jail inmates to mingle, to partake in unlimited recreation, to have unlimited visits, to work, to cohabit sexually. To each question I responded that I felt jail inmates should be permitted to do all these things and more, since their partaking in such activities need not detract from the ability of jail administrators to assure their presence at trial and to maintain the segregation of dangerous defendants from the free community. Once contained, they should be punished no more. After having led me down this path, the defense counsel, obviously pleased with his ability to push me into what he thought was an obviously untenable position, announced his surprise that an outsider to the local scene, a supposed expert, would make such outlandish, bizarre suggestions recommending practices which he felt would be considered exotic in his community. I was proposing, he said, no more than a kind of hotel for criminals. (p. 448)

Goldfarb defended the reasonableness of his ideas by noting that even a presidential commission had made similar recommendations. But that argument misses the point. Such reform proposals really *are* outlandish and bizarre, not because they are unworkable or inconsistent with concepts of justice and humanity, but simply because they are the opposite of what the public wants. The public does not want the rabble confined in

From John Irwin, The Jail: Managing Rabble in American Society, 1985. Shoestring Press, P. O. Box 4327, Hamden, CT 06514. Reprinted by permission of the author.

a hotel; it wants them to suffer in a jail. In our society, the jail will not change until we significantly reduce the size of the rabble class or significantly change our attitudes toward it. Unfortunately, the existence of both a rabble class and public hostility toward it seems to be firmly rooted in our society.

THE RABBLE: A PERMANENT UNDERCLASS

The rabble class is a product of many of our basic social processes. It is related to individualistic cultural values that promote estrangement. It is related to the continuing influx of nonwhite immigrants who are occupationally unprepared and vulnerable to discrimination based on strong racial prejudices. It is also related to the "suspended" social status of American youth. Young people are rarely admitted to adult social activities and institutions until they are in their twenties (for a thorough examination, see Matza, 1964). During this extended period of prohibition, they are freed from many adult responsibilities and offered a great deal of leisure time. But they do not spend this time passively, patiently waiting to be admitted to adult status. Instead, they invent their own social worlds. Some of these worlds are bizarre and deviant, and many of them, notably those in which drug use is prominent, recruit members into the rabble class.

Finally, the existence of the rabble class is related to persistent ("structural") unemployment among our least integrated citizens, especially among nonwhite minorities and black youth. . .

HOSTILITY TOWARD THE RABBLE CLASS

Negative attitudes toward the rabble are deeply embedded in the American social structure and its social processes. Historically, one primary source of the hostility is a generalized fear among conventional citizens that the rabble class collectively threatens the social order with riots, revolution, or at least corruption. Thus, at the end of the last century, when this fear was stronger, Charles Loring Brace (1880) could expect widespread agreement when he wrote: "Let the law lift its hand from [the dangerous classes] for a season, or let the civilizing influences of American life fail to reach them, and, if the opportunity offered, we should see an explosion from this class which might leave this city in ashes and blood" (p. 29). Although the fear of a revolution set off by the rabble class is no longer very strong, many people still believe that the rabble may occasionally explode into riot (as they did in the 1960s) and that they constantly assault the "moral fiber" of society.

Another source of hostility toward the rabble is the deep resentment that conforming individuals harbor toward deviants. In the late 1930s, in his book, *Moral Indignation and Middle-Class Psychology*, Svend Ranulf (1938) suggested that throughout modern history, middle-class persons, especially those from the lower middle class, have pursued the bourgeois virtues of frugality, hard work, and honesty at the expense of their expressive impulses so that they have endured unexciting and unsatisfactory lives. For this reason they have resented those who do not appear to be making the same sacrifices, and they have wanted to punish them for living a life of indulgence. This attitude, which has been described by American writers and artists for well over a century, remains part of our society's dominant culture. With considerable effort, most of us pursue conventional and usually materialistic goals, even though we suspect that they do little to change dull lives. Most of us are repulsed and frightened by the rabble, whom we see as indolent, dissolute, and immoral; and most of us, as Ranulf suggested, want to see them punished.

The appearance and behavior of the rabble, even when perfectly legal, threaten conventional citizens in a more fundamental and personal way. City dwellers manage to live among strangers by obeying the unspoken rules that govern almost every imaginable bit of public behavior. They put on a display of respectability that is composed of dress, speech, and gestures. When they do not recognize the same sort of display in others with whom they must mingle, they become nervous or even fearful because they cannot assume that things will run smoothly; their peace of mind, their dignity, even their lives may be in danger. . . . Members of the rabble incite fear and hostility in conventional people because the rabble regularly violate the rules of public life and display themselves in an outlandish, bizarre, repulsive, or threatening fashion.

Finally, America's perception of "the crime problem" draws hostile attention to the rabble. Many of the patterns listed above (individualism, competitiveness, consumerism, socioeconomic stratification), as well as our tolerance of successful but illegal monetary pursuits, have produced a very high crime rate in the United States. Statistically, rabble crime (or street crime, its rough equivalent) is only one of the problems; and most serious crimes—involving heavy property loss and physical harm or loss of life— are committed by "reputable" people from the middle and upper classes. Nevertheless, it is rabble crime that is most visible, inspires the most fear, and precipitates the most anger.

The police have been instructed by the public to do something about street crime. Because they have been unable to reduce it, no matter what they try, they have responded to the public mood by treating the rabble they arrest as if they were serious felons, though most of their crimes are petty. Some of them, moreover, receive prison terms—the full punishment intended for serious criminals.

WHY THE CAMPAIGN AGAINST THE RABBLE?

Even though the rabble are not responsible for a great deal of serious crime and even though they receive police attention more because of their disrepute than because of their crimes, the fact remains that they *are* bothersome, they *do* commit some crime, and they *do* inspire a great deal of fear among conventional citizens. Does this justify the longstanding campaign against them, even though the evidence suggests that it has had little impact on crime rates? Two students of the police, James Q. Wilson and George Kelling, conclude that it does; and their opinion should be noted since one of them, Wilson, has been a highly influential defender of conservative views on crime and police work (see esp. Wilson, 1975).

In an article about the use of foot patrols in a "dilapidated area in the heart of Newark," Wilson and Kelling (1982) admit that the return to this older police method, like other variations in police work, has little real impact on reducing crime. They claim, however, that it does serve to reduce fear by controlling disreputables: "We tend to overlook or forget another source of fear—fear of being bothered by disorderly people. Not violent people, nor, necessarily, criminals, but disreputable or obstreperous or unpredictable people: panhandlers, drunks, addicts, rowdy teenagers, prostitutes, loiterers, the mentally disturbed." Another benefit of the campaign against the rabble, they argue, is that it prevents neighborhoods from deteriorating. Tolerating the rabble is like neglecting broken windows (the title of their article), which leads to all the windows in a building being broken: "We suggest that 'untended' behavior also leads to the breakdown of community controls. A stable neighborhood of families who care for their homes, mind each other's children, and confidently frown on intruders can change, in a few years or *even* a few months, to an inhospitable and frightening jungle."

These justifications ignore several serious problems created by the campaign against the rabble. In the first place, it is undeniable that whim, prejudice, misunderstanding, and corruption influence the decisions about which forms of disreputable behavior and which disreputable persons should be controlled. Race, age, and social class—

factors independent of actual behavior—contribute significantly to the assignment of intolerable disrepute. For example, a group of noisy black teenagers on a street corner is much more likely to be perceived as threatening by white citizens and the police than a group of equally loud white teenagers. In a middle-class white neighborhood, a male stranger in scruffy work clothes is much more likely than a well-dressed man to be perceived as disreputable and possibly dangerous, even though one is an honest laborer walking to a garage-cleaning job, whereas the other is a swindler selling expensive but worthless house siding. Race often overrides all other visible qualities in the assignment of disrepute. Thus, a colleague of mine, a black professor at a major university, reports an incident in which he was walking at night down the sidewalk of an almost deserted business street in his college town when he saw a middle-aged white woman approaching. As they drew near, she looked at him and gasped: "Oh my God, is this it?"

The *Los Angeles Times* (1982a) documented how the police often treat respectable black males as disreputables:

There is a well-established rule of caution in the black community that says: If you are black, any contact with the police can unexpectedly become deadly. To Udell Carroll, what happened to him one night last February best illustrates that fear. Carroll, 36, an insurance salesman, pulled into the driveway of his home near 63rd Street and Crenshaw Boulevard after a brief ride through the neighborhood in search of his 16-year-old son. Carroll thought that the boy was out later than he should be; in fact, the boy was already home. Inside the three-bedroom house, family and friends were chatting amiably. His two youngest children were asleep in the back bedroom. As Carroll got out of the car [in front of his home], he noticed two policemen behind him. Suspecting he was a burglar, they had followed him. They ordered him to put his hands up. Carroll said he was confused but careful not to antagonize them. He said he raised his hands and then asked, "What's this all about?"

In the moments that followed, the scene turned violent. Carroll suffered a nasty head wound that required 18 stitches to close. Forced from the house, his family and friends stood shivering in the cold night air as police cars surrounded the house and a helicopter hovered overhead. The children watched in terror as white men in blue uniforms, guns drawn, dragged their father and their 16-year-old brother away in handcuffs. . . .

Roosevelt Dorn, now a Juvenile Court judge in Inglewood, said he was roughed up by two police officers who stopped him during a robbery investigation and did not take the time to ask him why he was carrying a gun. He was a deputy sheriff at the time.

Rep. Mervin Dymally (D–Los Angeles), then a state senator, said he was clubbed at a demonstration by a police officer who the congressman said refused to listen to his attempts to identify himself.

John Brewer, son of Deputy Chief Jesse Brewer, the highest ranking black in the Police Department, was forced to lie spread-eagle on the ground after a traffic stop.

Johnnie L. Cochran, Jr., then an assistant district attorney, said he was forced out of his car at gunpoint and ordered to put his hands above his head as his two crying children watched fearfully from the back seat. Cochran said the officers told him they stopped him because they believed the Rolls-Royce he was driving was stolen.

In reality, the police, who are given the task of actually controlling disreputables, consistently overextend the public's categories. This happens because the police tend to develop a simplistic view of society in which there are only good guys and "assholes" (or whatever is the currently fashionable police label for unworthy pariah). . . . The tendency to develop hate for increasingly broader categories of people will usually prevail unless it is checked by special processes that are not inherent in police work. In fact, the tendency is promoted when police are encouraged to control categories of disreputables.

Another serious problem with the campaign against the rabble and other disreputables is that it fails. . . . The deviance and petty crime (and even serious crime) that abound in certain neighborhoods are uncontrollable by any police campaign short of a Vietnam-style war effort. Knowledgeable and honest policemen admit this. Police Lieutenant Ron Flict tried for several years to rid Hollywood, California, of prostitution, an effort in which he used decoys, foot patrols, horse patrols, and even bicycle patrols. He remarked that prostitution is "like a water balloon. You squeeze it in one place and it squeezes out between your fingers somewhere else" (*Los Angeles Times*, 1982b)...

In fact, the campaign against the rabble not only fails, it makes matters worse. Focusing on disrepute blurs the distinction between actual crime and what is merely bothersome or offensive. Although some disreputables do pose a real threat to persons and property, their threat is usually not a serious one. For the most part, they steal or hustle small amounts of money or property, and they rarely inflict serious bodily harm (occasionally a purse-snatching or mugging does result in more serious injury). Wilson and Kelling argue that the skilled foot patrolman makes intelligent distinctions and keeps the merely bothersome or repulsive behavior within acceptable limits and scares off or arrests the persons who are real threats. My study has convinced me otherwise. Police officers consistently overextend the disreputable categories, and they gather up many persons who are merely bothersome or offensive and subject them to the harsh and alienating experiences of arrest, booking, and jail.

Finally, the campaign against the rabble is a political diversion. The public is deeply threatened by serious crime, mildly threatened by petty crime, and bothered by the rabble. The police cannot find many serious criminals, so they go after petty criminals and disreputables. Actually, the campaign against petty criminals and disreputables is a second-order diversion; to a great extent, the public fears petty crime because the mass media and politicians have systematically diverted attention away from our most serious crime problems. The "street crimes" that the public fears, in part because they are so heavily publicized—mainly stranger-to-stranger homicides, rapes and assaults,

robberies and burglaries—are not by any objective measure the country's most serious crimes. In recent decades criminologists have begun to discover that the most serious crimes, measured by loss of money and loss of life, are committed by reputable people whose actions are not usually scrutinized by policing agencies; these people are rarely prosecuted, and they almost never go to jail.

Reputable people also commit crimes or intentional acts that kill and injure many more people than street crime ever touches. In 1984 there were about 20,000 "traditional" murders in the United States. In the majority of these, the murderer was a friend, spouse, or acquaintance of the victim and was acting in a state of anger or rage. There were less than 8,000 occurrences of murder by a disreputable stranger. Physicians and drug companies are culpable for a much larger share of the nation's deaths than traditional murderers. Physicians continue to dispense drugs that have limited efficacy and present substantial risks to patients, and they recommend and perform surgeries that are unnecessary and result in a high death toll.* We ought to remember, when we think of crime, that more than 100,000 workers die every year from industrial diseases (not to mention industrial accidents, which claim another 15,000 lives). These deaths are not the unavoidable result of occupational risks; they are the result of intentional actions taken by reputable people. Several studies have shown that when medical researchers first identify an occupational disease, such as byssinosis (brown lung) or asbestosis, the industries involved invariably attempt to deny or suppress evidence related to the existence of the disease, its seriousness, or its link with the industry. When the evidence can no longer be denied, the industry successfully lobbies to manipu-

---

*In 1975 Dr. Sidney Wolfe, speaking before the House Commerce Oversight and Investigations Subcommittee, estimated that there were 3.2 million unnecessary surgeries performed each year, which resulted in 16,000 deaths; see *Washington Post*, July 16, 1975, p. A-3.

late the applicable laws or regulations so that it will have to make only minimal changes in its operations—even when there is substantial evidence that those modified operations will continue to result in substantial injury and loss of life. Finally, many industries persistently violate even the lenient laws and standards they have insisted upon, and then they cover up their violations (See Broeder, 1974; Page & O'Brien, 1973; Scott, 1974).

The most serious corporate crime, however, is turning out to be the pollution of water, land, and air with toxic chemicals. Gilbert Geis (1973), who for years has tried to shift the attention of criminologists and the public to "white-collar crime," wrote:

The efflux from motor vehicles, plants, and incinerators of sulfur oxides, hydrocarbons, carbon monoxide, oxides of nitrogen, particulates, and many more contaminants amounts to compulsory consumption of violence by most Americans. . . . This damage, perpetuated increasingly in direct violation of local, state, and federal law, shatters people's health and safety but still escapes inclusion in the crime statistics. "Smogging" a city or town has taken on the proportions of a massive crime wave, yet federal and state statistical compilations of crime pay attention to "muggers" and ignore "smoggers."

The data on white-collar crimes are not collected, categorized, tallied up in neat columns, and published in annual national reports such as the FBI's *Uniform Crime Reports*, which features frightening news about street crime. The deaths and injuries caused by law-breaking acts of respectable people—and by acts that *would* be crimes if other than powerful people committed them—are far more numerous than those caused by street crime, and many are just as gruesome. Yet the general public remains convinced that street crime is the greater threat. To a great extent, this public attitude is the creation of the mass media and opportunistic politicians. They have exaggerated its extent, decried the leniency of judges and courts toward it, and offered simplistic solutions. They have intentionally chosen to divert the attention of citizens

away from other social problems, such as unemployment, inflation, the energy crisis, the proliferation of atomic weapons, war in Central America, and crime committed by so-called reputable people. The reason for the diversion is that an increase in public awareness and understanding of these other problems might lead to ameliorative policies that require some suffering or sacrifice on the part of these reputable people. Street crime, on the other hand, is a safe issue. No powerful constituency is directly damaged by a campaign against it, even a campaign that drastically escalates penalties and the number of disreputables receiving them.

If the public has been systematically deluded on the issue of crime, as I contend it has, one may still ask, what is the harm in that? Couldn't it be true, as Wilson and Kelling argue, that the symbolic benefits outweigh the harm done? In other words, though crime and disrepute are not reduced by the ineffectual efforts of the police (and in fact are probably increased by them), isn't it good that the public is made to *feel* better by seeing the police patrolling neighborhoods and "rousting" undesirables, by hearing the media report on stiff sentences delivered to persons convicted of serious crimes, by witnessing the enactment of new punitive anticrime laws, and even by reading of the occasional execution of a murderer?

I would argue that it is not. These symbolic benefits are more than canceled out every time anger toward street crime is whipped up in support of another public policy "solution" that fails to solve anything. When nothing seems to reduce street crime and all the other distasteful and threatening forms of deviance—drug use, dereliction, prostitution, and petty property crime—a deep frustration is created in the public.

CONCLUSIONS

I believe that we are ready for an honest policy on crime control that goes beyond the criminal law and takes account of the following propositions:

1. Crime in America is not a pathological aberration of the American way, practiced only by a special category of people called criminals. It is widely and somewhat evenly spread throughout all social classes and is deeply rooted in basic American values and relationships.
2. The most serious crimes—the ones that cause great loss of money, personal injury or death, and the corruption of society's morals and political processes—are committed by reputable people.
3. Publicizing street crime committed by disreputable persons as the major crime problem in society is counterproductive in several ways:
   a) It encourages crime control policies that continually fail, and this failure creates a pervasive anger and frustration in society.
   b) It allows most serious crime to go unattended.
   c) It may even increase street crime because the disproportionately harsh treatment given to those who commit it tends to embitter and alienate them and to perpetuate the existence of a rabble class.

We can also begin to deal more effectively with crime and deviance and thereby indirectly influence jail policy by pursuing a new agenda:

1. We should concentrate police and penal attention on serious crime, which requires opening up the debate on what we want that term to mean.
2. In the short run, we should learn to tolerate a large number of the rabble.
3. We should work to reestablish informal, extralegal systems for controlling repulsive public deviance, particularly by taking measures that will foster a new sense of community among strangers.
4. In the long run, we should work to alter our basic values. Excessive materialism and individualism, for example, not only weaken and corrupt our personal relationships; they also help maintain a radically unequal distribution of wealth, opportunity, and prestige, which in turn produces high rates of crime and many forms of repulsive public deviance.

Progress on this agenda, if it occurs at all, will necessarily be slow. Reforming sluggish processes and static structures, particularly in the economic realm, is the work of decades, generations, even centuries. But that should not deter us, because no progress at all can be made on reforming the jail until we begin to reform our fundamental social arrangements. Until we do, the police will continue to sweep the streets of the rabble and dump them in the jails. By casting a broad net, they will snare a few disreputable persons whose crimes are serious, and these few will be punished severely. Crime rates will not be affected by these efforts; they will continue to rise and fall as they always have in response to changes in broader social arrangements. And the rabble will continue to suffer our harshest form of imprisonment, the jail—an experience that confirms their status and replenishes their ranks.

REFERENCES

Brace, C. L. (1880). *The dangerous classes of New York and twenty years' work among them* (p. 29). New York: Wynkoop and Hallenbeck.

Brodeur, P. (1974). *Expendable Americans.* New York: Viking Press.

Geis, G. (1973). Deterring corporate crime. In R. Nader and M. J. Green (Eds.), *Corporate power in America* (pp. 182–197). New York: Grossman.

Goldfarb, R. (1975). *Jails: The ultimate ghetto of the criminal justice system* (p. 448). New York: Doubleday.

Los Angeles Times. (1982a, August 27), pt. 1, pp. 1, 3.

Los Angeles Times. (1982b, August 21), pt. 2, p 1.

Matza, D. (1964). Position and behavior patterns of youth. In R. E. Faris (Ed.), *Handbook of modern sociology* (pp. 191–216).

Page, J., & O'Brien, M. W. (1973). *Bitter wages.* New York: Grossman.

Ranulf, S. (1938). *Moral indignation and middle-class psychology* (pp. 41–46). Copenhagen: Leven and Munksgaard.

Scott, R. (1974). *Muscle and blood.* New York: E. P. Dutton.

Wilson, J. Q. (1975). *Thinking about crime.* New York: Random House.

Wilson, J. Q., & Kelling, G. (1982, March). Broken windows. *Atlantic Monthly*, pp. 29–30.

34

The Pathology of Imprisonment
Philip G. Zimbardo

I was recently released from solitary confinement after being held therein for 37 months [months!]. A silent system was imposed upon me and to even whisper to the man in the next cell resulted in being beaten by guards, sprayed with chemical mace, blackjacked, stomped and thrown into a strip-cell naked to sleep on a concrete floor without bedding, covering, wash basin or even a toilet. The floor served as toilet and bed, and even there the silent system was enforced. To let a moan escape your lips because of the pain and discomfort . . . resulted in another beating. I spent not days, but months there during my 37 months in solitary. . . . I have filed every writ possible against the administrative acts of brutality. The state courts have all denied the petitions. Because of my refusal to let the things die down and forget all that happened during my 37 months in solitary . . . I am the most hated prisoner in [this] penitentiary, and called a "hard-core incorrigible."

Maybe I am an incorrigible, but if true, it's because I would rather die than to accept being treated as less than a human being. I have never complained of my prison sentence as being unjustified except through legal means of appeals. I have never put a knife on a guard's throat and demanded my release. I know that thieves must be punished and I don't justify stealing, even though I am a thief myself. But now I don't think I will be a thief when I am released. No, I'm not rehabilitated. It's just that I no longer think of becoming wealthy by stealing. I now only think of kiling—killing those who have beaten me and treated me as if I were a dog. I hope and pray for the sake of my own soul and future life of freedom that I am able to overcome the bitterness and hatred which eats daily at my soul, but I know to overcome it will not be easy.

This eloquent plea for prison reform—for humane treatment of human beings, for the basic dignity that is the right of every American—came to me secretly in a letter from a prisoner who cannot be identified because he is still in a state correctional institution. He sent it to me because he read of an experiment I recently conducted at Stanford University. In an attempt to understand just what it means psychologically to be a prisoner or a prison guard, Craig Haney, Curt Banks, Dave Jaffe, and I created our own prison. We carefully screened over 70 volunteers who answered an ad in a Palo Alto city newspaper and ended up with about two dozen young men who were selected to be part of this study. They were mature, emotionally stable, normal, intelligent college students from middle-class homes throughout the United States and Canada. They appeared to represent the cream of the crop of this generation. None had any criminal record and all were relatively homogeneous on many dimensions initially.

Half were arbitrarily designated as prisoners by a flip of a coin, the others as guards. These were the roles they were to play in our simulated prison. The guards were made aware of the potential seriousness and danger of the situation and their own vulnerability. They made up their own formal rules for maintaining law, order and respect, and were generally free to improvise new ones during their eight-hour, three-man shifts. The prisoners were unexpectedly picked up at their homes by a city policeman in a squad car, searched, handcuffed, fingerprinted, booked at the Palo Alto station house and taken blindfolded to our jail. There they were stripped, deloused, put into a uniform, given a number and put into a cell with two other prisoners where they expected to live for the next two weeks. The pay was good ($15 a day) and their motivation was to make money.

We observed and recorded on videotape the events that occurred in the prison, and we interviewed and tested the prisoners and guards at various points throughout the study. Some of the videotapes of the actual encounters between the prisoners and guards were seen on the NBC News feature "Chronolog" on November 26, 1971.

At the end of only six days we had to close down our mock prison because what we saw was frightening. It was no longer apparent to most of the subjects (or to us) where reality ended and their roles began. The majority had indeed become prisoners or guards, no longer able to clearly differentiate between role playing and self. There were dramatic changes in virtually every aspect of their behavior, thinking, and feeling. In less than a week the experience of imprisonment undid (temporarily) a lifetime of learning; human values were suspended, self-concepts were challenged, and the ugliest, most base, pathological side of human nature surfaced. We were horrified because we saw some boys (guards) treat others as if they were despicable animals, taking pleasure in cruelty, while other boys (prisoners) became servile, dehumanized robots who thought only of escape, of their own individual survival, and of their mounting hatred for the guards.

We had to release three prisoners in the first four days because they had such acute situational traumatic reactions as hysterical crying, confusion in thinking and severe depression. Others begged to be paroled, and all but three were willing to forfeit all the money they had earned if they could be paroled. By then (the fifth day) they had been so programmed to think of themselves as prisoners that when their request for parole was denied, they returned docilely to their cells. Now, had they been thinking as college students acting in an oppressive experiment, they would have quit once they no longer wanted the $15 a day we used as our only incentive. However, the reality was not quitting an experiment but "being paroled by the parole board from the Stanford County Jail." By the last days, the earlier solidarity among the prisoners (systematically broken by the guards) dissolved into "each man for himself." Finally, when one of their fellows was put in solitary confinement (a small closet) for refusing to eat, the prisoners were given a choice by one of the guards: give up their blankets and the incorrigible prisoner would be let out, or keep their blankets and he would be kept in all night. They voted to keep their blankets and to abandon their brother.

About a third of the guards became tyrannical in their arbitrary use of power, in enjoying their control over other people. They were corrupted by the power of their roles and became quite inventive in their techniques of breaking the spirit of the prisoners and making them feel they were worthless. Some of the guards merely did their jobs as tough but fair correctional officers, and several were good guards from the prisoners' point of view since they did them small favors and were friendly. However, no good guard ever interfered with a command by any of the bad guards; they never intervened on the side of the prisoners, they never told the others to ease off because it was only an experiment, and they never even came to me as prison superintendent or experimenter in charge to complain. In part, they were good because the others were bad; they needed the others to help establish their own egos in a positive light. In a sense, the good guards perpetuated the prison more than the other guards because their own needs to be liked prevented them from disobeying or violating the implicit guards' code. At the same time, the act of befriending the prisoners created a social reality which made the prisoners less likely to rebel.

By the end of the week the experiment had become a reality, as if it were a Pirandello play directed by Kafka that just keeps going after the audience has left. The consultant for our prison, Carlo Prescott, an ex-convict with 16 years of imprisonment in California's jails, would get so depressed and furious each time he visited our prison, because of its psychological similarity to his experiences, that he would have to leave. A Catholic priest who was a former prison chaplain in Washington, D.C., talked to our prisoners after four days and said they were just like the other first-timers he had seen.

But in the end, I called off the experiment not because of the horror I saw out there in the prison yard, but because of the horror of realizing that *I* could have easily traded places with the most brutal guard or become the weakest prisoner full of hatred

at being so powerless that I could not eat, sleep, or go to the toilet without permission of the authorities. *I* could have become Calley at My Lai, George Jackson at San Quentin, one of the men at Attica, or the prisoner quoted at the beginning of this article.

Individual behavior is largely under the control of social forces and environmental contingencies rather than personality traits, character, will power or other empirically unvalidated constructs. Thus we create an illusion of freedom by attributing more internal control to ourselves, to the individual, than actually exists. We thus underestimate the power and pervasiveness of situational controls over behavior because: (a) they are often nonobvious and subtle, (b) we can often avoid entering situations where we might be so controlled, (c) we label as "weak" or "deviant" people in those situations who do behave differently from how we believed we would.

Each of us carries around in our heads a favorable self-image in which we are essentially just, fair, humane, and understanding. For example, we could not imagine inflicting pain on others without much provocation or hurting people who had done nothing to us, who in fact were even liked by us. However, there is a growing body of social psychological research which underscores the conclusion derived from this prison study. Many people, perhaps the majority, can be made to do almost anything when put into psychologically compelling situations—regardless of their morals, ethics, values, attitudes, beliefs, or personal convictions. My colleague, Stanley Milgram, has shown that more than 60 percent of the population will deliver what they think is a series of painful electric shocks to another person even after the victim cries for mercy, begs them to stop, and then apparently passes out. The subjects complained that they did not want to inflict more pain but blindly obeyed the command of the authority figure (the experimenter) who said that they must go on. In my own research on violence, I have seen mild-mannered co-eds repeatedly give shocks (which they thought were causing pain) to another girl, a stranger whom they had rated very favorably, simply by being made to feel anonymous and put in a situation where they were expected to engage in this activity.

Observers of these and similar experimental situations never predict their outcomes and estimate that it is unlikely that they themselves would behave similarly. They can be so confident only when they were outside the situation. However, since the majority of people in these studies do act in nonrational, nonobvious ways, it follows that the majority of observers would also succumb to the social psychological forces in the situation.

With regard to prisons, we can state that the mere act of assigning labels to people and putting them into a situation where those labels acquire validity and meaning is sufficient to elicit pathological behavior. This pathology is not predictable from any available diagnostic indicators we have in the social sciences, and is extreme enough to modify in very significant ways fundamental attitudes and behavior. The prison situation, as presently arranged, is guaranteed to generate severe enough pathological reactions in both guards and prisoners as to debase their humanity, lower their feelings of self-worth, and make it difficult for them to be part of a society outside of their prison.

For years our national leaders have been pointing to the enemies of freedom, to the fascist or communist threat to the American way of life. In so doing they have overlooked the threat of social anarchy that is building within our own country without any outside agitation. As soon as a person comes to the realization that he is being imprisoned by his society or individuals in it, then, in the best American tradition, he demands liberty and rebels, accepting death as an alternative. The third alternative, however, is to allow oneself to become a good prisoner—docile, cooperative, uncomplaining, conforming in thought and complying in deed.

Our prison authorities now point to the militant agitators who are still vaguely referred to as part of some communist plot, as the irresponsible, incorrigible troublemakers. They imply that there would be no trouble, riots, hostages, or deaths if it weren't for this small band of bad prisoners. In other words, then, everything would return to "normal" again in the life of our nation's prisons if they could break these men.

The riots in prison are coming from within—from within every man and woman who refuses to let the system turn them into an object, a number, a thing, or a no-thing. It is not communist-inspired, but inspired by the spirit of American freedom. No man wants to be enslaved. To be powerless, to be subject to the arbitrary exercise of power, to not be recognized as a human being is to be a slave.

To be a militant prisoner is to become aware that the physical jails are but more blatant extensions of the forms of social and psychological oppression experienced daily in the nation's ghettos. They are trying to awaken the conscience of the nation to the ways in which the American ideals are being perverted, apparently in the name of justice but actually under the banner of apathy, fear, and hatred. If we do not listen to the pleas of the prisoners at Attica to be treated like human beings, then we have all become brutalized by our priorities for property rights over human rights. The consequence will not only be more prison riots, but a loss of all those ideals on which this country was founded.

The public should be aware that they own the prisons and that their business is failing. The 70 percent recidivism rate and the escalation in severity of crimes committed by graduates of our prisons are evidence that current prisons fail to rehabilitate the inmates in any positive way. Rather, they are breeding grounds for hatred of the establishment, a hatred that makes every citizen a target of violent assault. Prisons are a bad investment for us taxpayers. Until now we have not cared; we have turned over to wardens and prison authorities the unpleasant job of keeping people who threaten us out of our sight. Now we are shocked to learn that their management practices have failed to improve the product and instead turn petty thieves into murderers. We must insist upon new management or improved operating procedures.

The cloak of secrecy should be removed from the prisons. Prisoners claim they are brutalized by the guards, guards say it is a lie. Where is the impartial test of the truth in such a situation? Prison officials have forgotten that they work for us, that they are only public servants whose salaries are paid by our taxes. They act as if it is their prison, like a child with a toy he won't share. Neither lawyers, judges, the legislature, nor the public is allowed into prisons to ascertain the truth unless the visit is sanctioned by authorities and until all is prepared for their visit. I was shocked to learn that my request to join a congressional investigating committee's tour of San Quentin and Soledad was refused, as was that of the news media.

There should be an ombudsman in every prison, not under the pay or control of the prison authority, and responsible only to the courts, the state legislature, and the public. Such a person could report on violations of constitutional and human rights.

Guards must be given better training than they now receive for the difficult job society imposes upon them. To be a prison guard as now constituted is to be put in a situation of constant threat from within the prison, with no social recognition from the society at large. As was shown graphically at Attica, prison guards are also prisoners of the system who can be sacrificed to the demands of the public to be punitive and the needs of politicans to preserve an image. Social scientists and business administrators should be called upon to design and help carry out this training.

The relationship between the individual (who is sentenced by the courts to a prison term) and his community must be maintained. How can a prisoner return to a dynamically changing society that most of us cannot cope with after being out of it for a number of years? There should be more community involvement in these rehabilitation centers, more ties encouraged and promoted between the trainees and family and friends, more educational opportunities to prepare them for returning to their communities as more valuable members of it than they were before they left.

Finally, the main ingredient necessary to effect any change at all in prison reform, in the rehabilitation of a single prisoner or even in the optimal development of a child is caring. Reform must start with people—especially people with power—caring about the well-being of others. Underneath the toughest, society-hating convict, rebel, or anarchist is a human being who wants his existence to be recognized by his fellows and who wants someone else to care about whether he lives or dies and to grieve if he lives imprisoned rather than lives free.

PART VI

SOCIAL INSTITUTIONS

American social institutions, rapidly changing, have come under severe criticism from every side. As we cover in this part of the book, the medical institution presents a serious concern for many. Not only is improper treatment a major problem, so that many who are treated by physicians incur complications from that treatment, but others cannot even afford medical care. Similarly, education has severe problems, perhaps most poignantly indicated by armed guards patrolling our urban schools to prevent violence, and the graduation of illiterates from high schools that have retained but not taught them.

In this introduction, I shall concentrate on the American family, for it is an intricate part of the change occurring in our other social institutions and is itself undergoing fundamental change and painful adjustment. As the basic social institution (or the basic building block of society), the family always feels changes that occur in other parts of society.

Perhaps *the* fundamental change affecting today's family is the employment of women outside the home. This trend began with industrialization in the 1800s and, with the coming of World War II, gained quick momentum as large numbers of women did factory work to support the war effort. When the men returned from war, however, the day care centers—considered to be temporary, emergency measures—were shut down, and most women returned to the home.

What is new today is the extent of the change: For the first time in history, the number of married women who work for wages at least part-time outside the home is greater than the number who do not work outside the home. This change, in turn, has reinforced trends in divorce, reduced an already low birth rate, and led to complications in raising children, something that some think is *the* social problem of today's family. Although the movement of wives and mothers from the home is part of a gradual historical trend, it is so fundamental—forcing change in all family relationships—that it is sometimes called the "quiet revolution."

It is important to note that it is not simply the contemporary family that is changing. Our historical vision is usually much too limited, and we should see our current changes as adaptations by the family to both large-scale social events set in motion hundreds of years ago and current events of perhaps smaller magnitude. In one way or another, the family is always in transition, continuously reacting to changes in others parts of society. Not an independent unit, the family is forced to adapt for its very survival. Change in the economic sphere especially produces change in the family, for the family must provide for the economic well-being of its members.

The social changes to which the family has been forced to react have created "dislocations," severe problems for the family, indicating that its adjustments are far from complete. What are the problems facing the contemporary family, or, as some would phrase it, indications that the family is in trouble? I shall list ten:

1. For about every two couples happily married, another couple is not so happily having their marriage declared null and void.
2. While divorce may solve a problem for some adults, it disrupts the lives of over one million children each year (*Statistical Abstract*, 1988a). And that is in addition to what we can't put numbers on—the bitterness and rancor experienced by the million plus couples whose relationship has been fractured.
3. Somewhere between 300,000 and one million children run away from home each year, fleeing intolerable situations—incest, beatings, indifference, and other debilitating family conditions. Perhaps one in four has not so much run away as been shoved out by parents who no longer want them.
4. It is not uncommon for runaways and "pushouts" to wind up in prostitution. As Father Bruce Ritter, who founded shelters for runaways across the country, has noted: "Their alternative to starvation is to steal or to turn to the only thing they have—their bodies. Most get involved in prostituton and pornography when they tire of sleeping in doorways, have no money and no place to go."
5. Our overall rate of *illegitimacy*, births to unmarried women, doubled between 1940 and 1950 (perilous years, with wrenching mobilization for World War II and painful readjustment to peacetime), but by 1980 it had doubled again. Currently, our overall illegitimacy rate is almost *five times* what it was in 1940. This translates to *more than 800,000 babies* being born to unmarried women each year. Of all the children born in the United States, more than one of every five (22 percent) is now born to an unmarried woman. Illegitimacy has become so widespread today that by the age of 20, about one of every 10 unmarried American women has given birth to a child.
6. Poverty is closely related to single-parent families, which divorce and illegitimacy are creating by the millions. Children in single-parent families are more likely to give birth out of wedlock, to drop out of school, to become delinquent, and to end up on welfare.

7. Family violence is another indication that all is not well with the American family. In all, about 6 or 7 million children are harmed by parents or other family members, while in any 12-month period, in 1 of every 6 marriages a husband or wife is physically violent to his or her spouse (Straus & Gelles, 1988).

8. In the last two decades, the number of cohabiting couples has been on an unbroken line of increase, going from a half million in 1970 to two and a half million in 1987. Cohabitation has become so common that when hiring new executives, some corporations now pay for live-in partners to attend orientation sessions and also take them on house-hunting trips (*Wall Street Journal*, 1989).

9. *Incest,* forbidden sexual relations between siblings or with one's own children, is not uncommon. Sociologist Diana Russell (1986) interviewed a probability sample (from which one can generalize) of 930 women in San Francisco and found that before they turned 18, 16 percent had been victims of incest. Her definition was very broad, including any relative and not only sexual intercourse, but any unwanted sexual act from kissing to fondling of breasts, anus, or genitals. The police were informed in only 5 of 100 of these cases, which means official figures represent only a small fraction of the incest that actually occurs.

10. Finally, marital rape is much, much more common than most people realize. Sociologists David Finkelhor and Kersti Yllo (1989) found that 10 percent of 330 women in a representative sample of the Boston metropolitan area reported their husbands had used physical force to compel them to have sex. Based on a sampling technique that allows generalization, sociologist Diana E. Russell (1980) estimates that 12 percent of married women have been raped by their husbands. If these percentages come even close to the American population in general, we are talking about millions of married women who have suffered this form of sexual abuse.

It is important to note also that, rather than being isolated, family problems are likely to come as a bundle wrapped in the same package: Abuse of children, for example, is more likely to occur in families suffering from poverty and in those headed by only one parent (*Statistical Abstract*, 1988b). Similarly, juvenile deliquency is higher among children from broken homes, as are drug abuse and illegitimacy. In turn, children raised by one parent are more likely themselves to divorce than are children who are raised by both parents.

Others would include many other items to this list of trouble spots. Some observers would add that young people are postponing their first marriage, concluding that this is another sign that marriage and family are in trouble. There is no doubt that the postponement is true: Since 1950, the median age at first marriage has increased year by year. At 24.8 for males and 23.0 for females, males are now marrying for the first time two years later than in 1950, and females almost three years later (*Statistical Abstract*, 1989). For females, this is the highest average age at first marriage in over a century. In fact, it may be the highest in our history.

There is a question, however, about the interpretation of this change. Is it a further sign that the family is in trouble, that young people are so discouraged about the prospects of marriage that they now wait longer to get their courage up? Or is this, perhaps, merely a reflection of other changes in society, and a healthy one at that? I see no reason to conclude that it is a sign of trouble. Both young and old people are still eager to marry, as indicated by the rapid rate at which most divorced people rush back into marriage. Rather, I look at this change as due not to a desire to avoid marriage but to broader social changes: the lengthening of time young people spend in school and in preparing for careers, the uncertainty of the economy, stagnating wages in terms of inflation-adjusted dollars, spiraling costs of housing, and the freer availability of sexual relations outside marriage, including cohabitation. I believe another significant factor is also at work: an upgraded standard of living that has changed an entire generation's material expectations. This includes stronger desires to drive better cars, to travel more, to wear more expensive clothing, and to possess better furniture and better housing *before* one marries.

This postponement of age at first marriage can very well have far-reaching, healthy consequences for the family. I am convinced that most people marrying for the first time today have a lot going for them. On average, before they marry, young men and women have had two or three more years of dating experience than did their parents and grandparents. They have also gone farther in school and have more work experience. Consequently, they should be more certain of their goals in life. In addition, with this broadened background and having their first child at a later age, they should be more mature parents. A long-range, possible consequence of these shifting backgrounds due to being older at first marriage is that marriages may become more stable, for such persons should be less likely to divorce.

Although time will tell if this prediction comes about, it should be apparent that not all changes in the family are for the worse. It is *not* that marriage and family are about to fall apart. There are even strong indications that some aspects of marital life have improved dramatically. For example, husbands and wives talk things over much more today than they did a generation or so ago. Consequently, as they seem to be meeting deeper needs better, husbands and wives report *greater* satisfaction with marriage today than they did in the 1920s (Caplow et al., 1982).

In other words, it is difficult to paint American social institutions with a broad brush stroke. While some parts of a social institution may be doing poorly, and getting worse, other parts may be doing well, and even improving. While many families function well, for example, others fail to meet even the basic needs of their members. And, as in the example of American families, so it is with our other social institutions: It is always the poor who are hit the hardest with social problems.

REFERENCES

Caplow, T., Bahr, H. M., Chadwick, B. A., Hill, R., & Williamson, M. H. (1982). *Middletown families: Fifty years of change and continuity.* Minneapolis: University of Minnesota Press.

Finkelhor, D., & Yllo K. (1989). Marital rape: The myth versus the reality. In J. M. Henslin (Ed.), *Marriage and family in a changing society,* 3d ed. (pp. 382–391). New York: Free Press.

Russell, D. E. H. (1980). *Rape in marriage: A case against legalized crime.* Paper presented at the annual meeting of the American Society of Criminology.

Russell, D. E. H. (1986). *The secret trauma: Incest in the lives of girls and women.* New York: Basic Books.

Statistical Abstract of the United States. (1988a). Table 126. Washington, DC: U.S. Government Printing Office, 1988.

Statistical Abstract of the United States. (1988b). Table 277. Washington, DC: U.S. Government Printing Office.

Statistical Abstract of the United States. (1989). Table 130. Washington, DC: U.S. Government Printing Office.

Straus, M. A., & Gelles, R. J. (1988). Violence in American families: How much is there and why does it occur? In E. W. Nunnally, C. S. Chilman, & F. M. Cox (Eds.), *Troubled relationships* (pp. 141–162). Newbury Park: Sage.

The Wall Street Journal. (1989, January 11), p. B1.

35

Pregnancy as a Rite of Passage

Eileen White Read

A tiny, timid 15-year-old girl traipses into the health clinic here at Jordan High School and complains of dizziness. The staff soon discovers that she is four months pregnant.

A counselor, Hazel Black, makes the difficult phone call to the girl's mother. Then, she takes the teenager into a private room, closes the door and, in exasperated tones, tells her: "No, wonder your mother is hysterical; you've already had one baby for her to raise. Now, you're giving her another."

Fighting illegitimacy is a major problem in the ghetto. Teenage pregnancy—once taboo—has become a rite of passage for many children of the poor. "Back in the '60s, babies were mistakes. Now, if you haven't had a kid by the age of 18, [they think] there's something wrong with you," says Lannie Foster, a teacher and administrator at Jordan High for 22 years.

MAJOR IMPLICATIONS

The issue, although often cast in moral terms, is wider. Teenage motherhood hobbles social and economic advancement for the largely black and Hispanic population of poor neighborhoods. Generations of women have lost opportunities for education and work because of their own out-of-wedlock children and then their children's children.

Unwed black teenagers are nearly five times more likely to have a baby than are white teenagers, despite a slight overall decline in teenage births recently. About 80% of the black children of Watts, the Los Angeles ghetto seared by riots in 1965, are born out of wedlock. Many junior-high-school students here have babies. And at Jordan High, in the heart of this south-central Los Angeles community, the birth rate is stunning: One-fourth of the school's 1,000 girls have babies each year.

The problem of teenage pregnancy is national, and it is being addressed by organizations ranging from the NAACP to many churches to the White House. But it is schools that are on the front lines. The Los Angeles school board, searching for solutions, recently opened a free clinic at Jordan High. There's little talk of abstinence, although staffers say they favor it, and sex is treated forthrightly. The clinic both teaches students who are confused about sexual facts and counsels those who are knowledgeable but don't care. A team of counselors, including students acting as "peer" counselors, meets regularly with the most at-risk students to convince them that parenthood doesn't solve problems. Sexually experienced teenagers are urged to use birth control.

MORE FACILITIES PLANNED

Educators in many cities are taking this tack. There are about 120 such facilities; dozens more are planned. The Robert Wood Johnson Foundation, based in Princeton, New Jersey, has aided more than 40 clinics, including Jordan High's.

The clinics have sparked debate despite growing indications that they work. Roman Catholic clergymen object to distribution of birth-control devices and argue that the clinics encourage promiscuity. Church-related anti-abortion groups have picketed the facilities, deriding "contraceptives between classes." On the Jordan High clinic's opening day last September several dozen pickets paraded before television cameras in protest. Since then, they have been back to pressure the school board to close the facility.

Reacting to the emotional debate, the Jordan High clinic offers a variety of services. A clinic handbill advertises 11 of them, listing pregnancy tests and contraception ninth, well below things like dental care and treatment of minor diseases.

CLEAR PRIORITY

But the school board's priority is to bring down birth rates. Just down the hall from the principal's office, the suite of white-walled rooms, with their examining tables and detailed anatomical posters, is close to the clanging of students' lockers and the classrooms. Among cabinets of medical paraphernalia, aspirin, and unguents, counselors and other health professionals dispense birth-control pills, diaphragms, and condoms to children, many of whom aren't old enough to drive.

At a big wooden counter in the waiting room, an assistant—one of almost a dozen staffers—set up appointments. Students jostle with one another between classes and at lunch time. Parental permission is required to use the clinic, although parents rarely object.

Clinic staffers decline to disclose statistics, fearing that the numbers will help opponents. But after five months, the clinic is believed to be serving more than a third of Jordan's students—three times the number expected by this time.

A 16-year-old dressed in skin-tight jeans slips into the clinic on her first visit. Jeffrey Thompson, the physician's assistant, ushers her into an examination room for a physical. Shy at first, the girl slowly admits that she plans to sleep with her 23-year-old boyfriend and wants birth-control pills. When the physical is over, the girl must sit through a counselor's half-hour explanation of how the body's reproductive system—and the pill—works. The counselor gives her a month's supply of pills and an appointment for a follow-up visit.

Girls using the clinic outnumber boys and more often ask directly for contraception. Many boys visit for an athletic physical, not contraception, and, Mr. Thompson says, "I always have to bring it up." Few want condoms for birth control; so he urges their use to prevent acquired immune deficiency syndrome and gonorrhea. (No one has tested positive for the AIDS virus yet, but Jordan has one of the highest gonorrhea rates in the city's schools.)

The atmosphere here is friendly but direct, as the 15-year-old pregnant with her second baby discovers. Mrs. Black, the counselor, begins explaining various birth-control methods with the aid of plastic anatomical models and sample contraceptives. By school-district policy, any mention of abortion is taboo.

It's too late this time for this student, and Mrs. Black—suspecting a motive behind the second pregnancy—adds a stern admonition: "Don't think this boy is going to marry you—your first baby's father didn't." Then she softens it with a folksy recollection of teaching her own son about birth control when he was a teen-ager.

The teary-eyed girl says little and stares at the door; outside it, her boyfriend sits in the waiting room. In the hallway beyond, the shouts of students changing classes reverberate, reminding Mrs. Black that this soon-to-be mother of two needs an excuse to give her teacher for missing a class.

UNCONCERNED ATTITUDE

Shortly before the clinic opened, school officials took a survey and found that nearly two-thirds of the students who said they were sexually active had never used birth control. One, a 17-year-old with orange hair spiked upward like a crown and heavy eye makeup, contends, "Raising a baby isn't hard; with my baby, I don't need nobody else." She and her 16-year-old sister have three babies between them.

Bowing to reality, school officials have opened a day-care center to encourage teen-age mothers to stay in school. It cares for the babies of 22 students. but Patricia Connor, its 32-year-old manager, worries that it may only perpetuate a lifestyle that she wants to discourage. Looking over the toddlers, she says, "Their grandmothers are my age. They have five kids, all by different men, and they have no skills."

Fighting that cycle, the clinic staff hustles

for patients. The facility is run by the local Watts Health Foundation, and most of the staff members are from the area and familiar with its problems. Director Donzella Lee—a street-smart Watts native with a master's degree in public health—mixes with Jordan's students in the halls, in the school-yard, even at dances. "Kids won't come to a place they don't know, and they won't deal with adults they don't trust," she points out.

At times, the clinic happens on clients. One girl was brought in not long ago after an assistant principal found her scraping her arm with a knife in a fruitless effort to remove a tattoo. At the clinic, she said she had been sexually active for two years without birth control and had had one abortion. The clinic arranged a pregnancy test and birth-control counseling. However, she never showed up. Like two sisters before her, she dropped out of school.

MAKING A DIFFERENCE

Despite such failures, school clinics do make a difference. A project in St. Paul, Minnesota, has cut the birth rate at four high schools by two-thirds over a decade. More strikingly, a Baltimore clinic focusing on education and counseling changed younger teens' sexual habits and attitudes; a researcher found that participating girls postponed their sexual initiation an average of seven months.

But so strongly ingrained is the cycle of "babies having babies" that clinic officials expect to achieve only a 25% drop in pregnancy rates over the next six years. Poverty and hopelessness weigh heavily at Jordan, where police patrol the halls and fears of gang warfare are rampant.

Although the vast majority of teen pregnancies are unintended, researchers find that the girls most likely to become pregnant are those with few academic aspirations or job skills and little sense that pregnancy would blight their future. Some are trying to escape childhoods troubled by missing fathers or drug-addicted mothers. And the welfare system makes pregnancy seem almost like a job. Jordan has several adolescent welfare mothers, including two 16-year-olds who get a total of $1,040 a month and share their own apartment.

Many Jordan girls seem nonchalant about the risk of having sex without contraception. Asked whether they know they can easily get birth-control help, a pretty 15-year-old replies. "If I went to the clinic to get the pill, everybody would know I was having sex." What about caring for a baby? A 17-year-old giggles and shrugs, "My mother would take care of it."

PEER PRESSURE INTENSE

Peer pressure, too, is intense. "It's a put-down to a girl to say, 'You can't have no baby,' " says Miss Lee, the clinic's director. And in the macho folkways of Watts gang, fathering a child is proof of manhood—although child support has little cachet. Not far down the hall from the clinic, a 17-year-old gang member is bragging that his girlfriend is pregnant.

Grinning, he cradles the air with his arms and coos over and over again, "A baby, a baby." His 14-year-old girlfriend is in junior high school. He himself has no plans for the future.

Though the Los Angeles school board is expanding the clinic system to other schools, some leaders of the project are cautious. Robert L. Smith, the community health director at the Watts Health Foundation, worries about inflated hopes. Two decades ago, he says, "People thought busing was going to solve everything. What if people expect too much?"

36

Motherhood and Morality

KRISTIN LUKER

According to interested observers at the time, abortion in America was as frequent in the last century as it is in our own. And the last century, as we have seen, had its own "right-to-life" movement, composed primarily of physicians who pursued the issue in the service of their own professional goals. When abortion reemerged as an issue in the late 1950s, it still remained in large part a restricted debate among interested professionals. But abortion as we now know it has little in common with these earlier rounds of the debate. Instead of the civility and colleagueship that characterized the earlier phases of the debate, the present round of the abortion debate is marked by rancor and intransigence. Instead of the elite male professionals who commanded the issue until recently, ordinary people—and more to the point, ordinary women—have come to pre-dominate in the ranks of those concerned. From a quiet, restricted technical debate among concerned professionals, abortion has become a debate that seems at times capable of tearing the fabric of American life apart. How did this happen? What accounts for the remarkable transformation of the abortion debate?

The history of the debate provides some preliminary answers. Technological advances in obstetrics led to a decline in those abortions undertaken strictly to preserve the life of the woman, using the narrowly biological sense of the word *life*. These technological advances, in turn, permitted (and indeed forced) physicians over time to make more and more nuanced decisions about abortion and eventually brought to the fore the underlying philosophical issue that had been obscured by a century of medical control over abortion: is the embryo a person or only a potential person? Once this question is confronted directly, a unified world view—a set of assumptions about how the world is and ought to be organized—is called into play. World views are usually the product of values so deeply held and dearly cherished that an assault upon them is a deeply disturbing assault indeed. Thus the abortion debate has been transformed because it has "gone public" and in so doing has called into question individuals' most sacrosanct beliefs.

But this is only part of the story. This chapter will argue that all the previous rounds of the abortion debate in America were merely echoes of the issue as the nineteenth century defined it: a debate about the medical profession's right to make life-and-death decisions. In contrast, the most recent round of the debate is about something new. By bringing the issue of the moral status of the embryo to the fore, the new round focuses on the relative rights of women and embryos. Consequently the abortion debate has become a debate about women's contrasting obligations to themselves and others. New technologies and the changing nature of work have opened up possibilities for women outside of the home undreamed of in the nineteenth century; together, these changes give women—for the first time in history—the option of deciding exactly how and when their family roles will fit into the larger context of their lives. In essence, therefore, this round of the abortion debate is so passionate and hard-fought *because it is a referendum on the place and meaning of motherhood.*

Motherhood is at issue because two opposing visions of motherhood are at war. Championed by "feminists" and "housewives," these two different views of motherhood represent in turn two very different kinds of social worlds. The abortion debate has become a debate among women, women with different values in the social world, different experiences of it, and different resorces with which to cope with it. How the issue is framed, how people think about

it, and, most importantly, where the passions come from are all related to the fact that the battle lines are increasingly drawn (and defended) by women. While on the surface it is the embryo's fate that seems to be at stake, the abortion debate is actually about the meanings of *women's* lives.

To be sure, both the pro-life and the pro-choice movements had earlier phases in which they were dominated by male professionals. Some of these men are still active in the debate, and it is certainly the case that some men continue to join the debate on both sides of the issue. But the data in this study suggest that by 1974 over 80 percent of the activists in both the pro-choice and the pro-life movements in California were women, and a national survey of abortion activists found similar results.

Moreover, in our interviews we routinely asked both male and female activists on both sides of the issue to supply information on several "social background variables," such as where they were born, the extent of their education, their income level, the number of children they had, and their occupations. When male activists on the two sides are compared on these variables, they are virtually indistinguishable from one another. But when female activists are compared, it is dramatically clear that for the women who have come to dominate the ranks of the movement, the abortion debate is a conflict between two different social worlds and the hopes and beliefs those worlds support.

WHO ARE THE ACTIVISTS?

On almost every social background variable we examined, pro-life and pro-choice women differed dramatically. For example, in terms of income, almost half of all pro-life women (44 percent) in this study reported an income of less than $20,000 a year, but only one-fourth of the pro-choice women reported an income that low, and a considerable portion of those were young women just starting their careers. On the upper end of the income scale, one-third of the pro-choice women reported an income of $50,000 a year or more compared with only one pro-life woman in every seven.

These simple figures on income, however, conceal a very complex social reality, and that social reality is in turn tied to feelings about abortion. The higher incomes of pro-choice women, for example, result from a number of interesting factors. Almost without exception pro-choice women work in the paid labor force, they earn good salaries when they work, and if they are married, they are likely to be married to men who also have good incomes. An astounding 94 percent of all pro-choice women work, and over half of them have incomes in the top 10 percent of all working women in this country. Moreover, one pro-choice woman in ten has an annual *personal* income (as opposed to a family income) of $30,000 or more, thus putting her in the rarified ranks of the top 2 percent of all employed women in America. Pro-life women, by contrast, are far less likely to work: 63 percent of them do not work in the paid labor force, and almost all of those who do are unmarried. Among pro-life married women, for example, only 14 percent report any personal income at all, and for most of them, this is earned not in a formal job but through activities such as selling cosmetics to groups of friends. Not surprisingly, the personal income of pro-life women who work outside the home, whether in a formal job or in one of these less-structured activities, is low. Half of all pro-life women who do work earn less than $5,000 a year, and half earn between $5,000 and $10,000. Only two pro-life women we contacted reported a personal income of more than $20,000. Thus, pro-life women are less likely to work in the first place, they earn less money when they do work, and they are more likely to be married to a skilled worker or small businessman who earns only a moderate income.

These differences in income are in turn related to the different educational and occupational choices these women have made along the way. Among pro-choice

women, almost four out of ten (37 percent) had undertaken some graduate work beyond the B.A. degree, and 18 percent had an M.D., a law degree, a Ph.D., or a similar postgraduate degree. Pro-life women, by comparison, had far less education: 10 percent of them had only a high school education or less; and another 30 percent never finished college (in contrast with only 8 percent of the pro-choice women). Only 6 percent of all pro-life women had a law degree, a Ph.D., or a medical degree.

These educational differences were in turn related to occupational differences among the women in this study. Because of their higher levels of education, pro-choice women tended to be employed in the major professions, as administrators, owners of small businesses, or executives in large businesses. The pro-life women tended to be housewives or, of the few who worked, to be in the traditional female jobs of teaching, social work, and nursing. (The choice of home life over public life held true for even the 6 percent of pro-life women with an advanced degree; of the married women who had such degrees, at the time of our interviews only one of them had not retired from her profession after marriage.)

These economic and social differences were also tied to choices that women on each side had made about marriage and family life. For example, 23 percent of pro-choice women had never married, compared with only 16 percent of pro-life women; 14 percent of pro-choice women had been divorced, compared with 5 percent of pro-life women. The size of the families these women had was also different. The average pro-choice family had between one and two children and was more likely to have one; pro-life families averaged between two and three children and were more likely to have three. (Among the pro-life women, 23 percent had five or more children; 16 percent had seven or more children.) Pro-life women also tended to marry at a slightly younger age and to have had their first child earlier.

Finally, the women on each side differed

dramatically in their religious affiliation and in the role that religion played in their lives. Almost 80 percent of the women active in the pro-life movement at the present time are Catholics. The remainder are Protestants (9 percent), persons who claim no religion (5 percent), and Jews (1 percent). In sharp contrast, 63 percent of pro-choice women say that they have no religion, 22 percent think of themselves as vaguely Protestant, 3 percent are Jewish, and 9 percent have what they call a "personal" religion. We found no one in our sample of pro-choice activists who claimed to be a Catholic at the time of the interviews.

When we asked activists what religion they were raised in as a child, however, a different picture emerged. For example, 20 percent of the pro-choice activists were raised as Catholics, 42 percent were raised as Protestants, and 15 percent were raised in the Jewish faith. In this group that describes itself predominantly without religious affiliation, therefore, only 14 percent say they were not brought up in any formal religious faith. By the same token, although almost 80 percent of present pro-life activists are Catholic, only 58 percent were raised in that religion (15 percent were raised as Protestants and 3 percent as Jews.) Thus, almost 20 percent of the pro-life activists in this study are converts to Catholicism, people who have actively chosen to follow a given religious faith, in striking contrast to pro-choice people, who have actively chosen not to follow any.

Perhaps the single most dramatic difference between the two groups, however, is in the role that religion plays in their lives. Almost three-quarters of the pro-choice people interviewed said that formal religion was either unimportant or completely irrelevant to them, and their attitudes are correlated with behavior: only 25 percent of the pro-choice women said they *ever* attended church, and most of these said they do so only occasionally. Among pro-life people, by contrast, 69 percent said religion was important in their lives, and an additional 22 percent said that it was very important.

For pro-life women, too, these attitudes are correlated with behavior: half of those pro-life women interviewed said they attend church regularly once a week, and another 13 percent said they do so even more often. Whereas 80 percent of pro-choice people never attend church, only 2 percent of pro-life advocates never do so.

Keeping in mind that the statistical use of averages has inherent difficulties, we ask, who are the "average" pro-choice and pro-life advocates? When the social background data are looked at carefully, two profiles emerge. The average pro-choice activist is a 44-year-old married woman who grew up in a large metropolitan area and whose father was a college graduate. She was married at age 22, has one or two children, and has had some graduate or professional training beyond the B.A. degree. She is married to a professional man, is herself employed in a regular job, and her family income is more than $50,000 a year. She is not religiously active, feels that religion is not important to her, and attends church very rarely if at all.

The average pro-life woman is also a 44-year-old married woman who grew up in a large metropolitan area. She married at age 17 and has three children or more. Her father was a high school graduate, and she has some college education or may have a B.A. degree. She is not employed in the paid labor force and is married to a small businessman or a lower-level white-collar worker; her family income is $30,000 a year. She is Catholic (and may have converted), and her religion is one of the most important aspects of her life: she attends church at least once a week and occasionally more often.

INTERESTS AND PASSIONS

To the social scientist (and perhaps to most of us), these social background characteristics connote lifestyles as well. We intuitively clothe these bare statistics with assumptions about beliefs and values. When we do so, the pro-choice women emerge as educated, affluent, liberal professionals, whose lack of religious affiliation suggests a secular, "modern," or (as pro-life people would have it) "utilitarian" outlook on life. Similarly, the income, education, marital patterns, and religious devotion of pro-life women suggest that they are traditional, hard-working people ("polyester types" to their opponents), who hold conservative views on life. We may be entitled to assume that individuals' social backgrounds act to shape and mold their social attitudes, but it is important to realize that the relationship between social worlds and social values is a very complex one.

Perhaps one example will serve to illustrate the point. A number of pro-life women in this study emphatically rejected an expression that pro-choice women tend to use almost unthinkingly—the expression *unwanted pregnancy*. Pro-life women argued forcefully that a better term would be a *surprise* pregnancy, asserting that although a pregnancy may be momentarily unwanted, the child that results from the pregnancy almost never is. Even such a simple thing—what to call an unanticipated pregnancy—calls into play an individual's values and resources. Keeping in mind our profile of the average pro-life person, it is obvious that a woman who does not work in the paid labor force, who does not have a college degree, whose religion is important to her, and who has already committed herself wholeheartedly to marriage and a large family is well equipped to believe that an unanticipated pregnancy usually becomes a beloved child. Her life is arranged so that for her, this belief is true. This view is consistent not only with her values, which she has held from earliest childhood, but with her social resources as well. It should not be surprising, therefore, that her world view leads her to believe that everyone else can "make room for one more" as easily as she can and that therefore it supports her in her conviction that abortion is cruel, wicked, and self-indulgent.[1]

It is almost certainly the case that an unplanned pregnancy is never an easy thing for anyone. Keeping in mind the profile of the average pro-choice woman, however, it is evident that a woman who is employed full time, who has an affluent lifestyle that depends in part on her contribution to the family income, and who expects to give a child as good a life as she herself has had with respect to educational, social, and economic advantages will draw on a different reality when she finds herself being skeptical about the ability of the average person to transform unwanted pregnancies into well-loved (and well-cared-for) children.

The relationship between passions and interests is thus more dynamic than it might appear at first. It is true that at one level, pro-choice and pro-life attitudes on abortion are self-serving: activists on each side have different views of the morality of abortion because their chosen lifestyles leave them with different needs for abortion; and both sides have values that provide a moral basis for their abortion needs in particular and their lifestyles in general. But this is only half the story. The values that lead pro-life and pro-choice women into different attitudes toward abortion are the same values that led them at an earlier time to adopt different lifestyles that supported a given view of abortion.

For example, pro-life women have *always* valued family roles very highly and have arranged their lives accordingly. They did not acquire high-level educational and occupational skills, for example, because they married, and they married because their values suggested that this would be the most satisfying life open to them. Similarly, pro-choice women postponed (or avoided) marriage and family roles because they chose to acquire the skills they needed to be successful in the larger world, having concluded that the role of wife and mother was too limited for them. Thus, activists on both sides of the issue are women who have a given set of values about what are the most satisfying and appropriate roles for women, and they have made *life commitments that now limit their ability to change their minds.* Women who have many children and little education, for example, are seriously handicapped in attempting to become doctors or lawyers; women who have reached their late forties with few children or none are limited in their ability to build (or rebuild) a family. For most of these activists, therefore, their position on abortion is the "tip of the iceberg," a shorthand way of supporting and proclaiming not only a complex set of values but a given set of social resources as well.

To put the matter differently, we might say that for pro-life women the traditional division of life into separate male roles and female roles still works, but for pro-choice women it does not. Having made a commitment to the traditional female roles of wife, mother, and homemaker, pro-life women are limited in those kinds of resources—education, class status, recent occupational experiences—they would need to compete in what traditionally has been the male sphere, namely, the paid labor force. The average pro-choice woman, in contrast, is comparatively well endowed with exactly those resources: she is highly educated, she already has a job, and she has recent (and continuous) experience in the job market.

In consequence, anything that supports a traditional division of labor into male and female worlds is, broadly speaking, in the interests of pro-life women because that is where their resources lie. Conversely, such a traditional division of labor, when strictly enforced, is against the interests of pro-choice women because it limits their abilities to use the valuable "male" resources that they have in relative abundance. It is therefore apparent that attitudes toward abortion, even though rooted in childhood experiences, are also intimately related to present-day interests. Women who oppose abortion and seek to make it officially unavailable are declaring, both practically and symbolically, that women's reproductive roles should be given social primacy. Once an embryo is defined as a child and an abortion as the death of a person, almost everything else in a woman's life must "go on hold" during the course of her pregnancy: any attempt to gain "male" resources such as a job, an education, or other skills must be subordinated to her uniquely female responsibility of serving the needs of this newly conceived person. Thus, when personhood is bestowed on the embryo, women's nonreproductive roles are made secondary to their reproductive roles. The act of conception therefore creates a pregnant woman rather than a woman who is pregnant; it creates a woman whose life, in cases where roles or values clash, is defined by the fact that she is—or may become—pregnant.

It is obvious that this view is supportive of women who have already decided that their familial and reproductive roles are the major ones in their lives. By the same token, the costs of defining women's reproductive roles as primary do not seem high to them because they have already chosen to make those roles primary anyway. For example, employers might choose to discriminate against women because they might require maternity leave and thus be unavailable at critical times, but women who have chosen not to work in the paid labor force in the first place can see such discrimination as irrelevant to them.

It is equally obvious that supporting abortion (and believing that the embryo is not a person) is in the vested interests of pro-choice women. Being so well equipped to compete in the male sphere, they perceive any situation that both practically and symbolically affirms the primacy of women's reproductive roles as a real loss to them. Practically, it devalues their social resources. If women are only secondarily in the labor market and must subordinate working to pregnancy, should it occur, then their education, occupation, income, and work become potentially temporary and hence discounted. Working becomes, as it traditionally was perceived to be, a pastime or hobby pursued for "pin money" rather than a central part of their lives. Similarly, if the embryo is defined as a person and the ability to become pregnant is the central one for women, a woman must be prepared to sacrifice some of her own interests to the interests of his newly conceived person.

In short, in a world where men and woman traditionally have had different roles to play and where male roles traditionally have been the more socially prestigious and financially rewarded, abortion has become a symbolic marker between those who wish to maintain this division of labor and those who wish to challenge it. Thus, on an intimate level, the pro-life movement is women's version of what was true of peasants in the Vendée, the part of France that remained Royalist during the French Revolution. Charles Tilly has argued that in the Vendée, traditional relationships between nobles and peasants were still mutually satisfying so that the "brave new world" of the French Revolution represented more loss than gain, and the peasants therefore resisted the changes the Revolution heralded. By the same logic, traditional relationships between men and women are still satisfying, rewarding, and meaningful for pro-life women, and they therefore resist the lure of "liberation." For pro-choice women, however, with their access to male resources, a division of labor into the public world of work and the private world of home and hearth seems to promise only restriction to "second-class" citizenship.

Thus, the sides are fundamentally opposed to each other not only on the issue of abortion but also on what abortion *means.* Women who have many "human capital" resources of the traditionally male variety want to see motherhood recognized as a private, discretionary choice. Women who have few of these resources and limited opportunities in the job market want to see motherhood recognized as the most important thing a woman can do. In order for pro-choice women to achieve their goals, therefore, they *must* argue that motherhood is not a primary, inevitable, or "natural" role for all women; for pro-life women to achieve their goals, they *must* argue that it is. In short, the debate rests on the question of whether women's fertility is to be socially recognized as a resource or as a handicap.

To the extent that women who have chosen the larger public world of work have been successful, both legally and in terms of public opinion and, furthermore, are rapidly becoming the numerical majority, pro-life women are put on the defensive. Several pro-life women offered poignant examples of how the world deals with housewives who do not have an official payroll title. Here is what one of them said:

I was at a party, about two years ago—it still sticks in my mind, you see, because I'm a housewife and I don't work—and I met this girl from England and we got involved in a deep discussion about the English and the Americans and their philosophies and how one has infuenced the other, and at the end of the conversation—she was a working gal herself, I forget what she did—and she says, "Where do you work?" and I said, "I don't." And she looked at me and said, "You don't work?" I said "No." She said, "You're just a housewife . . . and you can still think like that?" She couldn't believe it, and she sort of gave me a funny look and that was the end of the conversation for the evening. And I've met other people who've had similar experiences. [People seem to think that if] you're at home and you're involved with children all day, your intelligence quotient must be down with them on the floor someplace, and [that] you really don't do much thinking or get yourself involved.

Because of their commitment to their own view of motherhood as a primary social role, pro-life women believe that other women are "casual" about abortions and have them "for convenience." There are no reliable data to confirm whether or not women are "casual" about abortions, but many pro-life people believe this to be the case and relate their activism to their perception of other people's casualness. For example:

Every time I saw some article [on abortion] I read about it, and I had another friend who had her second abortion in 1977 .. and both of her abortions were a matter of convenience, it was inconvenient for her to be pregnant at that time. When I talked to her I said, "O.K., you're married now, your husband has a good job, you want to have children eventually, but if you become pregnant now, you'd have an abortion. Why?" "Because it's inconvenient, this is not when I want to have my child." And that bothered me a lot because she is also very intelligent, graduated magna cum laude, and knew nothing about fetal development.

The assertion that women are "casual" about abortion, one could argue, expresses in a shorthand way a set of beliefs about women and their roles. First, the more people value the personhood of the embryo, the more important must be the reasons for taking its life. Some pro-life people, for example, would accept an abortion when continuation of the pregnancy would cause the death of the mother; they believe that when two lives are in direct conflict, the embryo's life can be considered the more expendable. But not all pro-life people agree, and many say they would not accept abortion even to save the mother's life. (Still others say they accept the idea in principle but would not make that choice in their own lives if faced with it.) For people who accept the personhood of the embryo, any reason besides trading a "life for a life" (and sometimes even that) seems trivial, merely a matter of "convenience."

Second, people who accept the personhood of the embryo sees the reasons that pro-abortion people give for ending a pregnancy as simultaneously downgrading the value of the embryo and upgrading everything else but pregnancy. The argument that women need abortion to "control" their fertility means that they intend to subordinate pregnancy, with its inherent unpredictability, to something else. As the pro-choice activists . . . have told us, that something else is participation in the paid labor force. Abortion permits women to engage in paid work on an equal basis with men. With abortion, they may schedule pregnancy in order to take advantage of the kinds of benefits that come with a paid position in the labor force: a paycheck, a title, a social identity. The pro-life women in this study were often careful to point out that they did not object to "career women." But what they meant by "career women" were women whose *only* responsibilities

were in the labor force. Once a woman became a wife and a mother, in their view her primary responsibility was to her home and family.

Third, the pro-life activists we interviewed, the overwhelming majority of whom are full-time homemakers, also felt that women who worked *and* had families could often do so only because women like themselves picked up the slack. Given their place in the social structure, it is not surprising that many of the pro-life women thought that married women who worked outside the home were "selfish"—that they got all the benefits while the homemakers carried the load for them in Boy and Girl Scouts, PTA, and after school, for which their reward was to be treated by the workers as less competent and less interesting persons.[2]

Abortion therefore strips the veil of sanctity from motherhood. When pregnancy is discretionary—when people are allowed to put anything else they value in front of it—then motherhood has been demoted from a sacred calling to a job.[3] In effect, the legalization of abortion serves to make men and women more "unisex" by deemphasizing what makes them different—the ability of women to visibly and directly carry the next generation. Thus, pro-choice women are emphatic about their right to compete equally with men without the burden of an unplanned pregnancy, and pro-life women are equally emphatic about their belief that men and women have different roles in life and that prenancy is a gift instead of a burden.

Abortion also has a symbolic dimension that separates the needs and interests of homemakers and workers in the paid labor force. Insofar as abortion allows a woman to get a job, to get training for a job, or to advance in a job, it does more than provide social support for working women over homemakers; it also seems to support the value of economic considerations over moral ones. Many pro-life people interviewed said that although their commitment to traditional family roles meant very real material deprivations to themselves and their families, the moral benefits of such a choice more than made up for it.

My girls babysit and the boys garden and have paper routes and things like that. I say that if we had a lot of money that would still be my philosophy, though I don't know because we haven't been in that position. But it's a sacrifice to have a larger family. So when I hear these figures that it takes $65,000 from birth to [raise a child], I think that's ridiculous. That's a new bike every year. That's private colleges. That's a complete new outfit when school opens. Well, we've got seven daughters who wear hand-me-downs, and we hope that sometime in their eighteen years at home each one has a new bike somewhere along the line, but otherwise it's hand-me-downs. Those figures are inflated to give those children everything, and I think that's not good for them.

For pro-life people, a world view that puts the economic before the noneconomic hopelessly confuses two different kinds of worlds. For them, the private world of family as traditionally experienced is the one place in human society where none of us has a price tag. Home, as Robert Frost pointed out, is where they have to take you in, whatever your social worth. Whether one is a surgeon or a ragpicker, the family is, at least ideally, the place where love is unconditional.

THE CORE OF THE DEBATE

In summary, women come to be pro-life and pro-choice activists as the end result of lives that center around different definitions of motherhood. They grow up with a belief about the nature of the embryo, so events in their lives lead them to believe that the embryo is a unique person, or a fetus; that people are intimately tied to their biological roles, or that these roles are but a minor part of life; that motherhood is the most important and satisfying role open to a woman, or that motherhood is only one of several roles, a burden when defined as the only role. These beliefs and values are rooted in the concrete circumstances of wo-

men's lives—their educations, incomes, occupations, and the different marital and family choices they have made along the way—and they work simultaneously to shape those circumstances in turn. Values about the relative place of reason and faith, about the role of actively planning for live versus learning to accept gracefully life's unknowns, of the relative satisfactions inherent in work and family—all of these factors place activists in a specific relationship to the larger world and give them a specific set of resources with which to confront that world.

The simultaneous and on-going modification of both their lives and their values by each other finds these activists located in a specific place in the social world. They are financially successful, or they are not. They become highly educated, or they do not. They become married and have a large family, or they have a small one. And at each step of the way, both their values and their lives have undergone either ratification or revision.

Pro-choice and pro-life activists live in different worlds, and the scope of their lives, as both adults and children, fortifies them in their belief that their own views on abortion are the more correct, more moral, and more reasonable. When added to this is the fact that should "the other side" win, one group of women will see the very real devaluation of their lives and life resources, it is not surprising that the abortion debate has generated so much heat and so little light.

NOTES

1. As might be imagined, it is not an easy task to ask people who are anti-abortion activists about their own experiences with a certain kind of unanticipated pregnancy, namely, a premarital pregnancy. Most pro-choice people were quite often open about having had such pregnancies; their pregnancies—and subsequent abortions—were central to their feelings about abortion. Pro-life women, by contrast, were deeply reluctant to discuss the topic. Several of them after acknowledging

premarital pregnancies, said that they did not want people to think that their attitudes on abortion were merely a product of their personal experiences. Thus we have no comparative figures about the extent to which the values represented here are the product of different experiences or just different opinions. We know only that unanticipated pregnancy was common among pro-choice women, and the interviews suggest that it was not uncommon among pro-life women. The difference in experience is, of course, that those in the first group sought abortions and those in the second group, with only a few exceptions, legitimized their pregnancies with a marriage.

2. In fact, pro-life women, especially those recruited after 1972, were *less* likely to be engaged in formal activities such as Scouts, church activities, and PTA than their pro-choice peers. Quite possibly they have in mind more informal kinds of activities, premised on the fact that since they do not work, they are home most of the time.

3. The same might be said of all sacred callings—stripped of its layer of the sacred, for example, the job of the clergy is demanding, low status and underpaid.

37

Marital Rape:
The Myth Versus the Reality

David Finkelhor
Kersti Yllo

For most people, forced sex in marriage has little to do with what they would call "real" rape. When they think of "real" rape, they think of a stranger, a weapon, an attack, a threat to a woman's life. Forced marital sex, on the other hand, conjures up an unpleasant, but not particularly serious, marital squabble.

This attitude toward marital rape as a rather innocuous event was vividly illustrated when we solicited fictitious descriptions of marital rape from over 400 university students. Here are some of the typical replies:

He wants to. She doesn't. He says, "That's tough, I'm going to anyway," and he does.

Husband and wife are newly separated. He comes for a short visit and forces her to make love because he really does love her and misses her.

The wife was unwilling to have sex and he forced himself on her.

These images of marital rape constitute what we call the "sanitary stereotype"— marital rape depicted as a petty conflict. People do not regard it as very serious because in their minds the action itself is not very dramatic. To most, it is a disagreement over sex that the husband wins. Their images are very bland: little graphic violence, little pain, little suffering. The coercion involved is abstract; people use neutral phrases like "he forced her" or "he makes her" to describe the rape.

These accounts contrast noticeably with the graphic descriptions one usually gets for scenarios of rape by a stranger. In these descriptions, a woman is often pictured walking home late at night when a man grabs her, drags her into an alley, pulls out a knife, and rapes her. The stereotype gives plenty of fodder for fear and outrage. One would hardly expect to hear a description of stranger rape that went: "They met on the street. He wanted to. She didn't." Even "He accosted her on the street and he forced himself on her" would be an unusually cursory description of rape by a stranger. But these were just the kind of flat accounts many of our respondents gave in picturing marital rape.

The sanitary stereotype that people conjure up when asked about marital rape is a product of ignorance and misinformation. Relatively few personal stories about raped wives have appeared on film or television, or even in the popular literature. Most that have make marital rape appear almost romantic.

Perhaps the most familiar movie imagery of marital rape comes from *Gone with the Wind*. There, a "healthily sexual" man, Rhett Butler (Clark Gable), overcomes the resistance of proper and frightened Scarlett O'Hara (Vivian Leigh), and carries her struggling upstairs to an outcome left to the viewer's imagination. The next scene shows Scarlett the morning after, preening and glowing with barely repressed exhilaration and love. *Gone with the Wind* presents a most dangerous image of marital rape, for it powerfully advertises the idea that women secretly wish to be overpowered and raped, and that, in fact, rape may be a good way to reconcile a marriage.

Coal Miner's Daughter offers a more current version of marital rape. There, young Loretta (Sissy Spacek) is carried off into marriage by a dashing—and obviously experienced—Mooney (Tommy Lee Jones). She knows little of what to expect from sex. As he roughly climbs on top of her, she senses that he is about to do something violent and awful. She tries to struggle and push him away, but he is so big that he overpowers her, and she is left frightened and sobbing.

Media images such as these mislead in their portrayals of marital rape as primarily about sex. Typically, the man is depicted as

having a healthy, if a bit overzealous, sexual appetite, while the women is seen as being repressed or squeamish. But even when the man is portrayed as a brute and his wife as a "healthily sexual" woman, the problem triggering the rape is still presumed to be a conflict over sex. We may disapprove of his methods, but we cannot help approving of his ends: conjugal relations.

Moreover, such media images present marital rape as a kind of trivial event, like an argument over what restaurant to go to. There is love underneath, even if passions get unruly, and it would be a travesty of the highest order if Rhett Butler or Mooney ended up facing a five-year jail term for their excess of passion. No wonder people are startled by the idea of criminalizing marital rape.

Fortunately, another verison of marital rape, a more realistic and alarming one, is bit by bit coming to supplant the sanitary renditions produced by Hollywood and the popular culture. As laws change across the country, stories of marital rapes are finding their way onto police blotters and sometimes into the newspapers. Through such stories, the myths of marital rape are being replaced with the reality of violation and brutality.

Sarasota, Florida, *Herald Tribune*—August 28

A 23-year-old Bradenton man has been formally charged by the state attorney's office with raping his wife, who is a paraplegic.

The man, who is not being named to protect the identity of his wife, was arrested for sexual battery after a neighbor in the couple's apartment complex on 26th Street West called police to report screams coming from a nearby apartment.

When the deputy arrived, the victim reported that she had been beaten a few days earlier and claimed she had lost several teeth. The deputy said he could see bruises on the woman's face.

The wife signed an affidavit alleging that her husband had committed anal and oral intercourse on her over a period of three days. The woman is reportedly paralyzed from her ribs to her toes. . . .

To the women we talked to in the course of our study, marital rapes were frightening and brutal events that usually occurred in the context of an exploitative and destructive relationship. This sexual abuse was only peripherally about sex. More often it was about humiliation, degradation, anger, and resentment. Women were left, if not physically disabled, then psychologically traumatized for a long time.

- one was jumped in the dark by her husband and raped in the anus while slumped over a woodpile;
- one had a six-centimeter gash ripped in her vagina by a husband who was trying to "pull her vagina out";
- one was gang-raped by her husband and a friend after they surprised her alone in a vacant apartment;
- one was raped at knifepoint by her estranged partner;
- one was forced to have sex the day after returning from gynecological surgery, causing her to hemorrhage and obliging her to return to the hospital;
- one was forced to have sex with her estranged husband in order to see her baby, whom he had kidnapped.

The list could go on. Our interviewees were not chosen because their assaults were especially severe. They were, for the most part, women at local family-planning agencies and battered-woman's shelters who admitted, when asked, that their husbands had forced them to have sex. The indignities they suffered are not unusual; they are the kind of marital rapes that show up when someone asks women to talk about the issue.

The sanitized image of marital rape routinely omits the component of terror. Many of the women we talked to told of marriages in which they had been beaten for years; of men who would turn on them unexpectedly at the slightest provocation; of homes they were afraid to leave. The quality of their lives was in some ways like a Grimm fairy tale: they lived with ogres whose violence, anger, and unpredictability kept them constantly in fear of where and when the next blow would come.

Shirley, a thirty-two-year old woman with three children, was working on the staff of a battered-women's shelter. She was referred to us by the other staff members.

Shirley had met her husband while he was in the military, and married him after knowing him for only a few months. He came from an affluent Southern family, his father was a doctor, and he had received a scholarship to a prestigious university.

She liked him at first because he was such a "perfect gentleman," the kind who opened doors, took her coat, and hung it up. He could be caring and playful, and they had had many good times together. But he had a Dr.-Jekyll-and-Mr.-Hyde quality. At times of stress, pressure would build up in him. His eyes would turn red, and he would explode. "It was like he turned into a different person," she said. She could sense it coming on, but the change itself might occur in seconds, with no connection to any alcohol or drug abuse.

At first his outbursts only occurred at work. (He had a steady job as a carpenter.) But then they began to involve her. For example, during his episodes he would force her to sit in a chair for hours on end while he watched her. If she looked at the clock, she got hit. If she said something he did not like, she got slapped or thrown to the floor.

One of these ordeals occurred when she was pregnant. He yanked her out of a chair and rammed her head into a cabinet. The concussion she sustained left her disoriented for five days, and she had a miscarriage. He abused their daughter, too. He had something against women, she felt, perhaps connected to his strong resentment to his mother.

In many ways. Shirley was a classic battered woman. Frequently black and blue, she was terrified of her husband's temper. And as a woman with little education and a number of children, she believed she could not survive without him. One time he spent all his earnings on his motorcycle and gave her five dollars for the week's groceries. Stunned, she spilled some milk on the floor as she protested that she could never feed the family on that small amount. He pushed her to the floor, poured the rest of the milk over her, and mopped it up with her hair and her clothes. . . .

The . . . rapes generally occurred during his tantrums, in the midst or at the end of beatings. She had a hard time saying exactly how frequent they were.

One particularly savage sexual assault occurred after they had had an argument and she had gone into the shower to try to put some distance between them. He came into the bathroom and kept ripping back the curtain. She slapped him, something she had never done before (and never did again: "That taught me"). He started socking her in the stomach, until she vomited. Then he forced her to have sex. Distraught, she thought she might finally get some assistance from her pastor and quickly dialed his number. Before she could tell him what had happened, however, her husband picked up the phone on another extension and shouted, "I just raped my wife! What are you going to do about it, pastor?"

She was finally able to get out of the marriage, but not unscathed. An acquaintance had given her the name of a shelter, and, at wit's end one day, she called up and demanded to be taken, even though the shelter had no room. While she was staying there, her husband found out its location and arrived at the door in a fury. She was frightened to death, she remembers, so immobilized that it was all she could do to crawl upstairs to safety on her hands and knees, "like a whipped dog with my tail between my legs." The staff at the shelter called the police, who came and removed her husband. . . .

Many marital-rape victims are, like Shirley, battered wives, and entrapment and terror are part and parcel of their lives. Her story illustrates many of the elements of the classic battering situation: the husband becomes increasingly brutal; his outbursts are capricious and unpredictable; he comes to dominate her life and makes threats to deter her from leaving or acting independently.

About half of the women in our sample of marital-rape victims were battered. Not all were as terrorized and brutalized as Shirley, but all had experienced repeated physical attacks, often connected to drunkenness. For the remainder of this chapter we will talk primarily about the rape experiences of these battered wives, and what their histories have in common. They were the most brutalized and terrorized of the marital-rape victims, and their stories are the ones that clash most starkly with the sanitary stereotype of marital rape.

Battered women are at especially high risk of sexual assault. Studies of battered women regularly show that anywhere from a third to a half of them are victims of marital sexual assault.

We noted certain common features in the marital rapes that occurred in battering relationships. First, the sexual violence in these relationships was another aspect of the general abuse. These men hit their wives, belittled them, called them names, took their money, and, as another way of humiliating and degrading them, resorted to sexual violence.

Often the sexual abuse was a continuation of the beatings. Husbands would find a pretext and start to attack. Beatings might last for an hour, or for a day. At some point, usually toward the end of the beating, the husband would either strip his wife or force her to disrobe and then have intercourse. Forty percent of the women we interviewed described one of these beating-plus-rape combinations.

When rapes followed physical assaults, two different patterns occurred. Sometimes, the hitting and the punching would continue throughout the sex, and the sex itself would be full of violence. In other cases, the men would act as though they were finished with the beating and wanted to make up with a little sex. The women, exhausted and in pain from the beating and hardly feeling close to their husbands, would not want to be touched. In these cases, the husbands would roughly push themselves on their exhausted partners or threaten them with more violence unless they complied.

Marital-rape incidents were not isolated episodes in these marriages. In the sanitary stereotype, a marital rape might be a once-in-a-relationship occurrence, something quite rare that happens under unusual circumstances. Exactly 50 percent of the women in our study said they had been sexually assaulted twenty times or more, and for the majority of the women we talked to, rape was a repeated occurrence. For some, assaults were so common they could not remember how often. "It happened half of the time we had sex during those three years," said one woman typical of this group. For most marital-rape victims, rape is a chronic and constant threat, not an isolated problem. The battered women, of course, were the most vulnerable of all to such repeated sexual abuse. Twice as many battered women suffered from chronic rapes (twenty times or more) as the other raped women. In addition to being punching bags, the battered women were also, as one woman put it, "masturbating machines."

A wife's leaving or threatening to leave her marriage frequently provokes a marital rape. In our study, over two-thirds of the women in our sample were raped in the waning days of a relationship, either after previous separations or when they were making plans to get out.

The rapists who attacked toward the end of the relationships or after separations obviously had retaliatory motives. These husbands, furious that their wives had gathered up the courage to leave, used the assault as a way to express their anger and punish their wives.

Some of the men seemed devastated at the thought of losing their wives and at seeing their connection and control disappearing. What they could not have willingly, they attempted to win back through a brute display of sexual power. "You know you're gonna like it. You liked it for that long. You're gonna like it again," one man screamed as he raped his wife, having learned she would not return to him.

Marital rapes are also quite common at the end of relationships because husbands feel they have nothing more to lose. One man, who knew his deteriorating marriage was headed for a break-up, tackled his wife and forced her to have anal intercourse—something he had always wanted but she had prevented in the course of the relationship. She commented, "I guess he realized that the relationship was over and he might as well have his way before we split up; sort of, I'll do it to you because it doesn't matter anymore!"

Twenty-one-year-old Katherine was interviewed at a battered-women's shelter where she had been living with her two-year-old son. She had recently escaped, for the second time, from her violent husband of almost three years.

Katherine remembered her family as a very nice one. Her parents did a great deal for her and her two siblings. There was never any arguing between them, and only once can she remember being spanked. Her father was a painter and a carpenter, while her mother took care of the family.

She met her future husband at a McDonald's. and they went together for a year before she got pregnant. He had just joined the army, but within two months he was out with a dishonorable discharge, and they married.

Their marriage was good at first but deteriorated suddenly and quickly. He was drinking a lot, and in the fifth month of her pregnancy he had an affair with another woman. Then, in the eighth month of her pregnancy, his violence came to the surface.

One night he knocked her out completely with a punch in the mouth. Another time he threw a knife at her. That same evening, in front of his parents, he threw her to the ground and kicked her in the head. He burned her with a cigarette. He locked her in their shed for an evening. His mother warned her to leave: "He's gonna kill you." Then, when she did so, the mother begged her to go back to him, because he was so distraught she thought he would commit suicide.

Four times he forced her to have sex in front of their child. One day, for example, when they were sitting on the couch while the child was in the room, he kept pushing her head down into his lap and telling her to fellate him. Even under regular circumstances, fellatio turned her off, but with her son there it seemed even more revolting. When she resisted, however, he got mad and smacked her. "It ain't gonna hurt him if he sees it," he said. "Just do it." She did, to keep him calm.

He also compelled her to have anal sex on one occasion. This time she says she went along with it because he made her feel that she was his wife and she was supposed to do what he wanted. "He had me brainwashed," she said.

After he had forced her, she would feel depressed and less like having sex with him. He would become distant and tell her, "Don't come near me. I don't want to see your face." Sometimes after beatings he would apologize, but never after the forced sex.

Although things were getting progressively worse between them and she did leave a few times, she kept coming back. "I had a child and wanted to have a happy family." He made resolutions to change and one time actually got a job; but he didn't change.

During one of their separations, she had an affair with another man, and this drove him to new heights of violence after she returned to him. One night he took a pair of pliers out of the drawer and told her, "I'm gonna rip out your vagina." He made her get on her hands and knees and beg him not to, but then he put the baby on the kitchen counter and said he was going to kill them both.

He was on a rampage. That night he woke her up several times and beat her, and also beat their child. She finally got away and had her mother take her to a shelter her father had told her about. But this did not end her husband's spree: he went to the place where she worked and pulled a knife on the people who worked there, then went to her mother's house and vilified her to her mother. The mother called the police.

His threat to rip out her vagina was one of the most terrifying incidents recounted in all the histories we took. Consistent with the incredible mania for violence this man displayed, his threat was an attempt to assert his ultimate ownership over her body. Her vagina was his and he would do what he wanted with it. If he could not have it, he was going to ensure that nobody else would, either.

The brutality that is displayed by the husband-rapists we have described in this section is not coincidental. Evidence from other researchers also suggests that among batterers, those who rape are among the most brutal and violent. It appears that there is a continuum of battering, that each batterer has his own limits. Whereas one man will only slap his wife around, another has no compunction about knocking her unconscious, or threatening her with a knife or gun; marital rape is apparently on the more violent end of this continuum.

The conventional stereotype of marital rape disregards the fact that a great many wives are forcibly subjected to a variety of sexual abuses in addition to, or sometimes in lieu of, forced vaginal intercourse. Wives are raped with objects. For instance, one woman's husband tried to rape her with a broomstick and several husbands had their wives insert things in their vaginas and then took pictures of them. Wives are raped anally and their genitals are mutilated. One woman said that her husband would bite her genitals until they bled, and another said she was burned with cigarettes. Wives are forced to have intercourse with their husbands' friends. Two of the women we interviewed said that their assaults had occurred when their husbands ganged up on them with some of their friends. One was able to escape, but the other was not so lucky.

One-third of the women we interviewed mentioned an episode of forced anal intercourse. A fifth told of forced oral sex. Nearly a quarter said they had been subject to sex in the presence of others—usually their children. These incidents are not disagreements over sexual positions; they are sexual humiliations inflicted on women.

Clare is a twenty-four-year-old woman from an affluent background who is currently three years into a second marriage. Her forced-sex experience had occurred with her first husband, to whom she had been married for three years while they were both in college.

The violent sexual episode took place at the very end of the relationship. Things had been deteriorating between them for a long time, to the point where they had not been talking to each other for two weeks. One afternoon she came home from school, silently changed into a housecoat, and started toward the bathroom. He got up from the couch, grabbed her, pushed her down on the floor with her face in a pillow, and, with his hand clamped over her mouth, proceeded to have anal intercourse with her. "It was very violent," she said. Despite the pillow, she screamed so loud that the neighbors heard. But he was very strong and had her pinned down with his full weight on top of her back; and nobody came to help.

When it was over, she found herself distraught, hateful, furious. "If I had had a gun there, I would have killed him," she said.

The victims of anal rape that we interviewed reported a great deal of pain and in some cases long-term damage as a result of these assaults. Clare said that for weeks afterward she had to defecate standing up, and that the injury took five years to heal fully. Another woman said that repeated anal rapes left her rectum torn and bleeding.

At first we were surprised by the number of anal rapes we heard about. But as we understood better the motives of the men who committed these assaults, the frequency of anal rape made more sense.

Raping a woman anally was an act by which the men expressed their anger, their control, and their desire to punish. Most of the women found it deviant and detestable, something they would not have consented to ordinarily.

The act in itself, when imposed by force, emphasizes the passivity, subservance, and impersonality of the victim. The woman takes no active part, as she would in fellatio. The man himself is not vulnerable, as he would be in either cunnilingus or fellatio. Because the man is facing the woman's back, the can avoid confronting her feelings and reactions in a way that would be difficult in ordinary vaginal intercourse. He can treat her as an impersonal object. This may help account for its frequent occurrence in forced-sex situations.

The image of marital rape as an unfortunate bedroom quarrel needs to be recast to encompass the full spectrum of the reality. Some rapes, of course, *are* little more than bedroom quarrels. But to think of marital rape solely in that way is to misunderstand the horrible reality of many women's experience.

38

Hospital Care for Profit

Geraldine Dallek

In 1961, four men set out for a game of golf. Two were real estate agents; two, young lawyers from a prestigious Louisville, Kentucky, law firm. That golf game was the beginning of what was to become an international corporation with $2.6 billion in annual revenue—Humana, Incorporated. Only a few years later, in 1968, two Nashville doctors met with Jack Massey, a founder of Kentucky Fried Chicken, and Hospital Corporation of America (HCA), the nation's largest for-profit hospital chain, was born. By 1984, HCA owned or managed 260 hospitals in 41 states and grossed more than $3.9 billion from its hospitals and nursing homes. By the mid-1980s, proprietary hospitals controlled 12 percent of the acute care hospital market in the United States, 21 percent in the South.

It is possible to understand the rapid growth and impact of these proprietary chains only by examining the environment that nurtured them. In many ways, the medical care industry is like the defense industry. First, the goals of each—protecting our nation and protecting our health—are intrinsically valued by our society. Second, medical care and national defense are extremely costly. We spend $300 billion on defense each year, three-fourths as much as the $400 billion spent on health care. Third, both industries, in what is clearly aberrant free-market behavior, have been permitted to set the price of the goods and services they produce. In defense, it is the weapons contractors who have been virtually given a blank check; in the medical industry, hospitals, nursing homes, drug manufacturers, and physicians have, until very recently, also had carte blanche to determine how much their product is worth. Given these factors, is it any wonder that both industries are highly profitable?

The ability to make money from the delivery of medical care is not new. In the late nineteenth century, as hospitals became

Reprinted by permission of Transaction Publishers from *Society*, Vol. 23, No. 5. Copyright © 1986 by Transaction Publishers.

safe and attractive places in which to care for the ill, small for-profit hospitals sprung up in the United States and Western Europe. In Europe, individual for-profit hospitals faded from the scene as government assumed more responsibility for ensuring the provision of health care. By contrast, the for-profit industry in the United States flourished.

In the early 1980s, for-profit chains were the darling of Wall Street with a 20 percent growth rate. During 1982, a recession year for most businesses, stocks of the top four hospital chains rose 30 percent. Profits of the twenty largest chains went up 38 percent in 1983 and 28.5 percent the following year. In 1984, HCA's chief executive officer was the second highest paid executive in the nation, and the head of National Medical Enterprises (NME) beat out the movie moguls as the highest paid executive in Southern California.

What accounts for the rapid expansion and huge profits of these new hospital organizations? Traditional reimbursement policies go far to explain the attractiveness of the hospital industry to enterpreneurs. Hospitals, until adoption of the new Medicare diagnosis related group (DRG) payment system in 1983, were generally paid by a retrospective cost-based reimbursement system. This open-ended system for paying hospitals, begun by Blue Cross plans (acting almost as agents for the hospitals) after World War II, was adopted by the federal government as the quid pro quo for the hospital industry's support of Medicare and Medicaid legislation in 1965. The potential for profits in this reimbursement system cannot be overstated. "It was hard not to be successful," commented the chief executive officer of National Medical Enterprises in a 1985 *Wall Street Journal* article. Profits could be made by simply buying existing hospitals and making sure that bills to both private and public insurers contained an add-on profit.

Hospitals could be bought easily in the 1970s and 1980s. For-profit chains' access to capital through the sale of stock gave them

an advantage over their nonprofit brethren for purposes of both building and buying hospitals. Because of their large revenue, assets, and equity base, they were viewed as sound financial risks.

The major growth of for-profit chains came from the purchase of financially troubled hospitals. Between 1980 and 1982, 43 percent of the growth of the six largest for-profit chains came from the purchase of other for-profit hospitals, mostly independent facilities. A third of the growth came from the construction of new hospitals, mostly independent facilities. A third of the growth came from the constructon of new hospitals and a fourth from the purchase of public and voluntary nonprofit hospitals. Following a for-profit purchase, ailing hospitals were brought back to health by building new facilities to attract physicians, substantially increasing charges, and reducing services to those who could not pay. Public hospitals owned and run by local governments were often receptive to being bailed out by for-profit chains. Faced with aging facilities, unable to attract privately insured patients, and confronted with increased numbers of the poor seeking care, public hospitals awash with red ink were all to happy to sell to for-profit chains.

In assessing the impact of the for-profit hospital industry, we must go well beyond the counting of beds. The industry has had a far-reaching impact on the cost of hospital care, the delivery of services to the poor, and the behavior of other health care providers.

COSTLY CARE

For-profit chains have often been viewed favorably because of their promise to bring managerial efficiency to the "wasteful" nonprofit sector. It does not appear that they possess superior managerial talents. After reviewing a number of studies on multihospital systems, Ermann and Gabel concluded in a May 1985 article in *Medical Care* that "There is little empirical evidence that [multihospital] systems have realized economies of scale of mass purchasing or use capital facilities more efficiently." Nor have chains served as a competitive catalyst to an industry grown fat by its insulation from free-market forces. Theoretically, competition and efficiency would lead to reduced costs. Judged by this standard, for-profit hospital chains also failed, as they increased, not lowered, the cost of hospital care.

For-profit chain costs have been higher than nonprofit hospital costs for three reasons: they mark up charges well above expenses; they use more expensive ancillary services than nonprofit facilities; and charges must cover their higher capital costs. According to several studies, the difference in costs between for-profit and not-for-profit hospitals is substantial. A comparison of charges at 280 California for-profit and nonprofit hospitals showed that for-profit hospital charges per admission were 24 percent higher than those of the voluntary hospitals and 47 percent higher than public hospital charges. According to this study—by Robert Pattison and Hallie Katz, reported in the August 1983 *New England Journal of Medicine*—huge profits were made in ancillary services such as pharmacy and laboratory services. The study also showed that despite the claims of administrative savings, costs for "fiscal services" and "administrative services" (which include costs to maintain corporate headquarters elsewhere) were 32 percent higher in for-profit chain hospitals than in voluntary hospitals. The authors concluded that the data "do not support the claim that investor-owned chains enjoy overall operating efficiencies or economies of scale in administrative fiscal services."

Results of a more recent study, by Lewin and Associates and health policy analysts at Johns Hopkins University, of eighty matched pairs of investor-owned chain and not-for-profit hospitals in eight states were remarkably similar to the Pattison and Katz study: prices charged by for-profit chain hospitals were 22 percent more per admission than those charged by matched not-for-profit hospitals.

For-profit hospitals also charge more for several procedures, according to a 1983 Blue Cross/Blue Shield of North Carolina study. Comparing charges for three commonly performed hospital procedures—gallbladder removals, hysterectomies, and normal deliveries of babies—at six for-profit hospitals and six matched nonprofit hospitals, the study found that in all but one case the average total charge was from 6 percent to 58 percent higher in the for-profit hospitals.

Patients have generally been insulated from higher for-profit charges by their third-party coverage. Nevertheless, at least one Las Vegas man found the cost of care at his local for-profit hospital upsetting. In a June 1985 letter to the *Las Vegas Review Journal,* the gentleman recounted how he had

... recently had the misfortune of requiring emergency room treatment at Humana Sunrise Hospital for kidney stone problems. This was my second encounter with this problem. The first encounter occurred last July, and I was treated at Southern Nevada Memorial Hospital.

As the treatment was almost identical, I have had the opportunity to compare the costs of the two facilities. I was not surprised to find that Humana hospitals were more expensive; however, I was shocked to discover that the cost was fully 50% above that of Southern Nevada.

As I was curtly informed by administrative personnel at Humana, the costs were higher because Humana is a "private" hospital, and Southern Nevada is a county hospital. Now this is a point well taken and probably could account for a 15 or 20% difference, but 50%—Come on, who does Humana think they are fooling?

For-profit hospitals have also increased health care costs indirectly by building unneeded hospitals. For example, primarily because of the growth of for-profit hospitals, twelve Florida counties, underbedded in 1972, had 6,600 excess beds three years later. The for-profit chains that had controlled 16.7 percent of beds in 1972 had built 60 percent of the new beds.

If efficiency is measured by maximum use of the physical plant, for-profit chains are once again found wanting. In 1985, average hospital occupancy rates for the four largest proprietary chains ranged from 46 percent to 56 percent. Empty beds were not as important under the old cost-based reimbursement system, as charges to insurers for patients in the occupied beds could be increased to cover the cost of unoccupied beds. This changed with Medicare's new reimbursement system which pays a flat rate based on a patient's diagnosis and vigorous cost-containment programs begun by Medicaid and private health insurers in 1983 and 1984.

The old cost-based reimbursement systems not only rewarded hospitals for providing extra services and hiking up prices but failed to penalize them for empty beds. Medicare's new flat-rate reimbursement scheme provides opposite incentives: it rewards hospitals for reducing services (the fewer services provided, the more money made) and penalizes them for their empty beds. This dramatic change in the way hospitals are paid would, it could be supposed, hurt most those hospitals that had taken greatest advantage of the old system. This seems to have happened. In October of 1985, announcements by the leading chains of flat or reduced earnings stunned Wall Street and resulted in a steep decline in their stocks.

In response to changes in hospital reimbursement and declining hospital revenues, chains began to diversify, investing in more lucrative areas of medical care, including nursing homes, insurance companies, health maintenance organizations (HMOs), neighborhood emergi-centers (often called doc-in-the-box), and home health agencies. Their proven ability to maximize profits from the provision of medical services will thus be tested in new arenas. Called a "managed system" approach, this vertical integration of the health industry gives proprietary chains added power to shape the future of health care delivery in this country.

Analysts may argue over the exact impact of the growth of the proprietary chains, but most agree that in subtle and not-so-subtle ways chains have irrevocably changed the milieu in which hospitals operate. Nowhere has the change been more profound than in the provision of hospital care to the poor.

TURNING AWAY THE POOR

Chains make no secret of their view that health care is nothing more than an economic commodity to be sold in the marketplace for a profit. One Humana senior vice president put it this way: "health care is a necessity, but so is food. Do you know of any neighborhood grocery store where you can walk out with $3,000 worth of food that you haven't paid for?" Chain spokesmen are also commonly heard to claim that their hospitals' commitment to the poor is taken care of by the payment of taxes. Given this view, it is not surprising that several state studies have found large disparities in the amount of care for the indigent provided by for-profit hospitals and voluntary and public hospitals. Typically, public hospitals provide the lion's share of uncompensated care; voluntary hospitals come in a poor second, with for-profit facilities running a dismal third.

Although for-profit hospitals constituted 32 percent of Florida's hospitals in 1983, they provided only 4 percent of the net charity care provided within the state. Florida's Hospital Cost Containment Board openly criticized for-profit hospitals as its 1983–84 annual report for their failure to share the burden of serving the uninsured poor. According to a report by the Texas Task Force on Indigent Health Care, for-profit hospitals made up 19.1 percent of the hospitals in that state in 1983, but provided less than 1 percent of the charity care and only 2.7 percent of the bad debt. Nonprofit hospitals, while making up 36.1 percent of the hospital facilities in Texas, provided 13.1 percent of charity care and 42.8 percent of the bad debt. Texas's public facilities provided most of the care of the poor: public hospitals, constituting 44.7 percent of the hospitals in the state, provide 86.9 percent of the charity care and 54.6 percent of the bad debt.

Some national data on provision of care for the indigent are available from the January 1981 Office of Civil Rights (OCR) survey of all general, short-term hospitals in the United States. An analysis of OCR data on inpatient and admitting practices showed that 9.5 percent of all hospital patients were uninsured in 1981; yet only 6 percent of patients treated at for-profit hospitals were uninsured, while 16.8 percent of those treated at hospitals owned by state and local governments were uninsured. Alan Sager also used OCR data in this study of hospital closures and relocation in 52 cities. He found that of the 4,038 patients categorized on admission as charity care patients (not to be charged) during the OCR survey, only 1 received care at a for-profit facility.

To some extent, the amount of charity care provided by for-profit hospitals is limited by their locations—in suburban white communities where few of the poor reside. When those hospitals are matched with similarly located nonprofit facilities, the amount of care to the poor differs little by ownership. However, geography does not explain why chain hospitals located in areas with significant numbers of uninsured populations provide so little in the way of charity.

The plight of one 56-year-old uninsured laborer described in a recent *Washington Post* article is a case in point. Mr. G. R. Lafon sought care for third-degree grease burns on his side and back at the hospital nearest his home, a for-profit facility. The hospital and two other for-profit hospitals refused him emergency care because he did not have a deposit ranging from $500 to $1,500. One of the hospitals did take the precaution of inserting an intravenous tube and a catheter to stabilize his liquids before sending him on his way. After seven hours and a 70-mile trek, Lafon arrived at Parkland Memorial Hospital in Dallas, the city's public hospital, where he was immediately admitted. Lafon required nineteen days of hospitalization and a skin graft for a cost of $22,000. Soon after discharge, he began receiving notices for an overdue hospital billl—not for the $22,000 owed to Parkland (that will be written off because Lafon is poor and uninsured), but for $373.75 from the for-profit facility to cover the cost of the catheter and intravenous tube.

Similar horror stories can be heard all over the South. In Memphis, for example, the city's largest HCA hospital threatened early in 1985 that it would stop chemotherapy treatments for a farmer with lung cancer when his family ran out of cash to continue the treatments. It was not until the day a suit was to be filed against the hospital claiming abandonment, denial of emergency medical care, intentional infliction of mental distress and extortion, that the HCA relented and agreed to continue treatment.

Voluntary hospitals and even some public hospitals also turn away the poor. What distinguishes the actions of for-profit chain hospitals from those of individual voluntary or public facilities is that the for-profit hospitals' policy of denying access is established at corporate headquarters and affects all their facilities throughout the nation. Although many voluntary hospitals are reducing their uncompensated care load in order to survive, others continue to view care for the poor as part of their mission.

The impact of care to the uninsured goes beyond the number of poor that proprietary chains do and do not serve. In the past five years, 180 public hospitals have been bought or managed by for-profit companies. This has resulted in an inexorable diminution of care to the poor: public officials do not sell hospitals in order to continue providing indigent care; they do so in order to relieve themselves from what they perceive as an onerous burden. These sales, in turn, add to the financial troubles of the public and voluntary hospitals which continue to serve the indigent population. Chains also have had one other far-reaching effect on the provision of care to the poor: they have caused what Louanne Kennedy of the City University of New York describes as "the proprietarization of voluntary hospitals."

BEAT 'EM OR JOIN 'EM

Nonprofit hospitals have long had a split personality, torn by the need to make money (their business side) and the need to succor the poor and sick (their humanitarian or social side). The rapid growth of for-profit chains forced nonprofit facilities to come to terms with this dichotomy. In the process, hospitals became more businesslike and less concerned with humanitarian goals.

Interestingly, for-profit chains did promote competition in the delivery of hospital services but not, as the supply/demand curve predicts, on the basis of price. In the middle and late 1970s, as the number of empty beds increased, hospital survival became increasingly predicated on attracting physicians who would admit their privately insured patients. In the competition for doctors, a hospital belonging to a large chain with easy access to capital had distinct advantages over the local voluntary and especially the public facility. A choice between a 30-year-old public hospital with its leaky roof, overcrowded emergency room (filled with poor people), and frequent equipment breakdowns and the spanking new Humana or HCA hospital with the latest in diagnostic equipment and nary a poor person in sight, was no choice at all.

Chains also had the money to recruit doctors to their hospitals. For example, an April 5, 1982, Humana recruiting letter to pediatricians offered the following inducements to join a five-physician multispeciality group in Springhill, Louisiana:

guaranteed income—$5,500 per month for the first six months; the lowest projected first-year income is $150,000;

rent-free office—absolutely no business or other overhead expenses the first year; this includes a paid nurse, secretarial and office equipment and furniture, free utilities, and more;

paid health/dental/life/malpractice insurance; company car; paid moving expenses; paid country club membership; paid on-site visit.

The most famous for-profit hospital recruit,

Dr. William DeVries, was brought to the Humana Heart Institute in Louisville, Kentucky, with the promise of 100 artificial heart transplants.

In the competition over physicians, chains did not ignore the patient. Although price was not a consideration, well-heeled patients were lured to specialized chain facilities which touted the latest in sports medicine, treatment of diet disorders, wine and candelight dinners for new parents, and free hairstyle with a "tummy tuck." If patients were to be appealed to directly, then chain products had to be merchandized, and so advertising budgets became part and parcel of the cost of providing medical care.

At the same time as voluntary hospitals were losing private, paying patients to the new hospital on the block, they were also getting less money for the private, paying patients still filling their beds. Generally, under the blank-check reimbursement system, hospitals simply passed on the costs of their nonpaying patients to their privately insured patients whose care was paid for through employer-subsidized insurance. Thus, employers were subsidizing care for the poor through higher insurance premiums. While hospital access for the poor has been far from universal, a great deal of service was paid for by this cost shift. The health insurance industry estimated that it was charged an extra $8 billion in 1983 to subsidize the provision of care to those who could not pay and were uninsured.

As hospital costs kept spiraling (in some years by 20 percent) and as the number of uninsured poor increased, commercial insurors and business interests became less willing to pay this cost shift or what they called a "sick tax." Arguing that they should only have to pay premium costs to cover care for their work force, not the nation's poor, employers demanded and got reductions in their premium costs and the beginnings of competition based on price.

Voluntary and public hospitals subsidizing the poor are at a distinct disadvantage in any game based on price competition because they are, according to policy analysts, playing on an "uneven playing field." To even stay in the game, they are forced to act like their opponents, which means toughening up their billing and collection practices and managing their indigent patient load. Unfortunately, "managing" is often synonymous with "excluding." An American Hospital Association study found that about 15 percent of nonprofit hospitals adopted limits on the amount of charity care they provided, and 84 percent increased billing and collection efforts.

There is no question that many tax-exempt charitable institutions provided little or no care to the poor well before the proprietary chains came on the scene. For these hospitals, for-profit chains made barring the poor an acceptable way of doing business. For nonprofit hospitals that took their charitable status seriously, the chains made it difficult and in some instances impossible for them to continue fulfilling their mission. The traditional behavior of tax-exempt hospitals that provide little or no charity care is being challenged in state courts. A decision by the Utah Supreme Court denied tax-exempt status to two nonprofit hospitals owned by Intermountain Health Care, a nonprofit hospital chain, because the hospitals did not meet their obligation to provide charity care.

"If you can't beat 'em, join 'em," was a slogan adopted by a large number of voluntary and public hospitals in the 1980s. In addition to conscious efforts to reduce services to the poor, nonprofit hospitals embarked on a mad scramble to buy nursing homes, establish home health agencies, "unbundle" hospital services (remove services such as pharmacy, laboratory, and X-ray from the hospital to get the higher reimbursement rates), specialize in highly profitable ventures such as sports medicine and wellness centers, structure patients care to achieve optimal reimbursement, consider terminating unprofitable services, and advertise.

While most hospitals argue that these changes are necessary for survival, others

maintain their efforts are directed toward continuing to subsidize charity care. This latter justification is commonly used by public hospitals which began in 1984 and 1985 to undertake corporate restructuring as an alternative to outright sale or transfer of management to a for-profit firm. While the exact configurations vary, the basic idea is to create several new nonprofit and for-profit subsidies. One of the nonprofits will lease the existing hospital for a nominal amount and operate it for the actual public owners, blurring what had once been a clear-cut distinction between for-profit and public hospitals.

Nonprofit hospitals copied the for-profit giants in one other way. Finding strength in numbers, voluntary hospitals began to form their own nonprofit chains. Although some chains of voluntary facilities (such as religious hospitals) predated the rise of for-profit chains, the impetus for increased horizontal integration among nonprofit hospitals in the 1980s was competition from the proprietary chains.

GOOD BUSINESS OR BASIC CARE?

It is likely that ten or so for-profit and nonprofit managed systems will compete with one another to serve the paying customer, while the few public hospitals left (primarily large inner-city facilities which cannot be closed for fear of adverse political repercussions) will continue their struggle to serve the impoverished of the nation. Is this the legacy of the proprietarization of American hospitals? The answer is no. The growth of for-profit chains was simply the natural development of a society that never viewed health care as a right, guaranteed to every citizen, and a government adverse to bucking the prevailing notion that medical providers should be left to their own devices to shape the nation's health care delivery system. If, in the shaping, no space was available for millions of Americans, so be it.

Uwe Reinhardt, a Princeton economist, argues that America's political ideology—its fear of big government—helped to create a medical system that tolerates "visible social pathos in our streets." This system accepts the existence of 35 million uninsured, most of whom are poor and near-poor; denial of prenatal and sometimes delivery care to poor women; the transferring or "dumping" of 500 patients a month from private Chicago hospitals to Cook County General, a public facility; excessive markups on drugs needed to control hypertension and other chronic illnesses; inhuman conditions in many of our nursing homes; and, lately, the premature discharge of elderly patients from hospitals when Medicare payments prove inadequate to cover the costs of care.

Our reponse to this social pathos depends in large degree on how we view the delivery of medical care. If, as for-profit hospitals maintain, health care is a business, if HCA and Humana are no different than a Mc-Donald's or a Macy's, then, our response is obvious: protect against the grossest anti-competitive behavior, but generally adopt a laissez-faire attitude and let market forces dictate the supply and a price of goods. If, however, we believe that health care is more than a business, but a societal good, then our response is different indeed. Laws will be needed to assure that prices are controlled, profits limited, and people guaranteed the provision of basic health care.

Which is it? To date, we have either ignored the question or, when forced to confront it, tried to have it both ways. This has led to ambiguous policies at best and huge holes in the nation's health care safety net. The "let's have it both ways" mentality is evident in the government's Medicare policies. Although the provision of medical care to the elderly and disabled is clearly seen as a societal good, the federal government's Medicare reimbursement policy with its substantial return on investment and unlimited passing through of capital costs resulted in huge profits for investor-owned hospital chains and more money going for fewer services. It is only recently, with the advent of DRGs and legislation to eliminate return on equity (over three years) and proposals to cap federal reimbursements for capital costs, that we have begun to realize that unlimited profits may be at odds with the nation's commitment to providing health care for the elderly.

States have not been any more certain of how to reconcile the needs of the ill and the needs of the medical care marketplace. A few northeastern states have controlled the growth of for-profit hospitals through hospital rate regulation; by limiting rates hospitals can charge, states limit the profits hospitals can make. These states also include payment for care of the indigent in their controlled rates. Other states have sought to require good citizenship of all their hospitals, for-profit and voluntary alike. Florida, South Carolina, and Virginia tax hospitals in order to pay for increased care of the indigent. Tougher emergency room laws in a few states, most notably Texas, have made it more difficult for hospitals to refuse emergency care to the poor or inappropriately transfer them to the nearest public hospital. Efforts have also been made, primarily through the health planning program, to require hospitals wanting to build or modernize to provide a small amount of charity care. North Carolina now requires for-profit hospitals that buy public hospitals to continue to provide care to the poor of the community.

Unfortunately, these efforts are too little, too late; the poor and, increasingly, the middle class with inadequate insurance are not guaranteed access to even basic hospital care when ill. Neither the federal government nor the states have been willing to limit profits made from providing hospital care, to require all hospitals to serve a minimum of uninsured and Medicaid recipients, or to provide health care coverage for all in need.

Unlike other Western industrialized nations, we treat medical care as a commodity to be bought and sold in the marketplace. This marketplace mentality is allowing corporate medicine to distort our medical care system into one that costs us a great deal even while it serves a diminishing share of our people.

39

Breaking the Cycle of Failure

George Melloan

Patrick F. Taylor might seem an unlikely educational reformer. He is the sole owner of Taylor Energy Co., an oil and gas company worth $300 million to $400 million. He likes fast boats and airplanes and wears expensive boots and heavy gold cuff links. He may be the richest man in Louisiana.

But he is more than that. Because he left his East Texas home at age 16 with 35 cents in his pockets and had to scrabble for a petroleum-engineering degree, he is a passionate believer in education. His interest has just led to a reform of Louisiana's system of higher education that will make college admission a greater academic challenge but at the same time remove financial obstacles for poor youths.

You might say that Pat Taylor is one of those thousand points of light George Bush talks about, a volunteer applying remedies of his own design to a serious social prob-

lem. He also may have rediscovered something obvious but often overlooked in all the theories about educational quality: the importance of self-motivation.

"I've heard all the arguments for better teachers, smaller classes—indirect lighting, for gosh sakes. But picture the learning process. You can have a teacher standing over every kid, a superlative teacher, and if that kid does not want to learn you can't force it into him. What does it take to learn? It takes daily effort. It takes getting up in the morning, going to school, paying attention, receiving the assignments, doing the homework. That has got to be from self-motivation."

Ideas from businessmen no longer are scoffed at by professional educators. The record of failure in public education is appalling. By one estimate, 18% of the nation's 18-year-olds are school dropouts and a similar number with high-school degrees are functionally illiterate. Business interest in doing something about the problem has been rising rapidly, and for good reason—there is a shortage of trainable workers. Business corporations have launched their own in-house remedial-education programs and increasingly are working with local school systems. Former Procter & Gamble Chairman Brad Butler is running a school-reform campaign by the Committee for Economic Development, primarily a business group.

Pat Taylor's interest in education has expressed itself several ways: direct aid to promising students, service on the Louisiana State University board of supervisors, the Taylor Merit Scholars Program at the University of New Orleans and, most recently, chairmanship of the governor's committee on college availability. His university reform was born out of a request that he visit a junior high in a rundown New Orleans neighborhood to serve as a "role model."

This was a familiar task. Mr. Taylor has been delivering inspirational talks to students and teachers on "Horatio Alger" days for some time. But he was warned that these kids were different. All 221 of them were either two or three years behind in school. They were in what was called a "transition class," a euphemism for salvage operation. They were 95% black, mostly children of single parents in a high-crime, high-drug area. It was estimated that 80% wouldn't finish high school. It was considered to be futile, and maybe even cruel, to talk to these kids about college.

"I didn't like what I'd been told," says Mr. Taylor. "I didn't enjoy the realization that these kids were different. So I made up my mind to try something. I was going to satisfy myself on whether in fact these kids placed no value on education.

"I laid it on pretty thick. I told them where I had come from and what I had, how I had succeeded—oil fields, gas fields, offshore, racing boats, airplanes, ranches—all that stuff. And I told them that I felt like I had had an advantage that most of their parents had not had in that I was born white, but that I personally did not think it was that much of a disadvantage to be black nowadays and that it frankly didn't make any difference.

"If they would stay in school, do their work and if they were a success, it was to their benefit. They were responsible. If they chose to drop out of school and end up on the streets, or on welfare, they could blame whomever they wished but it wouldn't make any difference. They would have to live with the results of that failure. But I didn't think it had to be that way.

"So I tried an experiment. I asked, 'How many of you kids would like to go to college?' The reaction was extraordinary. Every hand went up. Nobody looked around to see what the others were going to do. Every hand went up as if they all wanted to be the first ones to get their hands up. There was no lack of appreciation for education. Every kid knew that education was the way to succeed in our society.

"So I said, 'OK, here's how we're going to do this now.' While I was on the LSU board of supervisors, I had led the fight for LSU and later the University of New Orleans to adopt a 17½ core-credit curricula for admissions. At that time it was the only admission standards ever adopted in Louisiana. We've had open admissions. So I said. 'Your teachers know what these courses are. You kids stay in school and in your four years of high school complete these courses. If you make an A average you don't need me, the universities will snap you up. If you make Cs and Ds, I don't think you'll be qualified for college but you'll have a valid 12th grade education and you can go to vo-tech school or junior college and you can get a job. But if you make a B average, I'll see to it you go to college.' "

Mr. Taylor reached an agreement with three college presidents to waive tuition, room and board if his kids fulfilled his challenge. He arranged for the 83 eighth-graders to have a six-week summer course on the Loyola and UNO campuses, taking classes, attending cultural events, learning personal hygiene and working part time at paying jobs. Some did surprisingly well. He had "Taylor's Kids" T-shorts and blazers made up to create group peer pressures that would give the kids some protection from outside influences. Today, a year later, 172 of the original 221 still are in school, but the shrinkage results from family moves, not dropouts. One became pregnant. One got into trouble for a joy ride in a stolen car.

"I didn't pat them on the head and make them nice little boys and girls. I gave them something to risk. They now perceive that they have a future and they are not going to do those things."

Mr. Taylor wants all students to understand that they have to work in high school to make it to college. At his urging, 12 of the 15 state four-year institutions have replaced open enrollment with admissions requirements, including a high school grade point average of 2.5. But no qualified student will be denied admission because of financial circumstances.

Several lessons may be buried in the Pat Taylor experience: It's possible to motivate ghetto youths previously lacking in direction and hope; hope can be generated by living proof that poor kids still can become rich adults in the American system; the challenge-reward principle works with kids pretty much the way it works in the oil and gas business.

As Pat Taylor puts it: "You don't always get from individuals what you expect. But if you expect nothing, you're going to get nothing."

40

A Matter of Choice

Gary Putka

The schools of Cambridge, Massachusetts, didn't tell Lynn Chamberlain where her son Johnbryan would go to kindergarten. She told them.

Before enrolling Johnbryan last September, Ms. Chamberlain toured all 13 of the system's elementary schools. She became, as she says, a woman "obsessed"—grilling principals, sitting in on classes, and taking note of who treated her questions lightly. In the end, she enrolled Johnbryan in the Graham and Parks Alternative Elementary School, a loosely structured school where she has become active on parent committees.

"I'm delighted," says Ms. Chamberlain, a computer analyst. "The energy level here is astounding. If I'd had math classes like theirs I might have chosen it as a profession."

Enthusiasm for public education is on the rise in Cambridge, a pioneer in allowing parents a choice in where they send their children to public school. Originally adopted in Cambridge and elsewhere to foster desegregation, choice is now spreading rapidly throughout the nation on its merit as a school-improvement tool.

Minnesota is well on its way to requiring multiple options for all students by next year. A dozen other states from California to Maine, have adopted laws giving choices to some students—usually high-schoolers or dropout risks. At least 15 new state initiatives are under legislative consideration. Seattle, Chicago, Boston and other big cities have adopted or are formulating choose-a-school plans. Even President Bush has hopped on the bandwagon. He wants $100 million for establishing "magnet schools" that would give students and parents extra choices within the public school system.

"The idea is just taking off," says Joseph

Nathan, an educational specialist at the Humphrey Institute for Public Affairs in Minneapolis. In a recent report, the Denver-based Education Commission of the States called choice "the darling of new legislative ideas" in current school reform.

Though each plan varies, the fundamental principles are the same: Allow parents at least one alternative to their neighborhood school and reward schools that attract the most students. Schools forced to compete for students will improve, the argument goes. Parents and students who must choose would then become educational consumer activists, more demanding and more motivated.

The bad schools? Close them down, say disciples of choice. Or at least dismiss their principals and reorganize them.

"Choice is the best lever there is for really transforming schools and enhancing educational opportunity," says Mary Ann Raywid, a Hofstra University professor and educational consultant.

Surveys in Minnesota and Cambridge show that parents' satisfaction with schools rises when they are allowed to choose. Other evidence suggests that schools in competition for kids move rapidly to add embellishments such as advanced classes, computers, or fine arts.

But will the schools teach harder and better? Will students wind up knowing more algebra or history? Most choice plans haven't been around long enough to provide definitive answers. And some of the older ones are giving mixed signals.

In Cambridge, for instance, the public system has lost some students to private schools since the choice plan was introduced there in 1981. The number of students passing the basic competency test there has also slipped, to under 82% from 85%. (School officials says the results aren't strictly comparable, because the test has changed.)

Many educators remain deeply skeptical, even suspicious, of choice. They contend it could drain resources from inner-city schools and worsen their plight. Black educators, especially, argue that in practice, some plans give black students access only to inferior schools.

"Some blacks see the whole choice movement as a move by white people who used to be opposed to busing," says John O'Bryant, a black member of the Boston School Committee. "It may help a small number of students, but it won't do much good across the board," adds Willard Baker, former executive director of the Minnesota School Boards Association.

Whatever its merits, choice has snowballed—partly, it seems, out of frustration with the educational reform movement's accomplishments so far. The decade has seen virtually every state raise curriculum or promotion standards, a 29% real increase in spending on public schools and many new initiatives for those most at risk in the system—minorities, the urban poor, and the handicapped. But the tide of educational mediocrity, to paraphrase the 1983 report, "A Nation at Risk," hasn't appreciably turned.

After a period of modest recovery, Scholastic Aptitude Test scores fell again last year. Only marginal gains have been made in mathematics and science test scores; in science, students are still dumber than they were 20 years ago. Fewer than half the nation's high-school juniors know the year of D-Day or the plot line of "Julius Caesar." Most Americans between 18 and 24 can't find Britain or France on the map. All this while American battles Japan for primacy in a global economy that relies increasingly on creating, supplying, and applying knowledge.

Frustrated by the pace of improvement and confronted with new austerity in federal and state budgets, some educational policy makers are pushing a low-cost agenda that might be called educational deregulation—putting free-market forces to work in the public schools. In one manifestation, adopted in Washington State, Rochester, New York, Dade County, Florida, and elsewhere, school authorites are giving teachers and principals some budgetary and managerial autonomy in return for performance promises.

Choice, however, is spreading even faster. Boston's School Committee has adopted a school-choice plan for next fall to succeed the 1974 court-ordered desegregation plan that ripped the city apart racially. The new plan divides Boston into three zones. Parents would choose from among the schools in their zone in order of preference. Their selections would be honored, with some restrictions. The main one is that a school's white-to-minorities ratio can't vary from its zone's by more than 10%.

To reformers, the meat of the plan is what happens to schools that fail to attract enough students. In the first year of undersubscription, a school would have to devise its own self-improvement plan. If that doesn't help, the zone superintendent would intervene with his recommendations. After a third year of underenrollment, the zone superintendent or citizen's council could fire the principal, reduce school size, or close the school down.

A report commissioned by Boston Mayor Raymond Flynn calls the plan "a continuous public referendum on public schooling." Michael Alves, one of the plan's authors, predicts a turnaround for the troubled Boston system and a flowering of new ideas. "This is a concept that accommodates all the issues of school reform—desegregation, poor kids getting better access, more variety, and educational improvement," he says.

But choice has stirred old passions here, giving rise to charges that the city's white power structure would use it to disenfranchise black students. The School Committee's nine white members voted for the plan. All four black members voted against it, arguing that schools in heavily black neighborhoods are decrepit and couldn't compete fairly for students. Thomas Atkins, a lawyer for the plaintiffs in the school-desegregation case, says that the plan lacks adequate safeguards to prevent resegregation. He vows to haul the system back into court unless changes are made.

"We're concerned that you're really not giving people anything to choose from" says Mr. O'Bryant of the School Committee. Noting that Boston's plan doesn't provide for additional funding, he adds: "You can't do new programs and hire new staff without money.

One longstanding choice plan is in New York City's School District Four, in the *barrio* of East Harlem. In 1973, the district was at rock bottom: It ranked 32nd of 32 city districts in reading scores, with only 16% of its students reading at grade level or higher. Slowly, the district began introducing "alternative" middle schools—with specialities like performing arts or science—that students could elect instead of their regular schools. Now, choice has been extended to all 20 middle schools in the district, with each school competing for students.

At last count, 67% of the district's students read at or above grade level. Last year, some 300 middle-school students moved on to the city's prestigious, selective high schools, compared with about a dozen in the early 1970s. One middle school that didn't attract enough kids was shut down and reopened with a new program and principal.

Seymour Fliegel, a city school official who helped design the East Harlem system, says its success is evidence that choice works—so long as it is meaningful choice. "Schools need a mission, a dream, a vision," he says. "It's important to have choice—but choice is not enough. There must also be quality and diversity.

Choice has brought another, more tangible benefit to District Four, one of the city's poorest neighborhoods. Thanks to the growing reputation of its schools, the district now attracts 1,000 students from other parts of the city, along with extra state funding for each. Its waiting list includes many from the affluent Upper East Side and West Side of Manhattan.

Not long ago, schools in Prince George's County, Maryland, were reputed to be among the worst in the Washington, D.C., area. Enrollment, which peaked at 161,000 in 1972, plummeted to 103,000 in 1984, as racial tensions and safety fears caused parents to pull their children out of the system in droves. But now, Prince George's parents wait in line up to three days to get into the 44 magnet schools the county established in 1985 as part of its desegregation plan. The county's average scores on the California Achievement Test now exceed 70% of national norms, up from 50%. And enrollment has edged up a bit, partly because of net transfers from private schools.

Many parents, however, are still shut out of schools they want, leaving their children in non-magnet schools with less funding. A spokesman for the school system in Prince George's County says funds aren't available to raise each school's budget. He also notes that available magnet slots are decided on a first-come, first-served basis.

In Cambridge, about 75% of parents get their first-choice schools. Parent satisfaction and involvement have risen, surveys show, while program variety has increased. Unstructured classes, computers, and bilingual programs have proliferated.

At the John Tobin Elementary School, a modern building of bricks and carpeted concrete in West Cambridge, classrooms hum and tick with the noises of the modern office. Bobby, a brown-eyed first-grader, tentatively taps out a story about penguins on an Apple personal computer. Struggling to find the right keys, he fashions an ambitious, if imperfect, ending: "It look big in antarctca."

Tobin has flourished in the choice sweepstakes, partly because of an alternative computerized "School of the Future" curriculum. It attracts two-thirds of its 650 students from outside its neighborhood and has had to expand the number of kindergarten classes it offers.

To hook parents, Cambridge schools hold information nights and open houses. Each school has a "parent liaison officer" who becomes the school's salesman, arranging tours and talking up its strong points to interested parents.

"The choice system is really wonderful, because it encourages people to become involved with the school they choose," says Constance May, a Cambridge real-estate agent with two children in the system. After serving on parents' committees that help make hiring decisions and buy supplies, Ms. May considers choice's biggest plus to be the sense of control it gives parents over schools. She adds, "I feel empowered by it."

41

The "Cooling-Out" Function
in Higher Education
Burton R. Clark

A major problem of democratic society is inconsistency between encouragement to achieve and the realities of limited opportunity. Democracy asks individuals to act as if social mobility were universally possible; status is to be won by individual effort, and rewards are to accrue to those who try. But democratic societies also need selective training institutions, and hierarchical work organizations permit increasingly fewer persons to succeed at ascending levels. Situations of opportunity are also situations of denial and failure. Thus, democratic societies need not only to motivate achievement, but also to mollify those denied it in order to sustain motivation in the face of disappointment and to deflect resentment. In the modern mass democracy, with its large-scale organization, elaborated ideologies of equal

access and participation, and miminal commitment to social orgin as a basis for status, the task becomes critical.

The problem of blocked opportunity has been approached sociologically through means-ends analysis. Merton and others have called attention to the phenomenon of dissociation between culturally instilled goals and institutionally provided means of realization; discrepancy between ends and means is seen as a basic social source of individual frustration and recalcitrance.[1] We shall here extend means-ends analysis in another direction, to the responses of organized groups to means-ends disparities, in particular focusing attention on ameliorative processes that lessen the strains of dissociation. We shall do so by analyzing the most prevalent type of dissociation between

Revised and extended version of paper read at The Fifty-fourth Annual Meeting of the American Sociological Assn., Chicago, Sept. 3–5, 1959. Reprinted by permission of the publishers from *American Journal of Sociology*, 65 (1960).

aspirations and avenues in American education, specifying the structure and processes that reduce the stress of structural disparity and individual denial. Certain components of American higher education perform what may be called the cooling-out function,[2] and it is to these that attention will be drawn.

THE ENDS-MEANS DISJUNCTURE

In American higher education the aspirations of the multitude are encouraged by "open-door" admission to public-supported colleges. The means of moving upward in status and of maintaining high status now include some years in college, and a college education is a prerequisite of the better positions in business and the professions. The trend is toward an ever tighter connection between higher education and higher occupations, as increased specialization and professionalization insure that more persons will need more preparation. The high-school graduate, seeing college as essential to success, will seek to enter some college, regardless of his record in high school.

A second and allied source of public interest in unlimited entry into college is the ideology of equal opportunity.[3] Strictly interpreted, equality of opportunity means selection according to ability, without regard to extraneous considerations. Popularly interpreted, however, equal opportunity in obtaining a college education is widely taken to mean unlimited access to some form of college: in California, for example, state educational authorities maintain that high-school graduates who cannot qualify for the state university or state college should still have the "opportunity of attending a publicly supported institution of higher education," this being "an essential part of the state's goal of guaranteeing equal educational opportunities to all its citizens."[4] To deny access to college, then, is to deny equal opportunity. Higher education should make a seat available without judgment on past performance.

Many other features of current American life encourage college-going. School officials are reluctant to establish early critical hurdles for the young, as is done in Europe. With little enforced screening in the pre-college years, vocational choice and educational selection are postponed to the college years or later. In addition, the United States, a wealthy country, is readily supporting a large complex of colleges, and its expanding economy requires more specialists. Recently, a national concern that manpower be fully utilized has encouraged the extending of college training to more and different kinds of students. Going to college is also in some segments of society the thing to do; as a last resort, it is more attractive than the army or a job. Thus, ethical and practical urges together encourage the high-school graduate to believe that college is both a necessity and a right; similarly, parents and elected officials incline toward legislation and admission practices that insure entry for large numbers; and educational authorities find the need and justification for easy admission.

Even where pressures have been decisive in widening admission policy, however, the system of higher education has continued to be shaped partly by other interests. The practices of public colleges are influenced by the academic personnel, the organizational requirements of colleges, and external pressures other than those behind the open door. Standards of performance and graduation are maintained. A commitment to standards is encouraged by a set of values in which the status of a college, as defined by academicians and a large body of educated laymen, is closely linked to the perceived quality of faculty, student body, and curriculum. The raising of standards is supported by the faculty's desire to work with promising students and to enjoy membership in an enterprise of reputed quality—college authorities find low standards and poor students a handicap in competing with other colleges for such resources as able faculty as well as for academic status. The wish is widespread that college education be of the highest quality for the preparation of leaders in public affairs, business, and the professions. In brief, the institutional means of the students' progress toward college graduation and subsequent goals are shaped in large part by a commitment to quality embodied in college staff, traditions, and images.

The conflict between open-door admission and performance of high quality often means a wide discrepancy between the hopes of entering students and the means of their realization. Students who pursue ends for which a college education is required but who have little academic ability gain admission into colleges only to encounter standards of performance they cannot meet. As a result, while some students of low promise are successful, for large numbers failure is inevitable and *structured*. The denial is delayed, taking place within the college instead of at the edge of the system. It requires that many colleges handle the student who intends to complete college and has been allowed to become involved but whose destiny is to fail.

RESPONSES TO DISJUNCTURE

What is done with the student whose destiny will normally be early termination? One answer is unequivocal dismissal. This "hard" response is found in the state university that bows to pressure for broad admissions but then protects standards by heavy dropout. In the first year it weeds out many of the incompetent, who may number a third or more of the entering class.[5] The response of the college is hard in that failure is clearly defined as such. Failure is public; the student often returns home. This abrupt change in status and in access to the means of achievement may occur simultaneously in a large college or university for hundreds, and sometimes thousands, of students after the first semester and at the end of the freshman year. The delayed denial is often viewed on the outside as heartless, a slaughter of the innocents.[6] This excites public

pressure and anxiety, and apparently the practice cannot be extended indefinitely as the demand for admission to college increases.

A second answer is to sidetrack unpromising students rather than have them fail. This is the "soft" response: never to dismiss a student but to provide him with an alternative. One form of it in some state universities is the detour to an extension division or a general college, which has the advantage of appearing not very different from the main road. Sometimes "easy" fields of study, such as education, business administration, and social science, are used as alternatives to dismissal.[7] The major form of the soft response is not found in the four-year college or university, however, but in the college that specializes in handling students who will soon be leaving—typically, the two-year public junior college.

In most states where the two-year college is a part of higher education, the students likely to be caught in the means-ends disjuncture are assigned to it in large numbers. In California, where there are over 60 public two-year colleges in a diversified system that includes the state university and numerous four-year state colleges, the junior college is unselective in admissions and by law, custom, and self-conception accepts all who wish to enter.[8] It is tuition-free, local, and under local control. Most of its entering students want to try for the baccalaureate degree, transferring to a "senior" college after one or two years. About two-thirds of the students in the junior colleges of the state are in programs that permit transferring; but, of these, only about one-third actually transfer to a four-year college.[9] The remainder, or two out of three of the professed transfer students, are "latent terminal students": their announced intention and program of study entails four years of college, but in reality their work terminates in the junior college. Constituting about half of all the students in the California junior colleges, and somewhere between one-third and one-half of junior college students nationally,[10] these students cannot be ignored by the colleges. Understanding their careers is important to understanding modern higher education.

THE REORIENTING PROCESS

This type of student in the junior college is handled by being moved out of a transfer major to a one-or two-year program of vocational, business, or semiprofessional training. This calls for the relinquishing of his original intention, and he is induced to accept a substitute that has lower status in both the college and society in general.

In one junior college[11] the initial move in a cooling-out process is pre-entrance testing: low scores on achievement tests lead poorly qualified students into remedial classes. Assignment to remedial work casts doubt and slows the student's movement into bona fide transfer courses. The remedial courses are, in effect, a subcollege. The student's achievement scores are made part of a counseling folder that will become increasingly significant to him. An objective record of ability and performance begins to accumulate.

A second step is a counseling interview before the beginning of the first semester, and before all subsequent semesters for returning students. "At this interview the counselor assists the student to choose the proper courses in light of his objective, his test scores, the high school record and test records from his previous schools."[12] Assistance in choosing "the proper courses" is gentle at first. Of the common case of the student who wants to be an engineer but who is not a promising candidate, a counselor said: "I never openly countermand his choice, but edge him toward a terminal program by gradually laying out the facts of life." Counselors may become more severe later when grades provide a talking point and when the student knows that he is in trouble. In the earlier counseling the desire of the student has much weight; the counselor limits himself to giving advice and stating the probability of success. The advice

is entered in the counseling record that shadows the student.

A third and major step in reorienting the latent terminal student is a special course entitled "Orientation to College," mandatory for entering students. All sections of it are taught by teacher-counselors who comprise the counseling staff, and one of its purposes is "to assist students in evaluating their own abilities, interests, and aptitudes; in assaying their vocational choices in light of this evaluation; and in making educational plans to implement their choices." A major section of it takes up vocational planning; vocational tests are given at a time when opportunities and requirements in various fields of work are discussed. The tests include the "Lee Thorpe Interest Inventory" ("given to all students for motivating a self-appraisal of vocational choice") and the "Strong Interest Inventory" ("for all who are undecided about choice or who show disparity between accomplishment and vocational choice"). Mechanical and clerical aptitude tests are taken by all. The aptitudes are directly related to the college's terminal programs, with special tests, such as a pre-engineering ability test, being given according to need. Then an "occupational paper is required of all students for their chosen occupation"; in it the student writes on the required training and education and makes a "self-appraisal of fitness."

Tests and papers are then used in class discussion and counseling interviews, in which the students themselves arrange and work with a counselor's folder and a student test profile and, in so doing, are repeatedly confronted by the accumulating evidence—the test scores, course grades, recommendations of teachers and counselors. This procedure is intended to heighten self-awareness of capacity in relation to choice and hence to strike particularly at the latent terminal student. The teacher-counselors are urged constantly to "be alert to the problem of unrealistic vocational goals" and to "help students to accept their limitations and strive for success in other worthwhile objectives that are within their grasp." The orientation class was considered a good place "to talk tough," to explain in an *impersonal* way the facts of life for the overambitous student. Talking tough to a whole group is part of a soft treatment of the individual.

Following the vocational counseling, the orientation course turns to "building an educational program," to study of the requirements for graduation of the college in transfer and terminal curriculum, and to planning of a four-semester program. The students also become acquainted with the requirements of the colleges to which they hope to transfer, here contemplating additional hurdles such as the entrance examinations of other colleges. Again, the hard facts of the road ahead are brought to bear on self-appraisal.

If he wishes, the latent terminal student may ignore the counselor's advice and the test scores. While in the counseling class, he is also in other coures, and he can wait to see what happens. Adverse counseling advice and poor test scores may not shut off his hope of completing college; when this is the case, the deterrent will be encountered in the regular classes. Here the student is divested of expectations, lingering from high school, that he will automatically pass and, hopefully, automatically be transferred. Then, receiving low grades, he is thrown back into the counseling orbit, a fourth step in his reorientation and a move justified by his actual accomplishment. The following indicates the nature of the referral system:

Need for Improvement Notices are issued by instructors to students who are doing unsatisfactory work. The carbon copy of the notice is given to the counselor who will be available for conference with the student. The responsibility lies with the student to see his counselor. However, experience shows that some counselees are unable to be sufficiently self-directive to seek aid. The counselor should, in such cases, send for the student, using the Request for Conference blank. If the student fails to respond to the Request for Conference slip, this may become a disciplinary matter and should be referred to the deans.

After a conference has been held, the Need for Improvement notices are filed in the student's folder. *This may be important* in case of a complaint concerning the fairness of a final grade.[13]

This directs the student to more advice and self-assessment, as soon and as often as he has classroom difficulty. The carbon-copy routine makes it certain that, if he does not seek advice, advice will seek him. The paper work and bureaucratic procedure have the purpose of recording referral and advice in black and white, where they may later be appealed to impersonally. As put in an unpublished report of the college, the overaspiring student and the one who seems to be in the wrong program require "skillful and delicate handling. An accumulation of pertinent factual information may serve to fortify the objectivity of the student-counselor relationship." While the counselor advises delicately and patiently, but persistently, the student is confronted with the record with increasing frequency.

A fifth step, one necessary for many in the throes of discouragement, is probation: "Students [whose] grade point averages fall below 2.0 [C] in any semester will, upon recommendation by the Scholarship Committee, be placed on probationary standing." A second failure places the student on second probation, and a third may mean that he will be advised to withdraw from the college altogether. The procedure is not designed to rid the college of a large number of students, for they may continue on probation for three consecutive semesters; its purpose is not to provide a status halfway out of the college but to "assist the student to seek an objective (major field) at a level on which he can succeed."[14] An important effect of probation is its slow killing-off of the lingering hopes of the most stubborn latent terminal students. A "transfer student" must have a C average to receive the Associate in Arts (a two-year degree) offered by the junior college, but no minimum average is set for terminal students. More important, four-year colleges require a C average or higher for the transfer student. Thus probationary status is the final blow to hopes of transferring and, indeed, even to graduating from the junior college under a transfer-student label. The point is reached where the student must permit himself to be reclassified or else drop out. In this college, 30 per cent of the students enrolled at the end of the spring semester, 1955–56, who returned the following fall were on probation; three out of four of these were transfer students in name.[15]

This sequence of procedures is a specific process of cooling-out;[16] its effect, at the best, is to let down hopes gently and unexplosively. Through it students who are failing or barely passing find their occupational and academic future being redefined. Along the way, teacher-counselors urge the latent terminal student to give up his plan of transferring and stand ready to console him in accepting a terminal curriculum. The drawn-out denial when it is effective is in place of a personal, hard "No"; instead, the student is brought to realize, finally, that it is best to ease himself out of the competition to transfer.

COOLING-OUT FEATURES

In the cooling-out process in the junior college are several features which are likely to be found in other settings where failure or denial is the effect of a structured discrepancy between ends and means, the responsible operatives or "coolers" cannot leave the scene or hide their identities, and the disappointment is threatening in some way to those responsible for it. At work and in training institutions this is common. The features are:

1. *Alternative achievement.* Substitute avenues may be made to appear not too different from what is given up, particularly as to status. The person destined to be denied or who fails is invited to interpret the second effort as more appropriate to his particular talent and is made to see that it will be the less frustrating. Here one does not fail but rectifies a mistake. The substitute status reflects less unfavorably on personal capacity than does being dismissed and forced to leave the scene. The

terminal student in the junior college may appear not very different from the transfer student—an "engineering aide," for example, instead of an "engineer"—and to be proceeding to something with a status of its own. Failure in college can be treated as if it did not happen; so, too, can poor performance in industry.[17]

2. *Gradual disengagement.* By a gradual series of steps, movement to a goal may be stalled, self-assessment encouraged, and evidence produced of performance. This leads toward the available alternatives at little cost. It also keeps the person in a counseling milieu in which advice is furnished, whether actively sought or not. Compared with the original hopes, however, it is a deteriorating situation. If the individual does not give up peacefully, he will be in trouble.

3. *Objective denial.* Reorientation is, finally, confrontation by the facts. A record of poor performance helps to detach the organization and its agents from the emotional aspects of the cooling-out work. In a sense, the overaspiring student in the junior college confronts himself, as he lives with the accumulating evidence, instead of the organization. The college offers opportunity; it is the record that forces denial. Record-keeping and other bureaucratic procedures appeal to universal criteria and reduce the influence of personal ties, and the personnel are thereby protected. Modern personnel record-keeping, in general, has the function of documenting denial.

4. *Agents of consolation.* Counselors are available who are patient with the overambitious and who work to change their intentions. They believe in the value of the alternative careers, though of lower social status, and are practiced in consoling. In college and in other settings, counseling is to reduce aspiration as well as to define and to help fulfil it. The teacher-counselor in the "soft" junior college is in contrast to the scholar in the "hard" college who simply gives a low grade to the failing student.

5. *Avoidance of standards.* A cooling-out process avoids appealing to standards that are ambiguous to begin with. While a "hard" attitude toward failure generally allows a single set of criteria, a "soft" treatment assumes that many kinds of ability are valuable, each in its place. Proper classification and placement are then paramount, while standards become relative.

IMPORTANCE OF CONCEALMENT

For an organization and its agents, one dilemma of a cooling-out role is that it must be kept reasonably away from public scrutiny and not clearly perceived or understood by prospective clientele. Should it become obvious, the organization's ability to perform it would be impaired. If high-school seniors and their families were to define the junior college as a place which diverts college-bound students, a probable consequence would be a turning-away from the junior college and increased pressure for admission to the four-year colleges and universities that are otherwise protected to some degree. This would, of course, render superfluous the part now played by the junior college in the division of labor among colleges.

The cooling-out function of the junior college is kept hidden, for one thing, as other functions are highlighted. The junior college stresses "the transfer function," "the terminal function," etc., not that of transforming transfer students into terminal students; indeed, it is widely identified as principally a transfer station. The other side of cooling-out is the successful performance in junior college of students who did poorly in high school or who have overcome socioeconomic handicaps, for they are drawn into higher education rather than taken out of it. Advocates of the junior college point to this salvaging of talented manpower, otherwise lost to the community and nation. It is indeed a function of the open door to let hidden talent be uncovered.

Then, too, cooling-out itself is reinterpreted so as to appeal widely. The junior college may be viewed as a place where all high-school graduates have the opportunity to explore possible careers and find the type of education appropriate to their individual ability; in short, as a place where everyone is admitted and everyone succeeds. As described by the former president of the University of California:

A prime virtue of the junior college, I think, is that most of its students succeed in what they set out to accomplish, and cross the finish line before they grow weary of the race. After two years in a course that they have chosen, they can go out prepared for activities that satisfy them, instead of being branded as failures. Thus the broadest possible opportunity may be provided for the largest number to make an honest try at further education with some possibility of success and with no route to a desired goal completely barred to them.[18]

The students themselves help to keep this function concealed by wishful unawareness. Those who cannot enter other colleges but still hope to complete four years will be motivated at first not to admit the cooling-out process to consciousness. One exposed to it, they again will be led not to acknowledge it, and so they are saved insult to their self-image.

In summary, the cooling-out process in higher education is one whereby systematic discrepancy between aspiration and avenue is covered over and stress for the individual and the system is minimized. The provision of readily available alternative achievements in itself is an important device for alleviating the stress consequent on failure and so preventing anomic and deviant behavior. The general result of cooling-out processes is that society can continue to encourage maximum effort without major disturbance from unfulfilled promises and expectations.

I am indebted to Erving Goffman and Martin A. Trow for criticism and to Sheldon Messinger for extended conceptual and editorial comment.

UNIVERSITY OF CALIFORNIA, BERKELEY

NOTES

1. "Aberrant behavior may be regarded sociologically as a symptom of dissociation between culturally prescribed aspirations and socially structured avenues for realizing these aspirations" (Robert K. Merton, "Social Structure and Anomie," in *Social Theory and Social Structure* [rev. ed.; Glencoe, Ill.: Free Press, 1957], p. 134). See also Herbert H. Hyman, "The Value Systems of Different Classes: A Social Psychological Contribution to the Analysis of

Stratification," in Reinhard Bendix and Seymour M. Lipset (eds.), *Class, Status and Power: A Reader in Social Stratification* (Glencoe, Ill.: Free Press, 1953), pp. 426–42; and the papers by Robert Dubin, Richard A. Cloward, Robert K. Merton, and Dorothy L. Meier, and Wendell Bell, in *American Sociological Review*, Vol. XXIV (April, 1959).

2. I am indebted to Erving Goffman's original statement of the cooling-out conception. See his "Cooling the Mark Out: Some Aspects of Adaptation to Failure," *Psychiatry*, XV (November, 1952), 451–63. Sheldon Messinger called the relevance of this concept to my attention.

3. Seymour Martin Lipset and Reinhard Bendix, *Social Mobility in Industrial Society* (Berkeley: University of California Press, 1959), pp. 78–101.

4. *A Study of the Need for Additional Centers of Public Higher Education in California* (Sacramento: California State Department of Education, 1957), p. 128. For somewhat similar interpretations by educators and laymen nationally see Francis J. Brown (ed.), *Approaching Equality of Opportunity in Higher Education* (Washington, D.C.: American Council on Education, 1955), and the President's Committee on Education beyond the High School, *Second Report to the President* (Washington, D.C.: Government Printing Office, 1957).

5. One national report showed that one out of eight entering students (12.5 per cent) in publicly controlled colleges does not remain beyond the first term or semester; one out of three (31 per cent) is out by the end of the first year; and about one out of two (46.6 percent) leaves within the first two years. In state universities alone, about one out of four withdraws in the first year and 40 per cent in two years (Robert E. Iffert, *Retention and Withdrawal of College Students* [Washington, D.C.: Department of Health, Education, and Welfare, 1958], pp. 15–20). Students withdraw for many reasons, but scholastic aptitude is related to their staying power. "A sizeable number of students of medium ability enter college, but ... few if any of them remain longer than two years" (*A Restudy of the Needs of California in Higher Education* [Sacramento: California State Department of Education, 1955], p. 120).

6. Robert L. Kelley, *The American Colleges and the Social Order* (New York: Macmillan Co., 1940), pp. 220–21.

7. One study has noted that on many campuses the business school serves "as a dumping ground for students who cannot make the grade in engineering or some branch of the liberal arts," this being a consequence of lower promotion standards than are found in most other branches of the university (Frank C. Pierson, *The Education of American Businessmen* [New York: McGraw-Hill Book Co., 1959], p. 63). Pierson also summarizes data on intelligence of students by field of study which indicate that education, business, and social science rank near the bottom in quality of students (*ibid.*, pp. 65–72).

8. Burton R. Clark, *The Open Door College: A Case Study* (New York: McGraw-Hill Book Co., 1960), pp. 44–45.

9. *Ibid.*, p. 116.

10. Leland L. Medsker, *The Junior College: Progress and Prospect* (New York: McGraw-Hill Book Co., 1960), chap. iv.

11. San Jose City College, San Jose, Calif. For the larger study see Clark, *op. cit.*

12. San Jose Junior College, Handbook for Counselors, 1957–58, p. 2. Statements in quotation marks in the next few paragraphs are cited from this.

13. *Ibid.*, p. 20.

14. Statements taken from unpublished material.

15. San Jose Junior College, "Digest of Analysis of the Records of 468 Students Placed on Probation for the Fall Semester, 1956," September 3, 1956.

16. Goffman's original statement of the concept of cooling-out referred to how the disappointing of expectations is handled by the disappointed person and especially by those responsible for the disappointment. Although his main illustration was the confidence game, where facts and potential achievement are deliberately misrepresented to the "mark" (the victim) by operators of the game, Goffman also applied the concept to failure in which those responsible act in good faith (*op. cit., passim*). "Cooling-out" is a widely useful idea when used to refer to a function that may vary in deliberateness.

17. *Ibid.*, p. 457; cf. Perrin Stryker, "How to Fire an Executive," *Fortune*, L (October, 1954), 116–17 and 178–92.

18. Robert Gordon Sproul, "Many Millions More," *Educational Record*, XXXIX (April, 1958), 102.

PART VII

GLOBAL PROBLEMS

Many problems have expanded beyond national borders, and some have reached global proportions: Economic production, environmental destruction, disease (especially AIDS), and international violence in the forms of war and terrorism are examples that we shall cover in this final Part of the book.

THE ENVIRONMENT AND TECHNOLOGICAL CHANGE

Underlying the broad social problems of the environment and technological change is unenlightened self-interest. Biologist Garrett Hardin (1968) likes to make this point through what is known as *the tragedy of the commons*.

Let us picture a pasture open to everyone. The number of cattle exactly matches the amount of available grass. Each herdsman, however, will seek to maximize his own gain. He thinks to himself: "If I add a cow to my herd, I will receive *all* the proceeds from the sale of this additional animal. The little overgrazing that this extra animal causes will be shared by all the other herdsmen."

Naturally, the herdsman adds another animal to his herd. He eventually adds another . . . and another. And every other herdsman sharing the commons does the same. Each is locked into a system that rewards him for increasing the size of his herd. And therein lies the tragedy. The pasture is limited, and additional stress eventually causes it—and the civilization dependent on it—to fail. As each pursues his own interest, all rush to their collective ruin.

A second "push" behind these global problems is "rising expectations." Built into both capitalist and communist economies is the demand for an ever-increasing standard of living based on massive industrial output. For this standard of living to increase, industry must grow. Capitalist economies stimulate expectations by bombarding the public with advertising. Creating the "need" for specific items, the capitalist system creates the "demand" that stimulates its own growth. Without extensive advertising, but with the knowledge of what is attainable, consumers in communist countries also place increasing demand on their economies for more material goods.

If at the end of the year industrial output has not increased, capitalist governments may "stimulate" the economy. They may reduce interest rates in order to spur investment in factories, or cut taxes to provide more spending money for the products of those factories. In communist nations, central planners dictate production goals. In both capitalist and communist nations, leaders try to balance their people's demands for consumer goods with the need to produce the never-ending supply of weapons required by the international arms race.

A third push comes from the developing nations. They, too, want a share of the world's industrial abundance: the standard of living that not even royalty enjoyed in the past, accompanied by the world leadership that efficient factories bring. And since they are running the race from so far behind, they cannot afford the "luxury" of pollution control.

A refreshing counterbalance to these "pushes" toward environmental destruction is the arousal of citizens across the world over what they perceive as a needless threat to their own well-being. This environmental movement is not limited to the West, for Soviet citizens have also demanded better care of their environment, even engaging in protests over the threat to Siberian caribou from gas lines. This movement is a hopeful sign of the potential for a safer future. The danger, as conflict theorists would point out, is that the movement can be subverted by special interest groups, co-opted by the established powers and used for their own ends.

Where do you think the future lies?

WAR

For decades, the Soviets and the West have been caught up in an *arms race,* an escalating spiral of matching each other's war capabilities. Although the *cold war,* the protracted hostilities between these nations, thaws from time to time, the arms race has resulted in a stockpile of nuclear weapons so great that they threaten human existence. All previous catastrophes in human history would pale by comparison with the devastation of nuclear war. In a matter of seconds, major centers of population could be reduced to ashes, and the nuclear winter that scientists theorize would result could mean the end of all life on earth.

In spite of this alarming capacity for destruction, the world's nations continue to arm themselves. What is it about people that drives them to such behavior? While psychologists and psychiatrists look for answers *within* humans (such as aggressive instincts), sociologists focus on *external* (social) conditions, analyzing how a group's social organization and customs nourish or discourage aggression. Sociologists note that while human aggression and individual killing characterize all human groups, war does not. War is simply *one option* that groups may choose for dealing with disagreements, and not all societies choose this option. The Mission Indians of North America, the Arunta of Australia, the Andaman Islanders of the South Pacific, and the Eskimos of the Arctic, for example, have customary ways to handle aggression and quarrels (holding public contests that pit quarreling individuals against one another in head-butting, spear-throwing, or even singing duels, with the audience making its judgment about the quarrel known by its applause [Fromm, 1973]), but they do not have organized battles that pit one tribe against another. These groups do not even have a word for war (Lesser, 1968).

Such individualistic, non-war rituals, however, characterize only small, tribal groups. Modern society is organized in such a way that it encourages war preparations and the continuous threat of war. Why should this be? Conflict and functionalist theorists offer explanations that provide a good understanding of the *social* factors that underlie the situation that you and I now face on a daily basis—that although neither the United States nor the Soviet Union wants a war that will destroy themselves, and in spite of *glasnost* and various peace overtures, nevertheless each continually signals to the other that it is prepared for war, that it has developed some new weapon, or, as in the case of "Star Wars," a new defense system.

Conflict theorists stress that three major factors underlie war. The *first* is *the struggle for existence*, which they consider to be the central force in the human drama. Various groups competing for scarce resources are naturally in conflict with one another. War, then, is simply one of the forms that human conflict takes. Conflict theorists emphasize that war ultimately stems from the leaders of a nation utilizing its armed forces in order to expand their economic exploitation and political domination. At its essence, then, war is an attempt to enlarge wealth and power for the controllers of a society.

This leads to the *second* factor, *imperialism,* the pursuit of unlimited geographical expansion. In order to gain territory and markets, a government goes to war with another nation. Of special importance in capitalist nations are the business leaders—the manufacturers, financiers, investors, shippers, and exporters—who use war to try to gain greater wealth by expanding their markets (Hobson, 1902/1939).

Sociologist C. Wright Mills (1958) saw imperialism as the fundamental element underlying the relationship between the superpowers. He said that the goal of Soviet imperialism was booty—to gain political control over an area in order to extract from it raw materials and agricultural products. The West, too, seeks colonies for purposes of raw materials, but, in addition, it strives for profits by selling manufactured goods to those colonies. The greater the investments in a colony, the greater the need to use the military to protect colonial markets and investments.

The *third* factor is the *pressure* for war coming *from elites* in the military and the government (Schumpeter, 1919/1955). To bolster their authority and prestige, these elites build a military machine backed by a strong political organization. Once established, this machinery tends to lead to war, for it is there to be used, and it draws strength from continued warfare.

The interests of the military and industrial sectors of society, then, coalesce into a military machine. In the face of this power, politicians hand over the keys to the public treasury—in the name of financing war preparations. Mills concluded that these military machines now dominate modern society. He said that the constant push to prepare for war means that

War is no longer an interruption of peace; in our time, peace itself has become an uneasy interlude between wars; peace has become a perilous balance of mutual terror and mutual fright. (p. 2)

Functionalist theorists may disagree about some particulars, such as the role of the military machine, but their analysis blends well with that of the conflict theorists. Functionalists stress that war exists because it is functional, that it produces results that people want. Sociologist Robert E. Park (1941) found that war even brought the modern nation-states into existence, for our nations are the result of one group extending its political boundaries by subjugating other groups. The *first* major function of war, then, is the extension of *territory,* an enlargement of a group's political power.

Sociologist Lewis Coser (1956) identified *social integration* as a *second* function of war. War often creates peace within one's own border by providing conflicting groups with a common outside enemy. The factions close ranks and cooperate in order to repel the common threat. After they do so, however, they ordinarily turn on one anther to settle old scores and end unresolved issues (Blainey, 1973). An example is Afghanistan: The factions reluctantly cooperated to repel the Soviets, but after the Soviet withdrawal in 1989 they jockeyed for power—along religious, class, tribal, clan, and even family lines.

Sociologist Georg Simmel (1904) identified *social change* as a *third* function of war. For example, warfare stimulates the development of science and technology, as with Leonardo Da Vinci's designs of war machines. Today war and the threat of war stimulate new aerodynamic designs, the harnessing of nuclear energy, the development of new surgical techniques, and even the invention of "space age" products that we all use.

A *fourth* function of war is *economic gain*. This has traditionally included access to treasure, raw materials, trade routes, markets, and outlets for investment (Pruitt & Snyder, 1969). For today's industrialized societies it includes increased employment. For example, World War II put millions to work and helped lift the United States out of the Great Depression. Even the threat of war serves this function, for as Mills (1958) noted, "war readiness" requires high spending that benefits leading corporations.

A *fifth* function of war is *ideological*—the dissemination of a political or religious system or the suppression of an opposing system. Underlying current tensions between the West and the East are basic ideological differences in politics and economics. A *sixth* function is *venegeance* or *punishment*—teaching another nation "a lesson" in order to avenge an injury or insult (Pruitt & Snyder, 1969). Much of the warfare between the Arab states and Israel serves this function, although it cannot, of course, be separated from other functions. A *seventh* is achieving greater *military security*. A nation may not desire territory in and of itself, but attacks to prevent that territory from being strategically exploited by an enemy. This seems to have been the case in Israel's attack on Iraq's nuclear facility in 1981. An *eighth* function of war is to increase the *credibility* of a nation's threats or guarantees. By going to war, a nation demonstrates that it must be taken seriously, for it backs up what it says.

No war serves only a single function. The crusades, for example, began in 1095 when Pope Urban II exhorted Christians to go to war, promising that the journey to the Holy Land would count as full penance. Although ideological purposes dominated at first, the crusades also provided treasure and territorial enlargement (Bridgwater, 1953). Nine crusades and 200 years later, all nine functions of war could be seen.

As functionalists point out, war also carries the risk of dysfunction—the most obvious being defeat. A less apparent dysfunction arising from military victory is overdependence on the exploitation of subjugated peoples. When that subjugation ends, the subsequent economic adjustment can be quite painful, as Great Britain has been experiencing since the loss of her colonies.

Today, war carries more threat of dysfunction than at any time in history. The outcome of quarrels between the superpowers over areas of dominance is not limited to these powers alone. As I have stressed—a fact all of us are only too familiar with—the weapons the nations now possess can destroy the earth, or leave it in the hands of grossly deformed mutants.

If the functionalists and conflict theorists are right in their analysis, each nation faces strong social forces to put its war capacities to work. These socially produced tendencies of the world's leaders, then, must be counterbalanced by the people making their strong desire for peace apparent, for to counteract the social forces pushing towards war requires utter commitment and determination.

IN SUM

None of us is isolated. Although we may not see the connections between ourselves and others, we all are part of an extensive interdependent system that interrelates humanity, technology, and the environment. To think in terms of individual small units fails to do justice to the reality of the earth's interrelated societies. This principle applies to the pollution of a river in Minnesota, which has international consequences as the chemicals run into the Mississippi and from there make their way into the Atlantic. It also applies to war, which with today's extensive international economic and political interconnections, is difficult to keep localized. Nor does AIDS recognize national boundaries.

Our own world is an intricate part of the world of people across the globe. Although we don't know one another, what they do affects us, and what we do affects them. Those interconnections are either going to work in our favor toward a saner, safer world for ourselves and our children, or they will work against us toward our eventual destruction. The basic question, then, is how can we work for that saner, safer world? That, I believe, is *the* global question with which we, out of concern for the generations yet to come, must grapple.

REFERENCES

Blainey, G. (1973). *The causes of war.* New York: Free Press.

Bridgwater, W. (Ed.). (1953). *The Columbia-Viking desk encyclopedia.* New York: Viking.

Coser, L. A. (1956). *The functions of social conflict.* New York: Free Press.

Fromm, E. (1973). *The anatomy of human destructiveness.* New York: Holt.

Hardin, G. (1968, December). The tragedy of the commons. *Science, 162,* 1243–1248.

Hobson, J. A. (1939). *Imperialism: A study* (rev. ed.). London: G. Allen. (Original work published in 1902)

Lesser, A. (1968). War and the state. In M. Fried, M. Harris, & R. Murphy (Eds.), *War: The anthropology of armed conflict and aggression,* (pp. 92–96). Garden City, NY: Natural History.

Mills, C. W. (1958). *The causes of World War Three.* New York: Simon and Schuster.

Park, R. E. (1941, January). The social function of war. *The American Journal of Sociology, 46,* 551–570.

Pruitt, D. G., & Snyder, R. C. (1969). Motives and perceptions underlying entry into war. In D. G. Pruitt & R. C. Snyder (Eds.), *Theory and research on the causes of war.* Englewood Cliffs, NJ: Prentice-Hall.

Schumpeter, J. A. (1955). *The sociology of imperialism.* New York: Meridian. (Original work published in 1919)

Simmel, G. (1904). The sociology of conflict. *American Journal of Sociology, 9,* January, 490–525; March, 672–689; and May, 798–811.

Timasheff, N. S. (1965). *War and revolution,* J. F. Scheuer (Ed.). New York: Sheed & Ward.

42

AIDS: New Threat to the World

Lori Heise

Few tragedies in human history have captured the world's attention as has AIDS. No disease, past or present, has inspired an international response equal to the current AIDS mobilization of the World Health Organization (WHO). None in recent memory has provoked more anxiety, aroused such prejudice against the afflicted, or stimulated so many moral, ethical, and legal debates. And no disease has more pointedly forced societies to confront issues otherwise conveniently ignored: drug abuse, sexuality, and the plight of the poor.

THE PANDEMIC UNFOLDS

In 1981, astute physicians in California and New York began to recognize a strange clustering of symptoms among some of their male homosexual patients. Something was destroying the immune system of these individuals, rendering them susceptible to an odd assortment of opportunistic infections and cancers. Almost simultaneously, doctors in Central Africa, Europe, and Haiti began to note patients with similar conditions. By 1982, the new disease had a name: AIDS. And one year later, it had a cause: the human immunodeficiency virus, or HIV.[1]

HIV exhibits a unique combination of characteristics that makes it intrinsically hard to control. Like genital herpes, once caught, the virus stays with its carrier for life. Once disease develops, AIDS is almost always fatal—usually within two years. But instead of manifesting within, a few days or weeks, like most viral diseases. AIDS on average takes eight or nine years to develop. During this interval, carriers look and feel healthy but can pass the virus to others. Researchers now believe that most if not all individuals infected with HIV will eventually develop AIDS.[2]

The good news, however, is that compared with other viruses—such as polio and the common cold—HIV is fragile and relatively difficult to transmit. AIDS is overwhelmingly a sexually transmitted disease, communicated through body fluids and blood during vaginal or anal intercourse. To a significant but lesser extent, the virus is also transmitted through blood transfusions, through the sharing or reusing of contaminated needles, and from mother to child during pregnancy or birth. Contrary to widespread fears, AIDS cannot be caught through casual contact, sneezes, kissing, toilet seats, or insects.

Although the virus is transmitted the same way everywhere—through blood, through sexual intercourse, or from mother to child—the pattern of transmission and infection varies among regions. Indeed, the international AIDS picture can best be understood in terms of three broadly defined subepidemics, each with its own dynamic.

In North America, Western Europe, and certain Latin American countries, AIDS is mainly transmitted through homosexual intercourse and the sharing of needles among drug addicts. As a result, those infected are overwhelmingly male, and transmission from mother to child is limited. Less than 1 percent of the population is thought to be infected, but the infection rate among intravenous (IV) drug users and homosexual men exceeds 50 percent in some cities. Heterosexual sex is responsible for a small but increasing proportion of cases. Interestingly, despite its potential, sex with prostitutes is not a major mode of transmission.[3]

By contrast, in sub-Saharan Africa and parts of the Caribbean, AIDS is primarily a heterosexually transmitted disease, with women infected as often as men. Because so many women are infected, transmission from mother to child is disturbingly common. Blood transfusions—a route largely eliminated in the industrial world—remain a source of infection in many countries where blood supplies still are not screened. Since intravenous drug use and homosexuality are rare, these modes of transmission

are not significant, although reuse of contaminated needles by health workers remains a likely source of infection. In some countries, infection in the total population exceeds 1 percent, with 5–33 percent of sexually active adults in select urban areas infected. Male contact with prostitutes is thought to play; a major role in the epidemic's spread.[4]

In the third set of countries, HIV has been introduced only recently. Infection rates remain extremely low even among people with multiple sex partners, such as prostitutes. Most cases have originated outside of the country either through sex with a foreigner or through imported blood products contaminated with HIV. Although there is increasing evidence of in-country spread, no strong pattern of heterosexual or homosexual transmission has emerged. Asia, Eastern Europe, northern Africa, the Middle East, and most of the Pacific all fall in this category.[5]

These variations evolve from a combination of factors, including when and where the virus first entered the population and the different social practices and behaviors that exist among cultures. In Africa, for example, the epidemic involved the heterosexually active population first, whereas in the United States the epidemic was initially introduced and amplified in predominantly male populations: homosexuals, people with hemophilia, and IV drug users. Researchers also believe that the greater prevalence of untreated sexually transmitted diseases (STDs) in Africa has facilitated the spread of AIDS there and may largely explain the greater efficiency of heterosexual sex in transmitting the virus among Africans.[6]

It is becoming increasingly clear, for example, that chlamydia and STDs that cause genital sores (such as syphilis, herpes, and chancroid) make it easier for HIV to pass between sexual partners. Sadly, in developing countries where treatment is less accessible, STDs are far more endemic than in the industrial world. Laboratory evidence also suggests that an individual whose immune system has been activated by chronic infections might be more susceptible to HIV infection. This factor may operate to increase heterosexual transmission in the Third World, where viral and parasitic diseases are endemic.

Although scientists have mapped the virus's surface chemistry in minute detail, the world has only the vaguest notion of where HIV is and where it is going. As of December 1, 1988, 142 countries had reported a total of 129,385 AIDS cases to the World Health Organization. (See Table 1.) Due to gross underreporting and underrecognition, however, WHO suspects that the true global caseload is more than twice that figure. Moreover, AIDS cases represent only the tip of the iceberg: for every AIDS case, anywhere from 20 to 100 people may carry the virus but not yet show symptoms. All told, WHO estimates that 5 million to 10 million people worldwide may be infected with HIV.[7] (See Table 2)

TABLE 1.   Officially Reported AIDS Cases, Selected Countries, December 1, 1988

Country	Prevalance (cases)	Rate (cases per million population)
United States	78,985	321
Uganda	5,508	336
Brazil	4,436	31
France	4,211	75
Tanzania	3,055	126
Kenya	2,732	117
Malawi	2,586	336
West Germany	2,580	42
Italy	2,556	45
Canada	2,156	83
Mexico	1,502	18
Haiti	1,455	231
Burundi	1,408	271
Congo	1,250	568
Zambia	1,056	141
Rwanda	987	139
Switzerland	605	92
French Guiana	113	1,228
Japan	90	0.7
Bermuda	81	1,396
China	3	0.003

Sources: World Health Organization data base; Population Reference Bureau, *1988 World Population Data Sheet* (Washington, D.C.: 1988).

TABLE 2.   Estimated HIV Prevalence, Selected Regions, 1987/88

Region	Prevalence (number infected)
Africa	2–3 million
United States	1–1.5 million
Latin America	500,000–750,000
Europe	280,000–800,000
Asia	fewer than 100,000
World	5–10 million (probably closer to 5 million)

Source: Worldwatch Institute, compiled from various World Health Organization sources.

Because of the virus's long latency period, a country's current number of AIDS cases is actually a snapshot of the epidemic five to eight years ago, when those who now have AIDS first got infected.

Even more difficult than determining the world's current AIDS picture is predicting how the epidemic will evolve. The United States and Western Europe, for example, are now experiencing a second wave of epidemic among intravenous drug users. Whereas most AIDS cases used to involve homosexual men, evidence indicates that rates of new infection are declining among gay men but accelerating among drug addicts. In fact, in certain parts of Europe—including Italy, Spain, and Scotland—IV drug users now account for the majority of all cases.

This new pattern is important because of both its impact on the drug-using community and its potential to facilitate the spread of AIDS into the general population. Although it is too early to predict whether AIDS will move into the heterosexual mainstream in these areas, addicts could facilitate this process by communicating the virus to their sexual partners who in turn could infect people outside the drug community. Seventy percent of heterosexually transmitted cases in native-born U.S. citizens currently occur in partners of IV drug users.[8]

Indeed, it is difficult to overemphasize the role that drug abuse could play in the future of the American and European AIDS epidemic. Already, more than 70 percent of cases in American children are due to IV drug use by their mother or her sexual partner. Half of all AIDS cases in American women are related to drug use, with even higher proportions among black and Hispanic women (70 and 83 percent, respectively). Even among female prostitutes, the likelihood of infection is more closely linked to IV drug use than to prostitution itself.[9]

THE IMPACT IN THE THIRD WORLD

AIDS will have a profound impact in the Third World, and one that exceeds the impact in the West, where resources are more plentiful and basic infrastructure better developed.

A look at existing health care systems in the Third World provides a glimpse of the disadvantage that developing countries face in responding to AIDS. In 1984, Haiti had $3.25 to spend on health care per citizen; Mexico had $11.50. Rwanda's pitiful annual budget of $1.60 per person would not even buy a bottle of aspirin in the industrial world. By contrast, Sweden annually spends over $1,100 on health care per person and the United States invests more than $760. Yet meager Third World health budgets

must contend with existing epidemics of frightening proportion. Three million Third World children die each year from preventable diseases such as measles, tetanus, and whooping cough. In Africa alone, malaria annually claims 1 million lives.[10]

Data from countries already responding to AIDS confirm that the costs of prevention will be high. In 1988, for example, Brazil's prevention program was estimated to cost $28 million, $8 million of which went to screen blood at state-run blood banks. Health officials in Peru put the start-up costs of screening their national blood supply at $20 million in 1987, a sum that could otherwise cover the total annual health care bill for 1.5 million Peruvians. If borne alone by developing countries, these costs could derail already fragile and inadequate health care systems.[11]

Developing countries also have fewer options for treating AIDS patients than countries in the West do. Physicians in industrial countries largely respond by treating the secondary diseases, such as *Pneumocystis carinii* pneumonia, that accompany AIDS. It is an expensive ordeal that often involves frequent hospital stays. The only drug currently known to attack HIV directly—

Aids in perspective*

Other Epidemics

Bubonic Plague killed 17 million to 28 million people—one-third to one-half of Europe's population—between 1347 and 1350

Influenza killed 22 million in the 1917-1918 pandemic

Smallpox killed 400,000 Europeans at the height of the nineteenth-century epidemic

Polio killed 22,000 Americans of 400,000 infected between 1943 and 1956

*1981 to present: 72,504 cases reported worldwide. WHO estimates AIDS may kill 5 to 30 million people within the next decade.

Other Cause of Death

Measles kills at least 1.5 million people worldwide each year

Tuberculosis kills 500,000 people worldwide each year

Pregnancy and Childbirth kill 500,000 women worldwide each year

Ethlopian Famine killed 1 million people during 1984–85

Vietnam War killed 54,000 Americans between 1963–75. Killed 2,358,000 people total between 1960–75

Source: Compiled by Worldwatch Institute

zidovudine, commonly known as AZT—costs roughly $8,000 per patient annually, and causes anemia so severe that over a quarter of recipients require blood transfusions. In the Third World, where per capita incomes are measured in hundreds of dollars and blood is in short supply, a life-prolonging drug like AZT might as well not exist.[12]

Indeed, preliminary cost data from around the world suggest that the amount spent per AIDS patient roughly correlates with a country's gross national product (GNP). As with health care in general, poor countries are forced to spend less on each patient. If Zaire spent at a level comparable to the United States, the cost of treating 10 AIDS patients would exceed the entire budget of Mama Yemo, the nation's largest public hospital.

Given such constraints, AIDS naturally raises the question of triage. Where hospital space and medical supplies are scarce and where people regularly die of treatable illnesses, diverting resources to AIDS treatment may actually cost lives by crowding out patients who can be cured. From a quarter to half of precious hospital beds in some central African hospitals are occupied by patients who are infected with HIV; Costa Rican officials predict a similar situation by the mid-1990s. Already, AIDS patients are being discharged from some health facilities in Africa, Haiti, and Brazil to give preference to patients with curable illnesses.[13]

Not only does AIDS compete with other diseases for limited health budgets, HIV actually magnifies existing epidemics. By weakening the immune system of its host, the virus makes carriers more susceptible to renewed attack from other microbes lying dormant. For example, some 30–60 percent of adults in many developing countries are carriers of the tuberculosis bacteria, even though their bodies have conquered outward signs of the disease. By suppressing the immune system, HIV allows dormant TB bacteria to become active, leading to the contagious form of tuberculosis.[14]

It is in the area of child health, however, that AIDS has the greatest potential to erode hard-won health gains in the Third World. Over the last three decades, developing regions have inaugurated a "child survival revolution" through encouraging oral rehydration therapy for diarrhea, immunization, breast-feeding, and birth spacing. Together with economic growth and increased female literacy, these simple interventions have cut Third World child deaths by slightly more than half since 1955, with Southeast Asia making the greatest progress and Africa the least.[15]

Left unchecked, AIDS will undermine these gains as more and more pregnant women become infected and transmit the virus to their children *in utero*. Already 9–24 percent of pregnant women in some African cities—such as Kinshasa and Kampala—are infected. Up to half the children born to these women will contract the virus and die. Preliminary models of the most affected regions in Africa suggest that infant mortality could increase by more than 25 percent, eroding three decades of progress in infant and child death.[16]

Unlike other diseases that cull the weakest members of society—the sick, the old, and the very young—AIDS eliminates the most productive segment of a population. In Africa, HIV infection in women peaks during their third decade—the prime childbearing years—and for males during their fourth decade, the most productive years at work and in the community. Where the ranks of people with certain specialized skills and training may be small, the loss of even a handful of engineers, health planners, or agronomists can be debilitating.[17]

These economic disruptions come at a time when developing nations—especially in Africa—are already laboring under severe economic hardship. Per capita income is declining and foreign debt is mounting. Against this backdrop, AIDS threatens to further complicate balance-of-payment problems. Foreign exchange will be lost as governments seek to import items necessary to combat the epidemic, tourist dollars may decline in response to travelers' fears, and economic growth will slow as people and governments divert savings from investment to treatment. Indeed, in industrial and developing countries alike, the indirect economic costs of AIDS will far exceed any direct costs related to prevention or treatment.[18]

Yet the true costs of AIDS are both economic and personal. Economists can count up the direct costs and calculate the indirect cost of lost wages from disability and death. But what of the psychological toll on those left behind? Economic tally sheets cannot capture the pain of a child left without parents or of a generation whose future is shortchanged by AIDS.

PROGRESS TOWARD PREVENTION IN INDUSTRIAL COUNTRIES

For a world used to solving problems with a technical fix, AIDS is frustrating. Today, prospects for a vaccine or cure seem even more distant than they did two years ago, when scientists were reeling from the thrill of rapid discovery. The AIDS virus has proved a wily opponent: It hides within the very immune cells that the body normally uses to ward off invaders, making vaccines and treatments exceedingly difficult to devise. And it mutates at a furious pace—perhaps even faster than the influenza virus that requires researchers to alter the flu vaccine every year. Prevention will likely remain the world's primary weapon against AIDS for at least the next decade.[19]

In the industrial world, where transmission through blood transfusions has essentially ceased, stopping AIDS means getting people to change high-risk behavior. Risky behavior includes unprotected sex, especially with multiple partners, and the sharing of contaminated needles among drug addicts. The best way to avoid AIDS is to have a mutually monogamous sexual relationship with a partner known to be uninfected. Short of that, condoms provide good, although not foolproof, protection against HIV transmission. The spermicide nonoxyl-9 has also been shown to kill the

virus in laboratory tests, but its ability to prevent HIV transmission between sexual partners has yet to be proved.[20]

It is important to recognize that it is what people do, not who they are, that puts them at risk. As the Panos Institute has pointed out in its groundbreaking work *Blaming Others*, talk of "high-risk groups," such as Haitians, gay men, or prostitutes, tends to invite finger-pointing and erroneously suggests that anyone not in these groups is safe. Moreover, categorization fails to acknowledge that not all group members practice high-risk behavior. AIDS is not a "gay disease" or an "African disease" or a "disease of drug addicts." Anyone who engages in high-risk behavior can contract HIV.[21]

Given these risks, industrial countries have responded in a variety of ways, some constructive, others less so. The Soviet Union, Hungary, and Bavaria in West Germany, for example, all require testing of high-risk individuals, including prostitutes, drug addicts, and—with the exception of Bavaria—homosexuals. Yet health officials are unanimous in the view that mandatory measures merely drive underground those most in need of testing. In Charleston, South Carolina, the number of homosexual men seeking testing dropped by 51 percent after the state began requiring all those tested positive to be reported to the public health department. When anonymous and voluntary, however, testing, counseling, and partner tracing have proved to be useful and effective tools for AIDS prevention.[22]

So far it appears that among heterosexuals, prevention campaigns have increased knowledge but have changed sexual behavior only marginally. Change among gay men, however, has been dramatic and may well constitute the most rapid and profound behavioral response ever documented in public health. Studies throughout the United States and Western Europe have found that gay men have reduced their number of sexual partners, increased their use of condoms, and decreased their participation in unprotected anal intercourse. One review of 24 American and European studies concluded that, on average, gay men have 63 percent fewer sexual partners since AIDS. The incidence of receptive anal intercourse has similarly declined, by 59 percent.[23]

Unfortunately, studies on both continents confirm that a minority of gay men still engage in dangerous behavior despite understanding the risks involved. Risky behavior is most often associated with the use of uninhibiting drugs during sex, suggesting that programs aimed at alcohol and recreational drugs may be important for AIDS control. Moreover, gays living in lower risk areas do not seem to have modified their behavior as much, perhaps because they do not feel as personally at risk. It is unsafe to assume, therefore, that the entire gay male population in the United States and Europe has been educated and that attention is better placed elsewhere. Promising progress has been made, but much remains to be done.[24]

Intravenous drug users have also proved capable of change, although curbing HIV infection among drug addicts has received far too little attention, especially in the United States. Response has been hampered by debate over the moral and legal appropriateness of certain interventions, such as needle exchange programs, and the pervasive view that addicts somehow "deserve" AIDS. Inaction, however, is both inhumane to drug users and shortsighted, given that IV drug users are the most likely bridge between HIV and the general population.

For those unable or unwilling to break their addiction, programs aimed at safer injection are important for AIDS control. Needle-sharing is deeply ingrained in the drug culture, both as a form of social bonding and because new syringes are expensive, hard to obtain, and illegal to possess in many areas. But studies confirm that addicts will reduce their use of contaminated needles, especially if given the means to do so, either through needle/syringe exchange programs or through the provision of bleach for cleaning syringes between uses. Indeed, several studies suggest that supply-

ing the means to change behavior is critical; programs that provide information alone have tended to fail.[25]

While still controversial, other countries have been more willing than the United States to experiment with needle exchange programs. So far, Switzerland, Denmark, the Netherlands, the United Kingdom, and Australia have initiated programs and all report significantly less needle-sharing among addicts. France has also liberalized its policy by making needles available for sale at pharmacies without prescription or identification. Despite widespread concern that increased availability of needles would encourage drug use, there is no evidence that this is occurring.

Disturbing evidence indicates, however, that changes in sexual behavior among American and European drug addicts lag considerably behind changes in drug-use behavior. Even more distressing, the least amount of change has occurred within committed, heterosexual relationships, where HIV transmission is most likely to occur (because of frequency of intercourse) and where children are most likely to be conceived. Given that three fourths of American IV drug users are male and have a primary partner who does not use drugs, there is clearly need for more education on safer sex among addicts as part of an effort to prevent the spread of HIV.[26]

AIDS prevention programs to date have also been singularly ineffective at reaching U.S. minority communities. Studies show that blacks and Hispanics are less well informed than whites about AIDS and that they have not modified their behavior as much. This is particularly worrisome because blacks and Hispanics are at extremely high risk. Already they account for 41 percent of AIDS cases, even though they constitute only 19 percent of the U.S. population. Eighty-five percent of children who acquired AIDS from their mother and 71 percent of all women with AIDS are black or Hispanic.[27]

This pattern of infection is partly due to the fact that a disproportionate number of

IV drug users are black or Hispanic. But even among drug addicts, minorities are more likely to be infected than whites. The reasons for this are unclear, although for cultural and economic reasons, blacks and Hispanics may have less access to clean needles, drug treatment, and AIDS information. Particularly disturbing is evidence that blacks also account for a disproportionate share of new HIV infection occurring outside of big cities, where IV drug use would be less common.[28]

These trends emphasize the need for more culturally relevant AIDS information aimed at minorities. Recently, the Centers for Disease Control of the U.S. Public Health Service has attempted to fill this gap by earmarking almost $45 million for minority outreach projects in 1989, up from only $14 million in 1987. Experience suggests that initiatives arising from the minority communities themselves have the greatest chance of success.[29]

ALLIANCE FOR PREVENTION IN DEVELOPING COUNTRIES

Stopping AIDS in developing countries will take a worldwide alliance of professional skills, resources, and experience. Left unaided, the Third World would have to divert scarce resources from other essential development initiatives or be forced to accept ever-rising death tolls. Even industrial countries cannot fight this scourge alone. Barring a vaccine or a cure, no country can independently protect itself from HIV, for the disease respects no national boundaries. Like several of today's most pressing problems—global warming, ozone depletion, Third World debt—unless all nations work together against AIDS, there is little hope in acting separately.

Although nations have collaborated before on action aimed at disease control, there is no precedent for the level of cooperation that will be required to battle AIDS. HIV infection is invisible and insidious, and there is no vaccine. Stopping AIDS means getting people to change their behavior, a task that governments and international agencies are ill-prepared to do.

Although worth doing, screening blood will have a relatively small impact on the spread of AIDS because at least 80 percent of transmission in the Third World is through heterosexual sex. Thus, the bulk of prevention must come from encouraging fidelity and greater use of condoms. Also important is expanding access to treatment for other sexually transmitted diseases that may be facilitating the spread of HIV.

The best strategy for curtailing sexual transmission depends in part on whether HIV has infiltrated the general population or not. In countries where the virus is already widely dispersed, prevention activities must be broad in scope. But where HIV prevalence is still low, as in West Africa and Asia, countries have an opportunity to target interventions and thereby save vital resources. Experience has shown that HIV generally spreads outward from pockets of infection among individuals whose behavior increses their risk of contracting and transmitting the virus, such as prostitutes, men in the military, and IV drug users. By helping such groups to protect themselves, governments can prevent HIV from gaining a foothold in their country.[30]

The speed at which the virus can infiltrate unsuspecting populations argues persuasively for acting before HIV is an obvious problem. Studies in Bangkok, Thailand, for example, show that among the city's estimated 60,000 IV drug users, HIV prevalence rose from 1 percent in 1987 to over 30 percent by mid-1988. Had prevention programs been in place, this precipitous rise might have been avoided. These individuals now represent a large pool for spread of HIV both within the drug community and through sexual contact, outside of it.[31]

Even where HIV is already widespread, there is urgent need for more community-based programs designed to reach populations at highest risk: clients of STD clinics, long-distance truck drivers, and bisexual men in Latin America, among others. The message must be delivered in their own language and by a source they can trust. So far, programs that use peers as AIDS educators seem the most promising.

Consider the challenge of expanding condom use alone. Programs to supply condoms vary greatly in cost depending on how the condoms will be distributed and how actively they will be promoted. Even the least expensive option—subsidizing their sale through existing commericial outlets—costs roughly $12 per couple annually, half of which is the cost of the condoms themselves. Just to ensure that commercial channels supply enough condoms for one-third of all couples in the nine hardest-hit countries of Africa would cost $100 million annually, more than WHO's total AIDS budget for 1989.[32]

Yet the bigger challenge—both in terms of difficulty and expense—is getting couples to use condoms in cultures where birth control itself is not readily accepted and where condoms are especially disdained. In most African countries, less than 5 percent of married women practice any form of modern contraception and only 0.3 percent use condoms. Efforts to promote condoms throughout the Third World will have to overcome strong cultural and religious prohibitions as well as daunting logistical problems.[33]

The challenge ahead is to find new international funds for AIDS control with an eye toward helping the Third World develop the infrastructure and indigenous human talent necessary to sustain the effort over the long haul. So far donors have been forthcoming with development assistance to fight AIDS, but this money appears largely to have been subtracted from other development accounts. If AIDS control comes at the expense of other life-promoting initiatives, we will have won the battle but lost the war.

AIDS AS SOCIAL CRUCIBLE

AIDS is both a product of social change and its instrument. Rapid urbanization in Africa, the rise of gay liberation in the West,

and the advent of modern air travel have all fueled this pandemic. In turn, AIDS has already triggered profound changes in every aspect of human endeavor, from how we care for the dying to how we relate to the living. Perhaps most significant, AIDS compels societies to confront issues and aspects of the human condition that are otherwise easily ignored. While heightening awareness, the disease does not dictate our response. How societies choose to act on the issues raised by AIDS may stand as a key measure of our time.[34]

Like all crises, AIDS has brought out the best and the worst of human nature. The pulling together of the American gay community to respond to a crisis within its ranks, the generous and often courageous actions of thousands of professional and voluntary caregivers, and the outpouring of global resources and talent to fight the disease are all expressions of human compassion at its best. But if compassion has been at work, so too have fear and denial.[35]

The panic responses have been made worse by the fact that AIDS first struck already stigmatized populations—gay men, IV drug users, and foreigners in the West; prostitutes and those with multiple sex partners in developing countries. This has reinforced thinly veiled prejudices and encouraged scapegoating. Regrettably, the global mobilization against AIDS has been hampered by the human tendency to blame others for a problem rather than tackle the problem itself. AIDS has been blamed on everything from Western decadence to sexual promiscuity among Africans. Such accusations have merely bred resentment, encouraged denial, and thwarted the global cooperation so desperately needed to fight this disease.[36]

In addition to exposing human vulnerabilities, AIDS has thrown into sharp relief certain inadequacies and inequities in the existing social order. The crisis has underscored the dismal state of health infrastructure in the developing world, where even syringes are in short supply. It has highlighted the structural flaws in economic systems that fail to provide gainful alternatives to prostitution and drug dealing. And in the United States, it has made painfully obvious shortcomings in the nation's health care system: the underfunding of preventive health measures, the lack of care options for the chronically ill, and the plight of the poor and uninsured.

By highlighting these flaws and adding a sense of urgency, AIDS may galvanize societies to tackle the underlying problems that allow HIV to flourish. Stopping AIDS among drug users, for example, may have more to do in the long term with fighting unemployment, poverty, and welfare dependence than with needle exchange or more treatment. As Harvey Fineberg, Dean of Harvard's School of Public Health, observes: "Jobs, schools and housing . . . would go a long way toward creating the individual self-respect, dignity and hope for the future that can forestall the turning to drugs in the first place." Similarly, societies may come to realize that prostitution is seldom a profession of choice, but one of economic necessity. Already, a family planning association in Ghana is fighting AIDS by retraining prostitutes in other types of work.[37]

Ultimately, the power of AIDS lies in its ability to reveal ourselves to ourselves. AIDS raises the questions, and the quality of our response may define our humanity. What if scientists develop a solution to AIDS that works in industrial nations but is either impractical or too costly for the developing world? Will western nations consider further AIDS research a priority? Or will AIDS become like schistosomiasis and other Third World diseases that can be ignored because Americans and Europeans are not dying? What if AIDS becomes largely a disease of minorities and drug users? Will money for treatment and prevention still be forthcoming? As Jonathan Mann observes, "AIDS will . . . put our global conscience to the test." Let us hope that compassion and tolerance prevail.

NOTES

1. Renée Sabatier, *Blaming Others: Prejudice, Race and Worldwide AIDS* (Philadelphia: New Society Publishers, for Panos Institute in association with Norwegian Red Cross, 1988).

2. Observations about control from Dr. Malcolm Potts, "Preparing for the Battle," *People* (London), Vol. 14, No. 4, 1987; incubation period from Roy M. Anderson and Robert M. May, "Epidemiological Parameters of HIV Transmission," *Nature*, June 9, 1988; observation about progression to AIDS from Institute of Medicine, National Academy of Sciences, *Confronting AIDS, Update 1988* (Washington, D.C.: National Academy Press, 1988).

3. World Health Organization (WHO), "Global Programme On AIDS: Progress Report Number 3," Geneva, May 1988; role of prostitutes from Don C. Des Jarlais et al., "HIV Infection and Intravenous Drug Use: Critical Issues in Transmission Dynamics, Infection Outcomes, and Prevention," *Reviews of Infectious Diseases*, Vol. 10, No. 1, 1988, and from Bruce Lambert, "AIDS Among Prostitutes Not as Prevalent as Believed, Studies Show," *New York Times*, September 20, 1988.

4. Until recently, researchers commonly cited 5–20 percent of sexually active adults infected in major urban areas of East and Central Africa; see Jonathan M. Mann et al., "The International Epidemiology of AIDS," *Scientific American*, October 1988. New data from urban centers in the Kagera region of Tanzania reveal 32.8 percent of adults (aged 15–54) infected; see J. Killewo et al., "The Epidemiology of HIV-1 Infection in the Kagera Region of Tanzania," abstract of paper presented at the Third International Conference on AIDS and Associated Cancers in Africa, Arusha, Tanzania, September 14–16, 1988 (hereinafter cited as Arusha Conference). Prostitute observation from Peter Piot and Michel Caraël, "Epidemiological and Sociological Aspects of HIV-infection in Developing Countries," *British Medical Bulletin*, Vol. 44, No. 1, 1988.

5. Dr. Jonathan Mann, "Global AIDS: A Status Report," Testimony before the Presidential Commission on the Human Immunodeficiency Virus Epidemic (hereinafter cited as Presidential Commission), April 18, 1988.

6. Nancy S. Padian, "Heterosexual Transmission of Acquired Immunodeficiency Syndrome: International Perspectives and National Projections," *Reviews of Infectious Diseases*, September/October 1987; Sabatier, *Blaming Others.*

7. WHO computer printout and Mann et al., "International Epidemiology of AIDS."

8. *Report of the Presidential Commission on the Human Immunodeficiency Virus Epidemic* (Washington, D.C.: U.S. Government Printing Office, 1988).

9. Cases in American children from James W. Curran et al., "Epidemiology of HIV Infection and AIDS in the United States" *Science*, February 5, 1988; IV drug link to cases in American women from Donald R. Hopkins, "Aids in Minority Populations in the United States," *Public Health Reports*, November/December 1987; prostitutes' IV drug link from Dr. June E. Osborn, "Aids: Politics and Science," *New England Journal of Medicine*, February 18, 1988.

10. Figures on Haiti, Mexico, and Rwanda from Ruth Leger Sivard, *World Military and Social Expenditures 1987–88* (Washington, D.C.: World Priorities, 1987); Swedish figure refers to per capita health spending in 1984, as cited in ibid.; U.S. number refers to 1986 spending, from National Center for Health Statistics, U.S. Department of Health and Human Services, *Health, United States 1987* (Washington, D.C.: U.S. Government Printing Office, 1988); United Nations Children's Fund (UNICEF), *State of the World's Children 1988* (New York: Oxford University Press for UNICEF, 1988).

11. Hesio Cordeiro et al., "Medical Costs of HIV and AIDS in Brazil," paper presented at the First International Conference on the Global Impact of AIDS, London, March 8–10, 1988 (hereinafter cited as London Conference); Renée Sabatier, "The Global Costs of AIDS," *The Futurist*, November/December 1987.

12. AZT costs from Fred J. Hellinger, "Forecasting the Personal Medical Care Costs of AIDS from 1988 Through 1991," *Public Health Reports*, May/June 1988; anemia observation from Sabatier, *AIDS and the Third World.*

13. Hospital bed rates from Mann et al., "International Epidemiology of AIDS," and from Sabatier, *AIDS and the Third World*; patient discharge from J. Wilson Carswell, "Impact

of AIDS in the Developing World," *British Medical Bulletin*, Vol. 44, No. 1, 1988, and from Raisa Scriabine-Smith, unpublished manuscript prepared for the Hudson Institute, Indianapolis, Ind., 1988.

14. Slutkin et al., "Effects of AIDS on the Tuberculosis Problem and Programmes."

15. United Nations, *Mortality of Children Under Age 5: World Estimates and Projections, 1950–2025* (New York: 1988).

16. Figures on pregnant women from Carswell, "Impact of AIDS in the Developing World"; mother-to-child infection rate from T. Manzila et al., "Perinatal HIV Transmission in Two African Hospitals: One Year Follow-Up," abstract of paper presented at Arusha Conference; impact on child survival from Mann et al., "International Epidemiology of AIDS," and from Rodolfo A. Bulatao, "Initial Investigation of the Demographic Impact of AIDS in One African Country" (draft), World Bank, Washington, D.C., unpublished, June 15, 1987.

17. Carswell, "Impact of AIDS in the Developing World."

18. Indirect costs from Over, "Direct and Indirect Cost of HIV Infection," and from David E. Bloom and Geoffrey Carliner, "The Economic Impact of AIDS in the United States," *Science*, February 5, 1988.

19. Sharon Kingman and Steve Conner, "The Answer is Still a Condom," *New Scientist*, June 23, 1988; Marilyn Chase, "AIDS Virus in Infected People Mutates At a Dizzying Rate, Two Studies Show," *Wall Street Journal*, August 4, 1988.

20. Dr. Jeffrey Harris, AIDS Coordinator, AID, Washington, D.C., private communication, October 8, 1988.

21. Sabatier, *AIDS and the Third World* (1988).

22. Hungarian testing information from Radio Free Europe, February 23, 1987, as cited in Scriabine-Smith, unpublished manuscript; Bill Keller, "New Soviet Law Makes AIDS Testing Mandatory," *New York Times*, August 27, 1987; "Mandatory AIDS Test on Basis 'of Slight Suspicion' in Bavaria," *Nature*, June 10, 1988.

23. Marshall H. Becker and Jill G. Joseph, "Aids and Behavioral Change to Reduce Risk: A Review," *American Journal of Public Health*, April 1988; Office of Technology Assessment (OTA), U.S. Congress, *How Effective is*

AIDS Education? Staff Paper, Washington, D.C., May 1988; Robert R. Stempel and Andrew R. Moss, "Changes in Sexual Behavior By Gay Men in Response to AIDS," abstract of paper presented at Stockholm Conference.

24. R.R. Stempel et al., "Changes in Sexual Behavior by Gay Men in Response to AIDS," R. Stall et al., "Intravenous Drug Use, the Combination of Drugs and Sexual Activity and HIV Infection Among Gay and Bisexual Men: The San Francisco Men's Health Study," and M. Miller et al., "Relationships Between Knowledge About AIDS Risk and Actual Risk Behaviour in a Sample of Homosexual Men," all abstracts of papers presented at Stockholm Conference; Valle, "The Occurrence of STD's in a Cohort of Homosexual Men Prior To and After Repeated Personal Counselling." See also OTA, *How Effective is AIDS Education?* and C. Beeker et al., "Gay Male Sexual Behavior Change in a Low-Incidence Area for AIDS," abstract of paper presented at Stockholm Conference.

25. OTA, *How Effective is AIDS Education?*

26. OTA, *How Effective is AIDS Education?*; three fourths figure from Des Jarlais et al., "HIV Infection and Intravenous Drug Use."

27. Centers for Disease Control (CDC), "Weekly Surveillance Report," Atlanta, Ga., August 1, 1988; 19 percent figure from Martha F. Rogers and Walter W. Williams, "AIDS in Blacks and Hispanics: Implications for Prevention," *Issues in Science and Technology*, Spring 1987; rates for children and women from Dr. James Mason, Opening Address of the National Conference on the Prevention of HIV Infection and AIDS Among Racial and Ethnic Minorities in the United States, Washington, D.C., August 15, 1988.

28. "Needle Sharing and AIDS in Minorities," *Journal of the American Medical Association*, September 18, 1987; Rogers and Williams, "AIDS in Blacks and Hispanics"; black HIV infection outside cities from Lytt I. Gardner et al., "Race Specific Trend Analysis of HIV Antibody Prevalence in the United States," abstract of paper presented at Stockholm Conference.

29. "CDC Spends Over $30 Million to Prevent HIV Infection Among Minorities at Risk," press release from CDC, Atlanta, Ga., September 6, 1988; fiscal year 1989 funding information from Debbie Mathis, Budget Office, CDC, Atlanta, Ga., private communication, October 21, 1988.

30. Malcolm Potts, "The Imperative Intervention: Targeting AIDS Control Activities Toward High-Risk Populations," unpublished discussion paper from Family Health International (FHI), Research Triangle Park, N.C., undated; B. Auvert et al., "Characteristics of the HIV Infection in Kinshasa as Determined By Computer Simulation," abstract of paper presented at London Conference.

31. Chin, private communication.

32. In mid-1988 the total population in Burundi, Central African Republic, Congo, Kenya, Rwanda, Tanzania, Uganda, Zaire, and Zambia was an estimated 122.1 million, according to the Population Reference Bureau, Washington, D.C. In these nine countries, women of childbearing age (15–49) constitute on average 22.5 percent of the total population, according to age distributions available in United Nations, *World Demographic Estimates and Projections, 1950–2025* (New York: 1988). Thus the total number of people needing condoms is 27.5 million. Condoms cost about 4.4¢ apiece and an average couple uses 100–144 per year, according to Carl Hemmer, Chief of Commodity and Program Support Division, AID, Washington, D.C., private communication, October 12, 1988. Shipping adds 20 percent to cost and subsidizing their sale through commercial channels adds another 70 percent, making total costs roughly $12 per couple, according to Jerald Bailey, Deputy Division Chief of Research, Office of Population, AID, Washington, D.C., private communication, October 12, 1988. Community-based distribution or programs that actively promoted condom use through education, advertising, and so on would cost considerably more.

33. W. Parker Mauldin and Sheldon J. Segal, *Prevalence of Contraceptive Use in Developing Countries: A Chart Book* (New York: Rockefeller Foundation, 1986); condom use in Africa applies to married women of reproductive age, from John W. Townsend and Luis Varela, The Population Council, Testimony before Presidential Commission, April 18, 1988.

34. Harvey V. Fineberg, "The Social Dimensions of AIDS," *Scientific American,* October 1988.

35. Kenneth Presitt, "AIDS in Africa: The Triple Disaster," in Norman Miller and Richard C. Rockwell, eds., *AIDS in Africa: The Social and Policy Impact* (Lewiston, N.Y.: The Edwin Mellen Press, 1988).

36. For an excellent discussion of these issues, see Sabatier, *Blaming Others.*

37. Fineberg, "Social Dimensions of AIDS"; Ghana example from "Family Planners Define Their Role in Preventing Viral Spread," *New Scientist,* July 21, 1988.

43

Computers and Capitalism

JUDITH A. PERROLLE

The spread of computer technology is part of a transformation of the capitalist mode of production in the world's political and economic system (Perrolle, 1987). As Karl Marx argued in *The Poverty of Philosophy* (1973), the introduction of new machinery into the process of production requires a particular division of labor. The division of labor has consequences for the division of society into social classes, which in turn has political consequences. Although Marx is often misquoted as saying that the hand mill produced feudal society and the steam mill produced modern capitalist governments, his theory was not one of simple technological determinism. Before new machinery can be introduced into the workplace, work must be reorganized to accommodate the equipment by those who have the power to redefine tasks and products. It is from this reorganization of work in the new informa-

tion age that the social and political consequences of computer technology's "electronic mill" will emerge.

The modern computer has its origins in both the machinery of the early factories and the seventeenth-century mathematicians' and astronomers' fascination with computational and timing devices. For both industrialists and inventors, the rational organization of human activity was the means toward the desired goal of "progress." As the seventeenth-century mathematician Liebnitz wrote:

It is unworthy of excellent men to lose hours like slaves in the labor of calculation which could be safely relegated to anyone else if machines were used (Smith, 1959, pp. 156–164).

The "anyone else" was the person who operated the machine.

Charles Babbage, whose 1833 design for

the "analytical engine" was the prototype of the modern computer, owned factories organized around the principle that human labor was similar to capital and raw materials and should therefore be subject to similar controls.

The substitution of machinery for labor was an early part of the industrialization process. Marx (1973) agreed with Babbage's definition of a machine as a division of labor in which a single engine links particular operations performed by a single instrument. In this process factory workers became components of the machine as their work was first rationally divided into coordinated tasks. Later they were replaced by machines designed to do their specialized part of the operation.

The techniques which led to the eventual development of robots and other automated equipment appeared first on factory assembly lines, with manual workers serving as semi-automatic components. In fact, the word "computer" was first used to describe the jobs of women who performed calculations and wired hardware for the pioneering ENIAC computer. It only later meant the machine which replaced them. Such changes were not "because of" computers or any other technology. Rather, they occurred because those who had the power to decide how technology would be used reorganized the division of labor to accommodate the computer in ways they believed to be economically rational.

INFORMATION AS A COMMODITY

Theorists working in the Marxist tradition have tended to treat clerical, technical, and managerial workers quite distinctly from workers engaged in the production of *commodities*—items made by wage laborers in order to be sold at a profit. According to Harry Braverman's (1974) work on labor and monopoly capitalism, "commercial and financial labor add nothing to the value of the commodities represented by the figures or papers which they handle" (p. 414). Yet the industrial proletariat was considered a class by Marx not because it produced material objects, but because it was organized in a mode of production that systematically exploited the value of the labor of workers and added value to what the workers produced. By considering certain types of information as commodities, many of the theoretical insights of Marx's analysis of class can be more directly applied to the rapidly expanding proportion of the capitalist labor force who are in "computerized" jobs.

Information becomes a commodity when it is "made" by wage laborers and sold at a profit, and when the social and legal institutions of nations give such products the status of corporate property. The current legal trends in the advanced industrial countries toward the treatment of information as property are apparent in recent copyright cases and in laws designed to protect data from theft (Perrolle, 1987). Knowledge as private property based upon personal work is being replaced by information as private property based on wage labor. Throughout the world those who control the means of producing information products are also able to determine the social organization of the "mental labor" which produces them.

THE ALIENATION OF MENTAL LABOR

The history of capitalism has been a history of the reduction of thoughtful labor to routine, automatic processes. The skill and decision making of craftsmen were transformed in the factory to simple manual tasks. These in turn were gradually mechanized. Intellectual, or "white-collar," work was subjected to increasing bureaucratic organization, although it generally escaped automation. While the use of computers in management and the professions is being widely heralded as a technology for enhancing human skills, often it is a technology for the further routinization and in some cases actual automation of intellectual work (Perrolle, 1989).

When professional, managerial, and technical work becomes more organized and subject to the analysis needed to divide it into less skilled operations as part of production organized around computer-based information and control systems, an alienation process occurs. First, the technology physically removes the worker from the object of the work, as more and more labor is done on abstract information about the world rather than on material objects in the world. Second, the technology reduces the scope of a worker's activity to a small portion of a much larger product. In structured programming, for example, each programmer works on a small portion of a larger program according to specifications so rigid that in some cases computer programs are used to edit the work and remove any nonstandard lines of code.

Workers subjected to such conditions are "deskilled" (Cooley, 1980) in the sense that their labor requires less thought than before and gives them fewer decisions to make. If mental labor is increasingly organized for commodity production and if educational and intellectual institutions increasingly reflect capitalism's "need" for such deskilling, then even "creative" work may become a set of learned reflexes suitable for a machine environment. Work as a source of human satisfactions and social relationships will be further degraded, and education is likely to be redesigned in ways that blunt the intellectual and critical faculties of all but the elite.

THE DISTRIBUTION OF LABOR

In Industrial Revolution factories, people worked at a pace set by machinery and enforced by supervisors. While the temporal logic of factory machinery required a temporal discipline on the part of workers, in some new computer systems the machine can accommodate multiple tasks occurring at different tempos and in different sequences. The new technologies speed up the production process, shortening the time between design and product. They can also be used to coordinate work performed by individuals acting at their own pace and under their own direction. Communications and control technology also makes it possible to coordinate the work of people in different cities and countries. Work has been freed from the spatial requirement of the Industrial Revolution that people work together in the same factory or office building. The workplace can be anywhere.

The computer technology that maintains centralized control over workers who are physically distanced from their work and from one another facilitates a new international division of labor. Multinational corporations are increasingly able to integrate unskilled labor in the peripheral less-developed countries and deskilled labor in the core industrial countries into a geographically dispersed production system. This mode of production can be distinguished from earlier forms of international capitalist production by its centralized coordination of the scattered units. Labor is widely distributed while control remains centralized. In the periphery, new industrial locations take advantage of cheap unskilled labor in the militarily repressive states; in the core, runaway shops apply downward pressure to wages while the new "high tech" industries produce few "high tech" jobs and many low-paid, unskilled ones. Computer technology also supplies the automated equipment to dislocate the unionized and highly skilled industrial workers of the core and can create a return to nonunion piecework in "electronic cottage" arrangements. Already some clerical work is being distributed to part-time home workers in the United States. As telecommunications infrastructure improves, this sort of work can be done in almost any region which has been opened to electronic capital penetration.

Although proponents of telecommunications development stress the economic advantages that accrue to Third World nations through better communications facilities, the New World Information and Communication Order program proposed by UNESCO seems to some a "technological

Trojan Horse" through which the transnational corporations that monopolize communications technology can extend their control over the Third World (NACLA, 1982). If telecommunications is viewed as part of the computer technology base for a new mode of capitalist production, its consequences are clear. As the late Stephen Hymer (1972) observed: "To maintain the separation between work and control, capital has erected elaborate corporate superstructures to unite labor in production, but divide it in power" (p. 102–3). Computer technology provides the means for a global separation of work and control.

THE MACHINE AS MANAGER

Computer technology provides some capacity to relocate control over complex production processes from human decision makers to the machine itself. The field of "artificial intelligence" involves the design and production of computer systems and automated equipment with a limited capacity to behave in ways that at least resemble human thought processes. Although artificial intelligence is a new field and has so far shown very meager results, robots, expert systems, and the proposed new military "supercomputers" are being designed to replace the knowledge and judgment of human professionals with machinery. Although they have only just begun to appear as part of the capitalist mode of production, they represent a trend with enormous consequences for the social relations of production.

The main consequence of machine-embodied knowledge is a devaluation of the knowledge of human experts, especially at the lower technical and managerial levels (Perrolle, 1989). With the spread of artificial intelligence, we may expect a marked stratification between a small technocratic elite whose expertise is in the development of such systems and a massively deskilled middle class whose "professions" are increasingly subject to automation and computerized controls. Because the computer's

intelligence is limited by the narrow range of instrumental logic with which it has been endowed, decision making by computer can accelerate the dehumanizing effects already visible in bureaucratic organizations. In their military applications, decision-making machines increase the possibility of an accidental triggering of nuclear war. This is partially because the enormously complex technology is prone to failure. But it is also because the electronic reaction speeds of computer-controlled weapons greatly reduce the amount of time available to humans to plan, debate, and negotiate military situations (Perrolle, 1988).

The machine as manager permits a complex economic integration of manual and mental labor on a global scale and provides the technology for supervising and disciplining it. This "electronic mill," owned and controlled by multinational corporations and the military-industrial complexes of the core nations, represents a new force of capitalist production. Although now fettered by national economic and military interests, the electronic mill seems likely to give us a world-society dominated by multinational companies.

CLASS FORMATION

While the spread of computer technology is creating common working conditions for large numbers of individuals in the world-system, the conditions of computerized work do not facilitate the formation of class consciousness in the same way that the early industrial revolution situation of groups of workers in factories did. By allowing workers to be physically separate from their work and from one another (even across international boundaries at great distances), computer technology interferes with the linkages Marx observed between capitalist organization of industrial production and workers' political responses. If workers in the new international division of labor are to become organized into the sort of revolutionary class predicted by Marx, alternative means of creating common culture, easy communications among class members, and political organizations dedicated to economic transformation must develop. Computer technology provides some means by which this may occur, though it also provides means by which efforts to organize international workers can be severely inhibited by the dominant class. The fundamental changes being introduced by computers are occurring within the workplace, and are considered economic rather than political decisions. The impact of computers on centralized decision making will not occur as a direct use of computer systems in the political process but will occur through a restructuring of social classes.

Terence Hopkins (1977) and others have argued that a world capitalist class is consolidating across national boundaries and incorporating the elites of the Third World. Computer technology's contribution to this process is to improve production efficiency by consolidating production control into the hands of fewer but more expert managers, to eliminate large segments of the middle class, and to provide new forms of ideology and labor discipline. The information-society elite will contain a relatively small remnant of the managerial, technical, and professional occupations possessing both decision-making power and knowledge of computer technology.

The same computerized integration of production is occurring in socialist societies. Insofar as there exists a "new class" in the socialist countries, that class seems likely to become stronger and more international as computer technology is applied to international socialist economic integration. If, as Nyiri (1982) argues, the world-system incorporates both a capitalist world-economy and a socialist world-economy which are becoming more interdependent, then there may be some "blurring" of "the social differences between the two systems into some third form" (p. 21).

The spread of a world "corporate culture" of rather uniform patterns of electronically based production and ways of conducting international business may produce a worldwide information-society elite dedicated to the overthrow of nationalist political interference with their global accumulation process, to the incorporation of Third World and "socialist" ruling classes, and to the consolidation of social status and political power into their expert hands.

THE WORKING CLASS IN THE INFORMATION SOCIETY

One of the most visible signs of the progress of the second industrial revolution has been the automation of highly skilled jobs of the "labor aristocracy." These workers, largely through strong unions, had escaped many of the consequences of the proletarianization process of the first Industrial Revolution. Now that computerized industrial robots have been designed with enough "intelligence" to perform skilled manual operations on the assembly line, the unionized blue-collar worker's highly paid position in industrial society is seriously threatened. The significant feature of the robotics phenomenon is the use of expensive machines to replace expensive labor. Within a generation they will have broken the power of the industrial unions and restricted membership in the middle class by eliminating the high-wage blue-collar segment.

As the application of computer technology to traditional assembly lines reduces industrial wages, its application to office work is raising productivity and rationalizing working conditions. Many new automated offices are information factories; clerical and data-processing workers are the new information assembly line workers. In the beginning, the office automation phenomenon expands opportunities in the "pink collar" jobs traditionally held by women. However, eventually much of this work will be automated to the point where jobs can be eliminated. Already bank tellers and supermarket clerks are being replaced by machines; many types of office work can be similarly computerized. Downward pressure on pink-collar wages is provided by the trends towards "electronic cottage" piece-work (Mattera, 1983; Christensen, 1988) and the removal of clerical work to overseas locations.

Optimistic analysts of the computer revolution tend to dismiss the devaluation of blue- and pink-collar wages as a transitional phenomenon. They focus their attention on the promise of expanded opportunities for creative, highly paid jobs in the professions as a solution to computer-generated unemployment and worsening working conditions. However, one branch of computer science is threatening to make possible the automation of skilled mental work as well as the more routine forms of information handling. Expert systems, a type of "artificial intelligence" computer program, are bringing automation to the professions (Perrolle, 1989). Such programs can ask for needed information, can interpret information in terms of "best guesses" based upon their problem-solving experience, can draw inferences from data, and can modify their own behavior as a result of the outcome of their previous actions. The practical success of expert systems that play chess, infer chemical structures from molecular data, and diagnose illnesses indicate quite clearly that artificial intelligence is being put to work at industrial and professional tasks, despite theoretical objections (Dreyfus & Dreyfus, 1986) that what they do isn't really the same as human thought. The applications in which they are used are those in which the knowledge of human experts is characterized by great rationality; claims that they will eventually be able to perform in all areas of human expertise are essentially claims that all human knowledge can be made rational and automatable.

The computer software industry is often pointed to as a prime example of the new opportunities for creative work in high tech industry. Based on its rapid expansion in recent decades and its relative openness to women, software production was widely believed to be a positive example of the new employment pattern. Unfortunately, the U.S. pattern of employment discrimination

by race and gender persists in the information age (Fidel & Garner, 1987; Glenn & Tolbert, 1987; Kraft, 1977). Indeed, given our cultural beliefs about women's and minorities' lower capacities for mathematical and analytic thinking, we may find worsening job discrimination. Finally, a technological development called "structured programming" is being used to break large computer programming tasks into small interchangeable parts. Even as software production is thus being rationalized, expert systems are being designed to automate the programming itself.

In engineering and production control, computer-aided design and "embedded systems" are being designed to make production processes fully integrated and automated, from purchasing decisions through process design, production optimization, pricing, and marketing. These developments will also begin to eliminate managerial as well as technical functions.

As highly paid blue-collar workers lose their jobs, information workers are organized into production work, and even skilled white-collar workers find themselves downwardly mobile, the new information age working class is being formed. As competition for jobs requiring little skill becomes more intense, those already in the working class will suffer the brunt of the unemployment and declining benefits. The explanations and justifications for the decline of the middle class at the expense of the lower class will be terms of international competition, individual lack of "computer literacy," and the inevitability of progress. It is with great reluctance that the middle class population will identify itself by its new economic status; already an ideology is emerging to explain the new information society in ways which avoid any consideration of the basic economic transformation which is under way.

REFERENCES

Braverman, H. (1974). *Labor and monopoly capital: The degradation of work in the twentieth century.* New York: Monthly Review Press.

Christensen, K. E. (Ed.). (1988). *The new era of home-based work*. Boulder, CO: Westview Press.

Cooley, M. (1980). *Architect or bee? The human technology relationship*. Boston: South End Press.

Dreyfus, H., & Dreyfus, S. (1986). *Mind over machines: The power of human intuition and expertise in the era of the computer*. New York: Free Press.

Fidel, K., & Garner, R. (1987, August). *Computer professionals: Career lines and occupational identity*. Paper presented at the meeting of the Society for the Study of Social Problems, Chicago.

Glenn, E. N., & Tolbert, C. M., II. (1987, August). *Race and gender in high technology employment: Recent trends in computer occupations*. Paper presented at the meeting of the Society for the Study of Social Problems, Chicago.

Hopkins, T. (1977). Notes on class analysis and world system. *Review I*, 1, 67–72.

Hymer, S. (1972). The internationalization of capital. *Journal of Economic Issues, 6*(1), 91–123.

Kraft, P. (1977). *Programmers and managers*. New York: Springer-Verlag.

Mattera, P. (1983, April 2). Home computer sweatshops. *The Nation*, 390–392.

Marx, K. (1973). *The poverty of philosophy*. Moscow: Progress Publishers.

NACLA. (1982, July-August). Toward a new information order. *NACLA Report on the Americas* (Special Issue), *XVI*(4).

Nyiri, K. (1982, Summer). Towards an integrated international division of labor. The place of the world socialist economy. *Review VI*, 1, 15–23.

Perrolle, J. A. (1987). *Computers and social change: Information, property, and power*. Belmont, CA: Wadsworth.

Perrolle, J. A. (1988). *Risk and responsibility in a computerized environment*. Paper presented at the annual meeting of the American Sociological Association, Atlanta.

Perrolle, J. A. (1989). *White collar computers*. Paper presented at the annual meeting of the American Association for the Advancement of Science, San Francisco.

Smith, D. E. (1959). *A sourcebook of mathematics, Vol. 1*. New York: Dover.

44

Love Canal 10 Years Later

DAVID SHRIBMAN

The homes look much as they did that summer a decade ago: bungalows and ranch houses with basketball hoops in the driveways, swing sets out back and a plastic pink flamingo in the garden. But wait: 228 houses, two full streets' worth, have simply vanished, bulldozed into their basements or into holes in the ground.

Vanished, too, are nearly all of the people. Joann Hale, Barbara Quimby, Violet Iadicicco—all have moved away. Yellow "Hazardous Waste Area" signs are bolted to fences in the old neighborhood. Love Canal—or more properly, what remains of it—is whispery quiet now.

Yet it isn't quite gone. Ten years after the chemical crisis that transformed Love Canal from an anonymous subdivision into an ominous symbol, the 1,000 people who lived here still are victims. "We'll never get over this," says Mrs. Iadicicco, 54 years old. "The hurt is never going to go away."

Today she and her neighbors—working families who were drawn to the neighborhood because it seemed so safe—are bitter about government, distrustful of business, and worried about the future. Some suffer from nightmares, some still care for family members with birth defects, and many more can't stop wondering what new health problems may afflict their families. Marriages—many didn't survive—have undergone seismic shifts. The refugees from the Love Canal seem to have aged so much more than 10 years.

HARD TO GO ON

"Love Canal ruined a lot of lives," says Lois Gibbs, a homemaker who became the leader of the neighborhood group demanding action on the canal. "There are divorces, deaths, huge financial burdens, and a lot of children are still very sick. But the worst part of this is the fear of the unknown. It's really tough to continue life not knowing whether your kids are going to get sick and die."

Love Canal is still more than a story about chemicals. It is, most of all, a story about a few dozen homemakers who, as one of them remembered the other day, "baked cookies and stayed with the kids." They began to worry about birth defects and cancer and were transformed into sophisticated political activists who called nationwide attention to their plight and ultimately provided the impetus for the federal toxic chemical Superfund. Today, Love Canal is the story of women like Mrs. Quimby, caring for one child with breathing problems and another with a congenital eye defect and mental retardation, a woman told by her doctor that she had to be sterilized.

Mrs. Quimby, now 37, lived in the Love Canal neighborhood for the first 30 years of her life. She remembers how, as a child, she and her friends watched the sparks fly off the rocks they threw around the playground over the dump. Later, she raised her own children here.

BEAR CLAWS

"That neighborhood was the 'homemaker alley' of America," she says. "We were all Betty Crocker. We put our kids down to nap and we cleaned the house. But our bear claws came out with our cubs. It was a basic instinct. We wanted to protect our kids.

Their children suffered from birth defects, cleft palates, deformed ears and teeth, and retardation. One child was born with two rows of teeth, another with three ears, a third with only one kidney. Experts may never determine the extent of the link between the chemicals and the health disorders in the community, but the furor over the toxins, the months of living in hotels and military housing and the years of political battles prompted an extraordinary transformation of a blue-collar neighborhood and brought extraordinary stresses to ordinary families.

Ten years ago, Mrs. Hale, pregnant with her second child, attended worried and angry meetings at the 99th Street School. Today, the school is buried beneath a 22-acre clay cap intended to prevent human contact with the toxins, reduce the amount of water infiltrating the canal, and curtail air emissions. Mrs. Hale had her child, a daughter, but all of the child's teeth decalcified, she has a bone infection that can't be explained, and she has learning disabilities.

PSYCHOLOGICAL BURDEN

"There's no way to prove any connection" between these problems and the chemicals, says Mrs. Hale, a one-time homemaker who now works as a legal assistant counseling residents of other communities with toxic-waste problems. But she adds: "Tell me this [would] have happened if I didn't live there."

The damage to the lives of the Love Canal residents is just as difficult to measure.

"People who go through these sorts of things live with enormous uncertainty and feel they have little control over their own lives," says Michael Edelstein, an environmental psychologist at Ramapo College of New Jersey who has studied Love Canal and other communities with toxic-waste problems. "But they also look at the environment as a place where evil lurks and even feel at risk at home. A lot of them never stop feeling victimized."

They are people like Patricia Genzy, 36, who still dreams that she is being forced to move back to the Love Canal and says, "I don't think I'll ever stop having that dream." Or like Janice Alexander, whose husband grew up in the Love Canal area and who, as a young married woman, lived in the area for seven years.

"We don't know what to tell our kids," says Mrs. Alexander, who, like many of the Love Canal residents, now lives on Grand Island in the Niagara River between Niagara Falls and Buffalo. "I'm going to have to tell my son to have genetic testing. I would hold myself responsible if something went wrong with one of *his* kids. And we can only guess ourselves."

Laboratory analyses of soil and sediment samples taken from the Love Canal area showed the presence of more than 200 chemicals, including dioxin, considered one of the most toxic chemicals made by man; benzene, which has been linked to leukemia; and others that have been linked to nervous-system disorders, liver problems, respiratory distress, deafness, and cardiac arrest.

Between 1942 and 1953 Hooker Electrochemical Co., now known as Occidental Chemical Corp., had placed 21,800 tons of chemical wastes in a canal that had a visionary named William Love had hoped would provide cheap hydroelectric power for his model city. The canal was abandoned when alternating current was invented, eliminating the need for industrial plants to be located at power sites, and for years it was used as a neighborhood swimming hole.

Hooker, in a deed that warned that the land had been filled with "waste products," sold the property for $1 in 1953 to the Niagara Falls Board of Education, which a year later built a brick elementary school on the site. A neighborhood grew up in the area.

"The wastes at Love Canal were disposed of in a state-of-the-art fashion and the problems that were encountered happened only after control of the site had passed from the company," says John Stuart, Occidental Chemical's current director for public affairs in western New York. Nonetheless, by the end of the 1970s barrels of chemicals were surfacing, contaminated waste was turning up in backyards, and chemical smells were pervading the area.

SPEAKING UP

The ones who grew alarmed first and who took the initiative were the people like Grace McCoulf.

As a high-school student she was so withdrawn that if someone spoke to her she almost quivered, and in all the time she studied accounting at Niagara County Community College, she never remembers voluntarily speaking in class. When the Love Canal emergency broke in 1978 she was the sort of quiet mother of two best described as a homebody, but gradually she became angrier—and more vocal.

She screamed at state and local officials, she threw a microphone at the mayor, she was arrested. "My kids were getting sick," she says now, "and I wanted to kill."

A Love Canal chronology

1893 William Love announces plan for a model city on the Niagara Frontier.

1894 Work begins on canal to bring in hydroelectric power.

1910 Love's project sold at public auction.

1942-53 Hooker Electrochemical Co. uses canal as chemical dump.

1953 Hooker, warning of dangers, sells land to Niagara Falls school board for $1.

1978 New York state health commissioner declares emergency at Love Canal,

recommends relocating pregnant women and children under age 2. President Carter declares federal chemical emergency and state agrees to purchase homes affected by chemicals.

1979 State authorities broaden the evacuation area, remedial work begins.

1980 State files suit against Hooker and its parent corporation to recover damages, Carter declares second federal emergency at Love Canal and first homes purchased.

1988 State finds part of area habitable.

Her neighbors went through similar transformations. Mrs. Gibbs took on local authorities, Gov. Hugh Carey, Hooker—and eventually her own husband, ironically a chemical operator. In the process, clothes went unpressed, dinner was no longer on the table at five, her husband's lunch bucket wasn't filled. She never read any of the manifestos of the feminist movement; she wasn't a "women's libber," she told a reporter who spoke with her almost every day for two years; but she was changing, swiftly and irreversibly, almost before his eyes.

"It was bad for the men," Mrs. Iadicicco remembers a decade later. "They felt their homes were falling apart and their wives were standing up for the first time."

"I remember my husband saying he couldn't fight fires because he had to stay home with babies," says Mrs. Alexander, who had chosen the neighborhood in part so her husband, a volunteer fireman, could be near the fire hall. "He supported me, but it was a time of real strain."

A COMING OUT

The women not only were changing how the nation looks at chemical dumps—Love Canal set a precedent for a government granting benefits for victims of a man-made disaster—but they were also changing themselves.

"A lot of these women realized that if they could take on Love Canal, they could take on most anything," says Adeline Levine, a sociologist at the State University of New York at Buffalo. "They're more independent, more active. It was a watershed issue in their lives and in some of their marriages."

But Love Canal also robbed them of their innocence and their trust.

"People believed in what they learned in their civics classes," says Mrs. Gibbs, who was divorced from her first husband, married the man who was the liaison between the community and the state during the cleanup and now heads the Citizens Clear-inghouse for Hazardous Waste. "They believed in paying taxes, being law-abiding citizens, and now they question whether they should pay their taxes and whether the government is doing what it should."

Adds Marie Pozniak, 47, the wife of a tool-setter in a Chevrolet plant: "The whole experience has left me very bitter and distrusting of government. They made us struggle for three years to save our families."

Besides the $30,000 or $40,000 they were paid for their homes, the residents won $20 million in litigation against a number of Occidental Petroleum entitles and the city and county. The individual settlements were relatively small, from a minimum of $2,000 to a high of $400,000, and nearly 1,000 cases are still pending.

A COMMUNITY AGAIN?

This summer, two creeks north of Love Canal will be dredged. Occidental has offered to store and incinerate the contaminants, potentially saving the federal Superfund as much as $20 million. Last September, the state deemed part of the neighborhood north and west of the canal to be habitable, and 300 people have indicated an interest in moving into the area.

The discovery this month near the canal of chemicals that are suspected of causing cancer raised new questions about the study that led to the health department's decision. Indeed, a debate over whether and how to use the land still rages here. "I don't think the land should be written off forever," says the Rev. Donald Harrington, the president of Niagara University and chairman of the Land Use Advisory Committee examining the future of the canal area. "The challenge is to figure out how to use it well and safely."

A few Love Canal residents, in fact, never left. About 70 people still live in what is left of the neighborhood. Jerauld Wilson's grandchildren aren't allowed to drink the water when they visit, but he and his wife have lived here for 23 years. The state offered him $27,000 for his house but he rejected the offer. Today he has no neighbors. "They didn't offer me enough for my house," he says, "and now no one else would buy it."

Since August, however, one of his cousins, who lived in the house before he bought it, has been diagnosed with terminal cancer. His wife has had lumps removed from her breast and arm. "Right now I think we should have moved," says Mary Wilson. "Now, at 56, there's no place to run to."

Luella Kenney can never escape the Love Canal. Her son Jon died at age seven two months after the state declared a health emergency here. The diagnosis was nephrosis, a kidney disease, but Mrs. Kenney, a mother of two other children and a cancer research scientist for three decades, believes the cause was the Love Canal chemicals.

"I have an empty nest—the two others are gone—and I keep thinking Jon would still be here," she says. "You can't ever get over a child's death. I still can't get over the questions: What if he didn't play in the backyard? What if the chemicals weren't there?"

45

A World at Risk

Lester R. Brown
Christopher Flavin
Sandra Postel

The environmental era now dawning is distinguished by problems truly global in scale. Even while countries grapple with the more localized problems of acid rain, toxic waste, and soil erosion, global threats of unprecedented proportions are now overlaid upon them. The immediate challenge is to translate a common vision of a world at risk into the international alliances and bold actions needed to safeguard the earth.

CROSSING PERCEPTUAL THRESHOLDS

Social change occurs when people alter the way they perceive some of the elements constituting their world. Spurred by a dramatic event, a charismatic leader, or a gradual awakening through education, people cross a "perceptual threshold" that forces them to see and judge some aspect of their world in a new light. These perceptual shifts often have a decidedly ethical component. Witness the turning of slavery from an implicit right to a moral abomination, or the subjugation of women from common practice to—at least in some parts of the world—a reprehensible condition.

An effective response to the environmental threats now unfolding will require that humanity's perception of its relationship to the earth's natural systems cross a new threshold.

The explosion at the Chernobyl nuclear reactor in the Soviet Ukraine in early April 1986 did what hundreds of studies assessing nuclear technology could never have done: it made the dangers of nuclear power real. Fresh vegetables were declared unfit for human consumption in northern Italy. Polish authorities launched an emergency effort to get iodine tablets administered to children. The livelihood of the Lapps in northern Scandinavia was threatened when reindeer upon which they depend became too contaminated with radiation to bring to market. In the Soviet Union itself, 100,000 people in the vicinity of the reactor were forced to abandon their homes.

This single event shifted public attitudes so strongly against nuclear power that since then five countries have decided not to build more nuclear plants and two, Italy and Sweden, have decided to accelerate closings of existing plants. In the Soviet Union, at least five reactors have been canceled since the accident, and work has been suspended at several other sites.[1]

Rapid advances in recent years toward acid rain control in Europe stem in large part from the West Germans' sudden awakening to *waldsterben*, forest death. After a 1982 survey showed that trees in the fabled Black Forest and elsewhere were dying in large numbers—with suspected links to air pollution and acid rain—*waldsterben* rapidly emerged as a potent political and emotional issue.

Of course, perceptual shifts by themselves do not resolve problems. But such shifts are often prerequisites to effective responses, the sparks that ignite the processes of change. Indeed, crossing the perceptual thresholds needed to respond to ecological problems launches humanity toward a new moral frontier. A growing sense of the world's interdependence and connectedness takes shape—the recognition, for example, that automobile use anywhere threatens climate stability everywhere. The old business of pursuing narrow economic and political self-interest falls away, anachronistic and plainly untenable.

Without a strong sense that people favor the fundamental changes needed to respond to these problems, governments will not take the necessary actions. The immediate task, then, is for individuals everywhere to raise their understanding, concern, and voices to the point where political leaders are forced to respond. Scientists who not only convey the relevant facts but also articulate the consequences of political inaction

will play a crucial role in this process of education and mobilization. So, too, will the media.

Will societies cross these new perceptual thresholds soon enough to avoid major ecological backlash? A committed, active, vocal public is essential to bring about the policy changes needed to safeguard the earth's environment. The difficult choices that lie ahead will challenge our social institutions and personal values as never before. It will help to remember that progress is an illusion if it destroys the conditions needed for life to thrive on earth.

THE THREAT OF CLIMATE CHANGE

The warming of the earth's climate is an environmental catastrophe on a new scale, with the potential to violently disrupt virtually every natural ecosystem and many of the structures and institutions that humanity has grown to depend on. Although climates have shifted only slightly so far, the world faces the prospect of vastly accelerated change in the decades ahead. Conditions essential to life as we know it are now at risk.

The threat of climate change stems from the increasing concentrations of carbon dioxide (CO_2) and other "greenhouse gases" that hold heat in the lower atmosphere, allowing temperatures to rise. The burning of coal and of other carbon-based fuels such as oil and natural gas releases carbon as the basic product of the combustion, while the large-scale clearing of tropical forests adds additional carbon dioxide to the atmosphere. Just since 1958, when routine measurements began, the CO_2 concentration has gone from 315 parts per million to 352 parts per million—substantially above the highest concentrations experienced on earth in the past 160,000 years.[2]

Concentrations of other, more potent greenhouse gases—notably methane, nitrous oxide, and chlorofluorocarbons (CFCs)—are increasing even more rapidly. Based on current emission rates, they have as much potential as CO_2 to warm the atmosphere. While the carbon dioxide level has grown at a rate of 0.4 percent a year since 1958, these other gases are increasing at annual rates as high as 5 percent.[3] The United States is the largest contributor, but it may be passed soon by the Soviet Union and later by China. While carbon emissions are growing slowly in the industrial countries that account for two-thirds of the total, they are skyrocketing in the developing world. Deforestation in the Amazon and perhaps other tropical regions appears to have accelerated to frighteningly rapid rates.

Teams of British and American scientists have assembled series of global average temperatures going back 100 years. While experts still disagree about some of these numbers, the overall trend is clear. The global average temperature in the 1890s was 14.5 degrees Celsius, and by the 1980s it had climbed to 15.2 degrees. Temperatures leveled off between 1940 and 1970, but the accelerated rise during the eighties more than offset this lull. The five warmest years of the past century all occurred in the 1980s.[4]

The limited warming that has occurred so far is important to scientists, but not threatening to society. The danger lies in the acceleration of climate change that appears imminent. Between 2030 and 2050, average temperatures could be 1.5–4.5 degrees Celsius (3–8 degrees Fahrenheit) higher than they have been in recent decades, or warmer than the earth has been for the past two million years. If the spurt in global temperatures that began about 1970 continues, droughts, heat waves, and other unusual weather may increase by the late 1990s to the point where even nonscientists will notice the climate is changing.

The pace of climate change can be compared with nuclear war for its potential to disrupt a wide range of human and natural systems, complicating the task of managing economies and coping with other problems. Irrigation works, settlement patterns, and food production would be tragically disrupted by a rapid warming.

Trees are adapted to a narrow range of temperature and moisture levels, and cannot cope with rapid climate change. A temperature increase of 1 degree Celsius per decade in mid- to upper latitudes translates into a shift in vegetation zones of 60–100 miles northward. Terrestrial ecosystems cannot migrate that fast. Vast numbers of trees are likely to die, and new trees adapted to warmer temperatures are unlikely to be able to replace them rapidly. During such a disruption, huge areas of forest could die and, as they decay or burn, send large quantities of additional CO_2 into the atmosphere, accelerating the warming.

Biological diversity, already being reduced by various human activities, may be one of the chief casualties of global warming. Massive destruction of forests, wetlands, and even the polar tundra could irrevocably destroy complex ecosystems that have existed for millennia. Indeed, various biological reserves created in the past decade to protect species diversity could become virtual deathtraps as wildlife attempt to survive in conditions for which they are poorly suited. Accelerated species extinction is an inevitable consequence of a rapid warming.

Sea level rise is another threat. As ocean water warms, it will expand, and warming at the poles will melt parts of glaciers and ice caps. Studies conclude that a temperature rise of 3 degrees Celsius by 2050 would raise sea level by 50–100 centimeters. By the end of the next century, sea level may be up by as much as two meters. This would hurt most in the developing world, particularly in densely populated Asia, where rice is produced on low-lying river deltas and floodplains. Without heavy investments in dikes and seawalls to protect the rice fields from saltwater intrusion, such a rise would markedly reduce harvests. Large areas of wetlands that nourish the world's fisheries would also be destroyed.

In Bangladesh, sea level rise and subsidence caused largely by human activities could flood up to 18 percent of the nation's land area by 2050, displacing more than 17 million people. In Egypt, where only 4 percent of the land area can be cultivated, food production could drop and 8.5 million people could be forced from their homes. In these already crowded countries, there is no place for these people to go and no alternative land available on which to grow crops.

In the United States, a U.S. government-sponsored study has estimated the potential impacts of climate change on Cleveland, Miami, and New York. A few minor benefits are mentioned, such as lower snow removal budgets and winter heating bills, but the overall picture is bleak. In particular, many billions of dollars will likely have to be spent on improving already inadequate water supply systems, since demand will increase and supplies will be degraded as the climate changes.

In New York, for example, salt water could move up the lower Hudson River while more-severe droughts limit the amount of water available from upstate watersheds. In Miami, most of which was once below sea level, even extensive diking will not preserve its porous freshwater aquifer. If global warming continues, Miami could one day be reclaimed by the sea.

When air pollution and solid waste disposal first commanded attention in the 1970s, analysts were at least able to point to solutions to the problems and come up with 5- or 10-year action plans. One of the most disturbing things about global warming is that climate change has so much momentum behind it now that it can only be slowed, not stopped. Future generations will have to cope with a warmer and ever-changing world, one in which major investments are required simply to maintain the status quo. Global warming will hurt rich and poor, North and South alike. But those most at risk are the almost 4 billion people who live in the Third World, many of whom already face declining living standards and who lack the resources to protect themselves from spreading deserts and rising sea levels.

Indeed, climate change, like no other issue, calls the whole notion of human progress into question. The benefits of newer technologies, more efficient economies, and improved political systems could be overwhelmed by uncontrolled global warming. Some warming is inevitable, but unless trends are reversed, tragic changes could occur in just the next two decades. The challenge is to act before it is too late—which means before the scientific evidence is conclusive. The longer society waits, the more radical and draconian the needed responses will be.

A LOSS OF FOOD SECURITY

Climate change is being added to an already long list of environmental stresses and resource scarcities that are undermining global food security. Soil erosion, desertification, the salting of irrigated lands, and a scarcity of new cropland and fresh water are combining to lower the growth in food output below that of population in dozens of developing countries.

A dramatic 2.6-fold increase in grain production between 1950 and 1984 raised per capita consumption by nearly 40 percent. But since then growth has stopped. In 1987 and 1988, world grain production fell sharply, marking the first steep back-to-back annual declines on record. A monsoon failure in India in 1987 and drought-reduced harvests in North America and China in 1988 explain only part of the reduction. In several populous countries, including China, India, Indonesia, and Mexico, little or no progress has been made in expanding grain production since 1984.[5]

Continuing rapid growth of world population during the last few years combined with the reduced harvests has led to a record fall in per capita output of grain, the food source that accounts for half of world caloric intake when consumed directly and a sizable part of the remainder when consumed indirectly as meat, milk, and eggs. Between 1986 and 1988, production per person fell 14 percent, dropping back to the level of 1970.

This reversal in humanity's agricultural

fortunes has occurred rather abruptly. For those accustomed to reading of "a world awash with grain," the latest downturn in grain output may come as a surprise. Although not widely recognized at the time, the impressive growth in world production following the doubling of world grain prices in 1973 was achieved in part by plowing highly erodible land, and in part by drawing down water tables through overpumping for irrigation.

Farmers can overplow and overpump with impressive results in the short run, but for many the short run is drawing to a close. The result is a worldwide retrenchment in cultivated area and a dramatic slowdown in the spread of irrigation. As highly erodible cropland brought under the plow during the agricultural boom years of the 1970s is taken out of cultivation, and as falling water tables in key food-producing countries force a reduction in irrigated area, the growth in world food output is slowing.[6]

In Africa, the number of "food insecure" people, defined by the World Bank as those not having enough food for normal health and physical activity, now totals over 100 million. Some 14.7 million Ethiopians, one-third of the country, are undernourished. Nigeria is close behind, with 13.7 million undernourished people. The countries with 40 percent or more of their populations suffering from chronic food insecurity are Chad, Mozambique, Somalia, and Uganda. (See Table 1–1.) The Bank summarized its findings by noting that "Africa's food situation is not only serious, it is deteriorating."[7]

This deterioration is not limited to Africa. In Latin America, which exported more grain than North America did a mere half-century ago, per capita grain production has fallen 7 percent since reaching an all-time high in 1981. In its 1988 report "The Global State of Hunger and Malnutrition," the U.N.'s World Food Council reports that the share of malnourished preschoolers in Peru increased from 42 percent to 68 percent between 1980 and 1983. The Council summarized its worldwide findings by noting that "earlier progress in fighting

TABLE 1.1   Food Insecurity in Selected African Countries, 1986

Country	Number of People (million)	Share of Population (percent)
Ethiopia	14.7	34
Nigeria	13.7	13
Zaire	12.0	38
Tanzania	6.6	29
Kenya	6.2	29
Uganda	6.1	40
Mozambique	5.9	42
Algeria	4.1	18
Ghana	4.1	31
Sudan	3.4	15
Zambia	2.7	39
Mali	2.5	33
Chad	2.4	47
Morocco	2.4	11
Somalia	2.3	42

Source: World Bank, *Report of the Task Force on Food Security in Africa* (Washington, DC: 1988); World Bank, *World Development Report 1988* (New York: Oxford University Press, 1988).

hunger, malnutrition and poverty has come to a halt or is being reversed in many parts of the world."[8]

The effect of higher grain prices on consumers is much greater in developing countries than in industrial ones. In the United States, for example, a $1 loaf of bread contains roughly 5¢ worth of wheat. If the price of wheat doubles, the price of the loaf would increase to only $1.05. In developing countries, however, where wheat is purchased in the market and ground into flour at home, a doubling of world grain prices translates into a doubling of prices to consumers. For those who already spend most of their income on food, such a rise can drive consumption below the survival level.[9]

Already faced with a deteriorating food situation, the world is now confronted with climate change, an additional threat to food security. Though they remain sketchy, meteorological models suggest that two of the world's major food-producing regions—the North American agricultural heartland and a large area of central Asia—are likely to experience a decline in soil moisture during the summer growing season as a result of higher temperatures and increased evaporation. If the warming progresses as the models indicate, some of the land in the U.S. western Great Plains that now produces wheat would revert to rangeland. The western Corn Belt would become semi-arid, with wheat or other drought-tolerant grains that yield 40 bushels per acre replacing corn that yields over 100 bushels.[10]

On the plus side, as temperatures increase, the winter wheat belt might migrate northward, allowing winter strains that yield 40 bushels per acre to replace spring varieties yielding 30 bushels. A longer growing season would also permit a northward extension of spring wheat production into areas such as Canada's Alberta province, thus increasing that nation's cultivated area. On balance, though, higher temperatures and increased summer dryness will reduce the North American grain harvest, largely because of their negative impact on the all-important corn crop.

A study from the National Center for Atmospheric Research in Boulder, Colorado, suggests that a rise in average temperatures will also increase the probability of extreme short-term heat waves. If these occur at critical times—such as the corn pollination period—they can have a much greater effect on crop yields than the relatively modest average temperature increase of a few degrees might indicate.[11] This vulnerability of corn, which accounts for two-thirds of the U.S. grain harvest and one-eighth of the world's, can cause wide year-to-year swings in the world grain crop.

With the warming now apparently under way, hot dry summers will become more frequent. In the event of a disastrous drought, U.S. grain exports would drop dramatically. The world would face a food emergency for which there is no precedent in the decades since North America emerged as its breadbasket. There would be a desperate effort to corner available supplies as world grain prices soared to record levels. In such a situation, preventing starvation among the world's poor would re-quire affluent countries to reduce the amount of grain fed to livestock.

Asian and African countries, in particular, would find it impossible to feed their people without North American grain. Many of the world's major cities—Leningrad, Cairo, Lagos, Caracas, and Tokyo, for example—depend largely on grain from the United States and Canada. In an integrated world food economy, all countries suffer the consequences of poor harvests.

All available evidence indicates that the ranks of the hungry expanded during the late 1980s, reversing the trend of recent decades. Uncertainties and stresses from a changing climate are now being overlaid upon an already tightening food situation. In the absence of a major commitment by governments to slow population growth and strengthen agriculture, food insecurity and the social instability associated with it will preoccupy the political leaders of many countries during the 1990s.

WORLD WITHOUT BORDERS

The global commons—the oceans, the atmosphere, and tropical forests—are now at risk. Ozone depletion, climate change, and oceanic pollution simply cannot be solved at the national level. Indeed, a world in which countries go their own way may not be worth living in. Whereas the 1970s were marked by a series of national laws to address environmental problems, the 1990s may well be marked by comparable initiatives at the international level.

One encouraging sign is that East-West differences are being bridged. The Soviet Union has proposed a major strengthening of international institutions to deal with global problems. Addressing the U.N. General Assembly in September 1988, Soviet Foreign Minister Eduard Shevardnadze stated that "the dividing lines of the bipolar world are receding. The biosphere recognizes no division into blocs, alliances or systems. All share the same climatic system." Western leaders, still startled by the fading of Soviet intransigence, are daring to dream of a more unified world community. Protecting the biosphere is a new channel for the vast energies that have been directed to the cold war rivalry.[12]

Scientific cooperation is one aspect of environmental protection that has advanced in recent years. Most notable is the International Geosphere-Biosphere Program, also known as the Global Change Program. Established in 1986, it is intended to deepen understanding of the physical, chemical, and biological forces that affect the biosphere, using more extensive national monitoring, satellite reconnaissance, and advanced computer modeling.

International environmental cooperation has come furthest in Western Europe, where a score of countries are squeezed into a small area and trade pollutants back and forth across their borders via winds and rivers. Much of the region's environmental regulation is now done under the auspices of the European Economic Community.

The world community as a whole has also moved forward in protecting the atmosphere. During the 1970s, it became clear that air pollution was crossing borders and damaging forests. While countries are reluctant to make major investments to protect their neighbors' environments, all now have an interest in these kinds of agreements. Indeed, for Canadians and Scandinavians, imported air pollution has become a major foreign policy consideration.

The world's oceans are another global commons needing international protection. The activities of one country can endanger the open ocean as well as the coastal ecosystems of other nations. Water pollution, ocean dumping of waste materials, and overfishing are among the threats.

On April 30, 1982, after ten years of negotiations, the Convention on the Law of the Sea was signed by 119 nations, 35 of which have ratified it. Although 22 countries, including the Soviet Union and the United States, refused to sign, the Law of the Sea has already improved the way oceans are managed. It is in effect a consti-

tution for the oceans, stating that the oceans are "the common heritage of mankind," ensuring free navigation and limiting actions that despoil the seas. It provides a framework for future international agreements to protect this global resource.[13]

Central to the Law of the Sea are the 200-mile exclusive economic zones created around coastal nations, giving them the legal authority and international obligation to manage their coastal resources effectively. These now encompass 40 percent of the world's ocean area, and have led, for example, to a cut in the Northwest Atlantic cod catch by long-range fleets of at least 90 percent. The Law of the Sea also calls for national laws that reduce ocean dumping. Additional, stricter regulations of pollution are needed if oceanic resources are to be protected from the bewildering profusion of new toxic chemicals. The next decade will likely see a continuation of the growing array of oceanic agreements, some connected to the Law of the Sea and others independent.[14]

The international community also has a critical role to play in protecting the ozone layer. Although the United States and Scandinavian countries limited some uses of ozone-damaging chlorofluorocarbons (CFCs) as early as the mid-1970s, attempts to address the problem began in earnest in the 1980s.

Spurred by a dramatic annual thinning of the ozone over Antarctica, the United States led the push for CFC controls. In 1987, the Montreal Protocol was established and has now been signed by 35 countries. It freezes CFC production at 1986 levels and calls for a 50 percent cut by 1998 in industrial countries, but allows for some increases in the developing world.

Climate change is fast becoming the next arena for international environmental agreement, and solutions to the problem may have to break new institutional ground. Indeed, if climate change is to be minimized, international action may have to precede rather than follow national actions. Already, business and political leaders are arguing against stringent national policies on the grounds that by themselves such actions would hardly make a difference. This is particularly true for small nations that feel impotent in the face of global changes over which they have only a tiny influence.

The first step is scientific cooperation. In June 1988 at a world conference on The Changing Atmosphere: Implications for Global Security, held in Toronto, the final statement said that carbon emissions should be reduced by 20 percent by 2005.[15]

If such goals are to be achieved, an international treaty will probably be needed. Some have called for an international "Law of the Atmosphere" parallel to the Law of the Sea.[16]

Such a treaty must deal both with the industrial countries that have caused much of the problem so far and developing ones whose use of energy is growing rapidly and adding to global warming. Developing countries argue convincingly that if they are going to vastly improve efficiency and reforest millions of hectares, they will need funding from richer nations.

As with the other issues, unilateral commitments by individual countries may be the leadership spark needed to ignite international agreement. The governments of Canada, the Netherlands, and Norway are among those committed to international negotiations on global warming. The Soviet Union has expressed interest in it, and U.S. resistance is fading. Some have compared the scope of such negotiations to those of strategic arms talks. Indeed, similar approaches may have to be applied. For example, it may make sense to set up permanent negotiating teams in Geneva as a way to introduce and discuss approaches raised by various governments.

The next step is to move beyond agreements on CFCs, the oceans, and climate change to a more comprehensive rescue plan for the global environment. Among the issues now ripe for discussion of new international conventions or protocols are the preservation of biodiversity, the slowing of deforestation, and perhaps even family planning. This will require a strengthening of international institutions and a willingness to give up unilateral authority in some areas. Today these institutions are often fragmented and ineffective in dealing with global problems. But just as national governments themselves first emerged as tentative and weak efforts to unite diverse tribes or city-states, so international institutions may one day become far more robust and central to the issues of our time.

Maurice Strong, the first head of the U.N. Environment Programme, has pointed out that the world faces the challenge of developing effective mechanisms for governance, or management, at the international level: "People have learned to enlarge the circles of their allegiance and their loyalty, as well as the institutions through which they are governed, from the family to the tribe to the village to the town to the city to the nation state. We are now called upon to make the next and final step, at least on this planet, to the global level."[17]

This does not mean an end to national governments. Just as people did not give up allegiance to family or town when nation-states were created, so national governments can exist within a strengthened world community. The solutions to many problems are close to home—often within a local government or grassroots organization. All these levels of human organization can continue and even thrive as international cooperation is expanded.

WHAT WILL THE FUTURE BRING?

Whether the 1990s becomes a turnaround decade will depend heavily on the response of scientists and the communications media, for both play key roles in broad-based public education. As important as scientists' findings in their laboratories will be their ability and willingness to translate these findings into terms understandable by nonscientists. Similarly, the media will better serve the public's need for information when it begins reporting, for example, that deforestation rates are as important an indicator of societal health as inflation rates are.

Up until now, environmental organizations, both national and local, have provided the impetus for efforts to restore and protect the planet. Numerous citizens' groups have organized to remedy problems directly touching their lives, whether it be planting trees in a Third World village or opposing the siting of a toxic waste dump in a U.S. community. The challenge now is for other groups to get involved. Collectively, churches, civic groups, and professional societies represent an enormous potential for planetary reclamation.

Ultimately responsibility for the future rests with individuals. Our values, choices, and behaviors shape social and political change. Unless more of us join the effort, there is little hope of halting the planet's deterioration.

By the end of the next decade, the die will pretty well be cast. As the world enters the twenty-first century, the community of nations either will have rallied and turned back the threatening trends, or environmental deterioration and social disintegration will be feeding on each other.

The ultimate rationale for a massive social mobilization to safeguard the earth is summed up in a bit of graffiti painted on a bridge in Rock Creek Park in Washington, D.C. It says, "Good planets are hard to find."

NOTES

1. Christopher Flavin, "The Case Against Reviving Nuclear Power," *World Watch* (Washington, D.C.), July/August 1988; Bill Keller, "Public Mistrust Curbs Soviet Nuclear Power Efforts," *New York Times*, October 13, 1988.

2. World Resources Institute/International Institute for Environment and Development, *World Resources Report 1988/1989* (New York: Basic Books, 1988); Pieter Tans, Group Chief, Carbon Cycle Group, National Oceanic and Atmospheric Administration, Boulder, Colo., private communication, October 28, 1988;

Eric T. Sundquist, "Ice Core Links CO_2 to Climate," *Nature*, October 1, 1987.

3. V. Ramanathan et al., "Trace Gas Trends and Their Potential Role in Climate Change," *Journal of Geophysical Research*, June 20, 1985; F. Sherwood Rowland, "Chlorofluorocarbons, Stratospheric Ozone, and the Antarctic 'Ozone Hole'," *Environmental Conservation*, Summer 1988; Irving R. Mintzer, Senior Associate, World Resources Institute, Testimony before Subcommittee on Energy and Power, Committee on Energy and Commerce, U.S. House of Representatives, September 22, 1988.

4. Philip D. Jones et al., "Evidence for Global Warming in the Past Decade," *Nature*, April 28, 1988; James E. Hansen, et al., "Global Climate Changes as Forecast by the GISS 3-D Model," *Journal of Geophysical Research*, August 20, 1988.

5. U.S. Department of Agriculture (USDA), Economic Research Service (ERS), *World Grain Harvested Area, Production, and Yield 1950–87* (unpublished printout) (Washington, D.C.: 1988); USDA, Foreign Agricultural Service (FAS), *World Grain Situation and Outlook*, Washington, D.C., October, 1988.

6. USDA, ERS, *World Grain 1950–87*; "Farmers Turn Down the Irrigation Tap," *Farmline*, August 1988; Frederick W. Crook, *Agricultural Statistics of the People's Republic of China, 1949–86* (Washington, D.C.: USDA, ERS, 1988).

7. USDA, ERS, *World Grain 1950–87*.

8. U.N. Food and Agriculture Organization, *FAO Production Yearbook* (Rome: various years); USDA, ERS, *World Grain 1950–87*; WFC, "Global State of Hunger and Malnutrition."

9. Cost of the wheat in a loaf of bread calculated using a wheat price of U.S. $3 per bushel.

10. S. Manabe and R.T. Wetherald, "Reduction in Summer Soil Wetness Induced by an Increase in Atmospheric Carbon Dioxide," *Science*, May 2, 1986.

11. USDA, FAS, *World Grain Situation*; R.H. Shaw, "Estimates of Yield Reductions in Corn Caused by Water and Temperature Stress," in C. D. Raper and P.J. Kramer, eds., *Crop Reactions to Water and Temperature Stresses in Humid, Temperate Climates* (Boulder, Colo.: Westview Press, 1983); R.F. Dale, "Temperature Perturbations in the Midwestern and Southeastern United States Important for Corn Production," in ibid.

12. Eduard A. Shevardnadze, Minister for Foreign Affairs of the USSR, Statement before the Forty-third Session of the U.N. General Assembly, New York, September 27, 1988.

13. Information on signatories from U.N. Office for Ocean Affairs and the Law of the Sea, New York, private communication, October 11, 1988; Elisabeth Mann Borgese, "The Law of the Sea," *Scientific American*, March 1983; Department of Public Information, *A Quiet Revolution: The United Nations Convention on the Law of the Sea* (New York: United Nations, 1984).

14. Clyde Sanger, *Ordering the Oceans: The Making of the Law of the Sea* (London: Zed Books Ltd., 1986); Ann. L. Hollick, "Managing the Oceans," *The Wilson Quarterly*, Summer 1984; Karl Sullivan, "Overfishing and the New Law of the Sea," *OECD Observer*, July 1984; "United States Acceptance of MARPOL Annex Will Lead to Ban on Dumping Plastics at Sea," *International Environment Reporter*, February 10, 1988; "Global Stop to At-Sea Incineration Approved," *Multilateral Environmental Outlook*, October 13, 1988.

15. World Climate Programme, *Developing Policies*; "Conference Statement," The Changing Atmosphere.

16. Toufiq A. Siddiqi, East-West Center, Honolulu, Hawaii, "A Comprehensive Law of the Atmosphere as a Framework for Addressing Carbon Dioxide and Climate Change Issues," presented to the Workshop on Global Climate Change, Woods Hole, Mass., September 23, 1988; Brian Mulroney, Prime Minister of Canada, Speech at The Changing Atmosphere: Implications for Global Security, Toronto, Canada, June 27–30, 1988; Kilaparti Ramakrishna, "Steps Toward an International Convention for Stabilizing the Greenhouse Gas Composition of the Atmosphere" (draft), Woods Hole Research Center, Woods Hole, Mass., September 2, 1988.

17. Maurice F. Strong, "Beyond Foreign Aid—Towards a New World System," presented to the International Development Conference, Washington, D.C., March 19, 1987.

46

A World More Secure

Julian L. Simon

If we lift our gaze from the frightening daily headlines and look instead at wide-ranging scientific data as well as the evidence of our senses, we shall see that economic life in the United States and the rest of the world has been getting better rather than worse during recent centuries and decades. There is, moreover, no persuasive reason to believe that these trends will not continue indefinitely.

But first: I am *not* saying that all is well everywhere, and I do not predict that all will be rosy in the future. Children are hungry and sick; people live out lives of physical or intellectual poverty, with little opportunity for improvement; war or some new pollution may finish us. What I *am* saying is that for most relevant economic matters I have checked, aggregate trends are improving rather than deteriorating. Also, I do not say that a better future will happen automatically or without effort. It will happen because men and women will use muscle and mind to struggle with problems that they will probably overcome, as they have in the past.

LONGER AND HEALTHIER LIVES

Life cannot be good unless you are alive. Plentiful resources and a clean environment have little value unless we and others are alive to enjoy them. The fact that your chances of living through any given age now are much better than in earlier times must therefore mean that life has gotten better. In France, for example, female life expectancy at birth rose from under 30 years in the 1740s to 75 years in the 1960s. And this trend has not yet run its course (it was 76 in 1988).[1] The increases have been rapid in recent years in the United States: a 2.1-year gain between 1970 and 1976 versus a 0.8-

[1]*Statistical Abstract of the U.S.*, 1989, Table 1405.

year gain in the entire decade of the 1960s (from 1980 to 1987, the gain was 1.2 years).[2] This pattern is now being repeated in the poorer countries of the world as they improve their economic lot. Life expectancy at birth in low-income countries rose from an average of 35.2 years in 1950 to 49.9 years in 1978, a much bigger jump than the rise from 66.0 to 73.5 years in the industrialized countries.

The threat of our loved ones dying greatly affects our assessment of the quality of our lives. Infant mortality is a reasonable measure of child mortality generally. In Europe in the eighteenth and nineteenth centuries, 200 or more children of each thousand died during their first year. As late as 1900, infant mortality was 200 per 1000 or higher in Spain, Russia, Hungary, and even Germany. Now it is about 15 per 1000 or less in a great many countries.

Health has improved, too. The incidence of both chronic and acute conditions has declined. While a perceived "epidemic" of cancer indicates to some a drop in the quality of life, the data show no increase in cancer except for deaths due to smoking-caused lung cancer. As Philip Handler, president of the National Academy of Sciences, said:

The United States is not suffering an "epidemic of cancer," it is experiencing an "epidemic of life"—in that an even greater fraction of the population survives to the advanced ages at which cancer has always been prevalent. The overall, age-corrected incidence of cancer has not been increasing; it has been declining slowly for some years.

ABATING POLLUTION

About pollution now: The main air pollutants—particulates and sulfur dioxide—have declined since 1960 and 1970 respectively, the periods for which there is data in the United States. The Environmen-

tal Protection Agency's Pollutant Standard Index, which takes into account all the most important air pollutants, shows that the number of days rated "unhealthful" has declined steadily since the index's inauguration in 1974. And the proportion of monitoring sites in the U.S. having good drinking water has greatly increased since record-keeping began in 1961.

Pollution in the less-developed countries is a different, though not necessarily discouraging, story. No worldwide pollution data are available. Nevertheless, it is reasonable to assume that pollution of various kinds has increased as poor countries have gotten somewhat less poor. Industrial pollution rises along with new factories. The same is true of consumer pollution—junked cars, plastic wrappers, and such oddments as the hundreds of discarded antibiotics vials I saw on the ground in an isolated Iranian village. Such industrial wastes do not exist in the poorest preindustrial countries. And in the early stages of development, countries and people are not ready to pay for clean-up operations. But further increases in income almost surely will bring about pollution abatement, just as increases in income in the United States have provided the wherewithal for better garbage collection and cleaner air and water.

THE MYTH OF FINITE RESOURCES

Though natural resources are a smaller part of the economy with every succeeding year, they are still important, and their availability causes grave concern to many. Yet, measured by cost or price, the scarcity of all raw materials except lumber and oil has been *decreasing* rather than increasing over the long run.

Perhaps surprisingly, oil also shows downward cost trend in the long run. The price rise in the 1970s was purely political; the cost of producing a barrel of oil in the Persian Gulf is still only perhaps 15 to 25 cents.

---

[2]Ibid., Table 106.

There is no reason to believe that the supply of energy is finite, or that the price will not continue its long-run decrease. This statement may sound less preposterous if you consider that for a quantity to be finite it must be measurable. The future supply of oil includes what we usually think of as oil, plus the oil that can be produced from shale, tar sands, and coal. It also includes the oil from plants that we grow, whose key input is sunlight. So the measure of the future oil supply must therefore be at least as large as the sun's 7 billion or so years of future life. And it may include other suns whose energy might be exploited in the future. Even if you believe that one can in principle measure the energy from suns that will be available in the future—a belief that requires a lot of confidence that the knowledge of the physical world we have developed in the past century will not be superseded in the next 7 billion years, plus the belief that the universe is not expanding—this measurement would hardly be relevant for any practical contemporary decision making.

Energy provides a good example of the process by which resources become more abundant and hence cheaper. Seventeenth-century England was full of alarm at an impending energy shortage due to the country's deforestation for firewood. People feared a scarcity of fuel for both heating and the vital iron industry. This impending scarcity led inventors and businessmen to develop coal.

Then, in the mid-1800s, the English came to worry about an impending coal crisis. The great English economist William Stanley Jevons calculated then that a shortage of coal would surely bring England's industry to a standstill by 1900; he carefully assessed that oil could never make a decisive difference. But spurred by the impending scarcity of coal (and of whale oil, whose story comes next), ingenious and profit-minded people developed oil into a more desirable fuel than coal ever was. And today England exports both coal and oil.

Another strand in the story: Because of increased demand due to population growth and increased income, the price of whale oil used in lamps jumped in the 1840s. Then the Civil War pushed it even higher, leading to a whale oil "crisis." The resulting high price provided an incentive for imaginative and enterprising people to discover and produce substitutes. First came oil from rapeseed, olives, linseed, and pine trees. Then inventors learned how to get coal oil from coal, which became a flourishing industry. Other ingenious persons produced kerosene from the rock oil that seeped to the surface. Kerosene was so desirable a product that its price rose from 75 cents to $2 a gallon, which stimulated enterprisers to increase its supply. Finally, Edwin L. Drake sunk his famous oil well in Titusville, Pennsylvania. Learning how to refine the oil took a while, but in a few years there were hundreds of small refiners in the United States. Soon the bottom dropped out of the whale oil market: the price fell from $2.50 or more a gallon at its peak around 1866 to well below a dollar.

MORE FOOD FOR MORE PEOPLE

Food is an especially important resource, and the evidence indicates that its supply is increasing despite rising population. The long-run prices of food relative to wages, and even relative to consumer goods, are down. Famine deaths have decreased in the past century even in absolute terms, let alone relative to the much larger population, a special boon for poor countries. Per person food production in the world is up over the last 30 years and more. And there are no data showing that the people at the bottom of the income distribution have fared worse, or have failed to share in the general improvement, as the average has improved. Africa's food production per capita is down, but that clearly stems from governmental blunders with price controls, subsidies, farm collectivization, and other institutional problems.

There is, of course, a food-production

problem in the United States today: too much production. Prices are falling due to high productivity, falling consumer demand for meat in the United States, and increased foreign competition in such crops as soybeans. In response to the farmers' complaints, the government will now foot an unprecedentedly heavy bill for keeping vast amounts of acreage out of production.

THE DISAPPEARING-SPECIES SCARE

Many are alarmed that the earth is losing large numbers of its species. For example, the *Global 2000 Report to the President* says: "Extinctions of plant and animal species will increase dramatically. Hundreds of thousands of species—perhaps as many as 20 percent of all species on earth—will be irretrievably lost as their habitats vanish, especially in tropical forests," by the year 2000.

The available facts, however, are not consistent with the level of concern expressed in *Global 2000*, nor do they warrant the various policies suggested to deal with the purported dangers.

The *Global 2000* projection is based upon a report by contributor Thomas Lovejoy, who estimates that between 437,000 and 1,875,000 extinctions will occur out of a present estimated total of 3 to 10 million species. Lovejoy's estimate is based on a linear relationship running from 0% species extinguished at 0% tropical forest cleared, to about 95% extinguished at 100% tropical forest cleared. (The main source of differences in the range of estimated losses is the range of 3 to 10 million species in the overall estimate.)

The basis of any useful projection must be a body of experience collected under a range of conditions that encompass the expected conditions, or that can reasonably be extrapolated to the expected conditions. But none of Lovejoy's references seems to contain any scientifically impressive body of experience.

A projected drop in the amount of tropical forests underlies Lovejoy's projection of species losses in the future. Yet to connect these two events as Lovejoy has done requires systematic evidence relating an amount of tropical forest removed to a rate of species reduction. Neither *Global 2000* nor any of the other sources I checked give such empirical evidence. If there is not better evidence for Lovejoy's projected rates, one could extrapolate almost any rate one chooses for the year 2000. Until more of the facts are in, we need not undertake alarmist protection policies. Rather, we need other sorts of data to estimate extinction rates and decide on policy.

None of this is to say that we need not worry about endangered species. The planet's flora and fauna constitute a valuable natural endowment; we must guard them as we do our other physical and social assets. But we should also strive for a clear, unbiased view of this set of assets in order to make the best possible judgments about how much time and money to spend guarding them, in a world where this valuable activity must compete with other valuable activities, including the preservation of other assets and human life.

MORE WEALTH FROM LESS WORK

One of the great trends of economic history is the shortening of the workweek coupled with increasing income. A shorter workweek represents an increase in one's freedom to dispose of that most treasured possession—time—as one wishes. In the United States, the decline was from about 60 hours per week in 1870 to less than 40 hours at present. This benign trend is true for an array of countries in which the length of the workweek shows an inverse relationship with income.

With respect to progress in income generally, the most straightforward and meaningful index is the proportion of persons in the labor force working in agriculture. In 1800, the percentage in the United States was 73.6%, whereas in 1980 the proportion was 2.7%. That is, relative to population size, only ¹⁄₂₅ as many persons today are working in agriculture as in 1800. This suggests that the effort that produced one bushel of grain or one loaf of bread in 1800 will now produce the bushel of grain plus what 24 other bushels will buy in other goods, which is equivalent to an increase in income by a factor of 25.

Income in less-developed countries has not reached nearly so high a level as in the more-developed countries, by definition. But it would be utterly wrong to think that income in less-developed countries has stagnated rather than risen. In fact, income per person has increased at a proportional rate at least as fast, or faster, in less-developed than in more-developed countries since World War II.

THE ULTIMATE RESOURCE

What explains the enhancement of our material life in the face of supposed limits to growth? I offer an extended answer in my book, *The Ultimate Resource* (1981). In short, the source of our increased economic blessings is the human mind, and, all other things being equal, when there are more people, there are more productive minds. Productivity increases come directly from the additional minds that develop productive new ideas, as well as indirectly from the impact upon industrial productivity of the additional demand for goods. That is, population growth in the form of babies or immigrants helps in the long run to raise the standard of living because it brings increased productivity. Immigrants are the best deal of all because they usually migrate when they are young and strong; in the United States, they contribute more in taxes

to the public coffers than they take out in welfare services.

In the short run, of course, additional people mean lower income for other people because children must be fed and housed by their parents, and educated and equipped partly by the community. Even immigrants are a burden for a brief time until they find jobs. But after the children grow up and enter the work force, and contribute to the support of others as well as increasing productivity, their net effect upon others becomes positive. Over their lifetimes they are a boon to others.

I hope you will now agree that the long-run outlook is for a more abundant material life rather than for increased scarcity, in the United States and in the world as a whole. Of course, such progress does not come about automatically. And my message certainly is not one of complacency. In this I agree with the doomsayers—that our world needs the best efforts of all humanity to improve our lot. I part company with them in that they expect us to come to a bad end despite the efforts we make, whereas I expect a continuation of successful efforts. Their message is self-fulfilling because if you expect inexorable natural limits to stymie your efforts, you are likely to feel resigned and give up. But if you recognize the possibility—indeed, the probability—of success, you can tap large reserves of energy and enthusiasm. Energy and enthusiasm, together with the human mind and spirit, constitute our solid hope for the economic future, just as they have been our salvation in ages past. With these forces at work, we will leave a richer, safer, and more beautiful world to our descendants, just as our ancestors improved the world that they bestowed upon us.

47

How Technology Fuels the Arms Race
Matthew Evangelista

The thaw in superpower relations has raised hopes for a comprehensive U.S.–Soviet arms-control agreement. But amidst all the speculation about the elements of a possible settlement, observers have overlooked a central issue. The persistence of the arms race is deeply rooted in contrasting U.S. and Soviet approaches to weapons innovation, approaches that reflect the very different characters of the two societies.

The relative openness of U.S. society shapes the development of new weapons in this country. Compared to the Soviet Union, U.S. military research and development is widely decentralized, encouraging the free flow of information and rewarding low-level initiative. As a result, the process of weapons innovation takes place from the "bottom up" with scientists and technologists in government and the private sector playing a leading role. This process fosters the atti-tude that technological innovation is the surest guarantor of national security.

In the more closed Soviet Union, military R&D is highly centralized, hierarchical, and characterized by excessive secrecy and compartmentalization—all of which inhibit technological innovation. But these very same characteristics allow the Soviet Union to concentrate its resources from the "top down" and respond to U.S. technological initiatives by mass-producing weapons.

For decades these two systems have been locked in a vicious circle. The United States has depended on technological innovation to provide a decisive advantage over the Soviets. The Soviets have depended on the mass production of weapons to overwhelm U.S. technical quality with Soviet quantity. And whenever the Soviets have mastered an American innovation, they have been able to deploy it to negate the original U.S.

advantage, often posing an unforeseen and even more serious threat. The threat has served to justify further U.S. innovations, starting with the arms-race cycle all over again. In this way, U.S. technological innovation has ended up diminishing rather than enhancing Western security.

The vicious circle can be broken. The factors that have made for the spiraling arms race also hold the seeds for a fundamental U.S.–Soviet agreement on arms reduction—a trade-off of U.S. quality for Soviet quantity. Such a political compromise is the real hope of current negotiations. But achieving it will require the U.S. weapons scientists and technologists give up the false hope of attaining technological superiority once and for all.

In this country, the creation of a new weapons system generally begins when scientists in arms laboratories or military officials in close contact with them start to champion new technical possibilities in the government bureaucracy. The nuclear-powered submarine was largely the product of one such technical entrepreneur—Hyman Rickover. Starting in the mid–1940s as an unknown Navy captain with a background in engineering, Rickover persuaded his superiors at the Atomic Energy Commission and the navy's Bureau of Ships to support the development of nuclear propulsion for submarines. His efforts attracted the backing of influential members of Congress and eventually earned him the rank of admiral and the title of "father of the nuclear navy."

Similarly, the nuclear physicist Edward Teller was the patron behind the development of the hydrogen bomb in the early 1950s. While working on the Manhattan Project, Teller was preoccupied with the idea of a "superbomb" based on nuclear fusion rather than fission. After the war, he successfully lobbied Congress to establish a second nuclear weapons lab in Livermore, California, claiming that scientists at Los Alamos opposed hydrogen weapons. Even before coming up with the major design

breakthrough for the H-bomb, Teller was already trying to interest Air Force officials and lawmakers in the weapon. Thus began a long and remarkably successful career of influencing U.S. military policy through contacts in the Pentagon, Congress, and the military-technical community.

Sometimes, scientists will advocate a particular arms system as an alternative to weapons they oppose. Tactical nuclear weapons were developed in the early 1950s largely because some U.S. scientists, J. Robert Oppenheimer among them, disagreed with the prevailing policy of strategic bombing and Teller's plans for the H-bomb. At the height of the Korean War, Oppenheimer and his colleagues thought tactical warheads for actual use in combat were more relevant to U.S. military requirements. Ultimately, the United States developed both weapons.

Once a particular system gains the backing of enough civilian or military technologists, their enthusiasm can often keep it going under private sponsorship, even when high-level government officials try to eliminate it. In 1949, the Air Force decided to cut back on the Convair Corporation's research on ballistic missiles—weapons that threatened to undermine the Strategic Air Command's preferred reliance on bombers. But Convair simply continued research with its own funds until the Air Force resumed sponsorship of the program in 1951. The project eventually became the Atlas intercontinental ballistic missile (ICBM).

Such low-level initiative in the absence of high-level support has subsequently been institutionalized in the U.S. military research and development community, at a cost to taxpayers of several billion dollars a year. Under the Pentagon's Bid and Proposal (B&P) program, private corporations can charge the costs of preparing unsolicited proposals for additional new weapons as overhead on their Defense Department contracts. The Independent Research and Development (IR&D) program allows firms to recover the research-and-development costs of projects that they have initiated, without a prior government contract or any congressional oversight.

BUILDING CONSENSUS AND COUNTERING THREATS

Once a new technology is identified, its designers actively promote military applications by "consensus building." Creating a consensus around a weapons system starts with the military-technical community and gradually reaches to top military officials, members of Congress, and usually officials in the executive branch. Sometimes, it can take years or even decades.

Consider thee neutron bomb, a weapon that kills primarily with neutron radiation rather than with the blast, heat, and gamma radiation of standard fission and fusion weapons. The major conceptual breakthrough for the bomb occurred in 1958, a result of the work of physicist Samuel Cohen at the Rand Corporation. Over the next 20 years, Cohen, Teller, and other supporters went from the Air Force to the Navy to the Army in search of support for the weapon—at first with little success.

In 1973, however, when Congress turned down an army request for the development of a new nuclear artillery shell, the service somewhat reluctantly came to support the development of neutron warheads, in the belief that championing a new kind of tactical nuclear weapon was the only chance to get a new artillery shell. Five years later, President Carter ordered production of a neutron-bomb warhead for the Lance missile. And in 1984, Congress finally approved a program for a neutron-bomb artillery shell—in an obscure amendment attached to the Defense Authorization Bill and passed without a roll-call vote.

Consensus-building has an important influence on the design of U.S. weapons systems. For one thing, many related programs are often pursued at the same time so as not to exclude any potential supporters for a given technology. This leads to redundancy in weapons produced. The classic example is the development of intermediate-range ballistic missiles (IRBMs) in the 1950s. Both the Army and the Air Force worked on the weapons, ultimately producing two virtually identical systems—the Army's Jupiter and the Air Force's Thor.

A second common method for creating consensus is to incorporate all the technical features or capabilities desired by potential supporters into a system. The result is weapons of greater technical sophistication than is necessary or desirable for a given military mission. The F-111 aircraft was the unhappy product of such a logrolling consensus. Promoters designed the plane with variable-sweep wings on the theory that it could fill a variety of missions for both the Navy and the Air Force, including air-to-air combat, close-air support of ground troops, and long-range bombing. But because of persistent technical problems with this advanced design, the F-111 fulfilled none of these missions well and cost far more than anticipated.

Of course, as the neutron bomb example suggests, not all proposed weapons immediately win military or government approval. Often one branch of the military resists a particular innovation that it fears will jeopardize its own organizational traditions or mission. So, promoters of new weapons systems emphasize the inability of current weapons systems or organizational structures to deal with foreign threats. For example, the Air Force's interest in intermediate-range missiles during the mid–1950s was evidently triggered by concern that the army's IRBM program would yield a system that could replace aircraft in many important combat missions, such as deep interdiction attacks against major air bases and supply depots. Yet both services justified their programs by exaggerating the danger of a Soviet ballistic-missile threat.

Once a weapon has received sufficient support from the services and from key congressional committees to enter advanced

R&D, promoters frequently look for events to justify producing a prototype. The classic example is the Soviet Union's October 1957 launching of *Sputnik*. Although the Soviets had already tested an ICBM the previous August, the *Sputnik* satellite was a more dramatic demonstration of the technical capacity for launching long-range ballistic missiles. It spawned fears of a "missile gap" and transformed the U.S. ICBM from a project supported mainly by the Air Force and its contractors into a top-priority crash program.

This is not to say that factors like *Sputnik* actually *cause* the development of new weapons. Rather, they speed up a process already well underway. In fact, the weapons promoted as responses to such threats are often unsuited to them or unnecessary. In the case of the missile gap, President Eisenhower was confident that U.S. strategic bombers could adequately counter any emerging Soviet missile capability, and no crash program to mass-produce U.S. ICBMs was required. Nevertheless, the fear of a missile gap was used by the military services, arms manufacturers, and Democratic presidential candidates in 1960 to push for ICBM development and deployment. The Kennedy administration's missile buildup confirmed Eisenhower's worst fears and led to a major acceleration of the arms race.

Typically, U.S. weapons systems receive high-level political endorsement only at the final stage of the innovation process. Promoters seek wide public and congressional support so as to secure full funding for large-scale production of the weapon. Often under greater scrutiny than during earlier stages, the program generally must be justified with reference to a more specific threat or opportunity. But because promoters of the new weapon have already amassed considerable bureaucratic backing, their rationales need not be too realistic. President Kennedy's decision in early 1961 to accelerate deployment of 1,000 Minuteman missiles, even after it became obvious that the

missile gap was clearly in favor of the United States, constitutes a prime example.

At first glance, the most recent U.S. attempt at a major weapons innovation, the Strategic Defense Initiative (SDI), would seem to contradict the process outlined here. Surely, the argument goes, SDI was launched from the very top in President Reagan's March 1983 speech, at a time when the relevant technologies were immature at best. Pressure for strategic defenses has, however, been building up from the bottom for many years before the president's speech, and research was already proceeding at the rate of about $1 billion per year.

As with tactical nuclear weapons and the neutron bomb, the initiative for Star Wars came from physicists and weapons designers associated with government laboratories. Once again Edward Teller played a central role, as did some of his protégés at the Livermore Laboratory—most notably Lowell Wood, leader of the "O Group," which invented the nuclear-pumped X-ray laser. Starting more than a year before the Reagan speech, Teller promoted the laser and other defense technologies in meetings with members of Reagan's "kitchen cabinet" and with the president himself. What is different about the SDI case is that the scientific and military proponents of the system gained access to top political leaders before the process of consensus building in the military-technical community was complete.

CHURNING OUT MISSILES "LIKE SAUSAGES"

The Soviet Union enjoys a high level of scientific talent and devotes more resources to military R&D than any other country in the world, with the possible exception of the United States. In many respects, however, the Soviet pattern of arms development reverses the U.S. pattern. There is little technological innovation until the later stages of the development process, when foreign events spur high-level political intervention to pave the way by restructuring priorities.

This contradicts the conventional wisdom that the Soviet military's privileged status protects it from the shortcomings of the rest of the economy and makes it an island of innovation, employing the country's top scientists. But recent memoirs and descriptions by Soviet émigré scientists and engineers who have worked in military R&D suggest that the system's centralized, secretive nature, which is *strongest* in military research, acts to inhibit innovation.

For example, the secret nature of the work means that military scientists are not allowed many civilian advantages such as contact with foreign colleagues and the ability to publish articles and books in the open press. And even though salaries are sometimes higher in the military sector, they cannot be supplemented in the way that civilian salaries can—by fees from consulting, tutoring, writing, and lecturing. Therefore, the most ambitious and capable scientists often seek employment in the civilian sector.

Secrecy also severely inhibits how Soviet weapons labs function. Security personnel—members of the so-called First Department—rather than scientists and technologists determine work procedures and access to information. For instance, a researcher at a Soviet military design bureau who wants to visit a colleague at another establishment where classified work is conducted faces a daunting set of security procedures. To obtain permission for the trip requires considerable preparation and paperwork, the constant issuing and verifying of passes, the filling out of forms. Upon arriving at the colleague's institute, the researcher faces the same security practices as at the home institute, including the ban on retaining any notes. Notes must be written into prenumbered notebooks and presented to the First Department. The department then sends the notebooks by special mail to its counterpart at the home institute, where they are deposited in the researcher's classified portfolio.

This stultifying atmosphere shapes the Soviet innovation process. At first, Soviet weapons scientists devote some resources to keep up with research in a particular area, especially by monitoring foreign developments. Then, depending on events abroad, weapons labs and research bureaus may start to prepare a broad technological background that might prove useful later, should efforts ever be accelerated in response to an identifiable foreign threat. But in the absence of explicit political direction, work on particular weapons systems goes no further.

Consider tactical nuclear weapons. As early as 1946, when they first learned of the existence of the atomic bomb, some officers studying at Soviet military academies expressed interest in the impact of nuclear weapons on the battlefield. Yet while there was a widespread published discussion of this issue in the United States, Stalin's policy of strict nuclear secrecy did not even allow teachers to broach it in class. The Soviets focused instead on strategic uses for nuclear weapons.

Only after the United States deployed short-range atomic weapons in Europe in 1952 did the Soviet political and military leadership decide to reassess its priorities. In short term the Soviets restructured their air defense forces to respond to nuclear attack and began instructing soldiers in the effects of nuclear weapons. Then in 1953, Soviet leaders initiated programs to develop both tactical nuclear weapons and the delivery vehicles to carry them. They hedged their bets by ordering development of all the systems that they knew the Americans were working on—missiles, artillery, and aircraft.

Such a chain of events is typical of the Soviet system. In the final stages, when the Soviet leadership endorses an all-out effort to pursue a particular innovation, the change in priorities that allows the system to overcome its usual inertia becomes especially evident. To promote the development of missiles in the postwar period, Soviet leaders established a new network of research institutes, plants, and design bureaus. By 1948, some 13 scientific institutes and 35 major factories were involved in designing and manufacturing missiles, under the direction of Soviet rocket expert Sergei Korolev.

Although the specific character of new Soviet weapons programs is, to a certain extent, shaped by existing military organizations and technologies, the top leadership still retains the ability to intervene in the process of carrying out an innovation. In the late 1950s, Soviet leader Nikita Khrushchev canceled production of the expensive and technically unsuccessful "atomic cannon" in favor of an emphasis on missiles, and, to a lesser extent, aircraft. In the United States, by contrast, large atomic artillery pieces continued to be produced, despite serious criticisms of their capabilities.

The Soviet innovation process concludes when a particular weapons system moves into mass production. This normally corresponds to the first public evidence of a change in policy. In the case of ballistic missiles, Khrushchev announced in January 1960 that the Soviet Union believed a future war would inevitably be fought with nuclear missiles and that assembly lines at Soviet aircraft factories had therefore all been converted to missile production. Later the same year he announced the formation of a new military branch—the Strategic Rocket Forces—and boasted that the Soviet Union was churning out missiles "like sausages."

THE FALSE HOPE OF TECHNOLOGY

Khrushchev was bluffing when he made his claims about Soviet missile superiority. Yet in the wake of the Kennedy administration buildup and Soviet humiliation during the Cuban missile crisis, Khrushchev's successors were determined to overtake the United States in the major quantitative indi-

cators of strategic nuclear power—most notably intercontinental missiles. The Soviets had barely caught up when the United States inaugurated another key phase of the arms race by deploying the multiple, independently targetable reentry vehicle, or MIRV, that allowed a single missile to carry several warheads.

Adding MIRVs to U.S. missiles increased the number of deliverable strategic warheads from a couple thousand in the early 1970s to nearly 10,000 by the end of what Ronald Reagan has called "the decade of neglect" in U.S. military policy. But the Soviets eventually developed MIRVs as well and placed 10 warheads on each of their 308 "heavy" SS-18 missiles, thus posing the theoretical first-strike threat that has been a major source of concern among U.S. military planners and politicians ever since. The MIRV, which had once appeared to be a kind of technical panacea, is now understood, even by former proponents such as Henry Kissinger, to be perhaps the most dangerous and potentially destabilizing development in the Soviet-American arms race to date.

This pattern of escalation characterizes not only the past but possibly also the future of Soviet-American arms competition. We are now at a point where recent U.S. innovations such as cruise missiles, deep-strike conventional weapons, and SDI present the Soviets with crucial choices about how to respond. Certainly, they are capable of matching these innovations—whether through emulating U.S. initiatives or developing effective countermeasures to them. Either response would serve to diminish the security of both sides.

When the United States developed advanced cruise missiles during the 1970s, their promoters described them as another technical solution to the West's security problems, especially well-suited for negating Soviet quantitative advantages in air defense. But now the Soviets have developed their own cruise missiles. Unless restricted by verifiable arms-control agreements, they could be mass-produced and deployed on virtually any Soviet fishing trawler or commercial airliner—rendering any U.S. security gain chimerical.

The Soviets have also closely followed U.S. developments in the area of deep-strike weapons, ever since the relevant technologies—especially remote sensors, information-processing and target-acquisition systems, and cluster munitions—appeared during the Vietnam War. Prominent military figures such as Marshal Nikolai Ogarkov have argued that nuclear parity magnifies the importance of these high-tech systems for conventional warfare. Some Western observers believe that Gorbachev's economic reforms are specifically geared toward preparing the Soviet Union to compete in the realm of advanced military technology into the next century. If the Soviets develop deep-strike weapons in large quantities, and incorporate them into offensive military strategies, NATO's security will surely suffer.

Potential Soviet responses to a U.S. strategic defense system are already well known and need no further elaboration here. Whether the Soviets eventually try to create a defensive system of their own or simply offset any potential U.S. system by deploying countermeasures, SDI will render the United States less secure than it was before the program was ever proposed. SDI also poses an immediate threat to potential arms-reduction agreements. Without a U.S. commitment to abide by the 1972 Anti-Ballistic Missile (ABM) Treaty and refrain from deploying large-scale strategic defenses, the Soviets would be unlikely to carry out extensive reductions of their MIRVed and ICBM force—the best SDI countermeasure they have.

TRADING QUALITY FOR QUANTITY

The elements of a grand compromise to avert the next spiral in the arms race have been evident virtually from the moment Ronald Reagan announced the Strategic Defense Initiative in March 1983. SDI would be employed as a "bargaining chip" to get the Soviets to agree to substantial reductions in their force of MIRVed SS-18 missiles. Such an agreement would require each side to make sacrifices in its primary area of strength—for the United States, the ability to initiate technological innovations; for the Soviet Union, the ability to imitate those innovations and produce them in large quantity. Put another way, the arms-control deal that has received so much attention entails U.S. restraint in the next major technological innovation, strategic defense systems, in return for Soviet cutbacks in the previous major innovation, multiple-warhead ICBMs.

What appears to observers to be an ideal compromise may be perceived by the protagonists as giving up their sole source of strength. However, the treaty eliminating shorter- and medium-range missiles, signed in Washington in 1987, is in a sense just such a trade of comparative advantages, of quality for quantity. The SS-20 represented the Soviet Union's first successful, large-scale deployment of a technology—solid-fueled MIRVed missiles—that the United States had mastered years earlier. The new U.S. missiles, by contrast, are state of the art. In particular, the Pershing II is considered the world's most accurate ballistic missile. The treaty is largely the result of the Soviet Union's willingness to trade its numerical advantage in medium-range missiles in exchange for the United States relinquishing its technological advantage.

Gorbachev's recent initiatives suggest a preference for an alternative to the competition in military technology with the United States. During the mid-1980s, the Soviets took a number of actions intended to persuade the United States to agree to arms limitations. They maintained a unilateral moratorium on nuclear testing for over a year and a half, while the United States exploded more than 25 nuclear devices. They halted deployment of SS-20 missiles targeted against Europe and withdrew some 35 of them, even as the United States continued deploying Pershing II and cruise missiles. They refrained from testing anti-satellite weapons (ASATs), and they allowed unprecedented measures of on-site inspection to verify compliance with arms agreements. U.S. scientists were even permitted to set up seismic monitoring equipment adjacent to Soviet nuclear test ranges. The treaty removing missiles from Europe entails even more intrusive measures of verification, including monitoring of missile factories.

Soviet leaders seem to realize that although their nation has been able to match U.S. innovations and produce them in large numbers, these actions have served to justify new U.S. weapons developments. U.S. officials and scientists should recognize that unilateral U.S. advantages—especially in the realm of technology—are short-lived and provide no guarantee of security. In acknowledging the counterproductive nature of the technological arms race, both countries would open the way to cooperative agreements aimed at ending it.

How can this mutually advantageous outcome be achieved? In the tradition of the Soviet system, the initiative comes from the top. It clearly bears the mark of Gorbachev and his main advisers. In the United States, where the scope for low-level initiative has always been much greater, recent developments suggest that scientists are stepping in to promote serious measures of arms control despite the reluctance of their government.

The U.S. side of the agreement to monitor the Soviet nuclear test moratorium, for example, was a private initiative, organized by the Natural Resources Defense Council and funded by private donations: American scientists have been major participants in the movement to preserve and strengthen the ABM Treaty. Many of them have signed pledges refusing to conduct SDI-related research. Scientists have also put pressure on Congress to limit funding for ASATs so long as the Soviets maintain a moratorium on testing theirs. These efforts have contributed to averting a counterproductive and potentially dangerous ASAT race.

This is hardly the first time that scientists have taken a stand against an unconstrained technological arms race. The ABM Treaty itself testifies to past initiatives. Yet there remains much to do. Efforts to secure a comprehensive nuclear test ban should continue, in hopes that the Bush administration will reaffirm the longstanding formal U.S. commitment—broken only by the Reagan administration—to this goal. In addition, U.S. scientists could work with their Soviet counterparts to develop means of verifying limitations on sea-launched cruise missiles. Otherwise, these weapons threaten to open an enormous loophole in the European missile treaty as well as in any potential strategic weapons agreement.

The importance of such actions at the present time lies in the enhanced prospects for success. The international atmosphere has finally improved, and the increasingly frequent superpower summits suggest that U.S.-Soviet relations are on the way to normalization. The current leadership in the Kremlin recognizes the futility of the arms race and has made real concessions to demonstrate a serious intent to end it. All that remains is for the current American administration to demonstrate comparable flexibility and political will.

48

Will Terrorists Go Nuclear?

Brian M. Jenkins

My remarks will focus on the motives of political terrorists who might detonate or threaten to detonate a nuclear explosion.* In order to do so, they must first acquire a nuclear weapon. Can they do it?

There are several ways a terrorist group might acquire a nuclear weapon for its own use: They could steal a nuclear weapon from a military arsenal, attempt to bypass the elaborate devices that are designed to prevent tampering, and rearm it or use its components to construct a new weapon. Another way would be to steal weapons-grade nuclear material and use it to fabricate an improvised nuclear device. Either way would require attacking defended targets, something terrorists generally have not done. To avoid encountering defenses, terrorists could attempt to obtain the material surreptitiously by other means. These might include enlisting confederates within nuclear facilities who can supply the material or purchasing it on the black market, if such a market develops for nuclear material.

Assuming they had the necessary nuclear material, could terrorists make a nuclear bomb? This question remains a topic of debate within the nuclear community. I am not qualified to offer a judgment, so let me instead try to offer a consensus view. Although the ease with which a bomb could be made has probably been greatly exaggerated in the popular press, the notion that some group outside of government programs can design and build a crude nuclear bomb is certainly more plausible now than it was 30 or 40 years ago. At that time, the secrets of nuclear fission were closely guarded. However, much of the requisite

*A number of my colleagues and friends provided comments and advice in the preparation of my previous essays on the topic as well as this one. I would like to especially thank Konrad Kellen, Victor Gilinsky, Ariel Merari, and Paul Leventhal.

technical knowledge has since gradually come into the public domain. There are a growing number of technically trained people who understand these basic principles and who, without detailed knowledge of nuclear weapons design, theoretically could design such a weapon.

Actually building even a crude nuclear bomb, however, poses a greater obstacle. Experts argue about the number of persons needed, the mix of specialized skills, and the probability of success. They agree that it would involve considerable risks for its builders. Its detonation and performance would be uncertain. Its yield would be low, probably in tenths of a kiloton.

Few terrorists as we know them today possess the requisite technical skills identified by experts. There are a few engineers and a handful of scientists within the ranks of contemporary terrorist groups, but most terrorists come from the departments of social sciences or the humanities, which may help to explain why terrorists thus far have not carried out more technically demanding operations. One recent development, however, is changing this picture, and that is the increasing direct involvement of governments in the business of terrorism, not merely as political or financial supporters, but as participants in the direction, planning, and execution of terrorist attacks. State sponsorship puts at the disposal of the terrorists more resources: intelligence, money, sophisticated munitions, technical expertise. It also reduces the constraints on the terrorists, permitting them to operate at a higher level of violence.

It seems to me that the real arguments arise not so much in the area of theoretical capabilities as in the area of intentions. The public utterances of terrorists include very few references to nuclear activity. Terrorist groups in Western Europe have demonstrated their opposition to the deployment of new nuclear missiles, but they have done so with the traditional terrorist tactics of bombings and assassinations. Basque separatists have carried on a very effective terrorist campaign against the construction of

a nuclear power facility in northern Spain, again with traditional tactics.

In the late 1970s, the Red Brigades, in one of their strategic directives, reportedly urged action against nuclear power facilities in Italy, but the press account of this particular document could not be verified by Italian authorities. Puerto Rican separatists have also reportedly threatened action against nuclear facilities in the United States. Recognition that nuclear facilities may be attention-getting targets, however, does not readily translate into nuclear bomb threats.

Our insights into terrorists' contemplation of the use of nuclear weapons are limited to a few casual remarks, such as that of a former German terrorist who said that with a nuclear weapon, terrorists could make the chancellor of Germany dance on top of his desk in front of television cameras. This statement provides evidence that terrorists recognize the enormous coercive power a nuclear capability would give them. More recently, an "Armenian Scientific Group" warned that Turkey's largest cities would be destroyed by three small nuclear devices the group claimed to have at its disposal.* This raises an important point regarding motivation: Convinced that more than a million Armenians were the victims of Turkish genocide 70 years ago, some Armenians might now feel justified in using weapons of mass destruction in revenge, which is always a potent motive.

The obvious attraction to terrorists in going nuclear, however, is not that possession of a nuclear weapons capability would enable them to kill a lot of people. Simply killing a lot of people has seldom been one terrorist objective. As I have said on numerous occasions, terrorists want a lot of people *watching,* not a lot of people *dead.* Terrorists operate on the principle of the minimum force necessary. They find it unnecessary to kill many, as long as killing a few suffices for their purpose.

Statistics bear this out. Only 15 to 20

---

*Marmara, Istanbul, 14 January 1985.

percent of all terrorist incidents involve fatalities, and of those, two-thirds involve only one death. Less than 1 percent of the thousands of terrorist incidents that have occurred in the last two decades involve ten or more fatalities, and incidents of mass murder are truly rare.

We have to pause for a moment to define terms. By mass murder, I mean attempts to kill large numbers of persons in a single action outside of war. Let me set aside cases where governments have deliberately pursued genocidal policies, the cumulative body counts of terrorist campaigns, or the scores of serial murderers, not because I consider any of these things less reprehensible, but because they are not what we are talking about here.

Arbitrarily taking 100 deaths as the criterion, it appears that only a handful of incidents of this scale have occurred since the beginning of the century: a 1921 bombing in Bessarabia; a 1925 bombing of a cathedral in Sofia; a little-known attempt to poison German SS POWs just after World War II; the crash of a hijacked Malaysian jet airliner in 1977; the 1978 bombing of an apartment building in Beirut; a deliberately set fire that killed more than 400 in Teheran; the 1983 bombing of the U.S. Marine barracks in Beirut which killed 241. Lowering the criterion to 50 deaths produces a dozen or more additional incidents. To get even a meaningful sample, the criterion has to be lowered to 25. This in itself suggests that it is either very hard to kill large numbers of persons or very rarely tried.

Unfortunately, things are changing. Terrorist activity over the last 20 years has escalated, both in volume and in bloodshed. At the beginning of the 1970s, terrorists concentrated their attacks on property. In the 1980s, according to U.S. government statistics, half of all terrorist attacks have been directed against people. The number of incidents with fatalities and multiple fatalities has increased. A more alarming trend in the 1980s has been the growing number of incidents of large-scale indiscriminate violence: huge car bombs detonated on city streets, bombs planted in airline terminals, railroad stations, and hotel lobbies.

These incidents make it clear that terrorists have the means to kill greater numbers of people than they do now, if they wanted to. Because the constraints are not technological, we must search for other reasons. For years, I have been convinced that the actions of even those we call terrorists are limited by self-imposed constraints that derive from moral considerations or political calculations. The growing volume of testimony from terrorists interviewed while still at large, interrogated in prison, or testifying at trials has, I believe, borne out that notion.

Many terrorists consider indiscriminate violence to be immoral. They regard a government as their opponent, not the people. They may also wish to behave like a government themselves. They use the language of government to justify their actions: robberies are "expropriations," kidnap victims are subjected to a "people's trial," enemies of the people are "condemned" and "executed." Wanton violence, in their view, would imperil this image.

There are also political considerations. The capability to kill on a grand scale must be balanced against the fear of alienating perceived constituents (a population that terrorists invariably overestimate), provoking widespread revulsion, and unleashing government crackdowns that have public approval. The practical consideration of maintaining group cohesion also tends to impose limits on terrorist violence.

Attitudes toward the use of violence not only vary from group to group, but also may vary within the same group. We know now that within any terrorist group there are latent defectors who have lost faith in the cause or in the efficacy of terrorist tactics, or who find themselves repelled by escalating violence and would drop out or defect if the group goes too far. A proposal to indiscriminately kill on a grand scale might provoke sharp divisions among the terrorists, exposing the operation and the group itself to betrayal.

Obviously, not all groups share the same operational code. Subscribing, or at least paying lip service, to the philosophy that power comes from the people, left-wing terrorists generally target their violence against symbols and representatives of the state, taking care to avoid civilian casualties. However, not all left-wing terrorists share this caution—Marxist ideology, for example, did not prevent the Japanese Red Army from carrying out the Lod Airport massacre in 1972.

Right-wing terrorists generally regard the people as a disorganized, despicable mass that requires strong authoritarian leadership. These terrorist groups have shown themselves capable of "pure terrorism"—indiscriminate violence calculated to create panic and a popular clamor for a political strong man who will be able to impose order.

Certain conditions or circumstances also may erode the constraints. Like soldiers in war, terrorists who have been in the field for many years may be brutalized by the long struggle; killing becomes easier. A group may seek to avenge members who have been killed or a population that has been wiped out. Terrorists may feel compelled to escalate their violence in order to keep the attention of a public that has become desensitized by the growing volume of terrorism or to recover coercive power lost as governments have become more resistant to their demands. The composition of a terrorist group may change as the fainthearted drop out or are shoved aside by more ruthless elements. The lack of success or the imminence of defeat may call for desperate measures.

The threshold against mass murder may be lowered if the terrorists' perceived enemies and victims are members of a different ethnic group. As we have seen throughout history, the presumed approval of God for the killing of pagans, heathens, or infidels can permit acts of great destruction and self-destruction. In addition, state sponsors might covertly use terrorists to carry out a nuclear threat (although it is hard to imagine the scenario in which a state would relinquish a nuclear capability to terrorists without retaining direct control over its use). Some suggest that terrorists might overcome taboos against weapons of mass destruction by targeting a large industrial target, for example, an oil refinery where the loss of life would be minimal but the destruction of property and consequent disruption could be enormous. The annals of modern terrorism provide ample precedents for such targeting.

Several changes in the environment might increase the possibility of terrorists going nuclear. As nuclear programs expand, nuclear material suitable for use in weapons could become more widely available than it is now. Expanding commercial traffic in explosive nuclear fuel will increase the opportunities for diversion, which in turn could lead to a nuclear gray or black market where terrorists could acquire nuclear material as they now acquire conventional weapons. As knowledge of nuclear weapons design increases, so do the chances of terrorists gaining access to it.

Some developments could also alter incentives. A sudden rush by governments to acquire or to announce that they already possess nuclear weapons might persuade terrorists to attempt to do likewise. In one generation, China advanced from a guerrilla army to a nuclear power. Terrorists could try to take a shortcut. The use of a nuclear weapon in war would somehow seem to lower constraints against terrorists moving toward nuclear weapons, although I am not quite sure why. Certainly, it would depend very much on the circumstances and the results. Finally, an incident of nuclear terrorism, perhaps even an alarming hoax, would almost certainly increase the probability of other terrorists going nuclear.

The question often arises: Why would terrorists choose nuclear weapons over chemical or biological weapons, which evoke great fear and are technically less demanding? In several ways, these weapons also are less attractive. Terrorists imitate governments, and nuclear weapons are in the arsenals of the world's major powers. That makes them "legitimate." Chemical and biological weapons also may be found in the arsenals of many nations, but their use has been widely condemned by public opinion and proscribed by treaty, although in recent years the constraints against their use seem to be eroding.

But neither chemical nor biological warfare seems to fit the pattern of terrorist behavior. Terrorist attacks are generally intended to produce immediate, dramatic effects. Terrorist incidents have a finite quality—an assassination, a bombing, a handful of deaths, and that is the end of the episode. And the terrorist retain control. This is quite different from initiating an event that offers no bang but instead produces indiscriminate deaths and lingering illness, over which the terrorists would have little control.

If terrorists had a nuclear capability, they would be more likely to brandish it as a threat than detonate it, although one can conceive of a more emotional use of a nuclear weapon by an desperate group as the ultimate instrument of revenge or as a "Doomsday Machine." Translating the enormous coercive power that a nuclear weapon would give a terrorist group into concrete political gains, however, poses some difficulties. First, the terrorists would have to establish some credibility of the threat. The scenarists solve this problem by having them get away with a military weapon, thus removing the uncertainty of their possession, or by providing the terrorists with two weapons, one to be used as a demonstration.

Second, the terrorists would have to persuade the government that it has an incentive to negotiate. That may sound odd, given that they could threaten to cause thousands of casualties, but the "rules" of bargaining that have evolved from dealing with ordinary hostage incidents may not apply to nuclear blackmail. For one thing, we may assume that the terrorists' demands would be commensurate with the magnitude of the threat. Governments facing the threat of nuclear terrorism would paradoxically find it more difficult to refuse, yet more difficult to yield. Impossible demands—for example, that a government liquidate itself—could not be met even under a nuclear threat. Nor could terrorists enforce permanent policy changes unless they maintained the threat indefinitely. And if a government could not be assured that the threat would not be dismantled once the demands were met, it would have little incentive to negotiate. It thus becomes a matter not of concessions, but rather of governance. I am not suggesting that armchair extortionists cannot come up with solutions to these dilemmas—finite, irrevocable demands that governments could meet with adequate assurances that the threat would end once the demands are met. I *am* suggesting that it is not easy for terrorists, even if they are armed with nuclear weapons, to achieve lasting political results. They might find nuclear weapons to be as useless as they are powerful.

In a 1975 essay, I concluded that

Terrorists may not be interested in or capable of building a nuclear bomb. The point is, they do not have to. Within their range of resources and technical proficiency, they may carry out nuclear actions that will give them almost as much publicity and leverage, with less risk to themselves and less risk of alienation or retaliation. As the industry expands during the next few years, we will probably witness a growing number of low-level nuclear incidents. . . . There will be moments of alarm, but the inconvenience and political repercussions that these incidents produce will probably exceed the actual danger to public safety.

We did, in fact, witness more low-level incidents.

With regard to the possibility of serious nuclear incidents, I concluded that it would increase "at a far more gradual rate" if only because the opportunities for diversion and technical know-how would increase. "At some point in the future, the opportunity and capacity for serious nuclear terrorism could reach those willing to take advantage of it." But I did not see this as an inevitable development. Before then, the development of more effective safeguards could push that "point indefinitely into the future."

What do I conclude now? Despite the theoretical increase in opportunities as nuclear programs have grown, and the demonstrable escalation in terrorism, going nuclear still represents a *quantum juries* for terrorists, and one that is not impossible but by no means imminent or inevitable.

49

Dreams and Realities: Reflections On War

James M. Henslin

The Western world has become enchanted with Mikhail S. Gorbachev, the General Secretary of the Communist Party and the President of the Soviet Union. While his charming style captivated the media and his dramatic reforms at home captured the imagination of the public, his bold proposals for disarmament caught the world's leaders off guard.

In response to Gorbachev's proposals, President Bush attempted to gain the offensive and the world was treated to a spectacle it had not enjoyed before: the top leaders of the world's two superpowers attempting to "outpeace" one another. As one made a proposal to reduce armaments or troops in some part of the world, the other tried to grab world headlines with a counterproposal to reduce even more troops and armaments. This changing state of affairs has brought more than one international anomaly, including that of Sergei F. Akhromeyev

testifying before the U.S. Congress's House Armed Services Committee, where he presented details on Soviet military forces and spending—all in the attempt to persuade the United States to reduce its naval power ("Soviet Military," 1989). Consider that Akhromeyev is the former chief of the Soviet general staff (the Soviet's top military officer) and, not incidentally, Gorbachev's own military adviser.

Are these curious events the forerunners of "peace in our time"? Will we soon see a world without war? Will the United States and the Soviet Union cast their mutual suspicions aside and relegate intercontinental ballistic missiles to some soon-to-be-founded museum of modern warfare? Will the western and eastern blocs of the European nations forget their historical differences and join a pan-European economic alliance that will consummate in political unity? Will the world's economic powers then turn to the aid of the undeveloped nations so all can enjoy security within their own territories, united in a worldwide brotherhood/sisterhood? Is history about to usher in a new era in which men and women throughout the world will live in mutual tolerance, even respect, and the weapons of warfare will beat a hasty retreat into our memory banks? Ah, if only!

I do not wish to throw cold water onto anyone's dreams, and I acknowledge that dreams of a better world can be the precursor to that better world. But as a sociologist I must also acknowledge that understanding the world's problems and anticipating the likely path of world events require that one be firmly rooted in reality. Let us, then, see what indications of the future history might offer.*

First, have there ever been any periods of global peace, times when none of the world's nations were at war? Unfortunately, a search of the historical record draws a negative conclusion. A generation or so ago, sociologist Pitirim Sorokin (1937; 1941) set out to discover just how common war had been in human history. He recorded "all major interstate wars" from 500 BC to 1925 AD in the major European countries. He found that 967 wars had been fought during that time, an average of one every two to three years. Counting years or parts of a year in which a country was at war, Germany, at 28 percent, held the record for the lowest incidence of warfare, while Spain, at 67 percent, had the dubious distinction of having the highest. England was not much better, for since the time of William the Conqueror, who took power in 1066, England had been at war for 56 of each 100 years.

What about the superpowers, Russia and the United States? Sorokin found that during the entire previous thousand years, Russia, the land of his birth, had experienced

only one peaceful quarter-century. In a more recent study, Kohn (1988) reports that since 1850, the United States, a much younger country, has managed to average a military intervention somewhere in the world more than one time each year.

Of course, we like to think of our "military interventions" as gestures of peace—the same way the Soviets think of theirs. Neither of us likes to see ourselves as a belligerent of some sort, as a big bully threatening smaller nations, much less a ruthless warmonger. It is just that things have gotten out of hand in some part of the world in which we have legitimate interests. Consequently, to protect other people we must launch an invasion from time to time. (For us, invasions help "make the world safe for democracy," while for the Soviets, they "aid the people's repressed revolutionary forces.") Somehow, the role of our own interests in those military excursions seems to recede from view.

Hence, unbroken historical precedent would seem to dictate that we shall have continued warfare. And who am I to say this is not good? Perhaps, in some larger, grander scheme of things, war and military interventions help keep the world balanced. For example, no one can argue that the world's wars don't help check unbridled population growth!

This brings us to the second lesson of history: Whatever the label—military interventions, police actions, or wars—warfare is costly to human life. Physicist and mathematician Lewis F. Richardson (1960) found that between 1829 and 1949 there were:

- Seventy wars in which 3,000 to 30,000 people died
- Thirty-six wars resulting in 30,000 to 300,000 deaths
- Seven wars that claimed from 300,000 to 3 million lives
- Two world wars in which from 3 million to 31 million people were killed

An unfortunate side effect of industrialization is a greater capacity to inflict death.

---

*I have written more extensively on war elsewhere (Henslin, 1990). Some materials on the extent of war in history, war deaths, and the essential conditions for war are taken from that source.

For example, during World War I bombs claimed fewer than 3 of every 100,000 people in England and Germany. Technical advancements in human destruction, however, increased this toll 100 times—during World War II about 300 of every 100,000 people in those nations were killed by bombs (Hart 1957). Our more recent experiences with limited warfare also have proven to be costly in terms of human life. The seven painful years the United States fought in Vietnam cost 38,000 American lives and about 200,000 Vietnamese. The nine years the Soviet Union waged war in Afghanistan brought a death toll of about a million Afghanistani and perhaps 20,000 Soviet soldiers (Armitage, 1989). Iran and Iraq fought an eight-year war at a cost of 400,000 lives. Similarly, the excursion of Cuban mercenaries into Africa and South America have taken their tolls. Of course, the death toll of such wars would pale by comparison with the effects of any future nuclear war.

Surely the potential for destruction of lives and societies on a scale the world has never before known, perhaps even the eradication of civilization or of humanity itself, will encourage the world's nations to avoid conflicts that could lead to nuclear war. While one would hope so, we are far from such a present. To see why—and to gain understanding that may help avoid future warfare—we need to ask why wars are fought in the first place. Sociologist Nicholas S. Timasheff (1965) identified three essential conditions of war. The first is a *cultural tradition* which sets up expectations that encourage war when a country faces a serious conflict with another nation. The second is a *specific antagonistic situation* in which two or more states confront incompatible objectives—for example, competition for the same land or resource. The third essential condition is a *fuel* that heats the antagonistic situation to the point that both leaders and the people cross the line from thinking about war to engaging in war.

As Timasheff continued his studies, he was able to identify seven "fuels" which can ignite an antagonistic situation into warfare. The protagonist may see the opportunity to:

1. gain revenge or settle "old scores" from previous conflicts;
2. dictate its will to a weaker nation
3. protect or enhance its prestige or to save the nation's "honor";
4. unite rival groups within the country;
5. protect or exalt the position of leaders of the government or of the armed forces;
6. satisfy the national aspirations of ethnic groups (to incorporate "our people" who are living in another country);
7. forcibly convert others to religious and ideological beliefs.

The question, then, is: Are the three essential conditions of warfare still with us? Have the cultural traditions for war disappeared, the antagonistic situations been resolved, and the "fuels" dried up? If so, we shall be safe from war; if not, we shall have more wars—and continue to live under the threat of nuclear annihilation.

Let us examine these three conditions in reverse order. First, it is obvious from current events that the "fuels" are still present. Revenge is a high priority with some nations, the positions of top military leaders still become shaky, "national honor" continues to play a major role in world affairs, and so on. It is similarly the case with the second condition, for antagonistic situations continue to rear their ugly heads as nations confront incompatible objectives.

As to the essential background condition, the cultural tradition for war, have we maintained or eliminated it? Unfortunately, we know the answer far too well. While Bush, Gorbachev, Thatcher, Kohl, Mitterand, and the others talk peace, while they remove limited numbers of soldiers from some "hot spot" (to be held in reserve or simply moved elsewhere), while they reduce some armaments (only to replace them with fewer but more powerful ones), they show more interest in maintaining parity than in establishing peace. Not one of them eschews the use of military force to establish their objectives.

Moreover, while world leaders play their games of strategy, carefully moving soldiers and armaments about the world's face in the attempt to reach their objectives, the people themselves play their own culturally constructed war games. It is not encouraging to find that in their cultural ignorance people still clamor for war. In my own limited experience in Middle America, I see war movies acclaimed by the youth, the Vietnam debacle rethought by pundits (somehow we shall yet manage to turn it into a victory), Americans cheering as we invade a tiny island nation (Grenada) to overthrow communist punks, and common people from church members and college students to tavern habitues (not necessarily mutually exclusive categories) insisting that sending in the marines is the only way to solve problems in Nicaragua, Guatemala, El Salvador, Panama, and elsewhere.

In short, if history is any guide, and if I am correctly interpreting recent events, war remains an integral part of our cultural heritage and will continue. Currently, about 25 wars (including revolutions) are being fought, nearly all of them in developing nations ("The World's Wars," 1988). The antagonism between the Jews and the Arabs goes back thousands of years, and Israel and her Arab neighbors continue to follow one "preemptive strike" with another "retaliatory measure." Theirs is no mere rivalry or competition, but a deep death wish, directed outward, to which leaders on both sides devote precious energy and resources. In my estimation, sooner or later this millenia-old enmity will erupt into war and due to complicated treaties, cultural ties, and thinly disguised national aspirations, will ensnare the world's superpowers.

I dislike sounding so pessimistic (and I know that pessimists feel they are simply being realists!), but this is how I read history. Perhaps you can read it differently. Certainly the peace overtures being sounded between the East and West are refreshing, and many excellent things will come from them. However, I cannot help but consider that the basis of Gorbachev's proposals may be public relations, destined to be but another episode relegated to the footnotes of history. I note that Russia's economy, in shambles, is a bureaucratic quagmire, and that part of Gorbachev's peace overtures include a hand stretched out for economic aid and technological assistance. Perhaps the Soviets are simply manipulating the naiveté of the West—flowing from its almost desperate desire to avoid nuclear conflagration and the exhaustion that follows nearly fifty years of cold war—in order to neutralize the North Atlantic Treaty Organization, to shore up their sagging economy and rebuild their strength, and thus to emerge as an even more formidable adversary to a deeply divided West. I do not see that the Soviets have forsaken plans of global conquest, nor the conviction that communism is a morally superior system. Unfortunately, the basic contradictions and profound enmities of incompatible ideological-political-economic systems remain firmly entrenched in the world order.

Since, then, our deeply embedded mutual antagonisms remain, we need a healthy dose of reality, for dreams will only deceive. In this light, I find myself reluctantly agreeing with a man who for many years has headed my list of least favorite politicians, but who, in spite of his colossal failings and failures, does appear to have a firm grasp on the reality that underlies the present relationship between the superpowers. Richard Nixon (1988) contends that Gorbachev continues the basic goal of his predecessors: "to expand the influence and power of the Soviet Union"; that he has no intention of weakening the Soviet's military power; that if the Soviets reduce their military spending, it is only because their standard of living is declining; and that Gorbachev's orchestrated moves are designed only to strengthen the Soviet system.

In my more optimistic moments, however, I see the peace initiatives as sincere and as gradually percolating throughout the West and East, the Berlin Wall being dismantled, and the reduction of conventional and nuclear forces. And in my more wildly optimistic moments, I see those nuclear forces being relegated to the trash heap, the Iron Curtain being drawn aside to allow the free exchange of people, products, and cultural ideas, and the competition between the superpowers and industrialized nations being turned toward the peaceful sharing of technology for the betterment of people throughout the world. But such dreams are quickly shattered when I see the glorification of war in toys and movies, hear the clamoring from the citizenry around me for a stronger, more bellicose America, and smell the "fuels" of warfare ready to be ignited. I reawaken to a disturbing reality as I recall the history that encapsulates us all and enshrouds us in common destiny.

REFERENCES

Armitage, R. L. (1989, February 7). Red Army retreat doesn't signal end of U.S. obligation. *Wall Street Journal*, p. A20.

Hart, H. (1957). Acceleration in social change. In F.R. Allen, H. Hart, D. C. Miller, W. F. Ogburn, & M. F. Nimkoff (Eds.), *Technology and social change*. New York: Appleton.

Henslin, J. M. (1990). *Social problems*. Englewood Cliffs, NJ: Prentice-Hall.

Kohn, A. (1988, June). Make love, not war. *Psychology Today*, pp. 35–38.

Nixon, R. (1988, March 13). Dealing with Gorbachev. *The New York Times Magazine*, pp. 26–30, 66–67, 78–79.

Richardson, L. F. (1960). *Statistics of deadly quarrels*. Chicago: Quadrangle.

Sorokin, P. A. (1937, 1941). *Social and cultural dynamics* (4 Vols.). New York: American Book.

Timasheff, N. S. (1965). *War and revolution*. Joseph F. Scheuer (Ed.). New York: Sheed & Ward.

Soviet military adviser addresses House panel. (1989, July 22). *St. Louis Post-Dispatch*, p. 7A.

The world's wars. (1988, March 12). *The Economist*, pp. 19–22.

APPENDIX A

Topical Index

To the instructor: Because many articles have more than one theme, you may wish to present them in a different order than their presentation in this book. By classifying articles by major emphasis, this topical index is intended to be of aid in developing alternative organizations for classroom presentation.

Drugs
Morganthau: The Drug Gangs

Education
Clark: The "Cooling Out" Function in Higher
  Education
Melloan: Breaking the Cycle of Failure
Putka: A Matter of Choice
Read: Pregnancy as a Rite of Passage
Rodriguez: Searching for Roots in a Changing World

Energy
Brown, Flavin, & Postel: A World at Risk
Simon: A World More Secure

Environment
Brown, Flavin, & Postel: A World at Risk
Simon: A World More Secure

Family
Anderson: From Mafia to Cosa Nostra
Finkelhor: Sexual Abuse of Children
Finkelhor & Yllo: The Myth and the Reality of
  Marital Rape
Hiltz: Widowhood
Jackson: Alcoholism in the Family
Luker: Abortion and the Politics of Motherhood
Read: Pregnancy as a Rite of Passage

Homelessness
Coleman: Diary of a Homeless Man

Homosexuality
Kirkham: Homosexuality in Prison

International Stratification
Evangelista: How Technology Fuels the Arms Race
Gay: The "Patriotic" Prostitute
Heise: AIDS: New Threat to the World
Henslin: Dreams and Realities: Reflections on War

Labeling
Rosenhan: On Being Sane in Insane Places
Zimbardo: The Pathology of Imprisonment

Law
Attorney General's Commission: Sexually Explicit
  Materials
Irwin: Rabble, Crime, and the Jail
Michaud: The FBI's New Psyche Squad
Morganthau: The Drug Gangs
Quinney: Crime and the Development of Capitalism

Medical
Dallek: Hospital Care for Profit
Heise: AIDS: New Threat to the World

Mental Illness
Dobson Interview of Ted Bundy
Frymier: Teenage Suicide
Michaud: The FBI's New Psyche Squad
Rosenhan: On Being Sane in Insane Places

Military
Evangelista: How Technology Fuels the Arms Race
Henslin: Dreams and Realities: Reflections on War
Mills: The Structure of Power in American Society

Murder
Dobson Interview of Ted Bundy
Michaud: The FBI's New Psyche Squad
Morganthau: The Drug Gangs

Politics
Domhoff: The Bohemian Grove and Other Retreats
Evangelista: How Technology Fuels the Arms Race
Henslin: Dreams and Realities: Reflections on War
Mills: The Structure of Power in American Society

Pollution
Brown, Flavin, & Postel: A World at Risk
Shribman: Love Canal 10 Years Later
Simon: A World More Secure

Pornography
Attorney General's Commission: Sexually Explicit
  Materials
Dobson Interview of Ted Bundy

Poverty
Coleman: Diary of a Homeless Man
Dallek: Hospital Care for Profit
Domhoff: The Bohemian Grove and Other Retreats
Gans: The Uses of Poverty: The Poor Pay All
Irwin: Rabble, Crime, and the Jail
Henslin: Facing Old Age in American Society
Kotlowitz: Lords of the Slums
Morganthau: The Drug Gangs
Melloan: Breaking the Cycle of Failure
Read: Pregnancy as a Rite of Passage
Watson: Outlaw Motorcyclists
Wilson: The Black Underclass

Power
Domhoff: The Bohemian Grove and Other Retreats
Evangelista: How Technology Fuels the Arms Race

Henslin: Dreams and Realities: Reflections on War
Jenkins: Will Terrorists Go Nuclear?
Mills: The Structure of Power in American Society
Quinney: Crime and the Development of Capitalism
Scully & Marolla: Riding the Bull at Gilley's

Prostitution
Gay: The "Patriotic" Prostitute
Reichert & Frey: Bell Desk Prostitution

Racism
Rodriguez: Searching for Roots in a Changing World
Wilson: The Black Underclass

Rape
Dobson Interview of Ted Bundy
Finkelhor & Yllo: The Myth and the Reality of
  Marital Rape
Scully & Marolla: Riding the Bull at Gilley's

Resources
Brown, Flavin, & Postel: A World at Risk
Simon: A World More Secure

Sexism
Attorney General's Commission: Sexually Explicit
  Materials
Benokraitis & Feagin: Covert Sex Discrimination
Finkelhor & Yllo: The Myth and the Reality of
  Marital Rape
Scully & Marolla: Riding the Bull at Gilley's
Schwendinger & Schwendinger: Sexual Extortion
Watson: Outlaw Motorcyclists

Sexual
Attorney General's Commission: Sexually Explicit
  Materials
Dobson Interview of Ted Bundy
Finkelhor: Sexual Abuse of Children
Finkelhor & Yllo: The Myth and the Reality of
  Marital Rape
Gay: The "Patriotic" Prostitute
Kirkham: Homosexuality in Prison
Reichert & Frey: Bell Desk Prostitution
Scully & Marolla: Riding the Bull at Gilley's
Schwendinger & Schwendinger: Sexual Extortion

Social Inequality
Benokraitis & Feagin: Covert Sex Discrimination
Clark: The "Cooling Out" Function in Higher
  Education

Coleman: Diary of a Homeless Man
Dallek: Hospital Care for Profit
Domhoff: The Bohemian Grove and Other Retreats
Gans: The Uses of Poverty: The Poor Pay All
Henslin: Facing Old Age in American Society
Irwin: Rabble, Crime, and the Jail
Kotlowitz: Lords of the Slums
Melloan: Breaking the Cycle of Failure
Merton: Anomie and Social Structure
Mills: The Structure of Power in American Society
Quinney: Crime and the Development of Capitalism
Read: Pregnancy as a Rite of Passage
Schwendinger & Schwendinger: Sexual Extortion
Watson: Outlaw Motorcyclists
Wilson: The Black Underclass

Suicide
Henslin: When Life Seems Hopeless: Suicide in
  American Society
Frymier: Teenage Suicide

Technology
Evangelista: How Technology Fuels the Arms Race
Perrolle: Computers and Capitalism

Terrorism
Jenkins: Will Terrorists Go Nuclear?

Theoretical
Blumer: Social Problems as Collective Behavior
Gans: The Uses of Poverty: The Poor Pay All
Merton: Anomie and Social Structure
Mills: The Structure of Power in American Society
Quinney: Crime and the Development of Capitalism
Spector & Kitsuse: Social Problems as Claims-Making
  Activities
Sykes & Matza: Techniques of Neutralization
Watson: Outlaw Motorcyclists

Total Institutions
Anderson: From Mafia to Cosa Nostra
Irwin: Rabble, Crime, and the Jail
Kirkham: Homosexuality in Prison
Kotlowitz: Lords of the Slums
Rosenhan: On Being Sane in Insane Places
Zimbardo: The Pathology of Imprisonment

War
Evangelista: How Technology Fuels the Arms Race
Henslin: Dreams and Realities: Reflections on War
Jenkins: Will Terrorists Go Nuclear?

APPENDIX B

CORRELATION CHART

Sixteen basic social problems texts are listed alphabetically across the top of the correlation chart that follows. The chapters of those texts are located in the column to the left of the boxes. The numbers within the boxes refer to the articles in *Social Problems Today: Coping with the Challenges of a Changing Society.*

	1	2	3	4	5	6	7	8
Scarpitti & Andersen, Social problems, 1989.	1, 2, 3	6, 28, 30, 31, 32, 33, 34	9, 19, 29	7, 16, 17, 18	10, 11	4, 20, 21, 39	24, 25	8, 22, 23
Ritzer, Social problems, 2nd ed., 1986.	1, 2, 3, 4, 5, 6	31, 32	10, 11	12, 13, 14	17, 28, 29, 30, 33, 34	7, 9, 19, 35, 36, 37	26, 27	24, 25
Perillo, Contemporary social problems, 2nd ed., 1989.	1, 2, 3, 4, 5, 6	3, 32, 33	10, 11	7, 15, 16, 17, 18	6, 28, 29, 30, 31	9, 19, 29, 47, 48, 49	26, 27	24, 25
Pavalko, Social problems, 1986.	1, 2, 3, 4, 5, 6	22, 32	18, 44, 45, 46	16, 20, 32	41, 43	15, 20, 21	8, 9, 22, 23, 24	26, 27
Neubeck, Social problems: A critical approach, 2nd ed., 1986.	1, 2, 3	5, 15, 21	47, 48, 49	44, 45, 46	43	4, 5, 20, 21, 42	25, 39, 40, 41	24, 25
Lauer, Social problems and the quality of life, 4th ed., 1989.	1, 2, 3	4, 5, 6	7, 16, 17, 18	10, 11	12, 42	28, 29, 30, 31, 32, 33, 34	9, 13, 14, 19, 29	15, 20, 21, 38
Kornblum & Julian, Social problems, 6th ed., 1989.	1, 2, 3, 4, 5, 6	38, 42	12, 13, 14	7, 15, 16, 17, 18, 19	10, 11	28, 30, 31, 33, 34	9, 19, 29, 37	20, 21, 42
Jones, Gallagher, & McFalls, Social problems: Issues, opinions, and solutions, 1988.	1, 2, 3, 5	10, 11	38, 42	12, 13, 14, 19	27, 35, 36, 37	7, 9, 15, 16, 17, 18	4, 20, 21, 39	
Horton, Leslie, & Larson, The sociology of social problems, 9th ed., 1988.	1, 2	3, 4		5, 21, 47	6, 28, 29, 30, 31, 32, 33, 34	7, 35, 36, 37	45	
Henslin, Social problems, 2nd ed., 1990.	36	1, 2, 3, 4, 5, 6, 26, 27	7, 15, 16, 17, 18	10, 11	9, 19, 29	28, 30, 31, 32, 33, 34	20, 21, 39, 40, 41, 43	24, 25
Farley, American social problems: An institutional analysis, 1987.	1, 2	3	4, 20, 21	24, 25	8, 9, 22, 23	28, 29, 30, 31, 32	10, 11	7, 15, 16, 17, 18, 19
Eitzen, Social problems, 4th ed., 1989.	1, 2, 3	4, 5, 21	15	44, 45, 46	47, 48, 49	6, 20, 38	24, 25	8, 9, 18, 19, 22, 23
Currie & Skolnick, America's problems: Social issues and public policy, 2nd ed., 1988.	1, 2, 3, 4	5, 6, 15	20, 21, 39, 41		8, 9	7, 10, 35, 36, 37	43	
Curran & Renzetti, Social problems: Society in crisis, 4th ed., 1990.	1, 2, 3, 16	5, 18, 43, 47	21	4, 11, 15, 20, 21, 33	24, 25	8, 9, 22, 23	7, 10, 35, 36, 37	26, 27
Coleman & Cressey, Social problems, 4th ed., 1990.	1, 2, 3	15, 43	5, 47	39, 40, 41	35, 36, 37	4, 20, 21	24, 25	38, 42
Baker & Anderson, Social Problems: A Critical Thinking Approach, 1987.	1, 2, 3, 4, 5, 6				8, 22, 23	15, 20, 21, 39, 40, 41, 42, 43	24, 25	10, 11

9	38, 42	8, 16, 18, 22, 23	20, 21	7, 35, 36, 37	8, 9, 16, 18, 22, 23	26, 27	24, 25	24, 25, 26, 41	39, 40, 41	8, 22, 23	27, 35, 36, 37	26, 27	12, 13, 14, 38, 42	39, 40, 41	26, 27	28, 30, 31, 33, 34
10	12, 13, 14, 19	15, 20, 21, 39, 41	8, 22, 23	25, 39, 40, 41	26, 27	8, 22, 23	8, 22, 23	8, 22, 23	20, 32, 33	12, 13, 14, 38, 42	6, 43	16, 17, 42	44, 45, 46	12, 13, 14, 38, 42	8, 22, 23	11, 32
11	26, 27	43	35, 36, 37	38, 42	7, 35, 36, 37	24, 25	26, 27	6, 28, 29, 30, 31, 32, 33, 34	24, 25	35, 36, 37	26, 27	7, 35, 36, 37	11, 16, 17, 18, 19, 28, 29, 30, 31, 32, 33, 34	6, 17, 19, 28, 29, 30, 31, 32, 34	7, 16, 17, 18	45, 46
12	35, 36, 37	12, 13, 14, 38, 42	39, 40, 41	17, 19, 28, 29, 30, 31, 32, 33, 34	6, 19, 28, 29, 30, 31, 32, 33, 34	43	35, 36	45	8, 9, 22, 23, 26, 27	32	26, 45	43	48, 49	44, 46	47	43
13	5, 15, 47	22, 32	5, 47	12, 13, 14	12	39, 40, 41	39, 40, 41	44, 46	32	45	47, 48, 49	39, 40, 41	12, 13, 14	45	10, 11	
14	39, 40, 41, 43	45	12, 13, 14, 38, 42	10, 11	13, 14	35, 36, 37	43	47, 48, 49	10, 11, 13, 15, 16, 17, 18, 19	12, 14, 38, 42	5, 21, 43	28, 29, 30, 31, 32, 33, 34	10, 11	48, 49	6, 28, 30, 31, 33, 34	
15	44, 45, 46	44, 46	32		10	47, 48, 49			43	47, 48, 49	39, 40, 41	12, 13, 14	10, 11	45	9, 19, 29	
16		47, 48, 49	44, 45, 46		11	44, 45, 46	32	32	12, 14, 38, 42	43	33, 34	10, 11		32	45	
17			43				44, 45		43	44, 46	12, 13, 14, 38, 42				45	
18							47, 48, 49	47, 48, 49	44, 46					44, 45, 46		
19														47, 48, 49		